CONTEMPORARY

The Irwin Series in Marketing

Consulting Editor
Gilbert A. Churchill, Jr.
University of Wisconsin, Madison

CONTEMPORARY

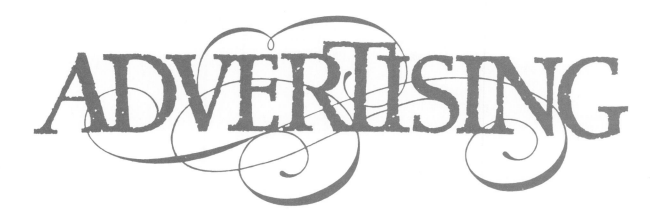

ADVERTISING

Second Edition

Courtland L. Bovée / William F. Arens

1986 **IRWIN** Homewood, Illinois 60430

Calligraphy by John Weber

Cover photo by David Bentley

ISBN 0-256-03302-1

Library of Congress Catalog Card No. 85–80275

Printed in the United States of America

1 2 3 4 5 6 7 8 9 0 D 3 2 1 0 9 8 7 6

To my family

—C.L.B.

To my parents,
John E. and Ruth H. Arens

—W.F.A.

CONTEMPORARY

PREFACE

British novelist Norman Douglas may have captured the essence of advertising's worldwide significance when he remarked: "You can tell the ideals of a nation by its advertisements." Indeed, while the advertising business was viewed as a particularly American institution in the first half of this century, that is certainly no longer the case. Today, everyone living and working in the modern world is under the influence of advertising. Thus, the study of advertising has taken on new importance, not only for the student of business or journalism—who may one day be a practitioner—but also for the students of sociology, psychology, political science, economics, history, language, art, or the sciences, all of whom will continue to be consumers of advertising.

There are six major reasons why students profit from studying advertising. It can help them to:

Understand the impact of advertising on our economy and the economies of foreign countries.

Comprehend advertising's role in fashioning society and, conversely, the impact of society on advertising.

See how advertising fits in the broader disciplines of business and marketing.

Learn how advertising relates to journalism and the field of communication.

Appreciate the artistic creativity and technical expertise required in advertising.

Discover what advertising people do, how they do it, and the career opportunities the field offers.

Our mission in the first edition of *Contemporary Advertising* was to present advertising as it is actually practiced. Our purpose is still the same. This text combines a strong managerial approach with a hands-on production orientation and includes the application of consumer behavior theory to marketing strategy as well as to effective copywriting and graphic design. In short, we believe advertising should be taught as it really is—as a business, as a marketing tool, as a creative process, and as a hybrid discipline that employs elements of the various arts and sciences—in a manner and a style relevant to the student of the 80s.

Our goal is to personally involve students with practical experiences while simultaneously giving them a solid understanding of advertising's role in marketing management.

In the pursuit of that objective, the second edition of *Contemporary Advertising* incorporates many minor and some major modifications. First of all, while we have tried to maintain the attractive, open feel of the book, both the text and the graphics have been tightened and redundancies eliminated.

Second, at the suggestion of adopters and practitioners alike, some chapters have been eliminated and other chapters added in an effort to better reflect the world of advertising in the late 80s and satisfy the needs of today's professors and students. Instead of seven parts, the text is now divided into five parts with no less than three and no more than five chapters in each part. This creates, we believe, a presentation that is both comprehensive and balanced while still following the traditional organization of topical material:

The historic, economic, and social aspects of advertising and the major segments of the advertising business (three chapters).

The elements involved in creating and evaluating the plans and strategies of marketing and advertising (four chapters).

The creative processes of copywriting, art direction, and advertising production (four chapters).

The print, electronic, direct mail, and out-of-home media alternatives available to advertisers (five chapters).

The special types of advertising including local, corporate, noncommercial, political, and international (four chapters).

This text is intended to put flesh on the bones of academic theory. To capture and hold student interest, the opening story of each chapter, written in a warm, narrative style, describes an actual situation that illustrates a basic concept in the study of advertising. In the second edition these stories are new or updated. Numerous real-life, behind-the-scenes vignettes tell what really happens in the advertising business. Each of the 20 chapters is heavily illustrated with current, award-winning advertisements and campaigns. All the major media are represented in a balanced manner—print, electronic, and outdoor. Artwork from the advertising agencies, much of it in full color, is used for most of the print and outdoor illustrations. Actual frames from television commercials, along with the dialogue, are shown. Several full-color "portfolios" of outstanding creative work are presented; and several complete case histories, from concept through final production, are developed—again, in full color. In-depth captions give all the illustrations a real-life tie-in to the basic concepts presented in each chapter. A comprehensive glossary of key marketing and advertising terms has been added at the end of the text as well as an extensive index. All these features give the student a familiar handle to aid in understanding the application and integration of advertising theory.

Active participation enhances learning, so in the first edition we introduced "Advertising Laboratories" into every chapter. In this edition we have created new Ad Labs and updated others. These highlighted sections of supplemental information serve as unique sidebars to the world of advertising. They include discussion questions to stimulate critical thinking and develop understanding of the concepts studied. All the Ad Labs, Checklists, tabular material, and technical illustrations are designed to make the information accessible with close integration to the text material.

Of course, a text for a survey course must be both thorough and substantive, and it must be built upon a sound academic foundation. The first edition of *Contemporary Advertising* was used in over 500 colleges, universities, and corporations in the United States and Canada; the second edition has been thoroughly reviewed by both the educational and professional communities. Students have cited several things they like about this text: the interest and enjoyment they experience from the material, the ease of reading and learning, the relevance of the examples and illustrations to their own experience, and the career orientation of the book which includes descriptions of job opportunities and prerequisites for specific positions in advertising or affiliated fields. Professors and students alike have found that the many checklists are a valuable teaching and learning aid in organizing thinking and facilitating decision making. We have maintained all these features in the second edition, clarifying or improving them wherever possible.

Contemporary Advertising was originally intended for the undergraduate student in business or journalism schools. Because of its approach, depth of coverage, and marketing management emphasis, it has also been found appropriate in university extension courses and courses on advertising management. The wealth of award-winning advertisements makes it a resource guide to the best work in the business for students in art and graphic design courses as well as for professionals in the field.

Many of the stories, materials, and techniques included in this text come from our own personal experiences as a college professor and a full-time marketing and advertising executive. Others come from the experiences of professional friends and colleagues. We hope that this book will be a valuable resource guide, not only in the study of advertising, but later on in the practice of it as well. In all cases, we hope that students feel like they are there—that they experience the feel and the humanness of the advertising world—whether they intend to become professionals in the business, to work with those who are practitioners, or simply to become more sophisticated consumers.

While the text itself is a complete introduction to the field of advertising, we have developed supplemental materials to assist the professor.

■ **Instructor's manual** This complete manual offers a wealth of opportunities for classroom lectures and discussions. Included are text-keyed references and answers to all discussion questions, course and subject outlines, and a completely new testing program to facilitate the administration of examinations.

■ **Testing systems** An extensive bank of objective test questions carefully designed to provide a fair, structured program of evaluation is available in several formats:

Irwin Computerized Test Generator System—a convenient and flexible question retrieval device for mainframe systems provides an extensive bank of test questions to use "as is" or with added questions of your own.

COMPUTEST—a microcomputer testing system provides convenient and flexible retrieval from an extensive bank of test questions to use "as is" or with added questions of your own.

COMPUGRADE—a microcomputer gradebook that stores and prints all grades by name or ID number. Capable of weighting and averaging grades.

TeleTest—a toll-free phone-in service to request customized exams prepared for classroom use.

Acknowledgments

We are deeply indebted to the many individuals in advertising and related fields for their personal encouragement and professional assistance. While we cannot begin to list all of them here, there are some whose contributions to our efforts must be acknowledged. These include Brad Lynch, Julianne Hastings, Charles Meding, Fred Posner, Ted Regan, and Agi Clark at N.W. Ayer; Klaus Schmidt, Alistair Gillett, and Lee Kovel at Young and Rubicam; Susan Irwin at Dancer Fitzgerald Sample; Phillippe Defechereux at Ogilvy & Mather; Terry Prindiville, Sid Stein, and Jim Ostreicher at J.C. Penney Company; Jack Donahue and Bill Wilkins at the Institute of Outdoor Advertising; Ed McCabe at Scali, McCabe, Sloves; Al Ries at Trout and Ries; Joel Baumwoll at Needham, Harper Worldwide; Joe Sosa at Chiat/Day; Elsie Behmer at McNeil Consumer Products Company; Lou Magnani at Marsteller; Paul Aass at MarkCom, Belgium; Rance Crain and his entire staff at *Advertising Age*; John O'Toole at Foote, Cone & Belding Communications; Nancy Coleman at the Union Tribune Publishing Company; René Gnam; E. S. Paccione; and Robert Posch. They, and all of the people who assisted us, gave us their best—the mark of true professionals in any industry.

In addition, we would like to thank E. L. Deckinger, Jorge Gutiérrez, Christopher Klein, Dan Maddock, Mark Stephen Martinez, Don and Deborah McQuiston, Tom Michael, Bob Oliphant, Marie Painter, Jane D. Pogeler, Bob Pritikin, Gene Rupe, Rob Settle, Terry Sherf, Roy Simon, Rebecca Smith, Don and Ann Ritchey, Homer Torrey, Laura Walcher, Lorene Ferris, and Tom Govea.

Special thanks goes to Ivan L. Jones, President; Eve Lill, Administrative Dean for Instruction; Michele Nelson, Dean, Business and Vocational Education; and Gerald Ashley, Department Chairperson for Business Administration, all at Grossmont College, for their encouragement and support.

We also feel it's important to recognize and thank the American Academy of Advertising, an organization whose publications and meetings provide a valuable forum for the exchange of ideas and for professional growth.

We are deeply grateful to the reviewers whose ideas and critical insights were invaluable in the preparation of this edition. They include: Isabella C. M. Cunningham, University of Texas at Austin; Linda C. Bateman, Glassboro State College; George Reinfeld, Glassboro State College; Valarie A. Zeithaml, Texas A & M University; Milton Richards, Mohawk Valley Community College; and Jack J. Tenge, San Francisco State University.

Finally, a project of this magnitude often places great stress on friendships and families. For their undying support, encouragement, and caring, a very special thank you to John V. Thill, Stanley L. Urlaub, and Olivia Reyes Arens as well as sons William and Christian Arens.

To all of you, thank you.

Courtland L. Bovée
William F. Arens

CONTENTS

3

THE ADVERTISING BUSINESS 68

PART II   Marketing and Advertising Plans and Strategies

4

ADVERTISING AND THE MARKETING MIX 116

5

CONSUMER BEHAVIOR AND MARKET SEGMENTATION 146

6

MARKETING AND ADVERTISING RESEARCH: INPUTS TO THE PLANNING PROCESS 176

PART III   Advertising Creativity

9

CREATIVE ART DIRECTION 282

10

CREATIVE PRODUCTION: PRINT MEDIA 308

11
CREATIVE PRODUCTION: ELECTRONIC MEDIA 338

PART IV   Advertising Media

12
MEDIA PLANNING AND SELECTION 372

PART V   Special Types of Advertising

19
NONCOMMERCIAL
AND POLITICAL
ADVERTISING 576

20
INTERNATIONAL
ADVERTISING 600

CONTEMPORARY

PART I   ADVERTISING PERSPECTIVES

1

THE EVOLUTION
OF ADVERTISING

A hundred years ago in Atlanta, Georgia, there was a pharmacist named John S. Pemberton. He was not particularly successful financially, but Dr. Pemberton was destined to develop something that would later become the most popular consumer packaged product in the world. In fact, it would revolutionize the beverage industry and create a new chapter in the history of marketing and advertising.

As legend goes, Dr. Pemberton was working over a three-legged pot in his backyard in 1886 when he produced a sweet-tasting brown syrup from the juices of certain plants and nuts. Mixed with soda fountain water, the syrup produced a remarkable sparkling taste. On May 8, 1886, Pemberton's new elixir was placed on sale as a soda fountain drink for five cents a glass at Jacobs' Pharmacy in downtown Atlanta (Figure 1–1). It was immediately popular. On May 29 a newspaper ad in the *Atlanta Journal* invited Atlantans to try "the new and popular soda fountain drink." The ad also proclaimed that Coca-Cola, as Pemberton called it, was "Delicious and Refreshing," a theme that continues today.

Following is a list of possible advertising slogans and headlines for Coca-Cola. Test your knowledge of advertising by trying to determine which ones were actually used by the Coca-Cola Company.

> The drink of quality.
> The great national temperance beverage.
> Whenever you see an arrow, think of Coca-Cola.
> Thirst knows no season.
> Around the corner from anywhere.
> The pause that refreshes.
> Universal symbol of the American way of life.
> Midsummer magic.
> Enjoy Coca-Cola.

In fact all nine slogans have been used by Coca-Cola. For the company's whole 100-year list of slogans, campaigns, and themes, see Ad Lab 1–A. The list chronicles not only the history of the world's most successful product but also the history of modern advertising and the American free enterprise system itself.

ADVERTISING DEFINED

What is advertising? According to McCann Erickson, Inc., the advertising agency that develops Coca-Cola's national campaigns, advertising is "truth well told." This philosophy is echoed by Coke's management:

> (Coke's advertising) should be a pleasurable experience, refreshing to watch and pleasant to listen to. It should reflect quality by being quality. And it should make you say, I wish I'd been there. I wish I had been drinking Coke with these people.[1]

That's what advertising is to Coca-Cola. But can the same be said for other products and services in the marketplace today? How do we define the advertising we see for those commodities?

Albert Lasker, who has been called the father of modern advertising, said that advertising is "salesmanship in print." That may well be. But he gave us that definition long before the advent of radio and television and at a time when the nature and scope of advertising were considerably different from what they are now.

Today, we all have strong concepts of what advertising is, and we also tend to have very strong opinions and prejudices about it. The definitions of advertising are many and varied. It may be defined as a communication process, a marketing process, an economic and social process, a public relations process, or an information and persuasion process, depending on the point of view.

In this text we shall use the following working definition of advertising:

> Advertising is the nonpersonal communication of information usually paid for and usually persuasive in nature about products, services, or ideas by identified sponsors through the various media.

Let's take this definition apart and analyze its components. Advertising is directed to groups of people and is therefore nonpersonal in nature. The group might be teenagers who enjoy rock music or men and women who watch soap operas or sporting events. But it is not personal or face-to-face communication.

In direct-mail advertising an attempt is often made to personalize the message by inserting the receiver's name one or more times in the letter. But direct mail is still nonpersonal; a computer inserted the name. And the signature on the direct-mail advertisement is written electronically.

Most advertising is paid for by sponsors. General Motors, K mart, Schlitz, and the local record shop pay for the advertisements we read,

FIGURE 1–1

Coca-Cola was first served at Jacobs' Pharmacy in Atlanta in 1886. Little did they know at that time that it would become the world's leading consumer packaged good.

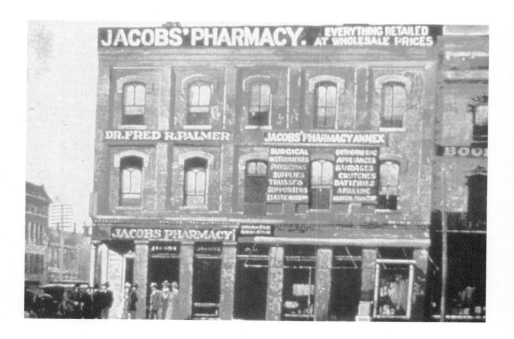

hear, and see. But some advertisements are not paid for by their sponsors. The American Red Cross, United Way, and American Cancer Society are only three of hundreds of organizations whose messages are customarily presented at no charge as a public service.

A company sponsors advertising in order to convince people that its product will benefit them. Most advertising tries to be persuasive—to win converts to a product, service, or idea. However, some advertisements, such as legal announcements, are intended merely to inform, not to persuade.

Advertising is not restricted to the promotion of tangible products such as soap and soft drinks. Advertising is also used extensively to

---

AD LAB 1–A   It had to be good to get where it is!

1886	Drink Coca-Cola.	1929	The pause that refreshes.
1904	Delicious and refreshing.	1932	Ice-cold sunshine.
1904	Coca-Cola . . . satisfies.	1932	Thirst come, thirst served.
1905	Coca-Cola revives and sustains.	1933	Bounce back to normal.
1905	Wherever you go . . . you'll find Coca-Cola.	1933	Don't wear a tired, thirsty face.
1906	The drink of quality.	1935	Coca-Cola . . . the pause that brings friends together.
1906	The great national temperance beverage.	1937	America's favorite moment.
1907	Coca-Cola is full of vim, vigor and go—is a snappy drink.	1938	The best friend thirst ever had.
		1938	Thirst asks nothing more.
1908	Get the genuine.	1939	Coca-Cola goes along.
1909	Whenever you see an arrow, think of Coca-Cola.	1939	Coca-Cola has the taste thirst goes for.
1911	Enjoy a glass of liquid laughter.	1939	Whoever you are, whatever you do, wherever you may be, when you think of refreshment, think of ice-cold Coca-Cola.
1917	Three million a day.		
1920	Coca-Cola . . . good things from 9 climes poured into a single glass.		
1922	Thirst knows no season.	1940	Within easy reach of your thirst.
1923	Enjoy thirst.	1940	America's year-round answer to thirst.
1925	It has the charm of purity.	1941	Work refreshed.
1925	With a drink so good . . . 'tis folly to be thirsty.	1941	Coca-Cola belongs . . .
		1942	The only thing like Coca-Cola is Coca-Cola itself.
1925	Six million a day.		
1926	Coca-Cola is the shortest distance between thirst and refreshment.	1942	Coca-Cola has that extra something.
		1942	The best is always the better buy.
1927	It had to be good to get where it is.	1942	It's the real thing.
1927	Around the corner from anywhere.	1943	Universal symbol of the American way of life . . . Coca-Cola.
1927	At the little red sign.		
1928	Coca-Cola . . . a pure drink of natural flavors.	1943	With a taste all its own.
		1945	The happy symbol of a friendly way of life.
1929	The best served drink in the world.		
		1945	Why grow thirsty?
		1946	The world's friendliest club . . . admission 5¢.

help sell services such as hair styling and motorcycle repairs. And increasingly advertising is used to sell economic, political, religious, and social ideas.

For a message to be considered an advertisement, the sponsor must be identified. Obviously, the sponsor usually wants to be identified—or else why advertise?

Most advertising reaches us through the mass media—that is, billboards, newspapers, magazines, radio, and television. But much advertising also reaches us through direct mail. Some advertising even reaches us through flyers hung on our doorknobs or placed under our windshield wipers at the shopping center.

1946	Yes.
1947	Coca-Cola . . . continuous quality.
1947	Continuous quality is quality you trust.
1947	The quality of Coca-Cola is a friendly quality you can always trust.
1948	Where there's Coke there's hospitality.
1949	Coca-Cola . . . along the highway to anywhere.
1950	Thirst, too, seeks quality.
1951	For home and hospitality.
1951	You taste its quality.
1952	What you want is a Coke.
1952	Coke follows thirst everywhere.
1953	Drive safely . . . Drive refreshed.
1953	Midsummer magic.
1955	Bright and bracing as sunshine.
1956	Coca-Cola . . . makes good things taste better.
1956	The friendliest drink on earth.
1956	Gives a bright little lift.
1956	Coca-Cola puts you at your sparkling best.
1957	Sign of good taste.
1958	The cold, crisp taste of Coke.
1959	Cheerful life of Coke.
1959	Relax refreshed with ice-cold Coca-Cola.
1959	Be really refreshed.
1959	The cold, crisp taste that so deeply satisfies.
1961	Coca-Cola refreshes you best.
1963	The big bold taste that's always just right.

1963	Things go better with Coke.
1963	Go better refreshed.
1964	Coca-Cola gives that special zing . . . refreshes best.
1965	Enjoy Coca-Cola.
1965	For extra fun—take more than one! Take an extra carton of Coke!
1966	Coca-Cola has the taste you never get tired of.
1968	Tells your thirst to go fly a kite.
1968	Wave after wave—drink after drink.
1968	For twice the convenience, bring home two cartons of Coke.
1968	It's twice time.
1970	It's the real thing.
1971	I'd like to buy the world a Coke.
1972	Coke . . . goes with the good times.
1975	Look up America, see what we've got.
1976	Coke adds life . . .
1980	Have a Coke and a smile.
1982	Coke is it.
1985	It's a kick; It's a hit; Coke is it.

Laboratory Applications

1. Which slogans would no longer be appropriate?

2. What new slogan might Coca-Cola use to reflect the 1980s?

FUNCTIONS OF

ADVERTISING

As soon as Dr. Pemberton had developed his new drink, he and his partner, Frank M. Robinson, came up with a name for it (Figure 1–2). They also decided to write the name in a unique way, using the flowing Spencerian script of the day. Later the name and script were trademarked with the U.S. Patent Office to ensure their sole usage by the Coca-Cola Company in its advertising and packaging. This demonstrates perhaps the most basic function of advertising—*to identify products and differentiate them from others.*

No sooner had they named the product than they ran an ad to tell people about it and where they could get it. Within a year, as more soda fountains began to sell the product, handpainted oilcloth signs with "Coca-Cola" began to appear, attached to store awnings. Then the word "Drink" was added to inform passersby that the product was a soda fountain beverage. Here we see another function of advertising—*to communicate information about the product, its features, and its location of sale.*

In 1888, the rights to Coca-Cola were bought for $2,300 by Asa G. Candler. Pemberton was in ill health and died in August of that year. Unfortunately, he was destined not to see the success his product would achieve.

Candler was a firm believer in advertising. He printed and distributed thousands of coupons offering a complimentary glass of Coca-Cola (Figure 1–3). As more and more people saw the advertisements and received free coupons, they tried the product and then tried it again. Another function of advertising is *to induce consumers to try new products and to suggest reuse.*

After more people tried the soft drink, liked it, and requested it, more pharmacies bought the product to sell to their customers. *Stimulating the distribution of a product* is yet another function of advertising.

Until then Coca-Cola had been sold only at soda fountains. One of the many functions of advertising, though, is *to increase product usage.* In 1899, the first bottling plant opened in Chattanooga, Tennessee. The second opened the following year in Atlanta. In 30 years these first two bottling plants increased to 1,000 with 95 percent of them locally owned and operated.

As with anything popular, however, there were many imitators, and the battle against these competitors has been continuous. An-

FIGURE 1–2

John Pemberton
F. M. Robinson

FIGURE   1–3

Coupons encouraged people to try the new soft drink in its early years. This is an example of one used in the 1890s.

other function of advertising is *to build brand preference and loyalty,* and Candler's use of a constant and consistent promotional campaign helped to do this.

In 1916, the famous Coca-Cola bottle with its distinctive contour design was introduced. This helped identify Coke and differentiate it from competitors to such an extent that the bottle was registered as a trademark by the U.S. Patent Office. In the meantime the bottle helped merchandise the company's other promotional efforts and also assured the public of the standardized quality of Coke with every purchase (Figure 1–4).

We see from this brief history of the beginnings of the Coca-Cola Company that advertising has many functions. Generally these functions could be grouped and categorized as marketing, communication, and education functions, as well as economic and social functions. We shall discuss each of these briefly.

Marketing Function

To make money, companies manufacture and sell products that compete in the marketplace. To increase their sales or profits, companies develop marketing strategies. The marketing strategy is determined by the particular way companies combine and use various marketing elements. This *marketing mix* includes a variety of options known as the four Ps and generally categorized under the headings of product, price, place, and promotion. Each of these will be discussed in Chapter 4.

Advertising falls in the promotion category and is part of the *promotional mix* along with personal selling, sales promotion, and public relations—all of which are used to sell or win acceptance of the company's products, services, or ideas.

Advertising involves presenting the message, usually through the mass media, to a large group of people known as the *target audience.* Through advertising, the cost of reaching a thousand people in your target audience is usually far less than the cost of reaching one prospect through personal selling.

For example, to make a personal sales call on every football fan who watches the Super Bowl game in order to sell each a bottle of Coke

FIGURE   1–4

Putting Coca-Cola in a bottle greatly widened its distribution. Bottles evolved over the years from the straight Hutchinson style used in 1899, and they have enjoyed decades of public acceptance. Management had great fear when it was suggested to add sizes larger than the traditional six-ounce container. Today, however, Coke is available in a wide variety of sizes.

would be unbelievably expensive. The McGraw-Hill Laboratory reports that the average face-to-face sales call now costs a company well over $170. If we multiply that by the 100+ million people who watch the Super Bowl, the cost is mind-boggling. However, you could buy a 30-second television commercial during the Super Bowl and tell those same 100 million people about Coca-Cola for only $525,000. That's a lot less. In fact, through advertising, you would be able to talk to a thousand of those prospects for only $5.25—about 3 percent of what it costs to talk to one prospect through personal selling.

Communication Function

All forms of advertising communicate some message to a group of people. As a communication function, advertising had its beginnings in ancient civilizations. Most historians believe the outdoor signs carved in clay, wood, or stone and used by ancient Greek and Roman merchants were the first form of advertising. Since the population was unable to read, the signs were symbols of the goods for sale, such as a boot for a shoemaker's shop (Figure 1–5).

Because early artisans took pride in their work, they placed their own marks on goods such as the cutlery, cloth, and pottery they produced. These trademarks enabled buyers to identify the work of a particular artisan, just as' trademarks do today, thus assuring consumers that they were getting the goods they wanted.

Today the communication of information is still one of the basic functions and objectives of advertising. Examples of advertising used primarily for communication are ads in telephone directories, newspaper classified ads, and legal notices published by various organizations and government bodies.

Education Function

People learn from advertising. They learn about the products that are available to them, and they learn how they can better their lives:

> Advertising, as an educator, speeds the adoption of the new and untried and, in so doing, accelerates technological advances in industry and hastens the realization of a fuller life for all. It helps reduce accidents and waste of natural resources and contributes to building a better understanding and appreciation of American ideologies.[2]

But advertising must be more than educational to be successful. It must also be persuasive to move people to action, whether that action is the purchase of a different brand of breakfast cereal or regular attendance at church. This persuasiveness usually has little in common with the impartiality of education.

What educational function do you think Coca-Cola advertising performs or has performed?

Economic Function

By making people aware of products, services, and ideas, advertising promotes sales and thereby commerce as well. As a buyer's guide, it provides consumers with news of new products or prices,

FIGURE 1–5

From a wall in Pompeii, this inscription promoted a contest of gladiators.

and it gives industrial buyers important information about new equipment and technology. By informing many people at once about available products and services, advertising greatly reduces the cost of distribution and eases the task of personal selling. This leads to lower costs and higher profits, which can be invested in more capital equipment and jobs.

The freedom to advertise enables competitors to enter the marketplace. This encourages the improvement of existing products and the development of new, improved models. These actions translate into increased productivity, higher quality, and the disappearance of products that don't measure up. Thus, as advertising invites people to try new products, it accelerates the success of good products and the failure of unacceptable products.

We shall discuss some of these far-reaching economic aspects of advertising later in this chapter.

■ Social Function

Advertising is one of the major forces that has helped improve the standard of living in this country and around the world. By publicizing the material, social, and cultural opportunities of a free enterprise consumer society, advertising has encouraged increased productivity by both management and labor.

By giving consumers an attractive picture of the products available to them, advertising motivates them to buy. For example, advertising has created a personality for each automobile make and model on the market. You, as a free individual, have the opportunity to select the product that best matches your functional or social needs.

Advertising serves social needs other than the stimulation of sales. Newspapers, magazines, radio, and television all receive their primary income from advertising. This facilitates freedom of the press.

Public services by advertising organizations also foster growth and understanding of important social causes. The Red Cross, Community Chest, United Way, and other noncommercial organizations receive continuous financial support and volunteer assistance because of the power of advertising (Figure 1–6).

Finally, advertising's effect on society has led to important social and legal changes. But, as we shall see in Chapter 2, advertising itself has been greatly affected by the very laws it has brought about.

The new drunk driving law, explained.

In California, convicted drunk drivers, even first offenders, must now spend up to 6 months in jail. Felony drunk drivers, even first offenders, can now be tried for murder. Need we explain more?

M.A.D.D.
Mothers Against Drunk Drivers

This message brought to you by the San Francisco Advertising Club

FIGURE 1–6

The San Francisco Advertising Club ran advertisements to support the efforts of Mothers Against Drunk Drivers. This is typical of the millions of dollars worth of advertising created and placed as a public service.

CLASSIFICATIONS OF ADVERTISING

The word *advertising* is often preceded by an adjective that indicates the kind of advertising being discussed. To understand what advertising is, it is helpful to classify it—and thereby learn some basic terminology.

■ Classification by Target Audience

Advertising is always aimed at a particular segment of the population. When you see ads that don't appeal to you, sometimes it is because the ad is aimed at a group of people to which you do not belong. For example, an advertisement on television for a new laundry detergent might have no meaning to a teenager. On the other hand, a homemaker with three small children may have very little interest in an advertisement for a rock concert coming to town. The *target audience* is generally defined as that group of individuals to whom the advertising message is directed.

There are many classifications of target audiences. The two major ones, though, are consumers and businesses.

Consumer advertising

Most television, radio, newspaper, and magazine ads are consumer advertisements. They are sponsored by the manufacturer of the product or the dealer who sells the product. They are usually directed at the ultimate consumer of the product or at the person who will buy the product for someone else's use. For example, a magazine advertisement for Coca-Cola may be aimed at both the purchaser and the consumer. A commercial for dog food on television, however, is aimed at the purchaser, not the consumer, of the product.

Only a few modes of transportation have proven themselves under the world's harshest conditions.

Over mountains. Across deserts. In the inner city and along rocky coastlines. Through the world's most difficult terrain and extremes of climate.
Has any carrier on legs or on wheels been as thoroughly tested around the world as a General

Motors locomotive?
Year after year, mile after mile, our locomotives have met the challenges of nature, impatient shipping companies and demanding engineers. No wonder, then, that GM Diesels are today at work in 57 countries worldwide.

From Australia to Zimbabwe, our customers have found that the simple design of our GM engines means there's less to go wrong.
And when something does go wrong, it's easier to fix. Much easier.
Our commitment to building locomotives that provide superior

performance and economy has given GM-powered locomotives the best in-service records in the railroad industry.
So if you want an affordable, fuel-efficient way of transporting people or freight from one point to another, contact us at the Elec-

tro-Motive Division, La Grange, Illinois 60525, U.S.A.
We'll put you in touch with one of our twelve manufacturing affiliates around the world for the GM-powered locomotives and the financing arrangements that will meet your specific needs.

Then you'll know even better why a GM-powered locomotive deserves a truly special place among the world's greatest beasts of burden.   **ELECTRO-MOTIVE**
Division of General Motors Corporation

FIGURE   1–7

Advertising aimed at business markets, such as this one for EMD locomotives, is rarely seen by consumers. It is usually placed in business publications directed to the specific audience the advertiser wishes to approach. In this case, that means people who purchase or influence the purchase of industrial goods.

Business advertising

Business advertising is often said to be invisible because, unless you are actively involved in some business, you are not likely to see it.

The majority of advertising you see as a consumer appears in mass consumer media. Business advertising, on the other hand, tends to be concentrated in specialized business publications or professional journals, in direct-mail pieces mailed to business establishments, or in trade shows held for specific areas of business. Until recently, business advertising was rarely seen in the mass media.

People in business who buy or specify products for use in business comprise the target audience for business advertising. There are four distinct types of business advertising: industrial, trade, professional, and agricultural.

Industrial advertising is aimed at individuals in business who buy or influence the purchase of industrial goods. Industrial goods include those products and services that are used in the manufacture of other goods (plants, machinery, equipment, etc.) or become a physical part of another product (raw materials, semi-manufactured goods, components, etc.). Industrial goods also include those that are used to conduct business and do not become part of another product, like capital goods (office machines, desks, operating supplies) and business services for which the user contracts (Figure 1–7).

Most advertising in such magazines as *Iron Age*, *Electronics*, and *Business Week* would be referred to as industrial advertising. In recent years, however, we have seen some of these products advertised in mass consumer media like radio and television, although the target audience is still businesspeople who are purchasers or users of industrial goods.

Manufacturers use *trade advertising*—the advertising of goods and services to middlemen—to stimulate wholesalers and retailers to buy goods for resale to their customers. An example of trade advertising is an ad promoting Coca-Cola to food store managers in a trade publication like *Progressive Grocer*. Some items advertised to the trade, such as office equipment, store fixtures, or specialized business services, might be bought for use in the middleman's own business.

However, the major objective of trade advertising is to obtain greater distribution of the product being sold. That may be accomplished by developing more sales outlets or by selling more products to existing sales outlets (Figure 1–8).

Individuals who are normally licensed and operate under a code of ethics or professional set of standards—such as teachers, accountants, doctors, dentists, architects, engineers, and lawyers—are called professionals, and advertising aimed at them is called *professional advertising*. Often the publications used for professional advertising are the official organs of professional societies such as the *Archives of Ophthalmology* published by the American Medical Association or the *Music Educators Journal* published by the Music Educators National Conference. Professional advertising has three objectives: (1) to convince professional people to buy items (e.g., equipment and supplies) by brand name for use in their work, (2) to encourage professionals to recommend or prescribe a specific product or service to their clients or

FIGURE 1–8

Advertising directed to wholesalers and retailers by manufacturers is called trade advertising. It is usually designed to promote wider distribution or increased sales of the manufacturer's product. Here, Hanes appeals to the retailer's sense of style and color to suggest the profitability of Hanes hosiery.

patients, and (3) to persuade the person to use the product personally.

Farming is America's largest single industry. Farmers are consumers, of course, but they are businesspeople, too, and as such they make up the audience for *farm (or agricultural) advertising*. The objectives of farm advertising are (1) to establish awareness of a particular brand of agricultural goods based on quality and performance, (2) to build dealer acceptance of the product, and (3) to create a preference for the product by showing the farmer how the product will increase efficiency, reduce risks, and widen profit margins. Publications such as *California Farmer* and *American Vegetable Grower* serve these markets.

Classification by Geographic Area Covered

The advertising for a dress shop would be most likely to run in the local area near the store. On the other hand, advertising for many other American products can be seen in foreign countries from Africa to Asia. There are four classifications of advertising based on geography.

International advertising

Travel to Europe and you might see advertisements for Crest in Norwegian. Go to Russia and you'll find the virtues of Pepsi-Cola extolled. Visit Brazil and watch an ad for Levi's on television (in Portuguese). International advertising is advertising directed at foreign markets, and as a field of study it has grown so fast and become so important that we have devoted an entire chapter (Chapter 20) to the subject (Figure 1–9).

National advertising

Advertising aimed at customers in various regions of the country is called national advertising, and its sponsors are called national adver-

FIGURE   1–9

Grey Advertising's campaign for BankAmerica Travelers Cheques, with the slogan "Known the World Over," talks to a worldwide audience with a common buying incentive. Using direct translations, this global campaign runs simultaneously in 27 countries.

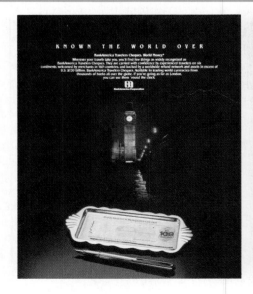

tisers. The majority of advertising we see on prime time network television is national advertising (Figure 1–10).

Regional advertising

Many products are sold in only one area or region of the country. The region might cover several states but not the entire nation. Publications such as *The Wall Street Journal* and *Time* sell space on either a national or a regional basis. Thus an airline that operates in only one part of the nation can purchase space in a regional edition of certain publications or buy television time on a regional rather than national network basis.

Local advertising

Many advertisers such as department stores, automobile dealers, and restaurants have customers in only one city or local trading area. Local advertising is often called retail advertising simply because most of it is paid for by retailers. It must be remembered, however, that not all retail advertising is local. Increasingly, retailers such as Sears, Roebuck and K mart are advertising beyond the local areas where their stores are located.

Although national and regional advertisements usually explain the merits and special features of a product, most local advertising tells consumers where to buy it. National and regional automobile commercials explain the durability, gas mileage, design, and other product qualities. Local advertising by automobile dealers emphasizes price, friendly salespeople, and other reasons to visit their dealership.

Classification by Medium

Advertising can be classified on the basis of the *medium* used to transmit the message. An advertising medium is any *paid* means used

FIGURE 1–10

ANNCR: Due to the nature of this Burger King commercial, viewers are advised to watch at their own risk.

SINGER: *Ohh, that hot and sizzling bacon.*

ANNCR: The Bacon Double Cheeseburger is for mature audiences only.

SINGER: *Two juicy, flame broiled burgers, melted cheese . . .*

ANNCR: This is your last warning.

CHORUS: *Aren't You Hungry? Aren't You Hungry? Aren't You Hungry For Burger King Now?*

ANNCR: The Bacon Double Cheeseburger has been rated PD. Perfectly delicious . . .

to present an advertisement to its target audience. It does not, therefore, include "word-of-mouth" advertising. The principal *media* (plural of *medium*) used in advertising are newspapers, magazines, radio, television, direct mail, and out-of-home, such as outdoor (signs, billboards) and transit (ads on buses, trucks). Thus there is newspaper advertising, magazine advertising, and so on.

Classification by Function or Purpose

Another way to classify advertising is on the basis of the sponsor's general objectives. Some advertising, for example, is designed to sell a product; some is not.

Product versus nonproduct advertising

Product advertising is intended to sell products and services. Nonproduct advertising is designed to sell ideas. When Exxon places an advertisement for the petroleum products it sells, it is a product ad. Advertising by companies that offer insurance services are also product advertisements. It should be pointed out here, by the way, that in this text the term *product* will refer to both products and services.

If Phillips Petroleum tells about its ability to drill for oil without disturbing or polluting the environment, the advertisement is selling the company rather than a particular product. This form of advertising is called *corporate, nonproduct,* or *institutional* advertising. Corporate advertising can have various objectives. Sometimes referred to as "image" advertising, it can be used in an effort to counter public criticism. In other instances it may be designed to promote noncontroversial causes, such as the arts or charities (Figure 1–11).

Commercial versus noncommercial advertising

A *commercial* advertisement promotes goods, services, or ideas for a business with the expectation of making a profit. A *noncommercial*

 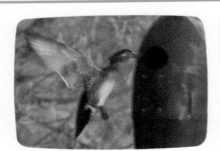 

FIGURE 1–11

ANNOUNCER VOICE-OVER:
The wood duck. One of nature's most beautiful waterfowl was once threatened by civilization destroying its nesting sites.

Then concerned citizens started erecting artificial nests. Like this one made of durable plastic invented by Phillips Petroleum.

So slick, it's almost predator-proof. It's helped the wood duck today become one of the most abundant species of waterfowl in North America.

Caring for your car and more. That's performance, from Phillips Petroleum.

FIGURE 1–12

This ad for Del Monte, prepared by McCann-Erickson/Canada, seeks a direct action on the part of the reader. By clipping the coupon, the reader can receive an immediate discount on the price of Del Monte's product.

advertisement is sponsored by or for a charitable institution, civic group, or religious or political organization. Many noncommercial advertisements seek money and are placed in the hope of raising funds. Others hope to change consumer behavior ("Buckle up for safety"). In Chapter 19 we will discuss noncommercial and political advertising.

Direct action versus indirect action advertising

Some advertisements are intended to bring about immediate action on the part of the reader. Mail-order advertisements, for example, fall into the category of *direct action* advertising. Likewise, some advertisements include a coupon for the reader to use to request catalogs or additional information. These ads are seeking an immediate, direct action from the reader (Figure 1–12).

Advertisements that attempt to build the image of a product or familiarity with the name and package are seeking an indirect action. Their objective is to influence readers to purchase a specific brand the next time they are in the market for that product.

Most advertisements on television and radio are indirect action. Some, however, are a mixture of the two. It is not uncommon to see a 60-second television commercial that devotes the first 50 seconds to image building and the last 10 seconds to a local phone number for a free demonstration.

Experienced advertisers, though, exercise caution in their use of direct action devices. The more they are used, the more they tend to detract from the image-building qualities of an advertisement. And that can have a very adverse effect on the advertiser's overall marketing objectives.

EVOLUTION OF MODERN ADVERTISING

As the world's industrial output has grown, so has the use of advertising. In the United States it is now a significant industry in relation to the total U.S. economy. In 1984 it made up 1.98 percent of the gross national product and represented a total expenditure of $66 billion (Figures 1–13 and 1–14). The media that received the most advertising expenditures (from high to low) were: newspapers, television, direct mail, radio, magazines, and outdoor. How did this industry grow to be so large?

Throughout history the purpose of advertising—to inform and persuade—has not changed. Although many people think of advertising as a modern process, it actually dates back many centuries. We have already seen how advertising as a communication function was born thousands of years ago. However, ancient civilizations had to depend on hand tools to produce goods. Because goods weren't produced in great quantity, the use of advertising to stimulate mass purchases of merchandise was not really necessary. At the same time, there were no mass media for possible advertisers to use.

Impact of Printing and Photography

The Chinese invented paper and Europe built its first paper mill by the year 1275. Perhaps the most important event that ushered in the

FIGURE   1–13   Leaders in national advertising
                     in the 1890s

Adams Tutti Frutti Gum	Heinz's Baked Beans
American Express Traveler's Cheques	Hires' Root Beer
Armour Beef Extract	Ivory Soap
Baker's Cocoa	Kodak
Beeman's Pepsin Gum	Lipton's Teas
Cook's Tours	Dr. Lyon's Toothpowder
Cuticura Soap	Mennen's Talcum Powder
Edison Mimeograph	Munsing Underwear
Elgin Watches	Oneita Knitted Goods
Edison Phonograph	Postum Cereal
Ferry's Seeds	Prudential Insurance Co.
Franco American Soup	Quaker Oats

era of modern advertising was the invention of movable type by Johannes Gutenberg in 1440. His invention made possible new advertising media and the first forms of mass advertising including printed posters, handbills, and newspaper advertisements. In London in about 1472 the first printed advertisement in English, tacked on church doors, announced a prayerbook for sale. The first newspaper advertisement, which appeared on the back of a London newspaper in 1650, offered a reward for the return of 12 stolen horses. Later, ads appeared for coffee, chocolate, tea, real estate, and medicines as well as "personal ads." The advertising was directed to a limited number of people who were customers of coffee houses where the newspapers were read.

Another major technological breakthrough was the invention of photography in the late 1880s. Before this time products in printed advertisements could be illustrated only by drawings. Photography added credibility to advertising because it showed products as they are, rather than as visualized by an artist.

Early U.S. Advertising

The first newspaper advertisements in the American colonies appeared in the *Boston Newsletter* in 1704. Later Benjamin Franklin made advertisements more readable by using large headlines and by surrounding the advertisements with considerable white space. He is credited with being the first American to use illustrations in advertisements.

The Industrial Revolution in the United States started in the early 1800s. For the first time manufacturers were able to mass produce goods with uniform quality. In order to mass produce, however, they needed mass consumption, which required vast numbers of people to purchase their products. They could no longer be content to sell only in their local area. Manufacturers soon realized the tremendous value of advertising as an aid in selling to the exciting frontier markets in the West as well as the growing industrial markets in the East. The Civil War and the victory of the industrial North over the agricultural South spurred the Industrial Revolution.

In July 1844, the first magazine advertising appeared in the *Southern Messenger*, a publication edited for a short time by Edgar Allen Poe. Magazines were the first medium used by manufacturers to reach the mass market and to stimulate mass consumption. Magazines made national advertising possible and thereby the sale of products nationwide.

Historians consider Volney B. Palmer, who started business in Philadelphia in 1841, to be the earliest advertising agent in the United States. He contracted with newspapers for large volumes of advertising space at discount rates and then resold this space to advertisers at a higher rate. The advertisers usually prepared the advertisements themselves. In 1890 N. W. Ayer & Son, another Philadelphia advertising organization, offered its services to advertisers. This company was the first advertising agency to operate as agencies do today— planning, creating, and executing complete advertising campaigns for clients in return for a commission paid by the media or for fees received from advertisers.

Other developments during the 19th century directly affected the growth of advertising. The population was growing rapidly, thus providing an increasingly large market for manufacturers. At the same time there was a substantial increase in the number of people who could read. The literacy rate was up to 90 percent by the late 1800s. This large reading public provided an audience that could understand advertising messages.

The development of a nationwide railroad transportation system quickly moved the United States into a period of spectacular growth. In 1896 the federal government inaugurated rural free delivery (RFD).

FIGURE 1–14   The leading advertisers by rank (millions of dollars)

Rank	Company	Advertising	Rank	Company	Advertising
1	Procter & Gamble Co.	$773.6	14	American Home Products Corp.	$333.5
2	Sears, Roebuck & Co.	732.5	15	Unilever U.S.	324.9
3	Beatrice Cos.	602.8	16	McDonald's Corp.	311.4
4	General Motors Corp.	595.1	17	Johnson & Johnson	295.3
5	R.J. Reynolds Industries	593.4	18	Mobil Corp.	294.9
6	Philip Morris Inc.	527.5	19	J.C. Penney Co.	292.5
7	Ford Motor Co.	479.1	20	Anheuser-Busch Cos.	290.6
8	American Telephone & Telegraph	463.1	21	Ralston Purina Co.	285.7
9	K mart Corp.	400.0	22	Coca-Cola Co.	282.2
10	General Foods Corp.	386.1	23	General Mills	268.7
11	Nabisco Brands	367.5	24	Colgate-Palmolive Co.	268.0
12	PepsiCo Inc.	356.4	25	Warner Communications	251.0
13	Warner-Lambert Co.	343.6			

FIGURE   1–15

Advertisements for health gimmicks and patent medicines in weekly newspapers in the 1880s were typical of the era. They exemplified the attitude of manufacturers at that time known by the Latin expression *caveat emptor* ("Let the buyer beware"). The result was the first consumer movement in this country leading to regulatory legislation (see Chapter 2).

Direct-mail advertising and mail-order selling flourished with mass production. Manufacturers had an ever-increasing variety of products for their catalogs. And they had a means of delivering their advertising (via newspapers and magazines) and their goods to the public.

The invention of important communications devices, including the telegraph, telephone, and typewriter as well as the phonograph and motion pictures, enabled people to communicate as never before. In short, advertising was growing with the country and helping to establish the nation's marketing system.

Advertising Enters the 20th Century

In 1800 the United States was agricultural, but it ended the century as a great industrial nation. During the first two decades of the 1900s, advertising underwent an era of reexamination. Unsubstantiated advertising claims, which caused widespread resentment, resulted in a consumer revolt. The focal point of the attack was the advertising for patent medicines and health devices. Regulation came from within the advertising industry and from the government (Figure 1–15).

In the 1920s, after World War I, the "era of salesmanship" arrived, and advertising truly became "salesmanship in print." Full-color printing was used lavishly by magazine advertisers. Testimonial advertising by movie stars became popular (Figure 1–16).

On October 29, 1929, the stock market crashed, the Great Depression began, and advertising expenditures were drastically reduced. However, perhaps due to desperation, false and misleading advertising continued to thrive. Several best-selling books exposed advertising as an unscrupulous exploiter of consumers, giving root to the consumer movement and resulting in further government regulation.

Because of consumers' sales resistance during the depression and the budget-cutting attitude of management, advertising turned to research to regain its credibility and effectiveness. A. C. Nielsen, Daniel Starch, and George Gallup founded research organizations to delve into the minds of consumers. The information they provided adver-

FIGURE   1–16

If you ever wondered where the name "Palmolive" (of Colgate-Palmolive) came from, here's the answer. A 1922 Palmolive shampoo ad says results come from "palm and olive oils, the softening, soothing cleansers discovered three thousand years ago in ancient Egypt." The company had not yet merged into Colgate-Palmolive.

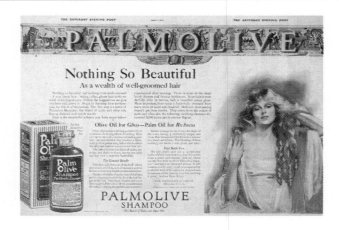

Says you're going places

1958 **EDSEL**

FIGURE 1–17

Ford Motor Company told us hopefully that the Edsel was here to stay. They were wrong. To the tune of $350 million, it was perhaps the largest single product marketing disaster in U.S. history.

tisers on public opinion, the performance of advertising messages, and the sales of advertised products through food and drug stores gave birth to a new phenomenon—the research industry.

Rise of Broadcast Advertising

A major, powerful new advertising medium, radio, started on November 2, 1920, in Pittsburgh, Pennsylvania. National advertisers used radio extensively because they could reach large, captive audiences that tuned into popular programs. In fact, it was their advertising agencies that produced the first radio shows. But then, radio became the primary means of mass communication. News arrived direct from the scene, and a whole new world of family entertainment became possible.

The most unusual expansion of any medium occurred after television was first broadcast publicly in 1941. At the end of World War II, the use of television advertising grew rapidly. In 1955 color TV was born. And today, television is the second largest advertising medium in terms of total dollars spent by advertisers.

Postwar Advertising

Since World War II the growth of both advertising and the money spent on it has been phenomenal. Postwar prosperity brought a boom of war babies eager to consume the products of the nation's manufacturers. As the war economy changed to a peacetime economy, the manufacturers of war equipment reverted to producing consumer products, offering greater luxury, style, and convenience through greater advertising.

The late 40s and early 50s were marked by a consumer society vigorously chasing itself up the social ladder in an effort to keep up with the Joneses. Ads of the era stressed social acceptance, style, luxury, and success. Rosser Reeves of the Ted Bates advertising agency introduced the idea that every advertisement must point out the product's USP—*unique selling proposition*. But soon there were so many imitation USPs that consumers couldn't take any more (Figure 1–17).

The transition to the image era of the 60s, therefore, was only natural. The Marlboro man created a macho image for male smokers, and Marlboro soared to the top of the sales charts where it has stayed for over 20 years (Figure 1–18). Cadillac became the *Cadillac* of luxury and the bourgeois symbol of success surpassed only by the aristocratic snootiness of Rolls Royce.

The positioning era

As Jack Trout and Al Ries pointed out in their famous treatise on the subject, just as the me-too (imitative) products of the 50s killed the product era, the me-too images of the 60s killed the image era.

The 70s saw a new kind of advertising strategy, where the competitor's strengths became as important as the advertiser's. This was called the *positioning era*, and Trout and Ries were its greatest advocates. Acknowledging the importance of product features and image, they insisted that what was really important was how the product ranked against the competition in the consumer's mind.

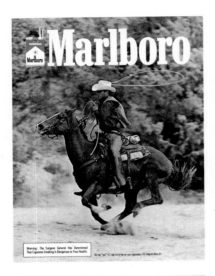

FIGURE 1–18

Until 1954 Marlboro had been a pink-tipped "women's" cigarette with sales to a restricted market. The ad claim had been "Mild as May," and the name Marlboro was written in delicate script. The restaged product included a flip-top box and a series of ads featuring rugged men, each with a tattoo on the back of his hand. Eventually the campaign settled on the now famous cowboy theme.

The most famous ads of the positioning era were Volkswagen ("Think small") (Figure 1–19), Avis ("We're only no. 2"), and 7UP ("The un-cola"). But many other manufacturers tried it with great success. Trout and Ries also pointed to product disappointments of the period and suggested that poor positioning was the reason.

The me decade

Trout and Ries did not address the consumer movement, which received its greatest impetus from the disillusioning setbacks of the Vietnam War, the Watergate scandals, and the sudden shortage of vital natural resources. These issues fostered cynicism and distrust of the establishment and everything traditional and gave rise to a morality that defended individual irresponsibility in the name of self-fulfillment and attacked corporate self-fulfillment in the name of social accountability.

By the beginning of the 80s Americans had already witnessed an avalanche of ads, especially in the toiletry and cosmetics industries, stressing the correctness of self-fulfillment to the me generation ("Kinda young. Kinda now. Charlie. Kinda free. Kinda wow. Charlie"). At the same time the nation's largest industrial concerns were spending millions of dollars on corporate advertising to extol their own righteousness for cleaning up after themselves and otherwise protecting the environment. Likewise a new phenomenon called *demarketing* appeared, as producers of energy and energy-consuming goods used marketing and advertising techniques to slow the demand for their products. Their strategy was to maintain customer goodwill even though customer demands for needed products could not be met (Figure 1–20).

Advertising Today

This brief history shows that advertising reflects the world we live in. Just as advances in technology are changing our lives, so will the

Think small.

FIGURE 1–19

Jack Trout and Al Ries called this "probably the most famous ad of the 60s." In their view it helped usher in the positioning era of the 70s. By opting for the "small" position, Volkswagen assumed a leadership rank that took many years and millions of competitors' dollars to overcome.

Nag. Nag. Nag.

Seems like that's all we've been doing lately, doesn't it?
Conserve this. Don't waste that. Turn it down. Turn it lower. Turn it off.
Well, for a change, we'd like to say something else.
Thank you.
You've been conserving a tremendous amount of natural gas. In fact, in 1977, over 23 billion cubic feet of natural gas was saved. That's equivalent to all the gas energy needs of 250,000 homes for one year.
An accomplishment like

that shows what real concern and cooperation can do even in an area as large and diverse as southern California.
Of course, the energy shortage won't just disappear. The need for conservation will always be a fact of life.
So remember, keep those showers short. Turn off your furnace pilot light during the summer. Lower the setting on your water heater. Wash and dry only full loads of...oops.
Sorry about that. Nagging's a tough habit to break.

Natural gas. It's too valuable to waste.

FIGURE 1–20

Demarketing, a new term in the 70s, described the efforts of utility companies and other energy providers to slow the demand for their limited products. The Southern California Gas Company won numerous advertising awards for its creativity in encouraging conservation.

actions and attitudes of special-interest groups, from big business to big labor, from progrowth advocates to environmentalists, from big religion to big cults. And although some groups fight progress all the way, they will all use the tools of progress to effect their aims. One of these tools will be advertising—in media yet to be conceived.

THE ECONOMIC IMPACT OF ADVERTISING

Earlier in this chapter we mentioned that one function of advertising is an economic one. By making people aware of new products and services, or by reminding people to repurchase existing products, advertising promotes sales and thus commerce.

■ The Billiard Ball Principle

The moment a company begins to advertise, like the opening shot in pool or billiards, a chain reaction of economic events takes place. Usually the extent of this chain reaction is impossible to measure. And, because it inevitably occurs at the same time as a host of other economic events, even the direction of the chain reaction is often in dispute.

For example, does advertising promote competition or discourage it? Does advertising raise or lower prices? What is the effect of advertising on the total demand for a product category? Does advertising affect consumer choice by widening it or narrowing it? How does advertising influence the business cycle? These are just some of the many questions frequently asked (and seldom answered) that relate to the chain of economic events caused by advertising.

To gain a deeper insight into the overall economic impact of advertising, a discussion of these questions is appropriate.

Microeconomic Impact of Advertising

What happened when Dr. Pemberton ran that first advertisement for his new soft drink back in 1886? Perhaps by focusing on this tiny microscopic event we can understand some broader concepts about the economic impact of advertising.

Impact on the product and medium

First, there was an impact on the product itself. Some people became aware of something new at Jacobs' Pharmacy, and they decided to try the new drink the next time they were there. Others forgot about the ad, but, when told at the pharmacy about the new drink, thought, "Oh, yes, I've heard about that." Others were interested only in selling the new drink: "What does Jacobs' have that we don't have?" In all cases the initial impact on the product was sales, or at least a new market attitude created by the advertisement that favored additional sales.

PEOPLE IN ADVERTISING

John O'Toole

Chairman and Chief Creative Officer
Foote, Cone & Belding
Communications, Inc.

John O'Toole, born in Chicago in 1929, began his writing career at 15 when his first poem was published. He went on to obtain his B.S. degree in journalism at Northwestern University and then served a tour of active duty in the Marines. After his discharge he interviewed with Foote, Cone & Belding (FCB) first, and he has been there ever since. He started as a copywriter under the guidance of the legendary Fairfax Cone, one of the agency's partners. He was promoted to creative director and then rose through the ranks to become president and chief creative officer.

In 1982, he was elected chairman of the board of Foote, Cone & Belding Communications, Inc. This corporate entity comprises 62 full-service advertising operations in 32 countries (5 of them in the United States) plus the offices of subsidiaries engaged in public relations, recruitment advertising, direct response, directory advertising, sales promotion, and financial and pharmaceutical advertising.

In a recent interview, portions of which were quoted in advertisements for *The Wall Street Journal,* O'Toole shared the following insights on advertising:

There is also an economic impact on the medium that carries the advertisement for the product—in this case the newspaper. Pemberton may have spent only $10 on his advertisement, but that was $10 the *Atlanta Journal* did not have before. That $10, mixed with the thousands of dollars from other advertisers, paid for the salaries, paper, and ink used by the newspaper that month.

Impact on the company

The second step in the chain reaction is the impact on the company that advertises the product. Pemberton was able to sell the stock in his company because investors were able to see sales occurring. As he advertised more and sold more, the company's stock became more valuable. At the same time, by advertising the availability of this new product, Jacobs' Pharmacy was able to attract new customers. This may have translated into increased sales of other products in the store, increased salaries for employees, and increased profits for the company.

Impact on competitors

Next is the impact on competitors. Other soft drink companies, seeing the advertisement for Coca-Cola, may have felt threatened by this newcomer. Their reaction might have been to lower their prices,

---

If I want to write to individual consumers, then I must know how they think, and live, and buy. So I believe it's essential to go beyond the statistics of public opinion, to look at what's happening in the real world. There's a new spirit of individualism, people seeking to satisfy their own goals, serve their ambitions, feed their individual appetites, find lifestyles to suit their needs. Small wonder there's such distrust of advertising that treats people as a homogeneous mass. Today's great advertising speaks to individual needs—to the strong drive to be yourself.

Also, there's an enormous amount of advertising and communication fighting for attention. So visibility is difficult to achieve. Yet, you must gain the eyes of the people you want to reach, or you haven't a chance of winning their minds. But making an ad visible means running risks. If an ad is provocative, interesting, intriguing, it's apt to create some adverse comments. Consider the alternative: advertising so bland there's no bite.

FCB is the third oldest, and sixth largest, advertising agency in the United States, and the eighth largest agency in the world. It has helped to turn Sunkist oranges, Hallmark cards ("When you care enough to send the very best"), Clairol hair coloring ("Does she or doesn't she?"), Dial soap ("Aren't you glad you use Dial?"), Zenith TV ("The quality goes in before the name goes on"), S. C. Johnson ("Raid kills bugs dead"), and hundreds of other products into universal habits.

In 1963 Foote, Cone & Belding made advertising industry history by offering its stock for public sale. Today FCB shares are held by some 4,000 stockholders throughout the world.

O'Toole is deeply dedicated to his trade. He has been Chairman of the American Association of Advertising Agencies and of the National Advertising Review Council. He has served as a director of The Advertising Council and as an original member of the National Advertising Review Board. His book, *The Trouble With Advertising,* was published in 1981, and his articles on advertising have appeared in *The Atlantic, Columbia Journalism Review,* and other magazines.

COCA-COLA ILLUSTRATES THE HISTORY OF MODERN ADVERTISING

A. Coca-Cola was already in wide distribution "at all (soda) fountains," before the Ford name became a household word. In those days only the wealthy could afford an automobile, and it was still considered quite avant-garde. Thus, it was an attractive and interesting association for Coke illustrated in this 1905 advertisement.

B. With the "charm of purity," a single Coke, one of 6,000,000 per day, was served by a white uniformed bellhop in this classic 1925 advertisement.

C. Coca-Cola discovered the benefits of merchandising very early. This 1934 tray with pictures of famous movie stars like Maureen O'Sullivan and Johnny Weissmuller (Tarzan) proved to be a delightful convenience to the fans.

D. While many ads of the 30s showcased movie stars, later advertising, such as this 1943 ad, reflected our involvement in World War II. At the same time Coke followed the troops with a total of 64 bottling plants shipped abroad during the war and set up as close as possible to combat areas in North Africa, Europe, and the Pacific. An order from Coca-Cola's president gave the assurance that "every man in uniform gets a bottle of Coke for 5¢ wherever he is and whatever it costs the company."

E. As Coca-Cola spread around the world, ads and news coverage in major American magazines continued to echo the themes of refreshment and availability. The *Time* magazine cover that appeared in the 1950s describes Coke as the world's "friend."

G. The campaign of the early 1980s captured the warm moments of everyday life with the "Coke Is It" series. Note the product's new container for Coke's new formula introduced in 1985.

F. "I'd like to teach the world to sing in perfect harmony. I'd like to buy the world a Coke and keep it company." A product such as Coca-Cola rarely changes; society, though, is constantly changing. Consequently, the advertising must change to reflect current lifestyles. An indication of Coke's success as the world's number one consumer product was the flashing sign at Times Square that greeted the Apollo astronauts returning from their moonflight: "Welcome Back to Earth, Home of Coca-Cola."

H. Some consumers insisted on keeping the traditional Coca-Cola formula. So, in the summer of 1985, the company reintroduced the original product as Classic Coke.

to change their product, to advertise more, or to do nothing and just watch. In reality, as Coca-Cola achieved more and more success, imitators appeared on the scene. This spurred Coca-Cola to concentrate on standardizing the quality of its product and to use more advertising designed to create brand loyalty.

Impact on customers

Just as competitors are influenced, so is the community of consumers in which the advertising takes place. Before the advent of Coca-Cola, consumers were restricted in their choice to whatever soft drinks were currently available. The moment he started advertising, though, Pemberton offered the consumers wider choice. Then, as imitators appeared, there was even greater consumer choice as advertising offered them selection alternatives.

Impact on the business community

Finally, advertising has an impact on the general business environment and on the business cycle. In a recent annual report, the Coca-Cola Company pointed out the effect on the local business environment of building a new bottling plant in some less developed countries:

> Setting up a bottling plant means virtually creating a system of local suppliers—putting into business everything from construction firms to build the plant to truck service garages to glass manufacturing plants. Mechanics and salesmen must be trained, and in many cases local craftsmen must be recruited to set up plants to make cases for bottles.
>
> A glass plant set in motion to produce bottles for Coca-Cola may also eventually produce bottles for milk, medicine and many other products that make contributions to the local economy.

Macroeconomic View of Advertising

Looking at the economic impact of advertising by one firm as we have just done gives us some simple answers to the complex questions raised earlier. But how realistic are these answers in the larger world of national and international economics?

Importance of mass distribution

Most economists agree that mass production has been a great stimulus to the success of our free enterprise system. Mass production has been given the credit for making tremendous selection alternatives available to American consumers, for maintaining low prices for most consumer goods, and for making possible the highest standard of living in the world.

However, the success of mass production depends on a system of mass distribution. It requires a huge network of warehouses, transportation facilities, wholesalers, distributors, dealers, packing plants, advertising media, salespersons, clerks, and stores to deliver the low-priced, mass-produced goods from the manufacturer to the consumer. This mass distribution system, which includes promotional activities like advertising, has drawn the most criticism from con-

FIGURE   1–21

SFX: *Wind and water sounds from the beach. Speakers being raised atop truck. Ice cubes dropping into glass, popping top. Echoing over beach. Fizzing soda is heard.*

BOY: (Drinking) Aah!
(Opens rear of van which contains hundreds of Pepsi cans and turns to crowd now gathered at van.) O.K. . . . who's first?
(Cut to scene of deserted beach.)

VO: Pepsi. The choice of a new generation.

sumer groups, legislators, and economists. The dirty words so often spoken—"middlemen's profits"—convey the implication of over-priced goods. Of course, the most conspicuous activity in the mass distribution system is advertising, and that visibility alone may contribute to advertising's role as a target of criticism.

While most people concede that advertising helps the individual firm, there is great disagreement about the benefits of advertising to the economy as a whole. The questions raised earlier should therefore be discussed from a macroeconomic point of view.

Effect of advertising on competition

The criticism is often heard that small businesses can't possibly compete with the huge advertising budgets of big businesses. For example, for many years it was said that a new automobile manufacturer could never compete in the United States because the big four American auto companies with their massive network of advertising had a monopolistic stranglehold on the consumer. Similarly, it has frequently been said that small beer companies have been driven out of business by the big breweries with their huge advertising expenditures.

For example, beer is one of the most highly advertised products. And the number of breweries has indeed been declining for more than a generation. Perhaps intense competition tends to reduce the number of businesses in an industry, but those that remain compete vigorously for consumer dollars. Or perhaps the firms eliminated through competition were those that served the consumers least effectively.

It is certainly true, in industries characterized by heavy advertising, that advertising may act as a barrier to market entry by new competitors. However, the necessity for heavy spending on plants and machinery is also a barrier to entry and usually a far more significant one than marketing costs. This is certainly borne out by the automobile industry. There are only four auto manufacturers in the United States, but the number of automobiles successfully marketed here by foreign manufacturers has steadily increased since 1950. The barrier to entry, therefore, has *not* been marketing costs but rather manufacturing costs.

Economists such as Galbraith and Samuelson have held that advertising creates industrial concentration. They point to the fact that companies that dominate particular industries invariably have the largest advertising budgets. But which came first, the chicken or the egg? Studies by Aaker and Myers to discover the relationship of advertising expenditures and industrial concentration concluded that "there is a positive relationship, but it is weaker than might be expected."[3]

Statements that attribute such great power to advertising are overly simplistic because they fail to admit the importance of such other significant influences as product quality, price, convenience, and customer satisfaction. Hershey chocolate candy bars, for instance, achieved and maintained market dominance for many years before spending any money on advertising (Figure 1–21).

Businesses compete in many ways—for personnel, plant and distribution locations, materials, customers, and so on. The most obvious and most public form of competition is advertising. But does intensely competitive advertising actually result in increased or decreased competition? As we have seen, this is a tangled question with no simple answer.

Competition occurs not only among companies in the same industry but also among companies in all industries. An auto manufacturer is obviously competing with other auto makers for consumer patronage. But the firm is also competing for the consumer dollar with companies that market boats, air travel, new homes, and other products. As the number and variety of products increase, interindustry competition also increases.

Moreover, no advertiser is large enough to dominate the whole country geographically. Regional brands of beer outsell national brands in many areas. Local oil companies compete very successfully with national oil companies on the local level. And nonadvertised store brands of food compete with nationally advertised brands on the very same shelves (Figure 1–22).

Therefore, heavy advertising actually encourages competition in some cases and discourages it in others.

Effect of advertising on the value of products

Why do most people prefer Coca-Cola to some other cola? Nationally, people buy more Cokes than Pepsis. Similarly, why do more women prefer Chanel No. 5 to some other unadvertised, inexpensive perfume? Is it because the advertised products are better products? Probably not.

Dr. Ernest Dichter, a psychologist known as the father of motivational research, has supported the view that the image of a product, which is produced partially by advertising and promotion, is an in-

FIGURE 1–22

During the two major energy crises of the 70s, the oil companies were frequently accused of "rigging" the crisis for monopolistic purposes. In one of the most effective issue-ads of the time, Union Oil pointed out the ineptitude of this "monopoly" which has given "the world's richest country some of the world's most inexpensive gasoline" and has let thousands of companies "horn in on the action" so that none has larger than an 8.5 percent share of the national gasoline market.

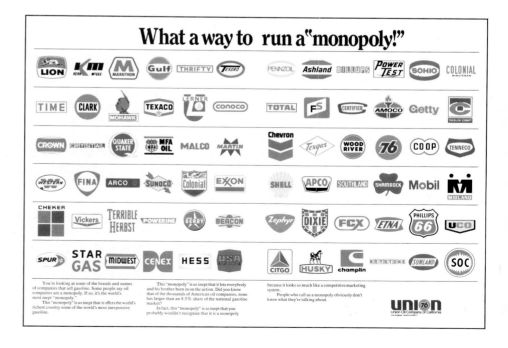

herent feature of the product itself. Image can add value to a product, making it more desirable to the consumer.

This fact was borne out in a famous court case between the Federal Trade Commission (FTC) and the Borden Company in the 1960s. The FTC accused Borden of selling milk of "physically identical and equal quality" at different prices. The Borden Company justified the price differences by pointing out that it sold the higher priced milk under a nationally branded label and the rest under private labels. In 1967 the U.S. Circuit Court of Appeals issued a decision saying, in effect, that the price differential represented the added value that had been given to the branded product through extensive advertising and promotion.[4]

Advertising can show consumers new uses for products. Arm & Hammer Baking Soda has done this effectively. Television commercials demonstrating its air-purifying qualities in refrigerators and its water-purifying qualities in swimming pools have added a new dimension to an old product.

Advertising can add value to a product in the consumer's mind. For example, what do you think most people would prefer: to buy an unadvertised brand of denim pants or Levi's?

Advertising can also add an economic value to goods and services. Brand quality can produce higher price levels for manufacturers. If all aspirin is the same, why do people pay more for Bayer than for an unadvertised house brand (Figure 1–23)?

One advantage of the free market system is that consumers can choose the values they want in the products they buy. If price is important, for example, they can buy an inexpensive economy car. If image and luxury are more important, they can buy a fancy sedan or a racy sports car. Many of our wants are emotional, social, or psychological rather than functional. Advertising allows us, as free people, the opportunity to satisfy those wants.

Effect of advertising on prices

If advertising adds value to products, then it follows that advertising also adds costs. Right? And if companies stopped all that expensive advertising, then products would cost less. Right? Wrong.

As we have just shown, there is no question that in some cases advertised products cost more than unadvertised products. How-

FIGURE   1–23

As prices have climbed steadily upward, many consumers have switched to unadvertised house brands to save money. Many others, though, prefer the convenience and confidence of buying nationally advertised brands. One of the benefits of our system is this freedom of choice.

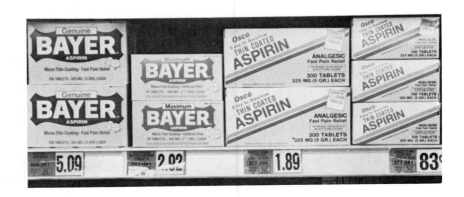

ever, there are probably just as many cases where the opposite is true. Timex watches, which are heavily advertised, cost less than most less-advertised brands.

For years Tylenol was not advertised. As an over-the-counter pain reliever, it was sold as a substitute for people who could not tolerate the side effects of aspirin. It sold for $2.85 per 100 tablets. Datril was then introduced and advertised as having an identical formula with identical results. It sold for $1.85 per 100 tablets. Tylenol immediately dropped its price and began to advertise. For some time thereafter the two engaged in heavy, competitive promotion, and prices continued to fall.

In recent years the Federal Trade Commission and the Supreme Court have ruled that professional people such as attorneys must be allowed to advertise because advertising has the competitive effect of keeping prices down. Therefore any broad, sweeping statements about the positive or negative effect of advertising on prices is likely to be too simplistic. There are several important points to understand, though, about the relationship of advertising and prices:

1. As one of the many costs of doing business, advertising is indeed paid for by the consumer who buys the product. The amount spent on advertising, though, is usually very small compared with total sales. Nevertheless, it may increase the cost of some products.

2. As pointed out earlier, advertising is just one element of the mass distribution system. This system enables many manufacturers to engage in mass production. The long, uninterrupted runs used in mass production lower the unit cost of products. These economies of scale can then be passed on to consumers in the form of lower prices. In this indirect way advertising may be credited with lowering prices.

3. Many industries, like agriculture, utilities, and oil, have been so heavily regulated by the government that advertising has had no effect on their prices whatsoever. In recent years the government has been deregulating certain industries in an effort to return free-market pressures on prices. In these cases advertising does affect price—usually downward.

4. Our economic system is complex and dynamic. We have a whole dictionary full of different market structures, including pure competition, pure monopoly, monopolistic competition, monopsony, discriminating monopoly, bilateral monopoly, and oligopoly. Marketing and advertising practices differ widely from one market structure to another. So the impact of advertising on prices also varies.

5. Price competition is perhaps most evident in retailing. However, even though prices are featured in many advertisements, there is less price competition than most people realize. Price is only one basis for competition. In retailing, store location, service, size of selection, reputation, clientele, and image are also very important. In manufacturing, companies attempt to market products that are different than those of competing firms. As a result, the main subject of competition and advertising is *product differentiation*—"Why our product is superior"—not price. In price competition, adver-

FIGURE 1–24

(MUSIC & VO): Tabu by Dana. It all begins with an embrace.

(MUSIC & LYRICS): *Embrace me—my sweet embraceable you!*

WHISPER VO: Tabu!

Embrace me—you irreplaceable you!

WHISPER VO: Tabu

(MUSIC)

(MUSIC)

My sweet embraceable you!

VO: Tabu

An embrace that lives forever. In a fragrance.

WHISPER VO: Tabu

tising forces prices down; in nonprice competition, advertising tends to hold prices up.

Effect of advertising on consumer demand

Critics of advertising sometimes accuse marketers of foisting unwanted products on the public—of creating consumer demand where none existed before—through massive advertising expenditures. The question of what effect advertising has on total consumer demand is extremely complex. Both economists and advertising professionals have puzzled over this relationship. Numerous studies show general agreement that promotional activity has some effect on aggregate consumption but no agreement as to the extent. More significant, though, is the effect of many other social and economic forces including technological advances, education of the masses, increases in population and per capita income, and revolutionary changes in lifestyle. These forces have a dynamic impact on the demand for different products.

For example, the demand for automobiles, mopeds, televisions, instant foods, and pocket calculators is expanding at a tremendous rate thanks in part to advertising, but especially to favorable market conditions. At the same time, advertising can do little to slow the decline in popularity of such items as men's and women's hats, train travel, fur coats, and home permanents.

We might conclude, therefore, that advertising can help to get new products off the ground by stimulating total consumer demand for the product class. But in declining markets, advertising can only hope to slow the rate of decline. We can also conclude that in growing markets advertisers generally compete for shares of that growth. In declining markets they compete for each other's shares.

Effect of advertising on consumer choice

If the greatest area of competition is product differentiation, then, logically, manufacturers are always looking for ways to make their products different, or at least make them seem different, in order to appeal to a greater number of consumers. As an example, look at the endless list of automobile models, sizes, colors, and features available to attract the most discriminating buyers. Similarly, grocery shelves may carry 15 to 20 different brands of breakfast cereals—something for everybody (Figure 1–24).

The freedom to advertise gives manufacturers an incentive to create new brands and improve old ones. When one brand reaches a point of market dominance, smaller brands may disappear for a short time. But, inevitably, the moment a better product comes along and is advertised skillfully, the tables suddenly turn and the dominant brand rapidly loses to the new, better product. As Walter Taplin points out, the consumer is the master, and "the producer and advertiser is the slave."[5]

Effect of advertising on the business cycle

The relationship between advertising and the gross national product (GNP) has been debated for years. Friends of advertising point with pride to this century's growth in GNP, disposable income (DI), and personal consumption expenditures (PCE). They boast that advertising has been the primary cause of all these blessings. Critical economists tend to see advertising as wasteful expenditures with little relationship to the overall business cycle.

Both sides make very strong points and back up their claims with numerous studies. The problem with most of these studies, however, is that there are so many uncontrollable social and economic factors constantly pushing and pulling on the economic system that studying the effects of one small element like advertising is nearly impossible. The results are always questionable.

The most positive study to date was conducted by Charles Y. Yang and published in 1964. He concluded that an increase in advertising expenditures of 1 percent over the rate of increase in the gross national product can produce an increase in consumption of 0.1 percent. Subsequent increases in investment and income are then generated, finally resulting in $16 of increased income generated by each $1 of increased advertising expenditure.[6]

This, of course, assumes increases in GNP. What about when GNP decreases? And, if what he says is true, why would GNP ever decrease if all we have to do is spend more advertising dollars? Again, we're left with the chicken and egg syndrome.

Historically, when business cycles dip, worried executives cut advertising expenditures. Numerous studies prove that businesses that cut their advertising expenses least during a recession fare better after the recession. But no study has ever shown that if everybody just kept advertising, the recessionary cycle would be turned around.

We must conclude, therefore, that when business cycles are up, advertising contributes to the increase. When business cycles are down, advertising may act as a stabilizing force, but the extent is currently impossible to measure.

Economic Impact of Advertising in Perspective

To individual businesses like Coca-Cola, Procter & Gamble, Sears, Roebuck, and the little appliance store on the corner, advertising pays more in results than it costs. If advertising did not pay, businesses and other institutions would not use it.

For the consumer, advertising costs less than most people believe. The various media that carry the advertisements we see are amazingly efficient. A bottle of Coke contains about a penny's worth of advertising. An automobile that costs $7,000 includes an advertising cost of less than $100.

To the economy as a whole the importance of advertising may best be demonstrated by the *abundance principle*. This states that in an economy that produces more goods and services than can be consumed, advertising serves two important purposes: (1) it keeps consumers informed of their selection alternatives, and (2) it allows companies to compete more effectively for consumer dollars.

The American economy produces an enormous selection for consumers. There are more than 10,000 different items on the average supermarket shelf. Each of the four American automobile manufacturers markets dozens of models. Clothing and shelter alternatives are seemingly endless. In short, the American economy is characterized by many suppliers competing for the consumer dollar. This competition generally tends to produce more and better products at similar or lower prices.

As a competitive tool, advertising has stimulated this phenomenon. Moreover, because American consumers have more income to spend after their physical needs are satisfied, advertising also stimulates the innovation and sale of new products to satisfy consumers' social and psychological needs.

However, no amount of advertising can achieve long-term acceptance for products that do not meet consumer approval. Less than a dozen of the 50 best-known automobile brands developed in this century are still with us despite major advertising expenditures. Only 2 of the nation's 10 largest industrial firms in 1900 remain in the top 10 today despite massive advertising.

As advertising has stimulated a healthy economy, it has also stimulated a financially healthy consumer who is more informed, better educated, and more demanding. And one of these demands has been for accountability by manufacturers and advertising, thus leading to an unprecedented level of social and legal regulation (see Chapter 2).

Summary

Advertising is defined as nonpersonal communication of information, usually paid for and usually persuasive in nature, about products, services, or ideas by identified sponsors through various media.

As a marketing tool, advertising serves several functions:

1. To identify products and differentiate them.
2. To communicate information about the product.
3. To induce the trial of new products by new users and to suggest repurchasing by existing users.
4. To stimulate a product's distribution.
5. To increase product use.
6. To build brand preference and loyalty.

Aside from marketing, advertising may also serve a communication function, an education function, an economic function, and a social function.

There are many different types of advertising. It may be classified by target audience (e.g., consumer, industrial), by geography (local, international), by the medium used (radio, television), and by its function or purpose (e.g., product advertising, noncommercial advertising, direct action advertising).

Advertising began in early times when most people could not read or write. The post–World War II era has been marked by the growth of television advertising, intense marketing competition, and increased attempts to differentiate products through positioning strategies or other techniques.

The economic impact of advertising can be likened to the opening shot in billiards—a chain reaction that affects the company that advertises as well as its competitors, customers, and the business community.

On a broader scale advertising is often considered the trigger on the mass distribution system that enables manufacturers to produce the products consumers want in high volume, at low prices, with standardized quality. There is disagreement, however, about whether advertising encourages or discourages competition, adds value to products, makes products more or less expensive, affects total consumer demand, and narrows or widens consumer choice, and whether it has any real effect on national business cycles.

While controversy surrounds most of these economic issues, the importance of advertising can best be understood by accepting the abundance principle. This states that, in an economy that produces more goods and services than can be consumed, advertising keeps consumers informed of their selection alternatives and helps companies to compete more effectively.

Questions for review and discussion

1. How do you suppose the advertising for the Child Abuse Council compares with the standard definition of advertising?
2. What examples can you give to demonstrate the primary functions of advertising today?
3. Is an advertisement for an office computer industrial advertising, trade advertising, or professional advertising?
4. What is the difference between the media used for local and for regional advertising?
5. How did the railroad affect the growth of advertising?
6. What examples can you cite of companies employing the concept of demarketing?
7. As a consumer are you more likely to save money by buying at a store that doesn't spend a lot of money on advertising? Explain.
8. How does advertising increase a product's value?
9. What is the overall effect of advertising on consumer choice?
10. How would the advertising for a new shopping center affect the local economy in your area? Are retailers in your area advertising more or less because of present economic conditions?

2

THE SOCIAL AND LEGAL ASPECTS OF ADVERTISING

On a recent flight from New York to Chicago, John O'Toole (profiled in Chapter 1), the chairman of Foote, Cone & Belding advertising agency, sat next to a woman who inquired what he did for a living. When he responded that he was in advertising, she stated somewhat scornfully, "I think advertising is destroying our language."

Because this is a common attack on the social impact of advertising, O'Toole debated whether to launch into his "case for national advertising as a preserver of clear, concise, colorful, and correct English." He refrained from that. Nor did this well-known poet tell her that advertising is "a portal for introducing new constructions and expressions into a constantly evolving language to enrich and renew it." He felt the flight would be far too short for such a long dissertation.

As he reported in one of his semiregular memos to the organization, he decided simply to cite an institution that, in his thinking, has done a far more thorough job of debasing language than advertising.

Regular readers of these memos will assume that I took out after the federal government, or Harvard Business School, or that perennial favorite, the legal profession. Not so.

I didn't have to look beyond the vehicle we were in to find a first-class miscreant: the airline industry.

I showed her this paragraph I had just read in the in-flight magazine.

"TWA is required by the federal government to ensure compliance with the regulations concerning smoking on board its flights. For the comfort and safety of all, we earnestly solicit each passenger's cooperation in strictly observing these rules. Persistent disregard could result in the offending passenger's disembarkation."

What I think they're saying, amidst all the passive and conditional gobbledygook (I like that one, too), is this:

"The government makes us enforce the no-smoking rules. Please obey them or we'll have to throw you off the plane."

Now being thrown off a plane, presumably in flight, is a disquieting prospect. So perhaps they deliberately obscured the thought with gratuitous verbiage to soften its impact. Whatever the motive, comprehension is the victim.

Pompous as it sounds, "disembarkation" is a more accurate word to describe getting off an airplane than the one they normally use: "deplaning." "We will be deplaning tonight," says the stewardess, "through the forward exit." I have an image of passengers standing at the forward exit picking tiny planes off their persons and dropping them out into the darkness. We are not deplaning. Actually the plane is depeopling. But what's wrong with just "getting off"? Then there's the matter of redundancy in airline talk. "For your own personal safety and convenience," for example. Or, "Be sure your seat backs and tray tables are returned to their original upright positions."

Compare that kind of language, which is the airline itself speaking, to the precision of advertising speaking for the airline: "Fly the friendly skies." "You're going to like us." "Doing what we do best."

Anyone who concludes advertising is the offender deserves to be disembarked.[1]

John O'Toole happens to be one of the most articulate "defenders of the faith" in advertising. However, the advertising industry has had to deal with a growing number of equally articulate critics who condemn it for a wide variety of sins far worse than the simple misuse of the English language. These attacks have led to a stream of actions on the part of consumer groups, business, and governmental bodies to regulate what advertisers say and do (Figure 2–1).

In this chapter we will discuss the major criticisms of advertising—some of which have stemmed from actual abuses of our freedom of speech. Then we shall examine the methods which have been used by business, government, and consumer groups to remedy those abuses.

FIGURE 2–1

Critics might attack this farm ad for its misuse of the English language (see the body copy). Worse, they might criticize the copywriter for stereotyping the audience. However, this ad won the highest awards from the advertising profession for its clever use of double entendre.

SOCIAL CRITICISM OF ADVERTISING

Advertising is the most visible activity of business. What a company may have been doing privately for many years suddenly becomes public the moment it starts to advertise. By publicly inviting people to try their products, companies invite public criticism and attack if their products do not live up to the promised benefits. Defenders of advertising say it is therefore safer to buy advertised than unadvertised products. By putting their names behind the goods, the makers of advertised articles stick their necks out and will try harder to fulfill their promises.

Because advertising is so public, it is widely criticized, not only for the role it plays in selling products but also for the way it influences our society. As a selling tool, advertising is attacked for its excesses. Some critics charge that, at its worst, advertising is downright untruthful and, at best, it presents only positive information about products. Others charge that advertising manipulates people psychologically to buy things they can't afford by promising greater sex appeal, improved social status, or other unrealistic expectations. Still others attack advertising for being offensive or in bad taste. Many argue that there is just too much advertising and that this overwhelming quantity is one reason it has such an impact on our society.

As a social influence, advertising is often charged, on the one hand, with contributing to crime and violence and, on the other hand, with making people conform. Critics attack advertising for perpetuating stereotypes of people, for making people want things they don't need and can't afford, and for creating insecurity in order to sell goods. Advertising, they say, debases our language, takes unfair advantage of our children, makes us too materialistic, and encourages wastefulness. Finally, by influencing the media, critics charge, advertising interferes with freedom of the press.

To adequately detail all the pros and cons of the charges against advertising would require volumes. However, it is important for the beginning advertising student to understand the essence of these attacks and the impact they have on advertising as it is performed today and tomorrow. Let's therefore examine some of the more common criticisms as they are usually expressed.

■ Advertising Debases Our Language

The very reasons John O'Toole likes advertising are the reasons defenders of traditional English usage don't like it. They feel advertising copy is too breezy, too informal, too casual, and therefore improper. Advertising, they believe, has destroyed the dignity of the language.

Grammar rules and especially punctuation rules are commonly broken by advertising copywriters, and this truly infuriates the critics. R. J. Reynolds Tobacco Co. introduced the line: "Winston tastes good like a cigarette should." The academic community created such a flap that the advertiser followed up with another commercial filmed on the steps of a university. When the student in the commercial voiced the famous slogan, another student in cap and gown quickly corrected her, saying: "Winston tastes good *as* a cigarette should." This temporarily quieted the critics, but the company continued to use the "like a cigarette should" slogan for many years.

Critics attack advertising's heavy use of punctuation (hyphens, dashes, periods, exclamation points, dots, and quotation marks) and are further offended by the use of multiple adjectives ("rich, full-bodied, heavy texture"). On the other hand, defenders suggest that today's advertising copywriters merely use the same license allowed in poetry for centuries. Examine any of Shakespeare's plays and note the use of alliteration, double adjectives and adverbs, broken sentences, and unusual punctuation:

> O! That this too too solid flesh would melt,
> Thaw and resolve itself into a dew;
> Or that the Everlasting had not fix'd
> His canon 'gainst self-slaughter! O God! O God!
> How weary, stale, flat, and unprofitable
> Seem to me all the uses of this world.
> (W. Shakespeare, *Hamlet*, Act I, Scene II)

The fact is that, to do its job, advertising must speak to people. Therefore it must be understandable and readable. Advertising research shows that people respond better to a down-to-earth, conversational tone than to a more dignified, correct tone. Therefore, good copywriters develop a style that is descriptive, colorful, and even picturesque, as well as warm, human, and personal. Because of the need for brevity, they try to use words that are simple, lively, and full of personality, and to use punctuation to build a conversational tone rather than to construct purely grammatical sentences.

However, not all copywriters are good copywriters; and literary license is a feeble excuse for what is sometimes just plain bad English.

Advertising Makes Us Too Materialistic

Critics claim that advertising adversely affects our value system because it suggests that the means to a happier life is the acquisition of more things instead of spiritual or intellectual enlightenment. Advertising, they say, encourages people to buy more automobiles, more clothing, and more appliances than they need, all with the promise of greater status, greater social acceptance, and greater sex appeal. For example, they point to the fact that millions of Americans own 20 or more pairs of shoes, several TV sets, and often more than one vehicle.

There is no doubt that we are the most materialistic society in the world. So the basic question concerning materialism is this: Is there a relationship between happiness and materialism? Does the acquisition of more goods and services contribute to contentment and the joy of living (Figure 2–2).

Philosophers and social scientists have debated the relationship between affluence and happiness for centuries, but they have reached no concrete conclusions. Defenders of advertising maintain that material comfort is necessary before a person can devote time to higher cultural and spiritual values. Therefore, they say, the stress on material things doesn't rule out spiritual and cultural values. In fact, they believe it may create a greater opportunity for it since the satisfaction of a person's higher desires is more likely when that person's lower, more basic desires have been met. They also like to point out

FIGURE 2–2

Johnnie Walker Black Label Scotch successfully appealed to status-seeking, upwardly mobile drinkers in this award-winning magazine ad. "On the way up the work may not be easier, but the rewards get better." This brief headline encourages ambition and rewards status while it builds an image for Johnnie Walker. Critics condemn this subtle form of persuasion as being psychologically manipulative.

that, through its support of the media, advertising has brought literature, opera, drama, and symphonies to millions who would never have seen them otherwise.

In reality, the first responsibility of advertising is to aid its sponsor by informing, persuading, and reminding the sponsor's customers and prospects. Most sponsors are frankly more interested in selling goods and making profits than in bringing about cultural changes or improvements. Sponsors find that advertising is most effective when it accurately reflects the society and the market to which it is targeted. Therefore, when culturally uplifting advertising copy sells goods, advertisers will use it. And some of them do. Likewise, if people want a more cultural approach to advertisements and respond to them, advertisers will probably be delighted to comply because it will be in their own best interest. Ultimately, the bottom line will prevail. The profit and loss in dollars and cents determine the advertising approach.

■ Advertising Manipulates People Psychologically to Buy Things They Don't Need

Advertising is often criticized for its power to make people do irrational things. The following are some suggestions based on variations of this criticism:

1. Advertising should be informative but not persuasive.
2. Advertising should report only factual, functional information.
3. Advertising shouldn't play on people's desires, emotions, fears, or anxieties.
4. Advertising should deal only with people's functional needs for products not their psychological needs for status, appeal, security, sexual attractiveness, or health.

Underlying all these criticisms is (1) a belief in the power of advertising to control customers against their will, or (2) an attitude that consumers simply have no freedom of choice when confronted with advertising persuasion.

Apologists for advertising point out that persuasion is a fact of life and so is our need to confront persuasion on a daily basis. We see it in every avenue of our existence, not just in advertising. Teachers try to persuade students to study. Students try to persuade teachers to give them better grades. Girlfriends persuade boyfriends; preachers persuade congregations; charities persuade donors; borrowers persuade lenders; stockbrokers persuade investors; kids persuade parents; and advertising persuades people. In short, we are all busy persuading or being persuaded in one way or another.

Second, they point out that when we persuade, we usually use a variety of tactics depending on the subject matter and the response of the listener. Sometimes the simple facts of our case are overwhelmingly persuasive. Other times we appeal to some other need or motive of our listener because the facts alone aren't persuasive enough. Should we use emotional appeals in persuasion? If not, say the defenders, then we are all guilty because we all do it.

Frankly, all of us have needs and desires beyond the basics of food, clothing, and shelter. One benefit of a free society is that we can choose to what degree we wish to indulge our desires, needs, and

FIGURE 2–3

According to the AAAA, advertising is just another word for freedom of choice. While that may be overstating their case a bit, the fact remains that advertising doesn't make us buy a product we don't want.

fantasies. Some people prefer a simple life without mortgage payments, fancy cars, and trips abroad. Others enjoy the material pleasures of a modern, technological society. There are advertising sponsors at both ends of that spectrum. Food companies offer natural products as well as convenience packaged goods. Shoe companies offer simple sandals as well as formal footwear.

Perhaps, if we recognize that advertising is persuasive by definition, then we can become better consumers and critics of advertising. All companies attempt to persuade consumers to try their products. Not all are successful, though. In spite of the fact that advertising techniques have become far more effective and efficient in recent years, there is still no black magic. The final reality is that many more products fail than succeed in the marketplace (Figure 2–3).

Advertising Is Excessive

One of the most common complaints about advertising is simply that there is too much of it. Consumer organizations protest "billboard blight" on the nation's highways. Local politicians criticize sign pollution in their communities. Advertisements reach us in cars, elevators, parking lots, hotel lobbies, subways, and in our homes on radio and television, in newspapers, and through the mail. According to most experts, the average American is exposed to over 500 commercial messages a day. Some give even higher figures. According to the advertising critics, we are awash in a sea of commercials that make life less pleasant than it might otherwise be.

There is no doubt that we live in an overcommunicated society. There are so many products from which to choose (over 10,000 in the average supermarket); and in a highly competitive society, goods must move in order to survive. Therefore companies must shout to be heard, and advertising is their megaphone.

Advertising professionals themselves are concerned about this. In an effort to control the noise level and make their advertisements more effective, most media impose voluntary restrictions on advertising volume. This, of course, limits the supply of space and time and contributes to the rising cost of media.

Consumers' tolerance of advertising in the print media seems to be greater than in the broadcast media. Readers can simply turn the pages and ignore the advertising if they so desire. Broadcast media tend to be more intrusive and therefore receive greater criticism.

However, because mass distribution supports our free enterprise system, advertising volume is here to stay and may be the price we have to pay for free television, freedom of the press, and our high standard of living.

Advertising Is Offensive or in Bad Taste

Many people find advertising offensive to their religious convictions, morality, or political perspective. Others find the use of advertising techniques that emphasize sex, violence, or body functions to be in bad taste. Certainly this is one of the most controversial issues. (See Ad Lab 2–A.)

Taste is highly subjective. Apologists point out that what is good taste to some is bad taste to others. And tastes change. What is considered offensive today may not be offensive in the future. People were outraged when the first advertisement for underarm deodorant was published in the *Ladies Home Journal,* but today no one questions such an advertisement. Some people find liquor ads offensive, while others find them simply informative. There has been some experimentation with advertising birth control products on television. Some feel this advertising supplies badly needed consumer information. Others feel that birth control is not a proper subject for a mass medium.

In the not-so-distant past, nudity was rarely seen in print advertisements. Today it is often featured in ads for grooming and personal hygiene products. Where nudity is relevant to the product being advertised, people are less likely to regard it as obscene or offensive.

Often the products themselves are not offensive, but the way they are advertised may be open to criticism. Advertising frequently emphasizes the sensational aspects of a product, particularly a book or

---

AD LAB 2–A   Jury Duty: Judge the guilt or innocence of these ads

Laboratory Application

Advertising Age sometimes devotes space to readers' submissions of "ads we can do without." The complaints about these ads range from "tasteless" to "repulsive." Judge them for yourself.

FIGURE   2–4

A few years ago, mentioning a competitor's name or product in an ad was considered taboo and in bad taste. Today the practice of comparative advertising is commonplace. In this example, Diet Pepsi compares its ingredients to Coke's ingredients in order to differentiate itself.

motion picture. Shock value may be used to gain attention, particularly by inexperienced copywriters. However, this sensationalism is often a reflection of the tastes and interests of the American people. If the advertisements don't attract the people they seek, the advertising campaign will falter and die. The audience, therefore, has the ultimate veto authority by ignoring offensive material.

It is unrealistic to assume that advertising, particularly mass advertising, will ever be free of this criticism. But reputable advertisers try to be aware of what the public considers to be tasteful advertising (Figure 2–4).

■ Advertising Perpetuates Stereotypes of People

Groups such as the National Organization for Women (NOW) protest that many of today's advertisements do not acknowledge the changing role of women in our society. One feminist says:

> Advertising is an insidious propaganda machine for a male supremacist society. It spews out images of women as sex mates, housekeepers, mothers, and menial workers—images that perhaps reflect the true status of women in society, but which also make it increasingly difficult for women to break out of the sexist stereotypes that imprison them.[2]

Consumer charges of ethnic and racial bias and of animal abuse in advertising were made to federal and business regulatory agencies for some time. The targets of these complaints included ads that showed a Japanese gardener at work and floor wax commercials that featured a black scrubwoman. Charges of animal abuse were made against beer commercials in which a dray horse was seen hauling a huge, old-fashioned brewery wagon. While none of these advertisements were illegal, all were objects of consumer efforts to halt their use, even to penalizing the advertisers.

Unfortunately, despite the efforts of many, there is still too much bias and sexism in advertising. The proper portrayal of women and minorities is still open to debate, however, and changes with the times (Figure 2–5).

FIGURE   2–5

Feminists have attacked advertising that portrays the traditional sexist roles of women dominated by men. In this amusing role reversal, it seems that women have won out. Who do you suppose is the target market for this ad?

Today it is especially important to portray women realistically, since they make so many important purchasing decisions. An area of vast change is the representation of minorities. Blacks, Hispanics, Italians, Chinese, American Indians, and others are now shown in favorable environments as a result of their upward mobility as well as organized pressure and threats of boycotts. New advertising agencies staffed with minority personnel are succeeding in reaching minority markets. Likewise, advertisers are taking special care to create advertisements that will neither offend nor alienate minority groups (Figure 2–6).

Advertising Is Deceptive

Perhaps the greatest attack on advertising has been and continues to be against the deceptive practices of some advertisers. This area has also received the greatest regulatory scrutiny, as we shall see in the next section.

Critics define deceptiveness not only as false and misleading statements but also as any false impression conveyed, whether intentional or unintentional. Advertising deception can take a number of forms, and many of these are highly controversial with no hard and fast rules. Common practices that are considered deceptive include those listed in Ad Lab 2–B.

Advertising must have the confidence of consumers if it is to be effective. Continued deception is self-defeating because, in time, it causes consumers to turn against a product.

Advertising puts the advertiser on record for all who care to look. Because of greater scrutiny by consumers and the government, it is in the advertisers' own interest to avoid trouble by being honest. The company that wants to stay in business over the long term knows it can do so only with a reputation for honest dealing.

FIGURE   2–6

Through its Hispanic advertising agency, Lionel Sosa and Associates, the Army targets families of Latin descent. The brilliance of this ad is accentuated by the headline, which captures the tendency of all bicultural families to speak a mixed idiom. In this case, "mi hijo" is Spanish for "my son," but it is also an expression of the special bond that often exists between a Latin father and his son.

DEFENSE OF ADVERTISING

Advertising professionals admit that advertising has often been used irresponsibly over the years. But they like to use the analogy of a high-powered automobile: if a drunk is at the wheel, there's going to be a lot of damage. The problem, though, is the drunk at the wheel, not the car.

In other words, they admit that advertising has been and sometimes still is misused. But they believe the abuse that has been heaped on advertising as a marketing tool and as a social influencer is no longer justified and is so excessive as to make all advertising appear bad. In support, they point out that of all the advertising reviewed by the Federal Trade Commission in a typical year, 97 percent is found to be satisfactory. Moreover, they say, the very critics who attack adver-

AD LAB 2–B   Unfair and deceptive practices in advertising

The courts have held that these acts constitute unfair or deceptive trade practices and are therefore illegal.

False promises Making an advertising promise that cannot be kept, such as "restores youth" or "prevents cancer."

Incomplete description Stating some, but not all, of the contents of a product, such as advertising a "solid oak" desk without mentioning that only the top is solid oak and that the rest is made of hardwoods with an oak veneer.

Misleading comparisons Making meaningless comparisons, such as "genuine antique reproduction" or "as good as a diamond," if the claim cannot be verified.

Bait-and-switch offers Advertising an item at an unusually low price to bring people into the store, and then "switching" them to a higher priced model than the one advertised by stating that the advertised product is "out of stock" or "poorly made."

Visual distortions Making a product look larger than it really is—for example, a TV commercial for a "giant steak" dinner special showing the steak on a miniature plate that makes it appear extra large. Or, showing a "deluxe" model that is not the same as the one offered at a "sale" price.

Testimonials Implying that a product has the endorsement of a celebrity or an authority who is not a bona fide user of the product.

False comparisons Demonstrating one product as superior to another without giving the "inferior" item a chance or by comparing it with the least competitive product available. For example, comparing the road performance of a steel-belted radial tire with an average "economy" tire.

Partial disclosures Stating what a product can do but not what it cannot do. For example, claiming that an electrically powered automobile will go "60 miles per hour—without gasoline" and not mentioning that it needs an eight-hour battery recharge every 100 miles.

Small-print qualifications Making a statement in large print (Any new suit in stock— $50 off!) only to qualify or retract it in smaller type elsewhere in the ad ("With the purchase of a suit at the regular price").

Laboratory Application

What examples have you seen of deception?

tising's excesses use advertising techniques themselves to sell their books and further their points of view.

Frankly, the sins of the past still haunt advertising today. What was once an unchecked, free-swinging business activity is now a closely scrutinized and heavily regulated profession. The excesses with which advertising has been rightfully or wrongfully charged have created layer upon layer of laws, regulations, and regulatory bodies. These are used by consumer groups, government, special-interest groups, and even other advertisers to review, check, control, and change advertising.

REGULATORS OF
ADVERTISING

A substantial amount of voluntary self-regulation has been achieved by the nation's advertisers in recent years. This reflects their desire for acceptance and growth in a competitive marketplace where consumer confidence is essential. Most large advertisers maintain careful systems of advertising review and gather strong data to substantiate their claims. Of all the regulators of advertising practices today, the greatest is, has been, and hopefully always will be voluntary self-regulation by the advertisers themselves.

PEOPLE IN ADVERTISING

Robert J. Posch, Jr.

Associate Counsel
Doubleday & Company, Inc.

Robert J. Posch, Jr., is associate counsel of Doubleday & Company, Inc., where he is responsible for ensuring legal compliance with governmental regulation of printed material.

His background in both law and marketing brings a unique perspective to this role. Posch received his degree in law from Hofstra University, then went on to obtain his MBA there and was elected to the National Honor Societies of Business and Marketing.

He has served in the legal department of Doubleday & Company for the past five years.

Posch believes that federal regulations governing advertising serve to protect both consumers and marketers. "The Federal Trade Commission," he explains, "seeks through these regulations to promote two objectives—to provide useful, truthful information to consumers and to maintain effective competition in the marketplace.

"One way the FTC does this," notes Posch, "is by enforcing minimal standards of advertising compliance. It will act against deceptive ads that influence consumers' buying decisions when such ads would harm either the consumer or the advertiser's competitor—and when it feels such action would be in the public interest."

We will discuss several major types of advertising regulators here. These include: regulation by government on the federal, state, and local levels; self-regulation by advertisers; regulation by the advertising profession and the media; self-regulation by industrial organizations; regulation by the business community; and regulation by consumers and consumer protection organizations.

■ Regulation by the Federal Government

The strictest advertising controls are imposed by federal and state laws and by judicial interpretations of these laws. Enforcement is the task of various government agencies. They must determine the scope and application of these laws and then act accordingly.

Federal Trade Commission

The FTC is the major, but not the sole, regulator of national advertising used to promote products sold in interstate commerce. Its efforts are largely directed toward consumer protection by policing the marketing done through the media. This includes monitoring false and misleading product advertising, which is defined as advertising that misleads through untrue statements or implications or by the omission of material facts. The FTC is concerned not only with truth in advertising but also with how consumers interpret such truth—

How does the FTC determine if an ad is deceptive? By reviewing it, says Posch, against these seven important standards.

1. Who is the audience? Ads directed at vulnerable groups, such as children, receive closer scrutiny from the FTC. So do ads aimed at the public at large, which includes many uninformed, unthinking, and gullible people. In making purchases, such people do not stop to analyze advertising. They tend to be influenced by appearances and by general impressions. Thus ads targeted to this mass audience usually are more subject to FTC review.
2. The FTC views an advertisement in its entirety. The total net impression is what counts.
3. Literal truth will not save an ad if it is misleading when read in its entire context. The advertiser must avoid deception by the use of half truths or by failing to disclose material facts.
4. An ad may be found to be false and deceptive if any one of two possible meanings is false.
5. Statements of subjective opinion, or puffery, may be actionable by the FTC if they give the impression of being factual or relate to material terms.

6. If an ad contains a mock-up that does not accurately represent the specific product or service it is selling, the ad may be found to be deceptive.
7. The advertiser has a continuing obligation to substantiate all material claims made in the ad, such as test results, price claims, and user endorsements.

Another way the FTC seeks to promote truth in advertising, says Posch, is by encouraging broader consumer information. "Since 1971," he notes, "it has actively encouraged truthful ads which make direct comparisons with competing products. The Avis 'We Try Harder' campaign launched this new era of comparative ads. Without the subsequent prodding of the FTC, however, ads probably would still be featuring 'comparisons' mostly with 'Brand X.'"

Posch has authored two legal guidebooks for marketers, *The Direct Marketer's Legal Advisor* and *What Every Manager Needs to Know about Marketing and the Law.*

His other writings include "Legal Outlook," a column in *Direct Marketing*, and articles in marketing publications such as the *Journal of Marketing* and *Fund Raising*.

and the effect particular advertising statements have on consumers. Because these efforts call for highly subjective judgments, FTC attempts to regulate the advertising industry are often controversial.

Federal regulations of advertising largely grew out of efforts to control unfair business practices through the Sherman Antitrust Act of 1890, amended by the Clayton Act of 1914. The Federal Trade Commission Act was also passed in 1914. It provided for the establishment of a five-member Federal Trade Commission with the power to en-

FIGURE 2–7   Federal laws affecting advertising

Year	Act	Provision	Year	Act	Provision
1890	Sherman Antitrust Act	Prohibited monopolies or attempts to monopolize and any contract, conspiracy, or combination involving restraint of trade.			products of like grade or quality unless such discounts are intended to meet competition or are based on the actual costs of servicing the customer.
1906	Pure Food and Drug Act	Outlawed shipment of misbranded or adulterated food or drugs in interstate commerce.	1938	Wheeler–Lea Amendment to the Federal Trade Commission Act	Expanded FTC jurisdiction. Prohibited advertising that was unfair or deceptive in its own right. No longer did the act have to injure competition to be illegal.
1914	Clayton Act	Prohibited price discrimination.			
1914	Federal Trade Commission Act	Made unfair methods of competition illegal. Established the FTC.			
1934	Communications Act	Established the Federal Communications Commission (FCC) giving it the power to license broadcast stations.	1939	Wool Products Labeling Act	Required that each product be labeled to show the total fiber weight of the wool; whether it is new, processed, or reused; the percent of nonwool filling; and the name of the manufacturer.
1936	Robinson–Patman Act	Amended the Clayton Act. Prohibited price discrimination that lessens competition or tends to create a monopoly. For example, anyone in interstate commerce cannot charge different customers different prices for	1947	Lanham Trade-Mark Act	Passed to protect slogans and brand names from infringement by competitors. Appointed the U.S. Patent Office to register slogans, brand names,

force the act. Today the commission is the leading federal regulatory agency for advertising (see Figure 2–7).

The FTC's procedure in monitoring claims is to compare the advertised product with what the advertising represents it to be. The FTC frequently asks advertisers to submit documentation and other proof of performance to substantiate their advertising claims. This proof includes not only claims of product quality or performance, but also claims about product safety, value, and uniqueness, as well as

Year	Act	Provision	Year	Act	Provision
		corporate or store names, and identifying symbols for brands or companies.			the FDA to remove dangerous products from the market.
1952	Fur Products Labeling Act	Required that the name of the animal, as well as manufacturing details, appear on the label of each item offered for sale.	1968	Truth-in-Lending Act	As part of the Consumer Credit Protection Act, it required creditors to make full disclosure of the cost of consumer credit in ads or no mention of it can be made.
1958	Automobile Information Disclosure Act	Required the manufacturer to show the suggested retail price of each new car itemized for base cost, extras, and freight.	1970	Public Health Cigarette Smoking Act	Made it illegal for broadcast media to accept money for cigarette advertising and required a health warning on all cigarette ads in the print media.
1960	Textile Fiber Products Identification Act	Required that labels on fiber items show the percentage of natural and synthetic fibers used in the manufacture of cloth and other materials.	1975	Magnuson–Moss Warranty— Federal Trade Commission Improvement Act	Empowered the FTC to protect consumers from deceptive warranties.
1966	Fair Packaging and Labeling Act	Established a "truth-in-labeling" law, requiring manufacturers to state the contents of the package, who made it, and how much it contains.	1978	Copyright Act	Extended copyright protection for the life of the owner of the copyright plus 50 years.
1966	Child Safety Act	Prevents the marketing of potentially harmful products and permits	1980	Federal Trade Commission Improvement Act	Provided for congressional review of the FTC as well as procedures by which the FTC could improve regulations and trade rules.

FIGURE 2–8

Listerine advertised for 50 years as a germ killer. In this 1941 scare approach, readers were admonished to gargle Listerine quick! In the 1970s the FTC held that the product did not relieve colds or sore throats, and it forced the company to include a corrective statement stating that the product was of no value in preventing colds and sore throats.

claimed contributions to the user's health or well-being. An FTC request for documentation prohibits further use of unverified claims by the advertiser. The FTC requires that advertising claims be adequately substantiated and that the advertiser possess such proof before these claims are made in advertising.

Consider the case of Acne-Statin, a product endorsed by singer Pat Boone. He said: "With four daughters, we've tried the leading acne medication at our house, and nothing ever seemed to work until our girls met a Beverly Hills doctor and got some real help through a product called 'Acne-Statin.'" The FTC said the advertising claims could not be substantiated and that celebrities, like companies that place the ads, must verify the claims before they go on the air or into print. As a result of this case, there is a clause in typical endorsement contracts that protect the endorser from claims made against the advertiser by third parties.

In a Campbell's Soup television commercial marbles were placed at the bottom of a bowl of soup. The marbles held the solid ingredients at the top so they would be more visible, giving the impression that the soup contained more ingredients than it actually did. Campbell's defense was that if they didn't use the marbles the ingredients would sink to the bottom; this would lead viewers to believe that there were fewer ingredients than was actually the case. Campbell's agreed to stop the practice.

In recent years the FTC has given increasing attention to bait-and-switch advertising. For example, the FTC filed a complaint stating that Sears, Roebuck & Company used bait-and-switch tactics to sell its sewing machines. Salespeople made disparaging remarks about an advertised model of sewing machine. They said there would be long delays in delivery, the sewing machines were noisy and had shorter guarantees than more expensive models, and they could not do certain types of stitching. Customers were then encouraged to buy more expensive models. Sears agreed to halt the practice.

The FTC has also expanded its emphasis on affirmative disclosure, whereby advertisers must disclose not only the positive qualities of their products but also the negative aspects, such as limitations or deficiencies. Examples of this are EPA estimates of gas mileage for automobiles, pesticide warnings, and statements that soft drinks made with saccharin may be hazardous to the consumer's health.

Also, endorsement of a product by an "expert" must be based on actual use by that expert. The endorser must be a bona fide user of the product. If an ad implies that the endorser has superior qualifications for making the judgment stated, the endorser's qualifications must bear this out. A spokesperson who doesn't speak on the basis of personal opinion but on behalf of the advertiser is not an endorser. Slice-of-life commercials are not considered endorsements but rather fictional dramatizations.

Complaints against advertisements usually come from consumers, brand competitors, and the FTC's monitors. After an investigation, the FTC may decide to issue a complaint against the advertiser. This may take any of several forms. For example, the FTC may issue a cease and desist order, prohibiting further use of the objectionable advertising. The advertiser may then sign an agreement to comply voluntarily. In other cases a consent decree may be issued. The advertiser may then agree, without admitting guilt, to halt the advertising and not indulge in such practices again. The FTC may also require corrective advertising, whereby a portion of the company's advertising for a period of time must be devoted to explaining that the previous advertising was inaccurate or misleading.

This occurred in a Profile bread advertisement claiming that each slice contained fewer calories than slices of other brands. However, the ad did not mention that slices of Profile were thinner than those of other brands. The company was ordered to devote 25 percent of its advertising for one year to correct this misleading statement. Ocean Spray Cranberry Juice used the words "high-energy food" to describe its product. The FTC charged that the words were misleading because, technically, high-energy food means calories, a fact that is not recognized by many consumers. The company was required to spend 25 percent of its advertising for one year to explain the meaning of "high-energy food" and to confess that it means calories. For many years Warner-Lambert advertised Listerine as a cold and sore-throat remedy based on tests they had conducted. The FTC proved the tests were invalid. Not only was Listerine required to stop making such claims, but it was called on by the court to run $10.2 million of advertising stating that "Listerine will not help prevent colds or sore throats or lessen their severity" (Figure 2–8).

Finally, in rare instances, the FTC may ask the attorney general to try the advertiser on a misdemeanor charge. Conviction carries a fine of not more than $5,000 or not more than six months in jail (Figure 2–9).

The advertiser has 30 days to respond to any of these actions. The company can agree to the action, or it can contest it by requesting a

FIGURE   2–9

The actions of the FTC caused many in the advertising industry to react with alarm to the restrictions on their creativity. In this famous tongue-in-cheek ad, Scali, McCabe, Sloves suggested that the Declaration of Independence itself would probably be considered misleading and deceptive by the FTC. Actually, the advertising agency is wrong, and their ad is incorrect in the point it pretends to make. The Declaration did not set forth an objectively verifiable product claim but an opinion, and opinions or ideas cannot be held false or deceptive.

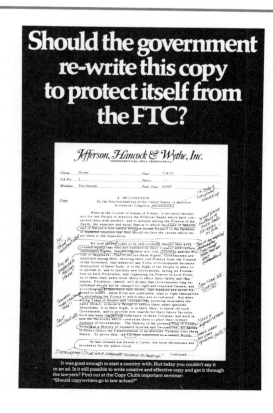

hearing before a trial examiner retained by the FTC. The findings of the examiner are considered by the full five-member commission, which rules on them by affirming or modifying the order or by dismissing the case. If the decision is adverse, the advertiser may appeal it again through the federal court system.

To prevent problems, the FTC is readily available to review advertising before it runs and to render "advance clearance" to the advertiser in an advisory opinion. The FTC also establishes advertising standards for the protection of consumers. To promote compliance with these standards, the FTC supplies advertisers, agencies, and the media with ongoing information about the regulations governing advertising in its *Industry Guides* and *Trade Regulation Rules*.

Federal Communications Commission

The seven-member Federal Communications Commission (FCC) was established as a result of the Communications Act of 1934. It has jurisdiction over the radio, television, telephone, and telegraph industries. Through its authority to license broadcasting stations and to remove a license or deny license renewal, the FCC has indirect control over broadcast advertising. This authority derives from the right of public domain over the airwaves and the mandate of broadcasting stations to operate in the public interest. The FCC stringently controls the airing of obscenity and profanity. It has restricted both advertising content and what products may be advertised on radio and television. Even before Congress banned cigarette advertising on television and radio (in the Public Health Cigarette Smoking Act of 1970), the FCC required stations to run antismoking commercials. The FCC has historically disapproved of the broadcast advertising of liquor, contraceptives, and lotteries. It has openly opposed commercials by medical doctors, clerics, and marriage and family counselors. Although this disapproval does not prevent stations from running such commercials, it exerts major influence. Stations that do not comply with FCC policies may risk losing their licenses.

The FCC has now dropped many of its rules and regulations for both radio and television stations, deciding marketplace forces can do an adequate job of keeping an eye on them. For example, the FCC no longer limits the amount of time that can be devoted to commercials. It has dropped minimum requirements for local programs and news/public affairs programs. And stations no longer have to maintain detailed program and commercial logs. However, stations still keep records of commercial broadcasts so that advertisers can be assured of value received for the advertising time they purchased.

Food and Drug Administration

A unit of the Department of Health and Human Services, the Food and Drug Administration (FDA) has authority over the advertising, labeling, packaging, and branding of packaged foods and therapeutic devices. It requires manufacturers to disclose all the ingredients on product labels, in all product advertising featured in stores, and in all accompanying or separately distributed product literature. The label must accurately state the weight or volume of the contents. Labels on therapeutic devices must give clear instructions for use. The FDA is

FIGURE 2–10

Adolph Coors Company filed a trademark infringement suit against Corr's. The latter agreed to change the name on its line of "natural sodas" to "Robert Corr" to lessen any possible confusion.

authorized to require warning and caution statements on packages of poisonous or otherwise hazardous products. It regulates "cents off" and other promotional statements on package labels. The FDA also has jurisdiction over the use of accurate words (such as *giant* or *family*) to describe package sizes. It regulates the size and placement of type to indicate the weight or volume of a package.

Patent and Trademark Office

A *trademark*, according to the Lanham Trade-Mark Act (1947), is "any word, name, symbol, or device or any combination thereof adopted and used by a manufacturer or merchant to identify his goods and distinguish them from those manufactured or sold by others." Ownership may be designated in advertising or on a label, package, or letterhead by the word "Registered," the symbol R, or the symbol TM. If a trademark is used illegally by another, the trademark owner can complain by notifying the violator in writing. If the illegal use continues, the trademark owner can ask the courts to order the violator to refrain from further infringement (Figure 2–10).

Ownership of a trademark can be lost for many reasons. Probably the most bitter and spectacular method of losing a trademark comes in court decisions that declare the trademark "generic," which means the term has come into common use and is now the dictionary name for the product. Advertising's very success may sometimes prove to be its failure. This is precisely what has happened to famous brand names like Thermos. They have become so thoroughly identified with a useful article or common function that the public uses them as the generic name. When a trademark ceases to indicate that the product derives from one particular source, exclusive legal rights to it are in jeopardy. Shredded wheat, yo yo, cube steak, and trampoline are examples of lost trademarks.

Owners of most trademarks take particular care to prevent their marks from becoming generic. They always see that the trademark is distinguished from surrounding words and always followed by the generic name of the product (Glad disposable trash bags, Kleenex tissues, Jell-O brand gelatin). They never refer to the trademark in the plural. It is not three Xeroxes but three Xerox copies (Figure 2–11).

It is useful to be familiar with trademark terminology, so we shall briefly discuss the important terms here.

Trademark and brand These are initials, words, or symbols such as IBM, or the globe for AT&T's products. They identify one particular product or line of products from a single source. Products may also have more than one trademark, such as Coke and Coca-Cola (Figure 2–12).

Trade name The name under which a company does business is its trade name. Two examples are Maxim (brand name) for General Foods (trade name) and Cadillac (brand name) for General Motors (trade name). In some instances, a company may use the same trade name and trademark, for example, Quaker Oats for the Quaker Oats Company.

"But Mr. Carruthers, you said you needed forty Xeroxes."

Mr. Carruthers used our name incorrectly. That's why he got 40 Xerox copiers, when what he really wanted was 40 copies made on his Xerox copier.

He didn't know that Xerox, as a trademark of Xerox Corporation, should be followed by the descriptive word for the particular product, such

as "Xerox duplicator" or "Xerox copier."

And should only be used as a noun when referring to the corporation itself.

If Mr. Carruthers had asked for 40 copies or 40 photocopies made on his Xerox copier, he would have gotten exactly what he wanted.

And if you use Xerox properly, you'll get exactly what you want, too.

P.S. You're welcome to make 40 copies or 40 photocopies of this ad. Preferably on your Xerox copier.

XEROX

FIGURE   2–11

Xerox advertises in order to protect its trade name and trademark.

House mark This is the name for a trademark used on all or most of the products of a particular company, as, for example, Nabisco, Vaseline, Del Monte, Farmer John, or Perdue.

Service mark When a service rather than a product is identified, the name or symbol is known as a service mark. For example, the Rock of Gibraltar identifies services rendered by The Prudential Life Insurance Company of America, while the initials "HFC" in a circle represent Household Finance Company.

Trade character Betty Crocker, the Green Giant, Aunt Jemima, the Marlboro man, Chiquita, and the Pillsbury dough boy are all famous examples of trade characters. They can be people, birds, animals, or other objects that may also be applied to the goods as a trademark. Trade characters are used because they can readily identify businesses and sources of products. They catch attention and sustain interest.

Certification mark These marks guarantee the origin, trade, or quality of the product. Teflon II, for example, certifies that cookware treated with Teflon nonstick coating meets Du Pont manufacturing standards. Cookware manufacturers therefore may use the mark in advertising if their products are treated with Teflon nonstick coating.

Collective mark A mark used to indicate membership in an organization is a collective mark. Members of the National Association of Electrical Contractors, for instance, may use the NECA symbol in their advertising.

Trademark laws also cover titles, catalogs, designations, slogans, designs, distinctive sounds, features, buildings, and personalities used in advertising.

Library of Congress

All copyrighted material, including advertising, is registered and protected by the Library of Congress. A copyright issued to an advertiser grants the exclusive right to print, publish, or reproduce the protected ad for a period of time equal to the life span of the copyright owner plus 50 additional years. An advertisement can be copyrighted only if it contains original copy or illustration. Slogans, short phrases, and familiar symbols and designs cannot be copyrighted. Although a copyright prevents a whole advertisement from being legally used by another, it does not prevent others from using the general concept or idea of the ad or from paraphrasing the copy and expressing it in another way.

The use of any original creative written, musical, illustrative, or other material by an outside source in an advertisement without the express written consent of its creator is an infringement of copyright that may constitute grounds for legal action. For this reason, advertisers and agencies obtain permission before they use creative material from any outside source.

Copyright is indicated in an advertisement by the word "Copyright," the abbreviation "Copr.," or the copyright symbol © near the name of the advertiser. An advertisement that has foreign or international copyright protection usually contains the year of copyright as well. These copyright marks are also used to denote protection in other forms of print advertising, including booklets, sales brochures, and catalogs.

See Figure 2–13 for a summary of federal regulators of advertising. The jurisdiction of these agencies is often overlapping, which makes the advertiser's task even more difficult.

■ Regulation by State Government

Much media advertising falls into the category of interstate commerce and is therefore regulated by federal agencies. Intrastate advertising, however, including local newspaper, radio, and television advertising, is under the jurisdiction of state laws and enforcement agencies. There is also a great deal of state legislation governing advertising, and it is often based on the "truth-in-advertising" model statute developed by *Printer's Ink*, the pioneer trade paper of the industry, which is no longer published. The statute holds that any maker of an advertisement that is found to contain "untrue, deceptive, or misleading" material shall be guilty of a misdemeanor. Today 46 states—with the exception of Arkansas, Delaware, Mississippi, and New Mexico—enforce laws patterned after this statute to control fraudulent and deceptive advertising.

FIGURE 2–12 Products' trademarks which have been in legal conflict

Trademark of successful product	Product	Name of losing product	Product
AWAKE	Frozen concentrate for imitation orange juice	ARISE	Liquid breakfast drink
BEER NUTS	Shelled and salted peanuts	BEER POTATO CHIPS	Potato chips
CORVETTE	Automobile	VETTE	Fiberglass repair panels for automobiles
KENTUCKY FRIED CHICKEN CORPORATION	Restaurants	OLD KENTUCKY HOME FRIED CHICKEN, INC.	Restaurants
OCEAN FREEZE	Frozen seafood	SEA FREEZE	Frozen seafood
Q-TIPS	Swabs made of sanitary absorbent cotton	QUICK TIPS	Manicure finishing spray
VANISH	Toilet bowl cleaner	BANISH	Room deodorant
WHOPPER and HOME OF THE WHOPPER	Burger-type sandwiches and drive-in restaurant services	WHOPPABURGER	Sandwiches

Regulation by Local Government

Many cities and counties, usually through consumer protection agencies, enforce laws regulating local advertising practices. These agencies function chiefly to protect local consumers against unfair and misleading practices by area merchants.

FIGURE   2–13   Federal regulators of advertising

Agency	Function	Agency	Function
Federal Trade Commission	Regulates all commerce between the states. Formed in 1914, the FTC is the leading federal regulatory agency for advertising practices and is the subject of the greatest criticism by the advertising profession.	Alcohol and Tobacco Tax Division	Has almost absolute authority over liquor advertising through its powers to suspend, revoke, or deny renewal of manufacturing and sales permits for distillers, vintners, and brewers found to be in violation of regulations.
Federal Communications Commission	Formed by the Communications Act of 1934, has jurisdiction over the radio, television, telephone, and telegraph industries. It maintains indirect control over advertising through its authority to license or revoke the license of all broadcast stations.	Office of Consumer Affairs	Is the chief consumer protection department in the federal government. Established in 1971, the OCA coordinates, maintains, and publicizes information on all federal activities in the field of consumer protection. Publications produced and circulated by the OCA include consumer education guidelines, monthly newsletters, and a consumer services column that is released to some 4,500 weekly newspapers.
Food and Drug Administration	Has authority over the advertising, labeling, packaging, and branding of all packaged goods and therapeutic devices. It requires full disclosure labels, regulates the use of descriptive words on packages, and has jurisdiction over the packaging of poisonous or otherwise hazardous products.	U.S. Postal Service	Has authority to halt mail delivery to any firm or person guilty of misusing the mails. The U.S. Postal Service maintains control over false and deceptive advertising, pornography, lottery offers, and guarantees which deceive or defraud.
Patent and Trademark Office	Regulates registration of patents and trademarks. It enforces the Trade-Mark Act of 1947.		
Library of Congress	Registers and protects all copyrighted material including advertisements, music, books, booklets, computer software, and other creative material.	Department of Agriculture	Closely monitors the distribution of misbranded or unregistered commercial poisons. The Department of Agriculture (USDA) works

Self-Regulation by Advertisers

Most large advertisers reflect a sense of social responsibility in their advertising. Falstaff Brewing Company, for example, specifically avoids implying that beer will give people "a lift." It also rejects any appeals to adolescents and children as well as any references to sex.

Agency	Function
	with the FTC to enforce regulations governing certain products. The USDA Grain Division has regulatory authority over false and deceptive advertising for seeds and grain products. The Grain Division of the U.S. Department of Agriculture is also empowered to initiate action against violators.
Civil Aeronautics Board	Regulates air traffic and advertising of all air carriers engaged in interstate commerce.
Securities and Exchange Commission	Was established in 1934 and has jurisdiction over all advertising of stocks, bonds, and other securities sold via interstate commerce. The SEC requires that public offerings of such issues contain full disclosure of all pertinent information on the company and the securities offered so that the prospective investor can make an informed buying decision. This disclosure must mention any negative elements that may affect the investment.
Department of Justice	Normally does not initiate legal action against persons or firms charged with violating the federal laws governing advertising. Instead, the Department of Justice enforces these laws

Agency	Function
	and represents the federal government in the prosecution of cases referred to it by other federal agencies.
Consumer Product Safety Commission	Was established in 1972 to develop and enforce standards for potentially hazardous consumer products. It derives its power from four acts: the Flammable Fabrics Act of 1954, the Federal Hazardous Substances Act of 1960, the Children Protection Act of 1966, and the Standard for the Flammability of Children's Sleepwear of 1972. It has jurisdiction over the placement of warning statements in advertisements and other promotional materials for products covered under these acts. Its authority extends to household products, toys, and hazardous substances that cause accidental poisoning. The Consumer Product Safety Commission actively investigates product advertising and labeling violations brought to its attention by consumers and consumer protection groups. Continued violations by product makers are grounds for prosecution and punitive action by the Attorney General.

FIGURE 2–14

The ad that changed history. Prior to the Bates ad, attorneys were not allowed to advertise. The case went all the way to the U.S. Supreme Court, which determined that state bar associations could not prohibit their members from advertising their services. Unfortunately, the moment the ban was lifted, we were treated to a plethora of attorney ads using some of the most deceptive advertising techniques known, including bait and switch. This caused great alarm among various professional advertising groups and prompted some to take action.

While efforts like these have improved the levels of advertising taste and integrity, they have not accomplished enough to satisfy the critics of advertising—notably some consumers and consumer advocate groups. These efforts also raise the following questions about consumer demands for self-regulation by advertisers:

1. Does self-regulation conflict with the free enterprise right of advertisers to conduct business as they see fit?
2. Does self-regulation impair free, open business competition?
3. Does the creation of consumer complaint departments encourage valid complaints or merely invite frivolous ones?
4. Does compliance with consumer demands result in excessive costs to advertisers and ultimately higher product costs?

Despite these considerations, self-regulation has increased in recent years. Today it is widely conducted by industry trade associations, professional organizations, advertising agencies, advertising associations and publications, media trade organizations and publications, business organizations, and the National Advertising Review Board (NARB). Together, these organizations include every segment of the advertising industry.

Self-Regulation by Industries and Professions

Many industries maintain their own advertising codes. These reflect an agreement by companies in the same industry to abide by certain advertising standards and practices. The codes establish a basis for complaints, whereby a member may ask the executive board of the association to review existing competitive conditions in terms of the advertising code to which all members have subscribed.

Some industry codes reflect a high degree of social conscience. The code of the national distilling industry prohibits liquor advertising on television and radio, outdoor advertising near a military or naval base, and advertising in any publication that bears a Sunday dateline. The Wine Institute code bars references to athletes, appeals to children, and inferences that wine is associated with religion.

Certain professions, such as legal, medical, and dental, also maintain advertising codes through their national, state, or local organizations. Since the 1977 U.S. Supreme Court decision declaring state bar association bans on member advertising to be in violation of the First Amendment right of free speech, attorneys are permitted to advertise their legal services, specialties, education and professional honors, office hours, fees, and credit arrangements (Figure 2–14). In some states dentists are also permitted to advertise. Recent actions by the Justice Department and the FTC may remove the bans on advertising by physicians, opticians, architects, and engineers. There has already been a relaxing of state laws that prohibit the advertising of eyeglasses and prescription drugs.

Codes like these are only as effective as the powers of enforcement vested in individual trade associations. Since enforcement may conflict with antitrust laws that prohibit interference with open competition, trade associations usually exert peer pressure on member companies that violate their codes rather than resorting to hearings or penalties.

Self-Regulation by Business

Several business-monitoring organizations provide effective controls over advertising practices, particularly at the local level. The largest of these organizations is the Better Business Bureau. Established in 1916, the Better Business Bureau (BBB) has national and local BBB offices funded by dues from over 100,000 member companies. It operates to protect consumers against fraudulent and deceptive advertising and sales practices. These bureaus, composed of advertisers, agency and media representatives, and laypeople, monitor advertising in their communities. They receive and investigate complaints from consumers and other advertisers. Violators are contacted and asked to revise their advertising. In many cases this is sufficient. The BBB also maintains files on violators, which are open to the public. Records of violators who do not comply are sent to appropriate government agencies for further action. The BBB often works with local law enforcement agencies to prosecute advertisers guilty of fraud and misrepresentation. Each year the BBB investigates thousands of advertisements for possible violations of truth and accuracy. All members of the BBB are pledged to uphold its stringent advertising standards.

The Council of Better Business Bureaus, Inc., is the parent organization of the Better Business Bureau and part of the National Advertising Review Council. One of its functions is helping new industries to develop standards for ethical and responsible advertising. It also provides ongoing information about advertising regulations and recent court and administrative rulings that affect advertising.

Self-Regulation by the Advertising Profession

Most advertising agencies monitor their own practices. In addition, professional advertising associations oversee the activities of their agency members to prevent any problems that may trigger government intervention. Advertising publications actively report issues and actions before the courts in an effort to educate agencies and advertisers about possible legal infractions.

Advertising agencies

Although information about a product or service is supplied to the agency by the advertiser, it is the agency's responsibility to research and verify all product claims and comparative product data before using them in advertising. The media may require such documentation before accepting the advertising. Substantiation also may be needed if government or consumer agencies challenge the claims. Agencies can be held legally liable for fraudulent or misleading advertising claims. For these reasons, most advertising agencies have legal counsel and regularly submit their advertisements for review. If any aspects of the advertising are challenged, the advertiser's attorneys are asked to again review the advertising and either confirm it is true or replace unverified material.

Advertising associations

The American Association of Advertising Agencies (AAAA) and two other national organizations—the Association of National Advertisers and the American Advertising Federation—are actively engaged in monitoring industrywide advertising practices.

The AAAA, an association of advertising agencies throughout the United States, controls agency practices by denying membership to any agency judged unethical. The AAAA *Standards of Practice* and *Creative Code* set forth advertising principles for member agencies.

The American Advertising Federation (AAF) is also a nationwide association of advertising people. The AAF helped to establish the Federal Trade Commission, and its early "vigilance" committees were the forerunners of the Better Business Bureaus. The AAF "Advertising Code of American Business" establishes standards for truthful and responsible advertising. Since most local advertising clubs belong to the AAF, it has been instrumental in influencing agencies and advertisers to abide by these principles.

The Association of National Advertisers (ANA) is composed of 400 major manufacturing and service companies that are clients of member agencies of the AAAA. These companies, which are pledged to uphold the ANA code of advertising ethics, work with the ANA through a joint Committee for Improvement of Advertising Content.

Advertising publications

Magazines and newspapers that serve the advertising industry maintain close watch over advertising practices. *Advertising Age*, the industry's leading trade publication, continually champions the cause of more ethical and responsible advertising.

The media

After an advertisement is approved by agency and advertiser, it is submitted to the media. Almost all media maintain some form of advertising review. They reserve the right to reject any material they regard as objectionable, even if it is not deceptive.

The strictest review is by the television networks. Advertisers are required to submit all commercials intended for a network or affiliated station to the broadcast standards department of that network. Commercial copy then goes simultaneously to each of the three networks for independent review.

National magazines monitor all advertising, particularly those by new advertisers and for new products. While newer publications that are eager to sell space may not be so vigilant, some established magazines, including *Time* and *Newsweek*, are highly scrupulous. *Good Housekeeping* tests every product before accepting advertising. If the tests do not substantiate the claims made, the ad is rejected. Products that are accepted, however, may feature the *Good Housekeeping* "Seal of Approval" on their labels and in advertising. If any such product is later found to be defective, *Good Housekeeping* promises to refund the money paid for it. A similar product seal and warranty are offered by *Parents Magazine*. *The New Yorker* will not accept discount retail store advertising or advertisements for feminine hygiene products or self-medication products. *Reader's Digest* will not accept tobacco advertising.

Newspapers also monitor and review advertising. Larger newspapers have clearance staffs that read every ad submitted. Most smaller newspapers rely on the advertising manager, sales personnel, or proofreaders to check ad copy. The advertising policies followed by most newspapers, set forth in *Newspaper Rates and Data* (Standard Rate and Data Service), include such restrictions as "No objectionable medical, personal, matrimonial, clairvoyant, or palmistry advertising accepted; no stock promotion or financial advertising, other than those securities of known value, will be accepted." Another rule prohibits the publication of any advertisement that simulates reading matter that cannot be readily recognized as advertising unless such an ad features the word "advertisement" or "advt."

Although some small newspapers have less stringent policies, large dailies like the *New York Times* and the *Chicago Tribune* are known for their strictness. Most newspapers closely monitor the comparative price claims made by their retail advertisers. A new-car dealer who advertises "greatest values anywhere" may be asked to change it to "compare our values."

National Advertising Review Council

In 1971 the National Advertising Review Council (NARC) was established by the Council of Better Business Bureaus, Inc., in conjunction with the American Association of Advertising Agencies, the American Advertising Federation, and the Association of National Advertisers. Its primary purpose is to promote and enforce standards of truth, accuracy, taste, morality, and social responsibility in advertising. Composed of members drawn from the leadership of these four organizations, NARC is regarded as the most comprehensive and effective regulatory mechanism in the advertising industry.

Under its direction, two regulatory divisions were established: the National Advertising Division (NAD), an investigative body, and the National Advertising Review Board (NARB), an appeals board for NAD decisions. The NAD monitors advertising industry practices. It reviews complaints received from consumers and consumer groups, brand competitors, Better Business Bureaus, NAD monitors, and others about objectionable advertisements. These complaints chiefly concern false or misleading advertising claims and ads that depart from taste, morality, or social responsibility (Figure 2–15). NAD does not reveal the identity of the challenger except with permission. When a complaint is found to be valid, the NAD contacts the advertiser's chief executive officer specifying the claims to be substantiated. The advertiser is also asked to furnish examples of all current national advertising containing similar claims in print, radio, or television. The advertiser is then asked to name its advertising agency, and a copy of the initial inquiry is sent to the agency's chief executive officer. No investigation is conducted if the claims in question are withdrawn prior to receipt of NAD's first inquiry or if they are the subject of litigation by a government agency. Once the investigation is concluded, and NAD is satisfied that the advertising claims are supported, it will close its file and advise the advertiser and the challenger. If NAD finds substantiation to be inadequate, it will request modification or discontinuance of the claims. Nearly half the national advertising cases reviewed by the NAD to date have resulted either in substantially revised advertising or in withdrawal of advertising by the advertiser.

If NAD and an advertiser reach an impasse in their discussions,

FIGURE   2–15

The NARB urges consumers to report advertisements they think are misleading, untruthful, or deceptive. They point out that the "NARB is self-regulation that works" since "not one advertiser has refused to modify or discontinue advertising found to be misleading."

either party has the right to review by a panel from the National Advertising Review Board. The NARB consists of a chairperson and 50 volunteer members: 30 national advertisers, 10 agency representatives, and 10 laypeople from the public sector. A five-member panel, composed of three advertisers, one agency representative, and one layperson, is then selected from this board to review the case. The

FIGURE   2–16   NARB panels: Complaints and decisions

Complaint

That Zenith Radio Corporation used misleading advertising in claiming in a television commercial that: "Every color TV Zenith makes is built right here in the United States by Americans like these." (The video showed Zenith employees at work.) At issue was the use of foreign-made components which investigation by NAD placed at as much as 14.5 percent of total components/parts, and approximately 9.5 percent of the value of a representative Zenith set. NAD, therefore, found the advertising misleading. Though the company cooperated fully throughout the investigation, it declined to change the advertising. NAD appealed to NARB. In the interim, Zenith reversed its earlier decision, and notified NAD that the commercial in question was being withdrawn from further use.

Decision

In light of the cooperative action by the advertiser, NAD asked the NARB panel to dismiss. The panel concurred and dismissed the matter.

That Volkswagen of America, Inc., used false and misleading advertising in selecting a single point from its warranty (i.e., a term of 24 months or 24,000 miles) and in comparing it with 12-month/12,000 miles terms in a selected list of 94 other cars. Complainant argued that the omission of other points in the warranties implied to the consumer that all were the same except for the terms compared. NAD had dismissed the complaint.

The panel's unanimous decision stated that while an advertiser has the privilege of selecting one or more points in his warranty to feature in advertising, if he does so he has the responsibility to point out that warranties differ in many respects, and that other features not cited may be of importance to the purchaser. Since this was not done in the subject advertising, the panel found it to be misleading and recommended that it be either modified or discontinued.

This action, initiated by NAD, deemed advertising by Ralston-Purina Company for "Chuck Wagon Dinner for Dogs" to be misleading in that it photographically depicted "tender juicy chunks" which appeared to be meat, but in actuality were made from soybeans. NAD referred the matter to NARB after a period of time in which it felt the advertiser had been given ample time to respond but had not. Subsequent to the referral, however, the advertiser did respond to NAD, stating that the advertising in question had been replaced with new copy removing the elements judged to be deceptive.

With assurances from the advertiser that the old advertising would no longer be used, and in the belief that the new advertising eliminated elements of possible misrepresentation, NAD requested that the matter be dismissed by the NARB. After a thorough review of the matter, the panel accepted the NAD recommendation and dismissed the complaint.

panel's decision is binding on NAD. If an NARB panel finds against an advertiser, and the advertiser refuses to modify or discontinue the advertising in accordance with the panel decision, NARB will refer the matter to an appropriate governmental authority and indicate the fact in its public record (Figure 2–16). In all its years of operation, no advertiser who participated in the complete process of an NAD investigation and NARB appeal has declined to abide by the panel decision.[3]

Both the NARB and the NAD issue monthly reports to help establish practicable standards for the advertising industry. The NARB also sponsors advisory panels to study such specialized topics as comparative advertising and women in advertising. The NAD is available to evaluate and render decisions about proposed advertising campaigns prior to their completion and placement in the media.

Regulation by Consumer Control

The greatest recent growth among the regulatory forces governing advertising has been that of consumer protection organizations. Starting in the 1960s, the consumer movement began to play an increasingly active role in fighting fraudulent and deceptive advertising. Consumers demanded not only that products perform as advertised but also that more product information be provided so that people can compare and make better buying decisions. The impact of the consumer movement and its growing pressure for more stringent advertising regulation soon gave rise to a new word: *consumerism*, or social action designed to dramatize the rights of the buying public. Since then, one fact has become clear to both advertisers and agencies: The American consumer has power.

The growing consumer movement has caused advertisers and agencies to pay more attention to product claims, especially those related to energy use (such as the estimated miles per gallon of a new auto) and the nutritional value of processed foods (such as sugar-coated breakfast cereals). Consumerism has fostered the growth of consumer advocate groups and regulatory agencies. It has also promoted more consumer research by advertisers, agencies, and the media in an effort to learn what consumers want—and how to provide it. Many advertisers agree that the creation of customer relations departments and investment in public goodwill ultimately will pay off in improved consumer relations and sales.

Consumer information networks

Several large organizations serve as mass communication networks for the exchange of consumer information. They enable consumers to express their views on advertising and marketing infractions. These organizations include the Consumer Federation of America (CFA), the National Council of Senior Citizens, and the National Consumer League. They have the following functions: (1) to serve as a central clearinghouse for the exchange and dissemination of information among its members; (2) to aid the development of state, regional, and local consumer organizations; and, (3) to work with and provide services to national, regional, county, and municipal consumer groups.

Consumer interests also are served by several private, nonprofit testing organizations like Consumers Union, Consumers' Research, and Underwriters Laboratories.

Consumer advocates

Consumer advocate groups focus on issues that involve advertising and advertisers. These groups act on complaints received from consumers as well as on those that grow out of their own research. Their normal procedures are to: (1) investigate the complaint; (2) if warranted, contact the advertiser and ask that the objectionable advertisement or practice be halted; (3) if the advertiser does not comply, release publicity or criticism about the offense to the media; (4) submit complaints with substantiating evidence to appropriate government agencies for further action; and (5) in some instances, file a lawsuit and seek to obtain from the courts a cease and desist order, or a fine or other penalty, against the violator.

Summary

As advertising has proliferated in the media, the criticism of advertising has also intensified. Detractors say that advertising debases our language, makes us too materialistic, and manipulates people unethically. Furthermore, they say, advertising is not only excessive but also offensive or in bad taste. It is frequently deceptive, and it perpetuates unrealistic stereotypes of people.

Defenders of advertising admit that advertising has been and sometimes still is misused. However, they point out that the abuse heaped on advertising is often unjustified and excessive. Moreover, the very critics who attack advertising, they say, use basic advertising techniques to sell their books and further their points of view.

One result of this criticism is the current large body of laws and regulations to restrict the use of advertising. Regulation comes in several forms: self-regulation by advertisers; regulation by the advertising profession and the media; regulation by local, state, and federal government agencies; self-regulation by industrial associations and the business community; and regulation by the consumer protection organizations.

The strictest advertising controls are those imposed by laws. Enforcement of these laws may come from the Federal Trade Commission (FTC), the Federal Communications Commission (FCC), the Food and Drug Administration (FDA), the Securities and Exchange Commission (SEC), and a host of other bureaucracies. The actions of the FTC have been criticized so much that Congress limited its jurisdiction in 1980. However, the growth of consumer advocacy groups in the last decade almost ensures continued pressure to further restrict what advertisers can say, show, and do.

Trademarks, trade names, house marks, service marks, trade characters, certification marks, and collective marks can be protected by the Patent and Trademark Office. Advertising can be protected by the Copyright Office of the Library of Congress.

The most effective body for self-regulation has been the National Advertising Review Council, which was formed by the Council of Better Business Bureaus, Inc., in conjunction with the American Association of Advertising Agencies, the American Advertising Federation, and the Association of National Advertisers. Through its investigative body, the National Advertising Division (NAD), complaints received from consumers, brand competitors, or local Better Business Bureaus can be reviewed and corrective measures suggested. Advertisers that refuse to comply are referred to the council's appeals body, the National Advertising Review Board (NARB), which may uphold, modify, or reverse the NAD's findings. It may also direct the advertiser to modify or withdraw the advertisement in question.

Questions for review and discussion

1. Is advertising's responsibility to lead or to reflect society? Explain.
2. What is the importance of the NARB to consumers and advertisers?
3. What is the relationship between the FTC and the advertising industry? Do you feel the FTC has overstepped its authority? Explain. Can you cite recent examples of FTC action against advertisers?
4. Why should advertisers be aware of the provisions of the Wheeler-Lea Act?
5. Do you believe advertising tends to create monopolies? How?
6. What roles do major organizations play in the self-regulation of advertising?
7. How does the FCC's power to license broadcast stations affect advertisers?
8. What effect, if any, does physician advertising have on the practice of medicine?
9. What is the importance of the trademark law?
10. Why have feminists been so upset about advertising? Is their displeasure reasonable?

3

THE ADVERTISING BUSINESS

F rank Perdue was being interviewed for an article in *Esquire* magazine. "I could say I planned all this," he says, "but I was just back there with my father and a couple of other guys working my ass off every day. I wasn't even sure for a long time that I even liked the chicken business. But my advantage is that I grew up having to know my business in every detail. I dug cesspools, made coops, and cleaned them out. I know I'm not very smart, at least from the point of view of pure IQ, and that gave me one prime ingredient of success—fear. I mean a man should have enough fear so that he's always second-guessing himself."

He pulls out a wrinkled clipping from his wallet. The words are Alexander Hamilton's: "Men give me credit for some genius. All the genius I have lies in this. When I have a subject in hand, I study it profoundly. Day and night it is before me. I explore it in all its bearings. My mind becomes pervaded with it. Then the effort I have made is what people are pleased to call the fruit of genius. It is the fruit of labor and thought."

Chickens are not a very glamorous business. And Frank Perdue didn't know anything about advertising. But when Madison Avenue learned that this chicken farmer from the Delmarva Peninsula (located between the Chesapeake Bay on the west and the Atlantic Ocean on the east) was ready to take a big plunge into advertising, everybody scrambled for the account. So many people were fawning all over Perdue that it made him uncomfortable. He pulled back for awhile.

To make sure that nobody put him at that disadvantage again, Perdue immersed himself in advertising day and night. He devoured great volumes on the subject, and he can still drop quotes by people like David Ogilvy and Rosser Reeves the way other people cite the Bible or Shakespeare. He haunted an advertising institute, studying all the pamphlets and textbooks. He called up advertising journalists and radio and TV station managers in New York, systematically trying to pick brains. Almost nobody knew him, but many helped simply because they were impressed by his inventive industry.

By the time he set himself up to be courted again by Madison Avenue, Perdue was an expert. Altogether, he interviewed almost 50 agencies. Eventually, he narrowed his list down to a championship flight of nine. Then he really went on the offensive, grilling, double-checking, interviewing. He called one very prominent agency and asked their representatives to have lunch with him in the Oak Room of the Plaza Hotel. The whole top executive force trooped over to the Plaza, licking their chops, convinced Perdue was going to tell them that he had selected their agency for his chickens. Instead, as soon as they settled at the table, Perdue informed them that they hadn't even made his final list, but he would appreciate it if they would rank the nine agencies that were still left in the running. Stunned and flabbergasted, the agency boys dived into another round of martinis and patiently did as he requested.

The losers were really the lucky ones. When Perdue called up Ed McCabe, the copy chief at Scali, McCabe, Sloves, for about the 800th time in a week, McCabe finally blew his cork. "You know, Frank," he said, "I'm not even sure that we want your account anymore because you're such a pain in the ass." McCabe recalls, "You know all he said to that? He just said, 'yeah, I know I'm a pain in the ass, and now that we've got that settled, here's what I want to ask you this time.'"

Sometime later Perdue picked McCabe's agency. One of the first commercials they shot, in a campaign built around Perdue himself (another idea he never cottoned to), won an award for excellence. Ed McCabe won more honors for his work on the Perdue campaign than any other copywriter in the nation that year. Frank Perdue became the biggest chicken man in the nation's biggest city, and a celebrity to boot (Figure 3–1).

The rest is history. Perdue's sales doubled every two years. By 1984 his company was selling over 260 million birds a year and realizing revenues of over $500 million. That makes Perdue Farms one of the top 50 private companies in the United States. But after appearing in over 70 commercials and spending untold millions of dollars to promote his birds, Frank Perdue may be as much in the advertising business as in the chicken business.

"I could write a book about advertising," he says matter of factly.[1]

The advertising business is comprised of three primary groups of organizations. There are the companies that advertise—the *advertisers*—which, like Perdue Farms, advertise themselves and their products or services. There are the *advertising agencies,* which plan, create, and prepare advertising campaigns and materials for the advertisers. And there are the *media*, which sell time and space to carry the advertiser's message to the target audience. In addition, there is another group known as the *suppliers* who assist both advertisers and agencies in preparing advertising materials.

By understanding who these various groups of companies are and what they do, we can grasp the breadth and complexity of the advertising business and also the career opportunities that exist in the business.

FIGURE   3–1

The Perdue campaign has been revolutionary in the business since it demonstrated that fresh meat could be branded and sold like packaged products. A large supermarket chain put Perdue side by side against a house brand selling for six cents a pound less. Incredibly, 40 percent of the customers chose Perdue at the premium price.

COMPANIES THAT ADVERTISE

Virtually every successful business uses advertising, and the majority of people who work in advertising are employed by those companies. The businesses range in size from small retail shops to multinational firms, or from small industrial concerns to large service organizations. All these companies have an advertising department of some sort, even if it is just one person like Frank Perdue who shares his company's advertising responsibility with many other job functions.

Naturally the importance of the advertising person in the company depends on several factors: the size of the company, the type of industry in which the company operates, the size of the advertising program, the role of advertising in the company's marketing mix, and top management's degree of involvement in the advertising function.

■ Company People Involved in Advertising

Most of us think of advertising people as the copywriters, art directors, or account executives—the people who work for advertising agencies. We will discuss them later in this chapter. But, in reality, people who work for the advertisers themselves are, like Frank Perdue, very much a part of the advertising business.

Company presidents and other top executives, who are usually very interested in how their advertising represents the company, are often directly involved in advertising decisions. Sales and marketing personnel, of course, have a direct relationship to advertising. They frequently provide input to the creative process, assist in deciding which advertising agency to use, and help evaluate proposed advertising programs.

Large companies may have a separate advertising department, employing from one to several hundred people and headed by an advertising manager or by a marketing director (Figure 3–2).

FIGURE 3–2

Because of their role as coordinators among clients, creatives, media, and suppliers, agency people are forever in meetings. Call a vice president at your favorite advertising agency in New York. Chances are that executive is in the meeting pictured above.

Product people like engineers and designers are often asked to make recommendations about product features or to help advertising by providing information about competitive products. Similarly, administrative people in accounting or purchasing are frequently asked to consider the impact of advertising programs on the company's financial status. They may help evaluate a campaign in progress or determine appropriate budgets for the next campaign.

Even clerical people can get involved in the advertising process by virtue of their position within the company. It is not unusual to see a secretary in a small firm promoted to administrative assistant and eventually to manager of the company's advertising activities.

Just about everybody who works for a company that advertises feels that the organization's advertising represents him or her in some way and therefore has some feeling about it. As a result, the more we can learn about advertising, how it works, and why it is prepared the way it is, the more help we can offer to the companies that employ us.

COMPANY ADVERTISING DEPARTMENTS

The ways advertising departments function are as varied as the companies that operate them. Many companies perform all their advertising activities themselves, whereas others hire outside advertising agencies or suppliers to help them. Regardless of the way responsibilities are divided, there are certain things all advertisers must do.

■ Functions Common to All Advertisers

Every advertiser, large or small, must have an understanding of and some expertise in communications to perform the basic functions necessary to a successful advertising program. These functions include administration, planning, budgeting, and coordination with other company departments and with outside advertising services. We will discuss each function briefly.

Administration

The advertiser must organize and staff the advertising department, supervise and control the department's activities, and select the advertising agencies to be used. These are normal administrative functions. An advertising manager (or committee in some companies) is also responsible for recommending specific advertising programs based on the company's marketing plans and budgets. It is imperative, therefore, that the advertising manager have a thorough understanding of all the major factors influencing the company's marketing activities. Advertising managers should establish an efficient procedure for handling inquiries, analyzing competitive advertising, and evaluating their own ads.

Planning

It is only occasionally necessary to draw up formal advertising plans for the approval of management, but the planning process is ongoing. Planning is a continuing process of defining goals and objectives, outlining advertising strategies, scheduling advertisements, and evaluating advertising results. The way marketing and advertising plans are developed will be discussed in greater detail in Chapter 7.

Budgeting

The advertising budget is usually determined annually or semiannually. The advertising manager's task is to formulate the budget and sell it to top management. But top management always has the last word on how much will actually be allocated to advertising functions. It is the advertising department's responsibility to see that the budget is followed and not squandered before all the advertising tasks are performed (Figure 3–3).

Coordination with other departments

The activities of business are usually divided into three categories: production, finance, and marketing. Advertising, like sales, is a marketing activity. Thus, the advertising manager must coordinate the department's activities with other marketing functions. The advertising department must also coordinate its work with the various departments involved in production and finance.

For example, both the sales and advertising departments sometimes find out and communicate to the production departments what product and packaging features may improve customer satisfaction.

The accounting department should be consulted for records on overhead, ad production, and media costs. Controlling costs is a joint responsibility of both these departments. Similarly, the legal department can help protect the company from trademark and copyright infringement and also keep it from inadvertently violating truth-in-advertising laws.

FIGURE   3–3

FRANK PERDUE: Hot dogs, only 25.

KID: Only 25 for a hot dog? How good could it be?

SFX: *Laughter*

PERDUE: I'm making it easy for people to try Perdue Chicken

Franks.

KID: (Makes a face) Chicken franks? Free would be a lot easier.

PERDUE: Perdue Chicken Franks cost less and have 25 percent less fat than regular hot dogs.

KID: All right, I'll bite.

PERDUE: So?

KID: Tastes as good as a real hot dog.

PERDUE: This kid's got good taste *and* good looks.

ANNCR V.O.: Try Frank's franks. They're good in every way.

Coordination with outside advertising services

The advertising department is the liaison between the firm and any outside advertising services it employs. These may include advertising agencies, the media, or other advertising suppliers. It has the responsibility of screening and analyzing the various services available, making recommendations to management, and frequently deciding which outside services to use. The advertising manager is then responsible for supervising and evaluating the work performed. (See the Checklist for agency review.)

Checklist for agency review

	Unacceptable	Marginal		Satisfactory		Excellent
	1	2	3	4	5	6
Art						
Overall quality of work	☐	☐	☐	☐	☐	☐
Well thought out to meet the creative strategy	☐	☐	☐	☐	☐	☐
More effective than competitive work	☐	☐	☐	☐	☐	☐
Production						
Faithful to creative concept and creative execution	☐	☐	☐	☐	☐	☐
Prepared on time, within budget	☐	☐	☐	☐	☐	☐
Control of outside services	☐	☐	☐	☐	☐	☐
Media						
Soundness of media research	☐	☐	☐	☐	☐	☐
Effective and efficient media strategy and alternatives	☐	☐	☐	☐	☐	☐
Achieve objectives within budget	☐	☐	☐	☐	☐	☐
Negotiates and executes program smoothly	☐	☐	☐	☐	☐	☐
Periodic review of plan and budget	☐	☐	☐	☐	☐	☐

Company reviewer_____

Title_____

Agency representative_____

Title_____

Period under review from_____ to _____

Division, department or product, if applicable_____

_____

Functions Performed by Some Advertisers

A small retail television or appliance store might have one person as its advertising department. That person would be responsible for performing the various administrative, planning, budgeting, and coordinating functions. But what else might be done? In most cases the person would also lay out newspaper ads, write much of the advertising copy, and select the media to be used. However, unless that person were also a commercial artist or graphic designer, it is unlikely that he or she would actually create the physical advertisements.

On the other hand, a large retail chain might have a complete advertising department staffed and equipped to provide a wide range of advertising services in-house. These activities generally fall into the categories of advertising production, media placement, and marketing support services.

Advertising production

If a firm does not use an advertising agency, the advertising department may be responsible for creating and producing all advertising materials. The department then has its own staff of artists, copywriters, and production specialists to produce the work (Figure 3–4).

Media placement

Advertising departments often perform the media function. They have to analyze and evaluate available media according to cost, services to advertisers, advertiser acceptability, circulation or reach, and editorial content. The department might also have to develop media schedules, purchase space and airtime, and verify affidavits of performance.

FIGURE 3–4

(A "fashion show" announcer and runway music effects an haute couture image in this in-house ad for Revlon. Open on models dressing in various elegant outfits. Music under).

1st VO: For long shirts/Short skirts/Satin PJ's/We've got your color/For wide cuffs/Straight legs/ New felt hat/We've got your color/For bare backs/Jet jewels and basic black/We've got your color.

2nd VO: Two hundred and sixty-nine gleaming Revlon shades for your lips. One hundred and fifty-six professional shades for your fingertips.

1st VO: We've got the Revlon color for you.

WOMAN: For me?

(The words "Revlon" and "Color" are comprised of tubes of lipstick and bottles of nail enamel.)

Other marketing support services

Often an advertising agency is retained to prepare product and corporate advertisements, while the company's advertising department performs other marketing support services such as the production of printed materials for distribution to managers, salespeople, dealers, and distributors.

Some advertisers produce their own product photography, technical films, trade show exhibits, and direct-mail campaigns. And there are many other functions performed by advertisers. The degree of responsibility depends on the company.

HOW LARGE ADVERTISERS WORK

Just as the size and the function of the advertising department depend on a variety of factors, so does the way in which the department is organized. No two firms, product lines, or markets are exactly alike. Therefore the method of organization depends on the unique circumstances of each company. The two basic structures used by companies are the centralized and the decentralized organization.

■ Centralized Organization

What do Lionel Trains, Wheaties, Betty Crocker, Parker Games, and Foot Joy golf shoes have in common? For one thing, they are a few of the many products that have been owned and marketed by General Mills, Inc., of Minneapolis, Minnesota. One of the 25 largest national advertisers, General Mills operates a vast advertising and marketing services department with 330 employees and a $269 million advertising budget.

Located at corporate headquarters in Minneapolis, Marketing Services (as the department is called) is really many departments within a department. As a centralized advertising department, it is responsible for administering, planning, budgeting, and coordinating the promotion of more than 50 different brands. In the process it supervises 26 outside advertising agencies and operates its own in-house agency for new or smaller brands.

Organized around functional specialties (e.g., market research, media, graphics, copy advisory), Marketing Services consults with General Mills brand managers and consolidates many of their expenditures for maximum efficiency. The Media Department, for example, is involved daily in all media plans and dollar allocations with the various marketing divisions. The Production and Art Services Department handles the graphic requirements of the in-house agency as well as package design for all brands. And Betty Crocker Kitchens provides promotional services for the various Betty Crocker marketing programs.

The result is a highly effective series of mostly unrelated advertising programs for a wide variety of products and brands, all directed from one central spot. This organization has the disadvantage of making it more difficult to provide a general overview of marketing strategies and execution. At the same time, however, it gives General Mills great efficiency in its advertising programs and provides appreciable savings.

The most common type of advertising department is the centralized organization like the one at General Mills. In smaller companies the advertising manager may report directly to the president. In larger firms the advertising manager usually reports to a marketing vice president. (See Ad Lab 3–A.)

AD LAB 3–A   Career opportunities in company advertising departments

Employment of advertising personnel is expected to increase faster than the average for all occupations through the 1980s. The growing number of consumer and industrial goods and increasing competition in many product and service markets will cause advertising expenditures to rise, thereby creating a need for more advertising employees. Because of the sheer number of advertising departments, the opportunities here are greater than with advertising agencies.

Company advertising departments need managerial personnel, but some need creative, media, and research people, too. Listed on the chart below are the titles of jobs commonly found in companies, the educational preparation required, the occupational experience helpful for gaining entry into the position, and salary information. The salaries vary considerably depending on the applicant's educational background and experience, the size of the company, and its geographic location.

Job title	Educational requirements	Occupational or related experience	Extracurricular activities	Salary
Public relations specialist	College degree with emphasis on liberal arts courses. English, journalism, and marketing courses helpful.	Journalism jobs even with small newspapers or specialized magazines. Selling, marketing, and advertising experience helpful. Military experience as a public information officer or writing experience with military publication or broadcasting.	Free-lance writing. Community organization work, election and fund campaigning. Public speaking.	$30,000 +
Copywriter for retail advertising department	B.A. preferred with courses in advertising, English, sociology, psychology, and languages.	Retail store sales or advertising. Newspaper, magazine, or broadcast writing.	Advertising or marketing clubs. Writing for school and community publications.	$18,000 (entry level)

There are several advantages to a centralized advertising department. Communication flows more easily within the organization. The need for a large staff of advertising specialists is reduced. Lower level personnel do not need to be exceptional because the firm's top management can take part in advertising decision making. And, unlike decentralized organizations, complete continuity can be built into the communications programs—at a substantial cost savings.

Other opportunities

Other positions offering career opportunities are: product managers, market researchers, production specialists, house organ editors/writers, audiovisual managers, marketing assistants, marketing directors, technical writers, technical illustrators, and sales promotion managers.

Laboratory Application

Select one of the "other opportunities" listed or choose an occupation not included in this box. Discuss what educational preparation, occupational or related experience, and extracurricular activities might assist you in obtaining such a job.

Job title	Educational requirements	Occupational or related experience	Extracurricular activities	Salary
Advertising manager	College degree with marketing Some positions require M.B.A.	Advertising and/or marketing department of a manufacturer or large retailer.	Participation in advertising and marketing clubs. Membership in off-campus organizations in contact with business community helpful	$30,000+
Artist for retail advertising department	B.A. desirable. Commercial art courses.	School newspaper or magazine experience doing layout illustration, or printing production.	Participation in community projects doing posters, brochures, direct mail, and advertising.	$18,000 (entry level)

Most centralized organizations are structured in one of five ways:

1. By product.
2. By subfunction of advertising (sales promotion, print production, TV/radio buying, outdoor advertising, etc.).
3. By end user (i.e., consumer products, industrial products).
4. By media.
5. By geography (i.e., western advertising, eastern advertising).

There are also numerous other ways that large advertisers with centralized departments can work, depending on the character of the management, the firm's marketing needs, and the nature of the company's customers and products.

■ Decentralized Organization

As companies become larger, take on new brands or products, acquire subsidiaries, and establish divisions in several parts of the country, a centralized advertising department becomes highly impractical. A company then begins to decentralize its advertising and establish departments assigned to the various divisions, subsidiaries, products, countries, regions, brands, or other categories that most suit the firm's needs. The final authority for each division's advertising, then, rests with the general manager of the particular division.

Commonly referred to as the nation's number one marketing practitioner, Procter & Gamble in Cincinnati, Ohio, is a $6 billion company that manufactures and sells over 70 different consumer products. These include many brands that are the leaders in their fields: Tide, Ivory soap, Crest toothpaste, Pampers diapers, Duncan Hines cake mixes, Crisco shortening, and Charmin paper products, just to mention a few (Figure 3–5).

For new recruits fresh out of college, P&G's brand manager development program is the legendary Marine Corps of marketing. Procter & Gamble has six consumer product divisions, five industrial product divisions, and four international divisions. Each division is set up almost like a separate company, and each has its own research and development department, manufacturing plant, advertising department, sales force, and finance and accounting staff. Likewise, every brand within each division has a brand manager, two assistant brand managers, and one or two staff assistants.

Each brand manager of P&G has his or her own advertising agency, which creates and places the brand's media advertising. The manager has the help of the division's advertising department for coordinating sales promotion and merchandising programs, and the support of the corporate advertising department's media and research supervisors who give statistical information and guidance.

Apprentice brand managers live with and learn the statistics of their brand's performance against competitors. They are assigned to work on store displays. They develop sales projections for their brand, help plan advertising budgets, and coordinate with other sections of the division's advertising department: media, copy, art and packaging, sampling and couponing, and legal. They learn how market research helps determine the packages, scents, sizes, and colors people want; how product research improves the brand in response

Figure 3–5

This example of Procter & Gamble advertising is a classic that has won the approval of the professional advertising community.

to competition; and how the division's sales force tries to muscle more shelf space for the brand in the supermarket.

When advertising is decentralized in large multidivision companies, it more easily conforms to the specific problems and needs of the division. Flexibility is increased, allowing quicker and easier adjustments in campaigns and media schedules. New approaches and creative ideas are introduced more easily. And the results of each division's advertising may be measured independently of the others (Figure 3–6).

There are certain drawbacks to decentralized advertising departments. Individual department heads sometimes tend to be more concerned with their budgets, problems, and promotions than with determining what will benefit the firm as a whole. The potential power of repetitive advertising is often diminished because there is no uniformity in the advertising among divisions. Rivalry between brand managers may become fierce and may further deteriorate into secrecy and jealousy. It is virtually impossible to standardize styles, themes, or approaches. After one multidivision company decentralized, it had difficulty just getting the product brand managers to use the same logo in their ads.

Of course there are advantages to both centralized and decentralized advertising departments. What works successfully in one market, though, may not work in the next. There are no constants in determining which form or organization is best. And no organization is pure. They are all different and individually designed to fit the needs of the particular company. (See the Checklist of ways to be a better client.)

In-House Agencies

Some companies, in an effort to save money and centralize all their advertising activities, have fired their advertising agencies and set up

FIGURE 3–6

KID: Mmmmm

SONG: *Chewy, gooey, chewy, gooey We love chewy gooey cookies made with homemade tastin' Duncan Hines Cookie Mix.*

ANNCR: If you love fresh, hot-out-of-the-oven homemade cookies, you're gonna love chewy gooey cookies made with Duncan Hines Cookie Mix.
Rich, chocolatey cookies that bake up chewy gooey homemade good.

SONG: *Oooh we love to mix 'em. Love to bake 'em. Love to eat 'em. Duncan Hines is chewy, gooey, homemade good!*

their own in-house advertising agencies wholly owned by the company. The "full-service house agency" is set up and staffed to do all the work of an independent full-service agency. Being fully self-contained, it is capable of developing and accomplishing every type of publicity, sales promotion, and advertising required by the typical manufacturing company.

The in-house advertising agency is basically a total-capability advertising department. All aspects of advertising creativity, production, and media placement are performed in-house. Operating as the company's advertising agency, it also retains any media commissions it earns.

There are several reasons advertisers set up their own agencies. Usually the most important is the hope of realizing savings by cutting overhead expenses and saving the 15 percent commission on space advertising that would normally be given to an advertising agency. With a house agency the company is not charged the standard print or art production markup, which ranges from 17.65 to 25 percent

---

Checklist for ways to be a better client

□ Look for the big idea. Concentrate first on positioning and brand personality. Too few products have either. Do not allow a *single* advertisement—no matter how brilliant—to change your positioning or your brand personality.

□ Learn the fine art of conducting a creative meeting. Deal with the important issues first. Strategy. Consumer benefit. Reason why. State clearly whether you think the advertisement succeeds in these areas. And if not, why not.

□ Cultivate honesty. Tell your agency the truth. Make sure your advertising tells the truth, and *implies* the truth as well. And never let creative people get away with excuses that honesty is "dull."

□ Be enthusiastic. When you like the advertising, let the creative people know you like it. Applause is their staff of life. After a really good presentation, send the copywriter a note. You may be amazed at the results.

□ Be frank when you *don't like the advertising.* Copywriters won't hate you for turning down an idea if you give them a *reason.* They may even agree with you.

□ Be human. Try to react like a person, not a corporation. Be human enough to laugh at a funny advertisement, even if it is off-strategy.

□ Be willing to admit you aren't sure. Don't let your agency press you by asking for the order *immediately* after a new copy presentation. You may need time to absorb what they've been thinking about for a long while.

□ Insist on creative discipline. Professionals don't bridle at discipline. A strategy helps creative people zero in on a target. But remember that rules are only a *starting* point.

□ Keep the creative people involved in your business. Successful copywriters want to know the latest market shares just as much as you do. Tell them what's happening, good *and* bad. Sales figures, consumer letters, a crazy idea from your research chemist—all can help.

□ Don't insulate your top people from the creative people. Agency creative people want to receive objectives directly—not filtered through layers. While most projects need not involve your top management, a valuable perspective can be provided by those not tied up in the day-to-day work. Good work is done in an atmosphere of involvement, not insulation.

when such items are purchased through an outside agency. Advertisers likewise feel they can receive more attention from their agency if the company is its only client.

In-house agencies can usually respond better to pressure deadlines because they can focus their full resources on the project. Although outside agencies may be able to produce just as quickly, they often have to hire free-lance help, thereby incurring potentially enormous overtime charges. Likewise, house agencies tend to have a greater depth of understanding of the company's products and markets. Also, services rendered to departments outside the normal advertising functions may be easily charged to those departments. This is particularly important for retailers. It enables the other departments to benefit from the talents of the in-house agency, and yet the true cost of the agency can be established. Finally, many companies feel they have better management control of and involvement in the advertising when it is done in-house. (See Figure 3–7.)

Despite these advantages, many full-service house agencies do not

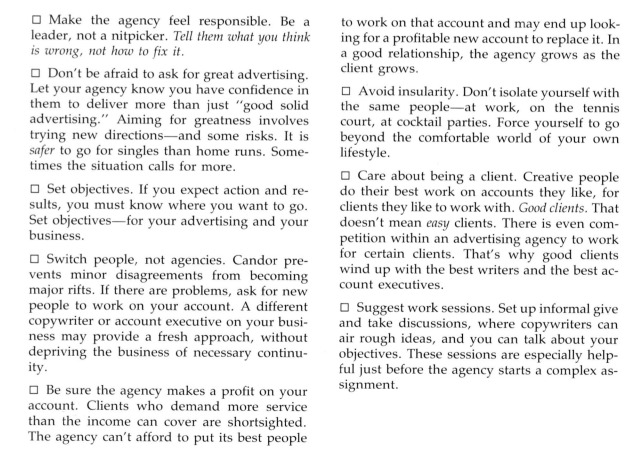

□ Make the agency feel responsible. Be a leader, not a nitpicker. *Tell them what you think is wrong, not how to fix it.*

□ Don't be afraid to ask for great advertising. Let your agency know you have confidence in them to deliver more than just "good solid advertising." Aiming for greatness involves trying new directions—and some risks. It is *safer* to go for singles than home runs. Sometimes the situation calls for more.

□ Set objectives. If you expect action and results, you must know where you want to go. Set objectives—for your advertising and your business.

□ Switch people, not agencies. Candor prevents minor disagreements from becoming major rifts. If there are problems, ask for new people to work on your account. A different copywriter or account executive on your business may provide a fresh approach, without depriving the business of necessary continuity.

□ Be sure the agency makes a profit on your account. Clients who demand more service than the income can cover are shortsighted. The agency can't afford to put its best people

to work on that account and may end up looking for a profitable new account to replace it. In a good relationship, the agency grows as the client grows.

□ Avoid insularity. Don't isolate yourself with the same people—at work, on the tennis court, at cocktail parties. Force yourself to go beyond the comfortable world of your own lifestyle.

□ Care about being a client. Creative people do their best work on accounts they like, for clients they like to work with. *Good clients.* That doesn't mean *easy* clients. There is even competition within an advertising agency to work for certain clients. That's why good clients wind up with the best writers and the best account executives.

□ Suggest work sessions. Set up informal give and take discussions, where copywriters can air rough ideas, and you can talk about your objectives. These sessions are especially helpful just before the agency starts a complex assignment.

FIGURE 3–7

A substantial amount of award-winning advertising has been created by the University of Utah's in-house graphic design group. This course catalog was prepared for the Division of Continuing Education.

CLASS EDITION

UNIVERSITY OF UTAH · DIVISION OF CONTINUING EDUCATION · PREVIEW OF FALL CLASSES 1982

succeed. In attempting to save as much of the independent agency's commission as possible, some companies sacrifice more than they anticipate. The benefit of the independent agency's objectivity is often lost along with much of its talent. Large, independent agencies provide experience, versatility, and a diversity of talent usually not available in in-house agencies. In-house agencies usually find it extremely difficult to attract the best creative talent. Part of the reason for this might be because of the slower wage-raise policy in some corporations. But, in addition, some creative people fear getting trapped in what they think might be a "stagnant" environment without the incentive and vitality of the stiff competition in the agency world. In addition, advertising production may suffer by becoming excessively company oriented rather than consumer oriented. By overly reflecting company policies and views, it can become too self-serving.

For years advertisers and agencies have squabbled over the pros and cons of in-house advertising agencies. Independent agencies consider in-house agencies interlopers and harbor a degree of bitterness toward the media that allow them the commission. It's not likely that the argument will be settled in the near future.

ADVERTISING
AGENCIES

Why would a shrewd businessman like Frank Perdue, who spends over $2 million a year advertising his chickens, want to hire an advertising agency? Couldn't he afford to hire his own advertising people and save money by doing his own advertising in-house? And why would he go all the way up to New York to find an agency? And how did Scali, McCabe, Sloves get a $2 million advertising account? Do all the agency's accounts have to be that big for an agency to make money? How do smaller agencies make money?

These and many other questions are logical ones for the beginning student of advertising. A discussion of the agency side of the adver-

THIS AD COULD SAVE YOUR LIFE.

Any ad that convinces people to drink less, to stop taking drugs, to follow life-saving medication can save a life. This ad offers organizations concerned with these causes the experience and excellence of our creativity. With it we will make advertising that helps convince people to live their lives more carefully.

If you're part of an organization that is interested in finding an advertising agency to help a good cause, save a life and give us a call.

Harris Carstens Amaral

444 Chesterfield Center, Chesterfield, Mo 63017 · 314–306-0206

FIGURE 3–8

In a self-promotion ad, this Missouri advertising agency offers to assist nonprofit organizations in their social causes. Many agencies have contributed substantial time, money, and manpower to advertising in the public interest.

tising business can shed some light on these issues and give a clearer understanding of the important role agencies play. We will first discuss what an advertising agency is and why so many advertisers use one.

The Role of the Advertising Agency

An *advertising agency* is an independent organization of creative people and businesspeople who specialize in the development and preparation of advertising plans, advertisements, and other promotional tools. The agency also arranges or contracts for the purchase of advertising space and time in the various media. It does all this on behalf of different sellers, who are referred to as its *clients*, in an effort to find customers for their goods and services.[2]

This definition gives us some good clues as to why so many advertisers hire advertising agencies. For one thing, agencies are *independent*, not owned by the advertiser, the media, or the suppliers. This independence allows them to bring an outside, objective viewpoint to the advertiser's business. And that is valuable because of the agency's depth of experience in working on a variety of marketing problems for their various clients. Independence also enables them to serve their clients' needs better when dealing with the media because their allegiance is to the client rather than to any particular medium.

The agency employs a combination of *creative people* and *businesspeople* who are specialists in applying the complex art and science of advertising to business problems. They include writers, artists, market and media analysts, researchers, and specialists of all sorts who apply their skills and talents to help make their clients successful. They have day-to-day contact with outside specialists and suppliers who illustrate advertisements, take photographs, set type, retouch art, film commercials, and record sound—all the steps required to produce quality work. They are able to stay abreast of the latest advances in technology, the most recent changes in prices, and the most current production problems (Figure 3–8).

By arranging and contracting for the purchase of broadcast time and magazine or newspaper space, the agency provides yet another service to the client. For one thing it saves the client money. Most media allow the agency to keep 15 percent of the gross amount of money placed in their medium. This *agency commission* reduces the amount of money the advertiser would otherwise have to pay the agency for its services. For its commission, the agency is expected to maintain an expertise in the various media available to the advertiser. This is no small task.

Finally, agencies work for a variety of different sellers to find customers for their goods and services. Agencies work for their clients, not for the media and/or the suppliers. Their moral, ethical, financial, and sometimes even legal obligation is to their clients—to find them the best prices, give them the best quality work, and help them grow and prosper. For much the same reason that a well-run business seeks professional help from an attorney, accountant, banker, or management specialist, advertisers use agencies because they are usually equipped to create more effective advertising—and select

AD LAB 3–B   How big is the agency business?

Although New York, Los Angeles, and Chicago are the three leading advertising centers in the United States, few cities with at least 100,000 people are without an advertising agency. Indeed, many small cities and towns support one or more agencies. Of 9,995 agencies, however, only 24 or 1 percent, have gross incomes of $5 million or more. These agencies represent approximately $34 billion in domestic billing—that is, the amount of client money the agency spends on media and equivalent activities. Interestingly, the top 10 agencies (which account for approximately one tenth of 1 percent of all agencies) handle 27 percent of the total volume of business.

An estimated 105,319 people are employed by United States–based advertising agencies today. Most agencies, however, have a low "body count" compared with that of other professions. When an agency staff is well balanced in skills and versatility, only five or six people can easily handle $1 million in annual billing. In agencies that bill $20 million or more per year, this ratio is usually even lower.

Basic information about advertising agencies in the United States can be found in the *Standard Directory of Advertising Agencies*. Known as the "Red Book" because of its cover color, this guide to the industry lists the names and addresses of most of the nation's agencies by state. It names the associations to which they belong, if any, and the media associations that recognize them for credit purposes. It also lists each agency's annual billings by media classification, the names and titles of its executives, and the names of its current accounts.

A related volume, the *Standard Directory of Advertisers*, lists the names of thousands of U. S. companies that advertise and the names and titles of their executives. Also cited are the names of their advertising agencies, their total annual advertising budget, and the principal media they use.

Laboratory Applications

1. How many agencies are listed on both tables? How many are on only one table? Can you explain why this is so?

2. From your library, obtain a copy of the agency "Red Book." Are there agencies in your town listed? If so, how many? If not, what is the town nearest you that has agency listings? How many?

Top ten U.S. agencies in U.S. income ($ millions)

Rank	Agency	1984
1	Young & Rubicam	$323.1
2	Ogilvy & Mather Intl.	270.5
3	Ted Bates Worldwide	263.2
4	BBDO International	235.0
5	J. Walter Thompson Co.	218.2
6	Foote, Cone & Belding	196.9
7	Leo Burnett Co.	163.2
8	Saatchi & Saatchi Compton	157.4
9	Grey Advertising	155.1
10	Doyle Dane Bernbach Intl.	154.1

Top ten U.S. agencies in world income ($ millions)

Rank	Agency	1984
1	Young & Rubicam	$480.1
2	Ted Bates Worldwide	424.4
3	Ogilvy & Mather Intl.	421.0
4	J. Walter Thompson Co.	405.8
5	BBDO International	340.0
6	Saatchi & Saatchi Compton	337.5
7	McCann-Erickson	325.2
8	Foote, Cone & Belding	268.5
9	Leo Burnett Co.	253.5
10	Grey Advertising	224.2

You can really fly
once you know where you're going.

We believe the sharpest advertising strategies provide the greatest creative freedom. Only when you know exactly where you're going can the imagination soar free, without fear or formulas.

YOUNG & RUBICAM INC.

FIGURE 3–9

Young & Rubicam Inc., the largest American advertising agency, uses beautiful imagery to illustrate a basic truth about advertising . . . and life.

more effective media—than the advertisers themselves can do. Today almost all sizable advertisers rely on an advertising agency for expert, objective counsel and unique creative skills.[3]

Yet, there are still many agency switches made every year. Likewise, many advertisers determine that it is in their best interest to work without an agency. Why is this so, if the agencies have all that independence, skill, expertise, and talent we just discussed?

Besides the obvious problems of personality conflicts and lack of communication that sometimes enter every human relationship, not every agency has all that much independence, skill, expertise, or talent. Likewise, an agency may produce outstanding results for one type of client and be totally incapable of grasping the problem or devising an appropriate solution for a different type. Some agencies lack the strength to remain truly independent and end up only trying to please the client rather than giving what is needed. Others are so arrogant in their approach that they forget to listen to the client. Some clients outgrow their agencies and need the additional services offered by larger firms. Some clients fail to see the expertise being offered and try to force their agencies to give them safe, but unexciting, advertising. Others make the honest mistake of giving their agencies incorrect information about their products, their markets, or their competitive strengths and weaknesses. In any of these cases the agency's work invariably suffers, the results received by the advertiser are less than desired, and either the agency or the client becomes restless and desires a change. (See Ad Lab 3–B.)

Types of Agencies

Advertising agencies are normally classified by one of two criteria: (1) the type of business they handle, such as consumer goods, industrial products, financial services, retail, and real estate, and (2) the range of services they offer, such as full service, media buying services, or creative services. We will discuss each of these major categories briefly.

General consumer agencies

A *general agency* is one that is willing to represent the widest variety of accounts. In practice, however, it concentrates on *consumer* accounts—that is, companies that make goods purchased chiefly by consumers. Soaps, cereals, automobiles, pet foods, and toiletries are examples. Most of the advertising produced by a general agency is placed in consumer media—television, radio, billboards, newspapers, and magazines—which are commissionable to the agency. As a result, the general agency has traditionally obtained most of its income from media commissions (Figure 3–9).

Industrial agencies

An *industrial agency* represents client companies that make goods to be sold to other businesses. Computer hardware, smelting furnaces, locomotives, and radium counters are examples of such goods. Although business and industrial advertising may not seem as glamorous as consumer advertising, it is a very important aspect of the business requiring highly developed technical knowledge as well as the ability to translate this knowledge into precise and persuasive advertising (Figure 3–10).

Most industrial advertising is placed in trade magazines and other business publications. These are generally commissionable, but their rates are far lower than those of consumer media. The result is that the commissions are not large enough to cover the cost of the agency's services, so industrial agencies frequently charge the client an additional service fee.

Full-service agencies

The modern *full-service advertising agency* is equipped to serve its clients in all areas of communication and promotion. Its services are essentially grouped in two categories—advertising and nonadvertising.

Advertising services include planning, creating, and producing advertisements, as well as performing research and media selection services. Nonadvertising functions include producing sales promotion materials, publicity articles, annual reports, trade show exhibits, and sales training materials.

PEOPLE IN ADVERTISING

Jay Chiat

Chairman of the Board, President, and Chief Executive Officer Chiat/Day, Inc.

Jay Chiat is chairman of the board, president, and chief executive officer of Chiat/Day, Inc., which has won more awards per client than any other advertising agency in the world. The 16-year-old agency commands annual billings of $350 million through its network of offices in Los Angeles, San Francisco, and New York City.

Chiat launched his advertising career as a copywriter at a small agency in Orange County, California. He soon rose to creative director of the firm's two-person creative department.

After serving two years in the Air Force, Chiat resumed his education. He graduated from Rutgers University, attended Columbia University's Graduate School of Broadcasting, and went on to graduate from the UCLA Executive Program. For three years, he taught advertising at the University of Southern California School of Journalism.

Chiat then launched his own agency. He attributes its success to these Chiat/Day rules for "How to Avoid Doing Bad Advertising":

1. Realize that your agency cannot work for everyone.
2. Recognize that there are no shortcuts. It's hard work to do great advertising.
3. Hire only those you believe can do the job better than you can. It makes the work brighter, and it makes you work brighter.

Media-buying services

In recent years, as the trend toward specialization has grown, there have been a number of offshoots from the agency business. Among these are the *media-buying services*. These are organizations of media specialists experienced in purchasing and packaging radio and television time. Such companies owe their success, in part, to the fact that radio and TV time is "perishable"; that is, a 60-second radio spot at 8 P.M. cannot be sold after that hour has arrived. For that reason, radio and television stations try to presell as much advertising time as possible and discount their rates to anyone who buys a large amount of time. Therefore, the media-buying service can negotiate a special discount rate with radio and TV stations. It then sells this time to advertising agencies or advertisers.

As part of their service, media-buying firms provide the prospective customer with a detailed analysis of the media buy. Once the media package is sold, the buying service orders the spots on each of the stations involved, verifies performance, sees to it that stations "make good" for any spots missed, and even pays the media bills.

The method of compensation used by media-buying services var-

---

4. Fire quickly those who do not measure up. They contaminate the agency by making good people question their judgment.
5. Recognize that all your people have creative capabilities, and demand creativity from all departments.
6. Make sure your account-management people are smart marketers. It takes brilliant marketing support to quiet client nervousness.
7. Never stop at the first creative solution. Explore alternatives.
8. Dig for the facts. Interview relentlessly. Your research must be unquestioned.
9. Know your target better than you know yourself.
10. Make sure a clear, concise, creative brief is written for every ad. Yes, *every* ad.
11. Treat all advertising as equal. The trade is as important as the TV commercial. Perhaps more so.
12. Do not permit "closet" accounts. If the work is not good enough to show to new-business prospects, the account is not good enough to keep.
13. Spend time training. Do not assume that people automatically understand what is expected of them.
14. Promote from within when possible. But do not hesitate to seek expertise elsewhere if it is lacking at the agency.
15. Treat everyone with the same level of dignity you expect yourself.
16. Perhaps most important, try to relax and have some fun.

Chiat, who has garnered gold and silver medals from the Los Angeles and New York Art Directors Shows, also has won several Andy Awards, numerous CLIOs, a shelf full of Belding Bowls, AAF "Best in the West" Awards, and CA Awards of Excellence. Named one of the "100 Top Creative People in the U.S." in *Ad Day* polls, Chiat has also had the distinction of being "Advertising Man of the Year" as designated by the WSAAA.

Similar top honors have gone to his agency. Chiat/Day was chosen "Advertising Agency of the Year" by *Advertising Age* in 1980 and, two years later, one of "the *Adweek* Eight " top creative agencies. In 1984, Chiat/Day won the Cannes "Grand Prix" Award.

Jay Chiat is an *Adweek* columnist, past president of the Advertising Industry Emergency Fund, and president of the Greater New York Cystic Fibrosis Association.

STRONG ADVERTISING CREATED HERE!

Glidden & Boyles is a business-to-business marketing and advertising agency that specializes in print media.
Trade magazine advertising, direct mail, sales brochures and catalogs are what we do best.

Our Elk Grove offices, close to our clients, help us to create their market communications on time and within budget.
For a free look at some very good samples, call Bill Boyles or Dick Glidden today!

GLIDDEN & BOYLES

MARKETING, ADVERTISING & GRAPHIC ARTS

1550 Higgins Road, Suite 108 • Elk Grove Village, Illinois 60007 • 312-228-6672

FIGURE   3–10

This Midwest agency promotes itself to business and industrial clients.

ies. Some receive a set fee. Others operate on an incentive basis, receiving a prescribed percentage of the money they save the client.

Creative boutiques

Just as some media specialists have set up media-buying services, some creative specialists like art directors, designers, and copywriters have set up creative services called *creative boutiques*. Working for advertisers and occasionally advertising agencies, their mission is to develop exciting creative concepts and to produce fresh, distinctive advertising messages.

Because advertising effectiveness largely depends on originality in concept, design, and writing, advertisers tend to value this quality highly. However, the creative services of the boutique are usually provided without the marketing and sales direction that full-service agencies offer. This factor tends to limit the boutique to the role of a creative supplier.

What Do Agency People Do?

The American Association of Advertising Agencies (AAAA) is the national organization of the advertising agency business. Its standards for membership are very high, and it has endeavored to be the most responsible speaker for the advertising industry. Its almost 400 members, representing the largest and oldest agencies in the business, place almost 80 percent of all advertising handled by all agencies in the United States.

In its Agency Service Standards, the AAAA explains that the purpose of an agency is to interpret to an advertiser's audience the advantages of a product or service. To accomplish this, the agency first conducts a study of the client's product or service in order to determine its strengths and weaknesses. Next it analyzes the present and potential market for the product. Then, using its knowledge of the channels of distribution and sales and of all the available media, the agency formulates a plan for carrying the advertiser's message to consumers, wholesalers, dealers, or contractors.

Finally comes the execution of the plan. That includes the writing and designing of advertisements, the contracting of space and time with the media, the proper production of advertisements and forwarding to the media, the verifying of media insertions, and the billing for services and media used.

The agency also cooperates with the client's sales force to ensure the greatest effect from advertising through package design, sales research and training, and production of sales literature and displays.[4]

To understand more fully the various functions just outlined, look at all the agency people involved in the case of Perdue Chickens presented earlier in this chapter. Scali, McCabe, Sloves was the agency Frank Perdue selected to handle his account. It was not one of New York's largest agencies. In fact, at the time it was one of the smaller shops, but it had piled up an impressive record of award-winning advertising with several other accounts such as Volvo and Dictaphone. As a full-service agency, Scali, McCabe, Sloves provides all the services suggested by the AAAA Service Standards (Figure 3–11).

Research

Before any advertising is created, research must be undertaken to study the uses and advantages of the product or service, to analyze the present and potential customers, and to determine what will influence them to buy. (See Chapters 5 and 6.) Sam Scali, the agency's creative director, has said, "We can't create on intuition. Give artists all the information they need to do a job—because advertising is based on information."[5]

Planning

The planning process actually begins before research and continues afterward. In the case of Perdue, Sam Scali, Ed McCabe, and Alan Pesky, the director of account services, were responsible for initiating this process with the client to determine his marketing and advertising objectives. They then met with the agency's market analysts, media planners, and other creative people to determine the appropriate advertising strategy. The results of research were considered, and the evaluation of the agency's planning team was then distilled into a detailed marketing and advertising plan. After the client approves this plan, it becomes the blueprint for the agency's creative and media program. (See Chapter 7.)

Creative services

Most advertising relies heavily on *copy*—the words that make up the headline and message of the ad. People like Ed McCabe who create these words are called *copywriters*. Their work requires skill, since they must be able to condense all that can be said about a product or service into just those points that are salient and pertinent to a

FIGURE 3–11

Many advertisers and agencies claim that award-winning advertising doesn't sell. Scali, McCabe, Sloves answers with the facts of Volvo's growth, Perdue's sales success, and testimonials from Dictaphone, all of whom had many award-winning ads. As they say, it's possible to do both.

**LAURIE JAGLOIS IS HAVING A BABY.
JOE SOSA IS HAVING A FIT.**

Laurie Jaglois is tops in all areas of print production.

She communicates with art directors, gets the most out of printers and keeps her head under the most ridiculous deadlines.

Unfortunately, Laurie also seems to be good at reproduction.

Which means we need a print production manager.

If you're interested, don't call. Send art director references and your best samples to Joe Sosa, Chiat/Day Advertising, 517 South Olive St., Los Angeles, CA 90013.

But only if you have three to five years experience and all of Laurie's qualities.

Except the craving for pickles and ice cream.   **CHIAT/DAY**

FIGURE   3–12

Production managers are responsible for making happen what the art director intended. Finding good production managers, though, is a difficult task, as this ad from Chiat/Day suggests.

given advertisement. Thus, what copywriters don't say is just as important as what they do say. (See Chapter 8.) Copywriters usually work closely with the agency artists and production staff.

The agency art department is composed of art directors, like Sam Scali, and graphic designers whose primary job is to *lay out* advertising—that is, to illustrate in sketches how the various components of an ad will fit together. When their assignment is to conceive a television commercial, the artists lay it out in a comic-strip series of sequential frames called a *storyboard*.

Most large agencies have their own art departments. Others prefer to purchase art services from independent studios or outside freelance designers. (See Chapter 9.)

Print and broadcast production

After the advertisement is designed and written and the client has approved it, it goes into production. This is the responsibility of the agency's print production manager or broadcast producers and directors. (See Chapters 10 and 11.)

For print advertising, the production department buys type, photographs, illustrations, and other components needed for the finished art. Production personnel then work with photoplatemakers, color separators, and other graphic arts suppliers to obtain the materials needed for the media (Figure 3–12).

If the ad is a broadcast commercial, the broadcast production personnel take the approved script or the storyboard and set about producing the finished product. Working with actors, camera people, and other production specialists, they produce the commercial on tape or records (for radio) or on film or videotape (for television).

Traffic

One of the greatest sins in the advertising agency business is to miss a deadline; and the whole business revolves around deadlines. If Scali, McCabe, Sloves intends to run an ad in a monthly trade magazine read by Perdue's grocers and they miss the deadline, they will have to wait another whole month for that ad to appear. That does not please clients.

The job of the agency traffic department, therefore, is to make sure that the work flow is smooth and efficient. It coordinates all the phases of production and checks to see that everything is completed on time and that all ads and commercials are received by the media before the deadline.

As the keystone position in the agency, the traffic department is often the first position for entry-level college graduates and is an excellent place to learn the operations of an agency. (See Ad Lab 3–C.)

Media

When Frank Perdue started advertising, the agency recommended subway posters as an initial medium for three reasons: it required only a small budget, the art could be used again in butcher-shop windows, and the message would be read by working mothers and lower- to middle-income groups. Later, as the campaign developed and more money became available, other more expensive media were considered and used.

The job of the media director is to match the profile of the desired target market with the profiles of the audiences of a wide range of media. The media are then evaluated according to efficiency and cost, and the media director recommends the best medium or media combination to use. (See Chapter 12.)

For the client, unbiased and authenticated media information is one of the most valuable services an agency can offer.

Account management

Scali, McCabe, Sloves's account management team is an essential part of the agency's organization. The *account executive* is the liaison between the agency and the client. Responsible on the one hand for mustering all the agency's services for the benefit of the client and on the other hand for representing the agency's point of view to the client, the account executive is often caught in the middle. The AE, therefore, must be tough, tactful, diplomatic, creative, persuasive, knowledgeable, sensitive, honest, and courageous—all at once.

Scali, McCabe, Sloves and other large agencies have many account executives who report to *management (or account) supervisors*. The management supervisors report to the agency's director of account services.

New business

To survive, agencies must grow. The best creative people always want to work for the "hot shops," the ones that are growing. Growth requires a steady flow of new business. Often this comes from new products developed by existing clients. In other cases clients seek out agencies whose work they are familiar with. Scali, McCabe, Sloves receives 15 to 20 calls per week, for example, because they are well

---

AD LAB   3–C   Career opportunities in advertising agencies

Why work for an advertising agency? In an agency you can specialize or work on a variety of accounts, plan a client's entire marketing program, or create the advertising itself. And because each project meets a challenge—to make your client's investment profitable, usually in the form of increased sales—you'll be competing with other bright people and cooperating with highly talented, experienced staff members.

Furthermore, unlike most other businesses, your work in an agency need not be limited to the affairs of one company or one industry. You could get involved in (and learn about)

fields as diverse as food manufacturing and financial institutions, the auto industry and air travel, retailing and restaurants. Thus, you can quickly gain a breadth of knowledge and experience about a variety of businesses.

Your own functions at an agency are determined partly by its size. In a small one with few accounts, you might handle several types of assignments. In a large international agency with hundreds of accounts, thousands of employees, and millions of dollars in business every year, you are likely to be assigned to one role at a time.

No matter what size agency you work for,

(continued)

AD LAB 3–C (continued)

you can be sure of one thing. If you are imaginative and quick-thinking, can work under pressure, and have a bent for solving problems, you'll find endless stimulation and satisfaction in agency work.

There aren't many businesses a person can hope to run while still young. Advertising agencies are different. In fact, more than one fifth of the agencies that belong to the American Association of Advertising Agencies are run by executives who were under 40 when they stepped up to the chief executive's chair.

If you want responsibility and are willing to work, you'll find faster advancement in an advertising agency than in many other businesses.

In addition to the six jobs listed, there are several other agency positions: market researcher, office manager, treasurer, secretary, billing clerk, bookkeeper, sales promotion specialist, film and television commercial producer, personnel manager, art buyer, casting specialist, television business affairs manager, talent reuse specialist.

Job title	Educational requirements	Occupational experience	Extracurricular activities	Average salary
Art director	B.A. desirable but not required. Degree from professional art school preferred. Community college courses. Visual arts courses.	Retail store advertising. Visual arts studio (portfolio required*).	Art director club. Communication arts group. Graphic arts group	$18,500 (assistant) $40,000 (senior)
Copywriter	B.A. with courses in advertising and marketing, English literature, sociology, psychology, philosophy, languages.	Intern in an agency. Retail store sales. Writing advertisements for newspapers, magazines, or broadcasters (portfolio required*).	Literary group. Press club. Public relations club. Journalism society. Communication arts group.	$18,000 (junior) $40,000 (senior)
Media buyer	B.A. with emphasis on marketing, economics, English, mathematics and statistics. M.B.A. desirable.	Retail store sales. Media sales. Media research. Assistant media buyer. Media trainee.	Ad club. Media organizations	$38,500 (media director) $25,000 (media supervisor) $18,500 (buyer of time and space)

Try your hand at applying for an agency position; turn to Figure 9–5.

For further information about advertising programs in four-year colleges and universities, write to Advertising Education Publications, 3429 Fifty-Fifth Street, Lubbock, TX 79413, enclose $1, and ask for a copy of *Where Shall I Go to Study Advertising*. Also available, free of charge, is *Advertising: A Guide to Careers in Advertising* from the American Association of Advertising Agencies, 200 Park Avenue, New York, NY 10017.

Laboratory Applications

1. From the list of positions, select one you might like to fill. Call a local advertising agency and see what you can find out about their requirements for that position, including salary paid, expected responsibilities, and other factors of importance.

2. Which of the positions offer, in your view, the greatest opportunity for growth and success? Why?

Job title	Educational requirements	Occupational experience	Extracurricular activities	Average salary
Account executive	B.A. in business. M.B.A. desirable.	Advertising and/or marketing department of a manufacturer or large retailer.	Participation in campus and community business organizations. Advertising club	$30,500
Traffic manager	B.A. not required but highly desirable for promotional purposes (commonly an entry-level position in an agency because it provides an acquaintance with the agency's functions and personnel).	Work experience in company advertising department. Media advertising departments.	Ad club. Marketing organization.	$18,000
Production manager	B.A. helpful but not essential with emphasis on graphic arts courses, visual arts courses, typography, design and layout.	Work experience with printers, photoengravers, paper merchants, typesetters, photostat houses, and art studios.	Printing club. Graphic arts group. Art directors club.	$27,600 (production manager) $20,000 (production assistant)

*A portfolio is a collection of your best work which you show during the job interview.

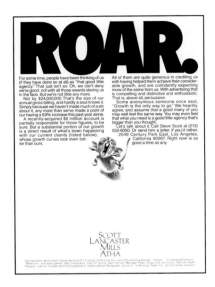

FIGURE   3–13

As agencies grow, they like to announce their successes. Scott Lancaster Mills Atha, for example, decided not to be mousy about their acquisition of a new $6 million account.

known for the work they have done on Perdue, Volvo, Maxell recording tape, and Nikon cameras, to mention just a few.

Most agencies keep a constant eye open for new business and have either "new business representatives" or agency principals assigned to target prospective clients and sell the agency's services (Figure 3–13).

Accounting

Scali, McCabe, Sloves receives invoices every day from radio and TV stations, magazines, newspapers, billboard companies, transit companies, type houses, platemakers, free-lance artists and illustrators, talent agencies, photographers, television production companies, sound studios, music producers, printers, and so on. These bills are totaled by the accounting department on periodic invoices to the clients. Client payments are received and recorded, and the accounting department has to pay all these outside suppliers.

Dealing with variations in media commissions, agency markups, errors in invoices, cash discounts, and the complex flow of large amounts of cash for dozens of clients requires a highly competent accounting staff. At the same time, the staff must monitor the agency's income and expenses and keep management informed of the company's financial status.

Additional services

What has just been described might be considered basic to the advertising agency business. Many agencies, however, provide a variety of other services and employ specialists to perform these tasks. Scali, McCabe, Sloves, for instance, has a highly regarded sales promotion department that is used by most of the firm's clients to produce dealer ads, window posters, point-of-purchase displays, dealer contest materials, and sales material.

Other agencies maintain public relations specialists, direct marketing specialists, home economics experts, package designers, or economists depending on the nature and needs of their clients.

How Are Agencies Structured?

How an advertising agency organizes its functions, operations, and personnel may vary greatly according to its size (gross billings or number of large accounts), the types of accounts it serves, and whether it is local, regional, national, or international.

In small agencies, daily business operations are usually supervised by the owner or president, who may be in charge of new business development as well. Client contact is generally handled by account executives. The account executive may also produce creative concepts for the clients and even write copy. Artwork may be produced by an inside art director or purchased from an independent studio or free-lance designer. Most small agencies have a production and traffic department or an employee who fulfills these functions. They also may have a media buyer, but in very small agencies the account executives also purchase media time and space for their accounts (Figure 3–14).

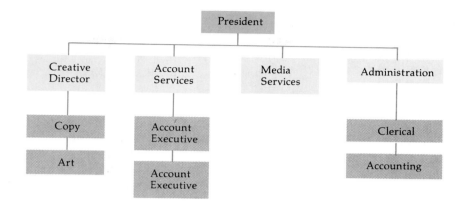

FIGURE 3–14

Typical organization of a small advertising agency.

In medium and large agencies, organization is generally more formal. Larger agencies are usually structured according to the departmental system or the group system.

In the departmental system each of the agency's varied functions—account management, creative services, media, traffic, and production—is set up as a separate department. Each department is called on as needed to perform its specialty. The account executive handles the client contact, the creative department writes the ad and lays it out, and so forth.

As agencies get larger, though, they tend to use the group system in which the agency is divided into a number of "little" agencies or groups. A group is composed of an account executive, a copywriter, an artist, a media buyer, and any other specialists that are needed. The group may be assigned to serve only one account—if the account is very large—or, as in most cases, three or four clients. A very large agency may have up to a dozen or more groups. It may even have separate production and traffic units to serve each one.

Each of these systems has its advantages. The organization that best enables the agency to provide its services effectively, efficiently, and profitably is the one that should be implemented.

■ How Do Agencies Make Money?

Like any other business, an advertising agency must make a fair profit on the services it renders. Inasmuch as the amount of service typically varies from client to client, agencies use a variety of compensation methods to arrive at an equitable financial arrangement. Basically, agencies make money from three sources: (1) media commissions, (2) markups on outside purchases, and (3) fees or retainers. We will discuss each of these briefly.

■ Media commissions

Agencies save the media considerable expense in sales and collections. So, historically, the major media have allowed recognized agencies to retain a 15 percent commission on any space or time they purchase for their clients. For outdoor advertising the commission is usually 16 2/3 percent. The way this system works is simple. Assume you plan to spend $1,000 for a magazine ad for your company. Working with you, your agency arranges to buy the space from the magazine, places the order for you, and delivers the ad to the magazine. When the ad appears, the magazine bills the agency $1,000. The agency then bills you $1,000. You pay the agency this gross amount, and the agency remits the money to the magazine *less* its 15 percent commission, as follows:

$$\$1,000 - (1,000 \times 0.15) = \$850$$

If you spent $1 million, the agency's commission would be $150,000, and it would remit $850,000 to the media. For large accounts, the agency normally provides its creative services, media services, and accounting and account management services for this fee. For smaller accounts, though, the commission is usually not enough to cover the cost of all these services, so additional compensation is required.

Many media also allow a 2 percent discount for prompt payment of their invoices (normally within 10 days). Agencies usually pass this savings on to their clients in the form of a bill reduction. In the advertising business, when the medium quotes rates to the agency, it describes this policy simply by saying, for example: "The ad cost is $10,000, less 15 and 2."

Markups

To create a magazine ad, the agency normally has to buy type, photography, illustrations, and a variety of other services or materials from outside suppliers. These suppliers do not normally allow the agency a commission, so the agency buys these services and adds a markup to the client's bill.

Traditionally agencies added a 17.65 percent markup to outside purchases. The reason for this figure goes back to the tradition of the 15 percent commission. When you add 17.65 percent to an invoice, the amount added becomes 15 percent of the new total, as follows:

$$\$8.50 \times 17.65\% = \$1.50$$
$$\$8.50 + \$1.50 = \$10.00$$
$$\$1.50 = 15\% \times \$10.00$$

FIGURE 3–15   Survey of percentages of costs and profits for 242 agencies

Rent, light and depreciation	7.22%
Taxes (other than U.S. income)	4.11
Other operating expenses	16.89
Total payroll	61.02
Payments into retirement plans	2.32
Insurance for employee benefit	1.71
Total expenses	93.27
Profit before U.S. income tax for all agencies	6.73
U.S. income taxes	1.64

Thus, the agency ends up with 15 percent of the total bill, which is the traditional agency commission. Some media, especially local newspapers, do not allow for an agency commission in their local rates. Therefore, agencies that use these media frequently use the markup formula to receive their commission. In this case, when your agency places an ad costing $1,000, the agency will bill you $1,176.50, keep the $176.50 markup, and remit the $1,000 to the medium.

In recent years many agencies found that 17.65 percent is not a sufficient markup to cover the cost of services they perform in dealing with outside suppliers. This is especially true on smaller accounts where the sums spent are minor. As a result, some agencies increased their markups to as much as 20 to 25 percent. (See Figure 3–15.)

Fees

Assume you are a small advertising agency with several local advertising clients. Perhaps your largest advertiser spends only $10,000 per month in commissionable media, yet you spend a lot of time servicing the account, providing in-depth media plans, staging in-store promotions, supervising press interviews, and developing posters and displays for windows and counters. Obviously the $1,500 per month you receive from the media commissions does not cover the amount of work you, your secretary, your artist, and your media person have to devote to this client. Nor does the $100 to $200 extra you pick up in markups offset the tremendous amount of time required plus the cost of your office overhead. You need to charge your client an additional fee for your work. How do you determine a reasonable amount?

Agencies that serve their clients on a fee basis frequently use one of two pricing methods. The first is a *fee-commission* combination. With this method, the agency establishes a fixed monthly fee for all its services to the client. If, during a given month, the agency earns any media commissions for time or space purchased for the client, it retains these commissions in addition to the fee.

The second method is a *straight fee* arrangement. This is frequently used for accounts in which the services needed—research or public relations, for example—produce no commission income, or in which any media commissions received are credited to the client against the fee. The straight fee is frequently called a *retainer* and is similar to the retainers paid to attorneys or accountants.

The retainer system is based on a cost-plus-fixed-fees formula. It assures the agency that it will receive a fair profit. Under this system the agency estimates the amount of personnel time required by the client, determines the cost of that personnel, multiplies by a factor of 2.5 to 3 for overhead and another factor (e.g., 0.5) for profit, and that total becomes the fee charged (Figure 3–16).

Using the data in Figure 3–16, you might decide to handle your client's account for a total monthly retainer of $3,000 and credit commissions against that fee. Or you might decide that the retainer will have to be over and above any commissions since most of the time you spend will be for noncommissionable work in public relations and sales promotion. In either case, it will be up to you to convince your client of the value of your services and to negotiate a compensation arrangement that will be fair for both.

FIGURE   3–16   How to compute a monthly retainer

Employee	Monthly salary	Hourly rate*	Billable rate†		Est. hours/ month	Total
1	$1,000	$ 7.69	$23.00	×	10	$ 230
2	$2,000	$15.38	$46.00	×	20	$ 940
3	$2,500	$19.23	$58.00	×	15	$ 870
4	$1,750	$13.46	$40.00	×	20	$ 800
						$2840

*Assuming approximately 130 hours a month.
†Using 3 as total factors.

How Do Agencies Get Clients?

To succeed, advertising agencies must have clients. But where do those clients come from? What can an agency do when it has a staff of artists, copywriters, account executives, media people, secretaries, and bookkeepers, but not enough billing to pay the salaries?

An advertising agency, like any other business, has a product or a service to sell. Clients come to an advertising agency, therefore, in much the same way as they come to an attorney, a doctor, a hairdresser, or a clothier: by referral, through advertising, because they were solicited, or because of reputation (Figure 3–17).

Referrals

Most good advertising agencies get their clients by referral. The president of one company asks the president of another company who does those great ads, and the next week the agency gets a call. If an agency feels a prospective client may pose a conflict of interest with an existing client, it will refer the new client to another agency.

In the case of local advertisers, representatives of the media frequently refer clients to an agency with whom they have a working relationship. It's important, therefore, for agencies to maintain good relationships with their existing clients, with the media, and with other agencies, and it is common practice for them to "put the word out" when they are looking for new business (Figure 3–18).

Solicitations for new business

An agency may decide to openly solicit new business by (1) advertising, (2) writing solicitation letters, (3) making "cold" calls on prospective clients, or (4) following up leads from sources within the business. Few agencies advertise their services. Considering the business they are in, one survey turned up some amusing answers as to why agencies don't advertise. Among the most common responses were:

"Advertising is not very effective."
"We have never been able to agree on an advertising theme."
"We have never budgeted for advertising."[6]

Our favorite worm stand.

As we look out on a string of tomorrows, we can be sure of at least one thing.

The great idea, put purely and simply, is going to remain our reason for being around.

It may be brought to you by satellite, laser or moonbeam. Or some other equally awesome thingamajig.

But reaching for ideas that touch both mind and heart is, and will continue to be, what Leo Burnett is all about.

By the way, you know why there's no little kid up there in our picture?

He's gone fishing. Sold out, you know.

LEO BURNETT COMPANY, INC.
ADVERTISING

FIGURE   3–17

The simplest ideas are often the biggest ideas. That message from Leo Burnett, offered with the sublime humor of understatement, makes an effective statement of this agency's philosophy of advertising.

THIS COMMERCIAL RAN JUST 17 TIMES. AND THAT'S GOSPEL.

Some people believe that in order for a commercial to be really effective, it has to run hundreds of times.

That's true. For most commercials.

The original 60-second Xerox "Monk" commercial ran a mere 17 times the first year.

After the very first airing the response began to be felt. We call that High Profile Advertising.

The kind of advertising we do for such clients as McDonald's, Honda, Parkay margarine and many, many more.

Call Joel Baumwoll in New York, Keith Reinhard in Chicago, or Brad Roberts in Los Angeles to find out how we do it.

NEEDHAM, HARPER & STEERS
High Profile Advertising

FIGURE 3–18

In Latin countries, there is an amusing expression about people who greet their friends by "tipping their neighbor's hat." This practice is quite common in American advertising agencies, who find it most effective to explain who they are by telling you who their clients are.

Most major agencies get their new clients by referral—either from existing clients, from friends, or simply because of their reputation. Other less-known agencies, though, must take a more aggressive approach, seeking new business through direct solicitation or any other means available.

The important task of soliciting new business usually falls to one of the agency's principals, since the rest of the staff is normally assigned to the work of existing clients. Once a new business prospect has been found, however, staffers may be called in to help prepare the presentation.

Public relations

Agencies frequently find that their best source of business is simply their good reputation. Although a good reputation normally takes a long time to develop, most agencies participate in activities that help raise their profile in the business community. Some work on charitable committees; others assist local politicians; and some are active in the arts, education, religion, or social circles. Some give seminars; others write articles in magazines; and many others become active in advertising clubs or other professional organizations. All these activities contribute to getting the agency known and respected in the community.

Presentations

Once an advertiser becomes interested in an agency, the agency may be asked to make a presentation. This may mean anything from a simple discussion of the agency's philosophy, experience, personnel, and track record to a full-blown audiovisual show complete with slides, films, sample commercials, or even proposed campaigns. In the profession, the latter is commonly, and somewhat disdainfully, referred to as a "dog and pony show."

Some advertisers ask or imply that they want the agency to make a *speculative presentation*. This means they want to see what the agency would do for them before they hire them. Most reputable agencies resist giving "spec" presentations because they generally consider it unethical and unprofessional, not to mention expensive. Smaller agencies think it gives larger agencies an unfair advantage. And large agencies do not like to invest money in presentations that allow clients to pick their brains for free. Likewise, many advertisers do not appreciate their agencies "wasting" the time and talent they are paying for on presentations to other clients. Thus, the practice is generally frowned on. However, when prospects get tough and business is scarce, spec presentations invariably appear.

Most agencies try to build their nonspeculative presentations around the work they have performed for other advertisers. In this way, they can demonstrate their versatility, philosophy, expertise, and depth of understanding of the marketplace and the client's business.

A simple fact, often overlooked, is that the presentation process allows the agency and the advertiser to get to know each other and find out if they like one another. Advertising is a very human business, and the advertiser-agency relationship is a peculiar kind of marriage. But, as in any marriage, there must be mutual friendship, trust, and communication.

THE MEDIA AND
SUPPLIERS

As a rambunctious student of the classics at Brown University, Robert Edward Turner III was suspended twice and barred from his fraternity. Nevertheless, he excelled at sailing and debating.[7] During college he was offered the chance to work and sail for the Noroton (Connecticut) Yacht Club, but his father, a strict disciplinarian who had often beaten Ted as a child, insisted he work for the family business.

Ted was nine years old when the family moved from Cincinnati to Savannah, Georgia. His father, Ed Turner, bought an outdoor advertising firm that became the Turner Advertising Company. During summers, Ted worked a 40-hour week cutting grass and painting poles for the company.[8] By the time Ted graduated, the business had expanded to several other southern cities. Ted's first position after college was as an account executive for the flagship company in Savannah, selling billboard space to local advertisers and advertising agencies. By the time he was 22, Ted was general manager of the Turner Advertising Company's branch in Macon.

Two years later his father overextended himself buying the General Outdoor Advertising Company in Atlanta, the biggest in the country. In the ensuing financial struggle to stay afloat, Ed Turner initiated plans to sell out, which greatly agitated Ted. When Ed suffered a nervous breakdown and shot himself, Ted immediately halted the sell-out and, against the advice of his financial consultants, set out to bring the debt-ridden business back to health. Through a series of complex financial dealings he rescued the company and regained the parts of the family business that had already been sold.

A few years later Ted again rejected his consultants' warnings and branched out into television, buying an independent UHF-TV station that was losing more than $500,000 a year. He immediately grabbed up five network shows that were not being shown on the local network affiliate station, sold sponsorships to local advertisers, and within three years turned Channel 17 into one of the first profitable independent UHF stations in the nation.

FIGURE 3–19

The "Mouth of the South," Ted Turner has an entrepreneurial spirit and flair for bombast, braggadocio, and promotion, which have catapulted him to riches and national prominence. As *Newsweek* says, his style may be the antithesis of boardroom decorum, but his formidable business acumen and knack for bringing off the near-miraculous have brought him wide professional respect. Several years ago he even found the time to win yacht racing's most prestigious America's Cup. But his antics earned him the title "Captain Outrageous."

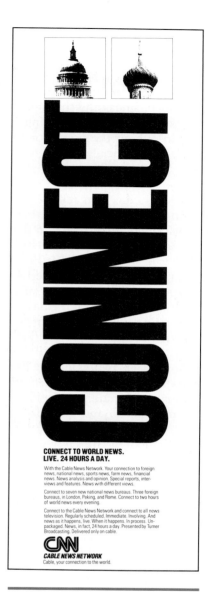

FIGURE   3–20

Ads in newspapers and magazines promote the independent news from CNN.

Turner wanted to televise major league sports, but he didn't want to pay broadcast rights. So he bought the Atlanta Braves baseball team and the Atlanta Hawks basketball team, both of which were in the cellar in their respective leagues and suffering from dismal attendance. As the teams' number one fan, Turner used his flair for promotion and bombast to boost attendance, sell advertising sponsorships, and catapult himself to national prominence as the "Mouth of the South" (Figure 3–19).

Turner's boldest stroke came in 1975 when RCA launched the Satcom satellite. He quickly built a $750,000 transmission antenna, formed a company to operate it, and in December 1976 began to distribute his local station's signal to cable TV systems in other states. With his "superstation that serves the nation," Turner immediately quadrupled his audience, picked up revenue from subscribing cable systems, and attracted the first of WTBS's 150 national advertisers. By 1980 Turner's WTBS superstation was reaching nearly 9 million cable homes in 48 states.

In June 1980, Turner struck again. Launching the Cable News Network (CNN), he suddenly enabled 2.2 million homes to plug into the state of the world at their convenience through television's first news-on-demand station. With seven domestic and three foreign news bureaus, a corps of network TV news veterans like Daniel Schorr and Reese Shonfield, and a wide variety of provocative commentators from Barry Goldwater to Ralph Nader, CNN took on the networks. Even more significantly, Turner provided an early demonstration of what is still to come in the 1980s and 1990s (Figure 3–20).

Within the next decade, it is predicted that the number of U.S. homes wired to receive cable systems will surge from one in five to more than half. As the dial becomes clogged with as many as 50 channels, broadcasters may survive only by emulating Turner and offering highly specialized fare—becoming, in effect, "narrowcasters" instead of broadcasters. Even the three major networks may be forced into cable casting as advertisers seek specialized markets for their products. Perhaps it was his recognition of this fact that led Turner to offer to buy the Columbia Broadcasting System in 1985.

Turner is showing the way. He receives a monthly fee from the cable-system operators who carry his service (about 20 cents per subscriber), and he reserves 12 minutes of time for advertisers (10 for CNN and 2 for the local cablecaster). With heavyweight sponsors such as General Mills, Sears, Time, Inc., and Bristol-Myers helping Turner launch the system, it's no wonder that this flamboyant southern folk hero boasts, "This will be the most significant achievement in the annals of journalism."

A sign on Turner's desk epitomizes his competitive drive: "Either Lead, Follow, or Get Out of the Way."

Media

The *medium* that carries the advertiser's message is the vital connection between the company that manufactures a product and the customer who wishes to buy it. It is the third link in the communication

"*What does The Post say?*"

When you want to know the latest
developments in Washington, Denver and around the world,
get the full story from the full-size newspaper.
THE DENVER POST
For home delivery call 820-1611.

FIGURE 3–21

This amusing cartoon ad
promotes the timeliness and
credibility of news from the
Denver Post. Research shows that
most people perceive newspapers
to be the most credible medium
of news and information.

chain. The media that are available today include the traditional print, electronic, out-of-home, and direct mail, and a variety of new, often untried, media that have been born of exploding technology. Due to recent media trends, those media are beginning to overlap.

For the student of advertising, it is important to understand the relationship of these media to the advertising business and the significance of current trends in the media world. For the person seeking a career in advertising, the media have often offered the first door to employment and the greatest opportunity for financial reward.

Print media

Traditionally *print media* refers to newspapers and magazines, but the term is used generally to describe any commercially published medium that sells advertising space to a variety of advertisers. In the United States today there are 1,745 daily and 7,602 weekly newspapers and 64,000 magazines. As we shall see in Chapter 13 (Print Media), this vast array of publications makes it possible for advertisers to pinpoint their messages to highly select markets in any of a variety of fields or geographic locations. Most of these print media are local, but some national newspapers and trade publications have become quite successful. Regional newspapers have also emerged (Figure 3–21).

Magazines, on the other hand, have long been national, and the trend is toward localization and specialization. The general category includes national consumer publications, national trade publications, local city magazines, regional consumer magazines, and local or regional trade and farm publications.

The print media also include directories, school or church newspapers and yearbooks, and programs used at sporting events and theatrical performances.

Electronic media

The electronic media of radio and television are frequently referred to as *broadcast media*. They include 726 local television stations, 7,000 local radio stations, several radio and TV networks, and the 4,000 local cable systems now blanketing the country and still growing. The electronic media are discussed in greater detail in Chapter 14.

Cable TV was just a lightweight medium yesterday, but is rapidly becoming a heavyweight contender. It offers the potential for big problems as well as opportunities for the nation's advertisers, although some cable networks carry no commercials, relying for revenue on viewer fees.

For the TV networks, the competition for viewers is increasing at an alarming pace. The number of viewers determines the rates that can be charged for advertising time, and that determines the revenues the networks receive. As audiences become more fragmented and turn to cable TV and noncommercial stations, the major networks will face new challenges to create revenue (Figure 3–22).

Out-of-home media

The major categories of out-of-home media are outdoor advertising (billboards) and transit advertising (bus and car cards). Most outdoor advertising plants are local firms, but much of their revenue comes from national advertisers. Both out-of-home media forms will be discussed in Chapter 15.

Out-of-home media also include colorful posters in bus shelters and train stations, creative billboards in airport lounges, stadium scoreboard ads, flying banners and lights, and skywriting.

Direct mail

When companies mail their advertisements directly to prospective customers, this is called *direct-mail advertising*. Often prepared by agencies that specialize in direct mail, these advertising messages may be simple letters with an offer or solicitation, or a complex package with coupons, brochures, samples, or other devices designed to stimulate response. As we will discuss in Chapter 15, direct mail is the most expensive medium on a cost-per-exposure basis. But it is often the most effective because the advertiser can target the customer directly and doesn't have to compete with other advertisers for attention.

Other media

With recent technological progress has come a host of new advertising media. Cinema advertising, long a favorite in European countries, is beginning to appear between movies in theaters around the country. Automatic telephone-dialing devices with recorded messages are another new direct advertising medium. Coptermedia (helicopters with lighted billboards) offer new opportunities for nighttime out-of-home advertisers. Even sound recordings can now be pressed into plastic sheets and inserted in magazines or mailed via direct mail.

As progress continues, so will the proliferation of new, yet unconceived media and so will the opportunities for those seeking their fortunes in the media.

FIGURE 3-22

MUSIC: (Eerie electronic tone)

SFX: *Ambient casino noises*

VO: Ladies and gentlemen, place your bets. Round and round and round they go. Who will get them? Nobody knows . . . round and round and round they go. Who will cure them? Nobody knows.

ANNCR V.O.: Diseases . . . for which there are no known causes or cures. What are the odds your number will come up? Find out. Watch "Mystery Illnesses." This week at six on Channel 7 (San Francisco).

■ Functions of the Media

Ted Turner's billboard company had one purpose—to carry advertising for its customers. Other media serve a variety of functions including communicating news or interesting information, offering mass or specialized entertainment, and disseminating advertising messages.

▨ News and information

When we speak of the news media, we naturally think of newspapers, magazines, radio, and television. Some of these have a stronger news orientation than others. The primary purpose of newspapers, for example, is to carry news. Most radio and television stations, however, devote only a small portion of their programming to news. The three major networks have historically presented only 22 minutes of news in prime evening time. For that reason many people like Ted Turner feel there is a potential for all-news stations like CNN.

The news carried by some media is very specialized. Weekly newspapers specialize in local community events, social notes, and high school sports. Fashion magazines specialize in fashion news. Trade publications specialize in news that is pertinent to their business.

In most cases the news we receive is gathered and reported to us in a very economical form. For only $5 or $6 we might receive thousands of pages of daily newspaper news every month. Many weekly papers, in fact, are distributed free, as are many colorful trade publications. The reason for this is advertising. The rates paid by advertisers enable the free press to operate without government interference. This more than anything else characterizes the news media in the United States.

▨ Entertainment

Television and radio, motion pictures, many magazines, and even some newspapers are classified as primarily entertainment media.

FIGURE   3–23

(Country music up and under)	VO: You play country music.	JOCK: Yep.
VO: So you're on the radio.	JOCK: Yep.	VO: But you don't talk much.
JOCK: Yep.	VO: But you don't talk much.	JOCK: Nope.
VO: But you don't talk much.	JOCK: Nope.	
JOCK: Nope.	VO: FM Stereo?	

Network movies, country western radio stations, and detective magazines are all designed to entertain us; that is their primary function. By entertaining us, they hope to attract a large enough audience to substantiate the rates they charge advertisers. If those rates are reasonable, advertisers will pay for the opportunity to deliver their message to that audience. The result for us is that the entertainment comes at a very low price (Figure 3–23).

Some entertainment media charge for the entertainment and carry little or no advertising. Home Box Office, for example, charges subscribers for movies and entertainment and carries no advertising. This allows the consumer to choose between free TV and fee TV.

Advertising

The out-of-home media (billboards, transit) tend to be strictly advertising media. Companies erect billboards and rent the space, or they contract for buses and rent that space. There is no entertainment or news value associated with these media, as their audiences are captive.

Some print media are strictly advertising, too. Weekly shoppers carry no editorials or entertainment, only advertising. Customers hoping to find bargains browse through the pages, and advertisers gain exposure.

Recently some effort has been made to begin all-advertising cable TV stations, and these attempts will probably multiply in the future with the increased availability of cable.

Media People in Advertising

Since advertising is one of the major functions of the media, most media people are involved to some extent in advertising. Television stations, for example, have camera people, directors, engineers, and audio technicians who spend as much or more time producing television commercials for local advertisers as they do preparing the nightly local newscast.

Radio station disc jockeys and production managers often spend their off-air time producing local radio commercials. It is common to see successful DJs quit their station jobs to become free-lance commercial voices.

Television and cable stations also employ copywriters, promotion directors, and traffic managers who write commercials, promote station activities, and schedule commercials within the daily programming. In addition, they all have sales staffs who call on advertisers and agencies, sell airtime, and write and produce commercial announcements.

Newspapers and magazines employ writers, graphic designers, production artists, sales promotion specialists, and merchandising personnel. All these people assist the medium's sales staff in writing, designing, or producing advertisements and promotions for the publication or its advertisers.

There are numerous opportunities in the media for people interested in advertising. Many of today's top advertising executives began by working in the traffic department of a local radio station or, like Ted Turner, by cutting grass around the billboards of a local outdoor advertising company. (See Ad Lab 3–D.)

Selling Media Advertising

Every advertising medium has an advertising sales department responsible for selling the medium's space or time. And the fact is that many of the highest paid people in advertising work in these departments. The way these departments are structured and the manner in which they function depend on the type of medium. Needless to say, these departments are very important since they normally provide the medium's primary source of income.

AD LAB 3–D   Career opportunities with the media and suppliers

A tremendous number of employment opportunities are available with the media and suppliers. The suppliers need personnel who generally have technical backgrounds and specialized skills. The list below give some idea of the types and variety of positions for which employees are needed:

Free-lance artists
Retouchers

Free-lance
copywriters

Paper merchants
Jingle creators
Mailing list brokers
Typesetters
Photographers
Premium promoters
Photoengravers
Packaging
designers

Film processing
specialists
Convention display
artists and designers
Printers
Market researchers
Film and
videotape producers
and directors

Job title	Educational requirements	Occupational experience	Extracurricular activities	Average salary
Photographer	B.A. from professional art school preferred	Photography studio. School newspaper, magazine, yearbook.	Photography club. Photo exhibit shows. Graphic arts club.	$24,000
Film and video tape producer or director	B.A. preferred but not required	Film or tape studio. Television station. Photography studio	National Academy of Television Arts and Sciences. Telecommunications and film organizations.	$18,300 (associate producer) $30,000 (broadcast producer or director)
Sales representative	B.A. preferred (but not required) with emphasis on business courses	Retail sales. Direct sales	Sales, ad, and marketing clubs. Print and broadcast organizations.	Variable (often highest paid position in the company) Commission against draw or guarantee.

Networks

The salespeople (account executives) who work for the networks concentrate on the national advertisers and their agencies who regularly purchase network radio or television time. In addition to selling network time, they frequently sell radio and TV time in individual markets or regions. That way, a company that doesn't have its product distributed nationwide can still buy television or radio time from the network on a per market basis.

Casting specialists   Free-lance public
Illustrators   relations writers

Laboratory applications

The advertising departments of the media are strongly sales-oriented:

1. Do any of these jobs look interesting to you as a career opportunity? Which ones? Why?

Sales representatives   Production specialists
Sales managers   Market researchers
Copywriters   Sales promotion
Artists   specialists

2. Choose one of the positions. What could you do to learn more about that job? Outline a plan to research the opportunities for obtaining such a job.

Job title	Educational requirements	Occupational experience	Extracurricular activities	Average salary
Jingle creator	B.A. preferred (but not required) with emphasis on music and business	Recording studio. Jingle production house	Ad club. Band, rock group, glee club or church choir.	$28,700
Market researcher	B.A., M.B.A., Ph.D. desirable with emphasis on writing, mathematics, statistics, sociology, and psychology.	Interviewer for research organization. Research trainee. Research assistant. Experience in company research department or research firm.	Research organizations.	$17,500 (research analyst) $35,500 (research director)

NETWORK TELEVISION HAS BEEN BITTEN.

Ouch! Cable has slithered into the picture and taken a big bite out of the networks' audience.
In 1979, the networks' share of prime-time viewers was 90%. A recent survey shows it has been nibbled down to 79%. And it's estimated that only 60% will remain by 1990.
The most painful part is that your advertising feels the bite, too.
Fortunately, there's a sure way to ease the pain. You can advertise more in magazines.

Magazine readership is stronger than ever in cable homes.
In fact, a national survey points out that readership is strongest in homes with cable availability. The biggest magazine readers are the people who watch network the least.
Put more teeth in your media schedule. Advertise more in magazines.

MPA   Magazine Publishers Association

MAGAZINES REACH PEOPLE YOU CAN'T GET THROUGH ORDINARY CHANNELS.

FIGURE   3–24

Taking advantage of cable television's intrusion into network audiences, the Magazine Publishers Association promotes the viability of magazines as an advertising medium.

To facilitate the sales effort, the network rep has a host of tools available. These include research data on the programs being offered, packaged programs for advertisers who are seeking sponsorships, and merchandising services.

Magazines

Most national magazines are headquartered in New York or Chicago and have extensive advertising departments to provide advertisers with research information and occasionally merchandising assistance. In addition magazines usually have sales offices or representatives in major U.S. cities to call on agencies and advertisers wherever they are located.

To assist the sales force, magazines frequently have a staff of writers, art directors, and sales promotion specialists who prepare direct-mail promotions and research reports for advertising managers and media buyers (Figure 3–24).

Most major publications subscribe to the reports of outside research firms like W. R. Simmons and Mediamark Research, Inc., which conduct extensive media audience studies. The sales staff uses these studies to prove the worth of their publication to the agencies. And the agency media buyers also depend on these studies to justify their media recommendations.

Newspapers

Newspaper advertising departments may vary in size from one person for a small weekly to several hundred people for a large metropolitan daily. Normally the advertising department is divided into retail advertising, general (or national) advertising, and classified, with a manager heading each group (Figure 3–25).

A newspaper offers a wide variety of services to entice advertisers. These include art and copy and also special promotions, publicity, market research, and planning assistance. To promote itself to advertisers, a newspaper frequently has a sales promotion department, an outside advertising agency, and a corps of salespeople to visit and assist advertisers and agencies. A merchandising department may even be staffed to assist national advertisers with local store promotions.

Newspapers usually contract with independent firms to represent them on the national level. The reps sell their newspapers' space by demonstrating to national advertisers that (1) the newspaper's audience has the right demographic profile for the advertiser's product, (2) the newspaper offers an economical alternative to competitive media, (3) the newspaper has excellent coverage of the market, and (4) the newspaper offers fringe benefits, such as merchandising assistance. For this service, newspapers pay the rep firm 10 to 15 percent commission or an agreed-on fee for large publications.

Radio and television

Local radio and television advertising departments are structured much like newspapers, with a local sales manager, a national sales manager, and a broadcast rep firm. However, these local sales departments are much smaller than those of daily newspapers.

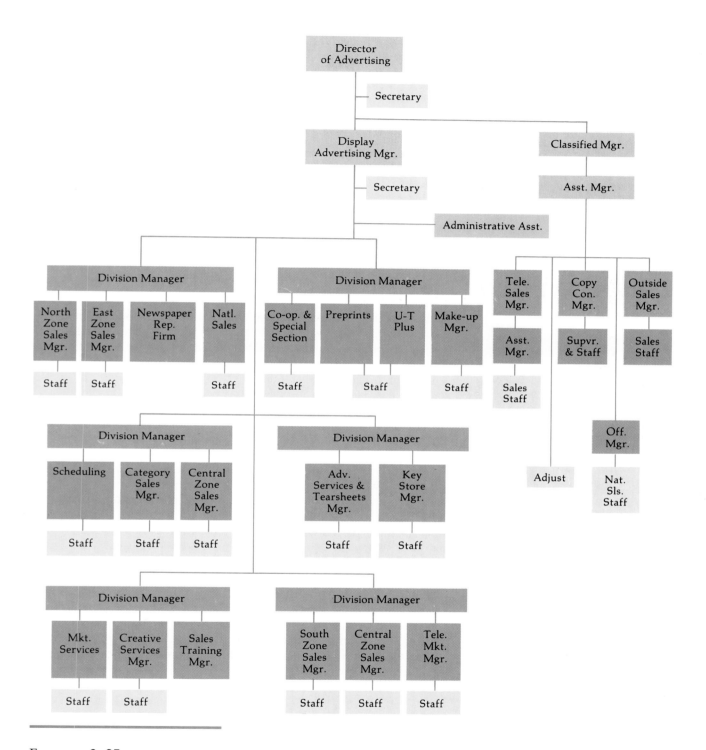

FIGURE 3–25

Organization chart for the Advertising Department of Union-Tribune Publishing Co., San Diego

To assist their advertisers, radio and television stations offer copy and production services, and many also offer merchandising and research.

Out-of-home

Local billboard company owners (called plant operators) lease promising sites from property owners, construct billboards on these sites, and then sell the space to local advertisers such as banks and shopping centers. National advertising is normally sold to agencies and advertisers through an industrywide organization.

Similarly, transit operators have a sales staff or contract with an independent sales organization to sell the space available on the sides and interiors of buses, taxicabs, and stations.

Local plant operators assist their customers with copy and art if needed as well as research data showing the most visible sites.

Suppliers

The people and organizations that specialize in some ancillary aspect of the advertising business are commonly referred to as the *suppliers*. Without their services it would be impossible to produce the billions of dollars' worth of advertising placed every year.

Although it is impossible to mention them all, we will briefly discuss at least some of the important ones here. These are the art studios, typesetters, printers, film and video production houses, and research companies.

Art studios

Art studios are used to design and produce artwork and illustrations for advertisements. They may supplement the work of an agency's art department or even take the place of an art department for small agencies. Art studios are usually small organizations with as few as three or four employees. Some large studios, though, may employ several art directors, graphic designers, layout artists, production artists, and sales reps.

Most studios are owned and managed by an artist or art director, and that person frequently serves as the organization's only salesperson. Calling on agencies and advertising managers, the artist has to sell the studio's services, take projects back to the office to be produced, and then deliver them for the client's approval. The work, therefore, is very time-consuming and requires a talent for organization and management.

Typesetters

Every printed advertisement we see uses type. The typesetter's job is to take the copywriter's words and the art director's layout and translate them into what appears in the ad. This requires a high degree of technical knowledge and skill and some artistic talent, too. (See Chapter 10, "Creative Production: Print Media.")

Speed and accuracy are critical to the success of a type house. Art directors are known for calling in type orders in the morning and requesting delivery by noon. The large typesetters are therefore computerized and systematized to function efficiently and economically. This, of course, requires a large capital investment and has resulted in increased labor and material costs as well as soaring prices for type.

As an exercise, make a photocopy of this page and take it to a typesetter near you for a price estimate. Be sure to say you want it set exactly as it is here. Then ask the typesetter how much it will cost to set just one of the sentences and deliver it to your residence. You may be amazed by what you learn. Many beginning advertisers are surprised the first time they encounter advertising production charges.

Printers and related specialists

The printers who produce brochures, stationery, business cards, sales promotion materials, and point-of-purchase displays are vital to the advertising business. Ranging from small instant print shops to large web offset operations, printers employ or contract with highly trained specialists who prepare artwork for reproduction, make color separations and plates (Figure 3–26), operate presses and collating machines, and run binderies.

As we will discuss in Chapter 10, printers may specialize in offset lithography, rotogravure, letterpress, engraving, or other techniques. The printers' salespeople have to be highly skilled to work with advertisers and agencies, but they often earn very large commissions.

Film and video production houses

Few agencies have in-house television production capabilities. Small agencies often work with local TV stations to produce commercials. But the large agencies normally work with independent production houses that specialize in film or videotape production, or both. Their services are usually bought on a bid basis, but some houses are sought out for their unique talent or capabilities.

FIGURE 3–26

Due to the special nature of their product, color separators have to take great care in preparing advertisements for themselves. Noral met that challenge with one of the most difficult tasks—printing the human face.

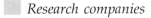 Research companies

Most major advertisers, agencies, and media include a research function as part of their marketing efforts. Advertisers are concerned about the attitudes of their customers, the size of potential markets, and the acceptability of their products.

Agencies, on the other hand, are anxious to know what advertising approaches to use, which concepts communicate most efficiently, and how effective past campaigns have been.

The media are concerned with the reading and viewing habits of their audiences, the desired markets of their advertiser-customers, and the perceptions of the public toward their own particular medium.

Research, therefore, is closely allied to advertising and an important tool of the marketing professional.

However, inasmuch as most firms do not maintain a fully staffed research department, there are thousands of independent research companies and consultants that can be employed to help. As we will see in Chapter 6, the range of services available from these suppliers is extensive.

Research firms come in all sizes, shapes, and specialties, and they provide employment for staff statisticians, field interviewers, and computer programmers as well as analysts with degrees in psychology, sociology, anthropology, economics, and marketing.

Summary

The advertising a company uses affects virtually every person in the organization. The advertising department is responsible for planning, administration, budgeting, and coordination with other departments or outside advertising services. In addition, some advertising departments take responsibility for ad production, media placement, and other marketing support services. Some firms have even developed in-house advertising agencies in hopes of saving money by keeping the normal agency commissions for themselves. However, they have sometimes saved money, but lost creativity.

Advertising agencies are independent organizations of creative and business people who specialize in the development and preparation of advertising plans, advertisements, and other promotional tools on behalf of clients.

To accomplish their task, agencies provide a wide range of services to their clients. These include research, planning, creative services, print and broadcast production, coordination of media and suppliers, account management, and accounting services, to name a few.

To make money, agencies may charge fees or retainers, receive commissions from the media, or mark up outside purchases made on behalf of their clients. Most agencies get their clients through referral or personal solicitation.

The medium that carries the message from the advertiser to the customer is the third and vital link in the communication chain. The major mass media available today are print, electronic, out-of-home (outdoor and transit advertising), and direct mail. Other media include cinema advertising, beetleboards, coptermedia, and scoreboard advertising.

Every medium has a sales department that calls on local advertisers and agencies to sell them space or time. In addition, most media can help the advertiser with production assistance, market research, sales promotion, or merchandising services. Most major media contract with a rep firm to sell their space or time to national advertisers.

In addition to the media, advertising suppliers are crucial to the growth of the industry. These suppliers include art studios, typographers, printers, photographers, film and video production companies, and market research firms. These companies, too, offer opportunities for specialized advertising careers.

Questions for review and discussion

1. If a company has an advertising agency does it still need an advertising manager? Why?
2. What are the advantages and disadvantages of an in-house advertising agency for a small retail chain?
3. In what ways can a full-service advertising agency help a manufacturer of industrial goods?
4. What do you think are the most important points for an advertiser to consider in selecting an agency?
5. Do you think an advertiser should change agencies on a regular basis? Why or why not?
6. Where do you think the most highly paid people in advertising work? With the advertisers, the agencies, or the media and suppliers? Why?
7. What is the best way to compensate an advertising agency? Explain.
8. What does media proliferation mean, and how will it affect the future of advertising?
9. How do the various media functions interrelate with advertising?
10. What methods can an advertiser or advertising agency use to locate suppliers and evaluate their services?

PART II

MARKETING
AND
ADVERTISING
PLANS AND
STRATEGIES

4

ADVERTISING AND THE MARKETING MIX

W|hile studying for his master's degree in mechanical engineering at Princeton University, Lido Anthony Iacocca began his automotive career as a student engineer at Ford Motor Company.

Less than four decades later, as the new chairman of the ailing Chrysler Corporation, he accomplished one of the most astonishing feats of "engineering" (and marketing) in the history of American business. And for that feat, the editors of *Advertising Age* named Lee Iacocca "Adman of the Year."

For several years, Chrysler teetered on the edge of collapse. Short of cash, saddled with huge overhead and inefficient plants, and overstocked with unwanted products, the company had to go begging to the U.S. government for a complex $1.2 billion bailout loan guarantee program.

Naysayers abounded. Many people were against the bailout program, and experts everywhere predicted the government guarantee would only prolong the agony by delaying the company's inevitable bankruptcy. And then, the very next year, Chrysler hit its low point, recording a $1.7 billion loss—the largest single-year loss in U.S. history.

Iacocca persevered.

Less than three years later the company paid back the total $1.2 billion loan and recorded record profits. In fact, the company made more money in the first three months of 1984 than in any year in Chrysler's history—$706 million.

Suddenly, Chrysler was once again a viable contender in its field. As *Advertising Age* reported, it had an array of trend-setting products in its stable (with more on the drawing board), a significantly more efficient operation, and a chief executive who broke new ground as a powerful advertising spokesman for his product—and, in fact, for American-made goods generally[1] (Figure 4–1).

How did he do it? Was Chrysler's sudden good fortune really due to its chairman's advertising skill?

To Iacocca, who naturally is very much guided by his engineering background, the product is king. To him the job of turning Chrysler around was a very difficult product task as well as a quality and productivity task.

Veteran marketing and advertising people see it differently, though. To them, what was accomplished at Chrysler smacks of marketing acumen of the first degree.

In this case, they're both right.

WHAT IS MARKETING?

Management usually divides the various functions of business into three broad areas: production, finance, and marketing. Students who major in business study many subjects that relate to one or all of these areas. For instance, courses in accounting relate to the finance area. Courses in purchasing, quality control, or manufacturing relate to the production category. And advertising is a specialty course in the marketing area.

FIGURE 4–1

After turning Chrysler around, appearing in America's living rooms as Chrysler's spokesman, and penning his own autobiography, Lee Iacocca's familiarity and popularity soared. Some even touted him as a presidential hopeful.

To be a good specialist in advertising, a person also needs a good general understanding of the marketing framework within which advertising operates. Marketing also includes other activities such as market research, product distribution, pricing, and sales, all of which also relate to advertising. The purpose of this chapter is to outline the subject of marketing and to discuss advertising's role in the marketing function.

■ Growth of the Marketing Concept

Unfortunately *marketing* may be one of the most misunderstood terms in business. In the past it was defined as "those various business activities which are used to direct the flow of products from the company that makes them to the people who use them." However, this definition tends to emphasize the activities of distribution and transportation, and today the field of marketing includes many other equally important activities.

A hundred years ago, when there were few products and many consumers, companies had to worry only about creating and producing more products to satisfy the huge demand. This was called the *production-oriented period*, and the emphasis in marketing was indeed on distribution and transportation.

After the introduction of mass production techniques, the marketplace was glutted with products. So business began to emphasize the selling function. The *sales-oriented period* was marked by extravagant advertising claims and an attitude of *caveat emptor* ("let the buyer beware") as companies tried to unload their products on the public.

The saturation point was eventually reached, and many companies found that no amount of high-pressure selling or slick advertising could move any more products. In the end, many companies lost substantial sums because of unsold inventories or falling sales.

In recent years companies have found it more profitable to determine in advance what customers want and then make products that will satisfy those desires. This is called the *marketing-oriented period*. Of course, many companies still operate under the sales-oriented concept or even the production-oriented concept. But they are constantly courting failure, and they risk experiencing their own Chrysler situations.

Chrysler's problems, according to Iacocca, were due in large part to the company's own disgraceful mismanagement. And marketing was one area where the mistakes seemed to be continuous. All too often the company was building the wrong cars for the wrong people. Chrysler buyers tended to be more conservative, older, blue-collar workers who were less inclined to buy cars loaded with high-profit options and who were most likely to get hurt in an economic downturn. Chrysler's products were often disappointing even to this market, and yet they never succeeded in attracting another one. In short, the company did not adequately determine the wants and needs of the car-buying public when new cars were designed. And so, as the company's president admitted, fully half the people buying a new automobile never even considered a Chrysler product.

In its broadest sense today, then, *marketing* refers to all business activities aimed at: (1) *finding out who customers are and what they want,* (2) *developing products to satisfy those customers' needs and desires,* and (3) *getting the products into the customers' possession.* The objective of marketing is to help the company make a profit by providing its customers with products or services that they want or need. Companies that operate under the marketing concept are concerned with shaping products to meet consumer needs rather than forcing consumers to buy what the manufacturer wants. As a result, they are intensely interested in the consumer's point of view, and they allow that point of view to dictate many company activities.

■ The Task of Marketing and Advertising

Under the marketing concept, the task of the marketing department is divided into three areas: (1) to discover, locate, and measure the demand for products; (2) to interpret this information for management so they can translate it into new services or products; and (3) to develop and implement a plan that makes the product available and informs prospective customers about the product's need-satisfying capabilities (Figure 4–2). Advertising is primarily concerned with the informing function, as well as with persuading and reminding customers about the product. But to be successful, advertising depends on the adequate performance of the other marketing activities as well.

As Chrysler showed, a company can spend millions and millions of dollars on advertising every year and still fail. The product must be what the consumer wants. The price must be acceptable. There must be a place where consumers can buy the product conveniently. And there must be people ready and able to sell the product to the consumer and coordinate all these other activities adequately and successfully. (See Ad Lab 4–A.)

FIGURE 4–2

The consumer-marketing cycle. The tasks of marketing management under the marketing concept are: (1) locating and measuring the demand for products; (2) interpreting this demand for management, which then develops products to satisfy the need; and (3) developing and implementing a plan that makes the product available and informs consumers about the product's capabilities. Marketing, therefore, begins and ends with the consumer.

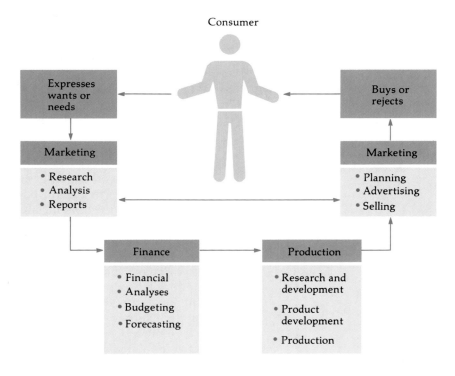

AD LAB 4–A Marketing Mac: Apple Computer's counterattack against IBM

The Macintosh is Apple Computer's latest weapon in the computer war being waged against the industry kingpin, IBM. The IBM Personal Computer caused Apple to lose its dominant share of all its markets—home, business, educational, and scientific. "Apple can't outsell or outservice IBM," says E. Floyd Kvamme, Apple's executive vice president for marketing and sales. "So we are out to establish and maintain a technological leadership position." And the company feels it has done that with Macintosh.

The Macintosh is an intriguing machine. Weighing less than 17 pounds, the Macintosh takes up only 10 × 10 inches of desk space. Information and documents on the display screen can be shown simultaneously in "windows," or boxes, and can be moved, expanded, or shrunk by means of a "mouse," a small hand-held pointing device. And on-the-screen "paper" can be shuffled, documents revised or discarded, and charts drawn, all with a few simple commands executed with the mouse. The Macintosh relies heavily on symbols and pictures on the screen to help people conquer computer phobia. It cost more than $100 million to develop. Apple spent another $20 million for a highly automated factory to build only the Macintosh.

Apple has a national sales team to penetrate the corporate market, but most of its sales come from retail dealers. The dealers are essential because no person is going to buy a computer without first reading about it, asking friends about it, and especially talking to a dealer about it. Apple feels that the Mac's best prospects will be small businesspeople and college students.

The advertising messages IBM and Apple are using to sell their personal computers are alike in one way: Both stress ease of use in order to allay buyers' fears about computers. Nevertheless, there is a big difference in the way Apple and IBM want to be seen as companies. IBM emphasizes dependability and trades on its name recognition value. As an IBM spokesperson explains it, "The PC product line has the excellent quality and service that are the hallmarks of IBM."

Apple, on the other hand, takes pride in being unique. "We want to be known as the innovators," says John Scully, Apple's president. "Apple is a gathering place for very bright people who have the opportunity and the resources to create significantly different products than what might be turned out in a larger, more structured environment."

Conventional wisdom maintains that computer buyers care less about achievement than about such factors as compatibility and customer support, prime virtues of IBM. In the volatile computer business, however, history has shown that significant technical achievements can attract customers away from the most deeply entrenched standards. Only time will tell whether Apple's Macintosh will provide another example of dubious conventional wisdom.

Laboratory Application

From your reading of the text so far and your knowledge of the Macintosh, what marketplace need or needs do you think the Macintosh was aimed at satisfying?

To explain the importance of these activities, we will briefly explore how markets are discovered, located, and measured. Then we will discuss the *four Ps*—product, price, place, and promotion—which are referred to as the *elements of the marketing mix* and which are used to accomplish the company's marketing objectives. The way in which a company decides to coordinate these elements has a profound effect on the advertising it uses. (Figure 4–3.)

First let's be sure we understand what a market is and where it can be found.

WHAT IS A MARKET?

At the annual convention of the Savings Institutions Marketing Society of America, delegates were shown a number of different advertisements that had been placed by savings institutions around the country. The savings bank officers in the audience were asked to grade each of the ads on a scale of 1 to 10. One ad presented was an outstanding example of tongue-in-cheek humor by Clearwater Federal Savings and Loan Association, a $450-million savings institution in Florida.

The ad pictured a millionaire standing in the hallway of his mansion before a large, ornately framed painting. The headline of the ad read: "I keep the family jewels in the safe behind the portrait of my first wife. I keep my money at Clearwater Federal." This was followed by a column of light, humorous copy, which told how rich the man was, how security-conscious, and how much he liked all the free services at Clearwater Federal that kept his money safe from his *second wife's* shopping sprees. The ad was signed: "Clearwater Federal. Where those who've made it keep it" (Figure 4–4).

Most savings and loan executives who viewed the ad gave it a very low rating, saying they didn't like it because it wouldn't appeal to everybody, only to the very rich.

FIGURE 4–3

In 1985 the board of directors of the American Marketing Association adopted a new definition of marketing reflecting the wide-ranging activities which fall under the marketing umbrella. How do you think this definition conforms to the concept of marketing presented in this text?

"Marketing is the process of planning and executing the conception, pricing, promotion, and distribution of ideas, goods, and services to create exchanges that satisfy individual and organizational objectives."

—AMA Board

FIGURE 4–4

Clearwater Federal targeted a very profitable market segment in this tongue-in-cheek ad. Wealthy people can afford to laugh at themselves, and the not-so-wealthy can enjoy the joke, too. Unfortunately, most savings executives viewing this ad failed to understand its sophisticated humor and marketing strategy, fearing it would not appeal to everybody. This is called the majority fallacy.

The Majority Fallacy

Their reaction is a typical example of the *majority fallacy*—a common misconception that, to be successful, a product or service must appeal to the majority of people. Sophisticated marketing and advertising people know that this is just not true. Often several products or services compete for the same customers, and therefore each is able to attract only a fraction of all the business. A new competitive product might do considerably better if it is specifically aimed at just one group of customers (like wealthy people) rather than at the majority of customers.

A market, therefore, does not have to include everybody. A market may include just one segment or group of potential customers who share a common interest, need, or desire. This group of customers must be able to use the product or service offered to some advantage, and they must be able to afford the purchase price. In its simplest terms, therefore, a market is people. Clearwater Federal actually did a good job of selecting a profitable market segment (i.e., wealthy people and those who would like to see themselves as wealthy) and catering to it.

There are five broad classifications of markets to which companies advertise and sell:

1. *Consumer markets* are composed of people who buy products for their own personal use.

2. *Industrial markets* are individuals or companies (like manufacturing companies) that buy products needed for the production of other products or services.
3. *Reseller markets* are individuals or companies that buy products for the purpose of reselling them, like retail stores and car dealers.
4. *Government markets* are governmental bodies that buy products for the successful coordination of municipal, state, federal, or other governmental activities.
5. *International markets* are any of the previously mentioned markets that are located in foreign countries.

■ Locating and Measuring the Market

The whole purpose of marketing and advertising is to find the right people and get them together with the right products. The advertisements we see every day are usually intended to appeal to a particular group of people called the company's target market. The better defined that market is, the better chance of success the company will have.

In the case of Clearwater Federal the target market was composed of those groups of individuals who were wealthy, were achieving wealth, or who liked to affiliate with the wealthy and who, therefore, were interested in security as well as high interest on their investments. A federally insured savings account that pays high interest

FIGURE   4–5

Stubbies sportswear segmented the youth market to appeal to those with the "California dream." Colorful ads showing beach scenes, kamikaze surfers, and leaping killer whales typify the feeling their agency wanted to create.

and comes complete with many free services is likely to be an attractive offer to these people.

Market segmentation

Markets for products may be selected according to a variety of classifications based on shared characteristics of customers. By categorizing customers into meaningful segments, the company can determine which group is potentially the most profitable market. It then designs products for that segment and aims all of its marketing activities at that group (Figure 4–5).

This process of dividing markets into meaningful groups is called *market segmentation* and will be more fully discussed in Chapter 5, "Consumer Behavior and Market Segmentation."

Market research

To select the most desirable segments, companies try to learn as much as they can about the various groups within the total market. Using *market research* techniques, companies first attempt to measure the size of the total market for the particular product. Then they try to estimate the size of the segments within the market. In the case of Clearwater Federal, they might have attempted to measure:

1. The total market for savings and loans and banks in Clearwater Federal's local area.
2. The size of the "wealthy people" segment in that area.
3. The size of the segment with "wealthy attitudes."

Next the company tries to measure the share of the market that it might attract by asking the following questions:

1. What is the potential share of the total market that Clearwater Federal might attract if it aimed at the majority market?
2. What is the potential share of the "wealthy people" segment that Clearwater Federal might attract if it aimed specifically at that market?

There are various methods used to measure the size of markets depending on the type of market being considered. For example, the methods used to measure consumer markets differ greatly from the methods used to measure industrial markets. These methods will be more completely described in Chapter 6, "Marketing Research."

Target marketing

Once the size and potential of the wealthy people segment are determined and the company selects that group as its *target market*, the planning of other marketing activities is greatly simplified. Special services catering to that segment may be designed, the price of services is determined, the number and location of branches needed become apparent, and the most suitable type of advertising can be prepared. Everything can be aimed at appealing to that target market. (See Chapter 7, "Marketing and Advertising Planning.")

If the wealthy people segment of the market had not appeared large enough to be profitable, Clearwater Federal would have had to select a different target market, and their other marketing and advertising activities would have been altered, too. (See Ad Lab 4–B.)

AD LAB 4–B   Marketing Mac: Who is the target market?

Review the Macintosh story in Ad Lab 4–A and relate that information to what you read in the text about locating and measuring the market for products.

Laboratory Applications

1. Is the Macintosh intended to appeal to all computer buyers or just particular groups? What groups?

2. Why do you suppose the Macintosh was aimed at the particular target groups you just identified? Explain your reasoning.

THE MARKETING MIX

Advertising, as the communications device in marketing, is just one of the many marketing tools used to help move goods or services from the company to its target market. However, the importance of advertising varies from business to business, depending on the nature of the company and the other marketing activities it uses. Every company has the option of adding, subtracting, or changing four elements in its marketing program to achieve a desired *marketing mix*. The elements that comprise the mix are called the four Ps: product, price, place, and promotion.

Consider two vastly different examples. First, a medical doctor wishes to increase the size of his or her practice. Some marketing-related communications might be business cards, a sign on the door, formal announcements, and direct-mail reminders to patients to come in for a checkup. Overall, though, due to professional ethics that have traditionally barred the use of promotion, media advertising may play little or no part in the doctor's business. Of greater importance are the physician's medical skill, experience, the cost of services, the location of the office, the size of the staff, and the physician's bedside manner.

On the other hand, how important is advertising in marketing a mail-order item? In this case, advertising may be the lifeblood of the business.

For 50 years Charles Atlas has marketed his body-building course and equipment through mail-order advertisements in magazines for boys and young men. In that time the company has made over $30 million in sales. Furthermore, the entire effort has been made through advertising, without the use of a single salesperson. In fact,

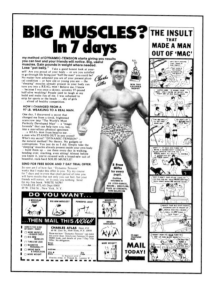

FIGURE 4–6

From this classic ad campaign came the famous question: "Do friends kick sand in your face?" Also came the classic concept of the "97-pound weakling." The basic ad remained virtually unchanged for 50 years, which reminds us of another famous line: "Stick with a winner."

Charles Roman, who created the series of ads first used in 1929, continued using basically the same ads for the next 50 years (Figure 4–6).

From these two examples, we can see that advertising plays vastly different roles in the marketing of various items. These differences are the result of company decisions about the appropriate mix of marketing activities that are used to promote its products or services.

In the case of the doctor, what would the marketing mix for the medical practice include? The doctor's product is the healing service or particular specialty. The place element is determined by the location of the office and the decision on whether to make house calls. Price is also a factor in marketing the services. Inasmuch as the doctor may not be allowed by the profession to advertise, what permissible promotional activities are most important to success? The sign on the door? Appointment cards? Or bedside manner? Now consider Charles Atlas. What do we already know about his marketing mix?

The remainder of this chapter will focus further on the relationship of each of these four Ps (product, price, place, and promotion) to the advertising a company may use.

Advertising and the Product Element

Companies use various means to distinguish their products from the products of their competitors. The way the product is advertised may be one of these.

Consider the ads for the Honda Civic and the Chrysler Laser in Figure 4–7. We see not only two very different styles of advertising but also two different ways of distinguishing products from one another. Look at the Honda ad first. What is the advertised uniqueness of the Honda? What features does the car have that make it stand out? How are those features important to the consumer? How would you answer the same questions for the Chrysler ad? Are they trying to sell something more than the functional superiority of the car? What?

What we learn from these two examples provides a clue to the answer to a basic marketing question: What is a product?

What is a product?

When you buy an automobile, what are you really buying? Is it the massive configuration of steel, plastic, rubber, and chrome you see? Is it the transportation it will deliver? Is it the better gas mileage you will realize? Or, on the other hand, is the product really the sleek, racy design of the car, the sense of speed you experience, and the self-esteem and confidence you have as people look at you admiringly in your gleaming, sexy machine? What is this product you are buying?

Today's marketers know that a product may be any or all of these things. A product represents a bundle of values or satisfactions to the consumer, depending on the individual consumer's particular needs and desires. The satisfactions the consumer receives, known as the *benefits,* may be simply functional, such as transportation, better gas mileage, or larger size. Or the satisfactions may be social, psychological, or emotional, such as beauty, self-esteem, pride, luxury, and sex appeal. By definition, therefore, *a product is a bundle of values encompassing functional, social, psychological, economic, and other consumer needs.*

FIGURE 4–7

VO: Chrysler creates . . . a more powerful Laser. Because the competition is always on our tail. And we intend to keep them there. We boosted turbopower. Zero to fifty Laser XE is faster than Toyota Supra. Front-wheel drive Laser beats Camaro Z28 in the slalom. And Laser XE has advanced electronics . . . Mark Cross leather available and the Chrysler Protection Plan. Laser XE. The competition is good. We had to be better. Chrysler. The best built, best backed American cars.

B. Honda's agency, Needham Harper Worldwide, chose a warm method to demonstrate graphically how the product had been enlarged.

When companies develop new products for specific markets, they first try to determine the functional and psychological needs of that market. The new products are then developed as complete *product concepts* with corresponding bundles of functional and psychological satisfactions in mind. This product concept is carried over into the way the product is designed, named, packaged, labeled, displayed, classified, and advertised.

Consider the names of various automobiles such as Volkswagen, Subaru, Chrysler, and Ford. Do you consider these functional names, or do they have some psychological connotations? Now consider these names: Jaguar, Mustang, Laser, El Dorado. Do these names imply functional benefits or psychological satisfactions?

The way a company classifies its product is also important in defining the product concept and its marketing mix. There are many ways in which products may be classified. They may be grouped by markets—that is, by who buys them. They may be classified by how fast they are used up or by how tangible they are. They may be grouped according to the purchasing habits of the people who buy them. Or they may be classified according to some physical description. (See the Checklist of product classifications.)

Product differentiation

Henry Ford is reputed to have said, "They can have any color they want as long as it's black." Marketers have since come to realize that if they don't offer customers what they want, the competition will. Therefore, the concept of product differentiation—building differences into products to satisfy consumer demand—has become a basic marketing strategy. The differences between products may be perceptible, imperceptible, or induced.

Perceptible differences When differences between products are visibly apparent to the consumer they are called *perceptible differences*. For example, automobiles come in a variety of shapes, colors, and sizes. Refrigerators are designed with right- and left-hand doors, single doors, double doors, and different colors and dimensions.

Imperceptible differences Not readily apparent are *imperceptible differences*, even though they may certainly exist. For example, without getting underneath the Honda, the consumer cannot perceive that its engine has no catalytic converter. Nor can one tell without lifting up the hood that the engine sits sideways and the car has front-wheel drive. Likewise, cigarettes look pretty much alike from the outside, but once people buy a certain pack and open it up they may discover a different shaped filter or a different color of paper. Once they light up, they experience differences in taste. The same is true with chewing gum and many food products. The differences may be imperceptible, or hidden, at first, but they do exist, and they may greatly affect the desirability of the product.

Induced differences In some products such as aspirin, gasoline, certain brands of cigarettes, and packaged foods, induced differences may be created by advertising. One of the most successful product introductions in recent years was L'eggs hosiery. The product itself was not differentiated other than through unique branding, packaging, distribution, merchandising, and advertising.

Checklist of product classifications

By Market

☐ Consumer goods. Products and services we use in our daily lives (food, clothing, furniture, automobiles).

☐ Industrial goods. Products used by companies for the purpose of producing other products (raw materials, agricultural commodities, machinery, tools, equipment).

By Rate of Consumption and Tangibility

☐ Durable goods. Tangible products which are long lasting and infrequently replaced (cars, trucks, refrigerators, furniture).

☐ Nondurable goods. Tangible products which may be consumed in one or a few uses and usually need to be replaced at regular intervals (food, soap, gasoline, oil).

☐ Services. Activities, benefits, or satisfactions offered for sale (travel, haircuts, legal and medical services, massages).

By Purchasing Habits

☐ Convenience goods. Purchases made frequently with a minimum of effort (cigarettes, food, newspapers).

☐ Shopping goods. Infrequently purchased items for which greater time is spent comparing price, quality, style, warranty (furniture, cars, clothing, tires).

☐ Specialty goods. Products with such unique characteristics that consumers will make special efforts to purchase them even if they're more expensive (fancy photographic equipment, special women's fashions, stereo components).

By Product Description

☐ Package goods. Cereals, hair tonics, etc.

☐ Hard goods. Furniture, appliances.

☐ Soft goods. Clothing, bedding.

☐ Services. Nontangible products.

▨ *Product packaging*

In the average supermarket more than 10,000 items compete for customer attention and dollars. Often the package is the major factor in this competition. Because of the emphasis on self-service, packaging is increasingly important not only in grocery stores but in drug, variety, and other retail establishments as well. The package quickly identifies the brand to current users and endeavors to convince nonusers to try its contents for the first time.

The five functions of packaging are (1) containment and protection, (2) identification, (3) convenience, (4) consumer appeal, and (5) economy. Since these functions may have a profound effect on the marketing of a product, we should discuss each of them briefly.

Containment and protection The basic purpose of any package is to hold and protect the product. Packages must keep the product fresh and protect their contents from shipping damage, water vapor (frozen foods), grease, infestation, and odors. Consumers don't want contaminated food, leaky packages, cut fingers, or tampering by criminals. Protection requirements are established by both the government and trade associations.

Identification A package must quickly identify the product by using the trade name, trademark, or trade character, or a combination of these devices. Packaging has become so important as an identification device that companies such as Heinz and Coca-Cola have adhered to the same basic bottle and label designs for years.

Consumers like high visibility and clear legibility in packaging. Since shoppers seldom wear their reading glasses, type should be easy to read, and color combinations should provide high contrast (Figure 4–8).

Convenience Packages must be able to survive storage and reshipment, and they must be easy to stack and display. This is why there are so few pyramid-shaped bottles. The retailer also looks for a full

FIGURE   4–8

Creative Software uses high contrast, bright colors, and bold graphics in the packaging of their computer software.

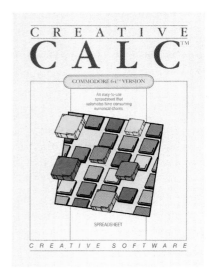

range of sizes to fit the customer's needs. Whether a store stocks an item is often influenced by these considerations.

Consumer requirements are similar. Consumers want packages that can be stored and opened easily. For this reason, when the package is designed it is important to know where the product will be stored. A package designed to fit on the shelf of a refrigerator will differ from one stored in a medicine cabinet or on a laundry room shelf. Products for a dresser table should be packaged so they don't spill or tip over easily. Shampoo bottles should be easy to grip.

Sometimes a customer's desire for convenience can interfere with protection. For example, cellophane wrappings permit easy inspection, but they may not always protect well. Spouts make pouring much easier, but they may limit the strength of the package.

Consumer appeal How well the package appeals to consumers can have a profound effect on the product's marketability. Appeal is the result of many factors—size, color, material, and shape. Even easy-to-read package instructions can create consumer appeal.

It is important to have a variety of sizes because users have different requirements and budgets. On the other hand, if a product is available in too many sizes, the retailer may not be able to carry all of them.

Color, too, is an important consideration. Louis Cheskin, a well-known researcher, has completed several studies suggesting that certain colors have special meanings to consumers. General Foods changed the Sanka package when it learned that its yellow label suggested weakness (Figure 4–9).

FIGURE 4–9

Color decisions in packaging are critically important for a product like fruit juice. The company wants to communicate freshness, naturalness, and healthfulness. What do the colors on the Welch's packages suggest to you?

The shape of a package may also offer special appeal. Containers of Janitor in a Drum and heart-shaped packages of Valentine's Day candy instantly tell what the product is and what it is used for.

Sometimes gift wrapping is used for special holidays. While often successful, it also increases the cost of packaging and poses problems if it doesn't sell out. Remaining items must be altered, offered at a discount, or held for the next holiday occasion.

The packaging of several items together may offer convenience as well as a discount price. Combination packaging also limits the waste that occurs with unit packaging.

The convenience that comes from secondary use can also add appeal to a package. For example, Kraft manufactures a cheese glass that, once emptied, can be used for serving fruit juice. Some tins and bottles even become collectibles. Liquor bottles can sometimes serve as decanters or vases. These packages are really premiums that give the buyer of the product extra value for the dollars spent.

Economy   Whether or not a package is used depends on its cost. Besides the obvious cost of materials and printing, the expense can

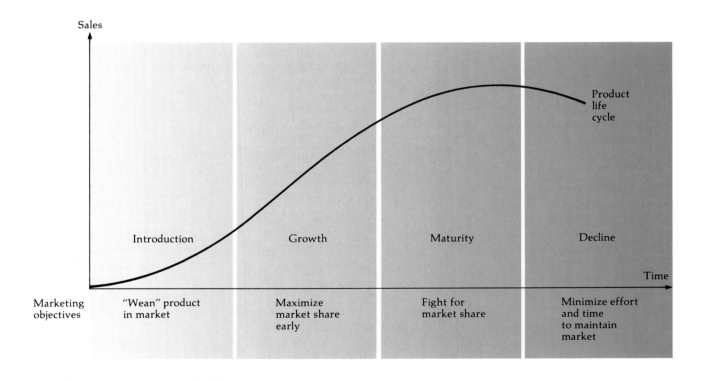

FIGURE   4–10

The product life cycle. Marketing objectives change as the product proceeds from one stage of the cycle to the next. So do marketing strategies. In the introductory and growth stages, promotional activities are aimed at creating product awareness and inducing trial. In later stages, efforts may be aimed at suggesting competition comparison or maintaining brand loyalty.

vary according to the amount of protection, identification, convenience, and consumer appeal.

Some of the factors that affect the cost of packaging are:

1. Cost of packaging materials.
2. Cost of manufacturing the package.
3. Cost of storage and shipping.
4. Cost of equipment used to manufacture and fill packages.
5. Cost of associated labor.

Sometimes a small increase in production costs may be more than offset by increased customer appeal. Aluminum foil and waxed paper boxes now come with cutting edges. Kleenex tissues became a hit with the introduction of a package that dispensed one tissue at a time. And many medicines are offered in "child-proof" plastic bottles. These benefits may make a considerable difference to the consumer and affect the way a product is advertised.

Product positioning

In 1959 Avis, Inc., the the car rental company, stunned the advertising world and the general public by openly acknowledging that it was only number two. "Therefore," their ad said, "we try harder." The Avis campaign was immensely successful. Why? Was it because of packaging? Was it because they tried harder? What was the real or perceived difference between Avis and the other car rental companies? The answer is one word: *positioning.*

Most products and services compete in a field of similar products and services. If the features or attributes of a particular product can be made distinct, the product will tend to occupy a particular product space, rank, or *position* in the consumer's mind. Part of the marketing effort, therefore, is determining what desirable positions are open in the consumer's mind and developing products to fill them.

There are many different ways to position products. They may be ranked in the consumer's mind by the benefits they offer, by a perceptible difference, or by some imperceptible or even induced difference.

How was Avis positioned? Avis had no product features that were significantly different from Hertz, National, or the other car rental companies. The product difference was, in effect, nonexistent. Hertz, on the other hand, was very distinct. It was the largest, and everyone knew it. Avis used this knowledge to position itself against Hertz as an alternative. By saying that it was number two, it separated itself from the pack and gained widespread recognition. (See People in Advertising.)

Product life cycle

Just as humans pass through stages in life from infancy to death, products also pass through a *product life cycle.*[2] Marketing and advertising people have identified four major stages in this cycle: introduction, growth, maturity, and decline. The advertising for a product depends to a great extent on where the product stands in its life cycle (Figure 4–10).

For example, when a major new product is invented and *introduced,* the company's objective may be to stimulate *primary demand*—that is,

PEOPLE IN ADVERTISING

Al Ries and Jack Trout

Chairman of the Board and President
Trout & Ries Advertising

Al Ries and Jack Trout are widely known for developing the "positioning" approach to advertising. Ries is founder and chairman of the board of Trout & Ries Advertising, a $25 million New York agency whose clients include Harrah's hotel/casinos, Western Union, and Monsanto. He was previously associated with Marstellar Advertising, Needham, Harper & Steers, and General Electric. Ries is board member of the Sales Executives Club and the Advertising Club of New York.

Trout, president of Trout & Ries, joined the agency in 1968 after serving as divisional advertising manager for Uniroyal. He was formerly with General Electric. A recent *New York Times Magazine* article credited Trout with changing the entire direction of the advertising industry with his unique "positioning" concept.

Positioning has received widespread attention in business, consumer, advertising publications. Articles have brought Trout and Ries more than 120,000 reprint requests and scores of speaking invitations. Their book, *Positioning, the Battle for Your Mind*, has become an industry text. As a result, *positioning* has become the buzzword of advertising and marketing people not only in this country but around the world.

What Is Positioning?

Positioning is a simple principle that can best be demonstrated by asking yourself some simple questions. Who was the first person to fly solo across the North Atlantic? Don't think it couldn't be Charles Lindbergh, because it was. Now who was the second person to fly solo across the North Atlantic? Not so easy to answer, is it? Who was the first person to walk on the moon? Neil Armstrong, right? Now who was the second? The first person, the first company to occupy the position in the prospect's mind is going to be awfully hard to dislodge: IBM in computers, Hertz in rent-a-cars, Coke in cola.

The Mind: A Memory Bank

Like a memory bank, the mind has a slot or position for each bit of information it has chosen to retain. In its operation, the mind is a lot like a computer. But there is one important difference. A computer has to accept what is put into it, whereas the mind does not. In fact, quite the opposite. As a defense mechanism against the volume of today's communications, the mind screens and rejects much of the information offered it. In general, the mind accepts only new information that matches its prior knowledge or experience. It filters out everything else.

For example, when a viewer sees a television commercial that says, "NCR means computers," he doesn't accept it. IBM means computers; NCR means National Cash Register. The computer "position" in the minds of most people is filled by a company called IBM (International Business Machines Corp.). For a competitive computer manufacturer to obtain a favorable position in the prospect's mind, it must relate its company to IBM's position.

To cope with advertising's complexity, people have learned to rank products and brands. Perhaps this can best be visualized by imagining a series of ladders in the mind. On each step is a brand name, and each different ladder represents a different product category. For advertisers to increase their brand preference, they must move up the ladder.

This is difficult, especially if the new category is not positioned against an old one. The mind has no room for the new and different unless they are related to the old. Therefore, if you have a truly new product, it's often better to tell the prospect what the product is not, rather than what it is.

The first automobile, for example, was called a "horseless" carriage, a name that positioned the concept against the existing mode of transportation. Words like "offtrack" betting, "lead-free" gasoline, and "tubeless" tires are examples of how new concepts can best be positioned against the old.

Number One Strategy

Successful marketing strategy usually consists of keeping your eyes open to possibilities and then striking before the product ladder is firmly fixed. The marketing leader is usually the one who moves the ladder into the mind with his or her brand nailed to the one and only rung.

Once there, what can a company do to keep its top-dog position? As long as a company owns the position, there's no point in running ads that scream "We're No. 1." It is much better to enhance the product category in prospects' minds. Notice the current IBM campaign that ignores competition and sells the value of computers—all computers, not just the company's types.

Number Two Strategy

Most companies are in the number two, three, four, or even worse category. What then? Hope springs eternal in the human breast. Nine times out of ten, the also-ran sets out to attack the leader. The result is disaster.

In the communication jungle, the only hope is to be selective, to concentrate on narrow targets, and to practice segmentation. For example, Anheuser-Busch found an opening for a high-priced beer and filled it with Michelob. Advertisers must assess the competitors. They must locate weak points in their positions and then launch marketing attacks against them. Savin developed small, inexpensive copiers and took advantage of a weakness in the Xerox product line.

Simply stated, the first rule of positioning is this:

You can't compete head-on with a company that has a strong, established position. You can go around, under, or over, but never head-to-head. The leader owns the high ground, the top position in the prospect's mind, the top rung of the product ladder.

In positioning, the name of a company or product is important. Allegheny Airlines was regarded as "small" and "regional" in consumers' minds until it changed its name to USAir. Similarly, if your corporate name is inappropriate for a new product you plan to market, create a new corporate name—and a new position. Singer Company put its name on business machines and lost $371 million. They committed the ultimate positioning mistake by trying to transfer a brand name to a different product sold to a different market.

Importance of Objectivity

To be successful in positioning, advertising and marketing people must be brutally frank. They must try to eliminate all ego from the decision-making process; it only clouds the issue. One critical aspect of positioning is objectively evaluating products and how they are viewed by customers and prospects. Successful companies get their information from the marketplace. That is where the program has to succeed, not in the product manager's office.

1. What position do we own?
The marketplace is where to find the answer

3. Whom must we out-gun?
Avoid a confrontation with marketing leaders

5. Can we stick it out?
Expect internal pressures for change

2. What position do we want?
Select a position that won't become obsolete

4. Do we have enough money?
Spend enough to accomplish the objective

6. Do ads match our position?
Creativity can often get in the way

consumer demand for the whole product category. To educate the consuming public about the new product, advertising will stress information about the what the product does and how it works. Promotion to the trade will also be used to encourage distributors and retailers to carry the new product. During this introductory phase, losses may be incurred as companies spend large amounts of money on research and development and on advertising and promotion in order to build widespread demand (Figure 4–11).

As sales volume begins to rise rapidly, the product enters the *growth* stage. New customers make their first purchases while earlier customers are already repurchasing. As the demand for the product class expands, stimulated by mass advertising and word-of-mouth, competitive products emerge and create even more purchase pressure on the marketplace.

At this point, sheer momentum may carry the product's sales upward, so the ratio of advertising expenditures to total sales will begin to decrease, and the firm may begin to realize substantial profits. In 1978, for example, more than half a million home videotape machines were sold—four times the number sold in the previous year. By 1985 as many as 20 percent of all U.S. homes had videotape machines, and many competitive brands with undifferentiated products had entered the scene to cash in on this growth.

In the *maturity* stage, industry sales reach a plateau as the marketplace becomes saturated and the number of new customers dwindles. As competition intensifies, profits also diminish. Promotional efforts are increased, but the emphasis is on *selective demand* to impress customers with the subtle advantages of one brand over another. At this stage, companies increase sales only at the expense of competitors. Therefore, the strategies of product differentiation, market segmentation, and product positioning become more important as companies fight for even the smallest increases in market share.

FIGURE 4–11

In this primary demand ad, Technics is comparing the new laser disc system to conventional stereo systems. Their goal is to promote the concept of this new package rather than to promote the benefits of their system over some competitor's laser disc system.

Do your teeth a flavor.

Aren't your kids worth Crest?

FIGURE 4-12

Crest shows the three formulations of their product, all containing their advanced formula Fluoristat. While Crest has experienced tremendous competition from other brands entering the health segment of the dentifrice market, it has played an effective number one positioning role, matching its competitors' moves with defensive moves of its own.

During the maturity stage, companies frequently take any of a variety of actions to try to extend the life cycle. These may be designed to (1) add new users, (2) increase the frequency of use by existing customers, (3) develop new uses for the product, or (4) change the size of packages, design new labels, or improve quality. Arm & Hammer baking soda, for example, extended its life cycle by promoting new uses for the product. It started as a cooking aid but later was promoted successfully as a bath water treatment and even as a refrigerator deodorizer.

Finally, as products eventually enter the *decline* stage due to obsolescence or changing consumer tastes, companies may choose to cease all promotion and phase them out quickly, as in the case of the Edsel automobile, or let them die slowly like old brands of cigarettes. They may also attempt to revitalize the product. In the case of Crest toothpaste, Procter & Gamble created a new "great-tasting gel" formulation and designed it into the product as a perceptible difference. In addition they developed their "advanced formula Fluoristat" and built that into the product as an imperceptible product difference (Figure 4-12). (See Ad Lab 4-C.)

■ Advertising and the Price Element

A product's price frequently has a tremendous bearing on its advertising. We see ads in newspapers regularly for retail goods that have been marked down for quick clearance. Advertising is used here to communicate the low price and motivate people to enter the store. On the other hand, many advertisements do not mention the price, but talk instead about other features of the product. And, finally, many premium-priced products are touted for the very fact that they do cost more. L'Oreal has excelled at promoting the expensive luxury of its hair products to the "me" generation.

■ *Influential factors*

Since price plays such an important role in product advertising, we must consider the factors that influence how a company determines the price for its products. Among the important considerations are market demand, production and distribution costs, competition, and corporate objectives. From these factors, companies may determine the appropriate pricing strategy. However, because of these factors, price is often the one element in the marketing mix over which the company has the least control.

Market demand Most people are familiar with the law of supply and demand. If the supply of a product stays the same and the desire (or demand) for it increases, the price tends to rise. If the demand decreases below the available supply, then the price tends to drop (Figure 4-13).

During the 1980 recession, Chrysler, and the other automobile manufacturers, too, were faced with a glut of unsold cars and low consumer demand. Iacocca offered factory rebates—in effect, a price cut. Chrysler sold more cars because of the lower price. In this case no amount of advertising or promoting would have had the same effect as simply cutting the price.

Production and distribution costs As pointed out in Chapter 1, American mass production and mass distribution techniques have enabled more manufacturers to produce and deliver more products to more consumers more inexpensively than in any country. The price of goods depends largely on the cost of production and distribution. As these costs increase, they must be passed on to the consumer, or the company will eventually be unable to meet its overhead and be forced to close its doors. If too many companies were forced out of business, products would become scarce and prices would soar even higher.

Chrysler faced this same problem when Iacocca took the reins. Because they sold fewer cars than either Ford or General Motors, they produced less. This meant that the production costs on each car were higher, making it that much more difficult to compete.

Competition Before the energy shortages of 1974 and 1979, price wars between gasoline service stations were common. As far as the consumer was concerned, gasoline was gasoline, and the most important consideration was price. If one competing station lowered its prices, the consumer switched without hesitation. This all changed during the energy shortages. Suddenly competition was no longer over price but over availability. With the short supply, long lines formed and prices skyrocketed. But the consumer didn't care as long as he or she could get a full tank of gas. Eventually, as prices doubled

---

AD LAB 4–C   Marketing Mac: Understanding the product

Steven Jobs, the 28-year-old chairman of Apple Computer, has said: "The Macintosh is my vision of what a personal computer *should* be. If Mac's sales are just average, then our vision of the world is significantly wrong."

Laboratory Applications

1. What do you think is the product concept of the Macintosh?

2. How would this product be classified?

3. How is the Macintosh differentiated from other computers?

4. What competitive position does the Macintosh occupy?

5. What stage of the product life cycle is Macintosh in? How can you tell?

FIGURE 4–13

If you plot the demand versus price and the supply versus price together, you get this figure. The demand curve is a schedule of the amounts demanded at various prices. The supply curve is a schedule of the amounts offered for sale at various prices. The point where the two curves cross is called the *market clearing price,* where demand and supply are in balance. It is the price that clears the market of supply.

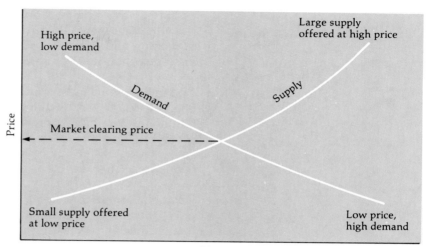

and tripled, demand dwindled, fuel consumption dropped, the supply increased, and price competition among service stations returned.

Corporate objectives Prices are also influenced by the objectives of the company. If a company is introducing a new product, it may set a high price to increase its short-term profits and thereby recover its start-up costs as quickly as possible. Or it may decide to enter the product as a premium or luxury-priced item aimed at a smaller target market.

As products enter the maturity stage of the life cycle, corporate objectives tend to be aimed at increasing share of market, and that tends to exert downward pressure on prices.

Figures 4–14 and 4–15 show two ads. How do you think corporate objectives relate to price in each case?

Other factors Also influencing the price of products and thus the advertising for those products are: consumer income, consumer tastes, government controls and regulations, and the supply of raw materials. Only after taking all these into consideration can the marketing manager determine pricing strategy.

Pricing strategies

The options a company has for determining its pricing strategy are numerous. Assume you are opening a retail stereo shop. You plan to sell hi-fi equipment, tape decks, car stereos, and peripheral products. One of your first decisions is how to price your merchandise. Consider the following alternatives.

Competitive pricing strategy You could run ads declaring: "We won't be undersold!" Your ads could show or list a wide variety of products with a large, bold price next to each item. This would mean lower profit on each item and would require constant monitoring of competitive prices. It would also make you vulnerable to retaliatory actions by your competitors.

Comparative pricing You could run ads for a new stereo system showing the regular list price and your special low price. By always comparing your low price with "normal" list prices, you might give the impression that your store offers discount prices on everything.

Skimming strategy If yours is the only stereo store in the area, you might decide to start with relatively high prices to quickly recover all the money you had to spend furnishing, decorating, stocking, and promoting the store. Your ads would probably feature convenience. Later you might decide to lower your prices if a competitive store opens up. What are the problems or disadvantages of this policy?

Penetration pricing Some stores open and immediately offer lower prices than they intend to have later on. Their hope is to penetrate the market quickly by creating immediate traffic and sales. As they develop regular customers, they gradually raise their prices to a more profitable level. Initial advertising might feature low prices, whereas later ads would promote store services, quality products, wide selection, or convenience.

Promotional pricing To introduce a new line of equipment or to clear out old lines, you might use promotional pricing techniques. Two-for-one sales or end-of-month sales are typical of retail efforts to maintain traffic, stimulate demand, or make room for new merchandise.

Loss-leader pricing A special promotional strategy common to retail selling is the loss-leader strategy. You might select one stereo package and advertise it at $100 below your cost. The purpose is to create store traffic and sell other regularly priced merchandise. This presents the problem, though, of bait-and-switch advertising, which

FIGURE 4–14

GUY 1: Hey, a whole week without women.
GUY 2: And no responsibility.
GUY 1: I think I'll grow a beard.
GUY 3: You think we'll survive?

GUY 4: It'll be tough.
GUY 1: Hey, no dishes to wash.
GUY 3: Fishing all day.
GUY 2: Yeah, cards all night.
GUY 5: And I feel lucky!!

GUY 2: Hi honey, ya miss me?
MUSIC AND LYRICS: *Reach out, reach out and touch someone.*

FIGURE 4–15

(MUSIC UNDER)
MAN: Have you been talking to our son on long distance again?
WOMAN: (NODS AND WHIMPERS)
MAN: Did he tell you how much he loves you?
WOMAN: (NODS AND WHIMPERS)

MAN: Did he tell you how well he's doing in school?
WOMAN: (NODS AND WHIMPERS AND CRIES)
MAN: All those things are wonderful. What on earth are you crying for?
WOMAN: Did you see our long distance bill?

(MUSIC)
ANNCR (VO): If your long distance bills are too much, call MCI. Sure, reach out and touch someone. Just do it for a whole lot less.

is illegal and unethical. If you offer loss leaders, you must have them in stock and be prepared to sell them without trying to talk customers out of them.

Prestige pricing Rather then competing on the basis of price, you might prefer to offer the finest stereo equipment available, the best service, free delivery, and friendly clerks in plush surroundings. In this case your ads might not mention prices at all. They would be aimed at a select clientele who could afford to pay your higher prices in exchange for convenience, service, and quality.

Which of these strategies would you select for your stereo store? Why? What are the advantages and disadvantages of each? (Figure 4–16.)

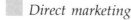 Advertising and the Place Element

If you manufacture a product, you must ask how and where the consumer or end user will buy it. At the factory? From a door-to-door salesperson? In a store? Before the first advertisement can be created, this question of place, or distribution, must be answered. There are two basic methods of distribution a company may use: direct or indirect.

 Direct marketing

Mail-order houses that communicate directly with consumers through mail-order advertisements and catalogs are one of the many types of companies engaged in direct marketing because they do not use the traditional channels of distribution. Rather, they build and

Be careful! That's Chivas Regal!

FIGURE   4–16

A minimum of words is all that is required to tell the reader that the extra value of Chivas Regal is worth its premium price.

maintain their own database of customers and use a variety of media to communicate with those customers directly.

Today, the use of direct marketing is growing rapidly as companies discover its primary benefits of accountability, cost efficiency, and control.

Indirect marketing

Most companies market their products through a distribution channel that includes a network of middlemen. A *middleman* is a business firm that operates between the producer and the consumer or industrial purchaser.[3] The term includes both wholesalers and retailers, as well as manufacturers' representatives, brokers, jobbers, and distributors. A *distribution channel* is composed of all the firms and individuals that take title, or assist in taking title, to the product as it moves from the producer to the consumer.[4]

To help the massive flow of manufactured goods, various types of indirect distribution channels have developed to make products available to customers more economically than the manufacturers could accomplish through direct marketing. National appliance companies, for example, contract with exclusive regional distributors who buy the products from the factory and resell them to local dealers, who in turn resell them to consumers. Many industrial companies market their products through reps or distributors to original equipment manufacturers (OEMs). The OEMs, in turn, may incorporate the product as a component in their own product, which is then sold to their customers.

Advertising and distribution strategy[5]

The advertising a company uses depends on its method of distribution. Much of the advertising we see is not prepared or paid for by the manufacturer but rather by the distributor or the retailer. Over the years the amount of promotional support given to manufacturers by members of the distribution channel cannot be overrated.

As part of their marketing strategy, manufacturers must determine what amount of market coverage is necessary for their products. Procter & Gamble, for example, defines adequate coverage for Crest toothpaste as almost every supermarket, discount store, drugstore, and variety store. Other products might need only one dealer for every 50,000 people. Consumer goods manufacturers traditionally use three types of distribution strategies: intensive, selective, and exclusive.

Intensive distribution   Soft drinks, candy, Bic pens, Timex watches, and many other convenience goods are available to purchasers at every possible location. This enables the consumer to buy with a minimum of effort. The profit on each unit is usually very low, but the volume of sales is high. For this reason, the sales burden is usually carried by the manufacturer's national advertising program. Ads appear in trade magazines to *push* the product into the retail "pipeline" and in mass media to stimulate consumers to *pull* the products through the pipeline. As a manufacturer modifies its strategy to either more push or more pull, special promotions may be directed at the trade or at consumers.

Selective distribution By limiting the number of outlets, manufacturers can cut their costs of distribution and promotion. Many hardware tools, for example, are sold selectively through discount chains, home improvement centers, and hardware stores. Manufacturers may use some national advertising, but the sales burden is normally carried by the retailer. In this case the manufacturer may share part of the retailer's advertising costs through a *cooperative advertising* program, and the retailer agrees to display the manufacturer's products prominently.

Exclusive distribution Some manufacturers grant exclusive rights to a wholesaler or retailer to sell in one geographic region. Automobile dealers are the best example of this. A town of 50,000 to 100,000 population will have only one Chrysler dealer or one Cadillac dealer. This is also common in the high-fashion business and in the marketing of some major appliance and furniture lines. What is lost in market coverage is often gained in the ability to maintain a prestige image and premium prices. Exclusive distribution agreements also force manufacturers and retailers to cooperate closely in advertising and promotion programs. (See Ad Lab 4–D.)

AD LAB 4–D   Marketing Mac: Price and distribution strategies

When the Macintosh was introduced, the company had to determine the most appropriate price and distribution strategies. In setting price, market demand had to be considered as well as the cost of producing and distributing the product. Competitive prices had to be analyzed, and, above all, Apple's corporate objectives for this product had to be weighed. Only then could price and distribution strategy be designed.

Laboratory Applications

1. Visit two or three stores where the Macintosh is sold. Can you determine what pricing strategy Apple is using?

2. Is Apple using intensive, selective, or exclusive distribution?

Golden Skillet Puts Teeth In Chicken.

Consumers' teeth, and lots of 'em. Which can put money in your pocket.
Starting as a small, family-run business fifteen years ago, Golden Skillet is now the third largest fast food chicken chain in the country. With over two hundred units in sixteen states, Canada, Japan and Puerto Rico. Return on investment! Thanks to a fully automatic patented cooking system, a Golden Skillet with

the same sales volume as the competition can operate with lower costs. Which means more profit for you. That's why we say, a leg in your hand will put a smile on your face. For complete franchise information, write Bud Granger, Golden Skillet Companies, 2819 Parham Road, Richmond, Va. 23229.

Golden Skillet Fried Chicken

Golden Skillet Companies is a member of the International Franchise Association and subscribes to the IFA Code of Ethics and Ethical Advertising Code.

FIGURE   4–17

The Golden Skillet Companies have used this award-winning ad in selected trade magazines to stimulate inquiries from businesspeople about purchasing a Golden Skillet franchise and thereby joining their vertical marketing system.

Vertical marketing systems[6]

To be efficient, members of the distribution channel need to cooperate closely with one another. This need has given rise in recent years to the development of various types of vertical marketing systems. These include *corporate systems* like Sears, Roebuck, which owns the manufacturers of many products sold in their stores; *administered systems* like Magnavox, which gains strong retailer support because of the brand's reputation; and *contractual systems* like I.G.A. Food Stores, which is a voluntary chain of independent members sponsored by a single wholesaler.

Other types of contractual systems include retail cooperatives, which set up their own wholesaling operations to better compete with chains, and *franchises* like McDonald's, in which dealers (franchisees) operate under the guidelines and direction of the manufacturer (Figures 4–17 and 4–18).

Vertical marketing systems enable both manufacturers and retailers to achieve substantial savings as well as continuity in advertising. A common store name and similar inventories mean that a single newspaper ad can promote all of the chain's retailers in the particular trading area.

Advertising and the Promotion Element

After the other elements of the marketing mix are determined, the company can add, subtract, or modify its promotional activities. *Promotion* may be defined as the marketing-related communication between the seller and the buyer. Activities usually considered part of the *promotional mix* include personal selling, advertising, public relations, sales promotion, and collateral materials. Since most of these elements are so closely related to advertising, they will be treated in this text as they concern our discussions of advertising principles and techniques. That includes all the activities outlined below except personal selling.

Personal selling

Selling is one of the oldest professions in the world; every product or service must be sold. However, the way in which personal selling is used may vary. Some products are sold by clerks in retail stores, others by salespeople who call on customers directly, and others by no salespeople, as in the case of mail order where advertising carries the entire sales burden.

Advertising

Advertising has been called mass or nonpersonal selling. As we discussed earlier, advertising is used to inform, persuade, and remind customers about particular products and services. Some products, of course, lend themselves to advertising more than others. Some positive factors are:

1. High primary demand trend for the product.
2. Chance for significant product differentiation.

3. High relative importance to the consumer of hidden qualities as opposed to external qualities.
4. The opportunity to use strong emotional appeals.
5. Substantial sums to support advertising.

Where these conditions exist, as in the cosmetics industry, large advertising expenditures are favored, and the ratio of advertising to sales dollars is often quite high. For completely undifferentiated products, such as sugar, salt, and other raw materials or commodities, the importance of advertising is minimal. In this case price is usually the primary influence. This will be discussed further in Chapter 7, "Marketing and Advertising Planning." The role advertising should play depends on many factors and is a major decision in the marketing planning process.

Public relations

Whereas advertising is paid-for communication, public relations usually has no clear or overt sponsorship. Many firms use public relations activities like publicity as supplements to advertising to inform various audiences about the company and its products and to help build corporate credibility and image. Public relations, as we will discuss in Chapter 18, is an extremely powerful tool that should always be considered in the design of a company's promotional mix.

Sales promotion

Sales promotion, the subject of Chapter 16, is a broad category that covers nonmedia advertising activities. Some items often included in sales promotion are free samples, displays, trading stamps, sweepstakes, cents-off coupons, and premiums. *Reader's Digest*, for example, is famous for its annual sweepstakes designed to increase circulation. Grocery manufacturers print and distribute over 130 billion coupons per year. Of these, only 6 billion are ever redeemed. But this 4.6 percent accounts for approximately $1.3 billion annually that manufacturers give their customers to try their products. Similarly, financial institutions spend untold millions on premiums to attract new accounts.

FIGURE 4–18   The six largest restaurant chains

Rank	Company	Sales ($ millions)	Units in chain	Share of market as a percent of sales among top six chains
1	McDonald's	$9,500	8,069	42%
2	Burger King	4,100	3,827	18%
3	Kentucky Fried Chicken	2,800	6,175	12%
4	Wendy's	2,496	2,995	11%
5	Hardee's	1,900	2,229	9%
6	Pizza Hut	1,870	4,350	8%

▨ Collateral materials

Collateral is a term used to refer to all the accessory advertising materials prepared by companies to help achieve marketing or public relations objectives. These may include booklets, catalogs, brochures, films, trade show exhibits, sales kits, annual reports, or point-of-purchase displays. (See Ad Lab 4–E.)

■ The Marketing Mix in Perspective

When we look at the promotional mix outlined above, we see that advertising is just one of the elements companies have the option of using. And the promotional mix itself is just one element of the whole marketing mix. These relationships are important to understand in order to keep the highly visible (and often controversial) subject of advertising in perspective.

As we will discuss in Chapter 7, marketing and advertising planning is a continuous process of analysis, planning, execution, review, and replanning. In this process, the decision to use any or all of the elements of the promotional mix is based on experience and judgment. And companies constantly reevaluate their promotional mix.

Since most of the promotional elements are so closely related to advertising, they will enter our discussions of advertising principles and techniques.

AD LAB   4–E   Marketing Mac: Deciding on promotion

As mentioned in the text, some products lend themselves to promotion better than others.

Laboratory Applications

1. What about the Macintosh? What opportunities exist for advertising? What about other promotional tools?

2. If you were the brand manager for the Macintosh, would you try to use public relations? Sales promotion? Collateral materials? How would you do it?

Summary

The term *marketing* refers to all business activities aimed at: (1) finding out who customers are and what they want, (2) developing products to satisfy those customers' needs and desires, and (3) getting those products into the customers' hands. In its simplest terms, marketing is the process companies use to satisfy their customer's needs and make a profit.

Advertising is concerned with the third step mentioned above. It is one tool marketers can use to inform, persuade, and remind customers about their products or services. To be successful, though, advertising depends on the adequate performance of the other marketing activities.

A *market* is a group of people who share a common need for a product or service and who can afford it. There are several classifications of markets: consumer, producer, reseller, government, and international.

To locate and measure potential markets, companies use market research and market segmentation. Based on common characteristics of customers, large markets are divided into smaller, more meaningful groups. Companies can then select from these groups a target market at which they will aim all their marketing activities.

Every company can add, subtract, or modify four elements in its marketing program to achieve a desired marketing mix. The elements of the marketing mix are referred to as the four Ps: product, price, place, and promotion.

Product, as a marketing term, refers to the bundle of values offered to the customer. These values may encompass functional, social, psychological, economic, or other consumer satisfactions. Marketing-oriented companies first try to determine what needs will be satisfied by their product. They then carry that concept into the product's design.

Thus, to satisfy their customers' needs and desires, marketers build differences into their products. Even the product's package is part of the product concept. The product concept may also be developed through unique positioning against competitive products in the consumer's mind.

Just as humans go through a life cycle, so do products. The location of a product in its life cycle determines to a great extent how it is advertised.

Price refers to what and how a customer pays for a product. There are many common pricing strategies. Some products compete on the basis of price, but many do not.

The term *place* refers to how and where the product is distributed, bought, and sold. Companies may use either direct or indirect methods of distribution. Consumer goods manufacturers use several types of distribution strategies.

Promotion refers to the marketing-related communication between the seller and the buyer. Elements of the promotional mix include personal selling, advertising, public relations, sales promotion, and collateral.

Advertising is considered nonpersonal selling and is most effective when there is a high demand for the product, a chance for significant product differentiation, an importance to the consumer of hidden product qualities, the opportunity to use strong emotional appeals, and substantial sums to support an advertising program.

Questions for review and discussion

1. What effect, if any, has the evolution of the marketing concept had on advertising?
2. How does advertising relate to marketing?
3. What is the most important factor to consider when determining the elements of the marketing mix?
4. What examples of different kinds of markets can you give?
5. What are examples of product positioning not discussed in this chapter?
6. What effect does the product life cycle have on the advertising a company employs?
7. How do corporate objectives relate to the product life cycle?
8. What factors influence the price of a product?
9. How do the basic methods of distribution affect advertising?
10. What product characteristics encourage heavy advertising? Little advertising? Why?

5

CONSUMER BEHAVIOR AND MARKET SEGMENTATION

D o you know Joe Shields? Chances are you do, although you may know him by another name. He's 21 years old, bigger than average, good-looking, sports a well-trimmed moustache, and has medium-length sandy brown hair. Joe dresses casually but well, and he loves to have a good time. You have probably seen him at football games, on the beach playing volleyball, or at the local pub with a beer in one hand and a pretty woman on the other. Actually Joe likes women a lot, and they like him.

He's not only big physically but has a strong personality, too. He hopes to be a lawyer one day, and he is already opinionated and has a way with words. He's not afraid to say what he wants, and he usually gets it. His friends look for his approval and tend to follow his lead. Joe's parents are definitely upper middle-class. His dad is a building contractor and knows everybody in town. And, of course, that helped the last time Joe was stopped for driving too fast.

With or without his parents, though, Joe does well. He's not at the top of his class, but his grades are well above average. He enjoys school and is conscientious about his work. But that doesn't stop him from having a good time. He's not a loner or a homebody. He likes to go out with both men and women. He likes parties where there are lots of music and talk, and women generally regard him as a bit of a swinger. But he's not at all rowdy. Actually he can be very quiet at times.

Joe looks forward to going away to law school, although he hasn't decided where yet. And he doesn't seem too worried about it. Perhaps "casual" is the best way to describe Joe, because even his personal relationships seem to be light and easy rather than heavy and serious. Marriage and a family are a long way off, at least until after law school. And, besides, Joe is having too much fun to be thinking seriously about that.

Do you know Joe? Do you know him well enough to describe what kind of car he'd like to buy? Do you think he eats a lot of fast foods, or does he prefer cooking for himself? What kind of beer does he drink? Does he smoke? What brand? What stores does he frequent? Does he own a stereo? What make?

In marketing and advertising, companies are constantly trying to match people with products. To succeed they need to understand what makes consumers like Joe Shields behave the way they do.

CONSUMER BEHAVIOR: DIRECTIONAL FORCE IN ADVERTISING

Some people regard advertising as an art. Others consider it a science. Actually it is a unique combination of the two. Advertising effectively blends the behavioral *sciences* (anthropology, sociology, psychology) with the communicating *arts* (writing, drama, graphics, photography, etc.) to motivate, modify, or reinforce consumer perceptions, beliefs, attitudes, and behavior. To accomplish this, marketing and advertising people try to be aware of consumers' attitudes, beliefs, likes and dislikes, habits, fears, wants, and desires. And since these factors are always changing, steps must be taken to monitor them.

As societies alter their attitudes toward dress, recreation, morals, religion, education, economics, or even other people, advertising techniques change, too. Why? Because the behavioral characteristics of large groups of people give the directional force to any advertising aimed at those groups. In short, advertising tries to use the trends in mass consumer behavior to effect changes in specific consumer behavior.

Look at the 1959 De Soto ad in Figure 5–1. What do you see? A young woman, white, affluent, dressed well and rather formally, concerned about stepping out of her new car "like a lady." Compare that with more recent automobile ads where we see young women, of various ethnic backgrounds, dressed according to modern trends, and enjoying the technical performance of their vehicles (Figure 5–2). Not only does the style of advertising reflect differences in accepted social behavior, but even the customer has changed considerably over the last 25 years. She thinks differently, acts differently, lives a different lifestyle, and seeks different product benefits than she used to.

There are two steps in understanding this relationship between consumer behavior and advertising. First, it is important to realize how complex human behavior is and how wide a variety of influences affect behavior. Second, we need to understand how these influences are used by marketers to categorize groups of consumers who tend to behave in the same way. At the same time, we will see how the tendencies or characteristics of these behavioral groups become the basis for advertising campaigns.

FIGURE 5–1

Automobile advertising then and now. In the 50s, Chrysler's DeSoto developed product attributes like swivel seats to suit feminine tastes. Notice the way the model is dressed and the thrust of the ad copy.

FIGURE   5–2

Today, tastes have changed. And so have fashions, as evidenced by the chic but casual ensemble worn by the model advertising the Ford Bronco. Similarly the style of advertising has also changed to reflect these newer values.

THE COMPLEXITY OF CONSUMER BUYING DECISIONS

When making even the simplest purchase, a consumer like Joe Shields goes through a complicated mental process. In Figure 5–3 we can view the typical anatomy of a purchase decision.

A company's marketing efforts join with various noncommercial sources of information (family, society, culture, subculture) to stimulate the purchase decision process. This process is also affected, though, by individual influences on consumer behavior such as motivation, personality, learning, and perception. In Joe's case, this process may stop if he loses interest or, after evaluating a product, decides not to buy. If he does make a purchase, though, then he has the opportunity to see whether the product satisfies his needs. If it doesn't, then he will probably discontinue using that product.

For us to fully appreciate the complexity of the consumer's buying decisions, we need to understand the variety of individual influences on consumer behavior; the impact of environmental factors such as family, social, and cultural influences on the consumer; and how these components are integrated in the consumer's mind.

■ Individual Influences on Consumer Behavior: the Importance of Your Inner Self

The effort of all advertising is to influence people's buying behavior, but it is difficult to foresee the success of planned advertising programs because human beings are all individuals. Each behaves differently, thereby making mass consumer behavior virtually unpredictable. Consider some of the contrasts in individual behavior patterns we see every day.

People vary in their persuasibility. Some are easily persuaded to do something; others are skeptical and difficult to convince.

Some people are "cool heads" and control their emotions. Others are "hot heads" and anger easily.

Some people are loners, whereas others like the security of a crowd.

Some people love their work and others hate it.

Many people are oriented toward the acquisition of material things. Some people are motivated mainly by spiritual matters.

Some people spend their money cautiously. Others spend their money more freely.

Other contrasts in people's behavior include sexual expression, interests in sports and hobbies, religious preferences, self-worth, goal orientation, color preferences, and musical expression. All affect consumers' buying decisions (Figure 5–4).

To further complicate the advertiser's goal of influencing consumer behavior, consider these observations. First, people's attitudes, beliefs, and preferences change. What we have liked for the last five years we may suddenly not like tomorrow or at some time in the future. That includes products, people, activities, and living conditions.

Second, individual behavior is inconsistent and difficult to predict from one day to the next. Joe Shields might react to an idea positively one day but negatively the next. He might enjoy going to a movie tonight, but he might prefer to stay home tomorrow.

Third, people are often unable to explain their behavior. A woman might say she bought a dress because she needed it and it was marked down 30 percent. The real reason may be quite different.

People often do not understand why they behave as they do. And if they do understand their true motivations, they may fear express-

FIGURE 5–3

Anatomy of a purchase decision.

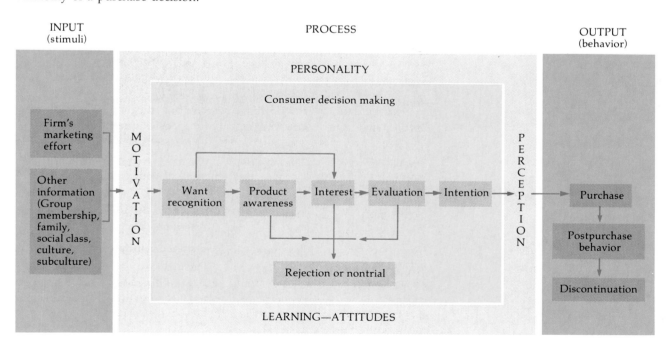

What becomes a Legend most?

Blackglama

BLACKGLAMA IS THE WORLD'S FINEST NATURAL DARK RANCH MINK BRED ONLY IN AMERICA BY THE GREAT LAKES MINK ASSOCIATION

FIGURE 5–4

Liz Taylor is one of a host of celebrities to pose for Blackglama fur ads. The campaign—simple and dogmatic—has itself become a legend. It has created an unequaled image of prestige and status, not only for the association of mink ranchers, which sponsors the label, but also for their customers and even the well-known models themselves.

ing them. For example, an executive who purchases a new Mercedes might be reluctant to admit it if the real reason for his purchase was severe insecurity as a child.

Needs and motives

In the study of consumer behavior, *motivation* means the underlying drives that contribute to the individual consumer's purchasing actions. These drives stem from the conscious or unconscious needs of the consumer. Unfortunately, though, motivations cannot be directly observed. When we see Joe Shields eat, we assume he is hungry, but that may not be correct. We eat for a variety of reasons besides hunger—to be sociable, because it is time to eat, because we are bored, or because we are nervous.

Often a combination of motives underlies our behavior in making a decision. The reasons (motives) a person switches an account from the City Bank to the Peoples Bank may be (1) the Peoples Bank is closer to work, (2) it agreed to give that person a loan, and/or (3) the personnel in the Peoples Bank are friendlier.

People have different needs and therefore different motivations. Understanding needs is very complex. One need might be satisfied in many ways. Likewise, the same product might satisfy different needs for different people, and it is not always clear which need or needs a product is satisfying.

Psychologists have tried to categorize needs to understand them better. Abraham Maslow developed the following widely used *hierarchy of needs* on the theory that the lower biologic or survival needs are dominant in human behavior and must be satisfied before higher, socially acquired needs become meaningful (Figure 5–5).

FIGURE 5–5
Promotional appeals and hierarchy of needs

Product	Need	Promotional appeal
Small home	Physiological	Inexpensive housing for the family; small but well-built
Smoke alarm	Safety	Could save your family's lives; think of your children and your spouse
Gold chain	Social	Show your sweetheart you care on Valentine's Day
Expensive luxury car	Esteem	Picture car in front of "gracious" home or club
Graphite golf clubs	Self-actualization	For the three-day-a-week golfer; for the golfer who is looking for only two strokes

1. Physiological needs—food, drink, oxygen, sex, and rest.
2. Safety needs—infantile dependency; avoidance of situations that are unfamiliar, threatening, or might lead to injury or illness; and economic security.
3. Social needs—friendship and affection, and a sense of belonging.
4. Esteem needs—self-respect, recognition, status, prestige, and success.
5. Self-actualization—living up to one's expectations (self-fulfillment).[1]

In affluent societies such as the United States, Canada, Western Europe, and Japan, most individuals pay little attention to such physiological needs as the availability of food or the safety of drinking water and waste-treatment facilities. They take these needs for granted. As a result, marketing and advertising campaigns for many premium products stress benefits related to self-esteem and self-fulfillment, and some even offer the rewards of better love relationships. (See Ad Lab 5–A.)

AD LAB 5–A   Using needs to stimulate motivation

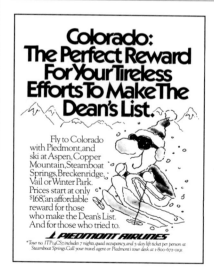 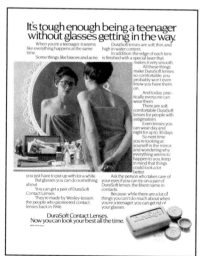 

Laboratory Application

Human needs are the basis for many advertisements. By referring to Maslow's hierarchy of needs described in the text, can you determine what motivations these advertisers are attempting to stimulate?

Although Maslow's hierarchy is a convenient way to classify human needs, it would be a mistake to assume that needs occur one step at a time. Usually people are motivated by a combination of needs.

The problem of analyzing motivations for marketing purposes is complicated by the fact that people are admittedly moved by both conscious and unconscious needs. To explore the depths of the unconscious, psychologists like Ernest Dichter have developed a discipline called *motivation research,* which, although limited to very small samples of consumers and hampered by analytical subjectivity, has offered some insights into the underlying reasons for unexpected consumer behavior. We will discuss this subject more thoroughly in Chapter 6 on marketing research.

Individual perception

While Joe Shields is motivated by his personal needs for self-esteem, love, or social recognition, his behavior is affected by his particular perception of himself and of the world around him.

AD LAB 5–B   Subliminal manipulation: Fact or fantasy?

Is it possible to manipulate people with subliminal advertising? This intriguing controversy started back in the 1950s when Vance Packard's bestseller *The Hidden Persuaders* described an experiment that appeared to show that if a message was perceived, perhaps unconsciously, at levels below the "limen," or perceptual threshold, it could motivate consumers.

The experiment involved showing movies while at the same time projecting the word "Eat Popcorn" and "Drink Coca-Cola" on the screen for 1/3,000 of a second. Sales figures jumped 57 percent for popcorn and 18 percent for Coca-Cola during the six-week term of the experiment. As expected, this finding caused quite a furor. Some states passed laws to prevent the practice. However, this study has never been replicated successfully. One reason perhaps was that a number of facts may have affected the results of the experiment. For example, the movie being shown during the experiment period was *Picnic,* which included many scenes of people eating and drinking in hot summer weather.

If subliminal advertising could persuade people "against their will," profound ethical questions would be raised. But there is general agreement that it is not possible. First, thresholds vary among individuals. Second, no galvanic skin response can be detected during subliminal-perception states. If a message is below the threshold of visual perception, then, in fact, it is not perceived at all. And even if a message were perceived, it could be easily distorted. "Drink Coke" might make a viewer "go smoke" or "think jokes."

The subliminal perception controversy has been rekindled with the publication of books that accused advertising people of planting hidden sexual messages in print ads— particularly in the ice cubes portrayed in liquor advertising.

Subliminal Seduction (subtitled "Here Are the Secret Ways Ad Men Arouse Your Desires to Sell Their Products) and *Media Sexploitation* include numerous examples of what the author (Wilson Bryan Keys) believes are sexual symbols, four-letter words, and pornographic pictures buried in the otherwise bland content of

Perception is the sensing of stimuli to which an individual is exposed—the act or process of comprehending the world in which the individual exists.[2] For example, when Joe looks at an automobile that he *needs* for transportation, he perceives more than a random collection of paint, tires, glass, and steel. He perceives an integrated entity designed to provide a variety of benefits—transportation, comfort, convenience, economy, and even status for the driver.

A person's perception of this integrated entity may be affected by the individual's self-concept, needs and motivations, knowledge, past experience, feelings, attitudes, and personality. As we suggested in Chapter 4 in the section on product concept, part of a person's past experience or attitude might also be shaped by the advertising he or she has seen. (See Ad Lab 5–B.) A number of years ago, for example, research showed that the general public perceived the Pontiac Grand Prix as a highly masculine automobile and the Volkswagen Karmann Ghia as a feminine one.[3] As an exercise, consider the various models of cars available today. What "masculine" cars spring to mind? What "feminine" ones? What has created their gender in your mind?

---

various ads. He concludes that such "hidden persuaders" were carefully contrived by major advertisers and their agencies to seduce consumers at a subliminal level.

But to people who work in ad agencies, there is a simpler explanation. Much photography for advertising art is sent to professional retouching studios, where artists correct photographic imperfections and add visual effects not captured by the camera. Ice cubes in ads, for example, are completely the work of retouching artists, since real ice cubes would melt under the hot lights of the photographer's studio. Retouchers, like most artistic people in commercial fields, want to add their own creativity to their work. Some even find it humorous to introduce carefully disguised sexual elements to an ad that must be puritanically straitlaced for the mass market.

Thus such concealed symbols and words in ads (and, indeed, there are a few examples) are most likely the work of individual creativity, boredom, or mischievousness rather than the cunning and insidious strategy of marketing decision makers as Mr. Keys suggests.

Interestingly, in more than 600 pages on the subject, Mr. Keys finds not a single individual willing to admit being involved in subliminal embedding.

Dr. Jack Haberstroh, professor in the School of Mass Communications at Virginia Commonwealth University, investigated Keys' charge that S-E-X is embedded on the face of Ritz crackers. His research even included a visit to a Ritz cracker factory. He concludes that the charges of S-E-X written on Ritz crackers in particular and of subliminal advertising in general are "preposterous, absurd, ludicrous, and laughable."

Laboratory Applications

1. Would words with sexual connotations hidden in an advertisement motivate you to purchase a product? Why?

2. Do you feel that appeals to the consumer's prurient interests can help sell products? Specifically, what kind of products?

Self-concept and roles We all carry images in our minds of who we are and who we want to be. If Joe Shields wants to appear masculine and a bit racy, he may favor an automobile that supports that image. On the other hand, if he wants to be regarded as solid and respectable, he may choose a type of vehicle that represents good engineering, safety, and economy. From the preceding statements about masculinity and femininity, we can understand why a woman who sees herself as young and attractive might be more inclined to favor one kind of car over another (Figure 5–6).

Marketers are very concerned with the perceptions consumers have of their products, because, to the consumer, the perception *is* the reality. As marketing consultant and psychophysicist Howard Moskowitz says, if the consumer wants a "natural taste" and if the consumer thinks lemonade with additives tastes natural, that's what we'll give her. "Lemon flavor is lemon flavor, whether you get it from a tree or from an artist flavorist. The constituents are different, but what is perceived as lemon flavor *is* lemon flavor. That's reality."[4]

Selective perception One of the major problems advertisers face is the fact that each of us exercises *selective perception*. As humans, we have the ability to select from the many sensations bombarding our central processing unit those that relate to our previous experiences, needs, or desires. The average adult is exposed to nearly 20,000 messages a day—twice as many as we received 10 years ago. Yet most people are hardly aware of most of these. We are limited not only by the physical capacity of our senses but also by our interests. We focus

PEOPLE IN ADVERTISING

Rena Bartos

Senior Vice President and Director of
Communications Development
J. Walter Thompson Company

Rena Bartos is perhaps advertising's best-known authority on the changing role of women and the effects these changes have on product marketing. Her major responsibility at J. Walter Thompson Company, America's fifth largest advertising agency, is to track these social changes and identify their impact on marketing strategies. Bartos works with all JWT offices in implementing her findings, and she consults with company clients worldwide. JWT clients include Eastman Kodak, Quaker Oats, Ford Motor Company, and Chevron. Bartos' unique function grew out of a research program she initiated to measure the changing roles of women. Her goal has been to forge a research link between female consumers and the advertising they see. Identifying women as "the moving target," Bartos declares that advertisers would be "better off aiming at where she's going than where she's been." Though many TV commercials portray women as idyllic housewives bent on achieving "the whitest, brightest wash in town" and dishes "you can see your face in," Bartos points out that 50 percent of the nation's women are employed and many others are in school or retired. Only 36 percent of American

attention on some things and avoid others. A single newspaper may contain hundreds of advertisements, but the average reader recalls only a small number of these and is influenced by even fewer. Thus, advertisers may spend millions of dollars on national media advertising, sales promotion, and point-of-purchase displays only to discover in later research that consumers have no knowledge of the product or promotion.

Moreover, research shows that new automobile buyers are more likely to read advertisements about the brands of cars they have already purchased than about competitive makes.[5] This selectivity makes it important for marketers to obtain satisfied customers and build brand loyalty, and for the product to fit the image created by advertising. Satisfied customers are less likely to seek new information about competing products and probably will not even notice it when it is forced on them.

Theory of cognitive dissonance Selective perception serves us in a variety of ways. Besides saving us time by filtering out irrelevant or uninteresting data, it protects us from facing unpleasant realities. Leon Festinger developed the *theory of cognitive dissonance*, which states basically that people strive to justify their behavior by reducing the degree to which their impressions or beliefs are inconsistent with reality (dissonance).[6]

For example, people may use Scope mouthwash because they believe that it's the most effective product on the market. However, if they see an ad that "proves" that Lavoris is even more effective, this

FIGURE 5–6

You know where you're headed, says American Express. And if you carry the American Express card, everyone else will, too, is the implication.

women are full-time homemakers. This makes traditional housewives a "minority group."

Bartos, a trained sociologist and professional researcher, also found that the women's market contains four distinct segments: career women, "just-a-job" working women, homemakers who plan to remain at home, and homemakers who plan to seek employment later. Women in each of these groups, she found, favor different products, shop differently, and use the media differently. They also have far more say about how family funds are spent than women did two decades ago. In fact, the major changes in women's lives over the past 20 years may have caused marketing programs to miss their mark, says Bartos, for these changes are not reflected in most of the ads we see today. Today's ads continue to portray women as full-time housewives, mothers, shoppers, cleaners, and cooks, and they minimize their roles in the working world and in community affairs.

Recently, Bartos said, "Marketing procedures and tools have never been more sophisticated and complex than they are today. Yet there is a curious gap between the realities of social change and the picture of society reflected in most marketing plans and advertising campaigns. Many marketing specialists who pride themselves on their pragmatism and realism have not related their day-to-day marketing activities to the facts of social change."

Bartos obtained her bachelor's degree from Rutgers University and did graduate work in sociology at Columbia University.

She has received a number of industry awards including the *Ladies Home Journal* Award as one of "America's 100 Most Important Women." She's also a recipient of the Matrix Award for outstanding achievement in advertising, the WEAL Achievement Award in advertising, and many others. She serves on the boards of directors of the Advertising Research Foundation, American Marketing Association, Educational Foundation of the American Association of Advertising Agencies, and the Travel Research Association. She is a member of the board of advisors of the American Woman's Economic Development Corporation.

Among the books Bartos has authored is *The Moving Target, What Every Marketer Should Know about Women.* Her articles have appeared in *Harvard Business Review, Madison Avenue, Marketing Times,* and *The Journal of Marketing.*

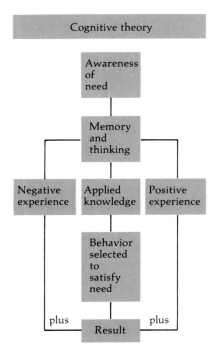

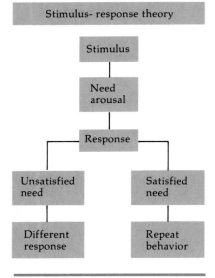

FIGURE   5–7

Two theories of learning.

exposure may create dissonance because of the gap between their previous thinking and the "new evidence." They may choose to ignore the Lavoris ad or subconsciously seek a reassuring Scope ad in order to reduce the dissonance. Or, they may accept the new evidence and reduce the dissonance by changing their purchasing behavior. Naturally, advertisers hope that their customers do not experience dissonance. But they also hope that consumers of competitive products do because those buyers might relieve that uncomfortable tension by switching to their product.

Consumer learning and habit development

Another individual influence on consumer behavior is the way consumers learn new information and develop purchasing habits. A major objective of advertising is to inform (teach) people about products and where to buy them. So advertisers are very interested in how people learn. Many psychologists consider learning to be the most fundamental process in human behavior. The advanced, "higher level" needs, for example, are learned. Learning produces our habits and skills. It also contributes to the development of attitudes, beliefs, preferences, prejudices, emotions, and standards of conduct.

By definition, *learning is a relatively permanent change in behavior that occurs as a result of reinforced practices.* Theories of learning are numerous, but most can be classified into two broad categories: cognitive theory and stimulus-response theory. *Cognitive theory* views learning as a mental process of memory, thinking, and the rational application of knowledge to practical problem solving.[7] This theory may be an accurate description of the way we learn in school. *Stimulus-response theory,* on the other hand, treats learning as a trial-and-error process whereby needs, motives, or drives are triggered by some cue or *stimulus* to cause the individual to *respond* in an effort to satisfy the need. Satisfaction, then, rewards or reinforces the response by reducing the drive and producing repeat behavior the next time the drive is aroused.[8] Figure 5–7 shows a simple schematic of these two theories.

Let's examine how the stimulus-response theory works in marketing. An advertisement is a stimulus, or *cue,* and a purchase is a response. The consumer's motivation is to satisfy various needs. If the product that the consumer purchases gives satisfaction, then there is some reinforcement. Additional reinforcement may be given through superior product performance, good service, and reminder advertising.

Through *repetition* of the cues (advertisements), the learning process, including memory, may be reinforced and repeat behavior encouraged. Learning may be further enhanced by engaging the consumer's *participation* in the process through the use of free samples or free in-home trials of the product. Finally, if learning is reinforced enough and repeat behavior is produced, a purchasing *habit* may result.

Habit is the natural extension of learning. It is the acquired or developed behavior pattern that has become nearly or completely involuntary. The old cliche "People are the creatures of habit" is true.

Why most consumer behavior is habitual There are three reasons why most consumer behavior is habitual. First, we resort to habit

FIGURE 5–8

A Canadian ad for Heinz ketchup uses Cole Porter tunes and a 1940s style jukebox to reinforce consumer habit of purchasing Heinz—the classic condiment that can be used on a variety of food types.

when we select products because it is *easy*. When we consider an alternative to an existing brand choice, we are forced to think, evaluate, compare, and then decide—and this is difficult for most of us, not to mention risky. We may be dissatisfied with a new choice or criticized by friends who disagree with our decision.

Second, we rely on habit because of *necessity*. Consider the person who purchases 50 items in a supermarket. To read all the labels of competitive brands would require hours of concentration, which almost no one has the time—or inclination—to do.

Third, we resort to habit because it is usually the *rational* thing to do. As we learn through trial and error which brands serve us well and which do not, we also learn which stores and service outlets satisfy us and which do not. When we find a product or a store to our liking, we continue to buy the product, or patronize the store, because it is the intelligent thing to do.

Interest of advertisers in habit Advertisers have three habit-related goals:

1. *Habit breaking*—To get consumers to *break* an existing purchase habit—that is, to stop buying their habitual brand and to try a new brand. Many devices are used to induce consumers to try a different product or visit a new store. These include giving away free samples of the product, announcing something new about the product, giving limited-time price reductions, and holding grand openings.
2. *Habit acquisition*—To get consumers to *acquire* the habit of buying their brand or patronizing their establishment. To build a product preference habit, advertisers may use "reassurance" advertising to remind customers of an earlier, satisfactory purchase response. Examples of advertising themes designed to encourage purchasing habits are: "Have it your way—at Burger King," "Tonight, let it be Lowenbrau," and "Once in the morning does it" (Scope).
3. *Habit reinforcement*—To convince current users to *remain* habitual purchasers or patrons. Each time a consumer uses the product and is satisfied, the habit of buying the product is reinforced. Continued satisfaction may reinforce the purchase habit to such a degree that the purchase decision is virtually automatic (Figure 5–8).

Much advertising is aimed at reminding consumers that a product they use satisfies their need. Examples of slogans used to help reinforce positive impressions in the minds of consumers are: "The king of beers for one hundred years. Budweiser," "Coke is it," and "I hate it. But I use it twice a day" (Listerine).

Of course, the overall objective is to produce the phenomenon in consumer behavior known as *brand loyalty*. Brand loyalty is the consumer's decision to repurchase a brand continually because the consumer perceives that the brand has the right product features or quality at the right price.[9] Measuring brand loyalty, or even defining its characteristics, is very difficult since so many aspects may be involved: consumer attitudes, perceptions, family pressure, friendship with the salesperson, and other factors. However, this is the usual long-term objective of marketers and a major goal in the study of consumer behavior.

Environmental Influences on Consumer Behavior:
The Importance of What's Around You

In addition to the numerous internal, individual influences we
have just discussed, many external, environmental factors influence
consumer behavior. The most important are the consumer's family,
social, and cultural environments.

 Family

Our attitudes toward right and wrong, religion, work, male and
female roles, political philosophy, sexual behavior, other races, ethical values, and economics are given their initial direction in the family
setting. This influence is usually strong and long lasting. Few people,
for example, who were brought up in one religion switch to another
when they mature. Nor are people easily persuaded to accept a radically different political outlook or social philosophy. If one is reared in
a capitalist or socialist environment, one will probably die a capitalist
or a socialist.

The family setting also affects our attitudes toward many products
and our purchasing habits. Food preferences in particular are shaped
to a considerable extent by what people eat when growing up. If Joe
Shields grows up eating turnip greens and corn bread, he will proba-

FIGURE   5–9   American social classes

Upper-upper class The upper-upper class is the
social elite. It consists of prominent people whose
families have been wealthy for generations. Less
than 1 percent of the population belongs to this
privileged class. People in this class live graciously
and quietly. They have great power but tend to use
it inconspicuously.

Lower-upper class This class is also small,
consisting of less than 2 percent of the population.
Sometimes referred to as the "Nouveau riche,"
members of this class include well-to-do
industrialists, business, and professional people.
People in the lower-upper class are not yet fully
accepted as the social peers of the people in the
upper-upper class.

Upper-middle class The upper-middle class
consists of about 10 percent of the population. Its
members are successful small businesspeople,
middle and upper level managers in business and
government, and professional people who are
moderately successful. Many people who make up
suburbia belong to this class. People in this class
tend to be very success-oriented and want to
improve their status in life.

Lower-middle class This class consists of
approximately 30 to 35 percent of the population.
Members in it work in nonmanagerial jobs, own
small business, and occupy low level positions in
government. The lower-middle class is strongly
motivated to win approval from their peers, has a
strong family orientation, and tends to be very law-
abiding.

Upper-lower class This is the largest social class,
consisting of an estimated 40 percent of the
population. Its members are unskilled or semiskilled.
Very few work in managerial positions or in the
professions. When we think of the "working class,"
we think of people in this category. The upper-
lower class strives less to "get ahead," "succeed,"
and "make more money" than the four classes
above it.

Lower-lower class This group consists of an
estimated 15 percent of the population. It is
characterized by low-level motivation, despair, living
day to day, lack of concern for education and
"getting ahead," and a whatever-will-be-will-be
attitude.

FIGURE 5–10

As an appeal to reference groups, the line "Brush often with Crest" is given new meaning in this ad aimed at the Hispanic market. The play is on the Spanish word "menudo," which is also the name of the very famous and popular Latin singing group pictured in the ad.

bly continue to enjoy them as an adult. Many other product preferences are formed in the family environment. Being programmed at an early age to know that the "right" headache relief is St. Joseph and the "right" name for appliances is General Electric goes a long way toward shaping the purchasing behavior of adults.

Society

The social community in which we live also influences the way we live. The social class we belong to, the leaders whose opinions we value, and the groups with which we identify all affect our views on life and the products we buy.

Social class Our society can be divided into social classes. People in the same social class tend to have similar attitudes, status symbols, and spending patterns. Which of the six social classes outlined in Figure 5–9 do you believe Joe Shields falls into?

We are a socially mobile society; members of our society can move upward or downward. Many middle-aged Americans have moved up one or two classes. Few, however, have moved up three or more. Some people fall back a class or two, but not many. It is significant that, with the exception of the upper-upper class and the lower-lower class, people in the other four classes are motivated to move up. The "get ahead," "better than your peers," "move up," and "win greater admiration" philosophy is a strong part of the American culture. Advertising people capitalize on the broad-based desire to "be the best you can."

Reference groups Whenever we are concerned with how we will appear in the eyes of other people, or whenever we attempt to emulate members of some group, we are demonstrating the significance of reference groups. Reference groups can be personal (family, fellow workers, neighbors) or impersonal (movie stars, professional athletes, business executives). A special form of reference group—our peers—exerts a great influence on what we believe or at least on the way we behave. To win acceptance by our peers (fellow students, fellow workers, colleagues, etc.), we purchase the right style of clothing, choose the appropriate place to live, and acquire habits that will earn us their approval (Figure 5–10).

Often an individual is influenced by two reference groups in opposite directions and has to choose between them. For example, to win peer approval, some young people may engage in behavior they believe (because of family influence) is wrong, such as taking drugs, smoking, or drinking.

Opinion leaders An *opinion leader* is someone whose beliefs or attitudes are considered right by people who share an interest in some specific activity. All fields (sports, religion, economics, fashion, finance, etc.) have opinion leaders. Our minds reason that "if so-and-so believes Spalding is the right tennis racket, then it must be so. She knows more about the game than I do." Or if Mr. Smith says natural fur is in again, then the consumer may reason, "I'm going to buy a coat made of real fur. After all Mr. Smith is the expert on fashion."

▧ Culture

Culture has an immeasurable influence on the consumer. Americans eat hot dogs, peanut butter, and apple pie. In Europe you may find a few hamburger outlets, but hamburgers won't taste the same. And you probably won't get a chocolate milk shake either.

In the United States and Canada the populations are made up of many subcultures. Some are based on race, nationality, religion, or simply geographic proximity. The advertiser must understand these subcultures because cultural differences may affect responses to products as well as to advertising. From generation to generation, these subcultures transfer their beliefs and values. Racial, religious, and ethnic groups all have backgrounds that affect their preference for styles of dress, food, beverages, transportation, personal care products, and household furnishings, to name a few (Figure 5–11).

Similarly, the social environment in a foreign country is also based on that country's particular language, culture, literacy rate, religion, and lifestyle. (See Chapter 20.) These cultural customs, traditions, attitudes, and taboos cannot be ignored by advertisers wherever they may be. (See Ad Lab 5–C.)

AD LAB   5–C   How understanding consumer behavior helps create effective advertising

Laboratory Application

Study the advertisements pictured here. What principles of consumer behavior does each exemplify? Discuss each ad from the viewpoint of individual influences on consumer behavior—namely, needs and motives, individual perception, or learning and habit development. Then discuss them from the viewpoint of environmental influences—namely, family, society, and culture.

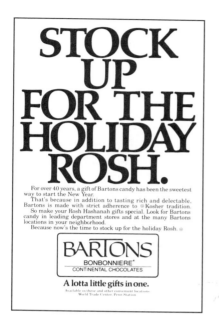

FIGURE   5–11

Barton's promotes its candy as the perfect holiday gift with an appeal to the culture surrounding the Jewish holiday Rosh Hashanah.

■ Integrating the Components of Consumer Behavior

We have seen in this chapter the wide array of influences on every consumer's purchasing decision. If Joe Shields needs a new shirt, his decision will be affected by many internal and external factors. To fully understand how Joe's purchase decision takes place, look back now at the purchase decision model in Ad Lab 5–A at the beginning of this chapter.

The shirt manufacturer may advertise or a local retail store may announce a sale on shirts. A friend of Joe's may have just bought a new shirt, or Joe's mother may have said she didn't like the shirt he was wearing. Any of these external influences might trigger the recognition by Joe that he needs or wants a new shirt. These external factors also influence the type or brand of shirt Joe selects.

At this point, however, Joe's decision to purchase a shirt is further influenced by internal forces. These include his needs and desires (which may be functional, psychological, or, most likely, a combination), his personality, his self-concept, his perception of the features or benefits of particular types of shirts, and the education or experience he has had which have contributed to his normal purchasing habits.

As all these forces converge within Joe's mental computer, he realizes the need, becomes aware of shirts and ads for shirts, develops an interest, evaluates what he believes he should do, forms an intention to buy, and eventually selects a shirt. This process may take several days, or it may occur in a few seconds if Joe happens to be in a store or passing a window display. It stands to reason that if we knew all the forces influencing an individual and could weigh the effect of each force, we would be able to predict the individual's probable purchase behavior.

A simplified decision matrix whereby we can look at many of the factors influencing Joe Shields' decision to buy a new car and determine his probable course of action is shown in Ad Lab 5–D. Before testing your understanding of Joe's purchase behavior, though, re-read the introduction to this chapter about Joe's personality and environment. Then see if you can figure out what car Joe would buy.

From the marketer's point of view, the more that is known about both the internal and external forces that influence Joe, the easier it is to create advertisements that will communicate with him.

MARKET SEGMENTATION

As we defined it in Chapter 4, *market segmentation* is the process of dividing a company's total market into smaller groups or segments to (1) locate target markets, (2) identify the needs of those target markets, (3) design products to fill those needs, and (4) promote the products specifically to those target markets. One of the major tasks of the marketing manager, therefore, is to determine what segments within the total market offer the greatest potential for profit after considering the company's capabilities and objectives. The second major task is to find more effective means of communicating with each segment. An understanding of consumer behavior will assist in both tasks.

AD LAB 5–D   The Decision Matrix: Can you predict consumer behavior?

Do you know Joe Shields well enough to predict what car he would be inclined to buy?

If we knew consumers well enough, we could theoretically construct a decision matrix to see what products they would be likely to purchase based on their personality and the forces that influence them. In the case of Joe Shields, we probably have some idea of the amount of influence each of the six decision forces would have on him. If we score those influences on a scale of 1 to 3 against different types of automobiles, we get a picture of how Joe might behave (1 = weak; 2 = moderate; 3 = strong).

Laboratory Applications

1. What needs does Joe have for transportation, economy, safety, sex appeal, self-esteem, status, or self-fulfillment? Which of these needs would be greatest? How strong would they be as motives in selecting the family sedan? An economy car? A personal sports car? A pickup or a van?

2. On the chart, score each car on a scale from 1 to 3 and total each column. Which car has the highest total? Is this result in line with the Joe Shields you know? Why?

Decision Forces		Considerations	Family Sedan	Economy Car	Sports Car	Van or Pick-up
Internal	Needs or Motives	Maslow's hierarchy: physiological; safety; security; belongingness, love; self-esteem, status; self-fulfillment.				
	Perceptions	The way external stimuli are sensed when modified by needs, personality, experience, attitude and feelings; selective perception.				
	Learning & Habits	How we learn in school and in life; what we learn; what we have experienced; the importance of habit in our lives.				
External	Family	Attitudes toward right and wrong, morality, ethics, religion. Male and female roles; safety; politics; sexual behavior; food; work; economy.				
	Social	Social class and class mobility; importance of reference groups: family, neighbors, peers; influence of opinion leaders.				
	Cultural	American customs, tradition, attitudes; subcultural influences based on race, religion, ethnicity, or geography; influences on taste and style.				
		Totals				

One of the most interesting cases of market segmentation occurred in the dog food business. General Foods conducted a major study to determine which types of consumers were likely to buy dog food and what kind of product would be most appealing to them. General Foods already manufactured Gaines and Gainesburger products, but it had no canned dog food in that $2 billion market.

Of the six basic types of dog owners classified by the study, two were found most likely to buy the most expensive kind of dog food. One of these groups tended to regard dogs as baby substitutes, were generally women, and tended to live in small apartments in the city. The other group included well-educated, high-income people concerned about nutrition who were willing to spend a lot of money to keep their dogs healthy.

General Foods targeted these two groups and introduced Cycle dog food in four different nutritional formulations. Cycle 1 was for puppies up to 18 months, Cycle 2 for young adult dogs, Cycle 3 for overweight dogs, and Cycle 4 for dogs over seven years old. Ads featured the differing nutritional needs of dogs as they grew older.[10] General Foods reached the market segments it targeted, but failed to reach the volumes it had hoped for in spite of massive expenditures for advertising and promotion.

Segmenting Consumer Markets

Despite its questionable success, Cycle dog food stands as an interesting example of psychographic segmentation. The dog owners targeted by General Foods all held a similar loving *attitude* toward their pets that implied that nothing was too good for them and that nutrition was a very important consideration. Marketers use a variety of methods to segment markets and identify behavioral groups (Figure 5–12). These methods generally fall into four categories: geographic, demographic, psychographic, and behavioristic.

Geographic

One of the simplest methods of segmenting markets is by their geographic location. People who live in one region of the country frequently have purchasing habits that differ from those in other regions. People in the Sunbelt states, for example, purchase more suntan lotion than people in the North or Midwest. Those in the North, though, purchase heavy winter clothing as well as special equipment for dealing with rain, snow, ice, sleet, and subzero temperatures. Figure 5–13 shows the most and least promising markets for a number of consumer products, based on a survey of 20 key cities.

When marketers analyze geographic data, they study sales by region, county size, city size, specific locations, and by types of stores. Many products sell well in urban areas but poorly in suburban or rural areas. On the other hand, the market for a swimming pool contractor is very small in center-city areas but considerably larger in suburban areas.

Even in local markets, geographic segmentation is important. A retailer may attract people from one part of town to his west-side store. Or, a local politician might send a mailer only to those precincts known to be supportive.

FIGURE 5–12   Methods used to segment consumer markets

Variables	Typical breakdowns	Variables	Typical breakdowns
Geographic			
Region	Pacific, Mountain, West North Central, West South Central, East North Central, East South Central, South Atlantic, Middle Atlantic, New England	City or SMSA size	Under 5,000, 5,000–19,999, 20,000–49,999, 50,000–99,999, 100,000–249,999, 250,000–499,999, 500,000–999,999, 1,000,000–3,999,999, 4,000,000 or over
County size	A, B, C, D		
Climate	Northern, southern	Density	Urban, suburban, rural
Demographic			
Age	Under 6, 6–11, 12–19, 20–34, 35–49, 50–64, 65+	Occupation	Professional and technical; managers, officials, and proprietors; clerical, sales; craftsmen, foremen; operatives; farmers; retired; students; housewives; unemployed
Sex	Male, female		
Family size	1–2, 3–4, 5+		
Family life cycle	Young, single; young, married, no children; young, married, youngest child under six; young, married, youngest child six or over; older, married, with children; older, married, no children under 18; older, single; other	Education	Grade school or less; some high school; graduated high school; some college; graduated college
		Religion	Catholic, Protestant, Jewish, other
		Race	White, black, oriental
Income	Under $3,000, $3,000–$5,000, $5,000–$7,000, $7,000–$10,000, $10,000–$15,000, $15,000–$25,000, $25,000 and over	Nationality	American, British, French, German, Scandinavian, Italian, Latin American, Middle Eastern, Japanese
Behavioristic			
Purchase occasion	Regular occasion, special occasion	Loyalty status	None, medium, strong, absolute
Benefits sought	Economy, convenience, prestige	Readiness stage	Unaware, aware, informed, interested, desirous, intending to buy
User status	Nonuser, exuser, potential user, first-time user, regular user		
Usage rate	Light user, medium user, heavy user	Marketing-factor sensitivity	Quality, price, service, advertising, sales promotion
Psychographic			
Social class	Lower lowers, upper lowers, lower middles, upper middles, lower uppers, upper uppers	Lifestyle	Straights, swingers, longhairs
		Personality	Compulsive, gregarious, authoritarian, ambitious

Demographic

Demographics is the study of the numerical characteristics of the population. It has long been used to divide or segment populations by sex, age, race, religion, education, occupation, income, and other quantifiable factors. For example, companies that sell products to middle aged people may find it useful to know the size of that market segment along with where they live and how much they earn. Similarly, a company planning to distribute a new Mexican food product might consider an area's latino population as a good primary target market and want to measure that group's size as well as distribution of income and age. How would you describe the demographic characteristics of the Cycle dog food market?

As consumers grow older, their behavior changes, as expressed by their demand for goods and services. The kind of products they buy therefore depends on what stage they are in in the human *life cycle*. Marketers have tried to chart this life cycle and draw some conclu-

---

FIGURE 5–13 Did you ever wonder? The best markets . . . and the worst

Merchandise purchased	The best	The worst
Beer and ale (percent of drinkers who consume)	Milwaukee (67.9)	Dallas/Fort Worth (44.2)
Canned chili (percent of homemakers who use)	Dallas/Fort Worth (72.7)	Boston (6)
Insecticides (percent of homemakers who use at least once a month)	Houston (61.9)	New York (26.4)
Life insurance (percent of adults who currently have)	Pittsburgh (80.3)	Miami (53.4)
Lipstick (percent of women using at least twice a day)	Seattle/Tacoma (58.2)	Cincinnati (35.6)
Panty hose (percent of women who bought in past month)	Houston (61.1)	Miami (39.7)
Popcorn (percent of adults who buy for home use)	Minneapolis/ St. Paul (54.3)	Miami (26.5)
Scotch whisky (percent of drinkers who consume)	New York (35.9)	Cincinnati (9.6)

sions about product appeals for each stage. However, these charts usually make assumptions that do not necessarily reflect the real world. For example, the illustrated Wells-Gubar chart assumes all people marry and have children. This is not true, especially today. Nevertheless, we can assume that as people grow older their responsibilities do change, and so do their interests in various products (Figure 5–14).

Demographics give us useful statistical information about markets, but they fail to provide us with much information about the psychological makeup of people who constitute markets. Not all people in one sex, one age group, or one income group have the same wants, attitudes, or beliefs. In fact, people in the same demographic segment may have widely differing product preferences.

Behavioristic

Many marketers believe that the best starting point for determining market segments is to divide consumers into product-related groups based on their knowledge, attitude, use, or response to actual products or product attributes.[11] This is generally called *behavioristic* (or product-related) *segmentation*. Behavioristic segments are defined by any of a large number of variables.

FIGURE 5–14   Heavy usage patterns of various age groups

Age	Name of age group	Merchandise purchased
0–5	Young children	Baby food, toys, nursery furniture, children's wear
6–19	School children (including teenagers)	Clothing, sports equipment, phonograph records, school supplies, food, cosmetics, used cars
20–34	Young adult	Cars, furniture, houses, clothing, recreational equipment, purchases for younger age segments
35–49	Younger middle-aged	Larger homes, better cars, second cars, new furniture, recreational equipment
50–64	Older middle-aged	Recreational items, purchases for young marrieds and infants
65 and over	Senior adult	Medical services, travel, drugs, purchases for younger age groups

Purchase occasion Buyers might be distinguished by *when* they use a product or service. Air travelers, for example, might fly for business or for vacation. Thus, one airline might promote itself as a business flyer while another targets the tourist market.

Benefits sought By determining the major benefits consumers seek in a product (high quality, low price, status, speed, sex appeal, good taste, etc.), marketers may design products and advertising especially around those particular benefits (Figure 5–15).

User status There are many types of product users into which markets can be segmented, including nonusers, exusers, potential users, new users, and regular users. By targeting one or another of these groups, marketers might develop new products or new users for old products.

Usage rate Also called *volume segmentation*, usage rates are used to define consumers as light, medium, or heavy users of products. In many product categories, 80 percent of the product is sold to only 20 percent of the people. Marketers are usually interested in defining that 20 percent as closely as possible. For example, 67 percent of the population doesn't even drink beer. On the other hand, 17 percent drinks 88 percent of all the beer sold. Logically, a beer company would rather attract one heavy user to its brand than one light user (Figure 5–16).

FIGURE 5–15

The strategy here relates to the old question of what to give the person who has everything. On the surface the appeal seems to be fun, pure and simple. But it could be argued that the whole point of the headline is to make Riva the ultimate status symbol.

Figure 5–16

Annual volume segmentation in several product categories.

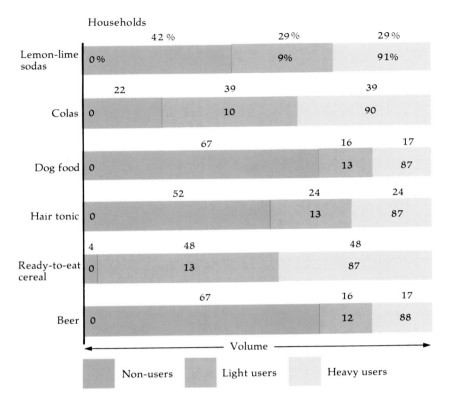

Marketers try to find common characteristics among heavy users of their products. In this way product differences may be more easily defined and advertising strategies more simply drawn. For example, heavy beer drinkers have been found to be primarily working-class men between the ages of 25 and 50 who watch more than three and one-half hours of television a day and prefer to watch sports programs.[12] What implications can a beer advertiser draw from that in determining an advertising plan?

Marketers of one product sometimes find that their customers are heavy users of other products, too. Therefore they can define their target markets in terms of the usage rates of those other products. Bowling alleys, for example, can target their markets to heavy beer drinkers and their families. Women who are heavy users of eye makeup have also been found to be heavy users of face makeup, lipstick, hair spray, perfume, cigarettes, and gasoline.[13]

By determining as many descriptive qualities of their markets as possible, marketers hope to end up with rich profiles that enable them to target all their marketing activities efficiently. In Figure 5–17 we can see how users of different toothpaste brands are segmented by benefits sought, demographics, behavioristics, and psychographics. Try making a similar chart for the four vehicles Joe Shields was considering.

Psychographic

Psychographics is a relatively new term which means the classification of consumers into market segments on the basis of psychological makeup—namely, personality, attitude, and lifestyle. Psychographics seeks to determine why they maintain their present attitudes. It classifies people according to their attitude toward life (workers, achievers, traditionalists) and their purchasing patterns (What newspapers do they read? Which magazines? Which brand of cigarettes do they buy? Which TV programs do they watch? What records do they buy?).

Marketers have attempted to categorize consumers by personality types in the hope of finding a common basis for making product appeals. Rogers studied consumer personalities by the way people adopt new products. He came up with five groups:

1. Innovators—Highly venturesome, cosmopolitan people who are eager to try new ideas and willing to accept the risk of an occasional bad experience with a new product.
2. Early adopters—People in the community with whom the average man or woman checks out an innovation; a successful and careful innovator, the early adopter is influential with those who follow.
3. Early majority—A group that tends to deliberate before adopting a product; its members are seldom leaders, but they are important in legitimizing and innovating.
4. Late majority—A cautious group that adopts ideas after the bulk of public confidence is already in favor of an innovation.
5. Laggards—Past-oriented people who are suspicious of change and of those who bring it; by the time they adopt a product, it may already have been replaced by yet another.[14]

This method of classification might be criticized as an oversimplification of consumer personalities and purchase behavior. There are so many influencing factors on the consumer's adoption process that an early adopter for one product might well be a laggard for some other, and vice versa. (See Ad Lab 5–E.)

Marketers have been able to create psychological profiles of the heavy users of various types of products, ranging from toothpaste to

FIGURE   5–17   Segmenting the U.S. toothpaste market

Benefit segments	Demographics	Behavioristics	Psychographics	Favored brands
Economy (low price)	Men	Heavy users	High autonomy, value-oriented	Brands on sale
Medicinal (decay prevention)	Large families	Heavy users	Hypochondriac, conservative	Crest
Cosmetic (bright teeth)	Teens, young adults	Smokers	High sociability, active	Macleans, Ultra Brite
Taste (good tasting)	Children	Spearmint lovers	High self-involvement, hedonistic	Colgate, Aim

AD LAB 5–E   Timex credits VALS for its products' success

Most marketers agree that, just as consumers may buy a particular product because they're 25- to 49-year-old heads of households with median incomes of $23,000, they may as easily buy that product because they detest authority, are looking for self-fulfillment, and tend toward introspection.

The latter are the buying motivations SRI International has tried to qualify since 1978 when it introduced its Values and Lifestyle (VALS) program. One client is Timex who uses VALS' psychographic categories to govern every aspect of a product's marketing strategy.

In 1982, Timex formed the Times Medical Products Corp., and in 1983 it introduced its first products: a digital scale, digital thermometer, and digital blood pressure monitor. For the maker of the Timex watch, the idea of moving into the $3 billion-a-year home health care market was a natural.

While Timex wanted to capitalize on the strengths of the Timex name and its reputation for dependability, the company suspected that the people who buy Timex watches would be unlikely to purchase state-of-the-art medical care products. It created the Healthcheck brand for the new market it set out to research. Initial demographic testing showed three distinct target groups for the Healthcheck products: for its digital thermometer, women 25 to 49 with children under 12, and adults over 60; for a digital scale, women between 18 and 49, especially women over 25; and for a blood pressure monitor, all adults over 35.

In the VALS vision of the world, consumers are typed by their psychological and sociological characteristics. VALS divides consumers into three broad groups: need-driven, outer-directed, and inner-directed. Within these three groups, there are a total of nine VALS types (see chart). These types are by no means fixed; people may change from one type to another as they mature, or they may fit into a combination of types.

Timex ranked each VALS group according to its likelihood to purchase or use Healthcheck

Value and Lifestyle Segments (VALS)

SURVIVORS: Old, intensely poor, fearful, depressed, despairing, far removed from the cultural mainstream, misfits.

I-AM-ME: Transition state, exhibitionistic, narcissistic, very young, impulsive, dramatic, experimental, active, inventive.

SUSTAINERS: Living on the edge of poverty, angry, resentful, streetwise, involved in the underground economy.

EXPERIENTIAL: Youthful, seek direct experience, person-centered, artistic, intensely oriented toward inner growth.

BELONGERS: Aging, traditional, conventional, contented, intensely patriotic, sentimental, deeply stable.

SOCIETALLY CONSCIOUS: Mission-oriented, leaders of single-issue groups, mature, successful, some live lives of voluntary simplicity.

EMULATORS: Youthful, ambitious, macho, show-off, trying to break into the system.

ACHIEVERS: Middle-aged, prosperous, able, leaders, self-assured, materialistic, builders of the "American dream."

INTEGRATED: Psychologically mature, large field of vision, tolerant, understanding, sense of fittingness.

products. In the end, the "societally conscious" and "achiever" groups as defined by VALS popped out as the likeliest targets for all three products in the line.

As VALS defines them, achievers tend to be middle-aged, prosperous, materialistic, and capable. The societally conscious are "mission-oriented," says VALS, and lead lives of voluntary simplicity. More specifically, the societally conscious can relate well to practical benefits like durability, accuracy, and ease of use. Achievers would tend to buy Healthcheck products as gifts, an important source of sales.

Timex next turned its attention to packaging the Healthcheck products, and again it used VALS. Each element of the packaging was designed to appeal to the two target groups. The thermometer packaging, for instance, features a mother and child outside in a natural setting to communicate the involvement and the inner-directedness of the relationship. In fact human interaction was a key element in all the packaging. Another package shows an older couple, their hands brushing lightly against each other—a nice little touch.

The clothing of the models on the packages was also carefully calculated to appeal to VALS achiever and societally conscious groups. They had to appear "natural looking" in muted tones, yet also "statusy enough." The models were also usually featured outside, often in activities such as riding bicycles or playing tennis.

While the front of the package with the photograph was designed to convey feelings of warmth and involvement with the product, the back of the package was filled with copy to explain the unique features of the products. Timex argues that because these two target groups love to read, they wouldn't be intimidated by a lot of details about the product.

The package design complete, the execution of each ad was then analyzed and reworked until it achieved harmony with its VALS audience. The models in the ads give off the self-satisfied vibes achievers can relate to; settings are usually upscale and yet natural and comfortable. When the models are inside a home, they are often surrounded by books and plants. Though there are differences between achievers and societally conscious consumers, the director of the VALS program says that they are subtle and that it is possible to appeal to both with one creative approach. Achievers are slightly older, more conservative and status conscious, while the societally conscious are younger and more concerned with taking control of their lives.

VALS also came into play in the media planning stage of Healthcheck. Timex's initial strategy was to use television to launch the brand and then to sustain it with print media. The strategy had to be enacted carefully, however. Achievers and the societally conscious generally don't watch television. VALS data show that when they do watch television, the two groups tend to concentrate on news, so Timex scheduled its introductory campaign during early and late news programs.

Whether or not Healthcheck's fortunes are due to its use of VALS is still debated—even among those who worked on putting together and carrying out its marketing strategy. What isn't debatable is the success Healthcheck has had to date. Each of the three products in the line moved to the top spot in its market within four months of its introduction.

Laboratory Applications

1. Which of the nine VALS categories do you fall into? Why?

2. What products can you name that appeal to a specific VALS group? Why?

3. What products could be redesigned or reformulated to fit certain VALS groups?

beer to air travel. For example, women who are heavy users of bank credit cards have been described as leading an active lifestyle, belonging to various social organizations, and being concerned with their appearance. They view the homemaking role more as managing and purchasing than the traditional concept of cleaning, cooking, and caring for children. They tend to be liberal and liberated, and they could be categorized as innovators, willing to take some risks and try new things.[15]

When marketers understand the attitudes, lifestyle, and personalities of people who tend to buy their products or services, the implications are considerable. Companies can better select potential target markets and match the image of their products with the type of consumer using the product.

Segmenting Business Markets

Business, or industrial, markets are composed of manufacturers, utilities, government agencies, contractors, wholesalers, retailers, banks, insurance companies, and institutions that buy goods and services to help them in their own business. These may be raw materials or parts that go into the product they produce, or they might be desks, office equipment, vehicles, or a variety of business services that are used in conducting their business. The products sold to business markets are often intended for resale to the public, as in the case of retail goods.

In all these situations, identifying prospective business market segments is just as important as identifying consumer market segments. In most cases we can use many of the same variables we discussed for consumer markets. Most organizations may be segmented by geographic location and by several behavioristic variables, such as benefits sought, user status, usage rate, and purchase occasion. Business markets have several distinctive characteristics, however—geographic concentration, a relatively small number of buyers, and a systematic procedure for making purchases.[16] These offer considerable implications for the companies seeking ways to segment their markets.

Market concentration

The market for industrial goods is heavily concentrated in the east north central and the mid-Atlantic states. The stylized map in Figure 5–18 shows that for manufactured goods, more than 50 percent of U.S. industry is located east of the Mississippi and north of the Mason-Dixon line. This fact greatly reduces the geographic target of most industrial marketing efforts made by companies.

Moreover, industrial marketers deal with a very limited number of buyers. Less than 2 percent of all the companies in the United States account for over 50 percent of all the manufacturing dollars. Thus, customer size is a critical basis for market segmentation. Companies may decide to concentrate all their marketing efforts on a few large customers or to target their products to the more numerous smaller customers. Steelcase, for example, manufactures office furniture and divides its marketing efforts between major accounts, on which its sales force calls directly, and dealer accounts, which resell their products to many small purchasers.

Business marketers can further break their markets down into who the end users are. Computers are now used in virtually every kind of business. If a firm develops a new computer-related product, it may decide to design it for use in one particular industry or field—banking, for instance.

■ *Business purchasing procedures*

The process businesses use to evaluate new products and make purchases is frequently far more complex and rigid than the consumer purchase process described at the beginning of this chapter. Marketers must design their communications programs with this in mind.

Large firms invariably have a purchasing department that acts as a professional consumer, evaluating the need for products, analyzing

FIGURE   5–18

The United States in proportion to the value of manufactured products.

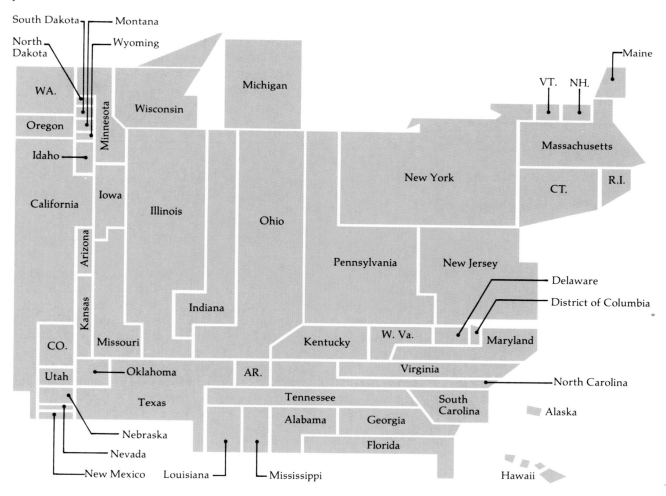

proposed purchases, seeking approvals and authorizations, making requisitions, placing purchase orders, and generally supervising all the product purchasing in the firm. The purchase decision, therefore, may take weeks, months, or even years before a sale is finally consummated. This is especially true in government agencies. Frequently, purchase decisions also depend on factors besides product quality—delivery time, terms of sale, service requirements, certainty of continuing supply, and others.

When analyzing market segments, many marketers consider the purchase decision process of various segments before determining the appropriate target market. Many new companies, for instance, target other small companies where the purchase decision can be made quickly and use commission-only representatives to call on larger firms that require more time to consummate the sale.

Standard Industrial Classification

The U.S. Department of Commerce classifies all businesses—and collects and publishes data on them—by *Standard Industrial Classification (SIC) codes*. These codes are based on broad industry groups which are then subdivided into major groups, subgroups, and detailed groups of firms in similar lines of business. In its reports, the federal government gives the number of establishments, sales volumes, and number of employees, broken down by geographic areas, for each SIC code. For those companies that can relate their sales to their customers' lines of business, these codes are a great help in segmenting markets and performing research (Figure 5–19).

FIGURE 5–19

Illustrative breakdown of SIC codes for selected businesses (product categories) in the apparel industry.

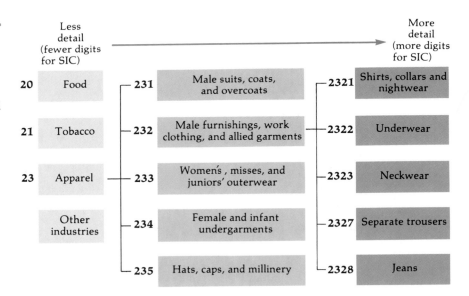

Summary

The objectives of advertising are to motivate, modify, or reinforce consumer attitudes, perceptions, beliefs, and behavior. This requires the effective blending of the behavioral sciences (anthropology, sociology, psychology) with the communicating arts (writing, drama, graphics, photography, etc.). Marketing and advertising people constantly monitor consumer attitudes, beliefs, likes and dislikes, habits, wants, and desires. The behavioral characteristics of large groups of people give the directional force to any advertising aimed at those groups. Thus, advertising uses changes in mass consumer behavior to affect changes in specific consumer behavior.

To be successful, advertising people must understand the complexity of human behavior and the variety of influences on behavior. As marketers become aware of group behavioral characteristics, they can use those characteristics to define new markets and develop advertising campaigns for those markets. Consumer behavior is affected by both internal, individual influences and external, environmental influences. Individual influences include the consumer's personal needs and motives, the consumer's perception of the world, the way the consumer learns, and habits that the consumer has developed. External environmental influences include the consumer's family, social structure, and culture. The way these influencing factors are integrated within the consumer determine how that consumer behaves.

The keen interest in consumer behavior today stems from the desire of marketers to find more effective means of communicating with their customers and to use common purchase behavior patterns as the basis for market segmentation. Market segmentation is the process of dividing a company's total market into smaller groups or segments for the purpose of (1) locating target markets, (2) identifying the needs of those target markets, (3) designing products to fill those needs, and (4) promoting products specifically to those target markets. Marketers use a variety of methods to segment markets and identify behavioral groups. The most common bases for segmenting markets are (1) geographic, (2) demographic, (3) behavioristic, and (4) psychographic.

Business markets are often segmented in the same way as consumer markets: by geographic location and by several behavioristic variables. In addition, they may be grouped by market concentration or by business purchasing procedures.

Questions for review and discussion

1. Why is consumer behavior called the directional force in advertising?
2. How do individual influences affect your behavior as a consumer?
3. What is the significance of Maslow's theory of human behavior to advertisers?
4. What examples can you give to demonstrate that "the perception is the reality"?
5. What is the importance of the theory of cognitive dissonance to advertising?
6. What significant purchasing habits do you have that may have been affected by advertising?
7. How do environmental influences affect your family's consumer behavior?
8. What is the importance of market segmentation to advertisers?
9. How could you use VALS to develop the marketing strategy for a product of your choice?
10. How is the segmentation of business markets different from that of consumer markets?

6

MARKETING AND ADVERTISING RESEARCH: INPUTS TO THE PLANNING PROCESS

Now it was up to Agi—and to the several creative teams working under her. The agency that came up with the best campaign would win the business and the lucrative commissions that go along with placing millions of dollars worth of advertising.

In the business, it was what they call a "plum" account—big and juicy—the kind every agency wants to get a crack at. In fact, just about every big agency in New York had tried to take a crack at it; but now the choice had been narrowed down to four finalists. Ayer was one of them—N. W. Ayer—the oldest agency in the United States. To win this $50 million plum, Agi (pronounced Ah-szhee) Clark and her people were going to have to win the client's confidence in Ayer and demonstrate that that confidence would not be misplaced. Their assignment was not a simple one—to come up with a new image for J. C. Penney that would be both honest and credible and would revolutionize the $200 billion-a-year department store industry.

The nation's third largest retailer, J. C. Penney had been struggling with image problems for a number of years. Was it a mass merchandiser of household commodities? Was it a nationwide discount retailer? Or was it a department store for fashionable apparel? Their customers said it wasn't. But then they really couldn't say *what* it was, either. Agi Clark's creative assignment was to find a way to change that—to communicate that J. C. Penney was indeed changing, that now it really did offer quality, fashion, and style but at the same time had not forgotten its traditional promise of high value, fair prices, and honest dealing with customers (Figure 6–1).

Clark's colleagues at Ayer provided her with reams of research about retail industry trends and Penney's position in the market. The agency's research and account teams analyzed sales data, tested consumer attitudes, and studied Penney's strengths and liabilities—all in an effort to find the best way to change Penney's image and boost its sales. They knew that to get customers to consider Penney's for their fashion purchases, they had to convince them that Penney's had changed. Somehow Penney's had to be connected to the modern, active lifestyle of upscale American consumers. Tie it to the way they work, the way they relax, the way they play. Make "human contact" (Ayer's slogan and advertising philosophy).

It wasn't the first time Clark played the high stakes game. A Fine Arts graduate from New York's Pratt Institute, she had joined Ayer 15 years earlier and worked her way up through the ranks. She had worked on liquor, ice cream, yogurt, tuna fish, cereals, lipsticks, travel, diamonds, soft drinks, pantyhose, hairsprays, and telephones. Now, as a senior vice president and executive creative director, she had already directed campaigns for several of Ayer's well-known clients—like DeBeers ("A diamond is forever"), AT&T ("Reach out and touch someone"), and others. While her years on the DeBeers account had given her invaluable experience working with outstanding photographers, directors, hair and makeup people, she had never really worked on an honest-to-goodness fashion account. She hoped that that very fact, along with her knowledge of the American consumer, would enable her to bring a fresh approach to this campaign.

In countless meetings with her teams of art directors and copywriters, the concepts began to evolve. As Penney's had changed, its advertising had to change, too. That meant a whole new look and feel. They came up with a design concept that was at once modern, fashionable, forward-looking, and simple. It could be used in magazine ads, newspaper ads, and even TV. OK. But what about the copy concept? What approach could they take that would be credible to the one third of women who make two thirds of the fashion purchases?

The ideas and proposed layouts started to pile up. They could tie Penney's to all the new brand names they were carrying. They could tell customers that Penney's changed its looks but not its values. They could compare J. C. Penney to other well-known department stores. Agi consulted with Chuck Meding, Ayer's senior VP and the management supervisor who headed the Penney's account team. Finally, they settled on four basic concepts.

"All right," Agi said, "let's send these over to research for testing." But instinctively she was sure which concept was right—the one that played off of Penney's long history of responding to their customer's needs. Tell them: "WE'VE CHANGED BECAUSE YOU'VE CHANGED."

THE NEED FOR MARKETING RESEARCH

As we discussed in Chapter 5, advertising people want to know what "makes you tick." When companies like J. C. Penney plan to spend $30 or $40 or $50 million on advertising, they don't want to risk losing it on ads or commercials that you won't notice or respond to. They also don't want to waste time and money by placing their messages on TV shows you don't watch, or in magazines you don't read, or on billboards if you don't drive a car.

Advertising is expensive. A single commercial on prime time network TV might cost $100,000—or more. A national magazine color

FIGURE 6–1

J. C. Penney saw its challenge as a positioning problem—to position itself as a "regional comparison retailer in competition with department and specialty stores similarly oriented." It wanted to be perceived by consumers as having appealing selections and a variety of styles, colors, and brands of good quality, fashionable merchandise with recognizable value. Most of all, it wanted consumers to have an enjoyable experience—so that they would feel good shopping at Penney's.

page might cost over $75,000. That is too much money to risk if you're not going to see the ad, or don't pay attention to it, or don't like it, or don't believe it, or forget it two minutes after it's gone. That's why advertising people need research—to cut the risks.[1]

Armed with the new concept from Ayer, a $22-million fall budget, and its own marketing and merchandising know-how, J. C. Penney launched an audacious assault on the department store industry in late 1984. The goal was simply to change the shopping habits of America.

Big bucks were at stake. Americans like clothes and fashionable merchandise. In fact, we spend more in department stores than many countries spend on food or national defense. And every year, for every man, woman, and child in this country, we consume an average of $1,000 worth of the type of merchandise sold in department stores. An increase of just 1 percent in share of this total market, therefore, means an added $2 billion in sales. A decrease of just 1 percent means a similar loss. These are high stakes; and the higher the stakes, the greater is the marketer's need to know.

THE SCOPE OF MARKETING RESEARCH

The American Marketing Association defines *research* as "the systematic gathering, recording, and analyzing of data about problems relating to the marketing of goods and services."[2] (See Ad Lab 6–A.)

Many decisions advertising people are forced to make cannot be made merely from intuition or knowledge of the product. In spite of her good instincts, Agi Clark, for example, would have had no assurance of what attitudes consumers had toward J. C. Penney or any of the other department stores without research data. Before she could start to develop that campaign, Clark needed to know how consumers perceived Penney's, what they thought were its strong points or liabilities, how that compared with competitive stores, and what image would likely be most credible for the company.

As Longman says:

> To be of benefit to us, research must be designed to maximize the probability of uncovering the facts about the marketplace that will affect our judgment about what to do. We will want to know whether people are aware of the existence of our brand or, in some cases, aware of the product class in which we compete. We would like to know whether those who are aware of our brand have a favorable opinion of it, and whether they think as favorably of our competitors. We will want to know how often our brand and competing brands are used, and whether they are used regularly or erratically. We will want to know what kinds of people use our brand and what kinds of people use competing brands. We will want to know how different kinds of people characterize our brand and competing brands. And we will want to know which consumers buy the product in which channels of distribution, what different uses are made of the product and on what different occasions the product is used.[3]

The importance of this information depends on the amount of risk involved in the decisions that are made. In Chapter 1 we mentioned the colossal failure of the Edsel automobile. The mistake of ignoring research findings cost Ford Motor Company $350 million and earned them the dubious award for the greatest marketing failure in history.[4]

Naturally, major marketers like J. C. Penney have no desire to take the record away from Ford. So, over the years, as the stakes in busi-

---

AD LAB 6–A   Market research versus marketing research: Xerox knew the difference

The difference between market research and marketing research is more than a semantic one. They can be distinguished on at least two substantive grounds. In the first place, they differ in scope. Market research is research about the market: its size, composition, structure, and so on. In contrast, marketing research is research about any problem in marketing, not just the market—for example, for sales personnel, compensation or channels of distribution. Thus, the term *marketing research* is much broader in scope, and is therefore preferable.

Another basis for distinction is that market research emphasizes measurement; it concentrates on quantitative dimensions. In contrast, marketing research emphasizes creativity; it concentrates on qualitative aspects. It seeks to discover unsatisfied consumer needs and wants; it tries to ferret out unsolved problems in the marketplace, the so-called holes in the market that offer significant opportunities for bringing innovation and change to it. The objective is to disturb the equilibrium in the market in the company's favor. The resulting increase in market share rebounds to the innovator as a reward for detecting problems, frustrations, difficulties or dissatisfactions, and then providing solutions which are perceived by the market as true solutions. This is the heart of the developmental type of research referred to previously. It focuses on what could be, rather than on what is.

The dramatic and successful entry of Xerox into the copying market of the late 50s is a classic example of the use of creative marketing research to discover and develop a huge, unexploited market opportunity. The two principal companies then in the market, Kodak (Verifax) and 3M (Thermofax), not only had inferior technology but required users to purchase their machines outright and to use only paper made exclusively by them. Defined this way, the market for copying machines (and copying) remained relatively small. If Xerox had used mere market research, it might have concluded, "The market is too small; why bother?"

However, its marketing research revealed the true potential for a company which could bring real innovation to the market, not only in technology (xerography), but in marketing strategy as well. It said, "We'll lend you our machine, and you can use any paper you wish!" The wedding of superior technology and superior marketing produced a striking synergistic effect; when copying was made easy, the market exploded! Xerox was not interested in what the market was but what it could be as a result of the constructive contribution Xerox could bring to it.

Laboratory Application

Explain how you could do market research for a fast-food chain in your area. Then explain how you could do marketing research.

ness have gotten larger, so has the dependence on sophisticated information.

Actually, marketing research is useful in all stages of the management process. Figure 6–2 shows the widespread application of research in a cross section of U.S. companies. Note how marketing research is used in fields like financial planning and economic forecasting even more than in traditional marketing areas like advertising.

For firms that operate under the marketing concept (discussed in Chapter 4), marketing and advertising research plays a key role in identifying consumer needs, developing new products and communication strategies, and assessing the effectiveness of marketing programs and promotional activities.

In this chapter, our objective is to understand the basic procedures and techniques used in marketing research today and the importance of research to the development of marketing and advertising plans and strategies. In addition we will want to look at the various ways research can be used to test the effectiveness of ads and campaigns both before and after they have run. When you complete this chapter you should have a greater realization not only of how research can help organizations cut their risks but also of how many limitations there are to research effectiveness.

FIGURE   6–2   Marketing research activities of 1,322 companies

Activity	Percent doing	Activity	Percent doing
Business economics and corporate research		**Corporate-responsibility research**	
		Studies on legal constraints on advertising and promotion	38%
Short-range forecasting (up to one year)	63%	Ecological impact studies	27
Long-range forecasting (over one year)	61	Social values and policies studies	25
Studies of business trends	61	Consumers' "right to know" studies	18
Pricing studies	56		
Acquisition studies	53	**Product research**	
Product-mix studies	51	Competitive product studies	64
Plant- and warehouse-location studies	47	New product acceptance and potential	63
Company-employee studies	45	Testing of existing products	57
Export and international studies	41	Packaging research: design or physical characteristics	44
Sales and market research			
Measurement of market potentials	68	**Advertising research**	
Determination of market characteristics	68	Studies of ad effectiveness	49
Market share analysis	67	Media research	44
Sales analysis	65	Copy research	37
Establishment of sales quotas, territories	57	Motivation research	33
Distribution channels studies	48		
Sales compensation studies	45		
Test markets, store audits	38		
Consumer panel operations	33		

BASIC STEPS IN THE RESEARCH PROCEDURE

The manager of marketing research and planning at J. C. Penney is Sid Stein. By 1980 he had been with the company for 15 years and, in that period, had seen significant management changes take place. But he was to play a key role in one of the largest repositioning efforts in corporate history. That was the year the chairman of the board appointed a committee of four to assess the competitive environment and to articulate a clear direction for the future of the company. Sid was one of the four; and over the next year the research performed by his department was going to make a significant contribution to the positioning strategy they were charged with developing.

■ Research Objectives and Problem Definition

The first step in the marketing research process is to define the problem and set research objectives (Figure 6–3). Sid was already well aware of the problem. His responsibility had been to conduct ongoing market research for the company and to develop a marketing information system. The company was not running blind, and he already had a good idea why Penney's position in the market seemed to be weakening.

During the 60s and early 70s Penney's marketing and merchandise mix had been very broad. Customers could expect to find everything they needed from automotive products to home furnishings and appliances. At Penney's you could get paint, hardware, lawn and garden supplies, home entertainment products, and apparel. The strategy had been one-stop shopping, "from a spool of thread to a refrigerator." During this period, as regional shopping centers emerged, Penney's followed the trend and ended up occupying more space in these regional malls than any retailer in the country. The company experienced tremendous growth, and its sales doubled or tripled in most categories. But Penney's research showed that they were steadily losing share of market, particularly in the highly profitable women's apparel department.

From their own studies, researchers believed that the "contemporary" woman was shopping at Penney's for commodity merchandise but not spending much of her fashion apparel dollars there. Yet, that group—about one third of the population—accounts for two thirds of women's apparel sales. Moreover, they discovered a perceptual gap between J. C. Penney and the department stores for fashionability and quality in women's apparel. It was becoming apparent that, in the process of trying to satisfy all consumers, Penney's had perhaps inadvertently neglected certain groups, especially the higher-spending segments. Since 1975 Penney's had tried to respond to these con-

FIGURE 6–3

Marketing research process.

sumer attitudes by adopting a segmentation strategy and upgrading the merchandise, but they had not done so fast enough. The competition seemed to be moving faster in upgrading products and images, so the perceptual gap had remained unchanged.

Thus, Stein was confronted with several problem *symptoms*. His first objective was to discover the *causes*, so the problem could be accurately defined and understood.

Schultz and Martin recommend writing a concise statement of the research problem and objectives at the beginning of any research project. The statement should contain three basic elements:

1. The information to be gathered must be measurable.
2. It must be relevant to the problem.
3. The various pieces of information or knowledge to be gained must be related.[5]

For example, the statement of Penney's problem and research objectives might have been written as follows:

> J. C. Penney's sales, while still increasing, seem to have lost their momentum and are not producing the profit expected by our shareholders. In the last year our share of the market has even slipped in several departments from X percent in the home

---

PEOPLE IN ADVERTISING

Jack J. Honomichl

President
Marketing Aid Center, Inc.

Jack J. Honomichl, who heads his own consulting firm, Marketing Aid Center, Inc., is an authority on the subject of marketing research and its use in the decision-making process.

A graduate of Kellogg School of Management at Northwestern University, Honomichl also obtained an A.M. degree in the social sciences from the University of Chicago.

He began his professional career in the marketing/advertising research department of the *Chicago Tribune*. Honomichl later was named vice president of Market Research Corporation of America. He then became vice president of Audits & Surveys, Inc.

His experience has included administrative responsibility for most types of data collection and analysis—diary purchase panels, store audit programs, and surveys—including large-scale studies funded by agencies of the federal government.

Honomichl has worked closely with the top marketing management of more than 30 major companies, chiefly in the development and marketing of new packaged goods products. These firms include Alpo Pet Foods, Inc.; Sears, Roebuck; Savin Business Machines; Star-Kist Foods; Foote, Cone & Belding; Arbitron Ratings Company; and Gallup & Robinson, Inc.

furnishings department to Y percent in the ladies apparel department. Is this slippage due to a decline in total shopping mall sales? Is it due to increased competition from specialty stores, small boutiques, or mass merchandisers? Or are sales lost to another department store in the same mall? If sales are lost to other department stores, which ones and why?

This hypothetical statement of the problem is specific and measurable, the questions asked are relevant to the problem, and the information requested is directly related.

■ Exploratory Research

The second step in the research process is to assess current knowledge through a number of information procedures. The objective of exploratory research is simply to learn more about the market, the competition, the business environment, and the problem before any formal research is undertaken. This may consist of discussing the problem with informed sources inside the firm; with wholesalers, distributors, or retailers outside the firm; with customers; or even with competitors. The two main tasks of the exploratory research stage are to analyze internal data and to collect outside secondary data.

The marketing research industry, says Honomichl, is undergoing some dramatic changes. These major trends, he believes describe the shape of its future:

1. There will be fewer specialists and more generalists. The focus will be more on problem solving and less on data-collection techniques.
2. The desire by top management for fewer studies—and for hand-tailored, creative programs—will cause a resurgence of small, highly personalized firms that both consult and execute projects.
3. Emphasis will shift back from exotic data manipulation to personal involvement with consumers—monitoring activity in supermarkets, doing pilot studies personally, and constructing humanistic questionnaires instead of those chiefly designed to facilitate data processing.
4. Growth will continue but not in traditional services. Instead, it will center on "information systems" data banks.
5. While machined research will continue, firms will discover that, instead of getting closer to the consumer, too much technology is building a wall. This will spur them to seek more humanistic approaches to research.

6. In-house research among client firms will accelerate, partly because of cost considerations, but chiefly because the integration of confidential internal data can greatly enhance the value of a research study. There are several prominent examples including General Foods, General Mills, Procter & Gamble, Pillsbury, and some advertising agencies. They have developed large, well-staffed internal research organizations. Proctor & Gamble spends about $10 million annually for in-house, do-it-yourself research. There are several reasons for doing research in-house including saving money, faster turnaround, confidentiality, use of internal facilities (like WATS lines), and more control.

Honomichl has published over 160 articles in professional and trade journals. He has also delivered more than 25 unpublished papers to numerous organizations including the American Management Association, the American Marketing Association, the American Research Foundation, and CASRO (the Council of American Survey Research Organizations.)

Utilizing internal data

Company records are often a valuable source of information. Types of internal data useful to a marketing manager include product shipment figures, billings to customers, warranty card records, advertising expenditures, sales expenses, correspondence from customers, and records of meetings with sales staffs.

In the case of J. C. Penney, which has a well-developed marketing information system, an analysis of sales data, a review of past tracking studies, and an examination of previous marketing research data signaled the problem the company faced. In another situation a marketing manager might discover from marketing expense data that certain customers or territories offer an unprofitable relationship of sales produced to the cost incurred to produce them.

Collecting secondary data

Secondary data are data that already exist somewhere, having been collected for another purpose.[6] Much information is available—usually free—if the researcher just knows where to look for it. It might be government-issued materials, such as census data or publications from the Department of Commerce, or published information from market research companies, trade associations, or various trade publications.

Generally, collecting secondary data is less costly than collecting primary data and requires less time. However there are problems with secondary data: (1) they may be obsolete; (2) they may not be relevant to the problem at hand; (3) they may not be valid or reliable information, depending on the way they were collected; or (4) the very wealth of information available for review may be overpowering relative to the size of the problem being studied. (See Ad Lab 6–B.)

Some of the most frequently used sources of secondary data are the following:

Library reference materials (e.g. the *Business Periodicals Index* for business magazines, *Reader's Guide to Periodical Literature* for consumer magazines, *Public Information Service Bulletin*, the *New York Times Index*, and the *World Almanac and Book of Facts*)

Government publications (e.g. the *Statistical Abstract of the United States*)

Trade association publications (e.g. annual fact books containing government data and information gathered by various industry groups listed in the *Directory of National Trade Associations*)

Research organizations publications (e.g. literature from university bureaus of business research, Nielsen retail store audits, MRCA consumer purchase diaries, etc., all available on a subscription basis).

When Sid Stein and his staff finished reviewing all the internal data and the outside secondary research on Penney's situation, they found that Penney's was *not* losing sales so much to the specialty shops and mass merchandisers, as to other department stores. But the fact that Penney's itself had a long tradition of mass merchandising created confusion in the minds of its own management and, most importantly, in the minds of its customers. Penney's management personnel at the store, district, regional, and corporate levels were not really clear about who the competition was. And consumers had difficulty describing just what kind of store J. C. Penney was. This all meant one thing to Sid Stein and his committee. More than anything else, they had to chart an unequivocal course for the company and communicate it clearly. Everyone—their 170,000 employees, the thousands of suppliers and vendors, the financial community, and the public—had to understand just what J. C. Penney stood for. Now the questions became: Who are our customers? Who are the department store's customers? What do they like and dislike about us and about our competitors? How are we perceived? And what do we have to do to clarify and improve that perception?

■ Performing Primary Research

The answers to these questions would become the foundation for Penney's evolving positioning strategy. That, in turn, would determine the kind of stores and merchandise the company would have and the kind of advertising and promotion the company could use. In short, it would set the company's course for years to come. Stein decided to do more primary research to get the answers.

■ *Basic methodology of quantitative research*

Once the researcher has concluded the exploratory research phase, he or she may discover a need to gain additional information directly from the marketplace. There are basically three methods in collecting this primary data: observation, experiment, and survey.

AD LAB   6–B   Using marketing research for new-product development

You are a marketing manager for a major manufacturer of ethical drug products, and management has indicated an interest in marketing a line of products to the proprietary market. After considerable brainstorming, you determine that your company has the research and development capability to produce a superior line of proprietary vitamin products which could be sold through your normal distribution channels.

The problem is to assess the opportunities to get into the over-the-counter vitamin business and to obtain volume share and profit levels consistent with corporate criteria.

The first step in obtaining the required information on the vitamin market is to consult available reference guides (see the chart). These will lead you to most of the important sources specific to the normal market. Additional information can be obtained through direct contact with qualified persons at the sources. In most cases they will lead you to less obvious data sources, which may turn up information of key significance to your overall findings. At this stage you will also reach the "industry experts" who may confirm (or deny) your assessment of the opportunities to participate in the vitamin market. Having systematically gone through all these steps, your search is completed. With 50 pounds of data, however, your real job has just begun. (*continued*)

Laboratory Application

What are the implications of this kind of research for the advertising activities that the company might use for its new product line?

AD LAB   6–B (*continued*)

A guide to obtaining information on the vitamin market

Sources	U.S. government	Trade and other organizations	Consumer/ business press	Publications
Reference guides	U.S. Government Organizational Manual Federal Statistical Directory Government reports and announcements	Encyclopedia of Associations	Business Publications Rates & Data Consumer Magazine & Agri-Media Rates & Data	Business Periodicals Index Funk & Scott Index of Corporations & Industries Index Medicus Thomas Register of American Corporations Pharmaceutical News Index Reader's Guide to Periodical Literature
Specific to the vitamin market				
Issues: Nature of the product Vitamins and how they are used New products and/or external issues influencing the market	National Technical Information Service (Department of Commerce) National Center for Health Statistics (HHS)	Vitamin Information Bureau American Dietetic Association National Science Foundation	Consumer Reports Today's Health Drug Topics Prevention Magazine American Druggist Product Marketing	Journal of the AMA New England Journal of Medicine FDA Reports (newsletter)
Role of government: Impact of existing and potential government rules and regulations	Food & Drug Administration (HHS) Reports of congressional committees	The Proprietary Association Pharmaceutical Manufacturing Association Consumer groups	Articles appearing in business and drug trade magazines and medical journals	Pharmaceutical News Index FDA Reports
Consumer behavior: Level of vitamin usage by consumers Consumers' perceptions and attitudes concerning vitamins	National Technical Information Service (Department of Commerce) National Center for Health Statistics (HHS)	Consumer groups	Prevention Magazine Readership studies of general consumer and trade magazines	Findex-Directory of Market Research Reports, Studies & Surveys

Sources	U.S. government	Trade and other organizations	Consumer/ business press	Publications
Specific to the vitamin market				
Competition:				
Nature of the competition and extent of leverage in the market	Form 10-K's (SEC)		Articles appearing in business and drug trade magazines	Moody's Industrial Manual
				Standard & Poor's corporation records
				Value Line Investment Survey
				Dun & Bradstreet Reports
				National Investment Library annual report
				Disclosure, Inc. annual report
				Thomas Register of American Corporations
Market trends and developments:				
Size of the market and growth rate	Census of Manufacturers (Department of Commerce)	The Proprietary Association	Product Marketing	Standard & Poor's Industry Surveys
Major vitamin categories and relative growth	Survey of Manufacturers (Department of Commerce)	Pharmaceutical Manufacturers Association	Drug Topics	Pharmaceutical News Index
Traditional distribution channels and the major retail outlets	Current industrial reports (Department of Commerce)		Supermarket Business	
Seasonal patterns or regional skews			Articles appearing in business and drug trade magazines	
Advertising:				
Kinds and levels of advertising support			Advertising Age	Leading National Advertisers
Creative strategies employed by advertisers			Marketing Communications	Publishers Information Bureau

Observation This method is used when researchers actually monitor the overt actions of the person being studied. It may take the form of a traffic count by outdoor billboard companies, a television audience count by means of an instrument hooked to TV sets, or a study of the way consumers react to products displayed in the supermarket.

The Pet Milk Company at one point radically changed its evaporated milk label and introduced the new label in the Detroit market. Researchers posted themselves near the evaporated milk section of supermarkets and observed how customers responded to the new label. Since it was apparent from observation that the label was causing a great deal of consumer confusion, and since retail orders were severely depressed, the label was withdrawn from distribution.[7]

Experiment This is a type of research designed to measure actual cause-and-effect relationships. Strict controls are used so the variable that causes the effect can be determined. This method is used primarily for test marketing new products in isolated geographic areas and in testing new advertising campaigns prior to national introduction. However, the method is expensive and not easy to use, since it is very difficult to control all the marketing variables.

Survey This is the most common way to gather primary research data. By asking questions of current or prospective customers, the researcher hopes to obtain information on attitudes, opinions, or motivations. The political poll is one of the most common surveys with which consumers are familiar. The three common ways of conducting surveys are by telephone, by mail, and by personal interview. Each of these has distinct advantages and disadvantages (Figure 6–4).

Sid Stein's department ran a continuous stream of consumer surveys in many locations around the country, asking shoppers to rate

FIGURE   6–4   Comparison of data collection methods

	Personal	Telephone	Mail
Data collection costs	High	Medium	Low
Data collection time required	Medium	Low	High
Sample size for a given budget	Small	Medium	Large
Data quantity per respondent	High	Medium	Low
Reaches widely dispersed sample	No	Maybe	Yes
Reaches special locations	Yes	Maybe	No
Interaction with respondents	Yes	Yes	No
Degree of interviewer bias	High	Medium	None
Severity of non-response bias	Low	Low	High
Presentation of visual stimuli	Yes	No	Maybe
Field worker training required	Yes	Yes	No

Penney's and competitive department stores on a variety of issues: quality, integrity, fashionability, stylishness, newness and oldness, selection, displays, store appeal, etc.

Around the country, shoppers said they thought J. C. Penney stood for honesty, integrity, and value. That was the good news. But they also said that Penney's stores were unexciting. And across the board they perceived that Penney's merchandise had less quality and was less stylish and contemporary than the merchandise carried by the department stores. That was the bad news. Moreover, the interviews convinced Sid and his committee that they *were* getting the same customers as the department stores, but that these customers were buying a disproportionately small amount of "fashionable" merchandise at Penney's. The problem, therefore, ran much deeper than women's, or even men's, apparel. It affected every department where product characteristics such as style, appearance, and timeliness were considered important by their target customers.

Elements of quantitative research

The three methods of data collection just described are used by market researchers primarily to develop hard numbers so they can completely and accurately measure a particular market situation. These *quantitative,* or descriptive, methods require formal design and rigorous standards for collecting and tabulating information. Only in this way can inaccuracies be minimized and the data considered *valid* and *reliable* for future decision making.

Assume a market contains 10,000 individuals, and you want to determine the attitude of that market toward a proposed new toy. You walk into a restaurant and show a prototype of the toy to five people, and four say they like it. If you then interpolate that to your entire market, you might predict an 80 percent favorable attitude. Is that test *valid?* Hardly. It is very doubtful that the results of your test reflect the true status of the market.

In addition, if you were to repeat your test with five more people in the restaurant, you might come up with an entirely different response. And if you repeated it again, you might come up with a third result. If that happened, it would show that your test also lacks *reliability.* For a test to be reliable it must be repeatable, producing the same result each time it is administered (Figure 6–5).

The validity and reliability of any research project, therefore, depends on several key elements. The most important of these are the sampling methods used, the way the survey questionnaire is designed, and the methods used for data collection and analysis. We will discuss these briefly.

Sampling theories   When J. C. Penney wants to know what consumers think about its products or its image, it cannot possibly ask everybody in the country. That would be too expensive and time-consuming. However, it is important that the results of the research accurately reflect the *universe,* or the entire target population, of department store customers. Marketing researchers therefore select a *sample* of the population that they expect will represent the appropriate targeted population. To accomplish this, they must make several basic decisions. Who is to be surveyed? How many people should be surveyed? How should the respondents be chosen?

A sample can be representative only if it reflects the pertinent characteristics of the universe the researcher wants to measure. Naturally, if we survey people who normally do not vote in an election, we are not going to get a result representative of the voters. The *sample unit,* or whom we survey, therefore, is very important.

Theories of sampling are drawn from the mathematical theories of probability. For a sample to be considered adequate, it must be large enough to achieve satisfactory precision or stability. Naturally, the larger the *sample size,* the more reliable are the results. However, adequate sample size has nothing to do with the size of the population. Good reliability can often be obtained with samples representing only a fraction of 1 percent of the population if the proper procedure is used. The two most commonly used *sampling procedures* are random probability samples and nonprobability samples. (See Ad Lab 6–C.)

Probability samples give every unit in the universe an equal and known probability of being selected for the research. If a researcher wishes to know the opinions of a community regarding a particular issue, all members of the community constitute the universe. Selecting various members of the community at random produces an unbiased sample and the most accurate results, but it also presents certain difficulties. It requires that every unit be known, listed, and numbered so that each has an equal chance of being selected. This is often prohibitively expensive, and sometimes impossible, especially in the case of customers for nationally distributed products. J. C. Penney annually participates in a national probability study conducted by

FIGURE 6–5

The reliability/validity diagram. Using the analogy of a dart board, the bull's eye in this example represents the actual average of some value among a population of people (e.g. average age). The marks of the darts thrown at the target are analogous to the averages that might be obtained by polling various sets of people in the population. The first column shows high reliability because the results are all very similar. The second column shows low reliability because the darts are randomly scattered on the target. The top row shows the pattern for high validity—because the marks are all centered on the bull's eye. The bottom row shows the effect of systematic bias and therefore low validity.

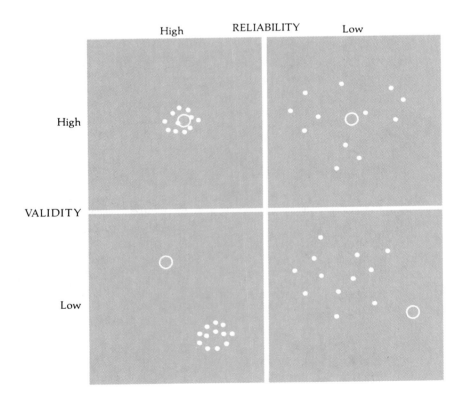

R. H. Bruskin Associates in order to identify the company's shopper base and to learn in what ways it resembles that of the targeted competition, i.e. department stores. These studies, when compared to earlier studies, provide an evaluation of how Penney's shopper base has changed over time.

AD LAB 6–C   How does sampling work?

Most expert statisticians could give you some very comprehensive answers to that question. Probably too comprehensive, in fact, for anyone but another expert statistician. So let's explain sampling by using a photograph of a child.

The first picture is composed of several hundred thousand dots. Let's consider these dots as our total population and draw several samples.

The other three pictures represent samples of 250, 1,000, and 2,000 dots. These samples represent a specific kind of sample design called "area probability sampling" because the black and white dots in the samples are distributed in proportion to their distribution in the original picture (more black dots in the hair, more white dots in the face, etc.). Think of homes (which add up to our population) instead of dots (which add up the pictures), and you have the sampling method used by Nielsen for arriving at national TV ratings.

Now . . . if you put the book down and step back a few feet, you'll notice a very interesting thing as you look at these small pictures. Your eye will adjust to the overall image and stop trying to "read" the dots. See how the 250-dot sample provides a recognizable picture? Rec-

ognizable, yes, but obviously not much detail. So, let's take a look at the 1,000 dot sample . . . again from a few feet away.

Now we find that the child is *very* recognizable; in fact, if all we wanted was a reliable idea of what she looked like, this sample would be quite adequate.

Another interesting thing about sampling. The 1,000-dot photograph is about twice as sharp as the 250-dot photograph because it has *four times* as many dots. And so it is with sampling: to double the accuracy, one must *quadruple* sample size.

These are some of the basic sampling laws followed in constructing Nielsen's 1,200-home television sample. Just as the 1,000-dot photograph provides a reliable idea of what the woman looks like, the television industry regards the Nielsen sample as adequate in size to provide a reliable estimate of national TV viewing habits and trends.

Laboratory Application

Under what circumstances could area probability sampling be used other than in determining TV ratings?

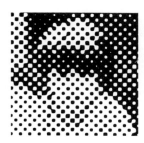
250

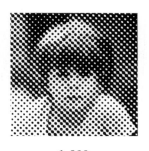
1,000

2,000

Nonprobability samples do not provide every unit in the universe with an equal chance of being included. As a result, there is no guarantee that the sample will be representative. Moreover, the probable magnitude of the sampling error cannot be measured as it can with random sampling. Nonetheless, nonprobability samples are used extensively because they are less expensive and less time-consuming and because random sampling is often not feasible. When only a general measure of the data is needed, nonprobability sampling can be very useful. Most advertising and marketing research studies use the nonprobability method. For example, in the case of J. C. Penney, the nonprobability method was sufficient to determine shopping preferences and image attitudes of its customers.

Questionnaire design The construction of a good questionnaire requires considerable expertise. Much research bias is blamed on poorly designed questionnaires. Typical problems include asking the wrong types of questions, asking too many questions, using the wrong form for a question, which makes it either too difficult to answer or too difficult to tabulate, and using the wrong choice of words (Figure 6–6).

FIGURE   6–6

J. C. Penney used a personal interview questionnaire similar to this (only much longer) to find out the feelings of shoppers toward the store, its merchandise, and its advertising.

1. Do you intend to shop at any J. C. Penney store between now and Sunday?
    Yes   1   No   2   (If no, skip to question 5).

2. Do you intend to go into J. C. Penney to buy something in particular or just to browse?
    Buy   1   Browse   2

3. Have you seen any of the items you intend to buy advertised by J. C. Penney?
    Yes   1   (continue)   No   2   (skip to question 5)

4. Where did you see these items advertised? Was it in a J. C. Penney advertising flyer included with your newspaper, a J. C. Penney flyer you received in the mail, on the pages of the newspaper itself, on TV, or somewhere else?

    Flyer in newspaper   _____
    Flyer in mail   _____
    Pages of newspaper   _____
    On TV   _____
    Somewhere else (specify) _____
    Don't recall   _____

5. Now, I would like you to rate the J. C. Penney advertising insert on the attributes listed below. Please place an "X" in the box at the position that best reflects your opinion of how the insert rates on each attribute. Placing an "X" in the middle box usually means you are neutral. The closer you place the "X" to the left or right phrase or word, the more you believe it describes the J. C. Penney insert.

Looks expensive								Looks cheap
Cleverly done								Unskillful
Appealing								Unappealing
Shows clothing in an attractive manner	1	2	3	4	5	6	7	Does not show clothing in an attractive manner

6. Please indicate all of the different types of people listed below that you feel this J. C. Penney advertising insert is appealing to?

    Young people   _____   Quality-conscious people _____
    Bargain hunters   _____   Low-income people   _____
    Conservative dressers   _____   Budget watchers   _____
    Fashion-conscious people _____   Older people   _____
    Rich people   _____   Middle-income people   _____
    Professionals   _____   Blue-collar people   _____
    High-income people   _____   Women   _____
    Men   _____   Office workers   _____
    Someone like me   _____   Smart dressers   _____
    Career-oriented women   _____   Other (specify):   _____

Consider the simple question: "What kind of soap do you use?" The respondent doesn't know what the word "soap" means. Is it hand soap, shampoo, laundry detergent, dishwashing soap, cleansing cream, or dishwasher detergent? And take the word "kind." Does that mean what brand, what size, or what use? Finally, what constitutes "use"? Does that mean what do you buy? You might buy one "kind" for yourself and another "kind" for your husband. You probably "use" several different "kinds." Answering the question accurately is impossible. Worse, if the question is answered, the researcher doesn't know what the answer signifies and will likely draw an incorrect conclusion. (See the Checklist for developing an effective questionnaire.)

Checklist for developing an effective questionnaire

□ Explain the research objectives. Be sure the reason for the study is clear. Listing the objectives helps to prevent the inclusion of extraneous material or questions that "would be interesting to know the answers to" but are not germane to the actual study.

□ Write the actual points to be determined by the questionnaire. Again, be sure the description of the desired information is clear and concise. Avoid long questionnaires that tax the patience of the respondent. When this happens, careless or flip answers often result, or the respondent finds reasons not to answer the questions fully.

□ Break the items to be determined down into specific questions. Questions must be stated so that they are clear to respondents and there is no chance for misunderstanding. Avoid generalities and ambiguous terms.

□ Write a rough draft first. Polish it after you've made all your points.

□ Use a short opening statement. Include your name, the name of your organization, and the broad purpose of the questionnaire.

□ Open with one or two easily answered, interesting, and inoffensive questions. This tends to put the respondent at ease.

□ Structure the questions so they flow logically and easily from one to another. Ask general questions before the more detailed ones.

□ Have as few "closed" questions as possible.

Use open-ended questions where possible, although there are some problems with them:

□ Open-ended questions let the respondent answer whatever comes to mind, but answers are difficult to tabulate.

□ Most open-ended questions can be closed by providing a list of anticipated answers for the interviewer to check off. This simplifies tabulation.

□ Avoid questions that suggest an answer or that could be considered "leading" questions. Let the respondent answer fully and honestly. Don't use words with strong favorable or unfavorable connotations. They tend to bias results.

□ Make the questions easy to answer. Don't use long, detailed questionnaires which may confuse the respondent.

□ When possible, include a few questions which will serve as a cross-check on earlier answers. This aids in ensuring validity.

□ Put the demographic questions (e.g., age, income, education) and other personal questions at the end of the questionnaire.

□ Pretest the questionnaire to get out the bugs. Your primary concern is to make sure the questions are being interpreted as intended and that all information being sought is included. Twenty to 30 persons in the proposed respondent group are usually a sufficient sample for a pretest.

Alreck and Settle suggest that effective survey questions have three important attributes: focus, brevity, and simplicity. They focus directly on the issue or topic of the survey. They are as brief as possible while still conveying the intended meaning. And they are expressed as simply and clearly as they can be.[8]

There are many ways to ask essentially the same question. Assume you are conducting a survey on J. C. Penney's advertising. Figure 6–7 shows four commonly used methods that might elicit responses about the quality of Penney's ads. There are many variations even within these four methods. For example, additional choices might be added to the multiple-choice format. Neutral responses might be added to the scale format. And there is obvious bias in the dichotomous question.

What is important is that the questions elicit a response that is both accurate and useful to the researcher's needs. For this reason, it is advisable that all questionnaires be tested on a small subsample to detect any confusion, bias, or ambiguities.

Data collection and analysis After all the research data have been collected, they must be validated, edited, coded, and tabulated. Answers must be checked to eliminate errors or inconsistencies. For instance, one person might answer a question "two years" while another says "24 months." These must be changed to the same units for

---

FIGURE 6–7   Different ways to phrase research questions

Type	Questions
Open-ended	How would you describe J. C. Penney advertising?
Dichotomous	Do you think J. C. Penney advertising is too attractive? ____ Yes ____ No
Multiple choice	What description best fits your opinion of J.C. Penney advertising? ____ Modern ____ Well done ____ Believable ____ Unconvincing ____ Old-fashioned
Semantic differential (scale)	Please indicate on the scale how you perceive J. C. Penney advertising? ― ― ― ― 1 2 3 4 Poor Excellent

correct tabulation. Some questionnaires may be rejected because the answers are obviously the result of misunderstanding. Finally, the data must be counted and summarized. For small studies, tabulation may be manual. But most research projects today use more sophisticated data processing equipment to count the answers and produce cross-tabulations of the data.

For example, many researchers want a cross-tabulation of product use by age group or other important demographic information. The researcher may take the raw data, apply advanced statistical techniques to them, and pass them through the computer again to seek additional findings. At this point, the cost of the research study can go through the ceiling if an unskilled marketer wants to see all the cross-tabulations possible. The researcher must use skill and imagination to select only those cross-tabulations that will show significant relationships.

Basic methodology of qualitative research

At this point in the research, Penney's wanted to understand its sales problem more clearly, especially since the company was rated so highly for honesty, integrity, and value. Penney's researchers initiated a series of *focus group* sessions to probe customers' perceptions of who were Penney's most frequent shoppers, who weren't, and why. They also held *in-depth interviews* with over 400 of Penney's management personnel at the store, district, regional, and corporate levels to understand their views and solicit their suggestions.

A variety of indirect research methods are used by marketers to understand the "why" of consumer behavior. No matter how skillfully posed, some questions are hard for the consumer to answer. As we discussed in Chapter 5, it is especially difficult for consumers to give the real reasons for their product choices. Thus qualitative research is used more and more to enable marketers to get a general impression of the market, the consumer, or the product. Some marketers refer to it as *motivation* research.

Qualitative research, according to Sampson, is usually exploratory or diagnostic in nature, involving small numbers of people surveyed on a nonprobability basis to gain impressions rather than definitions.[9] The methods used in qualitative research are usually described as intensive or projective in nature.

Projective techniques The idea behind this approach is to get an understanding of people's underlying or subconscious feelings, attitudes, opinions, needs, and motives by asking indirect questions or otherwise involving the consumer in a situation in which he or she can "project" feelings about the problem or product.

For example, when N. W. Ayer was vying for the J. C. Penney account, it conducted several studies of its own using a projective technique in a series of shopping center interviews. In one of them, Ayer personnel showed pictures of different types of shoppers to people in the mall and asked them where they thought these shoppers probably bought their clothes. This technique has long been used by psychologists for clinical diagnosis and is now being adapted to marketing use. These and many other types of projective techniques all require highly experienced researchers to be used correctly.

Intensive techniques Using this approach requires great care in administering the questions as it is an extension of the interview method of research. One type, called the *in-depth interview*, uses carefully planned but loosely structured questions to enable the interviewer to probe respondents' deeper feelings. The interviewer may talk to the subject for an hour or more in an informal setting to give the impression of an unstructured conversation and to set the subject at ease. Although these interviews are very helpful at discovering individual motivations, they are also very expensive, extremely time-consuming, and limited by the lack of skilled interviewers. In fact, the most important link in the process is the interviewer, who tends to be the least trained and lowest paid of all the professionals involved in the study. Recognizing this, many organizations prefer to use group techniques.

The *focus group* method is one of the most useful. Eight to 10 people, "typical" of the target market, are invited to a group session to discuss the product, the service, or the marketing situation. A trained moderator guides the often free-wheeling discussion for an hour or more, and the group interaction reveals the group's true feelings or behavior toward the product. These meetings are usually recorded and may even be viewed or videotaped from behind a one-way mirror. These groups do not offer sampling validity. However, participants' thinking can often be used prior to a formal survey to assist in questionnaire design.[10] Or, as in the case of Penney's, focus groups following a survey can put flesh on the skeleton created by raw data (Figure 6–8).

■ Interpreting the Findings

Marketing research is used to help solve management problems. Only if it does so is it worth the cost (Figure 6–9). The researcher, therefore, must prepare a complete analysis of the information gathered. Tables and graphs may be used, but it is important that these be explained in words management can understand. The use of technical jargon (such as "multivariate analysis of variance model") should be avoided or at least confined to an appendix. The report should state the problem and research objective, a summary of the findings, and the researcher's conclusions drawn from an unbiased analysis of

FIGURE   6–8

Focus group sessions are usually held in comfortable settings where participants can feel relaxed about discussing their attitudes and beliefs. The one-way mirror conceals recording or videotaping equipment and often agency or advertiser personnel viewing the proceedings.

FIGURE   6–9   How much does research cost using
                      professional firms?

Telephone: 500 20-minute interviews, with report	$12,000–$15,000
Mail: 500 returns, with report—33 percent response rate	$7,000–$8,000
Intercept: 500 interviews, four or five questions, with report	$15,000
Executive interviews (talking to business administrators): 20 interviews, with report	$2,500–$7,500
Focus group: One group, 8 to 10 people, with report and videotape	$2,500–$3,800

the data. The researcher's recommendations for management action should also be described, and the whole report should be offered with an oral presentation to allow for management feedback and to highlight important points. A description of the methodology, statistical analysis, and raw data on which the report is based constitute the report's appendix.

APPLYING RESEARCH TO MARKETING AND ADVERTISING STRATEGY

 Thus far, we have seen how Sid Stein and his department, in a step-by-step process, uncovered Penney's problem of declining market share, evaluated the company's competitive strengths and weaknesses, and measured consumer attitudes toward it. All this information was vital to the development of the company's positioning statement, marketing strategy, and subsequent advertising plans.

Developing Marketing Strategy

The pieces were all beginning to fit together. By the end of 1981 the J. C. Penney Stores Positioning Statement had the complete involvement and commitment of Penney's top management. The corporate direction for the decade was set. The nation's third largest retailer was going to change from a mass merchandiser to a fashion-oriented national department store.

To begin this evolution, two strategic moves were announced in 1982. The first involved major changes in the stores' merchandise mix. In all stores the automotive, paint and hardware, and lawn and garden departments would be discontinued. With the selling space thus made available, Penney's would make more dominant statements in its apparel lines by bringing in designer and higher taste-level private labels (Halston III, Stafford, Lee Wright, and others). It would also bring in the brands customers wanted, which would help improve the perception of quality and fashionability (Levi, Nike, Jordache, Adolfo, etc.).

Secondly, Penney's began a five-year, $1.5 billion modernization program to inject fashion and excitement into all its stores. In 1983, 38 stores were completely modernized, and 138 were remerchandised. In 1984, 34 stores were modernized and 200 remerchandised. By the end of the decade, virtually all Penney's metropolitan stores will be modernized.

The program was finally underway. The target market had been selected and the marketing strategy determined. Now it was time to start letting the public know. That meant advertising—and more research.

■ Developing Advertising Strategy

It is difficult to say where marketing research ends and advertising research begins since there is, admittedly, often quite an overlap. Overholser separates the objectives of advertising strategy research into three categories.[11] We will call these:

1. Product concept definition.
2. Target market selection.
3. Message-element selection.

Faison refers to these three categories as Stage 1 of advertising research—aimed at strategy determination. Stage 2, he suggests, is research designed for concept development; and Stage 3 includes the pretesting of ads and commercials.[12] We add a fourth stage—campaign evaluation—which is research designed to measure the effectiveness of a campaign after it has run (Figure 6–10).

At this point it is important to understand how advertisers apply the marketing research procedures we have discussed to basic advertising strategy and concept development (Stages 1 and 2).

We have already seen how J. C. Penney used its initial marketing research results to discover which consumers were currently shopping Penney's, which were not, and how the general market perceived Penney's position in the marketplace. Let's review for a moment the results of the Stage 1 research.

■ *Product concept definition*

Following its successful growth in the 60s and 70s and its emergence as a major shopping mall tenant, J. C. Penney was positioned in the consumer's mind as a major mass merchandiser of basic apparel, housewares, hardware, and basic commodities like bedding and towels. The attributes applied to it were honesty, integrity, and good value. But the characteristics of fashion, style, and quality were not associated with the Penney's name. Penney's was not where these same customers shopped for contemporary apparel, and it was not really perceived as a department store. In fact, in recent years, the consumer perception of the store's business had become unfocused.

Faison points out that it is usually easier to position a product in a manner consistent with consumer attitudes and perceptions than to reposition it by emphasizing other uses or attributes.[13] Trout and Ries, who wrote the book on positioning, would agree. However, the very fuzziness in the consumer perception of Penney's business could work to its advantage, and it is possible that Trout and Ries would agree with Penney's decision to change strategy. They believe it is virtually fruitless to try to dislodge a market leader unless the leader is making serious positioning mistakes. For many years, J. C. Penney's main competition had been with Sears, and Penney's was not really winning. It was still the number three retailer.

By repositioning itself as a fashion-oriented national department store with its traditional attention to value, Penney's would remove itself from competing head-to-head with Sears. Then, instead of being in a number three position, it could jump to number one—the largest fashion department store chain in the country.

To accomplish this task, though, Penney's knew they had to not only upgrade their stores and merchandise lines, but also gradually change and clarify the consumer perception of their stores. Repositioning any brand or product is an expensive and time-consuming process. To reposition a national chain of retail stores is an even more difficult and risky task. There are just too many elements involved for it to be accomplished overnight. And maintaining credibility with the consumer during the transition period is an absolute necessity. For this reason, Penney's was willing (and knew it had) to commit several years, many dollars, and a lot of fortitude to its new campaign.

FIGURE 6–10   Stages of research in advertising development

	Stage 1: Strategy determination	Stage 2: Concept development	Stage 3: Pre- testing	Stage 4: Post- testing
Timing	Before creative work begins	Before agency production begins	Before finished artwork and photography	After the campaign has run
Research problem	Product-class definition	Concept testing	Print pretesting	Advertising effectiveness
	Prospect-group selection	Name testing	Television storyboard pretesting	Consumer attitude change
	Message-element selection	Slogan testing	Radio commercial pretesting	Sales increases
Techniques	Consumer-attitude and usage studies	Free-association tests	Consumer jury Matched samples	Aided recall Unaided recall
		Qualitative interviews	Portfolio tests Storyboard test Mechanical devices	Sales tests Inquiry tests Attitude tests
		Statement-comparison tests	Psychological rating scales	

Target market selection

Penney's studies showed that, contrary to popular belief, the "traditional J. C. Penney customer" was the *same* as the "traditional department store customer." These consumers were attracted to regional centers where they could compare merchandise before buying. They were looking for fashionable apparel and home furnishings, and they wanted the opportunity to compare the offerings of several stores. Penney's heavy users, or "frequent" shoppers, were in the mall, but they were not shopping at Penney's as often as at the department stores.

Penney's mix of male and female shoppers was about the same as the department stores with a slight edge in men but a slight disadvantage in the high-spending, 18-34, female category. Yet this was the opportunity Penney's wanted—to appeal to this key, contemporary, fashion-buying segment with the offerings these customers wanted.

Message-element selection

At this point N. W. Ayer came into the picture. Penney's now needed to communicate a very important message to its customers. After all the advertising agency presentations were made, Penney's selected Ayer to help develop its message. According to Faison, studies on message-element selection are "concerned with the likes and dislikes of the consumers in relation to the brands and products being considered, focusing on the particular themes and claims that may be promising."[14]

In the attitude studies the agency had conducted and with the help of Agi Clark's creative group, Ayer discovered numerous possible message-elements that might be used: Penney's looks different, but the value's the same; You're changing, so is Penney's; etc. The agency decided to begin concept testing in order to discover which of the message-element options might prove most successful in the repositioning effort. This was the company's Stage 2 research aimed at advertising concept development.

Concept Testing

Ayer prepared four tentative advertising concepts, each with an illustration and a headline stressing a different Penney's appeal. The agency then gathered numerous focus groups of volunteer consumers into their unique "developmental lab," which combines intensive qualitative interviews with certain quantitative techniques. While a discussion leader moderated the conversation, each group was shown the series of ads and their reactions were measured as well as taped and observed by Ayer staff behind a one-way mirror (Figure 6–11).

The focus groups were nearly unanimous in their choice: the message that announced Penney's change but related it to the change in the customers themselves. The reason for their choice was clear: J. C. Penney was indeed changing. It did have more fashions than ever before. Why? Because *they*, the customers, had changed, and they needed more fashion than ever before. The message was logical and straightforward. The focus groups found it to be a believable position and a great promise. And that convinced Ayer to make it the back-bone of the new campaign.

Once the concept of how to announce the change was accepted, Ayer had to develop a campaign that would express the results and show the benefits of that change to the consumer. Agi Clark and her creative teams developed a series of ads for magazines and TV using the campaign idea: "YOU'RE LOOKING SMARTER THAN EVER." They believed that theme complimented the customer for looking and being smarter than ever and simultaneously made the promise that J. C. Penney would also be smarter than ever before.

FIGURE 6–11

The four layouts that were used in concept testing each stressed a different appeal. In a series of intensive interviews the reactions of shoppers to the various themes were monitored and measured. And the winner is. . . .

Bringing the two ideas together, the introductory ads read: "THERE'S A CHANGE IN PENNEY'S BECAUSE THERE'S A CHANGE IN YOU. YOU'RE LOOKING SMARTER THAN EVER. J. C. PENNEY." Ayer liked it. Penney's liked it. Now it was time to pretest to be sure this campaign would get the attention and recognition Penney's hoped for (Figure 6–12).

■ Testing and Evaluation of Advertising

When the nation's 100 leading advertisers spend $13 billion a year for advertising, its effectiveness is a major concern. In some instances advertising is the largest single cost in a company's marketing budget. Companies can't stop advertising, nor do they want to. But they *do* want to know what they are getting for their money— whether their advertising works.

Testing is the primary instrument advertisers have to assure themselves that their advertising dollars are being spent wisely. It may prevent costly errors in judging which advertising strategy and what media will produce the greatest results. And it can give the advertiser some measure (besides sales results) of a campaign's effectiveness.

FIGURE 6–12

The first ad in Penney's new campaign showed off the company's solid commitment to sophisticated style and fashion flair. It also demonstrated Penney's responsiveness to its customers. The campaign had two objectives. The first was to announce the change in Penney's from the perspective of the customer; and the second was to explain the benefits these changes would bring to the customer.

Objectives of testing

Pretesting, the third stage of advertising research, is used to increase the likelihood of preparing the most effective advertising messages. Pretesting can help advertisers detect and eliminate weaknesses or flaws that may ultimately result in consumer indifference or negative audience response. The fourth stage of advertising research, *posttesting*, is designed to determine the effectiveness of an advertisement or campaign *after* it has run. The findings obtained from posttesting can provide the advertiser with useful guidelines for future advertising.

Several areas of advertising that may be evaluated in pretesting include markets, motives, messages, media, budgeting, and scheduling. As we will see in Chapter 7, several of these variables are basic elements of the *creative mix* and are under the advertiser's control to add, subtract, or modify. Many of these same variables can be posttested. However, in posttesting the objective is normally to evaluate rather than to diagnose. The intent is not to make changes but rather to understand what has already happened.

Markets Advertisers may pretest advertising strategy and commercials against various market segments or audience groups to measure their reactions. In this process the advertiser may even decide to alter the strategy and target the campaign to a different market. In posttesting, advertisers are interested in determining the extent to which the campaign succeeded in reaching its target markets. Changes in awareness within the market segment may indicate successful advertising exposure, for instance. Or an increase in market share might give the same information.

Motives As we have already discussed, motivation research allows advertisers to learn why consumers behave as they do and what product benefits appeal to customers. In pretesting advertisements, the advertiser is interested in appeals that might cause people to buy based on their particular motives. The consumer's motives are outside of the advertiser's control, but the messages the advertiser uses to appeal to those motives are not.

Messages In advertising there are many message variables. Pretesting may be used to determine *what* a message says, or to determine how *well* it says it. The variables tested might be the headline, the text, the illustration, and the typography. Or the variables might be the message concept, the information presented, or the symbolism inherent in the ad.

Through posttesting the advertiser can determine to what extent the advertising message was seen, remembered, and believed. Changes in consumer attitude, for instance, indicate success in this area. Similarly, success might be measured by the ability of consumers to fill in the blanks in a campaign slogan or to identify the sponsor.

Media There are four levels of media decisions that can be affected through pretesting techniques: classes of media, subclasses, specific media vehicles, and units of space and time.

Classes of media are the broad media categories: print, electronic, outdoor, and direct mail. Subclasses are radio or TV, newsmagazines or business publications, and so on. The specific media vehicles involve deciding between the all-rock station or the middle-of-the-road music station in Albuquerque. And media units mean half-page ads or full-page ads, 30-second spots or 60-second commercials.

Likewise, numerous posttests are used to determine whether the media used were effective in reaching the target audience and in communicating the desired message. With the cost of media soaring, advertisers are always demanding greater media accountability.

Budgeting How large should a company's total advertising budget be? How much of this should be allocated to various markets and media? To specific products? Spending too little on advertising can be as hazardous as spending too much; but how much is "too little"— and how much is "too much"? Certain pretesting techniques are used to determine the optimum levels of expenditure before introducing national campaigns. (Refer to Chapter 7, "Marketing and Advertising Planning" for further information on budgeting.)

Scheduling Advertisers can test consumer response to a product ad during different seasons of the year or days of the week. They can test whether frequent advertising is more effective than occasional or one-time insertions, or whether year-round advertising of, say, a gift product is more effective than advertising concentrated in the Christmas gift-buying season.

Overall results Finally, advertisers want to measure overall results to evaluate the extent to which advertising accomplished its objectives. The results of these posttests might be used to determine how to continue, what to change, and how much to spend in the future.

All these tests are designed with the hope of discovering to what extent advertising is the *stimulus* and changes in consumer behavior are *responses*. Perhaps the greatest problem for the researcher, though, is to determine which, and how many, of these advertiser-controlled variables to measure and which consumer responses to survey.

Methods used to pretest print ads

Testing the effectiveness of an advertisement *before* it is run has obvious advantages. The advertiser can learn what results an ad is likely to have before spending what may be a large amount to produce it and place it in the media. Although no infallible means of predicting success or failure has been developed, certain popular pretesting methods can give the advertiser some useful insights if properly applied.

When J. C. Penney wanted to pretest Ayer's proposal for pre-printed newspaper advertising inserts, for example, they interviewed 250 women in shopping malls around the country. Respondents were asked direct questions such as: What does the advertising say? What do you think the advertiser is trying to tell you about their merchandise? Does the advertising say anything new or different about the store? If so, what? Is the advertising well done? Is it believable? What effect, if any, does it have on your perception of the store?

As a method of pretesting, *direct questioning* is designed to elicit a full range of responses to the advertising. From responses to questions like those just mentioned, researchers can infer how well advertising messages convey the key copy points. The researcher also takes note of verbatim comments made by the respondents, which often reveal more subtle but meaningful reactions to the advertisement. Direct questioning is especially effective for testing alternative advertisements in the early stages of development. Respondents are virtual participants in ad-making at a time when their reactions and input can best be acted on. During Penney's direct interviews, for example, the preprint format created by Ayer was compared to previous preprints created by Penney's own advertising department to evaluate the relative effect on shopper interest and Penney's image. Across the board the proposed new format was determined to be more effective (Figure 6–13).

In addition to direct questioning and focus groups, which we have already discussed, other techniques for pretesting print ads include order-of-merit tests, paired comparison methods, portfolio tests, mock magazines, and perceptual meaning studies. (See the Checklist of pretesting techniques.)

Methods used to pretest broadcast ads

A number of methods are used specifically to pretest radio and television commercials. The most common of these are central location tests, trailer tests, theater tests, and live telecasts. (See the Checklist of pretesting techniques.)

In *central location tests,* as the name suggests, videotapes of test commercials are shown to respondents on a one-to-one basis, usually

FIGURE   6–13

The preprint format proposed by Ayer (right) was compared to previous J. C. Penney newspaper inserts (left) in shopping center pretests. Across the board shoppers preferred the newer, more contemporary design.

in shopping center locations. Questions are asked before and after exposure to the commercials. J. C. Penney, for example, ran central location *clutter tests* of Ayer's television commercials in six dispersed markets before the campaign began. These tests had several objectives. By cluttering the Ayer commercials with other noncompetitive control commercials, Penney's could measure the effectiveness of the commercials in getting attention and increasing brand awareness; it could measure comprehension and resultant attitude shifts; and it could detect any weaknesses in the commercials. As expected, the commercials created by Agi Clark's team fared well in pretesting (Figure 6–14).

Additional pretesting techniques in common use fall into the general categories of sales experiments, direct-mail tests, and physiological testing. (See the Checklist for pretesting advertisements.)

Checklist of methods for pretesting advertisements

Print Advertising

☐ Direct questioning. Specific questions are asked about advertisements. Often used in testing alternative advertisements in the early stages of development.

☐ Focus groups. A free-wheeling discussion and interview is conducted with two or more people about a product, service, or marketing situation.

☐ Order-of-merit tests. Two or more advertisements are shown to respondents with instructions to arrange the advertisements in rank order.

☐ Paired comparison methods. Each advertisement is compared by respondents with every other advertisement in a group.

☐ Portfolio tests. Test ads are interspersed among other ads and editorial matter in an album-type portfolio. Consumers in an experimental group are shown this portfolio but without the test ads. Afterward members of both groups are questioned to determine their recall of the portfolio contents and the advertisements being tested.

☐ Mock magazines. An actual magazine is used instead of a portfolio. Test ads are "stripped into" the magazine, and it is left with respondents for a specified time. Respondents are then questioned about the test ads. Also used as a posttesting technique.

☐ Perceptual meaning studies. Ads are shown to respondents in timed exposures on a specially designed electronic tachistoscopic presentation instrument. Questions are given about recall of the product, brand, illustration, copy, and the main idea of the ad.

Broadcast Advertising

☐ Central location projection tests. Test commercials are run on a projector in a central location like a shopping center. Questions are asked before and after exposure to the commercials to determine brand awareness and to detect weaknesses in the commercials.

☐ Trailer tests. TV commercials are shown to people in trailers at shopping centers. Shoppers are then questioned about the commercials and are given packets of coupons that enable them to purchase products seen in the commercials at reduced prices. A matched sample of consumers who have not viewed the commercials are given identical packets of coupons. The impact of the commercials is measured in part by the difference in coupon redemption rates between the two groups.

The challenge of pretesting

By now it should be obvious that there is no one best way to pretest advertising variables. Different methods have been devised to test for different aspects of effectiveness. But each of the methods devised has its own peculiar set of advantages and disadvantages, thereby creating a difficult challenge to the advertiser.

Some of the methods are referred to as *laboratory methods*—where consumers are brought individually or in a group into a studio or auditorium. Laboratory testing offers the advantages of speed, economy, and a high degree of control. The researcher knows for sure that the subject has seen the test advertisement and in fact can control the way respondents are exposed to it. Responses can be measured immediately. Laboratory testing often produces some information that would be unavailable in other settings. The validity of laboratory

---

□ Theater tests. Electronic equipment enables respondents to indicate what they like and dislike as they view TV commercials.

□ Live telecast tests. Test commercials are shown on closed-circuit or cable television. Respondents are interviewed by phone to test their reactions. Commercials may also be evaluated by sales audits at stores in the areas where the commercials were run.

□ Sales experiments. Alternative advertisements are run in two or more different market areas to determine which ads are the most effective.

□ Direct-mail tests. Two or more alternative advertisements are mailed to different prospects on a mailing list. By keying each ad, the source of the orders can be traced. The ad that generates the largest volume of orders is presumed to be the most effective.

Physiological Testing

□ Pupilometric devices. Dilation of the pupil of the subject's eye is measured and presumed to indicate the subject's reaction to the illustration.

□ Eye-movement camera. Route the subject's eye travels is superimposed over an advertisement to show the paths it takes and the areas that attracted and held attention. Used to obtain information on the placement of headlines, proper length of copy, and the most satisfactory ad layout.

□ Galvanometer. A 25-milliampere current is passed through the subject, in at the palm and out at the elbow. When subject reacts to the advertisement, sweat gland activity increases, electric resistance decreases, and the current passes through faster. These changes are recorded on a revolving drum apparatus. It is assumed that the more tension an ad creates, the more effective it is likely to be.

□ Voice-pitch analysis. A tape recording is made of a consumer's explanation of his or her reaction to an ad. A computer is then used to measure the changes in voice pitch caused by emotional responses to the ad. This technique presumes a direct link between voice pitch and advertising effectiveness.

□ Brain-pattern analysis. A brain scanner monitors the reaction of the brain while ads are presented. Proponents of this approach believe that brain waves indicate whether people respond favorably or unfavorably to commercials.

FIGURE 6–14

TV commercials introduced Penney's new Wyndham collection of coordinated separates for the working woman. In a 30-second spot a fashion executive and her assistant are portrayed dashing to a presentation. The successful meeting ends with the supervisor giving credit to her hard-working assistant. All the commercials and print ads emphasized attractive people in real-life situations.

findings, though, may be highly questionable since forced exposure in a laboratory setting does not equate with real life.

Field testing, on the other hand, which may actually take place in the respondent's home or in a public place like a shopping center, still suffers from artificiality. Just as in the laboratory setting, the subject's response is actually a combined reaction to the test as well as to the advertisement.

Sales experiments, live telecasts, and direct-mail tests can actually approximate real-life conditions while still offering the necessary controls for experimentation. However, the depth of information available from these methods is usually more limited.

Thus, trade-offs are endless. Although pretesting is generally considered valuable in distinguishing very strong advertisements from very weak ones, there is still much controversy about the validity of other research findings. Even so, most advertisers are still interested in finding out whether an advertisement is interesting, believable, comprehensible, and memorable to the consumer. Verbatim responses from test subjects can even provide some useful copy ideas, and contact with consumers can give the advertiser or agency beneficial information on consumer buying habits.

But the limitations to pretesting are numerous, and advertisers should be aware of them. Besides the fact that the test itself is an artificial situation, test respondents may cease being typical prospects—many of them will assume the role of expert or critic and give answers that may not reflect their real buying behavior. Consumers who do not have strong opinions about the test ad are likely to invent opinions on the spur of the moment to satisfy the interviewer. Some do not want to admit they could be influenced by the advertisement. Others may try to please the interviewer by voting for the advertisements they feel they *should* like rather than those they actually do like.

Research also shows that when multiple opinions are sought on alternative advertisements—based on such factors as interest, personal pertinence, credibility, and comprehensibility—consumers are likely to rank the one or two ads that make the best first impression as the highest in all categories. This is called the *halo effect*. Also, whereas the most relevant area of such tests may be questions about the respondent's ultimate buying behavior, responses in this area may be the least valid. Behavior intent, in other words, may not become behavior fact.

Posttesting techniques

When Ayer launched its campaign for J. C. Penney in the fall of 1984, the client was anxious to know if customers saw it and paid attention to it, and what impression it made. So Ayer undertook a series of posttesting activities.

Posttesting is generally more costly and time-consuming than pretesting, but it permits advertisements to be tested under actual market conditions and without the unnaturalness of pretest conditions. Advertisers can reap the benefits of both pretesting and posttesting by running advertisements in a few select markets before launching a major nationwide campaign.

A variety of methods are used to determine what awareness or attitude changes have been achieved and what impact the advertising has had on sales. The most common posttesting techniques fall into five broad categories: aided recall, unaided recall, attitude tests, inquiry tests, and sales tests. Each of these has distinct advantages and limitations. (See the Checklist of posttesting techniques.)

Attitude tests usually seek to measure the effectiveness of an advertising campaign in creating a favorable image for a company, its brand, or its products. It is presumed that favorable changes in attitude predispose consumers to buy the company's product. The key factors attitude tests are designed to measure are consumers' general assessments of a given company, product, or brand, and their preference for, loyalty to, acceptance of, or intention to buy a given product or brand. The tests also seek to measure the comparative ratings of the company and competitors with regard to products, services, and other attributes (Figure 6–15).

Attitude tests are often conducted in conjunction with consumer awareness or recall tests. The Starch organization, for example, conducts ad impression studies because, after an advertiser has learned from readership data whether or not the advertisement attracted a satisfactory number of readers, the next logical questions are: Is the reader more favorably disposed toward the company, product, or service? What does the ad message mean to readers? Did the ad influence them, and do these readers now want to have the product or service or invest in the company?

In attitude tests a variety of measurement techniques are used, ranging from direct questions (Do you intend to buy this product?) to wholly unstructured questions or depth interviews. The semantic differential test (discussed earlier) is sometimes used to measure changes in respondents' attitudes after an advertising campaign. On

Checklist of methods for posttesting advertisements

□ Aided recall (recognition-readership). To jog their memories, respondents are shown certain advertisements. Questions are then asked to determine whether the respondents' previous exposure to the ad was through reading, viewing, or listening.

□ Unaided recall. Questions are asked of respondents without prompting to determine whether they saw or heard advertising messages.

□ Attitude tests. Direct questions, semantic differential tests, or unstructured questions are given to measure changes in respondents' attitudes after an advertising campaign.

□ Inquiry tests. Additional product information, product samples, or premiums are offered to readers or viewers in an ad. Ads generating the most responses are presumed to be the most effective.

□ Sales tests. Measures of past sales (comparing advertising efforts with sales), controlled experiments (using radio advertising in one market and newspaper advertising in another, for example, and auditing the results), consumer purchase tests (measuring of retail sales that result from a given advertising campaign), and store inventory audits (conducting an inventory of retailers' stocks before and after an advertising campaign in order to measure its effectiveness).

FIGURE 6–15

Bruzzone Research Company uses a direct-mail questionnaire to evaluate recall and attitude toward, in this example, a dog food commercial. Questionnaires are sent across the country to 1,000 households chosen at random from either auto registrations or telephone listings. Other users of this service include General Motors, Gillette, Holiday Inns, and Polaroid.

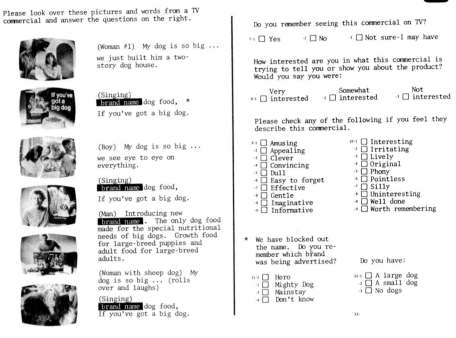

a regular basis, J. C. Penney uses lengthy questionnaires in shopping malls to determine shifts in attitudes as a result of its TV commercials and newspaper preprints.

The challenge of posttesting

Each posttesting method offers unique opportunities for advertisers to study the impact of their advertising campaigns. However, each also has definite limitations.

Recall tests are designed to measure specific behavior, not opinions or attitudes. They test advertising under natural conditions of exposure, so they are very helpful in determining whether advertisements are being read, how well the ads are working compared with competitors' ads, and the extent to which the ads have implanted ideas in consumers' minds. Recall tests indicate whether consumers got the point of the advertiser's message. They can also yield useful data on the relative effectiveness of different advertising components, such as size, color, or attention-getting themes. Aided recall tests are fairly simple to conduct and can be relatively inexpensive when their cost is borne in part by the media studied.

Recall tests do not measure advertising effect, however, but only what has been noticed, read, or watched (Figure 6–16). And readership or audience does not necessarily mean product sales. Although more audience members than nonmembers may ultimately buy the product, it does not necessarily follow that the advertisement was the sole motivating force. Recall tests are subject to the variations of individual memory. Some respondents have better memories than others. Some are better able to express what they remember. Respondents are often confused. Some may say they saw an ad merely to impress the interviewer. The techniques used may also encourage guessing.

Attitude tests are often a better measure of sales effectiveness than recall tests because an attitude change relates more closely to the purchase of the product. Such tests are fairly easy to conduct. They are low in cost because they can be made by phone or mail.

On the other hand, human attitudes represent a complex mix of feelings. Most researchers do not agree on precisely what an attitude is and what they have to measure. Many people find it difficult to determine their attitudes as well as to express them. Deeply entrenched attitudes, like those shaped by religious or philosophical beliefs, are resistant to change even by highly aggressive advertising efforts. Finally, a favorable attitude does not necessarily mean ultimate purchase of the advertiser's product or service (Figure 6–17).

Inquiry tests are fairly easy to conduct. They enable the advertiser to test the attention-getting value of advertisements as well as their readability and understandability. They also permit fairly good control of the variables that motivate reader action, particularly if a split-run test is used. Unlike some methods, the inquiry test can be effective in testing small advertisements.

Unfortunately, though, inquiry tests are valid only when applied to advertisements that can logically make use of an offer to elicit inquiries. When applied to an ad with more indirect purposes, it is questionable whether inquiry tests actually measure the ad's effectiveness or merely its ability to attract inquiries. Such inquiries, in fact, may not even reflect a sincere interest in the product or its purchase. Finally, inquiry tests can be time-consuming since the responses to a magazine offer, for example, may take months to receive.

FIGURE 6–16

A Starch readership report includes a copy of the magazine that has been rated. In this advertisement from *Ebony*, labels show readership of the ad-as-a-whole and component parts (headline, illustration, copy).

FIGURE 6–17

While advertisers continue to seek ways to measure advertising effectiveness, M. Wayne DeLozier has compiled a basic list of what does and doesn't work from his own research. While some may appear rather obvious (number 15), anytime is the right time to review the basics.

1. Unpleasant messages are learned as easily as pleasant messages.
2. Meaningful messages are learned more easily than unmeaningful messages.
3. Learning the conceptual idea is faster if massive advertising is followed by distributed advertising.
4. Products requiring mechanical skills are learned best if demonstrated in the ad as though the consumers were doing the task themselves.
5. Product benefits are learned best when presented at the beginning and end of a message.
6. Messages which are unique or unusual are better remembered than commonplace advertisements.
7. Rewarding the consumer who attends to a message enhances learning of the message.
8. Learning by consumers is enhanced when they are told the benefits they will receive from using the product.
9. Active participation in the message enhances learning.
10. Message learning is faster if previous or following messages do not interfere.
11. Repetition strengthens an older idea more than a newer idea.
12. Messages presented closer in time to an intense need are learned faster than those which are presented when the need is weaker.
13. The greater reward a consumer perceives from viewing (or listening to) an ad message, the faster his learning of the message.
14. The less effort required to respond to an ad, the faster learning occurs.
15. The more complex an ad message, the more difficult to learn.

Since the optimum goal of most advertisers is increased sales, *sales tests* are logically popular. Unquestionably, sales tests can be a useful measure of advertising effectiveness when advertising is the dominant element, or the only variable, in the company's marketing plan.

However, heavy reliance on sales tests has definite pitfalls. It is often difficult to gauge to what extent advertising has been responsible for sales since many other variables usually affect sales volume (e.g., competitors' activities, the season of the year, and even the weather). Sales response to advertising is usually long range rather than immediate. Sales tests, and particularly field studies, are often costly and time-consuming. And, finally, most of them are useful only for testing complete campaigns, not individual advertisements or the components of an advertisement.

Summary

Marketing research is defined as the systematic gathering, recording, and analyzing of data about problems relating to the marketing of goods and services. Marketing research is useful in identifying consumer needs, developing new products and communication strategies, and assessing the effectiveness of marketing programs and promotional activities.

In conducting research, there are several steps: first, to define the problem and set research objectives; second, to conduct exploratory research by analyzing internal data and collecting secondary data; then, to collect primary data. Primary research projects may involve observation, experiment, or survey and may be either quantitative or qualitative.

Quantitative research is used to accurately measure a particular market situation. Its success depends on the sampling methods used and the design of the survey questionnaire. The two sampling procedures used are random probability and nonprobability samples. Survey questions should have the attributes of focus, brevity, and simplicity.

Marketers use qualitative research to get a general impression of the market. The methods used in qualitative research may be projective or intensive techniques.

Advertising research is used to develop strategies and test concepts. Research results help the advertiser define the product concept, select the target market, and develop the primary advertising message elements.

Advertisers use testing to ensure that their advertising dollars are spent wisely. Pretesting is used to detect and eliminate weaknesses in a campaign. Posttesting is used to evaluate the effectiveness of an advertisement or campaign after it has run. Testing helps evaluate several variables including markets, motives, messages, media, budgets, and schedules.

There are many techniques used in pretesting including order-of-merit tests, paired comparison tests, portfolio tests, mock magazine tests, direct questioning, and perceptual meaning studies. To test broadcast advertisements, the most common methods are central location tests, trailer tests, theater tests, and live telecasts.

The most commonly used posttesting techniques are aided recall, unaided recall, attitude tests, inquiry tests, and sales tests. Each has opportunities and limitations.

Questions for review and discussion

1. If marketing research is so important to advertisers, why do so many succeed without using it?
2. What example can you think of that demonstrates the difference between marketing research and market research?
3. Do most advertisers prefer secondary or primary data? Why?
4. Have you ever used observational research personally? How?
5. Do people use quantitative or qualitative research to evaluate movies? Explain.
6. Which of the major surveying methods is the most costly? Why?
7. What example can you give of research that offers validity but not reliability?
8. What specific example can you think of where research could help in the development of advertising strategy?
9. How would the halo effect bias an effort to pretest a soft drink ad?
10. How would you design a controlled experiment to test the advertising for a chain of men's stores?

7

MARKETING AND ADVERTISING PLANNING

T om is standing at the door of the television repair shop when his father glances up from his work.

"Thought you had practice today," he says.

"No," replies the boy, "the field was too wet. Dad, do you have a minute?"

His father peers at him suspiciously over his glasses. "What's up?" He starts to pick up the TV he's been working on.

"Dad, I've decided . . . ." The static noise from the TV almost drowns him out. "I've decided to join the Army."

"Whoa," blurts his father as he quickly puts the set down.

"I think it's right for me," pleads the boy.

"What about college?" The man is scowling.

"I'm still gonna go to college . . . after the Army."

The man doesn't believe what he's hearing. "I thought you wanted to be an electrical engineer."

"I'll be learning about electronics and that'll help me with my engineering."

The boy is still pleading for his dad's approval, but the surprise and disappointment has not worn off his father's brow. He shakes his head. "That's a big step, Tom."

The boy argues, "Dad, listen. I can qualify for the Army College Fund. The government will help me pay for my tuition when I get out." His tone and expression suddenly change. With earnest warmth he says, "That way I can help *you* out for a change."

The man looks at his son, then picks up the TV and carries it to the back workbench. He turns, puts his hands in his pockets and, with his head cocked slightly to one side, sizes up the young man he has raised. "So, you're gonna be a soldier," he says gruffly.

"Yeah," the boy nods and smiles. "And an engineer," he promises.

The love sneaks back into the father's eyes as he looks at his boy. Suddenly, he clasps the young man to him in a fatherly bear hug and pridefully insists, "Be a good one."

As the commercial ends, the familiar tune is heard and the voice of a country singer: "Be all that you can be . . . you can do it . . . in the Army."

N. W. Ayer, the same agency that handles J. C. Penney (see Chapter 6), has been handling the Army's advertising since 1967. To Ted Regan, the agency's executive creative director responsible for the Army's advertising account, the "Be all you can be" campaign is the easiest campaign he's ever worked on. After all, he knows the value he himself got out of enlisting in the Army as a high school graduate— the opportunity to grow up, learn some valuable skills, travel, and get his education paid for by Uncle Sam. He also remembers the pressures he experienced to join and not to join. Creating effective, human advertising for the Army, therefore, just seems natural to him. And the unprecedented success of the "Be all you can be" campaign seems to bear witness to his belief.

However, the battle for young people's minds has not always been that successful. Recruiting for the volunteer Army has had its ups and downs in the face of changing economic and demographic conditions, varying social attitudes toward patriotism and the military, fluctuating budget allowances, and the resultant modification of marketing strategies (Figure 7–1). In fact, while one might consider the "Be all you can be" campaign to be the Army's best campaign ever, it would be more accurate to say that the Army's marketing strategy is the best ever, and the advertising accurately reflects that.

Marketing is war and the marketplace is the battlefield. (See Ad Lab 7–A.) The Army recruiting effort is no exception. Indeed, the late 70s witnessed a crisis that peaked in 1979. The military draft had ended six years earlier, and initial efforts to build a volunteer Army had met with some success. Numerical recruiting objectives were surpassed each year in spite of the negative legacy left by the Vietnam War. But the low proportion of high quality recruits caused considerable concern. Then, recruiting resources declined sharply, a healthier economic climate after the 1974–76 recession offered alternative employment opportunities, and popular incentive programs like the GI Bill were severely eroded. As a result, in 1979 the Army failed to reach its three-year recruiting objective, and, worse, nearly half the volunteers it did recruit came from the lowest acceptable mental categories.

To tackle this problem, therefore, required a new product, a new marketing strategy, very careful planning, an excellent advertising campaign, enough money to accomplish the objectives, and time. By 1984, the situation had completely turned around. In spite of a sharp decline in the size of the Army's primary target market (young people 17 to 20 years old), more than 210,000 men and women made the commitment to serve their country through the Regular Army and the Army Reserve. For four consecutive years the Army's numerical objectives were met or exceeded. More important, approximately 9 out of 10 new recruits were high school graduates, and more than 50 percent were in the top mental categories. Moreover, tracking studies

FIGURE   7–1

The famous picture of Uncle Sam pointing his finger at prospective recruits was the basic advertising poster for the U.S. Army for the first half of this century.

In Chapter 6, Jack Trout and Al Ries presented the concept of positioning. In this chapter, they share their latest advice—approach the marketplace as though it were a battlefield!

Much of the language of marketing has been borrowed from the military.

We launch a marketing campaign. Hopefully, a breakthrough campaign.

We divide people into divisions, companies, units. We report gains and losses. Sometimes we issue uniforms.

From time to time we go into the field to inspect those uniforms and review the progress of the troops. We have been known to pull rank.

In short, we have borrowed so many things from the military that we might as well adopt the strategic principles of warfare that have guided military thinking for centuries.

On War

Our "textbook" for marketing warfare is the classic book on military strategy, *On War*.

Written in 1831 by a Prussian general, Carl von Clausewitz, the book outlines the principles behind all successful wars.

Two simple ideas dominate Clausewitz's thinking.

First is the principle of force. Says Clausewitz, "The greatest possible number of troops should be brought into action at the decisive point."

Clausewitz studied all of the military battles of recorded history and found the vast majority of the time, the larger force prevailed. "God," said Napoleon, "is on the side of the big battalions."

The second principle is related to the first. It's superiority of the defense.

Take Napoleon at Waterloo. Napoleon actually had a slight superiority in numbers, 74,000 men versus Wellington's 67,000.

But Wellington had the advantage of being on the defense. And, of course, the defense prevailed.

So this year we predict that Crest will be the largest selling toothpaste and McDonald's the largest fast-food company—regardless of what the competition does and how much money it spends.

A well-established defensive position is extremely strong and very difficult to overcome.

The Strategic Square

So how do the principles of warfare apply to the marketing arena? It all comes down to what we call a "strategic square":

Out of every 100 companies

One should play defense	Two should play offense
Three should flank	And 94 should be guerrillas

Look at this strategic square from the point of view of the U.S. automotive industry.

General Motors	Ford
Chrysler	American Motors

General Motors is the leader and gets more than half the business. Its primary concern ought to be defense.

Ford, on the other hand, is a strong number 2. It's the only automobile company in a position to mount offensive attacks against GM.

Chrysler is a distant third and should avoid direct attacks. Rather, it should try flanking moves: smaller, bigger, cheaper, more expensive, and so on.

What can you say about American Motors? Head for the hills and become a guerrilla. The company should find a market segment small enough to defend. For AMC, the broad area of, say, "small cars" would be too much. But the Jeep business is distinctive and important enough to protect and make the most of. AMC's claim to that portion of the market should be further extended to include other four-wheel-drive vehicles.

Offensive Warfare

Let's look more closely at each of the four types of marketing warfare starting with offensive warfare.

Colgate had a strong number 1 position in toothpaste. But rival Procter & Gamble knew a thing or two about Carl von Clausewitz.

"Many assume that half efforts can be effective," said Clausewitz "A small jump is easier than a large one, but no one wishing to cross a wide ditch would cross half of it first."

P&G launched Crest toothpaste not only with a massive $20 million advertising budget but also with the American Dental Association "seal of approval."

Crest went over the top and is now the number 1 selling toothpaste in the country.

Overtaking the leader is not that common. Most companies are happy if they can establish a profitable number two position.

How can anybody topple Listerine, the king of halitosis hill?

With its "medicine breath" attacks on Listerine, Scope aimed straight for Listerine's weakest position. The campaign improved Scope's position and secured its long-term position.

But Listerine is still the leader, by a long margin. A well-established defensive position is extremely strong and very difficult to overcome.

To sum up, here are the rules of the road in waging offensive marketing warfare.

1. The main consideration is the strength of the leader's position. No matter how strong a number 2 or 3 company is in a certain category or attribute, it cannot win if this also is where the leader is strong.
2. The attack should be launched on as narrow a front as possible. The "full line" of products is a luxury only for leaders. Offensive war should preferably be waged with single products.
3. The attack should be launched at the leader's weakest position.

(continued)

AD LAB   7–A (*continued*)

Defensive Warfare

The battle of migraine mountain is an example of the advantages of quick response on the part of the leader.

Datril, as you might remember, opened up a war on Tylenol with a price attack.

Johnson & Johnson immediately cut Tylenol's price, even before Datril started its price advertising.

Result: It repelled the Datril attacks and inflicted heavy losses on the Bristol-Myers entry.

Here are the principles of defensive marketing warfare.

1. Defensive marketing warfare is a game only market leaders should play.
2. The best defense is a good offense. A leader should introduce new products and services before the competition does.
3. Strong competitive moves should always be "blocked." In a word, rapidly copy the competitive move. Too many companies "pooh-pooh" the competitor until it's too late.

Flanking Warfare

The third type of marketing warfare is where the action is for most companies.

Here's Clausewitz's suggestion. "Where absolute superiority is not attainable, you must produce a relative one at the decisive point by making skillful use of what you have."

In practice, this means attacking IBM where IBM is weak not where it is strong—as Amadahl is doing successfully on the high end and Digital Equipment Corporation is doing successfully on the low end.

Orville Redenbacher is successfully flanking the popcorn market leader with a high-priced brand.

And who won the marketing battle between Cadillac and Lincoln Continental?

Answer: Mercedes.

Here are the principles of flanking marketing warfare:

1. Good flanking moves must be made into uncontested areas. DEC introduced a small computer before IBM did.
2. Surprise ought to be an important element. Too much research will often snatch defeat from the jaws of victory by wasting time, the critical element in any successful flanking attack.
3. The pursuit is as critical as the attack itself. Too many companies quit after they're ahead.

Guerrilla Warfare

The fourth type of marketing warfare is guerrilla warfare. Most of America's companies should be waging guerrilla warfare.

The key attribute of successful guerrilla wars is flexibility. A guerrilla should not hesitate to abandon a given product or market if the tide of battle changes.

Here are the principles of guerrilla marketing warfare.

1. Find a market segment small enough to defend. It could be small geographically or in volume.
2. No matter how successful you become, never act like the leader.
3. Be prepared to "bug-out" at a moment's notice. A company that runs away lives to fight another day.

Laboratory Applications

1. Think of a successful product and explain its success in terms of marketing warfare.
2. Select a product and explain how marketing warfare strategy might be used to gain greater success.

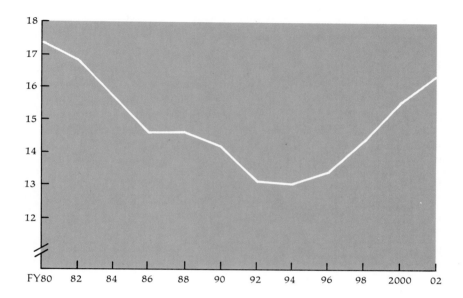

FIGURE 7–2

The shrinking market of 17 to 20-year-olds (in millions).

showed that the Army had become the second "most likely to enlist in" branch of the service, and the Army's "Be all you can be" campaign was the most recognizable of all military advertising programs (Figure 7–2).

For our purposes, the Army story demonstrates that advertising success usually depends less on creativity and more on strategy. Good advertising strategy depends on careful marketing planning. The process of marketing and advertising planning is the subject of this chapter and the means whereby we can bring together the topics of the last three chapters: marketing and advertising research, consumer behavior, market segmentation, and the various elements of the marketing mix—including advertising.

THE MARKETING PLAN

What did the Army do to successfully appeal to the upper segment of the youth market and carve out such a large share in so short a time? It didn't have nearly as much money to spend as either the soap or the beer companies.

Was it because of great advertising? Partly. But where did the ideas for the advertising come from? How did Ayer decide what to write the ads about, where to run them, and what to say?

The answer lies in one word: *planning.*

Yet, according to Richard Stansfield, author of *The Advertising Manager's Handbook,* "more money is poured down the drain—absolutely wasted—on advertising that doesn't have a ghost of a chance of doing its assigned job because of a dismal lack of adequate planning than for any other reason."[1]

What is a marketing plan? And what is an advertising plan? What is the difference, and what is their relationship? Let's deal with the first question first so we can better understand the overall success of the Army's campaign.

What Is a Marketing Plan?

Stansfield believes the written marketing plan is like a road map to the tourist. "It helps him find the right route, and once found, helps him stay on it." Inasmuch as marketing is the *only* source of income for a company (except possibly for investments), the marketing plan may be the most important document a company can possess.

The marketing plan serves a number of very important functions. First, it assembles all the pertinent facts about the organization, the

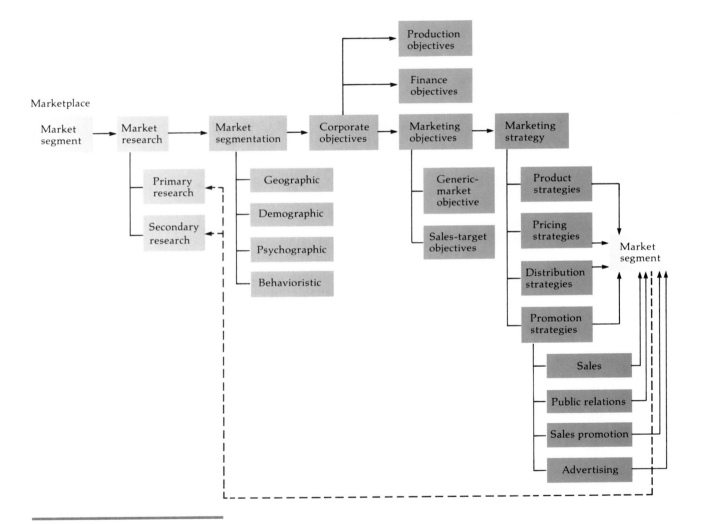

FIGURE 7–3

The marketing planning process model. Marketing planning is a continuous process that begins and ends with the consumer. Research locates and measures the needs of various market groups. Potentially profitable segments are selected. Corporate objectives are set, and these lead to the determination of production, finance, and marketing objectives. To accomplish these objectives, various strategies are developed— all aimed at the targeted market segments. Finally, research evaluates the success or failure of the marketing plan and suggests modifications, and the process starts over again.

markets it serves, its products, services, customers, competition, and so on, in one spot. It also brings all these facts up to date. Second, it forces all the functions within the company to work together: product development, production, selling, advertising, credit, transportation, and so on. Third, it sets goals and objectives to be attained within specified periods of time and lays out the precise strategies that will be used to achieve them. Thus, it musters the company's forces for the marketing battlefield (Figure 7–3).

■ Effect of the Marketing Plan on Advertising

If it truly does all these things, the marketing plan should have a profound effect on the organization's advertising programs. For one thing, the marketing plan enables analysis, criticism, and improvement of all company operations including past marketing and advertising programs.

Second, it dictates the future role of advertising in the marketing mix. It determines those marketing activities that will require advertising support as well as those advertising programs that will need marketing support.

Finally, it gives direction to advertising creativity, enables better implementation of advertising programs, and ensures continuity of all advertising activities.

■ Elements of the Marketing Plan

The written marketing plan must reflect the goals of the company's top management and still be consistent with the capabilities of the company's various departments. The plan should be prepared with four principal sections: situation analysis, marketing objectives, marketing strategy, and action programs.

In addition to these four sections, most marketing plans include a section on measurement, control, and review, a section on resource allocation, and a summary at the beginning to briefly state the contents of the whole plan. Where these subjects relate purely to marketing, they are beyond the scope of this text. As they relate to advertising, they will be discussed later in this chapter.

■ Situation analysis

The situation analysis section is usually the longest portion of the marketing plan. It is a statement of where the organization is today and how it got there. It should include all relevant facts about the company's history, growth, products or services, sales volume, share of market, competitive status, markets served, distribution system, past advertising programs, results of market research programs, company capabilities, and strengths and weaknesses.

The "Checklist for situation analysis" suggests some of the most important elements to be included. In addition, information should be gathered on key factors outside the company's immediate control. These might include facts on the economic, political, social, technological, or commercial environment in which the company operates. Only when these facts are completely gathered and agreed on can management hope to plan for the future successfully.

The introduction to this chapter presented some of the facts included in the Army's analysis of its situation in 1979. In addition, tracking studies on the attitudes of youth indicated that the Army's target market perceived the military services in terms of Physical/ Team benefits rather than personal challenge or Mental/Individual benefits (Figure 7–4). "Personal Challengers" were more oriented toward college and civilian pursuits. When asked about their likelihood of serving in the military, they tended to answer "probably" or "probably not," as opposed to "definitely" or "definitely not." The two "probably" groups, though, offered the greatest potential for growth in Army recruiting. Therefore, consideration had to be given to expanding benefits and creating appeals that would include the notion of intellectual and personal challenge. This, of course, would have a great bearing on the advertising employed later on.

Checklist for situation analysis

The industry

- ☐ Companies in industry: dollar sales, strengths, etc.
- ☐ Growth patterns within industry: primary demand curve, per capita consumption, growth potential.
- ☐ History of industry: technological advances, trends, etc.
- ☐ Characteristics of industry: distribution patterns, industry control, promotional activity, geographic characteristics, profit patterns, etc.

The company

- ☐ The company story: history, size, growth, profitability, scope of business, competence in various areas, reputation, strengths, weaknesses, etc.

The product or service

- ☐ The product story: development, quality, design, description, packaging, price structure, uses (primary, secondary, potential), reputation, strengths, weaknesses, etc.

- ☐ Product sales features: exclusive, nonexclusive differentiating qualities, product's competitive position in mind of consumer, etc.
- ☐ Product research: technological breakthroughs; improvements planned.

Sales history

- ☐ Sales and sales costs by product, model, sales districts, etc.
- ☐ Profit history.

Share of market

- ☐ Sales history industrywide: share of market in dollars and units.
- ☐ Market potential: industry trends, company trend, demand trends.

The market

- ☐ Who and where is market, how has market been segmented in the past, how can it be segmented in future, what are consumer needs, attitudes, and characteris-

■ *Marketing objectives*

Once the situation analysis is completed, the organization can lay down specific marketing objectives to be attained within the time covered by the marketing plan.

The Army, for example, determined specific marketing objectives every year, including numerical objectives for the Regular Army, the Army Reserve, and specific units within the Army (for example, the Nurse Corps), as well as quality objectives based on the mental aptitude of enlistees (Figure 7–5). For a manufacturer introducing a new product, though, marketing objectives might be expressed as follows:

1. Introduce the product to test markets and achieve a 10 percent share of market by the end of the first year.
2. Achieve total national distribution by the end of the second year.

---

tics? How, why, when, and where do consumers buy?

☐ Past advertising appeals which have proved successful or unsuccessful in speaking to consumer needs.

☐ Who are our customers, past customers, future customers? What characteristics do they have in common? What do they like about our product? What don't they like?

Distribution

☐ History and evaluation of how and where product is distributed, current trend.

☐ Company's relationship with and attitudes of members of the distribution channel toward product/company.

☐ Past policies regarding trade advertising, deals, co-op advertising programs, etc.

☐ Status of trade literature, dealer promotions, point-of-purchase, displays, etc.

Pricing policies

☐ Price history: trends, relationship to needs of buyers, competitive price situation.

☐ Past price objectives: management attitudes, buyer attitudes, channel attitudes, etc.

Competition

☐ Who is the competition? Primary, secondary, share of market, products, services, goals, attitudes. What is competition's growth history and size?

☐ Strengths of competition: sales features, product quality, size, etc. Weaknesses of competition.

☐ Marketing activities of competition: advertising, promotions, distribution, sales force, etc. Estimated budget.

Promotion

☐ Successes and failures of past promotion policy, sales force, advertising, publicity.

☐ Promotion expenditures: history, budget emphasis, relation to competition, trend.

☐ Advertising programs: review of strategies, themes, campaigns.

☐ Sales force: size, scope, ability, cost/sale.

3. Achieve a 10 percent share of market nationally by the end of the third year.

Naturally, the marketing objectives that are set must take into consideration the amount of money the organization has to spend, its knowledge of the marketplace, and its analysis of the competitive environment.

Marketing objectives should be logical deductions from the review of the company's current situation, its prediction of future trends, and its understanding of corporate objectives. *Corporate objectives* are usually stated in terms of profit or return on investment. Or they may be stated in terms of net worth, earnings ratios, growth, or corporate reputation. *Marketing objectives,* on the other hand, should relate to (1) the needs of specific target markets and (2) specific sales objectives. Kotler refers to the first as *generic-market objectives* and the second as *sales-target objectives.*[2]

The concept of a generic market is an attempt to shift management's view of the organization from a producer of products or services to a satisfier of market needs. For example, many people feel that one reason Penn Central Railroad went bankrupt was that it viewed itself as a railroad company rather than a provider of transportation. If it had adopted the latter view, it might have been able to

FIGURE 7–4

Life goal perceptual map. In order to make the Army more relevant to the young people seeking Mental/Individual benefits, advertising had to broaden the range of appeals to include the notion of intellectual and personal challenge.

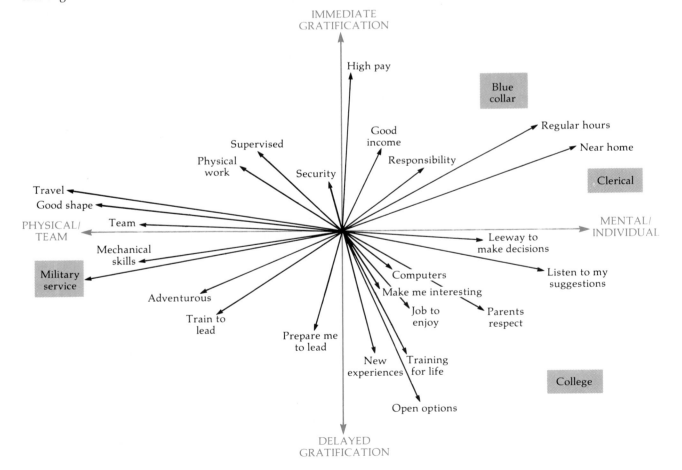

FIGURE 7–5

The Army offers a wide range of job opportunities in a variety of fields to both men and women. This ad for the Nurse Corps was aimed at teachers as well as students and promoted the fact that nurses in the Army could go right into intensive care without the normal wait associated with civilian hospitals.

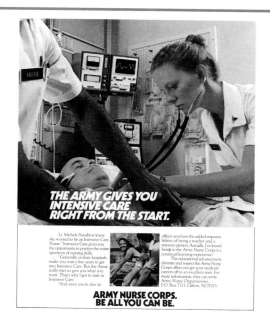

diversify into other more profitable techniques for providing transportation for people or freight. The broader view allows management to consider additional options for the company besides its traditional activities. Some oil companies are good examples of this view. They now see themselves as producers of energy, not just gasoline, and have diversified into natural gas, nuclear, and solar power.

Sales-target objectives should be specific, quantitative, and realistic. If the Army's marketing objective was to recruit more soldiers than anybody, the objective would be considered nonspecific, unquantified, and unprofessional. Rather, the objective needed to be stated in precise terms such as "attaining a 1.0 percent share for the Regular Army and a .3 percent share for the Army Reserves of the 16-million 17–20-year-old market each year for the next three years." This objective is specific as to product and market, quantified as to time and amount, and, judging by the results, realistic.

Objectives may be expressed in a number of ways. For instance, many marketing organizations set objectives by the following criteria:

1. Total sales volume.
2. Sales volume by product, market segment, customer type.
3. Market share in total or by product line.
4. Growth rate of sales volume in total or by product line.
5. Gross profit in total or by product line.

Many other objectives are used as well including: addition of new products; deletion of old products; development of new distribution channels or new policies regarding inventory control, pricing, and research; addition of marketing personnel; and retraining of field sales staff. Some firms today include objectives relating to social responsibility: statements concerning the preservation of natural resources, participation in community projects, and support of educational programs or institutions.[3]

As we will see in the section of this chapter on the advertising plan, specific marketing objectives also have an important impact on the way advertising objectives are set. Only by setting specific objectives can management measure the degree of marketing and advertising success it is achieving.

Marketing strategy

The next section of the marketing plan is the statement of how the company is going to accomplish its marketing objectives. The strategy is the total directional thrust of the company, the "how to" of the marketing plan. For example, if you decide you must travel from New York to Los Angeles, your objective is to get to Los Angeles. Your strategy might be to take the train, to take the plane, or to go around the Horn on a square-rigged schooner.

In marketing terms, the objectives are what you want to accomplish, while the strategy determines the methods.

People often confuse the terms *objectives* and *strategy*. This is understandable since, as Fred Posner, the director of marketing research for N. W. Ayer, points out, "the meaning will often depend on where

PEOPLE IN ADVERTISING

Barbara Gardner Proctor

President/Creative Director
Proctor & Gardner Advertising, Inc.

The impressive career of Barbara Gardner Proctor, founder and president of Chicago's Proctor & Gardner Advertising, Inc., has been shaped by a series of "firsts." In 1963 she was the first black person in agency advertising in Chicago. Seven years later she was granted the first service loan ever issued by the Small Business Administration. She transformed her business into the nation's first full-service advertising agency specializing in marketing to black communities, with a black woman as president. She built that agency into a $12.2-million business. Her client roster includes Alberto-Culver Company, Kraft Foods, and Sears, Roebuck and Co.

Before making her mark in advertising, Proctor was employed by VeeJay Records and gained acclaim as the person who brought the Beatles to the United States. She had joined the firm as a public relations writer and then became an international director. She developed as an international jazz critic, feature writer, and record reviewer for *Downbeat* magazine.

Proctor started in advertising in the early 1960s as a copywriter for Post-Keyes-Gardner/Chicago. Five years later she joined North Advertising Agency as a copy supervisor. During this period she realized advertising was not only challenging and rewarding but also a way to create positive changes in the lives of black people. In 1970 she decided to form her own agency.

you sit—whether you look at the marketing battlefield from a tank turret, a field command tent, or a computer console."

One person's strategy is another person's objective. The chairman of the board may have the objective of increasing the dividend. His strategies for accomplishing this may include increasing sales. To the marketing vp, the chairman's strategy, increased sales, becomes an objective. He, in turn, may decide that to increase sales he will use advertising to persuade his current users to use the product more often. That then becomes the agency's objective. The agency, in turn, concludes that its strategy is to make the product more appealing to its light users by defining more use occasions where the product is appropriate.

To be effective, a marketing strategy must stand the test of time. It must be an ingenious design for achieving a desired goal, and it must be result oriented. The particular marketing strategy a company selects will dramatically affect the advertising it uses. It will determine (1) the amount of advertising to be used, (2) the creative thrust of advertisements, and (3) which advertising media to use. In short, the marketing strategy will determine the advertising strategy.

Proctor has directed the advertising for dozens of accounts, including Gillette, Paper Mate, FTD Florists, Maybelline, and Jewel Food Stores, a midwestern supermarket chain. She writes everything that goes out the door of her chic, ultramodern, silver and white office high above the Chicago River. Before launching her agency, Proctor had never worked on promotion specifically for the black consumer market. Now most of her agency's output is directed to specialized black markets. But Proctor does not agree with the idea of a homogeneous black market. "There is no such thing as *the* black market," she says. "The black community is not one lump market, and that is the thing my agency deals with—segmenting the black community."

As to the advertising directed at blacks today, Proctor adds, "You would think that all we do is drink and smoke, that we eat only fast foods, and don't have much of a family life." Although these things are true of many Americans, she says, "It's primarily the way we're portrayed. You would not think from the ads, for instance, that a lot of blacks fly, despite the fact that we spend over $30 million a year going to conventions and meetings."

Likening her agency to an achievement in which all blacks can take pride, Proctor states, "I'm building a solid symbol, and black people are welcome to use it. I will be the best advertising agency in the business—and I will be black. I will have one of the best offices in the country—and I will be black."

When asked what advice she would give to students on how to succeed in business, Proctor said, "Concentrate your energies on developing curiosity, self-discipline, and flexibility. The ability to succeed in the future will require these characteristics as our world continues to demand incisive analysis, concentrated expertise, and rapid adaptation."

The recipient of nearly 40 awards, including the American TV Commercial Award and the International Film Festival Award, Proctor was named by *Business Week* as one of the "100 Top Corporate Women in America." She donates at least 15 percent of her agency's profits to charity. Proctor supports foundations that benefit blacks, women, and children. She is a member of the boards of directors of nearly a dozen national and regional organizations. President Reagan, in his 1984 State of the Union address to the nation, saluted Proctor's spirit of enterprise by referring to her as an example of one of the "heroes of the 80s."

In a recently published anthology of elite black Americans, Proctor was the only self-made millionairess included. All the other women had either inherited or married money, but Barbara Gardner Proctor has worked for her success.

FIGURE   7–6

There's just one place where you can go directly from high school to flight school—the U.S. Army. That's a very strong appeal to young people interested in a civilian flying career later on. To compete with the attractiveness of the Air Force, the ad points out that the Army has even more pilots than the largest airline.

Selecting the target market   Thus, the strategy a company develops is the means or direction for achieving the explicitly stated objective. And the strategy depends not only on those marketing objectives but also on the particular market being approached. The first step, therefore, is the selection of the *target market*. This is already accomplished to some extent through the market segmentation process before corporate objectives are even set. But the marketing director may pick more tightly defined target markets within the broader scope of the market segment.

For instance, the Army determined that it needed to recruit young people between the ages of 17 and 21 years old from the upper mental category. The Recruiting Command (or marketing manager for the Army) then had to select the appropriate target market within that segment. It might have been appropriate to select urban youth concerned about their inability to find jobs or other young people concerned about patriotism and the threat of aggression. Instead, the Army chose to target "young men and women 17 to 21 with primary emphasis on high school diploma graduates who ranked academically in the top half of their senior class and who were interested in the opportunity to be trained in the latest technology, particularly as it relates to civilian application." (See Figure 7–6.)

The Army itself appears to be designed specifically for the upper mental-category youth segment (because the whole organization is now technology based) *and* for the target market within that segment (because the "new technological Army" offers more than 270 military occupation specialties from which to choose, more than $20,000 for continuing education through the Army College Fund, and a variety of other enlistment bonuses).

Determining the marketing mix   The second step in the development of the marketing strategy is to determine a cost-effective marketing mix for *each* target market the company pursues. The mix will consist of particular levels of the four Ps (see Chapter 4): product, price, place, and promotion.[4]

What was the Army's marketing mix? First, a superior product—the new, modernized, technological Army. Second, a competitive pricing strategy—higher pay, education benefits, and enlistment bonuses. Next, an effective distribution system—2,000 recruiting stations throughout the 50 states, Puerto Rico, Guam, American Samoa, the Virgin Islands, and American communities in foreign countries. And finally, a promotional program that involved direct selling by thousands of Army recruiters, sales promotion programs in the form of sponsored scholar/athlete awards as well as sports clinics and demonstration films, and a heavy direct-mail and mass media advertising program consistent with share and volume objectives (Figure 7–7).

There are many common types of marketing strategies. For example, a company might decide to increase distribution, initiate new uses for a product, increase or change the product line, develop entirely new markets, or go into discount pricing. Each of these tends to emphasize one or more particular elements of the marketing mix.

Positioning strategies   To determine the appropriate marketing mix, Kotler suggests that the company first examine the wants of the market and the position of competitors and then decide on the competitive position it wants to occupy in the target market.[5]

David Ogilvy has said the first decision in marketing and advertising is also the most important: *how to position your product.* Ogilvy's agency (Ogilvy & Mather) developed the advertising for Lever Bros.' product, Dove. When Lever Bros. introduced Dove in 1957, the company decided to position the new product as a complexion bar for dry skin, not as a soap to get you clean.

> Dove's print and television advertising contrasted the effects of Dove and soap by showing pretty women taking the "Dove Face Test." Advertising promised that Dove "creams your skin while you wash," and supported that promise with a demonstration of the cleansing cream pouring into the bar.[6]

Dove maintained its position for a quarter of a century, and the strategy never changed. Every commercial still uses the same cleansing cream demonstration.

Companies usually have two choices in selecting a position. One is to pick a similar position next to a competitor and battle it out for the same customers. Another is to find a position that is not currently held by a competitor, a hole in the market, and quickly move to fill it.

In the early 70s, when Lever Bros. introduced Aim toothpaste, it decided to position the product against Crest and Colgate in the

FIGURE 7–7

The high-tech orientation of the new Army is beautifully illustrated in this full-color spread ad in magazines aimed at young men. The nonverbal aspects of this ad are probably even more powerful than the verbal aspects.

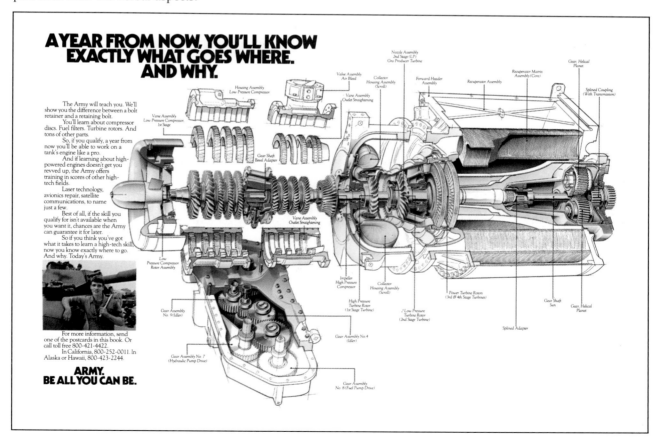

FIGURE   7–8

Lever Bros. broke its campaign with a call to mothers who had "cavity-prone children." Shortly thereafter, Colgate followed with its claim about children in the "cavity-prone years." What a coincidence!

health care segment of the toothpaste market and to use a *product differentiation* strategy to distinguish Aim in the eyes of potential customers. Product differentiation, as we discussed in Chapter 4, is the strategy companies use to build unique customer-satisfying differences or improvements into their products. Aim is an excellent example of product differentiation because it was the first really different fluoride toothpaste to take on Crest and Colgate. With its new gel formulation, fluoride ion activity was significantly higher than in Crest. Aim dispersed faster in the mouth than Crest. It was less abrasive than Crest, and taste tests showed a preference of two to one over both Crest and Colgate.[7] In short, Lever Bros. had come up with a significantly different product, so their primary task was simply to tell people about it and get them to try it (Figure 7–8).

Instead of positioning itself against the competition through product differentiation, a company might elect to position itself through *price/quality differentiation.* It could offer a better quality product at a higher price, like L'Oreal, and use the theme: "You deserve the best." Or it could advertise the same quality at a lower price, like Suave, saying: "Why pay more for the same?"

What was Ayer's strategy for positioning the Army? One of the ads in their campaign showed a squadron of paratroopers descending from a helicopter. The headline read: "Why should the Army be easy? Life isn't." Obviously, this was not as a life of travel and leisure.

Part of Ayer's strategy was to position the Army as a branch of the military that was admittedly tough (like life, itself) but challenging and personally rewarding with opportunities to reach and grow.

There are many variations of product differentiation strategies, price/quality strategies, positioning strategies, and segmentation strategies. Finding the best strategy calls for generating creative alternatives. These must then be evaluated in terms of satisfying the needs of the marketplace, securing advantages over the competition, and creating company profits.

Action programs

Once the overall marketing objectives and marketing strategy have been set, the company may determine what specific actions should be undertaken, by whom, and when, regarding each element within the marketing mix.

The *objectives* of a company indicate where it wants to go; the *strategy* indicates the general method and the intended route; and the *tactics* (or action programs) determine the precise details of the particular methods and routes it will use to get there.

In the case of a shoe company, a strategy may be to elect to produce a high-quality product, charge a premium price, sell only through better department stores, and rely heavily on advertising to promote the products. The action programs might then be to develop a shoe that will give two years of normal wear, be available at Bullocks and Macy's, sell for $55.95, and be supported by a $1.5 million advertising budget divided equally between television and magazines.[8]

It is in this world of action programs that advertising campaigns live. In the next section, therefore, we will discuss the process used for planning advertising.

THE ADVERTISING
PLAN

Richard Stansfield has decried the pervasive mediocrity of advertising. The fault, he feels, lies with inadequate planning, first on the marketing level and second on the advertising level. Advertising, he points out, is a natural outgrowth of the marketing plan. Once the marketing objectives and strategy have been determined, the advertising manager can begin to plan.

In fact, a company's communications or advertising plan is prepared in much the same way as the marketing plan. The company follows the same process of performing analysis, setting objectives, and determining strategy. From that strategy, specific tactics or advertising programs are conceived and created.

Review of the Marketing Plan

The advertising manager's first task is to review the marketing plan. It is important to understand where the company is going, how it intends to get there, and the role of advertising in the marketing mix. Therefore, the first section of the advertising plan is a premises or situation analysis section. This briefly restates the company's current situation, target markets, long- and short-term marketing objectives, and decisions regarding market positioning and the marketing mix.

Setting Advertising Objectives

Understanding the sales and market share objectives for particular products sold to particular market segments is essential to advertising planning. These objectives are designated as marketing objectives, not advertising or communications objectives. Marketing objectives must be set before the advertising manager can determine the specific tasks assigned to advertising.

Due to poor planning policies, some executives of large corporations have little idea of the specific tasks or objectives of their advertising programs. They rationalize the programs with such vague expressions as "keeping our name out in front" and "giving ammunition to the sales force." This ignorance may be the fault of advertising managers. By stating misty, generalized objectives, like "creating a favorable impression of the product in the marketplace in order to increase sales and maximize profits," the manager protects the program from ever being measured for effectiveness. Such vague gobbledygook serves only to reinforce the negative attitude shared by many executives about the large amount of money "wasted" on advertising. The statement commonly attributed to retailer John Wanamaker is typical of this misunderstanding of advertising objectives: "I know half of my advertising dollars are being wasted. I just don't know which half."

 Understanding what advertising can do

To define advertising objectives, we must have a clear understanding of what advertising can do. Most advertising programs hope to eventually cause some action on the part of prospective customers.

"I NEVER
CUT CORNERS
TO SAVE MONEY
ON MY CHICKENS.
BUT YOU CAN."

Frank Perdue

SAVE 25¢

FIGURE 7–9

Food manufacturers frequently use coupons in their ads to stimulate direct action by their customers.

Direct-action advertising attempts to induce the prospective customer to act immediately. This usually means clipping a coupon and mailing it in to order the product from the manufacturer (Figure 7–9).

However, only a very small percentage of those exposed to particular advertisements are expected to act right away. A number of very important steps must be accomplished before customers can be expected to act. *Delayed-action advertising,* therefore, seeks to inform, persuade, or remind its intended audience over an extended time about the company, product, service, or issue being advertised. This is the type of advertising generally used by retailers, manufacturers, banks, insurance companies, services, and associations.

The advertising pyramid

A simple way to understand the tasks advertising performs in preparing customers to act is to think of advertising as building a pyramid. Before a new product is introduced, the universe of prospective customers is in the desert of unawareness, totally oblivious to the product's existence. Thus, the first step for the pharaoh of advertising is to lay the foundation of the pyramid by making people aware of the product or service.

The next step is to give a portion of that foundation group enough information so they are aware of the product and also understand its purpose and perhaps some of its features. The general objective of the second step is to increase comprehension.

Next it is necessary to communicate enough about the product and its features so that a certain number of people will actually believe in its value. This is called the conviction block. Of those who become convinced, some can be moved to the block of people who actually desire the product. Finally, and only after all the preceding steps have been accomplished, a certain percentage of those who desire the product will actually go out and purchase it (Figure 7–10).

N. W. Ayer's creative director, Ted Regan, demonstrated how the pyramid works in his description of the effectiveness of Army advertising:

> Army advertising creates awareness, influences attitudes, corrects misconceptions, removes barriers, establishes credibility, and develops interest as a prospect moves from giving no consideration to the Army as an option for his or her future to seeking out a recruiter and taking action.

It's important to realize, though, that the pyramid is not static. The advertiser is actually working in three dimensions: numbers, dollars, and time. Over an extended time, as more and more dollars are spent on advertising, the number of people who become aware of the product increases. Likewise, more and more people comprehend the product, believe in it, desire it, and make the final action of purchasing it.

The objectives of delayed-action advertising, therefore, will change. At first the greatest effort might be spent simply to create awareness of the product. Later efforts might be centered more on creating interest and desire, or stimulating action.

In his book, *Defining Advertising Goals for Measured Advertising Re-*

sults, Russell H. Colley suggests that advertisers set objectives that are specific as to time and degree and objectives whose success can be measured by research studies and tests.[9] For example, a soap manufacturer might list the following advertising objective: "Among the 30 million housewives who own automatic washers, increase—from 10 percent to 40 percent in one year—the number who identify brand X as a low-sudsing detergent and the number who think that it gets clothes cleaner."

The problem is that this approach requires benchmark studies prior to the campaign and testing after the campaign, and it assumes that before and after results are simple and clear—a rarity in the real world. Furthermore, major changes in attitude and awareness can be created by many events besides advertising. And sometimes, changes *cannot* be affected by advertising at all. However, for our purposes in understanding the nature of advertising communication and the importance of trying to make advertising accountable, let's apply Colley's principles to the Acme footwear company.

Specific advertising objectives for the first-year introduction of the hypothetical Acme Company's new casual footwear line might read as follows:

1. Communicate the existence and availability of the Acme Casual Footwear line to 25 percent of the 10 million annual consumers of women's casual footwear between the ages of 15 and 49 who spend an average of $40 on each pair of shoes.
2. Inform 50 percent of the Aware group that Acme footwear is positioned as a high quality, premium-priced line available from select local retailers.

FIGURE 7–10

The advertising pyramid.

3. Convince 50 percent of the Informed group that the Acme line is very high quality, comfortable, stylish, and worth the price.
4. Stimulate the desire within 50 percent of the Convinced group to try on a pair of Acme casual shoes.
5. Motivate 50 percent of the Desire group to actually go to their local Acme dealer and test a pair of Acme shoes.

It's important to note here that these advertising objectives are both specific as to time and degree and quantified like marketing objectives. That means that, at the end of the first year, a consumer attitude study could be performed to determine *how many* people are *aware* of the Acme Company; *how many* people *know* what Acme makes; *how many* people *understand* the primary features of Acme casual footwear; and so on. If these results can be measured statistically, so can the effectiveness of the advertising program.

If Acme's advertising objectives are all achieved, and if we assume that all those who try the shoes buy them, Acme would gain approximately a 1.5 percent share of the targeted women's casual footwear market (or $3.75 million in sales) by the end of year one.

The second-year objectives might be to increase the percentage of women who are aware of the product, perhaps to 35 percent. Then greater emphasis could be placed on persuading more of them to believe in the product and eventually to try it.

Lever Bros. speeded up this process when they introduced AIM toothpaste. By using heavy sampling of the product, they were able to convert many people from being totally unaware one day to being users of the product the next. This is extremely expensive. However, many manufacturers use couponing and other sales promotion devices to accelerate the long-term effects of advertising (see Chapter 16).

In the case of Army recruiting, of course, sampling is impossible. Advertising objectives, therefore, were defined in terms of increasing awareness, improving image and attitude toward the Army, and generating inquiries from high-quality prospects.

Satisfied customers and the inverted pyramid

Once a certain percentage of people have actually made the purchase decision, a new advertising objective may be introduced: to stimulate some percentage of past purchasers to repurchase the product. As more and more people make the purchase and repurchase decision, our pyramid diagram can be changed. A new inverted pyramid can be built on top of the old pyramid to represent the growing number of people who join the action block and develop the habit of purchasing and repurchasing the product. At this point customer satisfaction and *word-of-mouth* advertising come into play. The greater the satisfaction, the more people are told about the product, and the faster the inverted pyramid will expand. While word-of-mouth advertising cannot be bought, *reinforcement* advertising can, and often is, to remind people of their successful experience with the product (Figure 7–11).

The problem with these types of models in real life is that they tend to oversimplify the complex phenomena of human behavior: how communication takes place, how learning is achieved, how needs and desires are stimulated, and how consumer purchasing actually happens. They also pay no attention to the dynamics of changing consumer tastes and preferences, to the activities of competitors, or to the fact that people can come into and leave the market continuously at various levels of the pyramid due to any of a million internal or external stimuli.

The hypothetical pyramid models, though, do give us a simple way of looking at the long-term building and reinforcing effects of media advertising. They also help us realize that as we find consumers at various levels of the pyramid, our communication needs, the objectives we can achieve, and our strategies for achieving them all change. For new products, building awareness will probably be our primary objective. For well-known, established products we will want to focus on building appeal. For well-known and well-liked products facing stiff competitive activity, we may want to promote additional use with ads that stress action. (See the Checklist for developing advertising objectives.)

■ Advertising Strategy

In the section on marketing planning, we learned that the marketing objective is where the company wants to be, whereas the marketing strategy indicates how it is going to get there. Similarly, the advertising or communications objective tells us where we want to be with respect to consumer awareness, attitude, and preference, whereas the advertising or creative strategy tells us how we are going to get there. Creative strategy is determined by the advertiser's use of the creative mix.

■ Creative mix

Marketing strategy refers to the way the marketing mix (product, price, place, promotion) is blended. Promotional strategy (see Chapter 4) refers to the way the promotional mix (personal selling, advertising, public relations, sales promotion, and collateral) is used.

FIGURE 7–11

The advertising pyramids. As more and more advertising impressions are made, and as more and more people purchase and repurchase the product, new blocks of ever-expanding numbers of customers may be built on top of the original pyramid.

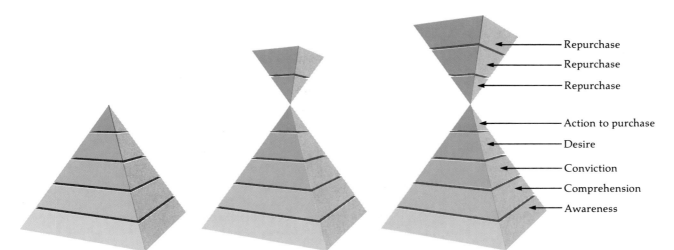

- Repurchase
- Repurchase
- Repurchase
- Action to purchase
- Desire
- Conviction
- Comprehension
- Awareness

Similarly, advertising strategy is determined by the *creative mix*, which is composed of those advertising elements that the company controls to achieve its advertising objectives. These elements include:

1. The product concept.
2. The target audience.
3. The communications media.
4. The advertising message.

The *product concept* refers to the "bundle of values" the product represents to the consumer. As discussed in Chapter 4, both the

---

Checklist for developing advertising objectives

To what extent does the advertising aim at closing an *immediate sale?*

☐ Perform the complete selling function (take the product through all the necessary steps toward a sale).

☐ Close sales to prospects already partly sold through past advertising efforts ("Ask for the order" or "clincher" advertising).

☐ Announce a special reason for "buying now" (price, premium, etc.)

☐ Remind people to buy.

☐ Tie in with some special buying event.

☐ Stimulate impulse sales.

Does the advertising aim at *near-term* sales by moving the prospect, step by step, closer to a sale (so that when confronted with a buying situation the customer will ask for, reach for, or accept the advertised brand)?

☐ Create awareness of existence of product or brand.

☐ Create "brand image" or favorable emotional disposition toward the brand.

☐ Implant information or attitude regarding benefits and superior features of brand.

☐ Combat or offset competitive claims.

☐ Correct false impressions, misinformation, and other obstacles to sales.

☐ Build familiarity and easy recognition of package or trademark.

Does the advertising aim at building a "long-range consumer franchise"?

☐ Build confidence in company and brand which is expected to pay off in years to come.

☐ Build customer demand which places company in stronger position in relation to its distribution (not at the "mercy of the marketplace").

☐ Place advertiser in position to select preferred distributors and dealers.

☐ Secure universal distribution.

☐ Establish a "reputation platform" for launching new brands or product lines.

☐ Establish brand recognition and acceptance which will enable the company to open up new markets (geographic, price, age, gender).

Specifically, how can advertising contribute toward increased sales?

☐ Hold present customers against the inroads of competition?

☐ Convert competitive users to advertiser's brand?

☐ Cause people to specify advertiser's brand instead of asking for product by generic name?

☐ Convert nonusers of the product type to users of product and brand?

☐ Make steady customers out of occasional or sporadic customers?

Chrysler and the Honda are medium-priced automobiles aimed at the American small-car market. However, the product concepts differ. One is conceived as a well-built, fast, fun, turbo sports car, whereas the other is conceived as sophisticated simplicity, practical, and easy to own.

When writing the advertising plan, the advertising manager should develop a simple statement to describe the product concept. To create this statement, the advertiser must consider the company's marketing strategy as it relates to the product. What is the product's intended position in the market? What is the company's intention rela-

---

☐ Advertising new uses of the product?

☐ Persuading customers to buy larger sizes or multiple units?

☐ Reminding users to buy?

☐ Encouraging greater frequency or quantity of use?

Does the advertising aim at some specific step which leads to a sale?

☐ Persuade prospect to write for descriptive literature, return a coupon, enter a contest.

☐ Persuade prospect to visit a showroom, ask for a demonstration.

☐ Induce prospect to sample the product (trial offer).

How important are "supplementary benefits" of end-use advertising?

☐ Aid salespeople in opening new accounts.

☐ Aid salespeople in getting larger orders from wholesalers and retailers.

☐ Aid salespeople in getting preferred display space.

☐ Give salespeople an entree.

☐ Build morale of company sales force.

☐ Impress the trade (causing recommendation to their customers and favorable treatment to salespeople).

Is it a task of advertising to impart information needed to consummate sales and build customer satisfaction?

☐ "Where to buy it" advertising.

☐ "How to use it" advertising.

☐ New models, features, package.

☐ New prices.

☐ Special terms, trade-in offers, etc.

☐ New policies (guarantees, etc.).

To what extent does the advertising aim at building confidence and good will for the corporation among:

☐ Customers and potential customers?

☐ The trade (distributors, dealers, retail people)?

☐ Employees and potential employees?

☐ The financial community?

☐ The public at large?

Specifically what kind of images does the company wish to build?

☐ Product quality, dependability.

☐ Service.

☐ Family resemblance of diversified products.

☐ Corporate citizenship.

☐ Growth, progressiveness, technical leadership.

tive to using a product differentiation or price/quality differentiation strategy? What stage of the product life cycle is the product in? How is the product classified, packaged, branded? All these influence the product concept.

What was the product concept for the Army? Functionally, the Army was the branch of the military that specialized in land battle—the infantry, the cavalry, the artillery. Conceptually, though, it was the "*modern* Army, where the Cavalry flies, the infantry rides, and the artillery can hit a fly in the eye 15 miles away—a printed-circuit, solid-state, computerized Army—that requires a special kind of young man or woman impatient for a challenge and hungry for responsibility."

The *target audience* refers to the specific people the advertising will approach. In the marketing plan for the Army, the target market was described as young men and women 17 to 21 years old in the upper mental categories with high school diplomas. In the advertising plan, however, the target audience differed slightly from the target market. The intended audience for the Army's advertising included the high school seniors and graduates described above, but the new challenge was to attract recruits from a larger pool of prospects—not just the "definitely-would-join" group, but also the "probably" and "probably not" groups. In addition, the target audience included their influencers—mothers, fathers, friends, coaches, counselors, business and civic leaders, clergy, and government officials—all of whom are considered important in the decision-making of potential recruits.

In determining the target audience, it is important to consider not only who the end user is but also who makes the purchasing decision and who influences the purchasing decision. Children, for example, may exert a strong influence on where the family decides to eat. So McDonald's concentrates much of its advertising spending on campaigns directed to children as a target audience.

Communications media refer to the method or vehicles used to transmit the advertiser's message. These may include radio, television, newspapers, magazines, or billboards. They may include direct mail, publicity, and certain sales promotion techniques such as sample

FIGURE 7–12

The impact of the Army's media campaign using broadcast national media and narrowcast local media.

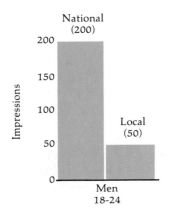
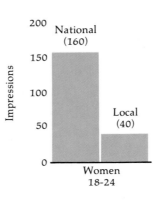
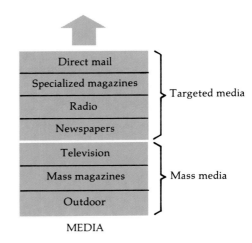

FIGURE 7–13

The Army demands total realism and accuracy in its ads. Commercials showing maneuvers and training sessions are filmed as they occur. And real soldiers are used in all ads and commercials. They are paid only $1 and can't be shown doing work they don't actually do in the Army. This adds to the credibility of the message.

packs or coupons. While most people are familiar with the Army's television campaign, much of its advertising is also placed in specialized publications aimed at narrowly defined audiences. Because its target audience was so broad, Ayer had to design an artful mix of media vehicles with broad and narrow coverage. In total, Ayer's media plan enabled the average 18-to-24-year-old male to see or hear an Army ad about 250 times a year (Figure 7–12).

Media considerations will be discussed more fully in Chapter 12. It's important to understand here, though, that the media to be used are determined by considering audience or readership statistics, potential communications effectiveness, relevance to the rest of the creative mix, and cost at the time the advertising plan is developed.

Look at the ad in Figure 7–13 and see how the Army decided to state its message. Can you see how the advertisement is a rational outgrowth of the marketing and advertising plan?

The *advertising message* is what the company plans to say in its advertisements and how it plans to say it—verbally and nonverbally. The Army wanted the message to center on "high technology" and "personal challenge" by showing actual recruits on the job, performing real-life Army tasks. Ted Regan has described the Army's advertising as an image campaign. In what it says and how it says it, it creates "an Army in the mind—an Army that is dynamic, contemporary, exciting. For prospects, it's an Army of high-tech skill training, personal growth, and financial aid for college. For the public at large, it's an Army of quality volunteers trained, equipped, and prepared to defend America."[10] In a nutshell, the copy, art and production elements used in this campaign comprised the agency's message strategy. (See Ad Lab 7–B.)

The advertising plan lays out the general direction of the campaign for the allotted time period. Then when it comes to creating the individual advertisements or commercials, the same process is repeated. The same questions are asked: What is the overall objective of the

---

AD LAB 7–B   Creative use of the creative mix

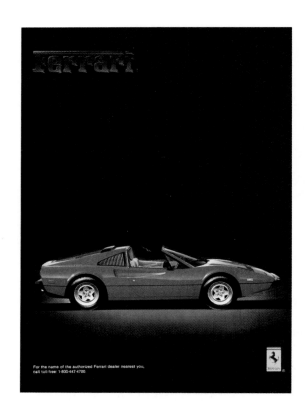

campaign? What is the overall strategy? What is the specific objective of this ad? What is the best way to do it? Who are we talking to? What media are we going to use? What do we want to say? How do we want to say it? Answering those questions will be the objective of the next two units of this text: "Advertising Creativity" and "Advertising Media."

(John Cleese, dressed as a corporate exec, is struggling to carry his bulky computer home for the night.)

VO: You're taking your computer home.

CLEESE: Yes, Mr. Prince wants my report in the morning.

VO: You know, Compaq Plus is portable.

CLEESE: Portable? Yes, but Mr. Prince says big computers do more.

VO: Compaq Plus does everything yours does and more.

CLEESE: Yes, but Mr. Prince says big computers store more.

VO: Compaq Plus stores 30 times more than yours.

CLEESE: Does it have a handle?

VO: Yes.

(Cleese "accidently" drops his computer.)

CLEESE: Oh, drat!

VO: Compaq Plus. It simply works better.

CLEESE: Mr. Prince, something terrible has happened!

Laboratory Application

Describe which elements of the creative mix are being emphasized in these advertisements.

ADVERTISING
INVESTMENT

In the late 1970s, the country experienced the first throes of the energy shortage. Cars lined up for blocks, sometimes miles, to buy gasoline at the one open station in town. Lights on Christmas trees were turned off. City halls and utility company buildings were dark at night. Plastics were in short supply. In fact, virtually everything made from petroleum or petrochemicals was back ordered, and prices for energy-related items skyrocketed. Companies called their suppliers, begging for products.

With demand for their products outstripping supplies, many executives marched into their company advertising departments and ordered the immediate cancellation of all ads. Many advertising budgets were cut to zero.

But as little as 12 months later, the executives were behind their desks worrying over why sales were down. And the stockholders were wondering how their companies had just lost several percentage points in market share.

■ Allocating Funds for Advertising

No advertising or marketing plan is complete without a discussion of what the program is going to cost and how the money is going to be spent. The advertising department has to convince management that the suggested level of expenditure makes good business sense.

Accountants and Internal Revenue Service agents consider advertising a current business expense. Consequently many executives treat advertising as a budget item that can be trimmed or eliminated like other expense items when sales are either extremely high or extremely low. Although this is certainly understandable, it is also regrettable.

■ An investment in future sales

The cost of a new plant or distribution warehouse is considered an investment in the company's future ability to produce and distribute products. Similarly, advertising, as one element of the promotion mix, should be considered an investment in future sales. Of course, advertising is used on a short-term basis to stimulate immediate sales, but it also has a cumulative long-range effect.

Advertising builds a consumer franchise and prompts goodwill. This in turn enhances the reputation and value of the company name. At first advertising may move a person to buy a new kind of potato chip, but it also affects that person's next purchase of potato chips, and the one after that, and the one after that. This same advertising may also influence the consumer to try the firm's other snacks.

Thus, while advertising may be treated as a current expense for accounting purposes, it can also be considered a long-term capital investment. For management to consider advertising as an investment, however, it must have some understanding of the relationship between advertising and sales and profits.

■ Relationship of advertising to sales and profits

Unfortunately, no one has come up with a reliable method to precisely determine the effect of advertising on sales. As we have shown in the last four chapters, there are many internal and external variables that influence a company's marketing and advertising efforts. Therefore, the research methodology that has been developed to measure the relationships between advertising and sales, as well as the relationship between sales and profit, is far from perfect and can give only rough estimates. However, enough data are available to verify certain facts:

1. Sales will increase if there is additional advertising. At some point, however, the rate of return will decline. (See Ad Lab 7–C.)
2. Sales response to advertising is spread out over a long period of time.

AD LAB 7–C   How economists view the effect of advertising on sales

Normally, the quantity sold will depend on the number of dollars the company spends advertising the product. And within reasonable limits (if its advertising program is not too repugnant), the more dollars spent on advertising, the more a company will sell—up to a point. Yet, even the most enthusiastic advertising agency will admit, reluctantly, that it is possible to spend too much on advertising.

To decide rationally how much to spend on this part of its marketing effort, management obviously should know just how quantity demanded is affected by advertising expenditure—how much more it will be able to sell per additional dollar of advertising, and when additional advertising dollars cease being effective. It needs to have, not a fixed number representing potential demand, but a graph or a statistical equation describing the relationship between sales and advertising.

Notice that in our illustration most of the curve goes uphill as we move to the right (it has a positive slope). This means that additional advertising will continue to bring in business until (at a budget of x million dollars) people become so saturated by the message that it begins to repel them and turn them away from the product.

Even in cases in which the saturation level cannot be reached within the range of outlays the firm can afford, the curve is likely to level off, becoming flatter and flatter as the amount spent on advertising gets larger and larger,

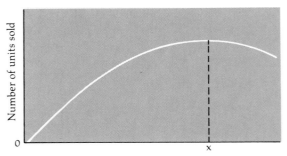

Advertising expenditure ($ millions)

and saturation is approached. The point at which the curve begins to flatten is the point at which returns from advertising begin to diminish. When the total advertising budget is small, even a $1 addition to the campaign may bring in as much as $10 in new sales and so be very much worthwhile to the firm. But when the market approaches saturation, each additional dollar may contribute only 30 cents in new sales, and that is not sound business.

Laboratory Applications

---

1. Can you give an example of when the advertising expenditure curve would have a negative slope?

2. Economists suggest that the quantity sold depends on the number of dollars the company spends on advertising. Is that a safe assumption? Discuss.

3. There are minimum levels below which advertising expenditures will have no effect on sales.
4. There will be some sales even if there is no advertising.
5. There are saturation limits imposed by culture and competition above which no amount of advertising can push sales.

To management, these facts, verified by numerous studies, might be interpreted into the following advice on how to allocate funds for advertising:

Don't advertise at all unless you are willing to spend enough to have some effect on sales. If you do decide to advertise, be willing to continue spending for an extended time. Do not expect immediate results, but keep your eye on the sales curve. Increase the advertising budget in stages until the effect on sales is noticed. At the point at which this effect is noticed, determine the effect on profits of the additional sales realized at this level of advertising expenditure. Next, continue increasing the level of advertising in gradual stages. At each stage, notice the volume of sales and determine the profitability. Continue increasing the advertising expenditure until (1) sales cease to be affected by additional advertising, or (2) the additional sales realized cease to be profitable. This is the upper limit and the point at which the advertising expenditure should be maintained.

This seemingly simple advice on how to set the appropriate level of advertising is actually full of complexities. It assumes, for instance, that advertising is the only marketing activity that affects sales. In reality, increased sales may be due to a better job of personal selling or to seasonal changes in the general business cycle. Furthermore, it assumes the company has a clear-cut way to determine the relationship between sales and profit. This is rarely true.

Moreover, what if the company sells many products? Then we have the problem of determining which advertising is contributing to which product, since all the company's advertising may help all the products.

One thing remains clear. Since the response to advertising is spread out over such an extended time, advertising should be viewed as a long-term investment in the company's future profits. Unfortunately, as long as management views advertising as a current expense, it attempts to keep those funds to a minimum. Naturally, like all expenditures, advertising should be evaluated for wastefulness. But, historically, companies that make advertising the scapegoat during periods of economic fluctuation invariably end up losing some share of market when the economy returns to stable growth.

The variable environments of business

Allocating funds to advertising is a very difficult task. Every business operates in several environments simultaneously. The way the company relates to these environments may determine its success or failure. Before attempting to determine the advertising allocation, therefore, the advertising manager must consider the status of the following:

1. Economic, political, social, and legal environment. The level of general economic activity, social customs and attitudes, as well as

the structure of tax rates affect both total industry sales and corporate profits on sales.

2. Institutional environment. What is the level of sales within the industry? The company can expect only a share of the total market demand.

3. Competitive environment. The various activities of competitors may either help or hinder the company from making sales and achieving profits.

4. Internal environment. The activities of the company itself in relation to its competitors and its markets will have a bearing on the effectiveness of advertising expenditures.[11]

These are just some of the problems facing advertising managers as they sit down to figure out their annual advertising budget. A thorough reappraisal of these factors at the time the advertising allocation is determined may have a profound effect on how much the company feels it can or should spend (Figure 7–14).

FIGURE 7–14

The black, white, and gray list identifies budget items and where they should be charged: to the advertising budget (white), items that are debatable (gray), and items that should not be charged (black).

White	Gray	Black
Space and time costs in regular media	Catalogs for consumers	Premium handling charges
Advertising consultants	Classified telephone directories	House-to-house sample distribution
Ad-pretesting services	Space in irregular publications	Packaging charges for premium promotions
Institutional advertising	Advertising aids for salesmen	Cost of merchandise for tie-in promotions
Industry directory listings	Financial advertising	Product tags
Readership or audience research	Dealer help literature	Showrooms
Media costs for consumer contests, premium and sampling promotions	Contributions to industry ad funds	Testing new labels and packages
Ad department travel and entertainment expenses	Direct mail to dealers and jobbers	Package design and artwork
Ad department salaries	Office supplies	Cost of non-self-liquidating premiums
Advertising association dues	Point-of-sale materials	Consumer education programs
Local cooperative advertising	Window display installation costs	Product publicity
Direct mail to consumers	Charges for services performed by other departments	Factory signs
Subscriptions to periodicals and services for ad department	Catalogs for dealers	House organs for salesmen
Storage of advertising materials	Test-marketing programs	Signs on company-owned vehicles
	Sample requests generated by advertising	Instruction enclosures
	Costs of exhibits except personnel	Press clipping services
	Ad department share of overhead	Market research (outside produced)
	House organs for customers and dealers	Samples of middlemen
	Cost of cash value or sampling coupons	Recruitment advertising
	Cost of contest entry blanks	Price sheets
	Cross-advertising enclosures	Public relations consultants
	Contest judging and handling fees	Coupon redemption costs
	Depreciation of ad department equipment	Corporate publicity
	Mobile exhibits	Market research (company produced)
	Employee fringe benefits	Exhibit personnel
	Catalogs for salesmen	Gifts of company products
	Packaging consultants	Cost of deal merchandise
	Consumer contest awards	Share of corporate salaries
		Cost of guarantee refunds
		Share of legal expenses
		Cost of detail or missionary men
		Sponsoring recreational activities
		Product research
		House organs for employees
		Entertaining customers and prospects
		Scholarships
		Plant tours
		Annual reports
		Outright charity donations

■ Methods of Allocating Funds

Business executives' attitudes toward the advertising budget are relatively simple to understand. They will spend more money as long as they can be assured it will bring in a profit. If it takes a dollar in advertising to produce one more penny of profit, it is worth the expense. The trick, however, is to determine when the dollar spent in advertising is not going to bring in a profit, but rather will result in a loss. That is hard to predict in advance, and advertising budgets must always be developed in advance.

In an effort to reduce the risk of overspending or underspending, a number of methods have been developed over the years to help companies determine how much to spend on advertising. Some businesspeople rely solely on one technique, while others use several in combination. Recently there has been a tendency to shy away from the simpler methods of the past, such as percentage of sales, and to use more sophisticated methods. However, no technique for allocating advertising funds is adequate for all situations. The methods discussed in this section are those used primarily to arrive at national advertising budgets. Additional techniques used by retailers, who operate under a different set of variables, are discussed in Chapter 17, "Local Advertising."

Percentage of sales

The percentage of sales method is one of the most popular techniques used to set the advertising appropriation. It may be based on a percentage of last year's sales, anticipated sales for next year, or a combination of the two. Businesspeople like this method because it is the simplest, it doesn't cost them anything, it is related to revenue, and it is considered safe (Figure 7–15).

Usually the percentage is based on an industry average or on company experience. Unfortunately, though, it is too often determined arbitrarily. The problem of basing the percentage on an industry average is that it assumes that the whole industry has similar objectives and faces the same marketing variables. When the percentage is based on company history, it assumes that the market is highly static, which is rarely the case.

There are some advantages to this method. When applied against future sales, it often works well. It assumes that a certain number of dollars are needed to sell a certain number of units. If we know what that percentage is, the correlation between advertising and sales should remain constant if the market is stable and competitors' advertising remains relatively unchanged. Furthermore, management tends to think in terms of percentages whether income or outgo. They think of advertising in the same way, so this method is simple. Also, because this method is common throughout the industry, it diminishes the likelihood of competitive warfare.

The greatest shortcoming of the percentage of sales method is that it violates a basic marketing principle. Marketing activities are supposed to stimulate demand and thus sales; they are not supposed to occur as a result of them. And if advertising automatically increases when sales increase and declines when sales decline, it automatically ignores all the other environments of business that might be suggesting a totally opposite move.

■ *Percentage of profit*

This method is similar to the percentage of sales method except that the percentage is applied to profit. It may be the past year's profits or profits expected in the coming year. Proponents of this method like it because they know they are dealing with profit dollars rather than with before-profit dollars. Furthermore, because they are working with only a percentage of the profit, they know there is an additional reservoir of profitable dollars to be used if necessary.

FIGURE 7–15   Percentage of sales allocated to advertising by the top 25 leading advertisers ($ in millions)

Category	Rank	Company	U.S. advertising expenditures	U.S. sales	Advertising as percent of U.S. sales
Food	3	Beatrice Cos.	$602.8	$ N/A	N/A
	10	General Foods Corp.	386.1	6,407.5	6.0
	11	Nabisco Brands	367.5	3,655.6	10.1
	16	McDonald's Corp	311.4	7,069.0	4.4
	21	Ralston Purina Co.	285.7	3,848.6	7.4
	23	General Mills	268.7	5,100.0	5.3
Automotive	4	General Motors Corp.	595.1	66,160.0	0.9
	7	Ford Motor Co.	479.1	33,000.0	1.5
Pharmaceuticals	13	Warner-Lambert Co.	343.6	1,822.0	18.9
	14	American Home Products Corp.	333.5	3,482.3	9.6
	17	Johnson & Johnson	295.3	3,600.0	8.2
Communications and entertainment	25	Warner Communications	251.0	2,715.9	9.2
Tobacco	5	R. J. Reynolds Industries	593.4	10,769.0	5.5
	6	Philip Morris Inc.	527.5	9,303.1	5.7
Wine, beer, and liquor	20	Anheuser-Busch Cos.	290.6	6,658.5	4.4
Soaps and cleaners	1	Procter & Gamble Co.	773.6	9,554.0	8.1
	15	Unilever U.S.	324.9	2,808.0	12.2
	24	Colgate-Palmolive Co.	268.0	2,200.0	12.2
Chemicals and gasoline	18	Mobil Corp.	294.9	23,900.0	1.2
Retail chains	2	Sears, Roebuck & Co.	732.5	32,637.0	2.2
	9	K mart Corp.	400.0	17,785.7	2.2
	19	J. C. Penney Co.	292.5	11,565.0	2.5
Soft drinks	12	PepsiCo Inc.	356.4	6,714.0	5.3
	22	Coca-Cola Co.	282.2	4,071.4	6.9
Telephone equipment	8	American Telephone & Telegraph	463.1	67,648.0	0.7

This method suffers many of the same deficiencies as the percentage of sales approach. Many forces other than current advertising affect profit, and it is even more difficult to evaluate profit effectiveness than sales effectiveness. A variation of this method was suggested at the beginning of this section where units of advertising funds were gradually increased until the marginal return of the last unit did not equal the marginal cost. As we said then, it's a nice, simple theory, but current advertising effectiveness cannot be precisely measured in most cases.

Unit of sale

This method, also called the case-rate method, is another variation of the percentage of sales technique. It has many of the same deficiencies. A specific dollar figure is set for each case, box, barrel, or carton produced or for each unit anticipated to be produced. For example, some automobile manufacturers set a figure of $40–$45 per car to be spent on advertising.

The unit of sale method has its greatest advantage in assessing members of horizontal cooperative programs and trade associations. Each member contributes equitably according to production. For example, when the Southern California Beef Association wanted to stimulate demand for California beef, it paid for advertising by assessing cattle feeders and packers 25 cents for each steer slaughtered.

Of course, this method cannot be used effectively for new product introductions. To overcome consumer inertia, spending must be much more than the usual unit of sale allocation. Another problem is that the amount assessed per unit often becomes set and the advertising program cannot respond to dynamic marketing problems.

Competitive parity

This method allocates advertising dollars according to the amounts spent by the firm's major competitors. We like to call it the self-defense method. It follows the line, "If they're spending that much, we'd better." Or conversely, "If that's all they're spending, there's no reason for us to spend any more."

Many businesspeople rationalize that if their leading competitors have been successful in capturing market share, they will be successful by emulating them. Furthermore, many companies determine the relative efficiency of their operations by comparing their firm's statistics in production and finance with their competitors. It's only natural that they would apply the same technique to preparing advertising budgets.

The fallacies of this rationalization should be obvious. Your competitors' objectives are rarely the same as yours. When your competitors make a mistake, so do you. Finally, many industries maintain a relatively low "noise level" of advertising. Just a moderate increase in one firm's advertising expenses could enable that particular company to stand out above the rest. As long as a company budgets defensively, however, it misses that opportunity.

Share of market

In industries where products are very similar, there is usually a high correlation between a company's share of the market and its share of industry advertising. Knowing this, some firms set a goal for

We're a part of and yet apart from the automobile business. They do things their way. We do things our way.

In 1949, their way was a garish, gas-guzzling hulk of sheet metal and chrome. The car.

Our way was a small, homely, humble attempt at good basic transportation. The Beetle.

It embodied our philosophy: Forget what looks best. Forget what sells best. What works best? Car makers scoffed.

Cars were expensive. The Beetle was economical. Cars were work to drive. Volkswagens were fun to drive. Cars were changed to look better. Volkswagens were changed to work better. Cars were built to self-destruct. Volkswagens were built to last.

Volkswagens became popular. Car makers became nervous. Especially in 1975 when we introduced the Rabbit. Today, it's still being copied.

So, after 35 years of turning our backs on every popular notion known to the car business, what's next?

A lot. We have a growing passion for the most practical, best performing, personal transportation our German engineering can build and almost anyone's money can buy.

We're raising more than a few eyebrows with two new Volkswagens: The 1985 Jetta and Golf.

They reaffirm our philosophy. As do the Quantum, Scirocco, GTI, Cabriolet, Vanagon and Camper.

We could follow the crowd. We could go with the flow. But that would be like trying to fit a round peg in a round hole. It's not a car. It's a Volkswagen.

Volkswagen.

FIGURE 7–16

Among auto manufacturers, Volkswagen spends the highest percentage of sales on advertising—over 7 percent. Whether advertising is accomplishing its task, though, is debatable.

a certain portion of the market and then apply the same percentage of industry advertising dollars to their budget.

This method has the advantage of being an aggressive attempt to achieve an objective. According to J. O. Peckham, executive vice president of the A. C. Nielsen Company, a company's best chance of maintaining its share of market is to maintain a share of advertising somewhat ahead of its market share. For example, if you have a 50 percent share of the market, you should spend 55 percent of the industry's advertising dollars.

One shortcoming is that there is no guarantee that your competitors will not increase their advertising budgets.

For new products, share of market is a common method. According to Peckham's formula, when a new product brand is introduced, the advertising budget should be about one and a half times the brand's expected share of market in two years. This means that if the company's two-year sales goal is 10 percent of the market, it should spend about 15 percent of the industry's advertising during the first two years.[12]

The share of market method assumes that to gain share of market, you must first gain share of mind. This is a logical approach to budgeting strategy. However, one hazard of this method is the tendency to become complacent. Companies compete on more than one basis, and advertising is just one tool of the marketing mix. Therefore, simply maintaining a higher percentage of media exposure may not be enough to accomplish the desired results. Companies must maintain an awareness of *all* the marketing activities of their competitors, not just advertising.

Task method

The task method is also known as the objective or budget buildup method. In recent years it has gained considerable popularity and is one of the few logical means of determining advertising allocations. It defines the objectives that are sought and how advertising is to be used to accomplish those objectives. It considers advertising a marketing tool used to generate sales rather than a result of sales.

The task method has three steps: defining the objectives, determining strategy, and estimating the cost. After specific, quantitative marketing objectives have been set, the advertiser develops programs to be used in attaining them. If the objective is to increase the number of coffee cases sold by 10 percent, the advertiser will have to determine which advertising approach will work best, how often ads are to run, and which media will be used. The proposed cost of this program is determined, and this becomes the basis for the advertising budget. Naturally, it is necessary to consider this budget in light of the company's financial position. If the cost is too high, the objectives may have to be scaled down and the strategy adjusted accordingly. Likewise, after the campaign has run, if the results are better or worse than anticipated, the next budget may require appropriate revisions.

The task method forces companies to think in terms of goals and whether they are being accomplished. The effectiveness of this method is most apparent when the results of particular ads or campaigns can be readily measured. Due to its nature, this method is adaptable to changing conditions in the market and is easily revised as dictated by past results (Figure 7–16).

Although it is easy to look back and determine whether money was spent wisely, it is often very difficult to determine in advance the amount of money that will be needed to reach a specific goal. This is the major drawback to the task method. Likewise, although techniques for measuring the effect of advertising are improving, they are still weak in many areas. As techniques become more exact, though, advertisers are using the task method more and more. Today it is probably the best basis for estimating the size of an advertising budget.

Additional methods

There are several other methods for allocating funds which advertisers use to varying degrees. The *empirical research method* uses experimentation to determine the best level of advertising expenditure. By running a series of tests in different markets with different budgets, companies determine which is the most efficient level of expenditure.

Since the introduction of computers, there has been a great deal of interest in the use of *quantitative mathematical models* for budgeting. A number of sophisticated techniques have been developed. However, for the most part these equations are not easily understood by line executives, and each relies on assumptions of data that are frequently unavailable or very expensive for the average business.

Some companies determine their advertising budget in an arbitrary manner. The *arbitrary method* is used primarily by small, inexperienced advertisers who have not realized the advantages of planned advertising and marketing strategy.

Others use the *all available funds method*. This "go for broke" technique is generally used by advertisers with limited capital who are trying to introduce a new product. Fortunately, this method is not used often because the available funds eventually exceed what is needed for advertising. When this occurs, the advertiser seeks another method such as the task method.

The Bottom Line

All these methods potentially assume one of two fallacies. The first fallacy is more obvious—that advertising is a result of sales. We know this is not true, and yet the widespread use of the percentage of sales method indicates that many businesspeople think advertising *should* be a result of sales.

The second fallacy is that advertising creates sales. Only in rare circumstances (where direct-action advertising is used) can advertising be said to create sales. Advertising locates prospects and stimulates demand. It may even stimulate inquiries. Salespeople likewise may locate prospects and stimulate demand. They also close the sale. But, in reality, only customers create sales. It is the customer's choice to buy or not to buy the product, not the company's choice.

The job of advertising is to inform, persuade, and remind. In that way, advertising affects sales. However, advertising is just one part of the whole, and advertising managers must keep this in mind when preparing their plans and their budgets for management.

Summary

The marketing plan may be the most important document a company possesses. It assembles in one place all the pertinent facts about a company, the markets it serves, its products, and its competition and brings all these facts up to date. It sets specific goals and objectives to be attained and describes the precise strategies that will be used to achieve them. Thus, it musters all the company's forces for the marketing battlefield and, in so doing, dictates the role of advertising in the marketing mix.

The marketing plan should contain four principal sections: (1) situation analysis, (2) marketing objectives, (3) marketing strategy, and (4) action programs. A company's marketing objectives should be logical deductions from an analysis of its current situation, its prediction of future trends, and its understanding of corporate objectives. They should relate to the needs of specific target markets and sales objectives. The sales target objectives should be specific, quantitative, and realistic.

The first step in developing marketing strategy is to select the target market. The second step is to determine a cost-effective marketing mix for each target market the company pursues. The marketing mix is determined by how the company uses the four Ps: product, price, place, and promotion. Advertising is one of the promotional tools companies may use.

Advertising is a natural outgrowth of the marketing plan, and the advertising plan is prepared in much the same way as the marketing plan. It includes a section on analysis, advertising objectives, and strategy.

Advertising objectives may be expressed in terms of moving prospective customers up through the advertising pyramid (awareness, comprehension, conviction, desire, action). Or they may be expressed in terms of generating inquiries, coupon response, or attitude change.

The advertising (or creative) strategy is determined by the advertiser's use of the creative mix. The creative mix is composed of the (1) product concept, (2) target audience, (3) communications media, and (4) advertising message. The product concept refers to the bundle of values the product is intended to represent to the consumer. The target audience is the specific group of people the advertising will approach. It may or may not be the same as the target market. The communications media are the vehicles used to transmit the advertiser's message. The advertising message is what the company plans to say in its advertisements and how it plans to say it.

There are several methods commonly used for allocating funds to advertising. Historically, the most popular method has been the percentage of sales approach. A similar method is called the percentage of profit approach. Other approaches include the share of market method, the competitive parity method, the empirical method, and the task method. The latter involves defining the advertising objective, determining the strategy, and estimating the cost to conduct that strategy.

Questions for review and discussion

1. Why should a marketing plan be created before any ads are designed?
2. What examples can you give to show the difference between generic-marketing objectives and sales-target objectives?
3. What are the elements of a marketing plan in outline form?
4. What is the most important consideration in developing any marketing strategy?
5. What are the elements of an advertising plan in outline form?
6. What examples can you give to show how one person's strategy might become another person's objective?
7. How might environmental factors affect an automobile company's expenditures for marketing and advertising?
8. What is the best method of allocating funds for advertising a real estate development? Why?
9. What types of companies would tend to use the competitive parity method? Why?
10. How could a shoe manufacturer use the empirical research method to determine its advertising budget?

PART III   ADVERTISING CREATIVITY

8

CREATIVE COPYWRITING

Suppose you are the advertising manager for one of the world's largest paper companies. Your boss, the marketing director, invites you in, asks you to sit down, and tosses a sheet of paper at you across the desk. You glance at it quickly. It's a summary of a recent consumer research study, and the bottom line is that people are reading less and less every year. Fewer books, fewer magazines, fewer newspapers. In fact, the study shows that literacy among America's youth is declining rapidly. Many who graduate from high school can barely read or write.

"Do you know what that means?" asks your boss.

You nod affirmatively. Your company is one of the leading suppliers of paper for books, magazines, newspapers, and commercial printing.

"I want you to give me a plan to attack this situation."

You are excused to start working on your problem. What would you do?

Unfortunately, this is not just a hypothetical situation. Literacy among youth has been declining for some years, and this problem has troubled parents, educators, and the International Paper Company. International Paper decided to try to do something about it. Together with its agency, Ogilvy & Mather, it created an unusual advertising campaign called "The Power of the Printed Word." The campaign was designed to help young people improve their verbal skills and thereby help International Paper's customers as well.

Speaking about the campaign, the agency's vice president/creative director said, "We did everything we could to make people want to read the ads." The language was simple and direct. Photos were used with captions to attract the reader's attention and add a bit of humor. And the ads were laid out in a very easy-to-follow style with editorial-type columns, several illustrations, boxes, bold type headings, and short paragraphs.

Consisting of seven "how to" articles, each written by a well-known and respected wordsmith, the campaign ran in youth-oriented and general interest magazines, some large metropolitan newspapers, and many small community newspapers. During the first four months, the company received over 1,000 letters a day and requests for 1 million reprints. The campaign was a smashing success—not because it could eradicate America's verbal problems, but because it generated a lot of interest and some concern. In the long run this concern could lead to a drive to improve the reading and writing abilities of America's future generations[1] (Figure 8–1).

COPYWRITING AND ADVERTISING STRATEGY

International Paper's primary advertising objective was simply to create awareness of the problem of declining literacy. In addition, the company hoped to stimulate interest and desire on the part of teachers and young people to do something about this problem—if not for others, then at least for themselves. The success of the company's efforts was indicated by the number of inquiries it received and requests for reprints of the ads. But what was the creative strategy that enabled International Paper to achieve that success?

A review of Chapter 7 reminds us that advertising or creative strategy consists of four elements:

1. The product concept.
2. The target audience.
3. The communications media.
4. The advertising message.

In this particular case, the product concept has seemingly very little to do with International Paper's primary functional product—paper. Instead of selling paper, the company is selling an idea: the power of the printed word—the concept that reading and writing are very important skills.

The target audience was young people—namely, high school students aged 15 to 18 and young adults aged 18 to 34. In the first year of the campaign, using print media like *Newsweek*, *Sports Illustrated*, *Rolling Stone*, *Ebony*, and *Seventeen*, International Paper reached 50 million young people with their message.

What is the message strategy? The message strategy is determined by what and how the company wants to communicate. International Paper wanted to convey the message that reading and writing skills are important. They can help your career, provide new opportunities in life, give pleasure and enjoyment to yourself and others, and help those around you. How to communicate those ideas involved developing a verbal and nonverbal presentation of the message that would be simple, interesting, informative, entertaining, enjoyable, and helpful. In Chapter 9, ''Creative Art Direction,'' we will discuss the nonverbal, graphic side of message strategy. The subject of this chapter, copywriting, concerns the verbal element of message strategy. The combined product of the art director and the copywriter is the creative nucleus, which is then translated through the production process into the final advertisement or commercial.

FIGURE   8–1

''How to write clearly,'' by Edward T. Thompson, editor-in-chief, *Reader's Digest*, was the subject of one ad in International Paper's award-winning series directed to young people. Others included ''How to write a business letter'' by Malcolm Forbes; Tony Randall on ''How to improve your vocabulary;'' and Bill Cosby on ''How to read faster.'' In all cases the authors of the ads worked closely with the advertising agency's art director and copywriter to ensure student readability and interest.

How to write clearly

Building the Message Strategy

Before the copywriter starts to think about writing an ad, he or she must understand the marketing and advertising strategies completely. This includes the message strategy. If the advertising plan has not spelled it out in detail (which is often the case), the copywriter should immediately build a message strategy, with the art director if

Checklist of product marketing facts for copywriters

Identity

- ☐ Trade name
- ☐ Trademark
- ☐ Product symbol
- ☐ Other copyrighted or patented information

Effectiveness

- ☐ Is there proof that it has been tested and works well?
- ☐ Are there any government or other regulations that need to be mentioned or observed?

Packaging

- ☐ Unit size or sizes offered
- ☐ Package shape
- ☐ Package design
  Styling
  Color
  Special protection for product
  A carrier for product
- ☐ Package label

Research

- ☐ What research about the product does the supplier have?
- ☐ Is research available?

Performance

- ☐ What does it do?
- ☐ What might it be expected to do that it does *not*?
- ☐ How does it work?
- ☐ How is it made or produced?
- ☐ What is in it?
  Raw materials   Preservatives
  Chemicals   Special ingredients
  Nutrients
- ☐ What are its physical characteristics?
  Color   Appearance
  Smell   Others
  Taste   Texture

Product image

- ☐ How do people view the product?
- ☐ What do they like about it?
- ☐ What do they dislike about it?
- ☐ Is it a luxury?
- ☐ Is it a necessity?
- ☐ Is it a habit?
- ☐ Is it self-indulgent?
- ☐ Do people have to have it but wish they didn't?

Life

- ☐ What is its life or use span?

possible, and get it approved before going any further. The fastest way to have an advertisement rejected is to write a brilliant piece of work that is off-strategy.

As a copywriter you need to review the research, analyze the facts, and study the market, the product, and the competition. (See the Checklist of product marketing facts for copywriters.)

How is the market segmented? How will the product be posi-

Competitive information

☐ Who are the competitors?

☐ Does it have any advantages over them?

☐ Does it have any disadvantages?

☐ Are they all about the same?

☐ Do rival products present problems that this one solves?

Manufacturing

☐ How is it made?

☐ How long does it take?

☐ How many steps in the process?

☐ How about the people involved in making it?

☐ Are there any special machines used?

☐ Where is it made?

History

☐ When was it created or invented?

☐ Who introduced it?

☐ Has it had other names?

☐ Have there been product changes?

☐ Is there any "romance" to it?

Market position

☐ What is its share of the total market?

Consumer use

☐ How is the product used?

☐ Are there other possible uses?

☐ How frequently is it bought?

☐ What type of person uses the product?

☐ Why is the product bought?
  Personal use
  Gift
  Work

☐ What type of person uses the product most (heavy user)?

☐ What amount of the product is bought by the heavy user?

☐ Where does the best customer live?

☐ What kind of person is a heavy user or buyer?

Distribution

☐ How widely is the product distributed?

☐ Are there exclusive sellers?

☐ Is there a ready supply or limited amount?

☐ Is it available for a short season?

tioned? Who are the best prospects for the product? Is the target audience different from the target market? What is the key consumer benefit? What support or reason does the consumer need to believe in that benefit? What support can you give? What will the product's image be? The answers to these questions help build the message strategy.

The next step is to determine the specific elements of the message strategy: copy, art, and production.

1. Copy—what you're going to say and how you're going to say it.
2. Art—what you're going to show and how you're going to show it.
3. Production—what you're going to create mechanically and how you're going to create it.

At this point, the results of research are important. Research identifies the best prospects; research identifies the best strategy; research can find the most important consumer appeals or product claims. *What* the advertising says may be more important than *how* it is said. Or the reverse may be true. So test the strategy.

■ Copy Platform

You are almost ready to start writing. Now review your strategy and write a specific statement about the most important issues that should be considered.

Who is the most likely prospect for the product? How tightly can you define and describe him or her in terms of demographic, psychographic, and behavioristic qualities? What would you imagine that prospect's personality to be like?

What wants or needs does that consumer have that you should appeal to? In Chapter 5 we discussed the innumerable types of appeals or approaches used by advertisers. The two broadest categories

---

FIGURE 8–2   Selected advertising appeals

Appetite	Sympathy for others	Novelty
Taste	Devotion to others	Safety
Health	Guilt	Courtesy
Fear	Pride of personal appearance	Rest or sleep
Humor	Home comfort	Economy in use
Security	Pride in appearance of property	Economy in purchase
Cleanliness	Pleasure of recreation	Efficiency in operation or use
Sex attraction	Entertainment	Dependability in use
Romance	Opportunity for more leisure time	Dependability in quality
Social achievement	Avoidance of a laborious task	Durability
Ambition	Enhancement of earnings	Variety of selection
Personal comfort	Style (beauty)	Simplicity
Protection of others	Pride of possession	Sport/play/physical activity
Social approval/approval of others	Curiosity	Cooperation

are rational appeals and emotional appeals. The former is an appeal to the consumer's practical, functional need for the product or service. The latter relates to the consumer's psychological, social, or emotional needs (Figure 8–2).

Other types of appeals used by advertisers, which may fall into one of these two broad categories, include positive and negative appeals, fear and sex appeals, and humor appeals. Depending on the message strategy, any or all may be used to gain attention, create a personality for the product or service, and stimulate consumer interest, credibility, desire, and action.

Next, write down what product features satisfy the consumers' needs. What support is there for the product claim? What is the product's position? What personality or image have you decided to create?

Then, what style, approach, or tone will you use in the copy? And generally what will the copy say? The answers to all these questions make up the *copy platform*, a document that will be your guide for writing the ad.

When the first ad is written, review the copy platform again. See whether the ad measures up. If it doesn't, reject it, and start again.

OBJECTIVES OF GOOD COPY

By 1910 Henry Ford had spent five years and thousands of dollars perfecting his new Model T. Now the first models were ready; it was time to advertise. But what sort of ad should he run? Ads at that time were mostly art or photos with few if any words. But Ford believed art alone couldn't sell his Model T. It had to be described—in detail.

A few weeks later readers of the *Saturday Evening Post* were startled to see a black and white ad, two pages long, that contained no pictures. Instead, it was all words!

"When Ford speaks the world listens." (Figure 8–3).

"Buy a Ford car because it is better—not because it is cheaper."

"The reason why can be given in a very few words . . . ."

The "very few words" totaled about 1,200. They told how Henry Ford invented the Model T. They detailed the financial condition of the Ford Company. And they listed its 28 factories, assembly plants, and branches.

The ad was a "first." It contained more words, or *copy*, than any ad of the day. It also caused some industry leaders to rebuke Ford. "Pictures sell cars," one said flatly, "not words." But Ford stood his ground and proved he was right. The ad soon produced more sales than any other auto ad in history. And it gave Henry Ford his first push toward what was to become, 10 years later, the largest and most profitable manufacturing company in the world.[2]

This example illustrates just one of many misconceptions about the creative function in advertising and the objectives of good copy.

The purpose of copywriting is usually to persuade or remind a group or groups of individuals to take some action in order to satisfy a need or want. But first people need to be made aware—either of their problems or, if they're obvious, that a solution exists. To create awareness you have to get people's attention.

FIGURE   8–3

This 1910 advertisement written by Henry Ford might have been the inspiration for E. F. Hutton's famous campaign: "When E. F. Hutton talks, people listen." Containing 1,200 words, the Ford ad contained the longest copy of any advertisement of its time. It also sold more autos than any previous ad in history.

Attention

Gaining attention is therefore the first objective of copywriting. The headline is usually the major attention-getting device. For example, an ad for Apple computers (Figure 8–4) has a news/information headline that uses a large number to catch the eye and makes a bold promise: "How to send mail at 670,000,000 mph." Other devices, such as the illustration, layout, color, size of the advertisement, unusual sounds or visual techniques, can be used to gain attention as well.

There are some factors over which the copywriter has no control. Obviously, the size of the advertisement influences whether it will be noticed, and the size is often determined before a copywriter is assigned to write the advertisement. The ad's position in a publication may determine who will see it. The copywriter must take all these factors into account before deciding on an attention-getting device. Also, the device used must relate to the product, to the rest of the advertisement, and to the intended audience. Headlines that promise something but fail to deliver will not make a sale; and, in fact, the advertiser may alienate a potential customer. For example, ads that use racy headlines or nude figures unrelated to the product or sales ideas may attract attention but will often lose sales.

Interest

The second step in writing an advertisement is to create interest. We've gotten our customer's attention. She's looking at our advertisement. But if we can't keep her interest, we're going to lose her. So we have to talk to her, about her, and about her problems and needs. We may want to use the word *you* frequently.

Interest is the bridge between attention and credibility. It is an important step. There are several effective ways to build and maintain interest. We might use cartoon characters, subheads, interior illustrations, storyline copy, or charts and tables. We will discuss some of these later.

 Credibility

The next step is to establish credibility. Consumers today are more sophisticated than in years past. To them the proofs offered in some advertisements are not only unbelievable but also insulting. In such cases product sales frequently suffer. As a result, if the advertiser offers test data, they must give honest support to the product claim and not be statistical manipulation.

Credibility is sometimes added to advertisements through the use of presenters. As a spokesman, comedian Bill Cosby has lent credibility to a variety of products including Jell-O and Coke because of his honest, personable, down-to-earth style.

 Desire

To heighten desire we need to inform the reader or the viewer of the benefits of our product or service. Each new benefit should heighten desire because it is matched with a real or perceived need of the customer. Even only one benefit must be presented in such a way that customers believe it and understand its application to their own situation. This is why knowing the customer is so important.

■ Action

We want to motivate the reader to take some action, to do something, or at least to agree with us. The action may be immediate or future. Action may be directly requested: "Come to our sale May 15." Action may also be indirect or implied in the copy.

FIGURE 8–4

The headline of this ad might have been "Now you can send mail fast" (which is informational) or "Now you can send mail at the speed of light" (which is provocative). This headline, though, with the large number and the "how to," is both informational and provocative, plus it's very attention getting.

The request for action must be in the copy. You're asking for the order. You're asking that the reader agree with you. Too many advertisements forget that readers are generally lazy or preoccupied; they need a course of action spelled out for them. That's the job of good copy (Figure 8–5).

UNDERSTANDING COPY TERMINOLOGY

All advertisements are made up of numerous elements or components. These elements may be moved, enlarged, reduced, reversed, changed, or eliminated until a new look or approach is achieved. To discuss copy we must understand what these elements are and what they do.

The key elements in print advertising are the headline, illustration, subhead, body copy, captions, boxes and panels, slogans, logotypes (logos), seals, and signatures.

In broadcast advertising, copy is normally spoken dialogue, so it is usually referred to as the *audio* portion of the commercial. The audio may be delivered as a *voice-over* by an announcer who is not seen but whose voice we hear. Or it may be *on-camera* dialogue by an announcer, a spokesperson, or actors playing out a scene. When words are shown on the screen, they are normally referred to by the same terms used in print advertising. Let's discuss each of those terms briefly.

Headlines

Many consider the headline the most important element in a print advertisement. The term *headline* refers to the words in the leading position of the advertisement—that is, the words that will be read first or that are positioned to draw the most attention. As a result, headlines are usually set in larger type than other portions of the advertisement.

A headline has six important functions. First, the headline must attract attention to the advertisement. The entire message is usually lost if no one reads the headline. To promote the eternity ring, DeBeers uses a highly effective headline statement: "You once said 'I do.' Now you can say 'I'm glad I did.'"

Second, the headline should select the reader; that is, it tells whether the subject matter of the ad interests the reader. Citibank's headline, "A word to the wealthy," means exactly what it says (Figure 8–6).

Audiences may be qualified by demographic (age, sex, income) or by psychographic criteria. A noted copywriter, Stan Freeburg, developed a headline for an airline advertisement that used psychographic qualification. The headline read: "Hey, you with the sweaty palms!" The campaign was short-lived. Research has since shown that airline passengers are subconsciously disturbed by airline advertisements concerned with safety. So care in advertising is essential; psychographic qualification can backfire, and the results can be devastating.

FIGURE 8–5

This all-copy ad directs the reader to "Ask for your personalized computer print-out telling exactly how the money would add up for you . . .", "Just send us the coupon below, or see an Allstate agent . . ." and "Yes! Tell me how Allstate Universal Life can give me insurance protection . . ."

— Third, the headline should lead the reader directly into the body copy. One good example is:

Headline: "What kind of man reads *Playboy?*"
Body copy: "He's a man who demands the best life has to offer . . . ."

—Fourth, the headline must present the complete selling idea. It may be intended merely to carry through a campaign theme, but it should tell the whole story. Marlboro accomplishes this in beautiful magazine and outdoor advertisements with nothing more than a western illustration, a cigarette pack, and the headline: "Come to where the flavor is. Marlboro Country." The headline creates the mood, suggests the image, asks for the sale, and states the brand name, all at once. Not only that, it is memorable and identifiable with the product. It therefore has the ability to trigger a recognition response in the consumer's mind. The DeBeers headline mentioned earlier accomplishes the same task.

David Ogilvy points out that on the average five times as many people read the headline as read the body copy. Therefore if you haven't done some selling in the headline, you've wasted 80 percent of your money. Ogilvy also suggests that advertisers should not be afraid of long headlines. Headlines that contain 6 to 12 words usually get the best results; and his best headline, he says, contained 18 words: "At sixty miles an hour the loudest noise in the new Rolls-Royce comes from the electric clock."[3]

—Fifth, the headline should promise the customer a benefit. The benefit should be readily apparent to the reader and easy to get.

Sixth, the headline should present product *news* of interest to the reader. Consumers look for new products, new uses of old products, or improvements on old products. Therefore words that imply newness increase readership and should be used whenever applicable.

FIGURE 8–6

The headline in this ad flags the target audience. Although neither the headline nor the visual tells the reader anything about the subject, the ad is still effective. The soft sell body copy is written in the same sophisticated tone as the headline. Also, the ad is beautifully designed and artfully produced in keeping with the institutional approach. In posttesting, the ad scored #1 in single-page Starch awareness, both in "noted" and "read most."

WE'LL GIVE YOU
A PERMANENT WITHOUT
MAKING WAVES IN
YOUR BUDGET.

At Prime Cuts, we don't think a great permanent should cost a great deal. That's why our permanents cost just $29.75. That's our everyday price, not a special. You'll find comparable savings on haircuts, makeup application and hair coloring, too.

Come in to Prime Cuts for a permanent. We'll put some curl into your hair. Without doing something kinky to your budget.

Prime Cuts

1314 S.E. 4th St./331-1218

FIGURE 8–7

A great example of how to do award-winning creative advertising on a small budget. The advertiser had the intelligence here not to destroy the simplicity of the layout or to insert superfluous information.

Examples are *new, now, suddenly, announcing, introducing, it's here, improved, revolutionary, just arrived,* and *important development.*

Copywriters and advertising academicians have been trying to classify types of headlines and body copy for years. There are probably as many different classifications and types as there are authors on the subject. Richard Stansfield, for example, has come up with 23 "basic" types of headlines for which he has developed names that range from "Teaser" to "So what?"

The advertising practitioner would probably say "so what?" to the whole subject. However, for the student of advertising and the businessperson with limited experience in the field, it is helpful if we briefly discuss certain common types of headlines and copy styles. This should facilitate understanding the role of copywriting and the skill required to write effective copy.

Generally, we can classify good advertising headlines into five basic categories: benefit, provocative, news/information, question, and command.

Benefit headlines make a direct promise to the reader. Two good examples are "Every time we race, you win" (Yamaha) and "We'll give you a permanent without making waves in your budget" (Prime Cuts haircutting salon) (Figure 8–7).

Some headlines are written to provoke the reader's curiosity. To learn more, the reader must read the body copy. Of course, the danger with *provocative headlines* is that the reader won't read on, and the headline won't have sold anything. For that reason, provocative headlines are usually coupled with illustrations that offer clarification or some *story appeal.* For example: "Dear American Tourister: I fell flat on my attache." The accompanying illustration shows the testimonial letter-writer tumbling down a flight of stairs and landing on his American Tourister briefcase. To know the rest of the story, the reader must read on.

News/information headlines include many of the "how to" headlines as well as headlines that seek to gain identification for their sponsors by announcing some news or providing some promise of information: "The Honda Civic. The car we designed around a shopping bag." Or Chivas Regal: "The most carefully poured Scotch in the world." This headline provides the reader with an enormous amount of information in a very short sentence. It tells the reader that Chivas Regal is precious and expensive. Neither of these facts is necessarily "hot news," but both provide information and are memorable.

Question headlines can be dangerous. If you ask a question that the reader can answer quickly, the rest of the advertisement may not get read. Imagine a headline that reads: "Do you like food?" The reader answers "of course" and turns the page.

An American Airlines advertisement with the headline "If you don't show your kids where America began, who will?" did not fall into that trap. It was designed to motivate thoughtful parents about future travel plans. It accomplished that objective.

A *command headline* orders you to do something and, therefore, might seem negative, yet we pay attention to such headlines. They motivate us through fear or emotion, or because we understand the inherent correctness of the command. For example, "Drive safely.

The life you save may be your own" is extremely well known and difficult to challenge. Similar appeals have extended to drunk driving: "Get the drunk driver off the road."

Other command headlines are more pleasant, such as "Listen to what you've been missing in cassette sound" (3M Company).

An ad for Wilson baseballs tells the reader to "Play with fire." (Figure 8–8).

Perhaps the best command headline ever written was: "Promise her anything but give her Arpege."

Classifying headlines into categories might take a lifetime and serves little purpose. We have only touched on a few in this brief discussion. Many headline categories are easily combined. Some work better with illustrations than others. Provocative headlines and question headlines, for example, usually require more support from definitive illustrations. A good exercise for the beginning copywriter is to keep a checklist of headline types and try to write several different types for each new project. That is one way to find the best solution to the problem at hand.

■ Subheads

Subheads are misnamed because they can appear above or below the headline. They can also appear in the body copy or the text of the advertisement. A subhead that appears above the headline is called a "kicker."

Subheads usually appear in a smaller type size than the headline. They are almost invariably larger than the body copy or text type size. Subheads may appear in boldface (heavier) type or in different ink color.

FIGURE 8–8

The headline and the blazing color photo make this ad a hit. The run is scored when the single line of body copy brings the promise home.

The purpose of the subhead is to transmit key sales points—fast! Most individuals read only the headline and subheads. The subhead should be reserved for important facts that may not be as dramatic or memorable as the headline information. Some may require more space than a headline because they communicate more information in more words.

The subheads should reinforce the headline and advertisement theme. Fidelity Federal's "Is your bank taking you to the cleaners?" is a headline well reinforced by the subhead, "If your bank isn't paying you interest on your checking account, no matter what your balance is, they're cleaning up. Instead of you." (See Figure 8–9.)

Body Copy

Body copy, or *text* as it is sometimes called, tells the complete sales story. It is a logical continuation of the headline and subheads. The body copy is set in smaller type than headlines or subheads. Body copy is also where the sale is closed.

The text should relate to the campaign appeal and to the reader's self-interest. It must explain how the product or service being adver-

---

PEOPLE IN ADVERTISING

John Caples

Vice President
Batton, Barton, Durstine & Osborn, Inc.

John Caples, famed master of advertising copy, is a vice president of Batten, Barton, Durstine & Osborn, America's seventh largest advertising agency. Creator of such classic ads as "They laughed when I sat down at the piano," Caples has written copy for scores of nationally advertised products in his more than 50 years of advertising. He has also taught advertising courses at Columbia University and at the Advertising Club of New York.

Noted for his research into scientific methods of testing advertising effectiveness, Caples has lectured extensively on these methods. He has also supervised advertising research for Du Pont, General Electric, U.S. Steel, Lever Bros., Goodrich Tire and Rubber, U.S. Navy, and other major organizations.

Born in New York City, Caples attended Columbia University. He was later nominated to the U.S. Naval Academy at Annapolis, where he earned a B.S. degree. While a student engineer with New York Telephone Company, Caples completed an advertising course at Columbia. He soon became a copywriter for Ruthrauff & Ryan. There he wrote the classic piano ad that was to launch an important new mail-order technique—and his advertising career.

In 1927 Caples joined Batten, Barton, Durstine & Osborn as a copywriter and account executive. He was named a vice president of BBDO in 1941, a

tised satisfies the customer's need. The text may concentrate on a single benefit or several benefits as they relate specifically to the target audience. Copy should be written as if the writer were conversing with one person. Some pointers follow.

1. Don't beat around the bush. Get straight to the point.
2. Be specific, factual. Don't generalize.
3. Avoid superlatives (people usually don't believe them anyway).
4. Be truthful and make the truth fascinating. Don't be a bore.
5. Be enthusiastic, friendly, and memorable. Tell the whole story and no more. When finished, stop.[4]

In writing copy we look for the techniques that provide the greatest sales appeal for the idea we are presenting. The advertising plan gives the direction for *what* to say. Now we're concerned with *how* to say it.

Copy styles fall into several categories. These include straight-line, narrative, institutional, dialogue/monologue, picture-caption, and gimmick.[5]

In *straight-line copy* the body copy begins immediately to explain or develop the headline and illustration in a clear attempt to sell the

---

position he still holds. In a recent interview, Caples made these observations about copywriting:

On word power: "Simple words are powerful words. Even the best educated people don't resent simple words. But they're the words many people understand. Write to your barber or mechanic or elevator operator. Remember, too, that every word is important. Sometimes you can change a word and increase the pulling power of the ad. Once I changed the word *repair* to *fix,* and the ad pulled 20 percent more!"

On humor: "Avoid it. What's funny to one person isn't to millions of others. Copy should sell, not just entertain. Remember there's not one funny line in the two most influential books ever written: the Bible and the Sears catalog."

On changing times: "Times change. People don't. Words like *free* and *new* are as potent as ever. Ads that appeal to a reader's self-interest still work. People may disagree about what self-improvement is important, but we all want to improve ourselves. Ads that offer news still work. The subjects that are news change, but the human curiosity to know what's new doesn't. These appeals worked 50 years ago. They work today. They'll work 50 years hence."

Praising these insights, David Ogilvy, chairman of the board of Ogilvy & Mather, International,

said of John Caples, "He is not only an indomitable analyzer and teacher of advertising, he is also a first-rate copywriter—one of the most effective there has ever been."

Ogilvy hailed Caples' book, *Tested Advertising Methods,* as "the most useful book about advertising that I have ever read." Caples has authored four other books on advertising: *Making Ads Pay, Advertising Ideas, Advertising for Immediate Sales,* and *How to Make Your Advertising Make Money.* Since 1972 he has been a featured monthly columnist in *Direct Marketing Magazine.*

Recipient of the annual award of the National Association of Direct Mail Writers and the Hundred Million Club Leadership Award, Caples was elected to the Copywriters Hall of Fame in 1973. Four years later he was named to the Advertising Hall of Fame. He is listed in *Who's Who in America.*

Slight and soft-spoken, Caples hardly fits the image of Madison Avenue's "man in the gray flannel suit." Yet, as his clients know, few surpass John Caples in the ability to induce people to buy products through skillful, persuasive advertising.

IS YOUR BANK TAKING YOU TO THE CLEANERS?

If your bank isn't paying you interest
on your checking account,
no matter what your balance is, they're cleaning up.
Instead of you.

Most of you aren't earning any interest on your bank checking
accounts. Maybe you didn't ask for it. Or maybe you thought you
needed a balance of $2,500 to get it.
But at Fidelity Federal, you always get the interest you deserve.
We offer only one kind of checking account. The kind you'll like.
It's our Money Market Plus/Checking Account. And it pays interest
all the time. No matter what your balance is.
And there are even more reasons to check into Fidelity Federal.
Like no monthly service charges if you maintain $3000 or more
in any of our savings accounts. Or if you're 62 years or older. We take
a personal interest in your other needs, too. (Ask about our $20
bonus interest on IRA's, for instance.)
So, come see us. It's high time someone showed you some
interest. Instead of leaving you high and dry.

FIDELITY FEDERAL
SAVINGS AND LOAN ASSOCIATION
Assets in excess of $2 Billion

Serving you in Southern California ... Arcadia 1400 S. Baldwin Av. 446-4455; Azusa/Glendora 1273 E. Alosta 335-1206; Bellflower 15908 Bellflower Bl. 925-9521; Beverly Hills 380 S. Beverly Dr. 553-3000; Big Bear Lake 42055 Sandalwood Dr. 866-7525; Blue Jay 27321 North Bay Rd. 337-2421; Buena Park 8480 La Palma Av. 527-7100; Corona Del Mar/Bayside 1111 Bayside Dr. 760-8611; Culver City 10784 Jefferson Bl. 559-7370; Fullerton 911 N. Harbor Bl. 879-7440; Glendale 600 N. Central Bl. 956-7100; Irvine 4482 Barranca Pkwy. 559-7997; Laguna Beach 310 Ocean Av. 497-3521; Lake Forest 25435 Trabuco Road 768-2946; Long Beach 525 E. Ocean Bl. 436-3271; Long Beach East 5767 Pac. Cst. Hwy. 597-6869; Newport Beach 1525 Westcliff Dr. 642-4090; North Hollywood 6350 Laurel Cyn. 985-2900; Northridge 19450 Plummer St. 993-6700; Palm Desert 73-040 El Paseo 340-4424; Placentia 301 E. Yorba Linda Bl. 524-8700; San Pedro 29000 S. Western Av. 832-7500; Santa Ana 1723 N. Main St. 547-9600; Seal Beach 15030 Seal Beach Bl. 598-7620; Sherman Oaks 14475 Ventura Bl. 788-2420; Stanton 12000 Beach Bl. 891-1711; Torrance 24600 Hawthorne Bl. 378-8374; Van Nuys 14545 Victory Bl. 781-4545; West Hollywood 8653 Beverly Bl. 657-4141.

FIGURE 8–9

This ad is a real attack on banks by the savings and loan. Its appeal goes straight to the customer's pocketbook, and, chances are, any bank customers reading it will feel they've been hung out to dry.

product. The product's sales points are ticked off in order of their importance. Straight-line copy is advantageous in industrial situations and for consumer products that may be difficult to use. Many camera advertisements, for example, use this straight, factual copy style to get the message across. The straight-line approach emphasizes the reason the consumer should buy something.

Narrative copy tells a story. It sets up a problem and then creates a solution using the particular sales features of the product or service. It may then suggest that you use the same solution if you have that problem.

Sometimes the advertiser will use *institutional copy* to sell an idea or the merits of the organization or service rather than sales features of a particular product. Often institutional copy is also narrative in style because it lends warmth to the organization. Banks, insurance companies, public utilities, and large manufacturing concerns are the most common users of institutional copy.

Dialogue/monologue copy can add the credibility that narrative copy sometimes lacks. The characters illustrated in the advertisement do the selling in their own words, either through a testimonial or quasi-testimonial technique, or through a comic strip panel. However, lay-people often have trouble writing this kind of copy. The copywriter who uses dialogue should have some playwriting experience. Unless it is done well, dialogue can be dull—not everything people say is interesting (Figure 8–10).

Sometimes it is easier to tell the story through a series of illustrations and captions than through the use of a copy block alone. Then *picture-caption* copy is used. This is especially true when the product is shown in a number of different uses or when it is available in a variety of styles or designs.

Gimmick copy depends on word-plays, humor, poetry, rhyming, great exaggeration, gags, and other trick devices. Don't downgrade gimmick advertising. A gimmick carried out rationally is believable. One institutional campaign featured a pink elephant as a product's speaker. Once readers accepted the pink elephant and laughed, they suddenly discovered themselves thinking about the product and not the speaker.

Humor is a popular form of gimmick copy, particularly in broadcast advertising. It is effective when the advertiser needs high memorability in a short time, and it may be used to destroy an outmoded attitude or use pattern that affects a product. However, humor is also very controversial and should never be used in questionable taste.

There are four basic elements to body copy: the lead-in paragraph, interior, trial, and close.

Lead-in paragraph

The lead-in paragraph is a bridge between the headline, the subheads, and the sales ideas presented in the text. It transfers reading interest to product interest.

Headline: "TV that puts itself to sleep."
Lead-in paragraph: "You don't have to get out of bed to turn off this Zenith portable TV. Just preset the time for up to 3 hours."

The lead-in paragraph may perform other functions as well. In short-copy advertisements (an increasing trend) the lead-in paragraph may also be the close. It may include both a promise and claim-support information.

Interior paragraphs

This is where we provide proof for claims and promises. Remember, a good advertisement not only has to be truthful, it also has to be believable in order to be effective. With educational levels constantly rising and with increased consumer awareness, proofs must be offered carefully. The key to the interior paragraphs is credibility. The proof offered may fall into the following categories:

1. Research: government or private studies.
2. Testing: by case history, testing firm, consumers, or the advertiser.
3. Usage: product market rank, case history, testimonial, endorsements.
4. Guarantee: trial offers, demonstration offers, free samples, warranty information.

Trial close

Interspersed in the interior paragraphs should be requests for the order. Good body copy asks for the order more than once in many cases. In mail-order advertisements particularly, it is necessary to ask for the order several times. Consumers may decide to buy without reading the entire body copy. The trial close gives them the option to make the buying decision before they get bored.

FIGURE 8–10

The drama expressed in the monologue copy brings home the important selling message of this ad. The problem is that after the crisis described has passed, you really don't feel like reading the selling message, most of which is unnecessary, anyway, because you already got the point.

COPYWRITER'S

PORTFOLIO

A. A clever play on words, the headline in this ad points out that Nikon is the preferred camera of professional photographers.

B. (Straw Hat asks for imagination in this daring commercial.)

VOICE OVER: We begin this commercial by closing your eyes. Now, imagine the sensual pleasures of pizza perfected. Straw Hat!
Rich . . . so rich. Tangy. And thick.
Oozing with . . .
Six melt in your mouth . . .
flavors. Mozzarella, Monterey Jack, Romano . . .
Smothered with things fresh . . .
So fresh . . . delicious.
Now . . . open wide. Hey.
You've been dreaming of Straw Hat Pizza. The best tasting pizza you can imagine.
Straw Hat.

C. (The utter simplicity of this copy is what creates its blatant sex appeal.)

SINGER: *Nuance says Yes. Yes. Yes.*

WOMAN 1: No.

SINGER: *Nuance says Yes. Yes. Yes.*

WOMAN 2: No.

SINGER: *Nuance says Yes. Yes. Yes.*

WOMAN 3: No.

SINGER: *Nuance says Yes.*

ANNCR (VO): Nuance says Yes. But you can always say No.

SINGER: *Nuance says Yes. Yes. Yes.*

WOMAN 1: Maybe.

D. Against the stunning backdrop of Everyman's sea-bound dream yacht, four little words say a lot.

E. The exaggerated illustration of the issue raised in the headline brings hilarious humor to this savings and loan ad, making it both attention-getting and unforgettable.

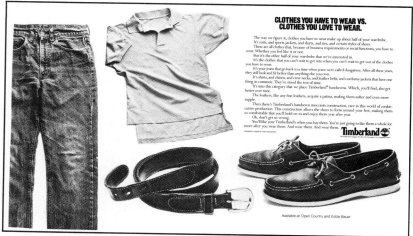

F. The warm, personal appeal of Timberland handsewn moccasins is highlighted by the concept of the clothes you like to wear and grow attached to—the torn, faded jeans, old shirts, and old sweaters. This award-winning campaign helped increase Timberland's sales 50 percent.

G. The brilliance of this ad for International Multifoods' croissants goes beyond the obvious French connection. The sophisticated humor accomplishes the most desirable of advertising tasks—forcing the reader to get involved in the message.

Close

An advertisement's close asks consumers to do something and tells them how to do it. This is the point in the advertisement when the sale is made. We use the word *sale* in its broadest sense. Not all advertisements sell products or services. We may be looking for a change in attitude, an understanding of our point of view, or a new preference for our product or service.

The close can be direct or indirect, ranging from subtle suggestion to direct command. English Leather men's toiletries uses an indirect close in its headline: "My men wear English Leather or they wear nothing at all." The last sentence of the body repeats the same line, suggesting indirectly that if you want to please a woman you will wear English Leather or, conversely, if you want to please a man, you will buy him English Leather. A direct close seeks immediate response. The response may be in the form of a purchase or a request for further details. Levi's ad directed to the trade closes with "Ask your Levi's representative for all the exciting details . . . and be sure to request a swatch of Premiere Corduroy . . ." (Figure 8–11).

The successful close simplifies the reader's response and makes it as easy as possible for the reader to order the merchandise, send for information, or visit a showroom. It makes reader action easy by providing a business reply card for mailing or including a toll-free telephone number. The close tells where to shop or what to send. In fact, everything the reader needs for action should be in the close or near it.

FIGURE 8–11

The dynamic graphics and the arresting headline make it easy to get hooked on this trade ad for Levis. The tight technical copy reinforces the implied benefit in the headline with specific objective information.

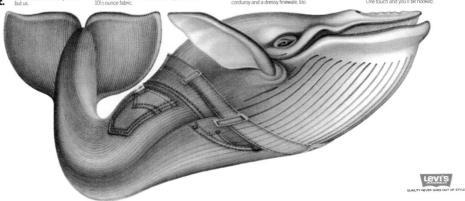

Boxes and Panels

Boxes and panels are generally used in advertisements that contain coupons, special offers, contest rules, and order blanks. The boxes and panels are used to set these features apart from the rest of the advertisement.

Specifically, a *box* is copy around which a line has been drawn. A *panel* is an elongated box that usually runs the whole length or width of an ad. Sometimes it may be shaded or completely black, with text or copy shown in reverse (white lettering).

Boxes and panels are used to draw greater attention to a specific element or message in your advertisement.

Slogans

Slogans (or tag lines) are similar to headlines. In fact, many of them began as successful headlines. They become standard statements for salespeople and company employees. They become a battle cry for the company. In fact, the word *slogan* comes from the Gaelic term for "battle cry."

Slogans have two basic purposes. The first is to provide continuity for a campaign. The second is to reduce a key theme or idea the company wants associated with its product or itself to a brief, memorable positioning statement. DeBeers ads, for example, still claim the famous premise in their tag line: "Diamonds are forever." On the other hand, Water Pik exclaims its promise: "You'll feel good about it" (Figure 8–12).

Slogans are like old friends who stay the same year after year. You recognize them instantly, and you feel you understand them. Some slogans endure because they encapsulate a corporate philosophy: "Quality never goes out of style" (Levi's).

Effective slogans are short, easy to understand, memorable, and easy to repeat. Good slogans help set the product apart from its competitors: "When it rains, it pours" (Morton Salt). Rhyme, rhythm, and alliteration are valuable copy aids to use when writing slogans.

Seals, Logotypes, and Signatures

The term *seal* is the subject of much confusion among advertising students. For some, it indicates the seals offered by such organizations as the Good Housekeeping Institute, Underwriters Laboratories, and Parents Institute. Seals are given only when a product meets standards established by these institutions. Since the organizations are all recognized authorities—and are trusted implicitly—it is beneficial to include the seals in an advertisement. The seals provide an independent, valued endorsement for the advertised product.

For others, the term *seal* refers to the company seal or trademark. These are actually called *logotypes*. Logotypes (logos) and signature cuts (sig cuts) are special designs of the advertiser's name or product name. They appear in all the advertisements and are like trademarks because they give the product individuality and provide quick recognition at the point of purchase. (See the Checklist for writing effective copy.)

Famous smiles depend on the Water Pik® Appliance.

TELEDYNE WATER PIK
You'll feel good about it.

FIGURE   8–12

This Water Pik ad gets attention through the use of a highly recognizable celebrity smile. The tag line promise has a double meaning—you'll be happy you bought it, and your mouth will feel better.

Checklist for writing effective copy

☐ Make it easy on your reader. Write short sentences. Use easy, familiar words.

☐ Don't waste words. Say what you have to say—nothing more, nothing less. Don't pad, but don't skimp. If it takes a thousand words, use a thousand words—as long as not one is excess baggage.

☐ Stick to the present tense, active voice—it's crisper. Avoid the past tense and passive voice—these forms tend to drag. Exceptions should be deliberate, for special effect.

☐ Don't hesitate to use personal pronouns. Remember, you're trying to talk to just *one* person so talk as you would to a friend. Use "you" and "your."

☐ Cliches are crutches: learn to get along without them. Bright, surprising words and phrases perk up readers, keep them reading.

☐ Don't overpunctuate. It kills copy flow. Excessive commas are the chief culprits. Don't give your readers any excuse to jump ship.

☐ Use contractions whenever possible. They're fast, personal, natural. People talk in contractions. (Listen to yourself.)

☐ Don't brag or boast. Everyone hates a bore. Translate those product features you're so proud of into consumer benefits that ring the bell with your readers. Write from the reader's point of view, not your own. Avoid "we," "us," "our."

☐ Be single-minded. Don't try to do too much. If you chase more than one rabbit at a time, you'll catch none.

☐ Write with flair. Drum up excitement. Make sure the enthusiasm you feel comes through in your copy.

COMMON PITFALLS IN WRITING COPY

The key point to remember about copy style is that it must reflect consumer tastes and values. Today's consumer is intelligent, educated, and discriminating. Generalizations are not convincing. The consumer is looking for specific information to form judgments and make purchase decisions. Being specific means leaving out the fancy advertising buzz words. *Amazing, wonderful,* and *finest* all fall into that category.

Words cost money. A print advertisement may cost $50 a word or $5,000 a word, depending on the medium. Every word must count at those prices. Words that do not sell cost more money than words that do. So use words that sell; and avoid the pitfalls that plague beginning copywriters and annoy customers.

● **Obfuscation** The fundamental requirements of any advertisement are that it be readable and understandable. Avoid $10 words (like *obfuscation*) that nobody understands. Write simply in the everyday, colloquial English that people use in conversation. (See the Ad Lab 8–A.) Use small words. You will get your point across better if you use words and phrases that are familiar to your reader. Use short sentences. The longer the sentence, the harder it is to understand. Compare these paragraphs:

AD LAB 8–A   Writing readable advertising copy: A self-test

The Gunning Fog Index is a measure of your writing simplicity. Here's how it works:

Take 100-word samples from any given piece of writing—at least five or six samples if possible.

Count the number of words to the end of the sentence nearest the end of the 100-word sample (this could be more or less than 100) and enter in column 1.

Count the number of sentences in the sample and enter in column 2.

Count the number of sentences in that sample and enter in column 2.

Enter the total in column 3.

Do *not* count:

1. Proper nouns—Chicago, Toronto, California, Jonathan.
2. Compound words made of simple words— bookkeeper, furthermore, nevertheless.
3. Words that become three syllables because of an added verb ending such as -ing or -ed— bargaining, donating, recanted, accounted.

Total each column.

Find the average number of words per sentence; divide the total number of words (column 1) by the total number of sentences (column 2).

Find the average number of words with three syllables or more; divide the total of column 3 by the number of samples.

Add the two averages, then multiply by 0.4. The result is the reading grade level—the Fog Index—for that piece of writing.

Laboratory Application

Select five or six pieces of your writing. Compute the Fog Index.

The Armco vacuum cleaner not only cleans your rugs and drapes, it's invaluable on hard surfaces such as vinyl floors, wood floors, even cement. You won't believe how incredibly smooth and quiet the machine is as it travels across your sparkling floors.

The Armco vacuum cleaner cleans rugs . . . drapes. It cleans hard surfaces like woods and vinyl floors. Even cement! The Armco vacuum cleaner is smooth . . . quiet. Try it! Make your floors sparkle with new cleanliness.

Thousands of advertisements compete for your reader. The more understandable your advertisement, the more likely it will be read.

● **Filibustering** We have discussed the importance of brevity. Look at this headline: "Winston tastes good like a cigarette should." Now imagine if it weren't concise: "Winston cigarettes taste exceedingly fine, the way every cigarette manufacturer wishes his cigarettes would taste."

Long-winded filibusters should be confined to the Senate. They are not allowed in advertising. Be complete, but be concise.

● **Me-me-me** To be effective the advertisement must appeal to the reader's self-interest, not the advertiser's. If you want to get your message across and persuade the reader, use the "you" attitude. Talk in terms of his or her needs, hopes, wishes, and preferences. In an industrial ad for Inter-Tel (Figure 8–13), note the use of you, your, and yourself. Talk about the reader and you are talking about the most interesting person in the world. For example:

Me	You
We are pleased to announce our new flight schedule from Cincinnati to Philadelphia which is any hour on the hour.	You can take a plane from Cincinnati to Philadelphia any hour on the hour.
We believe this vacuum cleaner to be technically superior to any other on the market.	Your house will be more beautiful because you'll be using the most powerful, easy-to-use vacuum we have ever offered.

FIGURE 8–13

Inter-Tel uses a surrealistic John Kleber illustration to break out of the clutter of telephone equipment advertisers swamping the pages of telecommunications trade magazines. This particular ad was specifically designed for one such publication—*Teleconnect*—which is known and liked for its avant-garde use of graphics and satirical editorial content. Amidst all the same-looking advertising for telephone push-buttons, bells, and whistles, Inter-Tel's agency, Phillips-Ramsey/Phoenix, hoped this unique approach would set their client apart. It did.

● **Cliches/triteness/superlatives** Overused expressions do nothing for copy. In fact, at least one study suggests that they harm readability. Most superlatives (greatest, large economy) and cliches (tried and true, a penny saved is a penny earned) were once exciting statements, but time has worn their value into rags.

Certainly cliches can communicate, and not all stock expressions are cliches. But cliches erode consumer confidence. They contribute to an out-of-date image.

● **Abstract/vagueness** Abstract words are words that do not provide a specific measurement, such as *good, fine, OK.* They are not easily understood or evaluated. Concrete words are specific and understood.

Good copy is concrete and tied in with the experience of the audience to which it appeals. Words should have concrete dollars-and-cents value. For example, in an industrial ad for a new piece of equipment, it would be better to be specific and say the machine "performs the work of five people" rather than to simply mention that it's a "work-saving machine."

● **The power of positive thinking** Think negatively, write negatively, and you may produce a negative response. Readers often respond more favorably to a positive viewpoint than to a negative one. Stress what things are or what they will be instead of what they are not or won't be. Remember that words have implications. They can provide a positive or negative response apart from literal meanings. Also, be aware that different people react to the same word in different ways. *Love*, that most beautiful word, may have a positive note for a single person and a negative connotation for a divorced person.

● **Euphemisms** To *euphemize* is to substitute an inoffensive, mild word for a word that is offensive, harsh, or blunt. When a copywriter euphemizes, he or she puts a good face on something. Calling toilet paper "bathroom tissue" doesn't change its appearance or function, but it may soften the mental impression for people. Other euphemisms are "resale cars" (for used cars), "package store" (for liquor store), "underarm wetness" (for sweaty armpits), "irregularity" (for constipation), and "midriff bulge" (for fat gut). But be careful in choosing euphemisms, they can be misleading, weaken your message, and, if considered fradulent, could invite investigation by the Federal Trade Commission.

● **Defamation** All advertising copy is governed by the laws of defamation. Making a false statement or allegation about a person or holding a person up to contempt is defamation. When this is done in print advertising it is called *libel*. In broadcast advertising or verbal statements it is called *slander*. Defamation occurs even when people's names are used or references are made to them in a libelous or slanderous manner. Size of audience is not a defense; a libelous statement, for example, need only be read by more than one person to be defamation.

CREATING NAMES

FOR PRODUCTS

Copywriters are sometimes called on to develop a name for a new product or a new name for an old product. Here are some ways in which names are chosen.

● **Personal names** One of the most common ways of labeling your product is to name it after yourself: Gerber baby foods, Hershey chocolate, Ford automobile. Problems occur, however, because people have similar names. Names can be easily copied, and it can be difficult to stop other people from using their own names on their products.

● **Geographic names** If a geographic name is used in an arbitrary manner, it may function as a trademark. However, if it identifies a product's place of origin or suggests where the product may have come from, it may not function as a trademark.

● **Coined or invented names** The most distinctive names are often coined or invented. Kodak was coined by George Eastman because he wanted a name beginning and ending with an infrequently used letter. Kleenex, Xerox, Betty Crocker, and Polaroid are other examples. They have an advantage because they are short, pronounceable, and arbitrary. It's unlikely others will use anything similar (Figure 8–14).

● **Initials or numbers** Some of the more common examples are IBM computers, RCA televisions, 7-11 stores, and A-1 steak sauce.

● **Company name** The company name is sometimes used also as a brand name—for example, Texaco, Gulf, Shell.

FIGURE 8–14

The Polaroid trademark was coined from the optical concept of polarization. The camera that carries the trademark was originally called the Polaroid Land camera in honor of its founder, Edwin Land.

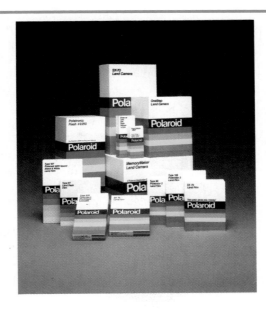

● **Foreign words** Perfume companies often use French words to project an image of romance (Vol De Nuit). Auto manufacturers use foreign words to add mystery and intrigue: Cordova, Biarritz.

● **Licensed names** Sometimes manufacturers license names for their marketability (Snoopy toothbrushes, Mickey Mouse watches). The prices are often steep, and the use of the name is subject to tight restrictions.

● **Dictionary words** Some of the most successful products have dictionary names: Tide detergent, Whirlpool appliances, Arrow shirts.

Arbitrary marks are dictionary words that have nothing to do with product identification. They are more easily protected than words that have some relationship to the product. Examples of arbitrary marks are Cheer and Bold detergents. Cars are often given names of animals: Mustang, Cougar, Jaguar, Barracuda.

Summary

Art is the visual presentation of the message strategy, and copy is the verbal presentation of the message. Before beginning to write, the copywriter must understand the intended marketing and advertising strategy. This usually requires a review of the marketing and advertising plan, an analysis of the facts, and an examination of the creative strategy. The copywriter should develop a brief, written copy platform that tells what the copy will say and how it will support the message strategy.

To create an effective advertisement, the copywriter seeks to gain attention, create interest, achieve credibility, heighten desire, and stimulate action.

The key copy elements in print advertising are headlines, subheads, body copy, captions, boxes and panels, slogans, logotypes, seals, and signatures. In broadcast advertising, copy is normally spoken dialogue and is referred to as the audio portion of the commercial. The copy may be delivered as a voice-over by an unseen announcer or on-camera by an announcer, spokesperson, or actor.

There are many types of headlines and copy styles. Good advertising headlines can generally be classified into five basic categories: (1) benefit, (2) provocative, (3) news/information, (4) question, and (5) command. Copy styles also fall into several categories. These are (1) straight line, (2) narrative, (3) institutional, (4) dialogue/ monologue, (5) picture-caption, and (6) gimmick.

The pitfalls for unsuspecting copywriters are many and varied. The most common ones are obfuscation, filibustering, cliches/triteness/superlatives, abstract/vagueness, me me me, negative thinking, misleading euphemisms, and unintentional defamation.

Copywriters may develop names for products. Personal names, geographic names, coined or invented names, initial or numbers, foreign words, licensed names, and dictionary words provide the basis for the selection of names of most products.

Questions for review and discussion

1. Based on an advertisement you have selected in this chapter, what is the advertiser's message strategy?
2. Based on an ad of your choice, how well has the advertiser achieved the five objectives of effective advertising copy? Explain.
3. Select a magazine advertisement you like. What functions are provided by the elements in the ad?
4. Choose an advertisement you don't like. How would you rewrite the headline using three different styles?
5. Find an advertisement with a tag line. What is its function, and what is your opinion of it?
6. Select an advertisement or commercial that you like. What issues did the advertiser have to consider in writing the copy platform? Discuss.
7. What are the six basic functions of a headline?
8. What are some of the most effective methods for making copy interesting?
9. Find an advertisement that you don't like. What is the message strategy? What type of headline is used? What is the copy style? Do you think the copy and headline reflect the strategy? What don't you like about the ad? Why?
10. If you had just invented a new soft drink, what would you name it? Why?

9

CREATIVE ART DIRECTION

J ohn Weiss still talks about that most risky and precious of opportunities he had—the chance to establish new standards in a new, uncharted market.

It all started just a few years ago when Godiva (the luxury chocolatier, not the mythical unclad equestrienne) came to him and John Margeotes of Margeotes/Fertitta & Weiss in search of promotional assistance. Unfortunately, the client was unable to give much help in formulating a campaign strategy because the luxury chocolate market was virtually nonexistent.

"It was really virgin territory," recalls Weiss. "We had no statistics as to who bought the chocolates or how much they were willing to pay."

With no established precedents to rely on, the Margeotes creative team journeyed to the source for inspiration—the Godiva plant. They toured the factory and saw people working with masks and gloves, discarding anything with a nick on it. They obviously had a love for the product.

The immediate challenge for Weiss, as the copywriter, and Margeotes, as the art director, was to translate this devotion into a commercially potent campaign.

For Weiss and Margeotes, and for all creative people, the first step in designing any advertisement or commercial is always the toughest. It's the long, tedious, difficult task of analyzing the problem, assembling any and all pertinent information, and developing some verbal or visual concept of how to communicate what needs to be said. This visualization process means establishing a mental idea or picture of the advertisement, commercial, or campaign before any copy is written or artwork begun.

The process may be called *visualization*, *conceptualization*, or *ideation*, and it is the most important step in planning the advertisement. It is the creative point where the search for the "big idea" takes place. In this process, 5, 10, 20, 100, or more ideas may come up, be considered, and then be rejected for any of a variety of reasons. Then it's back to the drawing board. Twenty more ideas. Some good, some not so good, some bad. No big ideas. Nothing clicks. That's when creative people recall the phrase: "Advertising is 10 percent inspiration, 90 percent perspiration."

In searching for the big idea for Godiva, Margeotes and Weiss worked through a wide variety of concepts. The stakes were high because, they believed, a lackluster effort would be completely obscured by the traditionally crowded field of upscale advertisers.

Weiss explains, "We wanted people to understand that Godiva's are more than just chocolates. They're exclusive, and they represent a chance for people to own something that's the best of its kind."

Finally they decided to present the chocolates in an elegant, dreamlike setting. As the dark of night bleeds off all sides of the page, a soft spot of light would fall upon the chocolates, creating a seductive, classy visual layout. Complementing this scene would be a brief, provocative headline and a short paragraph of exquisite copy using classic Shakespearean allusions or subtle wordplays ("Mint Summer Night's Dream") to lend a poetic mood to the ads. The copy would be enticing but never too sweet.[1]

That was it. The big idea. That inspired creative nutshell, out of which grow all the verbal and visual details of every great advertisement. It was this concept that would give birth to the Godiva mystique (Figure 9–1).

In this chapter we will discuss the visual details, the art in advertising—what it is, where it comes from, how it's done.

WHAT IS ART?

In advertising, *art* refers to more than what a cartoonist, a painter, or an illustrator does. The term refers to the whole visual presentation of the commercial or advertisement including how the words in the ad are arranged, what size and style of type are used, whether photos or illustrations are used, and, if so, how they should be organized. Art also refers to what style of photography or illustration is employed, how color is used, and how these elements are arranged in an ad and relate to one another in size and proportion.

In short, if copy is the spoken language of an ad, art is the body language. This is true for both print ads and television commercials. Art directors are as involved as copywriters in writing and producing the commercials we see on TV. In fact, many of the finest agencies even have their art directors help write radio commercials. Their feeling is that effective radio advertising combines sounds and words to create visual *word pictures* in the mind of the listener. To help orchestrate this visual side of the radio commercial, the art director can be very instrumental. Thus, every advertisement uses *art*—even if sometimes it is not good art.

FIGURE 9–1

Elegant poster-style layout and stunning photographic treatment of sculpted candies. The ad tells the price without ever mentioning it and demonstrates a broad departure from typical candy advertising.

ROLE OF THE
ADVERTISING ARTIST

There are several different types of people employed in advertising art. All of them may be called artists as a general description even though they may perform entirely different tasks. What is often surprising to nonadvertising people is that so many of these "artists" cannot draw. They have been trained for other artistic specialties.

Art Directors

Art directors are responsible for the visual presentation of the ad. They are therefore normally involved, with a copywriter, in the initial concept of the ad. They may do the initial sketches, or layouts, of what the ad might look like. But from that point on, they may not touch the ad again themselves, except to supervise its progress to completion.

The best art directors are strong conceptually in both words and pictures. They are usually highly trained in pure graphic design and experienced in various aspects of advertising and art, and they must be good managers of people. They may have a large or small staff under them, depending on the organization. Or they may work free lance, in which case they probably do more of the work that would normally be handled by assistants on agency art department staffs.

Graphic Designers

Graphic designers are responsible for the shape, dimension, and placement of the elements in an ad. The initial design of the ad dictates its artistic direction and eventually determines whether the ad is to be stunning, beautiful, a "work of art" or just another ad. To avoid the latter, graphic designers are employed.

Designers are precision specialists. They are preoccupied with the shape and form of things, and their effort in advertising is to arrange the various elements in the ad in the most attractive and effective way possible. Often the art director acts as the designer, too. Sometimes, however, a separate designer is employed to offer a unique touch to a particular ad (Figure 9–2).

FIGURE   9–2

The unusual design says "speed" in this spread for Volkswagen's sports car. The headline relates the perspective of the photo to the sensation you will get driving a Scirocco. The body copy ties it all together by talking about the car built for the no-speed-limit autobahns of Germany.

Illustrators

The artists who paint or draw the pictures we see in ads are called *illustrators*. One of the greatest illustrators in this century was Norman Rockwell, whose pictures brought life to the cover of the *Saturday Evening Post* every week.

Illustrators are specialists. They are so specialized, in fact, that many frequently concentrate on just one type of illustrating. Fashion illustrators, for example, specialize in drawing clothing. Their training enables them to catch a particular look and communicate the unique feel of a garment. Furniture illustrators do the same thing with home furnishings. They might draw a manufacturer's sofa, for example, in pencil or with watercolors, paying great attention to the fabric upholstery or wood veneer and showing it all off in a beautiful living room setting.

Illustration is such a specialty that most advertising illustrators work free lance. Very few agencies or advertisers retain full-time illustrators unless their work is of such a volume and so specialized that they require the continuous efforts of one type of illustrator (Figure 9–3).

Production Artists

Production or *paste-up* artists are responsible for assembling the various elements of an ad and mechanically putting them together the way the art director or designer indicated. Good production artists are fast, precise, and knowledgeable about the whole production process (see Chapter 10). In addition, they have the ability to stand the tedious task of bending over a drawing board all day assembling

FIGURE 9–3

Nocona boots uses a superb photo-realistic illustration to demonstrate the desirability of their product and create a super-macho image for the purchaser. Notice the detail of the stitching on the boots, the strands of hemp in the rein, the look of contempt in the horse's eye for the cowboy who is now upside down in mid-air, and even the subtle humor of the Let's Rodeo ring on the cowboy's fist. Note also the graphic design creating a gaze motion down through the ad ending right at the company logo.

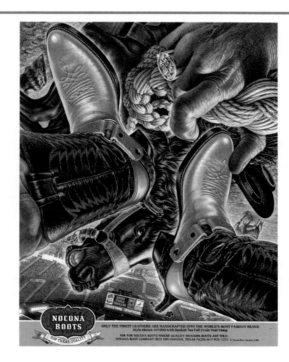

little pieces of type, drawing perfectly straight, clean lines with a pen, or cutting delicate photographs with a sharp knife.

Most art directors and designers start as production artists and work their way up. It's very difficult work, but it is also important, since this is where the ads actually come together in their finished form.

DESIGNING THE ADVERTISEMENT

The market for motorcycles in the United States and Canada is extremely large. It is also highly fragmented, with products from Germany, Italy, Sweden, England, and Japan successfully competing with American machines. To America's cyclists, many of these bikes might look alike. However, the manufacturers of Yamaha motorcycles felt that their Japanese bikes were superior to the rest in engineering, design, and performance. The question was how to communicate this.

Yamaha turned to its American agency, Botsford-Ketchum (San Francisco), for help. The agency responded with a campaign that not only won numerous awards for its excellent copy, art, and design, but also set a new international standard for motorcycle advertising.[2]

PEOPLE IN ADVERTISING

George H. Lois

President
Lois Pitts Gershon

George H. Lois, hailed by *The New York Times* as "perhaps the most outstanding art director in America," is president of Lois Pitts Gershon and has had an indelible influence on American advertising.

The son of Greek immigrant parents, born and raised in the upper Bronx, Lois attended P.S. 7, where his drawings were spotted by a teacher. She not only sent him to take the entrance exam for Manhattan's famed High School of Music and Art in 1945, but even gave him the dime for round-trip subway fare. Lois was accepted.

After high school Lois entered Pratt Institute to study art. A professor there decided Lois's talents were too advanced for what Pratt could offer and sent him to see design studio owner Reba Sochis. She examined Lois's portfolio and promptly hired him.

At 21 Lois became an art director at CBS. He then joined Lennen & Newell. That same year he created the first of the 92 brash, compelling covers he was to produce for *Esquire* magazine over the next 10 years. Lois was soon hired by Sudler & Hennessey. A year later he went on to Doyle Dane Bernbach. There his work captured three gold medals in the New York Art Directors Club annual

The campaign combined beautiful photography, sophisticated technical illustration, and straightforward, factual copy in a series of inviting, easy-to-read, full-color page ads and two-page spreads. Each ad supported the campaign theme: "When you know how they're built, you'll buy a Yamaha." The ads resembled the editorial format of slick specialty magazines. As such, the ads built great credibility with readers because readers were familiar with that editorial format in nonadvertising situations.

Over several years the ads grew in sophistication in both copy and illustration as readers became more familiar with the technical terminology associated with motorcycles. Unique features of Yamaha's superiority in engineering were shown with small *call-outs* or captions next to the photo illustrations. The illustrations became more intricate and diagrammatic as the agency introduced the design changes on new Yamaha models.

In test after test, the Yamaha ads consistently scored first or second in consumer memorability. Dealer feedback was excellent. And within two years Yamaha's share of market rose three points, placing it behind only Honda in the American market.

What set Yamaha's advertising apart was, again, the "big idea"—the same thing that sets all good advertising apart. In this case the big idea was the unique art direction, design, and execution in each ad in the campaign. Not only was the art concept unique and brilliantly

competition. After stints at several other agencies, he is today president of Lois Pitts Gershon.

Heralded by *ANNY* as one of America's "most promising new agencies," Lois Pitts Gershon has already achieved $35 million in annual billings. Today it occupies an entire floor of New York's prestigious Piaget building. Agency clients include *USA Today*, MTV, Nickelodeon, and Dreyfus Corporation. According to the LPG philosophy, "Great advertising not only conveys what has to be said about a product, but does so with a sense of theater and style." These two qualities—theater and style—describe the maverick, often outrageous creative output of George H. Lois.

Explaining Lois's unorthodox style, Bill Pitts, executive vice president of Lois Pitts Gershon, wrote, "Headlines must sound like the words and cadences people use. Copy has to read like images, not abstractions. But above all else," Pitts emphasized, "coming up with the unexpected always matters most."

Lois confirmed this when he told an audience recently, "Advertising should aim to be seemingly outrageous." The reason? Advertising must be *visible* to be effective. It can be made visible, Lois said, by following these 10 rules:

1. Make advertising human.
2. Believe in advertising as though your life depended on it.
3. Talk in prose that everyone relates to.
4. Create concepts, not ads.
5. Never settle for *almost* perfect.
6. Never try to please the trade ahead of the consumer.
7. Never be defeated by government or industry regulations.
8. Relate to the *real* world.
9. Take risks.
10. Listen to your heart—and respect your instincts.

Today Lois continues to create uncommon, often audacious campaigns. Arriving at his drawing table at 7:30 each morning, he works directly on every project, personally rendering each frame of his storyboards and tracing every word he sets in type.

Lois's 92 *Esquire* covers and numerous other triumphs of his prolific 30-year career are featured in his book, *The Art of Advertising: George Lois on Mass Communication*. He has been inducted into both the Art Directors and the Creative Halls of Fame.

executed, but, most important, it was also relevant to the subject matter, the audience, the objectives of the company, and the verbal presentation in the headline and the copy.

Laying Out the Ad

One of the most impressive features about the Yamaha ads is the layout and design. Note how the copy is set in neat, easy-to-read columns and yet works in and around the central, dynamic illustration. Note the attractiveness of the style of type used in the headline and body copy and the effective use of rules and lines to structure the ad and organize the reading material. Finally, notice the total unity and balance in spite of the number of elements in the ad. The Yamaha campaign is an appropriate demonstration of the importance of layout and design to advertising (Figure 9–4).

For print media, the first work from the art department is usually seen in the form of a *layout*, which is simply a pencil design of the advertisement within the specified dimensions. The term is used when referring to newspaper, magazine, and outdoor and transit advertisements. For direct-mail and point-of-purchase materials, which often require a three-dimensional presentation of the message, the layout is referred to as a *dummy*. For television, the script of a commercial is first seen as a layout in the form of a *storyboard*, which is a series of pictures or frames that correspond to the script.

The Use of Layouts

A layout is an orderly formation of the parts of the advertisement: headline, subheads, illustration, copy, picture captions, trademarks, slogans, and signature (or logotype).

The layout has two purposes. One is a mechanical function. The layout works as a blueprint, showing where the parts of the ad are to

FIGURE   9–4

One of a series of award-winning ads for Yamaha motorcycles. Notice the lack of company signature at the bottom of the ad. This was intended to impart an editorial feeling in order to build credibility for the product's quality and the company's engineering skill. The volume and intricacy of work on the Yamaha campaign required the full-time efforts of three art directors, each of whom supervised a staff of other art specialists.

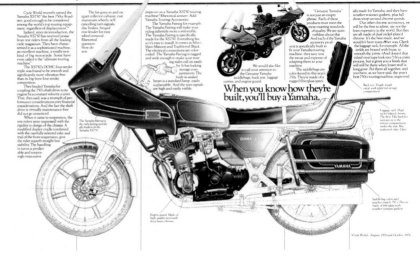

FIGURE 9–5

J. Walter Thompson used this approach to challenge would-be copywriters to complete a test of their skills and compete for a position at the agency. The ad, which ran in *The New York Times* and in college newspapers, was intended to allow job applicants to display their imagination. Note the interesting design with the bold headline and the wraparound type. As a fun exercise, try your hand at one or two of the test questions.

be placed. It guides the copywriter in determining the amount of copy to write. It helps the illustrator or photographer determine the size and style of pictures to be used. It helps the art director plan the size and style of type to be used. And it is also helpful in determining costs (Figure 9–5).

The second purpose of the layout is a psychological or symbolic function. As the Godiva story suggested, the ad's layout, as well as its execution, creates the feeling of the product. Depending on the way the layout is designed, it can be crucial in determining the image a business or product will present. For example, many food and drug stores lay their ads out in a cluttered, busy manner with rows and rows of items and bold, black prices. This is typical of bargain-basement advertising, and the purpose is to create the image of a store for bargain hunters. On the other hand, stores that offer higher quality merchandise, service, and status at higher prices will tend to use large, beautiful illustrations, often in color, small blocks of copy, and ample white space.

Both types of layouts communicate store image and provide blueprint directions for the production artist. Therefore, when designing the initial layout, the art director must be very sensitive to the desired image of the product or business and use a format that projects that image. (See Ad Lab 9–A.) In the case of Yamaha, that was one of the primary reasons for the combination of editorial and picture-caption layout. The ad presented a highly credible image instantly.

Steps in Advertising Layout

Each step in the layout process serves a particular purpose. For a specific ad, all or some of the steps may be performed. Layouts are relied on as guides in the development of the advertisement by those who are working on it and by those who must approve it (Figure 9–6).

AD LAB 9–A   Which ad would you select?

Laboratory Application

Assume you are the advertising manager for Hathaway shirts and your advertising agency brought you the pictured ad layouts for a new campaign. Which ad would you select? Why?

It takes courage to be a good advertising person. Mike Turner, the senior vice president of Ogilvy & Mather and managing director of OM's Houston office, offered this fictitious example of how a fearful agency account team systematically botched up a marvelous advertisement. Creating great advertising requires trust between the advertising manager and the creative team. Both must possess the courage to give the advertiser what is needed, rather than what he or she wants. The agency needs the courage to present it. The advertiser needs the vision to recognize its greatness and the courage to buy it.

In this example, ad 1 is the famous Hathaway shirt ad as it originally was conceived in the mid-1950s. The ad created an outstanding image for Hathaway and made the agency, Ogilvy & Mather, famous. However, an ac-count team terrified of taking risks nearly destroyed it at its birth.

When the ad was presented to an account executive at the agency, he added the ugly panel at the left (ad 2) and changed the strong, simple statement to a lackluster headline. Next in came a woman (ad 3) to add sex appeal. Then (ad 4), off went the "risky" eyepatch. Why? Because people might associate it with unpleasant eye diseases.

As Turner says, "this account team was so busy trying to outguess what the client wanted that they never gave one moment's thought to what was needed, and in the process a great advertisement was destroyed."

But what would you have done if the agency had presented these four layouts? Would you have had the courage to buy the "risky" ad? Or would you have taken the "safe" route?

Turner suggests that if an account person wants safety, he should go quickly and sign up as a tour guide on a cruise ship since he's great at the "at your pleasure" bit.

Thumbnail sketches

These are miniature sketches approximately one-fourth to one-eighth the size of the finished ad. They are used for trying out ideas. The best sketch can be chosen for further development.

Rough layout

The next step is the rough layout, which is drawn to the size of the actual ad. The headlines and subheads are lettered onto the layout, the artwork and intended photographs are drawn, and the body copy is simulated with pencil lines.

If the advertisement is to be a television commercial, the proposed scenes in the commercial are drawn in storyboard form—in a series of boxes shaped like TV screens. The copy corresponding to each scene is indicated underneath each frame along with a description of sound effects and music.

FIGURE 9–6

Thumbnails and rough layout—critical steps in creating the finished advertisement.

A. Thumbnail sketch.

B. Rough layout.

C. Finished advertisement.

Comprehensive layout

This is a facsimile of the finished advertisement and is prepared so the advertiser can gauge the effect of the ad. Copy is set in type and pasted into position. The illustrations are very carefully drawn. If a photograph will be included, it is pasted into position as well.

In national consumer advertising, the cost of producing layouts is often covered by the commission the agency receives from the media. It's not uncommon, though, for a client to be charged for the expense of a "comp" because comps are normally created for the client's benefit rather than for the agency's.

Mechanical

Once the type has been set and the illustrations created or photographs taken, these elements of the ad are pasted into the exact position where they will appear in the final ad. This *mechanical* (or *paste-up*) is then used as a direct basis for the next step in the reproduction process. (See Chapter 10, "Creative Production: Print Media.")

Dummy

For layouts of brochures and other multipage materials, a dummy is prepared. It is put together, page for page, to look just like the finished product. A dummy may go through the thumbnail, rough, comprehensive, and mechanical stages just as a regular layout does.

■ Which Kind of Layout Design Works Best?

Readership studies over the years indicate that the highest scoring advertisements usually use a standard layout with a single, dominant illustration that occupies between 60 and 70 percent of the ad's total area.[3] Next in ranking are ads that have one large picture and two more that are smaller. The illustration is there to stop the reader and arouse attention. Therefore, the content of the picture or pictures should also be interesting.

FIGURE 9–7

This stunning poster, created by free lancers Jim Newcombe and Bob Barrie as a public service for the Alumni Club of the University of Minnesota, also ran as an inside bus card. Reaction to it was so strong that other universities requested copies for their own use.

Headlines are also intended to stop the reader. Research shows that short statements in one line are best but that a second line is acceptable. The total headline area needs to fill only 10 to 15 percent of the ad, so the type does not have to be particularly large. Headlines may appear above or below the photograph depending on the situation (Figure 9–7).

Copy blocks should not be too long. Although long-copy ads can certainly be effective, research shows that readership drops considerably if ads have more than 50 words. Therefore, if the motive is to attract a large number of readers, copy blocks should be kept to less than 20 percent of the ad.

Finally, company signatures do not have to be particularly large. Most people who read ads also read who placed the ad. So company signatures or logos do not need to occupy more than 5 to 10 percent of the area. For best results they should be placed in the lower right-hand corner or across the bottom of the ad. (See the Checklist of design principles.)

ADVERTISING
ILLUSTRATION

Most people who are unfamiliar with advertising think that an artist is someone who paints or draws. As we discussed at the beginning of this chapter, many advertising artists have no talent for drawing at all. Their talent lies in the area of design or art direction, or in the mechanical areas of paste-up and production.

The artists who paint, sketch, and draw in advertising are called *illustrators*. The artists who produce pictures with a camera are called *photographers*. Together they are responsible for all the illustrations or pictures we see in advertising.

■ Purpose of Illustration

Most readers of advertisements (1) look at the illustration, (2) read the headline, and (3) read the body copy, in that order. If any one of these elements fails, the impact of the advertisement is decreased. The illustration, therefore, carries a great deal of responsibility for the success of an advertisement. Some advertisements have no illustrations because someone made a conscious decision that an illustration was not needed in order for effective communication to occur. However, if an illustration is used, it must do one or more of the following:

1. Capture the attention of the reader.
2. Identify the subject of the advertisement.
3. Qualify readers by stopping those who are legitimate prospects and letting others skip over the ad if they are so inclined.
4. Arouse interest in reading the headline.
5. Create a favorable impression of the product or the advertiser.
6. Clarify claims made by the copy.
7. Help convince the reader of the truth of claims made in the copy.
8. Emphasize unique features of the product.
9. Provide continuity for all advertisements in the campaign through the use of the same illustrative technique in each individual ad.[4]

Illustrative Techniques

Illustrations are chosen on the basis of their need, cost, the technical limitations of producing them, time required to obtain them, effect desired, printing process to be used, paper on which they are to be printed, and availability of the artist who can produce what is needed in the medium desired.

Checklist of design principles

Balance

☐ The reference point that determines the balance of a layout is the optical center. The optical center is about one eighth above the physical center, or five eighths from the bottom of the page. Balance is the arrangement of the elements as they are positioned on the page—the left side of the optical center versus the right, and above the optical center versus below. There are two kinds of balance, formal and informal.

☐ Formal balance. Perfect symmetry is the key to formal balance: *matched elements* on either side of a line dissecting the ad have equal optical weight. This is used to strike a dignified, stable, conservative image.

☐ Informal balance. By placing elements of *different* size, shape, intensity of color, or darkness at different distances from the optical center, a visually balanced presentation can be achieved. Just like a teeter-totter, an object of greater optical weight near the center can be balanced by an object of less weight placed farther from the center. Most advertisements use informal balance because it makes the ad more interesting, imaginative, and exciting.

Movement

☐ The principle of design that causes the reader of an advertisement to read the material in the sequence desired is called movement. This can be achieved through a variety of techniques.

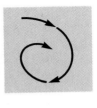

☐ Through the use of *gaze motion*, the placement of people or animals in the advertisement so that their eyes direct our eyes to the next important element to be read.

☐ By the use of mechanical devices such as pointing fingers, rectangles, lines, or arrows to direct attention from element to element or, in television, by moving the actors or the camera or by changing scenes.

☐ Through the use of comic-strip sequence and pictures with captions that force the reader to start at the beginning and follow the sequence in order to grasp the message.

☐ By using white space and color to emphasize a body of type or an illustration. Eyes will go from a dark element to a light, from color to noncolor.

☐ By taking advantage of the natural tendency of readers to start at the top left corner of the page and proceed on a diagonal Z motion to the lower right corner.

☐ By using size itself, which attracts attention because readers are drawn to the biggest and most dominant element on the page and then to the smaller elements.

The two basic devices for illustrating an advertisement are photography and drawn or painted illustrations.

■ *Photography*

There are several important contributions that a good photograph can make to an advertisement.

Proportion

☐ Elements in an advertisement should be accorded space based on their importance to the complete advertisement. For best appearance, elements frequently use varying amounts of space in some proportion, such as three or two, to avoid the monotony of equal amounts of space for each element.

Contrast

☐ An effective way of drawing attention to a particular element is with the use of contrast in color, size, or style. For example, reverse (white letters on a dark background), or a black and white ad with a red border, or an ad with an unusual type style creates contrast and draws attention.

Continuity

☐ Continuity refers to the relationship of one ad to the rest of the campaign. This is achieved by using the same design format, style, and tone for all advertisements, by using the same spokesperson in commercials, by incorporating an unusual and unique graphic element in all ads, or by the consistent use of other techniques such as a logo, a cartoon character, or a catchy slogan.

Unity

☐ Unity is the ad's bonding agent. It means that, although the ad is made up of many different parts, these elements relate to one another in such a way that the ad gives a harmonious impression. Balance, movement, proportion, contrast, and color may all contribute to unity of design. In addition, many other techniques can be used:

☐ Type styles from the same family.

☐ Borders around ads to hold elements together.

☐ Overlapping one picture or element over another.

☐ Judicious use of white space.

☐ Graphic tools such as boxes, arrows, or tints.

Clarity and Simplicity

☐ Any elements that can be eliminated without damaging the effect the advertiser is trying to achieve should be eliminated. Too many different type styles; type that is too small; too many reverses, illustrations, or boxed items; and unnecessary copy make layout complex and too busy. It makes the advertisement hard to read and hurts the overall effect desired.

White Space (Isolation)

☐ White space is the part of the advertisement that is not occupied by other elements (even though the color of the background may be black or some color other than white). White space can be used to focus attention to an isolated element. Put a vast amount of white space around a block of copy and it almost appears as if it's in a spotlight. White space has a great deal to do with the image the artist desires to create.

FIGURE   9–8

In this poster layout eye-stopper aimed at dancers, Danskin's agency, Grey Advertising, stretched its creative muscle and came up with an appealing photographic tribute to sinew and muscle.

Realism People like to see the "real thing" in their ads. Good color photography does wonders for all kinds of products, from gleaming cars to steaming bowls of soup. Just look at the food photography in any homemaker's magazine.

The feeling of "it's happening now" Photographs—especially news type photographs—put you right on the spot. You are standing on the goal line when the touchdown is scored. You are on the race-track approaching the finish line, and you get the checkered flag. You are personally involved in the action.

Making the "cartoon effect" come alive Photographers have done some wonderful things in taking cartoon situations and giving them the added dimension of realism. A drawing of the famous eye-patched Hathaway man, for instance, might be effective, but it would lack the dynamic realism of a photograph of the actual man.

Adding mood, beauty, and sensitivity A photograph can carry a tremendous emotional wallop—like the picture of a battered wife or an abused child. Some photographers, though, are able to achieve a high artistic level with their pictures—as in the case of Godiva chocolates or the Danskin poster at left (Figure 9–8).

Speed, flexibility, and economy A drawing or painting takes longer to complete than a photograph. In fact, several photographs can be taken at one session. And if the advertiser doesn't want to pay for custom photographs to be taken, *stock* photos of popular situations, people, and places can usually be purchased at reasonable cost.[5]

It is not unusual for a photographer to take hundreds of shots before being satisfied. The photographer may shoot a wide variety of poses at various angles and with various light settings. The negatives are then printed on a *contact sheet* in small size and in unretouched form. With the use of a magnifying glass, the art director finds the photo that is most suitable for use.

Photography offers flexibility since photographs can be cropped to any size or shape and retouched with a paint brush or airbrush to improve the image.

When a photograph is sold, whether it is a stock photo or a photograph taken by a commissioned photographer, a "legal release" is necessary. In the case of stock photos, the stock photo house will take care of legal releases. However, for photographs that are commissioned, any individuals who appear in the picture must sign a standard release (available from most stationery stores), which grants permission to the advertiser for the photo's use. For children, the release must be signed by the parent or guardian.

In addition, copyright laws restrict the rights of advertisers to use the work of photographers without compensating them equitably. The price a photographer charges, therefore, frequently depends on the intended use of the work. If the advertiser later decides to use the photograph in additional ways, the photographer usually has to be paid more money. These agreements are negotiable and should always be put in writing in advance.

Drawings

There are times when it is better to use drawn illustrations than photographs either because the advertiser wants to illustrate an event that has already taken place or one that will take place in the future, or because the drawing will produce greater impact.

Illustrators are limited only by their own skill. Unlike photographers, they have no need to find just the right setting or the right models. The artist has the freedom to create the impression or effect desired through personal style, as exemplified by Norman Rockwell. In this way, drawings, like cartoons, can exaggerate in ways a photograph cannot.

The Yamaha campaign used technical illustrators, who have the ability to work from blueprints if necessary, to create a precise picture of a product and its intricate components.

There are a number of techniques (media) illustrators use to produce drawings. These include (1) line drawings, (2) wash drawings, (3) scratchboard, (4) pencil, crayon, and charcoal, and (5) oil, acrylic, tempera, and watercolor.

Line drawings These are excellent for providing clear detail and sharpness. There are no shades of gray; everything is either black or white. Sometimes referred to as pen-and-ink drawings, line drawings are less costly than drawings with tonal values. Cartoons are frequently done as line drawings. Line drawings are used quite often for small illustrations or in small ads.

Wash drawings Sometimes it is too expensive or too time-consuming to photograph a situation. A wash drawing might then be used. As a painting done in various shades of one color, it can be almost as realistic as a black-and-white photograph. Moreover, it can overcome the limitations of a camera. There are two types of wash drawings: tight and loose. A tight drawing is quite detailed and is much more realistic than a loose drawing. It comes closest to a photograph as an illustrative technique. A loose wash drawing is more impressionistic. This technique is used extensively by fashion illustrators.

Scratchboard On a special paper with a surface specifically made for this art form, black ink is applied to the area of the illustration. With the use of a scratching device (a stylus or other sharp instrument), the ink is removed and a white line remains. The artwork is distinctive and different, and gives the impression of fine workmanship. It is also quite expensive.

Other illustrative techniques There are numerous other media used to draw illustrations. These include pencil, crayon, airbrush, and charcoal illustrations as well as oil, acrylic, tempera, and watercolor paintings. All these media are used for the individual effect each creates, but they are less common in advertising than either line or wash drawings. They are normally used when the artist wishes to convey an impressionistic feeling or create a solid, dignified image of quality (Figure 9–9).

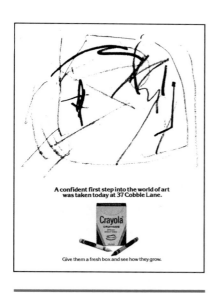

Figure 9–9

A clever use of crayon illustration to help sell Crayola crayons. Also an equally clever and subtle tug at parents' heart strings.

Choosing the Illustration

One dynamic aspect of advertising is the infinite number of illustrations that can be used to communicate the benefits of a product or service. The kind of illustration used is often determined during the visualization process. But frequently the desired illustration is not determined until the art director or designer is actually laying out the

---

Checklist for choosing illustrations

□ The package containing the product. This is especially important for packaged goods because it helps the consumer identify the product on the grocery shelf.

□ The product alone. Most advertising people point out the lower than average readership scores for ads that show the product alone. However, the Godiva ad is an excellent example of how this technique can be used to advantage.

□ The product in use. Automobile ads almost invariably show the car in use while talking about the ride, the luxury, the handling, or the economy. Cosmetic ads usually show the product in use with a close-up photograph of a beautiful woman wearing the mascara, the lipstick, or the eye shadow being advertised.

□ How to use the product. For food products, recipe ads featuring a new way to use the product historically pull very high readership scores.

□ Product features. The Yamaha campaign discussed at the beginning of this chapter is an excellent example of illustrating product features.

□ Comparison of products. One mouthwash compares itself with another, or one electric razor claims a closer shave than competitors A, B, or C.

□ User benefit. When Sylvania introduced its new 10-bulb flash cartridge, it illustrated user benefit through a series of 10 photographs of "Mona Lisa." The headline keyed the humor: "Now you have two more chances to get it right." It is often difficult to illustrate user benefits, especially intangible benefits. However,

salespeople know that the best way to get a customer's attention is to show the customer a way to benefit from the product.

□ Humor. There is no doubt that much advertising is entertainment. Humor in the right situations can make a positive, lasting impression. It can also destroy credibility if used incorrectly. Caution is always recommended when dealing with serious subjects. When appropriate, though, humor is like Pernod: "It grows on you."

□ Testimonial. A most common type of illustration is the photo of a star or a real person such as a teenager touting the product.

□ Before and after. This variation of the testimonial illustration has proved very effective for weight-loss products, skin care lotions, and body-building courses.

□ Negative appeal. Sometimes it is stronger to point out what happens if you don't use the product than if you do use it. Electricity, for example, is something we all take for granted, and illustrating it in use might be very difficult. Illustrating it not in use, however, is very simple—and compelling.

*A Talon zipper doesn't slip.
Even on a banana peel.*

If you want a zipper that doesn't take unexpected falls, choose Talon. Because Talon* zippers have the longest record of proven performance. They've been working reliably for over fifty years. In billions and billions of garments. So when you shop, always look for the Talon name. And protect yourself from an embarrassing slip. A Talon zipper says a lot about what it's in.

FIGURE 9–10

Talon, Inc., used this humorous approach for years to advertise its various zipper models to consumers and to the trade. Other ads include a photograph of a football with a zipper on it and even one of a kangaroo with a zipper on the pocket. An ingenious touch of humor drove the product feature home: "Trust your valuables to a Talon zipper."

ad. (For a list of the most common types of advertising illustrations used, see the Checklist for choosing illustrations.) Advertising managers or art directors frequently keep a similar checklist handy to help in the creative process of choosing the best type of illustration for their ad.

What if you're advertising a zipper? How exciting is a picture of a zipper? Do you show it on a man's pants or a lady's dress? Do you picture it opened or closed? Or do you picture something else, like the embarrassed face of a man whose zipper is broken? (See Figure 9–10.)

Selecting the appropriate photograph or illustration for an advertisement is a difficult creative task and is often what separates the great from the not-so-great. (See the "Art Director's Portfolio.")

Art directors have to deal with several basic issues in the selection of illustrations:

1. Is an illustration needed for effective communication to occur? Should it be black and white or color?
2. What should the subject of the illustration be, and is that subject relevant to the advertiser's creative strategy?
3. Should an illustrator or a photographer be used?
4. What are the technical and budgetary requirements needed to accomplish the desired illustrative solution?

Although these questions are very basic, they are unfortunately the most overlooked. They should be asked and answered in the initial planning stages of the advertisement, and they should be asked again when the advertisement is being produced.

Just as an exercise, thumb through any chapter in this book and study any one of the advertisements shown. Ask yourself the questions listed above as they apply to the ad you chose. On any day, in any given agency, top art directors perform this exercise routinely.

PACKAGING DESIGN

No discussion of advertising art direction can be complete without some attention to the way product packages are designed. Perhaps the best way to emphasize the importance of packaging design is by pointing out the money spent on it (over $50 billion in 1985). In fact, businesses spent more money on packaging than on advertising. A major reason for the heavy emphasis on packaging is the trend toward self-service. This requires that the package play a major role in both advertising and selling.

Packaging encompasses the physical appearance of the container and includes design, color, shape, labeling, and materials. In designing a package, consideration should be given to three factors: (1) how it communicates verbally and nonverbally, (2) the prestige desired, and (3) its stand-out appeal.

Packaging communicates both verbally and nonverbally. One bread manufacturer decided that a green wrapping would connote freshness. The only problem was that the customers associated it with fresh mold! Evidently the company chose the wrong shade of green—an easy mistake to make with green. (See Ad Lab 9–B.)

Even after consumers buy the product, they must continually be "sold" on it. A leading package designer, Walter P. Margulies, uses the cigarette package as a prime example. He stresses that it must be taken out 20 times and often placed in view of friends, intimates, co-workers, and strangers. Because of this, the design must "give consideration to what the user thinks others would regard as prestigious. Indeed cigarettes are a classic example of these so-called 'irrational products'' in which fancy, whim, and mystique all operate in place of rational choice."[6]

The package must stand out from the others on the shelf. This can be done by using shape, color, or size to indicate in-use application or just to grab the shopper's attention. The integrity of the manufacturer can be implied by the shape of the package. And regional preferences also play a role. For example, researchers determined in one study

---

AD LAB 9–B   The psychological impact of color

Reaction to color, says Walter Margulies, is generally based on a person's national origin or race. For example, "warm" colors are red, yellow, and orange; "these tend to stimulate, excite, and create an active response." Those from a warmer climate, apparently, are most responsive to those colors.

Violet and "leaf green" fall on the line between warm and cool. Each can be one or the other, depending on the shade used.

Here are some more Margulies observations:

Red Symbol of blood and fire. A runnerup to blue as man's "favorite color," but it is the most versatile; i.e., it's the hottest color with highest "action quotient." Appropriate for Campbell's Soups, Stouffer's frozen foods, and meats. Conveys strong masculine appeal—shaving cream, Lucky Strike, Marlboro.

Brown Another masculine color, associated with earth, woods, mellowness, age, warmth, comfort—i.e., the essential male; used to sell anything (even cosmetics), for example, Revlon's Braggi.

Yellow High impact to catch consumer's eye, particularly when used with black—psychologically right for corn, lemon, or sun tan products.

Green Symbol of health, freshness—popular for tobacco products, especially mentholated—i.e., Salem, Pall Mall menthol.

Blue Coldest color, with most appeal, effective for frozen foods (ice impression); if used with lighter tints becomes "sweet"—Montclair cigarettes, Lowenbrau beer, Wondra flour.

Black Conveys sophistication, high-end merchandise or used to simulate expensive products; good as background and foil for other colors.

Orange Most "edible" color, especially in brown-tinged shades, evokes autumn and good things to eat.

Laboratory Applications

1. Based on Margulies' observations, explain the moods or feelings that are stimulated by specific color advertisements or packages illustrated in this text.

2. Name products for which a redesign using different color combinations might make the product or package more attractive.

ART DIRECTOR'S PORTFOLIO

A. Mary McFadden. Mary McFadden uses a poster-style layout to let its product speak for itself.

B. Karastan. Floor covering advertising tends to be pretty monotonous. Remove the logo and the company signature and it's difficult to tell one ad from another. In fact, the furnishings in the ads are often more interesting than the carpet products. Karastan found an unusual way to break away from the pack and became the talk of the industry. The surrealistic effect in this poster-style ad was accomplished by building intricate sets and positioning photographs of birds in them. And there's no furniture to distract.

D. Sunkist. Utter simplicity creates instant communication in this outdoor ad for Sunkist.

C. Raging Waters. (The picture tells the whole story in this commercial for Raging Waters Theme Park.)

ANNCR V.O.: Don't just sit there. Raging Waters is coming.

SFX: *Crashing water.*

(*As water crashes through wall and envelops him, man just sits expressionless in his easy chair.*)

SUPER: Raging Waters. Coming June 18th.

E. Polaroid. Now you can shoot pictures of your little leaguer and be confident of 10 hits and no errors—or your money back. A great promise supported by a warm, human, graphic approach in picture-sequence layout form.

F. Arm & Hammer. George Lois (profiled in this chapter) designed this striking multiple-illustration ad for Arm & Hammer. By cramming tons of information and visuals into one ad with skill and beauty, Lois achieved an extraordinary result ideal for the many uses of Arm & Hammer Baking Soda. Notice the eye-catching technique of relating visuals to each other (e.g., the teeth and the cake).

G. Bulgari. Fabulous photographic illustration of stunning jewels shot against the embossed Bulgari name. What more needs to be said to create the image of the best?

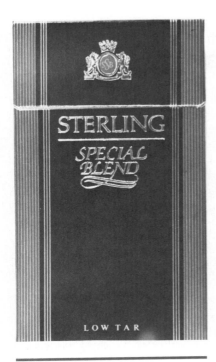

FIGURE   9–11

Attractive, targeted packaging may play the key role in the success of new brands of undifferentiated consumer products.

that people in the western part of the United States prefer margarine in an oblong package; the rest of the U.S. population prefers a square package (Figure 9–11).

Packages Come in Many Forms

Packages come in many forms including wrappers, cartons, boxes, crates, cans, bottles, jars, tubes, barrels, drums, and pallets. Packages are made of many substances, primarily paper, steel ("tin" cans), aluminum, plastic, wood, glass, burlap, and other fibers. Newer packaging materials include metal foils, which not only protect the contents but also add to the attractiveness of the package. Plastic provides a lightweight container as well as a safer one because it is unbreakable. Important improvements in packaging are occurring, such as wax wraps that keep products like cereals fresh and amber-green glass wine bottles that protect the contents from damage by light. The relatively new plastic film pouch for food products has become a substitute for tin cans and makes packages even more flexible, light, and compact.

Packaging Specialists

Management ultimately makes the final design decisions about packages and labels. However, because the right packages and labels have become increasingly important, numerous specialists have emerged to assist management in the decision-making process.

Because packaging is closely related to advertising, and because of the similar techniques used in advertising and packaging, the advertising department and the advertising agency usually play the most important role in package development. Advertising agencies design labels and packages and prepare the copy that goes on them. In many instances their help is vital because they coordinate their work with the overall theme of the advertising campaign that they have devised for the product. Most agencies consider packaging within the realm of their responsibilities. Packaging is now also considered part of the advertising and sales budgets of many manufacturers, who previously viewed it as a facet of production.

However, packaging problems have become so complex in recent years that packaging specialists are being used increasingly by advertisers and their agencies.

1. Consulting firms are used to provide package designs. These companies are staffed by designers and artists who are acutely aware of the effect of colors and shapes on consumer buying practices.
2. Design departments of larger corporations have their own personnel to work on packaging. In this case the same people who design the package probably played a role in designing the product as well.
3. Container manufacturers often provide help with package design as a service to their present and potential customers. It is considered part of the service that goes along with the sale of the package manufacturer's products of metal, paper, plastic, or other packaging materials.

FIGURE 9–12

Compare the old to the new. Graphics and quality production can make the difference between success and failure.

When Should a Package Be Changed?

There is an old saying: "If you build a better mousetrap, the world will beat a path to your door." Unfortunately, this is not always true. A better Swedish mousetrap was introduced into the U.S. market several years ago and immediately encountered problems. Called "The New Mousetrap," the product was packaged in a see-through polyurethane bag, but the graphics on the bag hid the product from view. In addition, the bag was difficult to handle and hard to open. The package was simply a poor marketing tool.

The manufacturer retained Selame Design Associates of Newton Lower Falls, Maine, to develop new packaging for the product. First Selame wanted to create a catchy name (no pun intended). "Get 'm!" was approved by the client, Wicander Enterprises.

Then, since minimizing costs was an important consideration, Selame created a highly practical and visible package using as little material as possible and incorporating the bright orange product itself into the design (Figure 9–12).

The orange tent card matched the mousetrap color. A *die-cut* opening in the front panel served to show the product and also hold it in place with a single staple. The graphic design of the rear legs and tail of a mouse showed how the trap works. The card was made of coated material and printed in only two colors, orange and black (for economy). The name was reversed out in white.

When it was introduced, the product immediately sold well. The self-selling, easily usable package apparently outweighed the mousetrap's higher price tag.

There are many reasons why even successful packaging gets changed. If a product is altered or improved, the packaging may change. New packaging may be necessitated by substitutions in materials, such as aluminum or plastic. Or competitors can influence alterations in the package.

A decision to stay with the present form can be as crucial as a decision to change it. Millions of dollars are spent in researching a new image and then promoting it. Margulies offers these caveats to determine whether packaging should be changed.[7]

1. Don't change because of a new brand manager's desire to innovate.
2. Don't change to imitate your competition.
3. Don't change for physical packaging innovation only.
4. Don't change for design values alone.
5. Don't change when product identification is strong.
6. Don't change if it may hurt the branding.
7. Don't change if it will weaken the product's authenticity.
8. Don't change if it will critically raise the product's price.

When a decision to change has been made, designers often change the packaging very gradually so consumers will feel comfortable and not suspect that something has happened to the product they have known and believed in for so many years.[8]

Even the familiar appearance of Betty Crocker has changed numerous times to keep the company looking up to date, but tender loving care has always been exercised there, too. (See Ad Lab 9–C.)

AD LAB 9–C   Bringing up Betty

"She's an all-American girl with blue eyes. She's a good cook, a good administrator, a good mother, civic-minded, she's good at everything." So illustrator Jerome Ryan, the artist of a 1972 portrait of the world's most famous cake baker, describes Betty Crocker.

Thousands of visitors to the Betty Crocker Kitchens in Minneapolis have learned over the years that their favorite maker of frosting, super-moist cakes, muffins, and nearly 200 other products is fictional. "They react like children finding out about Santa Claus," says a General Mills food publicist.

Betty, as she is known to her publicists, was born in 1921. Gold Medal Flour had run an ad that featured a jigsaw puzzle of a flour delivery at a corner store. Readers pasted down the completed picture to win a cookbook. The response was so large "they decided not to use the name of some researcher to answer the letters," General Mills says.

Whence B.C.? William G. Crocker was a popular, recently retired director of the Washburn Crosby Company (a forerunner of General Mills). The first Minneapolis flour mill had been called Crocker. The name Betty was also popular and suggested warmth.

Home bakers heard Betty before they saw her. In 1924, the Betty Crocker "Cooking School of the Air" became the first daytime radio food service program. It continued for 24 years, with over 1 million registrations from listeners who received recipes.

Betty's grandmotherly features did not grace cake boxes, however, until her 25th birthday in 1936, when Washburn commissioned a portrait from artist Neysa McMein. The features of several Home Service Department members served for the composite likeness that remained in use for almost 20 years.

But as the market changed, so did Betty. General Mills began selling more and more convenience foods, which were aimed at the younger women who would use them. In 1955, the company invited six artists to paint a new portrait, and asked 1,600 women to pick their favorite. Illustrator Hilda Taylor's Betty was deemed the best.

In 1972, Jerome Ryan, who had painted all the U.S. presidents for the backs of General Mills cereal boxes, was asked to paint a new portrait. "I didn't think Betty should be too beautiful," Ryan says. Mercedes Bates, head of the Kitchens at that time, was given a hand in modeling the new Betty, since she had to live with large reproductions of the portrait all over her office. Betty's outfit had already been decided. She would wear a trademark red David Crystal suit and a Monet pin, both made by subsidiaries of General Mills.

Betty was changed again in 1980 so that her hairstyle and dress reflected the changing lifestyle of America's consumers. This version incorporates the features of the 1965 face with softened, more casual coiffure and clothing.

Laboratory Applications

1. How would you compare the attributes of Betty Crocker with other trade characters currently used in the food field?

2. What do you feel are the benefits of using a trade character in food advertising?

Summary

Every advertisement uses art. In advertising, *art* refers to the whole visual presentation of the commercial or advertisement. This includes how the words in the ad are arranged, what size and style of type are used, whether photographs or illustrations are used, and how actors are placed in a television commercial.

There are many types of artists involved in advertising including art directors, graphic designers, illustrators, and production artists, to name a few. Each has been trained to handle a particular specialty.

For print advertising, the first work from the art department is seen in the form of a layout, which is a design of the advertisement within specified dimensions. The layout has two purposes. One is a mechanical function to show where the parts of the ad are to be placed. The other is a psychological or symbolic function to demonstrate the visual image a business or product will present.

There are several steps used in laying out an ad: a thumbnail sketch, rough layout, comprehensive layout, and mechanical. For brochures and other multipage materials the layout is referred to as a dummy. For television the layout is referred to as a storyboard.

A great deal of responsibility for the success of an advertisement is placed on the illustration. The illustration may be used to capture the attention of the reader, to identify the subject of the advertisement, to create a favorable impression, or for a host of other reasons.

The two basic devices for illustrating an advertisement are photography and drawings. Photography can make several important contributions to an advertisement, including realism; a feeling of immediacy; a feeling of live action; the special enhancement of mood, beauty, and sensitivity; and speed, flexibility, and economy.

Drawings may be used if the art director feels they can achieve greater impact than photographs. There are a number of techniques used in producing drawings. These include (1) line drawings; (2) wash drawings; (3) scratchboard; (4) pencil, crayon, and charcoal; and (5) oil, acrylic, tempera, and watercolor.

Selecting the appropriate photograph or illustration for an advertisement is a difficult creative task. Some common types of advertising illustrations are the package containing the product, the product alone, the product in use, comparison of products, user benefit, before and after, and the negative appeal of showing what happens if you don't use the product.

More money is spent on packaging than on advertising primarily because of increased emphasis on self-service. This requires the package to play an important role in both advertising and selling.

Factors that should be considered in packaging design are (1) how the package communicates verbally and nonverbally, (2) the prestige desired, and (3) the standout appeal required.

Package design is often changed because of a desire to (1) align the package more closely with the product's marketing strategy, (2) emphasize the product's benefits, (3) emphasize the product's name, or (4) take advantage of new materials.

Questions for review and discussion

1. Choose any television commercial shown in this text. How would you describe the "art" in that commercial?
2. Select a print ad of your choice. What do you suppose the art director contributed to that advertisement?
3. What is a layout? What is its purpose?
4. What do you think is the best color to stimulate sales? Why?
5. What is a mechanical? How is it used?
6. What color is white space?
7. What is the purpose of an illustration in an advertisement? When would you not use an illustration?
8. Select an advertisement with a photograph in it. What are the advantages and disadvantages of using a photograph in that ad?
9. Select an advertisement with a drawn illustration in it. What advantages and disadvantages does that illustration present?
10. What are five criteria for selecting illustrations? Which do you think is the most important? Why?

10

CREATIVE PRODUCTION: PRINT MEDIA

Everyone is familiar with the efforts made by big cities to clean up their skid-row areas. If you gave a photograph of those slums to a retoucher like Emilio Paccione, he could perform a miracle of urban renewal—transforming run-down shacks into freshly painted, beautifully renovated historic landmarks replete with green lawns, flowering gardens, and majestic trees.

The role of the retoucher, whose accomplishments, style, and sensitivity help make the art director look good, is surprising to many. Most people don't realize that almost every photograph we see for a national advertiser, or on the covers of national magazines, has been worked on by a retoucher to some degree.

For example, *Esquire* magazine was preparing a full-page color shot of an actor costumed and made up as George Washington. On stage and distanced from the audience, he might have resembled the father of our country. But under the merciless scrutiny of the close-up camera, he just looked like a poor old actor with a terribly wilted wig, drooping eyelids, and a pitifully painted putty nose that was more than just a few shades darker than the rest of his face. They called for Paccione.

Working over the weekend, with a 102-degree temperature, Patch (as his friends call him) treated the photograph with various dyes and bleaches and then, with paintbrush and airbrush in hand, used his artist's skill to bring forth a finished product that looked uncannily like the famous portrait on the $1 bill (Figure 10–1).

"I think I could have been a great plastic surgeon," Patch says with a modest smile.

Most of Paccione's business comes from advertising agencies preparing print campaigns for such big name advertisers as Clairol, Avon, Dr Pepper, Volkswagen, and General Foods. (See the Creative department: From concept through production of a magazine advertisement.) In one case, Ron Travisano, the president of Della Femina, Travisano & Partners, called on Patch to assist him in a very special and sensitive ad for a public action program called The Hunger Project, the professed aim is to end world hunger by the year 2000.

The object was to show an undernourished skeletal child gradually progressing to a smiling, healthy youngster. Paccione worked in reverse. Taking four prints of a single 35mm frame, Patch carefully bleached and shaded each print. What he created was a remarkable series showing the progressive stages of starvation, the child's eyes receding into the skull and skin stretching across protruding cheekbones and ribs (Figure 10–2).

"It was almost like animation," Paccione says, and the humanitarian point of The Hunger Project could not have been made clearer—or more striking.

Sometimes the retoucher's job is relatively simple, correcting blemishes on a model's face or straightening out the wrinkled crease in a pant leg. Other times the task is far more complex, requiring the skill of an experienced painter or illustrator.

Says Paccione, "Our job is to correct the basic deficiencies in the original photograph." In truth, he adds an element to photography that photographers themselves often cannot provide — in effect, to improve on the appearance of reality.[1]

THE PRODUCTION

PROCESS

The average person who reads advertisements has no concept of the intricate, detailed, technical stages those printed announcements go through from start to finish. Yet the entire advertising effort can be affected by the outcome of the production process. An otherwise beautiful ad can be destroyed by a poor selection of type, by a less-than-interesting photograph, by improper manufacture of printing material, or simply by an incorrect procedure used to reproduce photographs or artwork on a particular paper stock.

Any person who is connected with advertising should, therefore, have some basic knowledge and understanding of production procedures. A fundamental grasp of mechanical production saves a lot of money and disappointment in the long run.

In recent years it has become more difficult and complex to gain a thorough knowledge of these production procedures. There has been enormous technological progress in the graphic arts, due, in particular, to the revolutionary application of electronics. Much of the work performed by Paccione, for example, can now be accomplished by computers and *electronic pagination systems* (see Figure 10–3). As a result, knowledgeable and experienced print production professionals are extremely important to today's major advertisers and advertising agencies.

In Chapter 9 we looked at the award-winning ads Botsford-Ketchum created for Yamaha motorcycles. We discussed the editorial design of the ads, the interesting combination of illustration and photography, and the unity of the art concept with Yamaha's campaign theme: "When you know how they're built, you'll buy a Yamaha."

During the time Botsford-Ketchum handled the Yamaha motorcycle account, Joe Sosa was the agency's production supervisor. He became intimately involved in the campaign after the concept was developed. His responsibility was to ensure that the final advertisement printed in the magazine reflected exactly what the art director had intended.

This was no small task inasmuch as each advertisement presented numerous production complexities. These included the reproduction of fine technical illustrations in full color, the precise specification and

FIGURE 10–1

These amazing "before" and "after" pictures show the portrait power of a great retoucher.

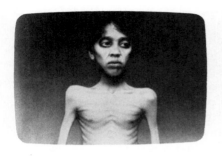
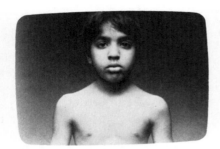

FIGURE   10–2

The power of this commercial for The Hunger Project is delivered through the heart-rending visual of a poor, starving, emaciated child gradually becoming healthy right before your eyes—all in 30 seconds. No words are necessary to tell or sell the story.

placement of type around the illustrations, and the need to have all printing materials checked, approved, duplicated, and shipped to the magazines in time for a specific deadline.

PLANNING PRINT PRODUCTION

After an advertisement has been laid out and the artwork and copy approved, it is under the supervision of the print production manager and a staff of production artists and assistants. The print production department specifies type, creates camera-ready mechanicals and orders printing materials, and gives any necessary technical instructions to outside production specialists.

The manager must decide at the earliest possible time what is most important for a particular project: speed, quality, or economy. The answer may determine which production methods are used; one will surely be sacrificed at the expense of another. In the Yamaha ads, what do you think was considered most important?

Working backward from the closing dates (deadlines) of the publications, the production manager schedules when each step of the work must be completed in order to meet the deadline. Deadlines can vary from months to hours.

The production manager acquaints the art director and copywriter with the opportunities and limitations of various production techniques and keeps them abreast of the progress of each job. In the case of Yamaha, this meant coordinating with three teams of art directors and writers for just the one account.

Finally, the production manager must check all proofs for errors, obtain all necessary approvals from agency and client executives, and release the approved advertisements to the publications.

For the production process to run smoothly, it is important that all concerned have a working knowledge and understanding of production procedures. Consider the problem of correcting errors. After the advertisement has been delivered to the typographer, photoplatemaker, printer, or publication, it costs substantially more to make any changes than before the actual production begins. For example, the cost of changing a single comma after the copy has been typeset is well over $10.

As a result, advertisers as well as the personnel in their agencies should develop a sensitivity to art, graphics, and type and learn all they can about typography, platemaking, printing, and color.

TYPOGRAPHY

Turn back to Chapter 9 and look carefully at the Yamaha ad in Figure 9–4. Now look at the Yamaha ad in Figure 10–4. It was created a year or two later by Yamaha's new agency, Chiat-Day Advertising in Los Angeles. What major differences do you notice between the two ads? Both use an illustrative technique to talk about the unique features of the bikes. Both use a somewhat similar design. Yet the ads look considerably different, and some people think they create a very different feeling.

The major difference, of course, is the use of typography. Figure 9–4 uses a headline set in a very pretty, traditional typeface called Goudy (pronounced "gow-dee") Old Style. Notice the characteristics of this typeface: delicate curved serifs (tails) on each letter; variation in the thickness of the letter strokes; and the clear, easy-to-read roundness of style.

FIGURE 10–3

The advertiser asked for drastic work: create a two-door car from the left photograph. To do this a highly skilled technician, using new electronic equipment, manipulated the computer-stored data scanned from the original photograph. Working with the image projected on a cathode ray tube the operator can remove part of the image, clone or duplicate part of the image, and alter the data to create a different image. In the left picture, the retoucher was asked to: (1) remove the rear door and replace the metal trim around it, (2) roll down the front window, (3) add fog lamps, (4) remove the back door vent windows, (5) change the background, keeping the soft shadows under the car, and (6) add a burglar alarm on the front fender.

Figure 10–4, on the other hand, uses a larger, sans serif (no tails) headline typeface called Futura Bold. This typeface is characterized by no serifs on the letters; uniform thickness of strokes; wide, thick letters; and a bold, round, "newsy," announcement-style presentation.

Consumers differ in the styles they prefer. Art directors, therefore, try to select type styles that suit the objectives and strategy of the campaign and communicate well with the target audience.

Which of these type styles do you prefer? Do you find one easier to read? Is one more attractive than the other? Does one communicate news value better? Which attracts your attention more quickly? Do you get different feelings, or a different impression, from the two type styles? Does one offer a greater feeling of credibility than the other? Considering all these things, if you were the art director would you prefer one of these type styles over the other?

◼ Classes of Type

Type can be divided into two broad classes: display type and text type. *Display type* is larger and usually heavier than text type. It is used in headlines, subheads, logos, addresses, and wherever there is a need for emphasis in an advertisement. For body copy in an advertisement, the smaller *text type* is used.

◼ Type Groups

There are thousands of typefaces available, and type designers are continually developing new ones. Typefaces are classified into vari-

FIGURE 10–4

The Yamaha campaign, as executed by Chiat-Day, featured a continuation of the illustrative techniques already in use by Yamaha with the addition of bold, newsy, action-oriented headlines. Many art directors feel this is more in tune with the intended audience of the ads—motorcycle enthusiasts.

ROMAN TYPE

Garamond (OLD STYLE)

Plantin

Palatino

Caledonia (TRANSITIONAL)

Baskerville

Zapf Book (MODERN)

Tiffany

SANS SERIF TYPE

Helvetica

Spartan Book

Eurostyle

Franklin Gothic

SQUARE SERIF TYPE

Serifa 55

Rockwell

Lubalin Graph Medium

Memphis Medium

SCRIPT TYPE

Snell Round Hand

Bank Script

Kaufman Bold

ORNAMENTAL TYPE

HELVIN

Karnac

NEON

Orbit-B

FIGURE 10–5

The five major type groups.

ous groups because of their similarity in design. There is no reason to learn the names of all the faces because each typesetting house or printer has only a limited number of typefaces, depending on requirements and the kind of equipment it uses. Except for people who wish to become specialists in the field, an understanding of the five major type groups is sufficient (Figure 10–5).

Roman

This is the most popular type group. It offers the greatest number of designs, so contrast can be achieved without a basic design change. It is also considered the most readable. The two most distinguishing characteristics of roman type are (1) the small lines, tails, or serifs that cross the ends of the main strokes and (2) variations in the thickness of the strokes. Roman type comes in a variety of sizes and has dozens of subclassifications that differ from one another on the basis of thickness of the strokes, the way the letters are designed (letterforms), and the size and regularity of the serifs.

Sans serif

This is the second most popular type group. It is also referred to as *block, contemporary,* or *gothic.* This large group of typefaces is characterized by (1) the lack of serifs (thus the name, sans serif) and (2) the relatively uniform thickness of the strokes.

In text type sans serif typefaces are usually not as readable as roman faces. However, they are widely used because of the simple, clean lines, which give a modern appearance.

Square serif

A combination of sans serif and roman are the square serif faces which have the same uniform thickness of strokes as sans serif faces. Square serif is similar to roman in that it has serifs, but the serifs have the same weight and thickness as the main strokes of the letters.

AD LAB   10–A   How to use type as the major graphic design element

Type—and type directing—reaches its apex when the art director chooses it as the sole or major design element as illustrated in the following figures.

Type is used in many ways today, and nowhere is that more apparent than in headlines. Serifs, sans serifs, verticals, slants, condensed, expanded, across-the-gutter, loose, tight, all caps, upper and lowercase, small, huge, elegant, powerful, quiet, screaming, colored, dropped-out, plain, fancy—this is the type story today.

Art directors are not only using all possible headline styles, but they're also working *with* them—their directing reflects solid, effective judgment, with type matched to art to fulfill ad objectives.

Laboratory Application

Discuss these ads with reference to the impact of type selection on the design concept and the execution.

■ *Cursive or script*

These typefaces resemble handwriting. They are rather difficult to read and are used primarily in headlines. The letters are often connected and convey a feeling of femininity, formality, or beauty. They are commonly used in cosmetic and fashion advertising.

■ *Ornamental*

This group of typefaces includes designs that provide novelty and are ornamental or decorative. They are used for special effects but are difficult to read.

■ Type Families

Within each major type group, there are type families. A type family is made up of related faces identified by such names as Cheltenham, Futura, Goudy, Souvenir, Bodoni, and Caslon. The basic design remains the same within a family, but there are variations in the proportion, weight, and slant of the characters. These variations make up a family and commonly include light, medium, bold, extra bold, condensed, extended, and italic (Figure 10–6). All these variations may not be available in a particular type family. These differences, however, enable the typographer to provide contrast and emphasis in an advertisement without changing type styles. For any typeface and size of type, a font consists of a complete assortment of capitals, small capitals, lowercase letters, numerals, and punctuation marks.

In an effort to control the exclusivity of their advertising, some advertisers have a unique type style designed. The Volvo ad in Figure 10–7, for example, shows a bold, sans serif headline set in Volvo's own type style designed by John Danza, the creative director at Scali, McCabe, Sloves, Volvo's advertising agency.

Other advertisers might go in the opposite direction for uniformity. They may tailor their advertisements to blend well with the typography and design elements of the magazines in which they are to run. In this way, a truly editorial look is given to the ads, and the advertiser hopes credibility (or at least interest) is thereby enhanced.

FIGURE 10–6

Meet the Cheltenham family. Note the variety of looks that can be used without changing families. Art directors may use a boldface in the headline, lightface in the copy, as well as different sizes or even italics for emphasis. Most art directors try to use only one type family in a single ad, and they rarely use more than two.

Cheltenham
Cheltenham Italic
Cheltenham Bold
Cheltenham Bold Italic
Cheltenham Bold Condensed
Cheltenham Bold Condensed Italic
Cheltenham Bold Extra Condensed
Cheltenham Nova
Cheltenham Bold Nova
Cheltenham Light
Cheltenham Light Italic
Cheltenham Book
Cheltenham Book Italic

Cheltenham Bold
Cheltenham Bold Italic
Cheltenham Ultra
Cheltenham Ultra Italic
Cheltenham Light Condensed
Cheltenham Light Condensed Italic
Cheltenham Book Condensed
Cheltenham Book Condensed Italic
Cheltenham Bold Condensed
Cheltenham Bold Condensed Italic
Cheltenham Ultra Condensed
Cheltenham Ultra Condensed Italic

Figure 10–7

Volvo has owned its own typeface for many years. Used in the headline and tag line of all ads, it guarantees an exclusive continuity to the company's advertising campaigns.

Type Structure and Measurement

Several terms must be explained in order to understand type structure and measurement.

Points

Points measure the depth (or height) of the type. There are 72 points to the inch, so one point equals 1/72 of an inch. This term refers to the vertical measurement of a line of type measured from the bottom of the descenders (extensions downward from the body of the type) to the top of the ascenders (extensions upward from the body of the type).

The most common type sizes used in advertising have traditionally been 6, 8, 10, 11, 12, 13, 14, 18, 24, 36, 42, 60, 72, 84, 96, and 120 points (Figure 10–8). However, with new, computerized phototypesetting equipment, any type size is possible. The smaller sizes, 6 through 14 points, are used for text type. The larger sizes are normally used for display type.

Pica

The unit of measurement for the horizontal width of lines of type is the *pica*. There are six picas to the inch (Figure 10–9) and 12 points to the pica. The width of a single letter of type depends on the style of the typeface and whether it is regular or bold, extended or condensed. It also depends on the proportions of the letter. But averages for each type style and size have been established and are provided by the manufacturer of the type.

Upper and lowercase

Capital letters are called *uppercase,* and small letters are called *lowercase.* The terms came about when type was set by hand and compositors stacked the two cases containing the capital and small letters one above the other.

Type can be set using all caps, caps and small caps, or caps and lowercase. Note from the material you are now reading how much easier it is to read a combination of upper and lowercase. Advertising copy set in lower case is more readable than copy set in all capitals. That goes for headlines as well as body copy. Type set in solid capitals can be used for emphasis, but this should be done very sparingly.

Type Selection

The art of selecting and setting type is known as *typography.* Because almost every advertisement has some reading matter, type has tremendous importance in advertising. The typeface chosen affects the advertisement's general appearance, design, and readability. Although type cannot compensate for a weak headline, poorly written body copy, or a lack of appropriate illustrations, it can create interest and attract readers to the advertisement.

Knowledge of the effects and symbolism of typefaces requires great expertise. There may be fewer experts who can accurately interpret how a typeface will influence an ad than any other kind of expert connected with the advertising business. This art requires experience

FIGURE   10–8

Sample variations in type size.

text type		display type	
SIZE of type	6 POINT	SIZE of type	16 POINT
SIZE of type	8 POINT	SIZE of type	18 POINT
SIZE of type	9 POINT	SIZE of type	20 POINT
SIZE of type	10 POINT	SIZE of type	24 POINT
SIZE of type	12 POINT	SIZE of type	30 POINT
SIZE of type	14 POINT	SIZE of type	36 POINT

and skill and should not be left to the layperson. Among local advertisers, however, it is often the most overlooked aspect of advertising creativity.

There are four important points to consider in the selection of type: readability, appropriateness, harmony or appearance, and emphasis. We shall discuss each of these briefly.

Readability

Factors that contribute to readability include type style, boldness, size, length of the line, and spacing between the words, lines, and paragraphs. An advertisement is printed to be read, and a reduction in readability kills interest. Difficult-to-read typefaces should be used sparingly and only to create special effects.

Naturally, large, bold, legible typefaces are the easiest to read. However, we are limited by the amount of space in the advertisement and the amount of copy that must be written. Readability is also affected by the length of the line in which the copy is set. Newspaper columns are usually less than two inches wide, magazine columns slightly wider. For advertisements, columns of copy less than three inches (18 picas) wide are usually recommended.

The way lines of type are spaced also influences readability. Between lines of type there is always a small amount of space to allow for *descenders* (j's) and *ascenders* (d's). When this is the only space between lines, type is "set solid." Sometimes an art director decides to add extra space between the lines to give a more "airy" feeling. In this case, *leading* (pronounced "ledding") between lines is called for. The term dates back to when thin metal strips were actually inserted between lines of metal type.

Type that is set in 10-point with 2 points of space (leading) between lines is specified as "10 on 12," or "10/12." This same terminology is used whether the type is set in metal or by photocomposition, to be discussed later.

Appropriateness

A typeface must be appropriate to the product being advertised. With many varieties of type available in terms of both style (typeface) and size, a host of moods and feelings can be conveyed quite apart

PICA INCH

FIGURE 10–9

In the printing industry, picas and points are common units of measurement. One inch equals six picas or 72 points. Thus, type set at 36 points would be ½ inch tall; and an 18-pica column of type would be three inches wide.

from the meanings of the words themselves. Some typefaces suggest ruggedness and masculinity, while others give a feeling of delicateness and femininity. A typeface can whisper "luxury," while another can scream "bargain." A typeface that conveys the feeling of something old-fashioned obviously would be inappropriate in an advertisement for a space-age electronic watch. (See Ad Lab 10–B.)

■ Harmony/appearance

A common mistake of advertising novices is the mixing of typefaces. This normally results in disharmony and a feeling of clutter. Type should harmonize with the other elements of an advertisement—including the illustration and the layout. Therefore typefaces should be chosen which belong to the same family or are closely related.

■ Emphasis

Emphasis with type selection can be achieved by using contrast. One method is to use more than a single type style, or to use italic versus roman or upright type, lowercase versus uppercase, or small-size versus large-size type. Care must be taken because an effort to emphasize *all* the elements in an advertisement will only result in emphasizing *none* of the elements.

■ Type Specification and Copy Casting

Type must fit into the space designated for it in the layout. So before the type can be selected, the number of characters in the copy has to be determined, or "cast off."

There are two ways used to fit copy to a particular space: the word-count method and the character-count method. With the word-count method, the words in the copy are counted and then divided by the number of words per square inch that can be set in a particular type style and size, as given in a standard table.

With the character-count method, there is greater accuracy. An actual count is made of the number of characters (letters, word spaces, and punctuation marks) in the copy. In a type specimen book or chart provided by the typographer, the average number of characters per pica is given for each typeface and type point size. From this information it is relatively simple to determine how much space a given type will use.

Copy sent to a typographer or publication should be marked with the type specifications written beside the copy. Usually the copy is accompanied by a layout. When specifying type, the typographer should be provided with at least the following information: (1) the typeface by name, (2) the type size and the leading, and (3) the width of the line of type in picas.

The specification of type in advertising agencies is handled by art directors, type directors, or the print production staff. However, it is also important for copywriters and account executives to understand the basics of type specification and copycasting since copy must often be written to fit a particular space in an advertisement. Otherwise, the ad risks looking either overly crowded or too empty—thereby impairing its visual impact.

AD LAB 10–B   The most unforgettable characters you will ever meet

AIRKRAFT   ROCO   PICCADILLY   traffic
Locomotive   Shamrock   YAGI LINK DOUBLE   YANKEE
STRIPES   BUSTER   Cathedral   SUPERSTAR
FAT SHADOW   ELEFONT   Shatter   Thalia
GALADRIEL   Masquerade   Neptun   Octopuss
Magnificat   BABY TEETH   L'Auriol   BLOW UP
GOOD VIBRATIONS   GLASER STENCIL   Knightsbridge   Fino
Motter Ombra   oxford   Harlow   Quartermaine
Pluto Outline   SINALOA   CALYPSO   STOP

Laboratory Application

Choose five of these type styles and discuss them from the standpoint of readability, appropriateness (give examples of products), harmony/appearance, and emphasis.

TYPESETTING
METHODS

In the last decades, technology has revolutionized typesetting methods. The old method of metal type composition (letters were formed by pouring molten lead into brass molds) is obsolete and has virtually disappeared. The "hot-type" era included a variety of composition processes with such names as Linotype, hand-setting, Monotype, and Ludlow; but it has yielded to a new "cold-type" era characterized by high-speed electronic photocomposition equipment and operators schooled in computer technology. This new era, which really began in the 1960s, has brought tremendous changes in the tools available to art directors, designers, and writers. As a result, they can achieve more faster and for less cost.

Today's typesetting methods generally fall into two broad classifications: strike-on composition and photocomposition.

 ### Strike-On Composition

Strike-on or *direct-impression composition* can be done on either a regular typewriter or on the new breed of intelligent electronic typewriters and word processors. These have microprocessors, can perform basic text-editing functions automatically, and also offer storage capabilities. This equipment is often used in typesetting direct-mail advertising, catalogs, and house organs.

The drawback to this method is that there is only a limited range of typefaces available, and these machines produce only text, not display type. However, this means of composition offers substantial savings and is primarily used when economy is the overriding consideration. Because the price of the equipment is relatively low, organizations can afford to have the equipment in-house, which offers the advantage of getting material set quickly when the need arises.

Strike-on composition is being used less often because it is being replaced by laser printers and other technologies that permit digital data files to be output in low-resolution typographic quality.

■ Photocomposition

A combination of computer technology and electronics, *photocomposition* is the most dominant method of producing advertising materials today. It offers an almost unlimited number of typefaces and sizes, faster reproduction at lower cost, and improved clarity and sharpness of image.

The basic function of all phototypesetting machines is to expose photosensitive paper, or film, to a projected image of the character being set. The most commonly used equipment operates photo-optically, by cathode-ray tube (CRT) technology, or by laser exposure (Figure 10–10).

▪ *Photo-optic typesetters*

This typesetting equipment uses an electromechanical method of generating characters. Character fonts are stored on film grids, discs, drums, or on a film strip matrix. The matrix is then rotated mechanically until the desired character is in the proper position. A xenon

FIGURE   10–10

Typesetting methods used today.

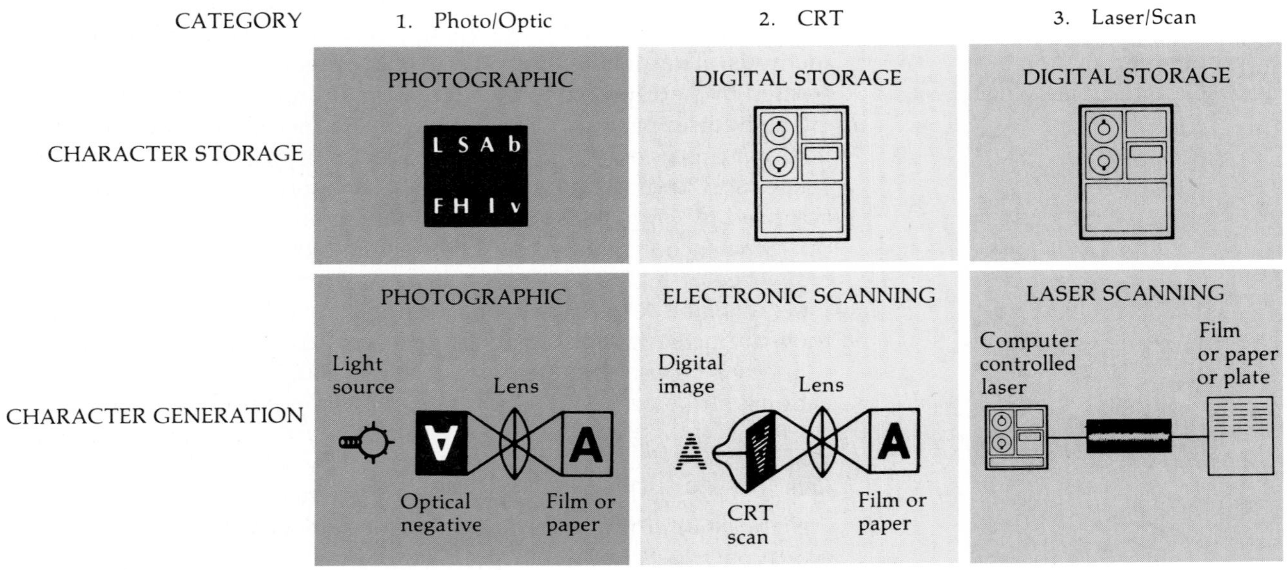

FIGURE 10–11

The on-screen layout of the Comp/Edit from AM Varityper gives a visual presentation of the typeset layout before the type is set. The final typeset output has all elements in position so there is little or no need for paste-up in straight-copy advertisements.

lamp flashes, and the light image of the character is projected through a lens, which magnifies it to the desired size. This image is then reflected off a mirror onto the photosensitive paper or film, thus setting the character. Photo-optic typesetters are no longer manufactured but are still very common in the graphic arts field.

CRT typesetters

In cathode-ray tube techniques, characters are stored digitally. They are retrieved from the computer's memory and passed to a print CRT (similar to a television receiver tube) where they are lined up and then exposed through a lens system onto the photosensitive paper or film. Since they are generated electronically, the characters can be modified (condensed, heavied, slanted, etc.) at the operator's command. These versatile machines can store hundreds of fonts and have extremely high speed capabilities. Digital typesetters are rapidly replacing photo-optic machines.

Laser typesetters

With new computer-laser technology, type fonts and software programs can be stored digitally in a computer. As the computer turns the laser on and off, the laser beam "writes" onto (exposes) the output paper or film. No cathode ray tube is necessary. Extremely high speeds are possible as well as great reliability and versatility. In addition, laser typesetters are usually able to even put out graphics and halftones as well as type.

The Typesetting Process

Typesetting is a series of separate steps, including inputting (keyboarding), hyphenation and justification, typesetting by one of the processes explained above, developing the exposed photographic material, proofreading for errors and omissions, correcting and resetting, and makeup. Modern equipment available today ranges from equipment that performs only one step in the process to complete *direct-entry* systems, which have the input and output capabilities in one device. Some of these devices are able to "paginate" (make up) entire pages of copy (Figure 10–11).

Direct-entry phototypesetters became affordable at the end of the 1970s. Now many advertising agencies, studios, and clients have them in-house, facilitating fast, cost-effective, do-it-yourself typesetting, something previously provided only by large, outside type houses.

THE PRINTING PROCESS

The transfer of an image from one surface to another is the objective of all printing methods. There are basically four major methods by which printed advertising materials are reproduced today: letterpress, rotogravure, offset lithography, and screen printing.

We will discuss each of these methods shortly. But first, let's examine some basic principles of printing.

65-line screen.

100-line screen.

150-line screen.

FIGURE 10–12

Halftone screens. Three examples of the same photograph show the effect of varying the screen fineness.

Preparing Materials for the Press

For all of today's modern, high-speed presses, whether the method is letterpress, rotogravure, or offset lithography, printing plates are required. A process called *photoplatemaking* is used to create the printing surface on the plates.

The photoplatemaking process can easily be compared to taking a picture with your own camera. When you take a picture, you produce a negative. The picture is then made by laying the negative on sensitized paper and exposing it to light. Photoplatemaking also begins with a picture. However the negative of the image photographed is printed in reverse on a sensitized metal plate rather than on paper; this plate is then used for printing.

Before this plate can be made, though, the artwork has to be prepared properly.

Line films

Unlike a piece of photographic paper, which prints its image in black, white, and any variety of shades of gray, a printing plate can only print or not print—black or white. That's fine if the artwork is simply typeset copy, pen and ink drawings, or charcoal illustrations. In that event, the artwork is simply photographed to create what is called a *line film*. From that, a *line plate* is produced for printing. (In the letterpress process, these are also known as line cuts, line etchings, and line engravings.)

However, a photograph or other illustration requiring gradations in tone cannot be reproduced on a plate without using an additional process—namely, a halftone screen.

Halftones

Whereas line plates print lines and solid areas (like type), halftone plates print from dots. The key element in making such a plate is the *halftone screen,* which breaks up continuous-tone artwork into dots. The screen itself is glass or plastic, crisscrossed with fine black lines at right angles like a window screen. This screen is placed in the camera between the lens and the negative holder, which, in effect, converts the artwork being photographed into a series of black dots.

In the dark areas of the (halftone) photograph the dots are large; in the gray areas they are small; and in the white areas they almost disappear. The combination of big and little dots with a little or a lot of white space between them produces the illusion of shading in the photograph. The human eye, seeing minute dots of black and white, mixes them and perceives them as gradations of tone. But, in reality, the screened illustration is made up of only two tones, black and white.

The fineness of the halftone screen determines the quality of the illusion. A fine screen has more lines and thus more dots per square inch. Screens generally range from 50 to 150 lines to the inch each way, and the printed halftone may be described as a 65-line or a 110-line screen, for example. Variation in the fineness of the screen is necessary because the quality of the paper on which the halftone is printed may be smooth and glossy or coarse and ink-absorbent. Halftones printed on newsprint must be screened coarsely, whereas fine

Two-color texture.

Random line.

Mezzo tint.

Wavy line (dry brush).

FIGURE 10–13

Many special effects are possible through the use of different special line screens. All these processes use the same principle as the dot screen. They use lines, scratches, or some other technique, and require much more careful photo work.

quality magazine paper can take fine-screen halftones. Note that with a coarse screen the dots can be seen clearly with the naked eye (see Figure 10–12).

Different types of screens may also be used for artistic effect. Figure 10–13 demonstrates the result of using different screens to reproduce the same photograph.

Stripping

To make the printing plate, a single negative must be made of all the line and halftone artwork. The type and line art is first photographed separately from the halftone illustrations. Then, through a process known as *stripping*, the various negatives are carefully cut and taped together into one single negative which is used to make the combination plate.

Methods of Printing

Few agencies or advertisers maintain all the necessary capital equipment and personnel required for producing printed materials. As a result they hire outside print production companies who work at their direction. The suppliers may include a typesetting house, a photoplatemaker, a printer, or a duplicating house for newspaper material. All these sources are particularly important when media schedules include publications that print by different methods or when it is desirable to convert material from one printing process to another to save time and money.

Now that we understand some of the basics of printing, let's discuss the major printing methods used today (Figure 10–14).

Letterpress

For many years, letterpress was the major method of printing around the world.

The process is similar to the way a rubber stamp works. In letterpress printing the ink is applied to a raised (relief) surface and transferred to the paper. Like a stamp, the image to be transferred is backward ("wrong reading"). The printing is done from a metal or plastic printing plate, usually on a rotary press.

The rotary press is designed for high-speed work and for economy in long press runs. Both the paper (in a continuous web) and the printing surface are on cylinders. The printing plate is curved so that it will fit the cylinder. Printing takes place as the two cylinders strike against each other.

To produce the letterpress plate, the negative of the photographed image is laid on top of a sensitized plastic or copper plate and exposed to light. Since everything on a negative is in reverse, the image areas on the negative are transparent. This allows light to pass through the negative to the plate which has been treated with a light-sensitive emulsion. The emulsion hardens in the areas exposed to the light and thereby forms an acid resistant protective covering over the image area of the plate. The plate is then placed in an acid bath. This etches away the nondesign areas—leaving the desired printing image raised on the surface of the plate.

The result is the line plate we discussed earlier. Sometimes a plastic

LETTERPRESS
Relief printing

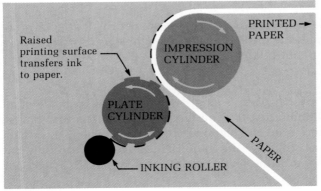

GRAVURE
Intaglio printing

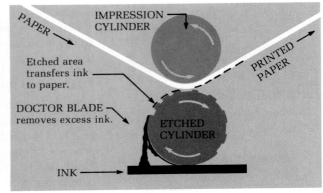

OFFSET
Surface printing

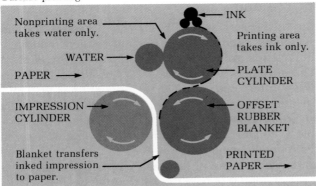

SILKSCREEN
Surface printing

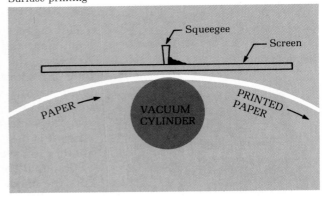

FIGURE   10–14

Comparative illustrations of the major printing processes in use today. To complement your understanding of these processes, visit a local printer and ask to see the processes at work. It will be interesting and worthwhile.

plate may be used, in which case a photochemical process called *photopolymerization* followed by a simple washout is used to produce a relief plate.

In the past, letterpress was used in the reproduction of newspapers and many magazines that needed good quality with sharp contrast. However, due to the advent of newer, higher quality methods, very little letterpress printing is done in the United States today

Rotogravure

The process used in rotogravure is different than letterpress. First, two separate films are made—one for all type and line illustrations and the other for halftone illustrations. The negatives are combined into a single film "positive." In the gravure process, though, even type and line art are screened.

Then, instead of printing from a raised surface as in letterpress, the rotogravure process prints from a depressed surface. Like letterpress, the image to be transferred is backward ("wrong reading"). The design is etched or electromechanically engraved into a metal plate or cylinder, leaving depressions one or two thousandths of an inch deep. As the plate is inked and wiped clean with a metal blade, ink is left in the tiny depressions. It transfers to the paper by pressure and suction.

Because preparing the printing plates or cylinders is time-consuming and costly, rotogravure is practical and economical only for long press runs. Sunday newspaper supplements, mail-order catalogs, many major magazines, packaging, and other materials requiring a great number of photographs are well suited for this method. Rotogravure is noted for its good reproduction of color on both newsprint and quality paper stocks.

Offset lithography

Offset lithography employs the same line and halftone processes used to make letterpress plates. However, to the naked eye, the image on the lithographic printing plate appears to be flat instead of raised, as in letterpress, or depressed, as in rotogravure. Unlike letterpress and rotogravure, the image on the plate is "right reading."

The principle underlying lithography is that oil and water do not mix. To start, a photograph is made of the material to be printed. The negative from the photograph is laid on top of a zinc or aluminum printing plate and exposed to light. Chemicals are applied to the plate after the exposure, and the image takes the form of a greasy coating. The plate is then attached to a cylinder on a rotary printing press, and water is applied with a roller. The greasy-coated image repels the water, but the blank portions of the plate retain it. As the plate is inked with an oily ink, the moist blank portions of the plate repel the ink. The greasy-coated image retains the ink for transfer to an intermediate rubber surface called a blanket, which comes in contact with the paper and enables the image to be printed.

Today lithography is the most popular printing process in the United States. The printing plates cost less than for other printing methods, the printing can be done on rougher paper than can letterpress, and the preparation time is short. Because the process is photographic, it meshes well with the most popular form of typesetting, photocomposition. Advertisers simply have to provide camera-ready paste-ups or film.

Lithography is used extensively for inexpensive advertising materials prepared at "instant" printing shops. Most newspapers and magazines are printed by this process, as are most books (including this one), direct-mail materials, and catalogs. Because it is suitable for printing on metal, most packaging, including beer and soft drink cans, is also printed by lithography (Figure 10–15).

FIGURE 10–15

The high-speed Heidelberg five-color offset press is used for printing magazines. The first four units are used for four-color process printing, while the fifth may be used to varnish the printed page or to lay down a specific fifth color. Some art directors, for example, may want a "company blue," which is a specific colored ink rather than a combination of process colors.

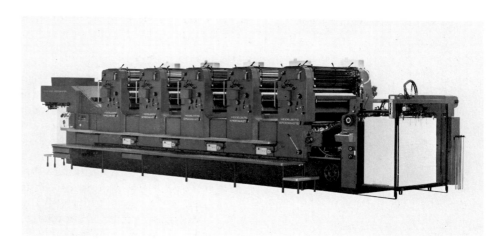

Screen printing (serigraphy)

The signs and billboards we see along the highway often illustrate the use of screen printing. Billboards use sheets of paper that have historically been too large for many printing presses. Also the quantities required for many outdoor advertising campaigns, especially local ones, are so small that it is often uneconomical to use other printing processes, like offset, which might be used for national campaigns.

Screen printing, an old process based on the stencil principle, requires no plates. A special screen is stretched tightly on a frame. The frame is placed on the surface on which the message or image is to be printed. A stencil, either hand cut from film or photographically prepared, is used to block out areas that are not part of the image to be printed. Ink is squeezed through the screen by a squeegee (rubber rollers) sliding across the surface, thus reproducing the desired image. For printing in color, a separate stencil is made for each color.

Printing stencils are made of nylon or stainless steel mesh. Originally, silk was used, hence the old term *silk screen*. Today automatic presses for screen printing are also available, making the process economical for even longer runs.

PEOPLE IN ADVERTISING

Klaus F. Schmidt

Senior Vice President and
Director of Creative Support
Young & Rubicam Inc., New York

Klaus F. Schmidt is senior vice president and director of creative support at Young & Rubicam Inc., New York. In this capacity he is responsible for the company's print production, art buying, audiovisual facilities, and art studio. Prior to his appointment in 1968 Schmidt served as type director and then as director of print operations for Young & Rubicam.

Born in Germany, where he received his graphic arts training, Schmidt came to the United States in 1951 as a union compositor and printer. He obtained a B.A. in advertising and marketing at Wayne State University in Detroit. Schmidt went on to become type director of Mogul, Williams & Saylor and then of Doyle Dane Bernbach Inc., both in New York, before joining Y&R in 1961.

Print production, says Schmidt, is the "vital step" that transforms an advertising concept into the final printed result. He notes that while account executives "need not become expert" in the technical complexities of typesetting, photoplatemaking, and printing, they "should understand at least the basics of graphic arts technology and print production procedures." Only with this working knowledge, Schmidt explains, can account executives expect to communicate successfully with their clients.

Emphasizing that print production people "are not merely technically knowledgeable purchasing

■ Printing in Color

The method for printing color advertisements with tonal values, such as photographs and paintings, is the full-color process. This process is based on the principle that all colors can be printed by combining the three primary colors—yellow, magenta (red), and cyan (blue)—plus black (which provides greater detail and density as well as shades of gray).

All the printing processes we have discussed can print color. However, a printing plate can print only one color at a time. Therefore, if a job is to be printed in full color, the printer must prepare four different printing plates, one for each color.

The artwork to be reproduced is photographed through color filters that eliminate all the colors except one. For example, one filter eliminates all colors except red and extracts every light ray of red to be blended into the final reproduced picture. An electronic scanning device may also be used to make these color separations. Thus, four separate continuous-tone negatives are produced to make a set of four-color plates: one for yellow, one for magenta, one for cyan, and one for black. The resulting negatives are in black and white and are called *color separation negatives*.

---

agents assigned to buying typesetting, printing image carriers, paper, and other graphic arts services and commodities," Schmidt points out that "they are, beyond that basic purchasing function, you and your client's graphic arts consultants, production planners, and production liaison people—internally, with the creative, traffic, media, and account management areas, and externally with graphic arts vendors and with the print media."

Schmidt notes that, at Young & Rubicam, New York, the print operations group includes the following:

1. *Art buyers,* who are versed in various forms of photographic/illustrative techniques. They know the available talent and make all business arrangements with photographers, model agencies, illustrators, retouchers, photo labs, and others, in close cooperation with art directors.
2. *Type directors,* who are trained in the creative as well as the technical aspects of typography. Working with art directors they select, specify, mark up, and purchase all typesetting.
3. *Print producers,* who coordinate all print production activities with the traffic, account management, and creative groups. They purchase image carriers for the various printed media from photoplatemaking houses and provide the vital contact with publication production departments.
4. *Printing buyers,* who specialize in the production planning and buying of outdoor and transit advertising, newspaper and magazine inserts, and collateral printed material from brochures to elaborate die-cut direct-mail pieces. A printing buyer's knowledge reaches into properties of paper and ink and into the capabilities of printing, binding, and finishing equipment.

Schmidt, who has written numerous articles for both American and European graphic arts magazines, has been the recipient of the Typomundus Award of the International Center for the Typographic Arts and the International Book Exhibition Award.

Cofounder and former board chairman of the International Center for the Typographic Arts, Schmidt has also served as chairman of the American Association of Advertising Agencies' Subcommittee on Phototypography and of the Gravure Advertising Council of the Gravure Technical Association. He is a member of the American Association of Advertising Agencies Subcommittee on Newspaper Formats and past president of the New York Advertising Production Club, president of the Type Directors Club, and vice president of the Art Directors Club.

These color separations are photographed through a halftone screen to make a set of screened negatives from which the plates are made. In photographing the color separations, the halftone screen is rotated to a different angle for each separation. As a result the dots do not completely overlap because the four plates superimpose the dots over one another during printing. On the printed page tiny clusters of halftone dots of the four colors in various sizes give the eye the optical illusion of seeing different colors of the original photograph or painting. In printing, transparent inks are used, so people can see all colors through the four overlapping coatings of ink on the paper. For example, even though green ink is not used, green can be reproduced by a yellow and a cyan dot, each overlapping their respective colors on paper in the form of halftone dots. Dark green would have larger blue halftone dots than yellow. (See Creative Department: From concept through production of a magazine advertisement.)

Recently developed electronic scanners perform two- or four-color separations and screening in one process, along with enlargement or reduction. In a single operation, an operator can achieve highlight/shadow density changes, contrast modification, color change, or removal of an area or a whole piece. All this can be done in several minutes instead of the hours or days needed for camera work and hand-etching in the process camera operation described previously. Lately scanners have grown into color pagination systems which perform in a digital manner all positioning of illustrative and text elements as well as electronic retouching.

For letterpress printing, the four-color halftone plates are made the same as for black and white halftones, except four plates are sent to the publication instead of one. For rotogravure and lithography, color-separated positive or negative film is furnished instead of plates. From this film, publications make their own printing plates or cylinders.

FIGURE   10–16

The impact of color is accentuated by the contrast against the black and white surrounding art. Great concept, well executed.

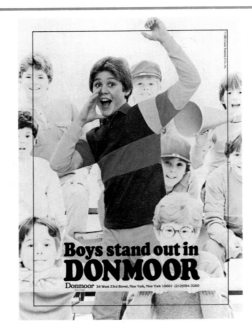

CREATIVE DEPARTMENT

From Concept through
Production of a Magazine
Advertisement

Marketing considerations

Traditionally, Dr Pepper targets two distinct markets with its promotional activities. One is the consumer of its product—young people of high school and college age. And the other is the local bottler whose enthusiasm and support is vital to the company's marketing efforts.

As a result Dr Pepper's marketing strategy includes substantial advertising to the youth market on targeted television programs and MTV as well as in college yearbooks and other specialized media. In addition the company lends support to the efforts of local bottlers by providing advertising materials and dollars on a selective basis. The company also does substantial amounts of sales promotion—sponsoring rock concerts, floats in major parades, and self-liquidating advertising premiums that merchandise the fun aspect of their product.

In 1985 Dr Pepper celebrated its 100th anniversary. In keeping with its traditional strategy, the company decided to sponsor a float in the Rose Parade and participate in the events surrounding the Cotton Bowl game. To support these activities Dr Pepper asked its advertising agency, Young & Rubicam, to prepare an ad that would appear in the official programs of the Rose Bowl and the Cotton Bowl.

Creative concepts

As an advertising medium, football programs are not usually taken very seriously by either advertisers or their agencies. In fact the ads that appear in them are frequently bought as a courtesy by the various sponsors—a simple thank you and congratulations. The fact is, though, that these programs often enjoy a fairly wide distribution within a very specific target market and are frequently kept for their souvenir value. Recognizing this, and in light of its client's anniver-

A. Rough layout.

sary, Young & Rubicam decided not to do just an ordinary ad. Instead it wanted to do something fun and very special.

Readers of these programs would tend to be young football enthusiasts as well as the local bottlers affected by the Bowl game activities in their areas. Y&R decided to create an ad that would play off that enthusiasm and merchandise the 100th anniversary in a fun manner. It decided to show a portrait of a football team from a century ago enjoying a Dr Pepper after their game. The copy would be light—just enough to mention the 100th anniversary and play off the fun of football without getting heavy-handed. But the most compelling aspect of the ad would come from the production values employed. Everything would be as authentic looking as possible, thereby making it more interesting and fun to the readers. (See A. Rough layout.)

Shooting the ad

The key to the creative concept was the production, and this would require great attention to detail. The agency searched photo archives for pictures of old football teams from a hundred years ago, and a stylist was employed to match the pictures in every way. The stylist bought authentic costumes from the period and found all the other props, too—an old football, an oaken bucket, a handpainted oil backdrop, even hay for the floor to suggest the fall season. Models were carefully selected to be handsome but not too pretty, and hairstyles were matched to the period. To top it all off, the picture would be shot in full color, but then the color would be reduced to create a sepia tone portrait, typical of the period, leaving only the Dr Pepper cans in full color. This, the agency felt, would make the product look even more appetizing.

The photographer was selected because of his unique ability to light and shoot this type of shot; and the art director had experience as a portrait photographer. Nothing was left to chance either before or on the day of the shoot. Just to arrange the props, light the set, stage the models, and perform the shot required a full day.

$2\frac{1}{4} \times 2\frac{1}{4}$

B. Transparency selected.

Preparation for production

After processing the film from the shoot, the photographer submitted the 2 × 2 transparencies to the art director and art buyer for their approval and selection. After choosing the picture that best captured the concept of the ad, the art buyer proceeded with the preparation of the print. (See B. Transparency selected.)

Both the main illustration of the football players and the small product shot were sent to a color lab for dye transfers. (See C. and D. Unretouched dye transfers.) The football dye transfer was specially filtered to reduce all the color in the picture and to create the brown or "sepia" tone. The dye transfer of the cans was processed normally to match the actual color of the cans. Both these prints were then given to a retoucher to adjust them to the art director's requirements and to prepare them for reproduction.

On the football print, all the color on the cans was restored to match that of the actual product. Selective bleaching and repainting ensured that all elements in the print achieved the necessary creative quality and compensated for whatever loss in fidelity would occur in the color separation. (See E. Retouched dye transfer.)

D. Unretouched dye transfer of product shot.

C. Unretouched dye filtered print (sepia).

E. Retouched dye transfer with cans in color.

On the print of the cans, the cans and shadows were carefully silhouetted and the lettering on the cans cleaned up and emphasized with retouching so that the brand name would read easily in a small size. (See F. Retouched product shot.)

Typesetting

Meanwhile, the copy and rough layout, drawn on an artist's tracing pad, were submitted to the agency type director by the art director. Together the art director and type director selected a suitable type style. (See G. Rough sketch in color.) The type director determined the size of the headline and carefully marked up the copy for style of typeface, spacing, and size. (See H. Marked copy for typesetter.)

F. Retouched product shot.

G. Rough sketch in color.

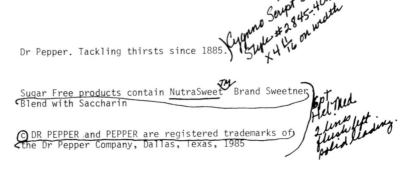

H. Marked copy for typesetter.

At this point the copy with layout was sent to the typographer, who set the headline with photodisplay equipment. From the film output of the equipment, a photomechanical was made up as indicated on the rough tissue and then proofed. The copywriter, art director, and type director reviewed the proofs and made whatever aesthetic or technical adjustments were required. The ad was submitted to the client in this form for preliminary approval. (See I. Photomechanical.)

When all adjustments and corrections in copy and artwork were compiled, an adjusted "paper" mechanical was returned to the typographer. The corrected photomechanical was then contacted to a negative line film and delivered to the photoplatemaker.

Photoplatemaking

The photoplatemaker prepared offset lithography separation films to SWOP (Specifications for Web Offset Publication) standards in order to fill the needs of the publications involved on the media list. Then continuous-tone separations were made. After photocomposing the elements together, the job was screened to provide the necessary printing dots. (See J. dot screens.) After screening, an off-press proof was produced to check the colors. Then the job was dot etched to make the color more closely related to the supplied artwork.

I. Photomechanical.

Dr Pepper. Tackling thirsts since 1885.

J. A greatly enlarged section of the final printed advertisement showing how the process colors are combined to produce continuous color tone.

K. Progressive proofs (color separations).

The line negative of the typographic elements, sent by the type shop, was incorporated with the screened separations. A set of four-color offset plates was made and placed on the press. A set of proofs and progressive proofs showing the single colors and combination of colors was pulled and sent to the agency for approval. (See K. Progressive proofs.) Minor corrections were handled by the photo-platemaker through dot etching of the offset film masters.

After client and agency product group approval, the master films were duplicated by the platemaker, and the necessary quantity of films, proofs, and progressive proofs were sent to the publications involved. The proofs were to be used by the publications as a guide for color at the press to be sure that a faithful reproduction would be achieved. (See L. Completed ad.)

L. Completed ad.

Preparing Materials for Publications

Most local media, newspapers, and magazines are very willing and able to work with advertisers to help produce their advertisements. Frequently this service is free. The local dress shop or furniture store works with the newspaper's ad salesperson and provides the copy and illustrations, and the newspaper's production department takes care of the rest.

At some point in their growth, advertisers decide to exercise more control over the production process to assure consistency and quality. Major agencies always like to maintain complete control over the preparation of materials used for reproduction rather than giving the media that responsibility.

Media schedules frequently contain numerous publications that will run the advertisement at about the same time. This requires the advertiser to provide duplicate materials to each publication.

Production specifications can be obtained directly from the publication. It is often more convenient, however, to use the Standard Rate and Data Service *Print Media Production Data* directory, which contains critical information on the printing material and mechanical measurements (dimensions of advertising space accepted) of every major publication.

For publications printed by rotogravure or offset lithography, duplicate materials consist of duplicate sets of film positives (for gravure) or photographic copies of the mechanical and screened art (for offset lithography). These photographic copies may be in the form of *photoprints* (a screened print or a Velox) or contact *film negatives*, depending on the requirements of the particular publication.

Selecting Papers for Printing

When preparing materials for printing, it is important to know the kind of paper on which the advertisement will be printed. Some advertisers are so concerned about the appearance of their advertisements that they have them printed on a higher quality of paper stock than that used in the regular pages of a newspaper or magazine. They will then ship the printed material to the publication for insertion or binding.

Paper used in advertising can be broken down into three categories: writing, text, and cover stock.

Writing paper This is commonly used in letters and other direct mail pieces. Bond writing paper is the most durable and also the most frequently used.

Text paper Many different types of text paper are available. Major classifications—news stock, antique finish, machine finish, English finish, and coated—range from less expensive, very porous, coarse papers to very smooth, expensive, heavier papers used for industrial brochures and fine quality annual reports.

Cover paper Because of its tough, durable quality, cover paper is used for softcover book covers and sometimes for direct mail pieces. Advertisers can choose from many finishes and textures.

Summary

The production process in print advertising is so critical that if it is not handled correctly, an otherwise beautiful ad can be destroyed. A fundamental understanding of production techniques, therefore, can save a lot of money and disappointment.

The print production manager's job is to ensure that the final advertisement reflects what the art director had in mind. That is often a difficult task as the print production manager must work within the limited, specified confines of time requirements, quality objectives, and acceptable budgets.

The typeface chosen for an advertisement affects its appearance, design, and legibility. Type can generally be divided into two broad classes: display type and text type. In addition, typefaces can be classified by their similarity of design. The major type groups are roman, sans serif, square serif, cursive or script, and ornamental. Within each group are many type families, such as Bodoni, Futura, Goudy, and Caslon. In a type family the basic design remains the same, but variations of weight, slant, and size are available.

Type is measured in terms of points and picas. Points measure the vertical size of type. There are 72 points to an inch. Picas measure the horizontal width of a line of type. There are six picas to an inch. Type may further be referred to as uppercase (capital letters) and lowercase (small letters).

There are four important points to consider when selecting type: readability, appropriateness, harmony or appearance, and emphasis. The process of determining how much type will fit a specified area in an advertisement is called copy casting. There are several methods used to cast copy today.

There are also several methods used to set type. The most important of these are the various photocomposition techniques including photo-optical methods, cathode-ray tube (CRT) techniques, and laser exposure.

Printing processes have undergone great technological changes in recent decades. Today the most common printing methods are letterpress, rotogravure, offset lithography, and screen printing. Each method has its unique advantages and disadvantages.

Preparing plates for printing involves exposing an image to a sensitized metal plate. Two types of plates are used for printing: line plates and halftone plates. Line plates print only two tonal values—black and white. For gradations of tone, as in an illustration or photograph, halftone plates are used. These print a series of black dots of various sizes, thus producing an optical illusion of tonal grades.

When full-color is required, four halftone plates are used, one for each primary color plus black. These print the colored dots in tiny clusters, creating the illusion of full color.

Questions for review and discussion

1. What are the characteristics of the five major type groups?
2. What does type casting mean? Explain the ways in which it is done.
3. What is the importance of these terms: readability, appropriateness, harmony/appearance, emphasis?
4. What do these terms mean: point, pica, uppercase, lowercase?
5. The two broad classifications of display type and text type have basic differences. Explain what they are. Give some examples in which display type may be used.
6. What are the types of photocomposition, and what advantages does photocomposition offer?
7. What are the major differences between rotogravure and offset lithography?
8. What is a halftone? How is it produced?
9. How are color photographs printed? What are the potential problems with printing color?
10. What role is played by one of the typical production suppliers of advertising?

11

CREATIVE PRODUCTION: ELECTRONIC MEDIA

D ick Wilson, at 68 years old, has been an actor for almost half a century. He has appeared in over 300 television roles and has played major parts in several series. But it wasn't until he started playing the finicky grocer, Mr. Whipple, that people began asking for his autograph.

Twenty years ago Wilson got a call from his agent. Shortly thereafter, Wilson found himself promoting bathroom tissue at a studio in—appropriately—Flushing, New York. His role was to simply whine, "Please don't squeeze the Charmin," in a commercial for Procter & Gamble. Two decades later Charmin is the best-selling bathroom tissue in America. Wilson clearly delights in his odd calling, which he pursues with professionalism and disarming zeal. "People ask me if I mind being called Mr. Whipple all the time, and I respond, 'no,' because they call me Mr. Wilson at the bank." Mr. Wilson earns more than $100,000 a year. For that tidy sum he spends some 16 days a year taping and the rest of the year praying to live to 100. That's how long the advertiser has promised to keep using him.[1]

When Virginia Kraft goes home to the little village in Iowa where she was born, she's the queen of the parade. The old water tower in the small Swedish community of 700 has been changed into a giant coffee pot with a spout, a handle, and painted flames at the bottom. They've painted it white with little flowers and a written Swedish poem on it. All this to honor the lady who has the stage name of Virginia Christine but whom we all know and recognize as Mrs. Olsen of Folger's Coffee fame (Figure 11–1).

Dick Wilson and Virginia Christine are just two of the many continuing personalities we have seen on TV's commercial circuit. The list of others includes Madge the manicurist for Palmolive Liquid, Old Lonely the Maytag repairman, and Rosie the counter lady for Bounty paper towels, to name just a few.

These continuing commercial presenters, according to most advertisers, produce fantastic goodwill and product identification. They attract attention, identify the brand immediately by their familiarity, act as friendly authority figures for the consuming public, and guarantee advertising continuity over the years to the brands they support. As such, they are an important consideration in the development of product advertising campaigns and in the production of commercials for electronic media.

PRODUCING TELEVISION COMMERCIALS

Advertisers produce more than 50,000 television commercials every year in an effort to sell their goods and services. No one knows exactly how much is spent in the production of all these commercials, but most estimates are in the many hundreds of millions of dollars.

Producing commercials for television is expensive. For a local advertiser a simple spot might cost anywhere from $500 to $10,000. For national quality spots, though, the costs are considerably higher. The lowest figure is probably around $15,000 with the highs in the hundreds of thousands.

As the technology of electronic commercial production has soared, so have the costs and the complexity. This has resulted in the specialization of those involved in commercial production. Major agencies, for example, used to maintain complete production facilities in-house. Not any more. The trend for several decades now has been toward the use of outside producers, directors, production companies, and other technical suppliers.

As a result, it has become more difficult to gain an expert knowledge of electronic production. However, a broad understanding of basic production concepts is still a must for anyone interested in advertising today. This includes an understanding of: how commercials are written; which types of commercials are most commonly used, and which are most effective; what the basic terms and techniques are for producing a commercial; and how is the production process organized.

For the student of advertising, an understanding of these concepts will explain how commercials are made, why commercial production is so expensive, and what methods can be used to cut costs without sacrificing quality or effectiveness.

■ Writing the Commercial

How did Dick Wilson, for instance, get to be Mr. Whipple and Virginia Christine become Mrs. Olsen? And where do those characters come from anyway?

Put simply, they are usually born in the minds of the men and women who conceive of the original commercial—the art director, the copywriter, and the creative director.

Initially, the concept may call for an actor to play a part. Or, the creative team may decide they want to use a well-known celebrity to present the product. At the time the commercial is written, the casting of characters is a major consideration. And the most important consideration in casting is relevance to the product. It might be unwise, for example, to use a known comic to sell financial services—or mortuary services for that matter.

As the copy is written and the storyboard laid out, the creative team develops the personalities of their characters and usually writes a brief but detailed description of them. These descriptions are used in casting sessions as guides in the selection of prospective actors to be interviewed, auditioned, and considered for the roles. Sometimes a Dick Wilson or Virginia Christine will be discovered—solid, believable actors who go beyond a simple role and actually create a personality or image for the product.

FIGURE 11–1

As commercial presenters, Dick Wilson and Virginia Christine have played Mr. Whipple and Mrs. Olsen successfully for years.

Mechanics

A television script is divided into two portions. The right side is the *audio*—indicating sound effects, spoken copy, and music. The left side is the *video*—indicating camera action, scenes, and instructions. (See the script for the commercial in the "Creative department: From concept through production of a television commercial" later in this chapter.)

After the script has been approved by the person in charge of the account, the writer and art director prepare a storyboard. The typical storyboard is a sheet preprinted with a series of 8 to 20 blank television screens (frames). The frames are sketched in by the art director to represent the video. The audio, plus instructions for the video, are typed underneath. Due to space limitations, many abbreviations are used. See Figure 11–2 for some of the more common ones.

A storyboard helps in estimating the expense, visualizing the message, revealing any weakness in concept, presenting for client approval, and guiding the actual shooting. At best, the storyboard is an approximation of what the commercial will be. Actual production

FIGURE 11–2   Cut, zoom, and wipe, please!

CU:	Close-up. Very close shot of person or object.
ECU:	Extreme close-up. A more extreme version of the above. Sometimes designated as BCU (big close-up) or TCU (tight close-up).
MCU:	Medium close-up. Emphasizes the subject but includes other objects nearby.
MS:	Medium shot. Wide-angle shot of subject but not whole set.
FS:	Full shot. Entire set or object.
LS:	Long shot. Full view of scene to give effect of distance.
DOLLY:	Move camera toward or away from subject. Dolly in (DI), dolly out (DO), or dolly back (DB).
PAN:	Camera scans from one side to the other.
ZOOM:	Move rapidly in or out from the subject without blurring.
SUPER:	Superimpose one image on another—as showing lettering over a scene.
DISS:	Dissolve (also DSS). Fade out one scene while fading in another.
CUT:	Instant change of one picture to another.
WIPE:	Gradually erase picture from screen. (Many varied effects are possible.)
VO:	Voice-over. An off-screen voice, usually the announcer's.
SFX:	Sound effects.
DAU:	Down and under. Sound effects fade as voice comes on.
UAO:	Up and over. Voice fades as sound effects come on.

sometimes results in many changes in lighting, camera angle, focal point, and emphasis. The camera sees many things the artist didn't see, and vice versa.

Sometimes, to aid and supplement the storyboard, a commercial is roughly taped using the writers and artists as actors. Or the storyboard sketches may be photographed on a film strip and then accompanied by the audio portion synchronized on tape. This is called an *animatic*.

Writing effectively

In Chapter 8 the fundamentals of writing advertising copy were presented. The writing of television commercials demands that additional attention be given to credibility, believability, and relevance. That goes well beyond the use of words.

Millions of dollars spent on TV commercial research have resulted in the following principles:

The opening should be a short, compelling attention-getter—compelling in action, drama, humor, or human interest.

Situations should be believable—authentic and true to life. Demonstrations should never appear to be a camera trick.

The commercial should be in good taste—ethically and morally—and not offend or step on any toes.

The entertainment should be a means to an end and not interfere with the message.

The general structure of the commercial and the copy should be simple and easy to follow. The video should carry over half the weight, with the audio merely supporting.

Characters should be appealing and believable.

These are only some of the principles research has shown to be true. See the Checklist for creating effective TV commercials for more.

To illustrate these principles, look at the 30-second award-winning Jarman shoes commercial, "Manhole," illustrated in Figure 11–3. Created by The Bloom Agency in Dallas, this is a classic example of a well-written, simple, interesting, credible, and entertaining commercial. It's also relatively inexpensive.

First, look at the commercial as a whole. There is one dominant mood throughout and a single, unified impression. The number of people is kept to a minimum. The whole commercial is shot in *close-up*. Everything not relevant to the commercial's objective has been deleted. The situation is high in human interest and believable. The structure is *simple* and easy to follow. The presenter is *appealing*, authoritative, and credible. The entertainment value is high but perfectly *relevant*. The *sales points* are demonstrated smoothly, and the product *name* is given sufficient mention. Finally, there is a strong *closing identification* illustrating the name and the product.

Looking at some of the mechanics, note that there seems to be only one scene throughout. There are in fact four different camera setups. But the *unity* is so strong and the flow so smooth that the changes are hardly noticeable.

Examine the opening scene. Before one word is spoken, we know who the man is and what he's doing. He looks the part and acts the part. In 12 words he has established the whole context of the commer-

Checklist for creating effective TV commercials

□ The opening should be pertinent, relevant, and not forced. It should permit a smooth transition to the balance of the commercial.

□ The situation should lend itself naturally to the sales story—without the use of extraneous, distracting gimmicks.

□ The situation should be high in human interest.

□ The viewer should be able to identify with the situation.

□ Generally hold the number of elements to a minimum.

□ Present a simple sequence of ideas.

□ The words should be short, realistic, and conversational, not "ad talk." Sentences should be short.

□ Words should not be wasted describing what is being seen.

□ The words should interpret the picture and prepare the viewer for the next scene.

□ Don't jump too far ahead in the audio by describing one feature while showing another. Synchronize audio and video.

□ Keep the audio copy concise—without wasted words. Fewer words are needed for TV than for radio. Less than two words per second is effective for demonstrations.

□ Remember, 60-second commercials with 101 to 110 words are most effective. Those with more than 170 words are the least effective.

□ Allow five or six seconds for the average scene, with none less than three seconds.

□ Provide enough movement to avoid static scenes.

□ Scenes should offer variety without "jumping."

□ The commercial should look fresh and new.

□ Any presenters should be properly handled—identified, compatible, authoritative, pleasing, and nondistracting.

□ The general video treatment should be interesting.

cial and is into the sell. By the second frame of the storyboard he has already said the product name once and made a case for the popularity of the product. By the third frame he's proving his first sales point and is into the second—style. Then he hits the name again. Two frames later he hits it again and then there is a third sales point—comfort. One more frame and he hits the fourth sales point—price. Then he hits the name again and the fifth point—for men only. Finally, a touch of human interest humor is handled in exceptionally good taste, and the closing frame shows the shoes, the name, and the strong tag line: "Style to fit your style."

In all, the commercial contains only 76 words, yet it says so much. That's what makes a commercial memorable.

As an exercise, take a few moments to compare some of the other television spots illustrated in this text to that Jarman commercial. How many can you find that are as concise? As simple? As appealing? And as credible? These are the qualities that make commercials effective.

FIGURE 11–3

Jarman shoes.

SFX: CITY STREET SOUNDS. ON CAMERA: At this level, it's easy to become an expert on shoe styles.

Know what I see a lot of? Jarman.

Take those.

Look European?

They're Jarman.

Those boots and slip ons...

Both Jarman.

That one too. Looks comfortable doesn't it?

And they're not that expensive either.

Yes sir, when it comes to style,

I'd say Jarman's got a style to fit everybody.

Well, just about everybody.

Hello there, how are you?

You need a cab? (WHISTLES)

TYPES OF TELEVISION COMMERCIALS

The advertisements we have discussed have all been "presenter" commercials, where one person or character presents the product and carries the whole sales message. Sometimes these presenters are celebrities, like Bill Cosby for Jell-O and Ford or John Houseman for Smith Barney. Other times they are corporate officers of the sponsor, like Frank Perdue for Perdue Chicken or Lee Iacocca, the chairman of the board of Chrysler Corporation. In the case of Jarman, we see an actor playing a role and simultaneously acting as a spokesperson. Other commercials, like Bank of America, use an actor to play a straight, unidentified spokesperson. The variations are almost limitless.

There are many types of commercials in addition to the presenter format. Actually there may be as many ways of classifying television ads as there are television advertisers. The six basic categories, though, in addition to the presenter category, are: the straight announcement, demonstration, testimonial, slice of life, lifestyle, and animation. These groupings often overlap and should not be considered ironclad.

We will next discuss each of these types briefly before considering the more practical subjects of production techniques and procedures.

■ Straight Announcement

This is the oldest type of television commercial. An announcer delivers a sales message directly into the camera or off-screen while a slide or film is shown on screen. It is a safe method and can be effective if the script is well written and the announcer convincing. The appeal may be either "hard sell" or relaxed. It is a relatively simple approach and needs no elaborate facilities, so the advertiser saves money. It may be combined with a demonstration.

Few commercials are made this way today. The chief holdouts are late-night TV programs, local advertisers, and ads for nonprofit organizations.

■ Demonstration

Studies have shown that a demonstration convinces an audience better and faster than an oral message. Memorable demonstrations have been used to show the product advantages of car tires, ballpoint pens, and paper towels, to mention just a few. Such products may be demonstrated in three ways—in use, in competition, or before and after.

These techniques enable the viewer who sees the utility and quality of a product to project what its performance would be like if he or she owned it. Therefore, the theme of the demonstration should be as clear, simple, graphic, and as *relevant* as possible. It doesn't make any sense to demonstrate a point that is not important to the customer (Figure 11–4).

PEOPLE IN ADVERTISING

Joe Sedelmaier

**Founder and President
Sedelmaier Film Productions, Inc.**

Joe Sedelmaier, whose hilarious, offbeat TV commercials for Wendy's and numerous other companies have made him today's hottest—and most controversial—TV commercial director, is the president of Sedelmaier Film Productions, Inc., in Chicago.

His TV spots are instantly recognizable—the fast-talking man for Federal Express, the Jartran commercial with the roomful of multiplying rabbits, the Aamco ad in which appliances blow up just as their warranties expire, and the Mr. Coffee spot in which hordes of disgruntled coffee drinkers hurl their coffee pots out their windows. "They are by far the strangest commercials on TV," writes an industry observer. "They may also be the best."

Sedelmaier, born John Josef Sedelmaier on May 31, 1933, in Orrville, Ohio, graduated from Chicago's Art Institute and the University of Chicago. He entered advertising in 1956 as an art director/producer for Young & Rubicam in Chicago, then served in the same capacity at Clinton Frank and J. Walter Thompson there.

During these years, Sedelmaier directed and produced several short films. *Mrofnoc* ("conform" spelled backwards) and *Because That's Why* netted him top awards including the Golden Lion at the

FIGURE 11–4

The aerial acrobat is fast approaching the Fuji film blimp. Then, suddenly, she crashes into

it. But, no, it's just a huge, enlarged photo of the blimp, and she has broken through the

paper. As the script says, Fuji offers "a real break-through"—in commercial demonstration.

 Testimonial

People are most easily persuaded by the opinions of individuals they respect. This holds true whether the "product" is a political candidate or a bar of soap. It makes TV testimonials highly effective.

Figures from all walks of life endorse products—from big-name stars and personalities to unknowns and nonprofessionals. The per-

---

Cannes Film Festival and the Mannheim Film Festival's Golde Ducat.

Launching his own production company in 1967, Sedelmaier soon became known for his comic TV commercials for clients such as Del Taco, Dunkin' Donuts, Alaska Airlines, PSA, and American Motors.

What do Sedelmaier's commercials have in common? They are funny. They are odd. They focus on everyday human anxieties. Most people have been victims of postal neglect, of awful fast-food chicken, of screwed-up cars. Sedelmaier sells through this human dread. Watching his commercials is oddly comforting, yet unsettling. You relate, you identify. And then you laugh.

Sedelmaier feels that casting is 50 percent of his job. He is famous for the group of mostly nonactors—former bricklayers, cabbies, CPAs, even former manicurist Clara Peller—who spark his commercials. If a face strikes him as evocative or funny, he'll use it. And he likes to let the people he chooses inspire his comic direction. "If an actor has some distinctive quality, I'll write him or her into the spot. Casting can change everything."

So can Joe Sedelmaier, as his clients attest. He takes total control over the commercials he directs,

from idea to final print. Typically, he begins by dispensing with the client-approved storyboards for the commercial. Then he changes dialogue, alters sequence, adds characters. He revamps the entire commercial and leaves only the original idea intact. Sedelmaier likes things a certain way—his way—and his TV spots reflect this determination.

Sedelmaier is the only TV commercial director who works exclusively in comedy. While many in advertising claim that humor just doesn't sell, Sedelmaier's commercials suggest otherwise. They helped to shoot Federal Express from obscurity to number one in overnight delivery. And Wendy's sales reportedly climbed 15 percent after Sedelmaier's "Where's the beef?" spots first aired.

"The reason I've always held to comedy," explains Sedelmaier, "is that there's not much to be serious about. How can you be serious about toilet paper?"

The notion has paid off—for Joe Sedelmaier. He shoots 75 to 80 TV commercials a year, which reportedly earn him about a million dollars. His commercials have won over 50 Clio awards, the Golden Hugo award at the Chicago Film Festival, and top honors from The One Show, the Art Directors Club, and the Hollywood IBA.

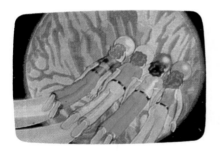  

FIGURE 11-5

Computer animation is used to enhance the flavor fantasy of Bubblicious bubble gum. The well-executed effect blows the viewer away.

son used usually depends on the product. One research firm found that a little girl's endorsement on a cake mix carried more weight than that of a chef. The viewer felt confident he or she could handle any cake mix a little girl could, but perhaps not one recommended by a chef.

Using celebrities to endorse a product gains attention. But they must be believable. The product and copy must fit their mannerisms and style.

Satisfied customers also provide excellent testimonials. They're often camera shy, but their natural sincerity is usually persuasive.

Slice of Life (Problem Solution)

The slice-of-life commercial is a little play that portrays a real-life situation. It usually starts with just plain folks before they discover the solution to their problem. The situation is usually tense, often dealing with something of a personal nature—bad breath, dentures, dandruff, B.O., or yellow laundry. Usually a relative or a co-worker drops the hint, the product is tried, and the next scene shows the result—a happier, cleaner, more fragrant person off with a new date or finally able to bite into an apple. Such commercials are often irritating to viewers, but their messages still break through and sell, which is why you keep seeing them.

The key to effective slice-of-life commercials is simplicity. The ad should concentrate on one product benefit and make it memorable. Often a *mnemonic device* is used to dramatize the product benefit. Users of Imperial Margarine suddenly discover a crown on their head, or the doorbell rings for the Avon lady. Creative people as well as consumers find these corny, but they make a commercial memorable.

Believability is difficult to achieve in slice-of-life commercials. People don't really talk about "ring around the collar," so the actors must be highly credible to put the fantasy across. For that reason, most local advertisers don't use the slice-of-life technique. Creating that believability takes very professional talent and money.

Lifestyle

When they want to present the user rather than the product, advertisers frequently use the lifestyle technique. Miller Beer targets its messages to young, contemporary men working and playing in a variety of different occupations and pastimes with the simple musical message: "Welcome to Miller time." Likewise soft drink advertisers frequently target their messages to active, outdoorsy, young people, focusing on who drinks the brand rather than specific product advantages.

Animation

The use of cartoons, puppet characters, or animated demonstrations can be very effective in communicating especially difficult messages or with specialized markets like children (Figure 11–5).

Herbal Essence shampoo developed a unique art style for its packaging and print advertising, which it animated for its television commercials. This created a mood, personality, and unity that were evident in every communication about the product.

The way in which aspirin or other medications affect the human system is difficult to explain. Animated pictures of headaches and stomachs, however, can simplify the subject and make a demonstration understandable.

PRODUCTION TECHNIQUES

Animation is more than just a category of commercial. It is also a major production technique that has recently experienced startling technological progress. When Levi's spent a quarter of a million dollars to produce a single animated TV commercial, it was called "a milestone in television advertising" by columnist Harry Wayne McMahan in *Advertising Age*.[2] The commercial did indeed make history—in more ways than one:

It set a new record at the time for the production cost of just one commercial.

It chalked up the highest test score in Burke's (a major advertising research company) experience, with a score of 59—two to four times as high as "normal" commercials.

It pioneered radically new and effective techniques in communication—especially with young people.

It continued to build the sales momentum of this 130-year-old firm, which in 1985 used more than 10 percent of all the cotton grown in this country.

The commercial—created by Levi's agency, Foote, Cone & Belding/Honig, San Francisco—was 60 seconds long and titled "Brand Name." When the Disney organization saw the storyboard, they turned down the production assignment at any price. Then the production house of Robert Abel & Associates in Hollywood came into the picture. Their experience with new lighting and photography techniques convinced them they could produce the commercial within budget.

The resulting commercial must be seen to be appreciated because it is so visually outstanding. Part of its success is due to the use of technical and electronic effects described as "luminetics" or "drawing with light on film," an entirely new approach to film making. According to Robert Abel, the techniques, similar to those used in the feature film *Star Wars*, "stimulate the subconscious or dream levels of perception—the area of fantasy."[3]

One psychiatrist described the style and technique of the commercial as penetrating directly to the subconscious section of the brain to become "reality" and to be retained in "permanent memory."

The commercial starred the red Levi's logo as the doggy blanket on a fantasized puppy on a leash, barking and leading its owner down a lengthy San Francisco street (Figure 11–6). Although the set was only 52 feet long, its unique design and perspective made it appear to stretch out to infinity.

The key to the effect was an intricate and specially built electronic crane and dolly. This made it possible for the camera to travel on a track. It could pan, tilt, stop, and go from scene to scene in what appeared to be one continuous take of the puppy "trademark" being walked down the street. The camera was automated electronically to totally repeat the same movements in identical continuous sequence time after time. As many as 42 separate exposures could be put on the same film negative. Thus one take could cover the puppy, another an old miner petting him, another a woman shopper, another a translucent "android," another a boy on a skateboard, and so on.

Animation was combined smoothly with live action in several scenes. In one, when the "puppy" jumped through a window, the strings holding the doggy blanket logo would of course not go through the window frame, and several frames of animation were added to bridge the gap.

FIGURE 11–6

Photoboard and script of Levi's commercial.

MALE (VO): C'mon old Trademark, time for your walk. Where will you take me? Sure wish you could talk.

I know what you'd tell me. How your family began with

the same Levi's blue jeans worn by this man.

Hey, here come more Levi's; red, yellow and blue.

Free wheeling kiddos are wearing them, too!

And what a surprise! Look who's been window shopping for clothes.

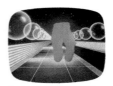

Yeah, a gal in her Levi's instinctively knows of your special appeal. Enough of this kissing, little Register Mark.

Time that we meet some guys by the park. Dressed in your newest addition. Sums it up right there: Levi's Sportswear.

Hey, Trademark, this looks like the place where tomorrows begin.

Your family's future — sure looks like it should.

That's right, little Trademark —

Levi's don't have to be blue — just have to be good!

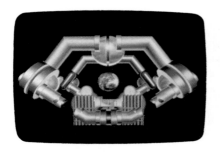 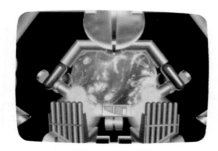 

FIGURE 11–7

A commercial for a children's role playing game, "Star Frontiers," offers endless horizons and weird geometric sights, a strangely angular city only the most imaginative person could dream of. *Art Direction* magazine likens Digital Productions' computer-generated effects to stepping off the edge of this world . . . and into a vastly different one.

In all, over 40 people took part in the production—in specialties ranging from choreography and costuming to optical design and puppeteering. It took six people for the ingenious system engineering and design.

Apparently the commercial was worth it—considering all the word-of-mouth publicity and image-building it gave to Levi's. After viewing the commercial during the Burke test, several people said: "Levi's must be better, the commercial is so well done."

While this Levi's masterpiece opened the door to untold innovations in commercials, historically there have been relatively few basic types of executions. Possibly this is because the selling idea is generally considered more important than the way it is presented.

■ Animation Techniques

The Levi's commercial is an example of the new style of modern, computerized, laser light animation. Even more advanced animation techniques using computer generated graphics and simulation produce scenes that appear to be filmed from live action (Figure 11–7). However, the more traditional animation techniques involve the use of cartoons, puppets, and photo animation.

■ Cartoons

This technique often has the highest viewer interest, the longest life, and the lowest cost per showing, but many viewers consider it childlike. There are several animation styles—Disney, contemporary, psychedelic, and others. Cartoons are sometimes supplemented by live action, especially when a serious purchase decision is to be made and the product benefits are described.

The technique is achieved by drawing illustrations of each step in the action and photographing them one frame at a time. Projecting the film at 24 frames per second gives the illusion of movement.

■ Puppets

Frequently puppets or dolls are used instead of illustrations. Special kinds of action can be portrayed, such as the journey of a drug through the body.

■ Photo animation

This technique uses still photography instead of illustrations or puppets. Making slight movements of the photos from one frame to the next creates the animated illusion. This technique is especially effective for making titles move. However, it is considered a very low-budget technique.

FIGURE   11–8

Poppin' Fresh, the Pillsbury
doughboy, has been the
continuing central character of
that company's commercials for
many years. Made of rubber with
flexible arms and legs, the
doughboy can seemingly be made
to walk, talk, laugh, and point
through the marvel of stop-action
photography.

Stop-motion

This is another animation technique whereby objects and animals
come to life—walk, run, dance, and do tricks—by means of stop-
motion photography. One of the most famous special-effect creations
is the charming, giggling Pillsbury Doughboy (Figure 11–8). The
Doughboy is a flexible rubber figure with movable joints. The arms
and legs can be bent to simulate walking or pointing. Each frame of
film is shot individually. An arm may be moved only 1/32 of an inch
on each frame, but when the frames are assembled the effect is
smooth and natural. Since film is projected at 24 frames per second,
this means 1,440 frames must be shot for each minute of activity by
the Doughboy.

Live Action

The basic production technique that portrays people in everyday
situations is called *live action*. It gives the greatest realism but sometimes lacks the distinctiveness of animated commercials or commercials that use special effects.

Special Effects

Memorability is often achieved by using dramatic sound, music, or
photography. Pepsi-Cola, for example, used striking shots of the sun,
unusual colors, slow motion, and new camera techniques to project
the image of a youth-oriented drink. It was reinforced by young actors and a contemporary musical theme. Such special effects often
attract viewers and win awards. But if the sales message is complex or
based on logic, another technique would be more successful. The
obvious precaution is not to let your technique so enthrall the audience that they don't remember your product.

Most special effects don't go this far. They are usually limited to
one fantasy or mnemonic device: a jolly green giant, a white tornado,
or the Imperial crown. In these cases the fantasy is directly related to
the product's claims, and heavy repetition makes strong impressions
on the viewer.

THE PRODUCTION PROCESS

The Tom Thumb-Page stores in Dallas planned a promotion to sell
Thanksgiving turkeys and talk about the store's money-back guarantee. Its advertising agency, KCBN, had developed a very simple concept for a television commercial. A live turkey would be shown in an
extreme tight close-up. As the announcer spoke off-screen, the camera would slowly zoom back, showing the turkey bobbing his head
and occasionally gobbling at the announcer's words. Finally, as the
announcer promised to give any unsatisfied customers their money
back—or another turkey—the turkey was supposed to run offstage.

In concept it was a very simple spot, but in the production process
it turned into a frustrating but hilarious farce reminiscent of the Keystone Kops. Many producers talk about the production problems of
working with kids. They should try working with a turkey!

FIGURE   11–9

Profits jumped 27 percent for Cullum Companies thanks, in part, to Tom Thumb TV spots.

KCBN found a "trained" turkey in upstate New York. That was fine since they had already decided to go to New York to produce the commercial to assure top-quality production.

On the day of shooting everybody was at the studio. The agency account and creative people had flown in from Dallas, and the trained turkey had been trucked in from upstate. The agency had been assured that the turkey would gobble on command and, with a simple hand signal, would run off-stage.

The lighting was set up, tested, and checked. The announcer practiced his pitch in the sound booth. The audio and video levels were adjusted and checked. Everything was ready to go. The trainer picked up the turkey, carried him onto the set, and deposited him on the marked spot in front of the camera and stepped out of camera range.

The lights blazed, the film rolled, the red camera lights went on, the director called for action, and the announcer read the script. At just the right instant, the trainer gave the turkey his cue to go. The turkey didn't move an inch.

"Cut!"

"OK. Let's try it again. Take two."

On the second try the turkey just sat there again.

"I don't understand it," said the trainer. "He's never done this before."

Five takes later, the turkey was still sitting there. By this time the trainer had abandoned his hand signals and was starting to shout at the bird, clapping his hands, screaming, stamping his foot. The pitch of his hysteria was rising rapidly. But the turkey just sat there. And the lights were getting hotter and hotter.

Finally, the trainer came on the set with a long broom handle.

"This'll do it," he said. There seemed to be a slight tone of hostility in his voice.

"Action," shouted the director.

Just as the announcer got to the cue in the script, the trainer lunged with the broom handle, stabbing the unsuspecting fowl in the belly. With a horrendous squawk, the turkey bolted from the set, crashed into one light stand and then another, toppling them over. He landed on top of one lamp, and as the searing heat scorched his wings, he squawked off in frenzied half-flight only to get tangled in more lights, cables, cameras, and props. All the while, the trainer and crew were chasing him around the set trying to capture him.

Finally they subdued the terrified bird and spent an hour calming him down while they relit the set. But, of course, when they were finally ready to start up again, the turkey now knew what was out there. And there was no way on earth he was going to move. He just sat absolutely still—terrified.

When all seemed lost, somebody got a bright idea. They decided to tie a line to his ankles and string the line off-camera. When the cue came, they gently jerked the line, pulling the bird's feet out from under him. Frightened by this sudden turn of events, the turkey flapped his wings, squawked, and struggled to regain his footing. In the process, he moved sideways just enough to go off-camera, and the effect was finally achieved. The director and crew, the agency, the trainer, and, most of all, the turkey all heaved a huge sigh of relief (Figure 11–9).

Costs

Roman and Maas list 14 factors that add to the cost of a commercial:[4]

1. Children and animals (including turkeys).
2. Location shooting.
3. Large cast.
4. Superstar talent.
5. Night or weekend filming.
6. Animation.
7. Involved opticals, special effects, stop-motion.
8. Both location and studio shooting for one commercial.
9. Expensive set decoration.
10. Special photographic equipment.
11. A second day of shooting.
12. Legal requirements.
13. A single word or sentence of dialogue.
14. An extremely simple, close-up commercial.

About the last factor, they point out that the extremely simple close-up is the kind of commercial that frequently requires a whole day just to get lighting right. We might add: "or to get the turkey to move."

There are three stages or steps in the process of producing a television commercial:

1. Preproduction—which includes all the work prior to the actual day of filming including casting, arranging for locations, estimating costs, obtaining necessary permissions, selecting technical suppliers and production companies, and finding props and costumes.
2. Production—the actual day (or days) that the commercial is filmed or videotaped.
3. Postproduction—all the work done after the day of shooting to finish the commercial including editing, processing film, recording sound effects, mixing audio and video, and duplicating final films or tapes.

Each step has a dramatic impact on the eventual quality of the commercial and its cost. We shall discuss each stage briefly (see Figure 11–10).

 Preproduction

After the advertiser approves a storyboard and budget, the production begins. Few people have the background to handle the entire production from start to finish. For this reason the commercial is a group effort. The team includes a writer, art director, producer, director, and sometimes a musical composer and choreographer. The person responsible for completion on schedule and within budget is the producer, either in-house or free lance.

The producer seeks competitive bids, usually sending copies of the storyboard to three studios. The bids include the services of a director, camera operators, electricians, and other technicians. The studio may edit the film or tape, or it may be sent elsewhere for editing.

After the studio has been chosen, the cast is selected by audition or through talent agencies, and an announcer, if needed, is chosen. Next the set is built, and the crew and cast rehearse under the director's supervision.

The greatest waste of money in commercial production inevitably occurs because of a lack of adequate preproduction planning. The converse is also true. The greatest savings can be effected by proper planning before the day of production.

Casting, for example, is a crucial decision and must be completely settled before the day of shooting. Children and animals are unpredictable and often cause production delays. Rehearsals before production, therefore, are a must.

Shooting days are expensive. The cost of studios, casts, crews, and equipment are normally figured on a full-day basis. Therefore, any unnecessary delays that could throw the production into an unex-

FIGURE 11–10

Production process for film and videotape commercials.

Film commercial

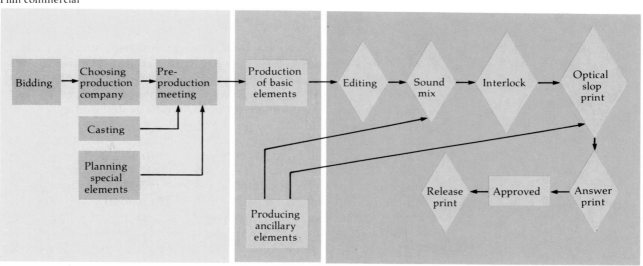

Videotape commercial

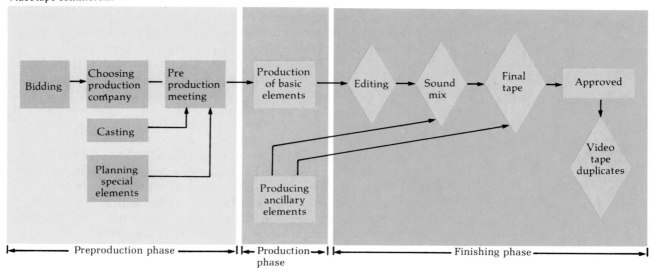

CREATIVE DEPARTMENT

From Concept through
Production of a
Television Commercial

Marketing background

From the restaurant chain's inception in 1969 until 1978, Wendy's basic menu consisted of hamburgers, chili, french fries, and their trademarked Frosty Dairy Dessert. By 1978, Wendy's recognized that Americans were becoming increasingly fitness and health conscious, and decreasing their red meat consumption. To capitalize on this lifestyle shift, Wendy's introduced a self-serve salad bar and a chicken sandwich. Other hamburger and nonhamburger fast-food chains followed suit, and by 1984, consumers could find a chicken product on most fast-food menus. Wendy's chicken sandwich no longer seemed unique or newsworthy. The challenge to Dancer Fitzgerald Sample, Wendy's national advertising agency, was to distinguish Wendy's chicken from the clutter and convince consumers to go to Wendy's when hungry for chicken rather than to the competition.

Creative strategy

The first step was to identify the target audience for the advertising. Wendy's research indicated that young adults were the heaviest consumers of the chicken sandwich and held the best potential for sales increases. All advertising would be targeted at this group. Second, a sales message, or key thought, had to be determined to motivate the target audience to go to Wendy's for chicken rather than to the competition. The agency easily recognized a major product advantage that could be used for a key thought: each Wendy's chicken sandwich is made with a pure, boneless breast of chicken that maintains its natural form through the cooking procedure. Several competitive chicken products are not served in this natural state; instead, a variety of chicken parts are combined together and processed into a convenient serving shape. The agency believed that this point of difference could separate Wendy's from the competition and interest the target audience in Wendy's product. Also, such a message would reinforce Wendy's corporate philosophy of providing high-quality products to the customer.

The agency and Wendy's also determined that the tone of the advertising should be directly competitive against other fast-food restaurants in compliance with Wendy's ambitious corporate goals.

The chicken advertising campaign would be exposed to the public through selectively targeted media vehicles, including television, radio, and in-store print materials.

Creative concept

Once the creative strategy was completed and approved by the client, a DFS creative group began to develop an executional concept. They created several strategically sound storyboards, but the one they ultimately presented to the account group and then to the client was a humorous storyboard depicting a customer victimized by "some other" hamburger restaurant. This executional style had previously worked well for Wendy's hamburger advertising in commercials such as "Where's the Beef?".

In the recommended chicken storyboard (titled "Processed

A. Storyboard.

Chicken"), the customer at "some other" restaurant asks the crew people "what parts" of the chicken were used in their chicken product. The customer never receives a satisfying, appetizing answer at the other restaurant. In the middle of the storyboard, an off-camera Wendy's announcer interrupts the customer discussion to describe the superiority of Wendy's chicken (as appetizing Wendy's food appears on-camera).

This storyboard was accepted by the account group since it delivered the key thought in a humorous and competitive manner. In addition, the "Processed Chicken" concept could be easily adapted to radio and in-store merchandising materials. (See A. Storyboard.)

Storyboard, script, production estimate

DFS presented the 30-second TV storyboard to Wendy's and recommended that Joe Sedelmaier direct the commercial. It was agreed to single-bid the job to this one director and his production company since DFS and Wendy's believed Mr. Sedelmaier was essential to the success of the storyboard. This same director had worked successfully on "Where's the Beef?" and its campaign predecessors and was well known for his humorous portrayal of victimized consumers. The approved storyboard was forwarded to the director for his production and postproduction estimate. The director returned his estimate along with possible copy and scene revisions to increase the humor of the commercial. These suggestions were approved by DFS and Wendy's, and the storyboard was revised accordingly. (See B. Script.)

 Dancer Fitzgerald Sample, Inc.

Television Copy

Client: WENDY'S

Product: CHICKEN

Traffic No: WOFH-4329

Date Typed: 10/29/84

Type: :30

Show & Date:

Subject: "PROCESSED CHICKEN - REVISED"

Video	*Audio*	
	ANNCR:	Those nuggets some hamburger places serve are actually processed chicken.
	CUSTOMER #1:	Excuse me, but what was that in there?
	CREW PERSON #1:	It's chicken.
	CUSTOMER #1:	Chicken?
	CUSTOMER #2:	Processed.
	CUSTOMER #1:	Pr-Processed?
	CREW PERSON #1:	That's like when they take a lot of chickens and assemble the respective parts.
	CUSTOMER #1:	What parts?
	CREW PERSON #1:	What parts?
	CREW PERSON #2:	Different parts.
	CREW PERSON #1:	Parts is parts.
	ANNCR:	Wendy's Chicken Sandwich is pure boneless breast of chicken. Moist and perfect, and not processed.
	CREW PERSON #1:	As I hear tell, all the parts are crammed into one big part.
	CREW PERSON #3:	Fused.
	CREW PERSON #1:	Yeah, then the one big part is cut up into little pieces parts. And parts is parts.
	ANNCR:	Pure boneless breast of chicken for Wendy's kind of people.

B. Script.

Preproduction

The next step was to select a cast to portray the customers and restaurant crew. The director referred to his talent files and then presented photographs of his recommendations, which included seven on-camera principles and seven on-camera extras. This cast was recommended for their facial expression range, which was critical for the humor of the commercial. This cast was approved by DFS and Wendy's.

Since the director, his production facility, and much of the cast were located in Chicago, DFS and the director agreed to shoot the commercial there. The DFS storyboard specified a generic fast-food restaurant setting, so the set designer hired by the production company had to choose between building a false restaurant interior on a stage or renting and converting the interior of an existing establishment. After discussions with the director and DFS, the set designer opted to use an existing location so that the camera angle could include an outdoor view. While location scouting, the set designer found an unfinished computer shop with a glass front that opened onto a parking lot and busy street. The owner agreed to rent the computer shop to the production company to construct an interior restaurant set.

Once all parties approved this recommendation, the production company began construction of the set including a restaurant counter and doors leading to an off-camera kitchen. Props such as cash registers, dining tables and chairs, and a menuboard with humorous product names such as "Bunburgers" and "Cluckers" were brought in to complete the effect.

The production company then hired a stylist to costume the cast. The restaurant crew members needed custom-made "uniforms," and restaurant customers needed street clothes. In a preproduction meeting, the stylist presented a prototype uniform, which was approved. It was further agreed that restaurant customers would provide their own street clothes.

The week before the shoot, a Wendy's operations representative met with the home economist hired by the production company to discuss food scenes in the commercial. It was decided that the home economist would furnish the tomato and lettuce sandwich toppings, while Wendy's would supply the chicken breasts, breading, and buns. The home economist also agreed to arrange for cooking equipment and utensils for the shoot.

Shooting the commercial

Client representatives and the agency account, creative, and TV production teams assembled in Chicago the day before the two-day shoot for a final preproduction meeting. The director intended to film the performers on day one and the food on day two. On the set the morning of day one, the performers blocked out the shots so that they would be rehearsed when filming began. The morning of day two, the home economist prepared food to be filmed while the director and crew arranged the lighting and background for the upcoming shots. Two tabletop food situations were scheduled: a shot of a chicken breast being cut open and a beauty shot of a whole chicken sandwich.

During the lunch break on day two, the director provided a screening of the day one dailies for the agency, client, and production crew. The director arranged to have a sample music track played during the screening so the dailies would more closely resemble a finished commercial. It was apparent that the previous day's filming successfully covered the talent portion of the storyboard.

Dailies to distribution prints

The day after filming was completed, the creative group and producer met with the director to select the best takes of each scene. From these recommended takes, a soundless 35-mm rough cut of the film was assembled. Voice-over announcer and music scratch tracks were combined with the 35-mm rough cut to become an "interlock," or preliminary version of the commercial, which was then transferred to ¾-inch videocassette to present to the agency account group. Once this process was completed, all parties agreed that the appearance of the food could be improved. The director and producer reshot the food sequences. The best takes were then spliced into the interlock to replace the original food footage, and a ¾-inch videocassette interlock was presented to the client. The interlock approved, the director, producer, and postproduction personnel completed color corrections and opticals on the 35-mm film to create the final optical negatives. At the same time, Wendy's preferred voice-over announcer recorded the final announcer track, which would later be combined with final music and sound effects. After the final mix of the 35-mm optical negative and full-coat audio reel, a final film-to-tape transfer was scheduled which provided a one-inch videotape master of the completed commercial. Once DFS and Wendy's approved a ¾-inch videocassette duped from the master, it was shipped to Wendy's broadcast materials fulfillment supplier who used it to duplicate prints for test market television stations.

Campaign results

Test markets using the "Processed Chicken" commercial proved that the advertising contributed to significant increases in sales and advertising awareness. As a result, the decision was made to air the commercial on network television. Prior to the network air date, the voice-over track was re-recorded to increase the competitive tone of the copy. This new track was then remixed with the commercial's video, a new one-inch videotape master was made, and the commercial was retitled "Parts is Parts" to avoid confusion. Under the director's guidance, a 20-second version was edited from the "Parts is Parts" 30-second footage. This version aired simultaneous to the network schedule in markets where a local message (such as a special promotion) was required in addition to the chicken sandwich message. (See C. Picture board with script.)

During the scheduled five-week network flight (November/December 1984), Wendy's chicken sandwich sales exceeded projections. With sales and publicity so positive, Wendy's authorized DFS to purchase two additional weeks of network time to maximize the campaign results.

ANNCR:
Those nuggets some hamburger places serve are actually processed chicken.

CUSTOMER
Excuse me, but what was that in there?

CREW PERSON
It's chicken.

CUSTOMER
Chicken?

CREW PERSON #1:
Processed.

CUSTOMER
Pr-Processed?

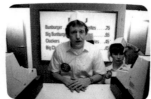

CREW PERSON #1:
That's like when they take a lot of chickens and assemble the respective parts.

CUSTOMER
What parts?

CREW PERSON #1:
What parts?
CREW PERSON #2:
Different parts.
CREW PERSON #1:
Parts is parts.

ANNCR:
Wendy's Chicken Sandwich is pure boneless breast of chicken. Moist and perfect, and not processed.

CREW PERSON #1:
As I hear tell, all the parts are crammed into one big part.

CREW PERSON #3:
Fused.
CREW PERSON #1:
Yeah, then the one big part is cut up into little pieces parts. and parts is parts.

ANNCR:
Pure boneless breast of chicken for Wendy's kind of people.

C. Picture board with script.

pected second shooting day must be avoided. This also suggests a problem for location shooting. Weather must be considered. Locations should be selected close to home whenever possible. Extra days on location are extremely expensive.

All these factors should be taken into consideration during the preproduction phase, and every aspect of the commercial production discussed, decided, and approved by the client, agency, and production company prior to the shooting day.

During these preparatory steps, a preproduction meeting should be held by the producer and include the agency account executive, the writer, art director, studio director, possibly the advertiser, and anyone else deemed important to the production. At this time they iron out any last-minute problems, review the storyboard, and make final decisions on the actors and announcer. The music, sets, action, lighting, and camera angles are all reviewed. The more details that are settled at this time, the better. A 60-second commercial takes only 90 feet of film, but the shooting often requires several days and from 3,000 to 5,000 feet of film.

The soundtrack may be recorded before, during, or after the actual production of the film or videotape. Recording the sound in advance assures that the commercial will be neither too long nor too short. This technique is used when the subject of the commercial has to move or dance to a specific rhythm. Sometimes, though, music or voice-over is recorded after the shooting.

■ Production

The actual shooting day (or days) of a commercial can be very long and tedious. Starting very early in the morning, the crew may take several hours just to light the set to the director's liking.

When the scenes are being shot, it may be necessary to try several "takes" to get them right. During this time the lighting may be readjusted several times as unexpected shadows pop up. The director usually requires two or three good takes of every scene. In addition each scene is probably shot from two or three different angles: one to establish the characters, one to show only the person speaking, and one to show the reaction of the person listening.

Scenes are not necessarily shot in order. For example, scenes with no synchronized sound are usually shot last since they don't require the full crew.

Between the shootings of each scene, a long interval may be required to move the camera, reset the lights, reposition the actors, and pick up the action, sound, and look to match the other scenes. This is extremely important since each piece of action must match what comes before and after. Otherwise the commercial will contain disconcerting jumps that can potentially destroy the credibility of the message (Figure 11–11).

■ Postproduction

The postproduction phase is where the commercial is actually put together. It is also the stage that usually determines how good a commercial is. At this point the responsibility of the film editor, sound mixer, and director is enormous.

The visual portion of the filmed commercial is first assembled on one piece of celluloid without the extra effects of dissolves, titles, or *supers* (words superimposed on the picture). The sound portion of the film is assembled on another piece of celluloid. This is called the *work print* stage (also called *rough cut* or *interlock*). At this time, scenes may be substituted, music and sound effects added, or other last-minute changes made.

Next the external sound is recorded. The announcer records the voice-over narrative. The music is recorded by musicians and singers, or prerecorded stock music may be bought and integrated into the commercial. Sound effects such as doorbells ringing or doors slamming are mixed. This includes the actors' voices, the announcer, the music track, the singers, and the sound effects.

The finished sound is put on one piece of celluloid, which, combined with the almost-completed visual celluloid, is called the *mixed interlock*. When these two are joined, along with all the required optical effects and titles, a print is made called the *answer print*. This is the final commercial. If it receives all the necessary approvals, *dupes* (copies) are made and delivered to the networks or TV stations for airing.

 ## Film versus Tape

Today very few commercials are done live. Even those that look live are usually videotaped, and most commercials are made on color film. Film projects a soft texture that live broadcasts and videotape do not have. Because film is the oldest method of showing moving pictures, there is a large pool of skilled talent in this field. Also film is extremely flexible and versatile. It can be used for numerous optical effects, slow motion, distance shots, mood shots, fast action, and animation. The film size normally used for national commercials is 35 mm. If some rough-test commercials are to be run, 16 mm is some-

Figure   11–11

Preparing the set for a Whirlpool commercial may take hours to get the lights, products, and talent in the most attractive and effective positions. Each time the scene or a camera angle changes, the lights may have to be reset to maintain continuity.

times used because it is much less expensive. Likewise, local commercials usually use 16 mm for lower cost. Duplicate film prints are also cheaper than videotape dupes.

On the other hand, recording a commercial on one- or two-inch magnetic videotape offers a more brilliant picture and better fidelity than film. It certainly looks more realistic and appears to have a "live" quality. Tape is also more consistent in quality than film stock. The chief advantage of tape, though, is that it can provide an immediate playback to the take. This permits the work to be checked and redone while the props and actors are still assembled. Computerization has cut editing time by up to 90 percent of the time involved in film. Videotape can be replayed almost forever, but a film commercial can be run only about 25 times.

Some directors shoot their commercials on film to gain the advantages of texture and sensitive mood lighting. Then they dub their processed film onto videotape to do their editing. This is more costly, but it gives them the advantage of faster finishing and the opportunity to see the optical effects instantly as they are added. Most directors, however, still prefer to edit on film because of the wider range of effects possible, thereby achieving a higher level of "creative story telling." (See "From concept through production of a television commercial.")

PRODUCING RADIO COMMERCIALS

Blue Nun was the best selling imported wine in the United States in 1980. But it wasn't always that way. In fact, until a few years ago, sales of Blue Nun were fairly static at about 70,000 cases per year. The wine was positioned as a gourmet selection and advertised only in sophisticated gourmet magazines via small-space ads.

Then Della Femina of Travisano & Partners got into the act. This agency was known for its highly creative and unusual approaches to marketing and advertising problems. In the case of Blue Nun, it lived up to its reputation.

The agency recommended repositioning the brand as an "all-purpose" wine that was perfectly suited to all meals and foods. It also suggested selling Blue Nun as a packaged goods item rather than a specialty good. This strategy put Blue Nun squarely against the leading all-purpose rosé wines such as Mateus and Lancers. The most interesting part of the strategy, though, was the suggestion to use radio exclusively to deliver Blue Nun's message. The agency felt that radio could be used best to target the intended market (men, high middle- to upper-class demographics) and simultaneously deliver the large audience numbers required for a packaged goods product.

Because of the uniqueness of the brand identification, it was decided to feature the Blue Nun name as the easiest way to order a premium wine for any meal.

The agency selected the husband/wife comedy team, Stiller and Meara, to deliver a series of humorous slice-of-life vignettes of the problems couples face while ordering and serving wine. The agency assigned an art director and copywriter, Mark Yusting and Kay Kavanagh, to develop the scripts.

Locking themselves in an office for several days, Yusting and Kavanagh hammered out the first series of radio commercials, which would eventually catapult Blue Nun into market leadership. Simultaneously, these commercials repositioned radio as an action medium for advertisers in need of results.

The tone and manner of the commercials set a trend for the next decade of Blue Nun advertising by playing off the brand's name with sophisticated wit and humor (Figure 11–12).

Blue Nun no longer sells 70,000 cases per year. By 1980 the figure exceeded 1.2 million cases per year and was still climbing. Blue Nun became this country's best-selling imported wine, beating out Lancers and Mateus, and its brand image equaled or exceeded those two previous leaders in all its advertised markets.

FIGURE   11–12   Blue Nun radio commercial

Stiller:	Excuse me, the cruise director assigned me this table for dinner.
Meara:	Say, weren't you the fella at the costume ball last night dressed as a giant tuna? With scales, the gills and the fins?
Stiller:	Yeah—that was me.
Meara:	I recognized you right away.
Stiller:	Were you there?
Meara:	I was dressed as a mermaid so I had to spend most of the night sitting down. Did you ever try dancing with both legs wrapped in aluminum foil?
Stiller:	No, I can't say I have. Did you order dinner yet?
Meara:	I'm having the filet of sole.
Stiller:	Hmmm. The filet mignon looks good. Would you like to share a bottle of wine?
Meara:	Terrific.
Stiller:	I noticed a little Blue Nun at the Captain's table.
Meara:	Poor thing. Maybe she's seasick.
Stiller:	No, Blue Nun is a wine. A delicious white wine.
Meara:	Oh, we can't have a white wine if you're having meat and I'm having fish.
Stiller:	Sure we can. Blue Nun is a white wine that's correct with any dish. Your filet of sole. My filet mignon.
Meara:	Oh, it's so nice to meet a man who knows the finer things. You must be a gourmet?
Stiller:	No, as a matter of fact, I'm an accountant. Small firm in the city. Do a lot of tax work. . . . [*fade out*]
Announcer:	Blue Nun. The delicious white wine that's correct with any dish. Another Sichel wine imported by Schieffelin & Company, New York.

Producing radio commercials is similar to producing television commercials in several aspects. Radio uses the same basic techniques as television—namely, testimonials, slice of life, straight announcements, or music, and generally follows the same developmental pattern as television. Only the details differ.

Writing Radio Copy

Radio listeners usually decide within the first five to eight seconds whether they want to pay attention to a commercial. Therefore radio copy must be intensive. It should get the listener's attention and hold it to the end. To accomplish this, many techniques and devices can be used. Creativity knows no limits. (See the Checklist for creating effective radio commercials.)

The radio listener is often busy driving, washing dishes, or reading the paper. Therefore the message should be catchy, memorable, and never dull. In the effort to gain attention, though, care must be taken to avoid jarring the listener offensively. That can cause resentment. A friendly approach wins more friends than a bloodcurdling scream. The style should be kept personal, relaxed, and cheerful.

Humor can be one of the best attention-getting devices and is being used with increasing success. But beware! It is difficult to master. Poorly done humor is worse than none at all.

Some additional rules of thumb follow:

Mention the advertiser's name often—at least three times.

If the name is tricky, spell it—at least once.

Be conversational. Use easy-to-pronounce words and short sentences. Avoid tongue twisters.

Keep the message simple. Omit unneeded words.

Concentrate on one main selling point. Don't try to crowd in too many ideas. Make the *big* idea crystal clear!

Create a visual image. Paint pictures with the words. Use descriptive language. Familiar sounds, such as a fire engine siren or a car engine, can help paint the picture.

Stress action words rather than passive words.

Emphasize the product benefits repeatedly—with variations.

Make the script fit the available time. The average announcer normally reads about 125 words per minute, with the range running from 100 to 150 words.

A good rule of thumb for the number of words in a commercial is as follows:[5]

10 seconds—20–25 words
20 seconds—40–45 words
30 seconds—60–70 words
60 seconds—125–140 words

And be sure to *ask for the order*. Try to get the listener to *do* something. The story is told that Martin Block, an early announcer on radio station WNEW, once made a bet. Figuring that many women drove from New Jersey to New York to shop, he bet that he could persuade some of them by radio to turn around, go back through the tunnel,

Checklist for creating effective radio commercials

☐ Identify your sound effects. A sound effect is only effective when the listener knows what it means. The sound of rain falling in the forest is the same as the sound of bacon sizzling, of a shower running, and of static. Unless you identify the sound effect, you may confuse your listener, or the sound effect may go barely noticed.

☐ Don't be afraid to use music as a sound effect. The commercial will work if the meaning of the music sounds are clearly explained.

☐ If you use a sound effect, build your commercial around it. By the time you explain what the sound effect means and play it for a while, your listener will be focused on it. So it pays to make the message all about the relationship of the sound effect to your product. All about the sound of a crisp new cracker, for example. Or all about the thundering power of a new kind of bank account.

☐ Give yourself time. Media planners love to run numbers through a computer and tell you that a 30-second commercial will be twice as efficient as a 60-second commercial. But it's difficult, and often impossible, to establish your sound effects in 30 seconds and still relate them to product benefits. You need time in radio to set a scene and establish a premise. A 30-second commercial that nobody remembers has zero efficiency. Fight for 60s.

☐ Consider not using sound effects. A distinctive voice, or a powerful message straightforwardly spoken can be more effective than noises from the tape library. People love to hear a good story. Can you spin a compelling yarn about your product and just let someone narrate it?

☐ Beware of comedy. Professional funnymen devote their lives to their art. Even so, a miniscule percentage of them succeed—often after 20 years of struggling. It's rare for anyone else to sit down at a typewriter and match the skill of the best comedians.

☐ If you insist on being funny, begin with an outrageous premise. The best comic radio commercials begin with a totally ridiculous premise from which all subsequent developments logically follow. An example of a ridiculous premise: A man puts on his wife's nightgown at 4 A.M. and goes out to purchase *Time* magazine—and the cops catch him. The premise may have been weird, but the events that grew out of it were perfectly rational under the circumstances.

☐ Keep it simple. Radio is a swell medium for building awareness of a brand. It's a rotten medium for registering long lists of copy points or making complex arguments. You can mention copy points until the clock runs out, but nobody will remember them, and the blabber and jabber will weaken the intrusiveness of your message.

☐ What one thing is most important about your product? That is what your commercial should spend 60 seconds talking about.

☐ Tailor commercials as to time, place, and specific audience. Radio is a local medium. So if your commercial is running in Milwaukee, you can write it for Milwaukee, about familiar places and faces. You can adjust your commercials to talk in the lingo of the people who will hear them and to the time of day in which they'll be broadcast.

☐ Presentation counts a whole lot. Most radio scripts—even the greatest radio scripts—look boring on paper. Acting, timing, vocal quirks, and sound effects make them come alive. If you can possibly produce a demo of a commercial, do so. Happily, studio time and demo fees aren't nearly as costly as television production.

and buy their dresses from his New Jersey sponsor. He did, they did, and he won the bet. The women told his sponsor![6]

Types of Radio Commercials

Although not all radio commercials can be rigidly cataloged, the wide range of possibilities was considered by Wallace Ross and Bob Landers who came up with 17 creative categories. (See Ad Lab 11–A.) For our discussion here, we will consider four basic types: musical, slice of life, straight, and personality.

AD LAB 11–A   Creative ways to sell on radio

Product demo Telling how a product is used or the purposes it serves.

Voice power Where the power of the commercial is in the casting of a unique voice.

Electronic sound Synthetic sound-making machines create a memorable product-sound association.

Customer interview A product spokesperson and customer discuss the product advantages—often spontaneously.

Humorous fake interview Variation of the customer interview in a lighter vein.

Hyperbole or exaggerated statement Overstatement arouses interest in legitimate product claims that might otherwise pass unnoticed; often a spoof.

Sixth dimension Compression of time and events into a brief spot involving the listener in future projections.

Hot property Commercial adapts a current sensation—a hit show, performer, or song.

Comedian power Established comedians do commercials in their own unique style, implying celebrity endorsement.

Historical fantasy Situation with historical characters revived to convey product message.

Sound picture Recognizable sounds used to involve listener by stimulating imagination.

Demographics Music or references appeal to a particular segment of the population, as an age or interest group.

Imagery transfer Musical logo or other sound reinforces the effects of a television campaign.

Celebrity interview Famous person endorses product in an informal manner.

Product song Music and words combine to create musical logo selling product in the style of popular music.

Editing genius Many different situations, voices, types of music, and sounds are combined in a series of quick cuts.

Improvisation Performers work out the dialogue extemporaneously for an assigned situation; may be post-edited.

Laboratory Applications

1. Select three radio commercials with which you are familiar and discuss which creative techniques they use.

2. Select a radio commercial with which you are familiar and discuss how it could have been more effective by using a different creative technique.

Musical

Jingles, or musical commercials, are among the best and the worst advertising messages produced. If done well, they can bring enormous success—well beyond that of the average nonmusical commercial. Likewise, when done poorly, they can waste the advertising budget.

Musical commercials have several variations. The entire message may be sung, jingles may be interspersed throughout the copy, or orchestras may play symphonic arrangements. A growing number of producers use music that has no lyrics as a background theme. After hearing several such announcements, the listener gradually begins to associate the product with the music. This is called a *musical logotype.*

Advertisers have three principal sources of music. They can buy the use of a tune from the copyright owner, which is usually expensive. They can use a melody in the public domain, which is free. Or they can hire a composer to write an original tune. Several of these original tunes, including the Coke song, "I'd like to teach the world to sing . . . ," discussed in "Coca-Cola Illustrates the History of Modern Advertising" in Chapter 1, have turned into hits.

Slice of life (problem solution)

As in television, the slice of life is a situation commercial in which professional actors discuss a problem and propose the product as its solution. Played with the proper drama, it can get attention and create interest. "Slice" commercials can be produced straight or for humorous effect. In all cases the story should be relevant to the product and simply told.

Straight announcement

The straight commercial is probably the easiest to write. Delivered by one person, it can be designed as an *integrated commercial*—that is, woven into a show or tailored to a given program. There are no special sound effects as a rule. The only music, if any, is played in the background. It is adaptable to almost any product or situation and is therefore used frequently. Getting and holding the listener's attention is probably its greatest problem (Figure 11–13).

Personality

It is sometimes desirable to have a disc jockey or show host express the message in his or her own style. When such a commercial is done well, it is almost always better than anything the advertiser could supply.

The advertiser surrenders control of the commercial, however, and turns it over to the personality. The main risk, outside of occasional blunders, is that the personality may criticize the product. Even so, this sometimes lends a realism that is hard to achieve otherwise.

If the advertiser decides to use this technique, the personality is supplied with a sheet highlighting the product's or the company's features. This gives the main points to be stressed and the phrases or company slogans to be repeated. Most of the specific wording, though, and the mode of delivery are left up to the discretion of the announcer.

FIGURE 11–13

Radio commercial for a radar detector.

Anncr: If you listen carefully for the next 30 seconds, you may never have to pay another speeding ticket. This message is about a dependable little electronic device called "The Snooper XK." It sits on your dash like a watchdog. The moment it detects radar . . .

SFX: BEEP BEEP BEEP

DAU: it flashes a warning and beeps, reminding you to check your speed. You get plenty of advance warning, whether the radar beaming device is on the roadside, in the sky, or hidden in a tree.

THE RADIO PRODUCTION PROCESS

A radio commercial is quicker, simpler, and less expensive to produce than a television commercial (Figure 11–14).

Live commercials require that the station be sent a script and a recording of music, or special effects, if any is to be used. Care must be taken to ensure that the material is accurately timed for length. A live commercial script should run about 100 to 120 words per minute. This enables the announcer to deliver the message at a normal conversational pace.

The disadvantage of live commercials is that announcers may not be consistent in their delivery. In addition, the use of sound effects is quite limited. Obviously, if uniformity of delivery of the commercial is crucial, a recorded commercial must be used.

An agency may assign a radio producer from its staff or, as is often the case, hire a free-lance producer to develop the commercial. The radio producer first estimates the costs and then presents a budget to the advertiser for approval. Next, for recorded commercials, the producer selects a studio and a casting director.

The casting director casts professional actors for roles if it is a slice-of-life commercial or finds the right "voice" if there is only an announcer. If the script calls for music, the producer decides whether to use music already recorded or to hire a composer. The producer may also hire a music director, musicians, and singers. This is often done after hearing audition tapes of the recommended talent. Depending on the script, sound effects may be created or taken from prerecorded sources.

Next, a director supervises rehearsals until everything falls into place. Then the commercial is recorded several times, and the best take is selected. Music, sound, and vocal are usually recorded separately and mixed. In any case, the final recording is referred to as the *master tape*.

From the master tape, duplicates of the commercials, called *dubs*, are recorded onto 1/4-inch magnetic tape and sent to radio stations for broadcast.

FIGURE   11–14

The process for producing a radio commercial.

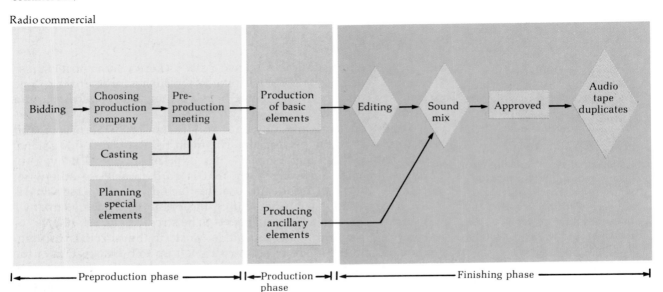

Radio commercial

Summary

Understanding broadcast production means knowing how commercials are written, the types of commercials that are most effective and most commonly used, the basic techniques for producing commercials, and the important steps in the production process.

A television script is divided into two portions. The right side is the audio for sound effects, spoken copy, and music, and the left side is the video for camera action, scenes, and instructions. On a sheet preprinted with a series of blank television screens, the writer and art director prepare a storyboard of the script. The video is sketched in by the art director, and the audio is typed underneath.

The six basic types of television commercials are straight announcement, demonstration, testimonial, slice of life, lifestyle, and animation. Animation techniques can be further categorized by whether they use cartoons, puppets, photo animation, or the new computerized laser light methods.

Producing a television commercial involves three stages or steps: preproduction, production, and postproduction. The preproduction stage includes all the work prior to the actual day of filming—casting, arranging for locations, estimating costs, finding props and costumes, and other work. The production stage is the actual time that the commercial is filmed or videotaped. Postproduction refers to the work done after the day of shooting. This includes editing, processing film, recording sound effects, mixing, and duplicating final films or tapes.

Most commercials are shot on film. Film is extremely flexible and versatile, it can be used for numerous optical effects, and film prints are cheaper than videotape dubs. In recent years, though, many more commercials are shot on tape. Videotape offers a more brilliant picture and better fidelity than film, it looks more realistic, and tape quality is more consistent than film stock. The chief advantage of tape, though, is that it can provide an immediate playback of the scene that was shot.

Producing radio commercials is similar to producing television commercials in several aspects. It uses the same basic techniques and generally follows the same development pattern. Only the details and the cost differ.

Radio offers a wide range of creative possibilities. The radio listener is often busy doing something else while the radio is on, so the message should be catchy, memorable, and simple. Radio commercials should be written to create a visual image in the mind of the listener. Action words should be used rather than passive words. The copy should fit the available time. The four basic types of radio commercials are musical, slice of life, straight announcement, and personality.

The radio production process is similar to television production, only simpler and less costly. The final commercial is dubbed onto 1/4-inch tape for distribution.

Questions for review and discussion

1. What is the benefit of a continuing commercial presenter?
2. Why is an understanding of broadcast production techniques important for people involved in advertising today?
3. What is an animatic, and how is it used?
4. What is the importance of unity to a television commercial?
5. What are the advantages and disadvantages of using animation in television advertising?
6. What leads to the greatest waste of money in broadcast commercial production? Explain.
7. Is it better to use film or tape in producing a television commercial?
8. Why is radio often described as theater of the mind? Explain.
9. What are the four basic types of radio commercials? Describe them. Which is most effective, and why?
10. Select a radio commercial of your choice. What, in your mind, makes it effective? Explain.

PART IV ADVERTISING MEDIA

FOSTER and KLEISER

12

MEDIA PLANNING AND SELECTION

Just a decade ago, the market for cameras in the United States was neatly divided between amateur and serious photographers. The amateur market was the target for inexpensive, cartridge-loading Instamatic snapshot cameras or Polaroid "instant" cameras. These were advertised via mass media to the broad range of amateur snapshot consumers. The more expensive 35-mm cameras were advertised predominantly in photo-buff magazines to the smaller, more specialized market of serious and professional photographers.

In 1976 the little Japanese optics maker, Canon, had just gone through some hard times but was on its way to becoming a billion-dollar, diversified, precision instrument concern. Its two major products were copiers and 35-mm cameras. However, it still lagged behind the other well-known 35-mm camera manufacturers (Minolta, Olympus, and Pentax) in U.S. sales. That year Canon introduced its new, fully automatic, AE-1 single-lens reflex (SLR) camera and simultaneously made marketing history.

At that time, less than 10 percent of U.S. consumers owned 35-mm cameras. Canon believed that the market was wide open for an aggressive marketing approach. Research showed that 80 percent of the people who bought SLR cameras were upscale, college-educated men between the ages of 18 and 45. Most were married, and about half had children. Canon felt this group would make an ideal market for the new automatic camera if they could just see how easy it was to operate.

Canon decided to use network television to introduce its new product to the masses. Hiring Grey Advertising in New York to create the campaign, Canon spent a modest $1.5 million in prime-time TV in the fourth quarter of 1976, just in time for Christmas. With tennis pro John Newcomb as the spokesman, Grey used the theme, "The Canon AE-1 is so advanced it's simple." Consumers could see the camera demonstrated, step by step, right on their TV screens in live action sequences that no form of print advertising had paralleled. The results were immediately successful.

In 1977 Canon increased its television spending to $3 million with heavy emphasis in the spring and fall months. Magazine advertising, handled by Dentsu Advertising, likewise rose to $1.7 million. The next year the total budget shot up to $9.6 million with over $6 million of that in network and spot TV. The magazine lineup, which reflected the TV campaign, included regular insertions in leading consumer magazines with heavy male readership. These included *Time, Newsweek, Playboy, Sports Illustrated, Road and Track, Skiing, Golf, Tennis,* and *Esquire.*

The TV scheduling included heavy sports programming such as "Monday Night Football" and the World Series. Leading sports personalities were hired to show how simple the AE-1 was to operate, even for a novice photographer (Figure 12–1).

To top it all off, Canon joined the host of other manufacturers sponsoring the Winter Olympics in 1980 and again in 1984 by becoming the official camera of the games. The company used the Olympic logos in all advertisements and created a special series of corporate Olympic ads featuring the whole Canon line.

The success of Canon's media plan was evidenced by the fact that, within a year, Canon came from behind and took over the 35-mm sales lead. Immediately the other manufacturers jumped into the fray with new product introductions and hefty television buying. But they were too late. TV spending for all 35-mm cameras exploded to $50 million within two years. In 1978 Minolta was the largest TV spender. But a year later they were still $50 million behind Canon in sales.[1] In three short years Canon captured a 32 percent share of the market. Quickly following with other product introductions aimed at particular niches within the market, Canon moved into the number 3 spot in 1981 behind Kodak and Polaroid in camera and photo supply advertising expenditures.

In short, Canon scored a huge marketing success, not so much because of what people usually call advertising creativity but because of extraordinary media planning and selection.

The decisions made in media planning frequently involve as much creativity as the decisions made by senior art directors and copywriters. As we shall see in this chapter, media decisions, like good art and copy ideas, are made in the context of the larger marketing and advertising framework. They must be based on sound marketing principles and research as well as experience and intuition.

MEDIA PLANNING

Each of the major media—newspapers, magazines, radio, television, direct mail, outdoor, transit advertising, and others—has unique capabilities and unique audience characteristics. Each therefore appeals to the needs of certain advertisers. The advertiser and agency must *plan* which media to use to convey the message to those consumers identified as their target audience. Then the task of the media planner is to *select* from those media the particular radio stations, TV programs, newspapers, etc. that will reach the target audience most effectively. The media function, therefore, involves two basic processes: media planning and media selection (Figure 12–2).

In this chapter we will examine how a media plan is developed, what terms are used to express media objectives, and what alternative media strategies are available to the advertiser to accomplish those objectives. Finally, we will analyze the criteria used to select particular media vehicles, schedule the appearance of advertisements and commercials, and measure the relative effectiveness of one medium over another.

FIGURE 12–1

The Canon AE1—so advanced it's simple. And the same holds true for its commercials.

◼ Role of Media in the Marketing Framework

As we discussed in Chapters 4 and 7, advertising is a promotional activity, and promotion is just one of the four Ps that companies may use to achieve their marketing objectives. The others are product, price, and place.

By the time Canon made the decision to try television advertising, it was already exercising a very new marketing plan with major changes in the product and price elements. The new, inexpensive Canon AE-1 automatic single-lens reflex camera was a great departure from the bigger, more complex, and more expensive 35-mm cameras of the past. In developing the marketing plan for this new product, Canon analyzed the marketing situation, determined realistic marketing objectives, before developing a unique marketing strategy.

◼ Marketing objectives and strategy

Before media planning can begin, the marketing objectives for the product, brand, or service must be precisely determined by the advertiser and the agency. These may include a decision to expand the market for the product—for example, by advertising 35-mm cameras not only to serious photographers but also to hobbyists. The marketer may seek to extend distribution into new geographic markets or income groups. Or the objectives may be to resell current users—by advertising a camera with "new, more advanced" capabilities to current camera owners.

Consider the risk that was involved for Canon. Less than 10 percent of the people in the United States owned a 35-mm camera. To most marketers that would indicate little interest in the product class

FIGURE   12–2   Advertising volume in the United States, 1984 ($ millions).

Medium	Volume Total	Volume Share	Percent of total	Percent of share	Medium	Volume Total	Volume Share	Percent of total	Percent of share
Newspapers	17,694		26		Magazines	3,858		6	
National		2,452		14	Weeklies		1,659		43
Local		15,242		86	Monthlies		1,147		30
Business					Women's		904		23
papers	1,876		3		Farm		148		4
Television	14,329		22		Outdoor	721		1	
Network		6,210		43	National		465		64
Spot		4,360		31	Local		256		36
Local		3,759		26	Miscellaneous	13,113		20	
Radio	4,670		7		National		7,067		54
Network		255		5	Local		6,046		46
Spot		923		20	Total	66,580		100	
Local		3,492		75	National		37,785		57
Direct mail	10,319		15		Local		28,795		43

and would discourage them from considering any mass marketing techniques. Obviously, at some point, some optimistic person at Canon looked at those figures in reverse and said, "If only 10 percent of the people have a 35-mm camera, then there is still 90 percent we can sell to. What a wonderful opportunity!" That was right. But in another situation it might have been wrong.

Consider the other related risks. How much would it cost to develop and produce a new, untried camera for the small market that then existed? How would a lower priced camera fare in a market that was used to paying high prices for high quality? How much would it cost to manufacture enough of these untried cameras to make it profitable even if they did sell well? How would camera retailers accept these new 35-mm cameras that sold for less and gave them less profit? Would the beginning photographer pay even that much for a first camera?

All these questions had to be answered satisfactorily before marketing objectives or a marketing strategy could be developed. Once that was accomplished, advertising objectives could be determined and advertising strategies considered.

Advertising strategy

In Chapter 7, "Marketing and Advertising Planning," we defined the advertising strategy as the manner in which the advertiser blends the elements of the creative mix. Those elements are: (1) the product concept, (2) the target audience, (3) the communications media, and (4) the advertising message. How did Canon combine these elements?

Canon's plan targeted a whole new market—upscale men between the ages of 18 and 45 who were amateur photographers buying their first or second cameras. The men in this group were upper income, active, educated, and family oriented, for whom good photography would be a useful, enjoyable, recreational activity. This was definitely a large, mass market and a new target audience for 35-mm camera advertising.

This audience would be offered not just a new product but also a new product concept—a camera that offered ease and simplicity of operation, like the pocket cameras, along with the historic, professional quality of 35-mm cameras.

The price would be new, too—higher than the pocket cameras to be sure, but less than other 35-mm cameras and still affordable.

The message strategy was to be authoritative and positive, almost dogmatic, and as simple as the camera: "The Canon AE-1 is so advanced it's simple." And this would be demonstrated by well-known, believable personalities who were not professional photographers.

By this time the media choice appeared obvious. A mass market, the ability to demonstrate in live action, the audience desired, and the opportunity to tie in with relevant sporting events all dictated using television as the mainstay of the media plan with the support of special-interest magazines. How this media plan was developed depended, like a marketing or advertising plan, on two things: objectives and strategy.

Defining Media Objectives

The media plan begins with a statement of objectives. These are determined by defining the primary target audiences and then setting goals for communicating with those audiences (Figure 12–3).

Target audience

In the initial stages of marketing planning, the company's target markets are defined and prioritized. Similarly, defining target audiences is an essential step in determining media objectives and strategy. The whole media effort will be wasted if the right people are not exposed to the ads in the campaign.

As we will see in the section on media selection and scheduling, media vehicles are selected according to how well they "deliver" an audience that closely parallels the desired target audience. Advertisers like Canon are always concerned about wasting money on ads that reach consumers who are not likely to need or want the product or who are not important buying influences.

How media objectives are expressed

After the target audience is defined, specific objectives may be set. These should be stated precisely so that, once the plan is under way, the results can be measured against the objectives. The purpose of media objectives, according to Sissors and Petray, is to translate marketing objectives into goals that media can accomplish. For example, for a new product introduction, a simple statement of media objectives might be written as follows:

> Reach at least 75 percent of the primary target audience an average of six times and 50 percent of the secondary target audience an average of four times during the first six weeks of advertising.

Media planners use special terms to develop and express media objectives. These include *reach, frequency, impressions,* and *gross rating points,* as well as *continuity, flighting,* and *pulsing.* We shall discuss each of these briefly here.

Reach The term *reach* refers to the number of *different* people or households that are exposed to an advertising schedule during a given time, usually four weeks. For example, if 80 percent of a total of 10,000 different radio listeners hear the Super Soap commercials on radio stations CBA and XYZ at least once during a four-week period, then the reach is 8,000 people. Reach, then, measures the *unduplicated extent* of audience exposure to a media vehicle and may be expressed either as a percentage (80) or as a raw number (8,000).

Frequency *Frequency* refers to the number of times an advertising message reaches the same person or household. Across a total audience, frequency is calculated as the *average* number of times individuals or homes are exposed to the advertising. The figure is used to measure the *intensity* of a specific media schedule.

For example, suppose 4,000 of our 10,000 radio listeners heard the Super Soap commercial *three* times during a four-week period and another 4,000 people heard it *five* times. To determine the *average frequency* the following formula would be used:

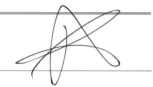

FIGURE 12–3   The scope of media planning activities.

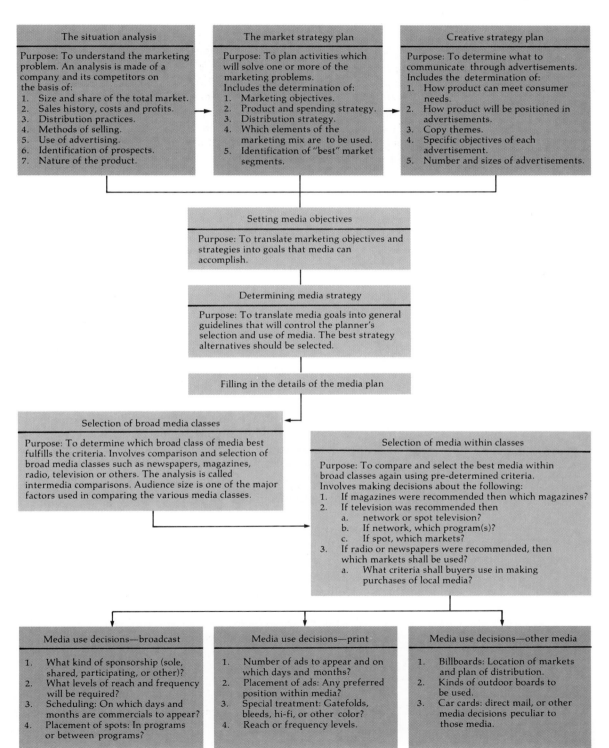

$$\text{Average frequency} = \text{Total exposures} \div \text{Audience reach}$$
$$= [(4{,}000 \times 3) + (4000 \times 5)] \div 8{,}000$$
$$= 32{,}000 \div 8{,}000 = 4$$

Thus, for the 8,000 listeners reached, the average frequency or number of exposures was four. Frequency, then, is an important planning tool because it offers a measure of the repetition that can be achieved by a specific media schedule.

Impressions *Impressions* are the total of all the audiences delivered by a media plan. In the example above, it would be the same as *total exposures*. It is calculated by multiplying the number of people who receive a message by the number of times they receive it—in this case, 32,000. If the same schedule ran for another four weeks, what do you think would be the total number of impressions? What would be the average frequency?

Gross rating points The total audience delivery or weight of a specific media schedule might be expressed by counting the total number of impressions. However, the more common method of expressing this is in *gross rating points*. GRPs are computed by multiplying the reach, expressed as a percentage, by the average frequency. In our example, 80 percent of the radio households heard the Super Soap commercial an average of four times during the four-week period. To determine the gross rating points of this radio schedule, we use the following formula:

$$\text{Reach} \times \text{Frequency} = \text{GRP}$$
$$80 \times 4 = 320 \text{ Gross rating points}$$

It is important to understand that gross rating points are used to describe the total message weight of a media schedule, without regard to audience duplication, over a given period of time. For broadcast media, gross rating points are often calculated for a week or a month. In print media they are often calculated for the number of ad insertions in a campaign. And for outdoor advertising, they are calculated on the basis of daily exposure.

Continuity, flighting, and pulsing These terms refer to the length of an advertising campaign and the manner in which it is scheduled and sustained. For example, the Super Soap commercial might be scheduled on radio stations CBA and XYZ for an initial four-week period. But then, to maintain *continuity* in the campaign, additional spots might be scheduled to run continuously every week through the year on station XYZ.

On the other hand, the advertiser might decide to introduce the product with a four-week *flight* and then to schedule three additional flights to run during seasonal periods later in the year.

A third alternative would be a mixture of the continuity and flighting strategies. The advertiser could maintain a low level of advertising all year but heavy up with periodic *pulses* during peak selling periods. Obviously, the difference between flighting and pulsing is a subtle one; and, in fact, in the advertising business, the terms are usually used interchangeably.

Naturally the continuity of a campaign will affect the number of people who can be reached and the number of times they can be reached. It will also affect how well the message is remembered over time. The ideal in most cases, of course, would be achieved if a company could simply advertise heavily all year long.

However, the reach, frequency, and continuity of a media plan all depend on the advertiser's media budget. Because all budgets are limited, so are the media objectives that may be attained. It should also be understood that these objectives have an inverse relationship to one another within the limits of the budget (Figure 12–4). To achieve greater reach, some frequency may have to be sacrificed. Likewise, to gain greater continuity, short-term reach and/or frequency must be sacrificed. The goal of the media planner, therefore, is to optimize these objectives by getting enough reach, enough frequency, and the proper continuity to make the media plan work for the advertiser.

Once the correct media objectives have been determined—that is, the best mix of reach, frequency, and continuity—the media strategy, discussed in the next section, can be developed. (See the Checklist for developing media objectives and strategies.)

Considerations in Developing Media Strategy

The media strategy describes how the advertiser will achieve the stated media objectives. The strategy reflects the specific course of action to be taken with media: which media will be used; how often each will be used; how much of each will be used; and when will they be used.

Generally, media strategy decisions fall into one of two broad areas: selection of media class or choice of media use. Should the advertiser, for example, use television, radio, magazines, or some combination? Should it run three commercials per week for 52 weeks a year? Or should 16-page, full-color inserts be used once every three months?

These decisions are based on a wide variety of factors, some of which we shall discuss here.

FIGURE   12–4

Reach and frequency have an inverse relationship to each other. For example, for the same budget, it might be possible to reach 6,000 people 1 time, 3,000 people 5.5 times, or 1,000 people 9 times.

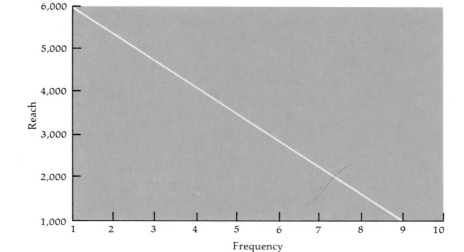

Checklist for developing media objectives and strategies

Considerations	Reach	Frequency	Continuity	Pulsing
Message needs:				
New or highly complex message, strive for	■	■	■	
Dogmatic message, surge at beginning, then				■
Reason-why messages, high frequency at first, then			■	
Emotionally oriented messages				
When message is so creative or product so newsworthy, they force attention	■			
When message is dull or product indistinguishable, strive for		■		
Consumer purchase patterns:				
To influence brand choice of regularly purchased products		■		■
As purchase cycle lengthens, use		■		
To influence erratic purchase cycles, strive for				
To influence consumer attitudes toward impulse purchases		■	■	
For products requiring great deliberation, alternate	■	■	■	
To reinforce consumer loyalty, concentrate on				
To influence seasonal purchases, anticipate peak periods with	■	■		
Budget levels:				
Low budget, use			■	
Higher budgets, strive for				■
Competitive activity:				
Heavy competitive advertising, concentrate on		■		
When competitive budgets are larger, use				■
Marketing objectives:				
New product introductions to mass market	■			
To expand share of market with new uses for product	■			
To stimulate direct response from advertising		■		■
To create awareness and recognition of corporate status	■		■	

■ *Scope of target audience*

A key strategic decision relates to the breadth of the media plan. That is determined by where the target audience is located and who comprises the target audience.

Normally, advertising should be limited to areas where the product is available. A *local* plan may be used, for example, if the product is available in only one city or if that market has been chosen to introduce or test-market a new product.

A *regional* plan, on the other hand, may cover several adjoining metropolitan areas, an entire state, or several neighboring states. Regional media objectives can be achieved by using local media, regional editions of national magazines, or spot television and radio. Regional plans are also used to accommodate sectional differences in taste or preference that affect product sales. For example, more instant coffee is sold in the Midwest than in New England.

Advertisers who want to reach consumers throughout the country generally use a *national* plan. The media used in a national plan are usually network television, network radio, full-circulation national magazines, and nationally syndicated Sunday newspaper supplements. Figure 12–5 shows the media used by the 25 largest national advertisers.

The scope of the media plan might also be based on something other than geography. If the target audience comprises people in specific income, educational, occupational, social, or ethnic groups, the

FIGURE 12–5   Media expenditures of 25 leading advertisers in 1984 (in measured media only, $ in millions)

Rank	Company	Total measured advertising expenditures	Newspaper	Magazines	Farm publications	Spot tv	Network tv	Spot radio	Network radio	Outdoor
1	Procter & Gamble Co.	$650.4	$ 9.8	$ 40.2	$—	$229.2	$366.7	$ 2.8	$ 1.5	$ .2
2	Sears, Roebuck & Co.	224.4	—	33.6	—	29.3	145.0	5.5	10.6	.3
3	Beatrice Cos.	221.7	17.2	50.2	.5	46.0	97.6	5.3	.5	4.4
4	General Motors Corp.	449.0	88.6	89.0	1.7	25.7	201.4	29.1	9.4	4.2
5	R.J. Reynolds Industries	469.7	112.3	155.1	—	39.6	69.9	3.9	—	88.9
6	Philip Morris Inc.	462.0	65.3	140.4	—	50.4	128.2	22.5	—	55.2
7	Ford Motor Co.	365.5	49.6	80.3	3.4	37.9	172.3	13.0	7.2	1.8
8	American Telephone & Telegraph Co.	359.1	72.0	61.3	—	41.3	146.6	27.9	9.5	.4
9	K mart Corp.	49.7	—	11.0	—	10.0	23.5	4.9	—	.2
10	General Foods Corp.	284.8	4.2	33.4	—	73.0	170.1	2.3	1.7	.07
11	Nabisco Brands	125.5	6.2	9.2	—	22.1	82.0	1.0	4.7	.4
12	PepsiCo Inc.	222.7	6.0	3.9	—	121.8	74.0	14.2	.9	1.9
13	Warner-Lambert Co.	132.3	1.5	7.3	—	39.4	74.6	1.7	7.8	—
14	American Home Products Corp.	223.0	1.8	21.3	.6	32.1	161.4	1.9	3.9	—
15	Unilever U.S.	184.9	4.7	13.0	—	55.8	110.3	.3	.7	.05
16	McDonald's Corp.	193.4	—	.2	—	105.0	80.9	2.0	.8	4.3
17	Johnson & Johnson	168.0	2.0	23.2	.4	9.2	131.3	.3	1.6	—
18	Mobil Corp.	42.3	7.0	3.9	.8	20.8	7.2	2.4	—	.05
19	J.C. Penney Co.	70.2	—	19.7	—	18.1	31.9	.2	—	.2
20	Anheuser-Busch Cos.	242.6	4.2	10.9	—	59.4	116.5	40.7	6.9	4.0
21	Ralston Purina Co.	158.7	3.2	14.6	1.7	35.7	94.4	8.8	—	.3
22	Coca-Cola Co.	192.5	6.0	8.6	—	70.7	95.9	8.0	—	3.3
23	General Mills	253.1	5.6	25.5	—	113.0	100.3	6.2	2.4	.2
24	Colgate-Palmolive Co.	103.8	1.7	8.5	.2	29.6	59.9	3.9	—	—
25	Warner Communications	156.0	15.7	25.6	—	27.4	84.2	2.2	.5	.3

advertiser may want to use a selective media plan. The advertiser, for example, may want to use trade media that reach electrical engineers or television stations that reach middle-income, Hispanic consumers. Or, as in the case of Canon cameras, the goal may be to reach upscale, active sports enthusiasts.

Nature of the medium and the message

An important determinant in media strategy is the nature of the media themselves. Some media lend themselves better to certain types of messages or creative approaches than others. For an understanding of the creative advantages and disadvantages of each of the major media, see Ad Lab 12–A.

AD LAB 12–A   Media selection: As the creative person sees it

	Creative Disadvantages	**Creative Advantages**
Newspapers	Loss of fidelity, especially in reproduction of halftone illustrations. Too many ad-format variations among newspapers. Variance in column widths. Difficulty in controlling ad position on page.	Almost any ad size available. Impact of black against white (still one of the most powerful color combinations). Sense of immediacy. Quick response; easy accountability. Local emphasis. Changes possible at short notice.
Magazines	Size not as large as those of newspapers or posters. Long closing dates, limiting flexibility. Lack of immediacy. Tendency to cluster ads. Possible difficulties in securing favorable spot in an issue.	High-quality reproduction. Prestige factor. Accurate demographic information available. Graphic opportunities (use of white space, benday screen, reverse type). Color.
Television	No time to convey a lot of information. Air clutter (almost 25 percent of broadcasting is nonprogramming material). Intrusiveness (TV tops list of consumers' complaints in this respect). Capricious station censorship.	Combination of sight and sound. Movement. A single message at a time. Viewer's empathy. Opportunity to demonstrate the product. Believability: "What you see is what you get."
Radio	Lack of visual excitement. Wavering attention span (many listeners tune out commercials). Inadequate data on listening habits (when is the "listener" really listening?). Fleeting nature of message.	Opportunity to explore sound. Favorable to humor. Intimacy. Loyal following (the average person listens regularly to only about two stations). Ability to change message quickly.

Advertising messages differ in many ways. Some are very simple, dogmatic messages: "When E. F. Hutton talks, people listen." Others are based on an emotional attitude, appealing to people's needs for safety, security, social approval, love, beauty, or fun: "Reach out and touch someone." Many advertisers use a reason-why approach to explain their product's advantages: "Lite. Everything you always wanted in a beer. And less." Some messages are complex, requiring considerable space or time for explanation. Others announce a new product or product concept and are, therefore, unfamiliar to the consuming public. In each of these circumstances, the media strategy will be considerably affected.

A message that is either new or highly complex, like the ad for

	Creative Disadvantages	**Creative Advantages**
Direct mail	Damper of state, federal, and postal regulations on creative experimentations. Censorship often unpredictable. Formula thinking encouraged by "proven" direct-mail track records.	Graphic and production flexibility, such as use of three-dimensional effect (folding, die-cuts, pop-ups). Measurable. As scientific as any other form of advertising. Highly personal.
Posters	Essentially a one-line medium with only a limited opportunity to expand on the advertising message. Inadequate audience research, especially in transit advertising.	Graphic opportunities. Color. Large size. High-fidelity reproduction. Simple, direct approach. Possibility of an entirely visual message.
Point of sale	Difficulty in pinpointing audience. Failure of retailers to make proper use of material submitted to them.	Opportunities for three-dimensional effects, movement, sound, and new production techniques.

Laboratory Application

1. What creative disadvantages and advantages can you add to the list?

2. From the list of leading advertisers in Figure 12–5, select one, and explain why the primary medium they use is specifically advantageous for their product from a creative point of view.

Paine Webber, requires greater frequency to be understood and re-membered (Figure 12–6). A dogmatic message, like that for Canon or E. F. Hutton, may require a surge at the beginning to communicate the idea. But then it is usually advantageous to maintain low fre-quency and strive for greater reach.

Reason-why messages, like the ad for Worcester Controls, may be complex to understand at first (Figure 12–7). But once the explanation is understood, a pulsing of advertising exposures at irregular inter-vals is often sufficient to remind customers of the explanation. On the other hand, emotionally oriented messages are usually more effective if spaced at regular intervals to create a continuing feeling about the product.[2]

Consumer purchase patterns

While the nature of the medium and the messages are important considerations in developing media strategy, so are the normal pur-chasing habits of customers for the product. For example, seasonal products such as snow tires or suntan lotion require concentrated exposures just before peak buying periods.

Some products are purchased at very regular intervals, and the advertising function is to influence the customer's brand choice. If this is the case, we want to reach prospects regularly and especially just before they make their next purchasing decision. Situations of this type call for relatively high frequency and high continuity, de-pending on the length of time of the purchasing cycle. As the pur-chasing cycle gets longer, the pulsing of messages becomes more appropriate.

In some cases, the purchase cycle is erratic but susceptible to influ-ence by advertising. In these situations we try to space advertising exposures using periods of high frequency followed by periods of very low exposure. The purpose is to try to reduce the length of time between purchases.

Some products are bought on impulse and therefore require steady, high-frequency advertising. Others, that are bought after great delib-

FIGURE   12–6

In this commercial for Paine Webber, an investor client—with the help of the broker's

employees—soundly defeats Jimmy Connors in a round of tennis. The message comes

through that, as team players, Paine Webber people are a match for the best.

FIGURE 12-7

This ad presents "quite a chilling argument" for Worcester Controls through the use of extensive technical copy and simple but clear tech art. A fine example of reason-why industrial advertising, this ad should be given heavy exposure at first and then irregular pulsing to remind customers of the explanation.

eration, may require pulsing with alternately high and low frequencies depending on market conditions and on competitive activity.

Products with a high degree of brand loyalty can usually be served with lower levels of frequency, allowing the advertiser to achieve greater reach and continuity. (Review the Checklist for developing media objectives and strategies.)

Mechanical considerations

Considerations of how to use the media we select may greatly affect our overall media strategy. For example, greater attention can usually be gained from a full-color ad than from a black-and-white ad. Likewise, a full-page ad attracts more attention than a quarter-page ad (Figures 12–8 and 12–9). With limited advertising budgets, though, larger units of space or time cost dearly in terms of reach, frequency, and continuity.

Is it better for a small advertiser to run a full-page ad once a month or a quarter-page ad once a week? Should television advertisers use occasional 60-second announcements or a lot of 10-, 20-, and 30-second commercials? The answers to these questions are not simple. Some messages require more time and space to be explained. Competitive activity often dictates more message units. The nature of the product itself may demand the prestige of a full page or full color. On the other hand, the need for high frequency may demand smaller units. It is sometimes better to run several small ads consistently than to run one large ad occasionally.

Other mechanical considerations include using the preferred posi-

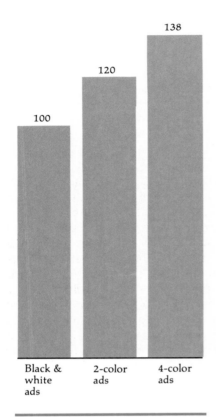

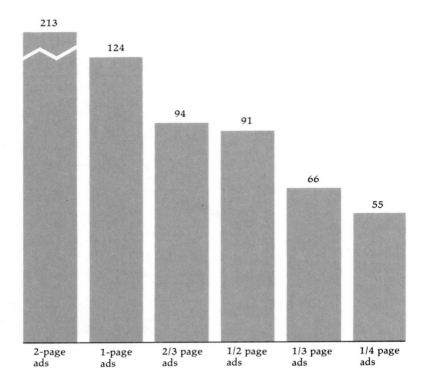

FIGURE   12–8

How is advertising readership
influenced by the addition of
four-color? Four-color significantly
increases the average advertising
readership score beyond both
two-color and black and white.

FIGURE   12–9

How is advertising readership
influenced by ad size? As the size
of an advertisement increases, the
readership score increases; but,
depending on the publication, the
additional readership may not
offset the additional cost.

tions of magazine advertisements on front and back covers or sponsoring prime-time television shows. Special positions, sponsorships,
and other mechanical opportunities are usually sold at a premium by
the media. The media planner must therefore weigh the benefits of
these extra costs in terms of the potential sales impact against the loss
of reach and frequency.

Competitive strategy and budget levels

Media strategy must consider what competitive advertisers are
doing, particularly if their advertising budgets are larger. The general
rule is to bypass media that competitors dominate and to choose,
instead, those that offer a strong or dominant position. An exception
to this is when a campaign has such a unique creative approach that it
will stand out, regardless of competitive advertising.

As we've said before, the reach, frequency, and continuity of any
media plan are greatly limited by the advertising budget. Of great

importance to most small advertisers, therefore, is an understanding of how to use their budgets most effectively. Generally the smaller the budget, the more pulsing is required. In this way, even with a low budget, the advertiser can sometimes attract as much attention as bigger competitors in the product class. As the budget grows larger, greater continuity can be sought by spreading advertising messages more evenly.

■ Stating the Media Strategy

A written statement of the media strategy is an integral part of any media plan. Without one, it is very difficult to analyze the logic and consistency of the overall media schedule that is recommended. Generally, the strategy statement should tell what types of media will be used, how they will be used, and the rationale for the choices made. It should start with a brief definition of the target audiences and the priorities for weighting them, and it should outline specific reach, frequency, and continuity goals. The nature of the message should be explained. Then, it should provide a breakdown of the various types of media to be used over the period of the campaign, the budget for each, and the cost of production and any collateral materials. Finally, the intended size of message units, along with any timing considerations, should be stated as well as the effect of budget restrictions.

MEDIA SELECTION AND SCHEDULING

After the media strategy has been developed, the task of selecting the specific media vehicles and scheduling their use falls to the media planner.

In the development of its media strategy, Canon decided to use television sports programming to reach upscale young men. But which sports programs should be used? Boxing? Bowling? Golf? Baseball? Football? Basketball? "Wide World of Sports"? The choices seem endless. Which golf tournaments? Which football games? Should ads also be run in horse show programs or baseball scorecards? How about an ad on the scoreboard at these events?

As always, budgets are limited. The media planner must take many factors into consideration to make the most efficient media selection and then weigh a variety of other criteria to schedule these media appropriately.

Considerations in Selecting Individual Media

The media planner's job is to match the right media vehicles with the right audiences at the right time in the best environment and the most logical place so that the advertising message will not only achieve the desired exposure but also attract attention and motivate customers to some action. And the planner must do this with cost efficiency so that the reach, frequency, and continuity goals can be met.

Therefore, in considering specific media vehicles for use, the planner must first study several influencing factors: (1) overall campaign objectives and strategy; (2) size and characteristics of each medium's audience; (3) geographic coverage; (4) attention, exposure, and motivation value of the media being considered; (5) cost efficiency; and (6) the various approaches available for media selection.

Overall campaign objectives and strategy

When the selection process begins, the media planner's first job is to review the nature of the product or service, the intended objectives and strategies that have been developed, and the primary and secondary target markets and audiences. These all influence the media selected (Figure 12–10).

The nature of the product itself may suggest the type of media to be used. For example, when a product—such as a fine perfume—has a distinct personality or image, it might be advertised in media that have personality traits that reinforce this image. Some magazines, for instance, are regarded as feminine or masculine, high-brow or low-brow, serious or frivolous.

If the objective of the marketing and advertising campaign is to gain greater product distribution, the media selected should be those that influence both consumers and potential dealers. For example, if the goal is to stimulate sales of a nationally distributed product in certain isolated markets, we will want to concentrate our advertisements in the local and regional media that penetrate those markets rather than in national media. On the other hand, if our goal is to elevate product image or company reputation, we may be willing to sacrifice the sales potential of popular local programming in favor of the prestige of high quality programs on network television.

The price of the product and the pricing strategy may influence media choices, too. Pricing is often a key consideration in product positioning. For example, a premium-priced product may require the use of prestigious or "class" media to support its market image.

Thus, the media planner must carefully assess the objectives and the strategy of the campaign in order to select the most suitable media (See Ad Lab 12–B).

Likewise, reviewing the product's target market and the campaign's target audience is another vital step in media selection. The more the media planner knows about the market, the better the media selections are likely to be. Data gathered on the nature of the target market should include its size, location, and demographic profile, such as age, sex, education, occupation, income, and religion. Psychographic characteristics should also be included, such as lifestyle, personality, and attitudinal traits. Behavioral characteristics should be studied, too, such as purchase cycles, benefits sought, and other product use habits.

The task of the media planner is then (1) to select from these data the characteristics most relevant to the acceptance, purchase, and use of the product (e.g., the most relevant characteristics for ladies dress shops are sex, age, and lifestyle) and (2) to match these data to the characteristics of the audiences reached by the specific media vehicles under consideration.

FIGURE 12–10 Comparative evaluation of advertising media

	Spot television	Network television	Spot radio	Network radio	Consumer magazines	Business publications	Farm publications	Sunday supplements	Daily newspapers	Weekly newspapers	Direct mail	Outdoor	Transit	Point of purchase
Audience considerations														
Attentiveness of audience	⊗	⊗	⊗	⊗	⊗	⊗	⊗	⊗	⊗	⊗	⊗	○	○	○
Interest of audience	⊗	●	⊗	⊗	●	●	●	●	●	●	○	○	○	○
Avoids excess selection by audience	⊗	⊗	⊗	⊗	○	○	○	○	○	○	○	○	○	○
Offers selectivity to advertiser	○	○	⊗	⊗	●	●	●	○	○	○	●	○	○	○
Avoids waste	○	○	○	○	●	●	●	⊗	○	○	●	○	○	○
Offers involvement	⊗	●	⊗	⊗	⊗	●	⊗	⊗	⊗	⊗	○	○	○	○
Avoids distraction	⊗	●	⊗	⊗	●	●	●	⊗	⊗	⊗	○	○	○	○
Avoids resistance	N	N	N	N	N	N	N	N	N	N	N	N	N	N
Provides impact	V	V	V	V	V	V	V	V	V	V	V	V	V	V
Offers prestige	⊗	●	○	⊗	●	●	⊗	●	⊗	○	○	○	○	○
Good quality of audience data	⊗	⊗	⊗	⊗	●	●	⊗	⊗	⊗	○	⊗	○	○	○
Timing factors														
Offers repetition	●	●	●	●	⊗	⊗	⊗	○	⊗	○	V	●	●	⊗
Avoids irritation	○	○	○	⊗	⊗	⊗	⊗	⊗	⊗	⊗	⊗	⊗	⊗	⊗
Offers frequency	●	●	●	⊗	⊗	⊗	⊗	○	⊗	○	●	●	●	●
Offers frequency of issuance	●	●	●	●	V	V	○	○	⊗	○	V	N	N	N
Offers flexibility in scheduling	●	●	●	●	V	V	○	○	⊗	○	V	N	N	N
Long life	○	○	○	○	●	●	●	⊗	○	⊗	○	○	○	○
Low mortality rate	○	○	○	○	●	●	●	⊗	○	⊗	○	○	○	○
Avoids perishability	○	○	○	○	●	●	●	⊗	○	⊗	○	○	○	○
Allows long message	⊗	⊗	⊗	⊗	●	●	●	●	●	●	●	○	○	○
Provides product protection	V	⊗	V	⊗	⊗	⊗	⊗	⊗	V	V	●	○	○	⊗
Geographic considerations														
Offers geographic selectivity	●	○	●	○	⊗	⊗	⊗	●	●	●	●	⊗	⊗	●
Offers proximity to point of sale	○	○	○	○	○	○	○	○	○	○	⊗	⊗	⊗	●
Provides for local dealer "tags"	⊗	○	⊗	○	⊗	⊗	⊗	⊗	●	●	●	⊗	⊗	●
Creative considerations														
Permits demonstration	●	●	○	○	⊗	⊗	⊗	⊗	⊗	⊗	●	○	○	●
Provides impact	●	●	⊗	⊗	●	●	⊗	⊗	⊗	⊗	●	○	○	⊗
Permits relation to editorial matter	⊗	⊗	○	⊗	●	●	●	⊗	⊗	⊗	●	N	N	N
Competitive factors														
Light use of medium by competitors	○	●	○	●	○	●	●	⊗	⊗	●	⊗	⊗	●	●
Low amount of total advertising	○	○	V	●	⊗	V	●	⊗	⊗	⊗	●	⊗	○	●
Control considerations														
Advertiser control of media content	○	⊗	○	⊗	○	○	○	○	○	○	●	N	N	N
Favorable environment	○	⊗	○	⊗	○	○	○	○	○	○	●	○	○	●
Advertiser control of location		●		●	⊗	⊗	⊗	○	○		●	○	○	⊗
Amount of government regulation	○	N	○	N	N	N	N	N	N	N	○	○	N	N
Number of other restrictions	○	○	○	○	V	V	V	V	V	V	○	○	○	○
Mechanical and production factors														
Ease of insertion	⊗	●	⊗	●	●	●	●	⊗	⊗	○	●	⊗	⊗	○
High reproduction quality	⊗	⊗	⊗	⊗	●	●	●	●	V	V	●	V	V	●
Flexibility of format	⊗	⊗	⊗	⊗	●	●	●	○			●	⊗	○	○
Avoids vandalism	N	N	N	N	N	N	N	N	N	N	N	○	○	○
Financial considerations														
Low total cost	⊗	○	⊗	○	○	○	○	⊗	●	●	○	⊗	⊗	⊗
High efficiency	⊗	●	●	⊗	⊗	⊗	⊗	⊗	⊗	○	●	●	●	○

Note: N = not a factor for this medium, V = varies from one vehicle to another with the medium, ○ = weak, ⊗ = medium, ● = strong.

AD LAB   12–B   Off-the-wall media that pull customers off the fence

Advertising via Telephone

You can purchase 30-second messages in which the advertiser supplies the company with relevant sales points. They can be taped, introduced by a live-pitch person, or both. "Where to Buy" telephone services identify retailers of specific products from consumers' inquiries.

Aerial Banners and Lights

Banners, usually more than 30 feet long, are pulled by low-flying planes. After dark, traveling aerial lights can display messages of up to 90 characters.

Balloons

The advertiser's message is imprinted on the balloons. Airborne heights vary from 200 to 800 feet.

Coptermedia

This method uses thousands of light bulbs mounted on a 40-by-8-foot billboard frame on a slow-flying helicopter. The effect is that of a brilliant flying electric sign floating about 500 feet above ground.

Handbills

Handbills are simple sheets of paper with brief advertising messages which may be slipped under windshield wipers or hung on door knobs. Distributed by agents, they are one of the least expensive methods of advertising a local service or retail business.

Litter Receptacles

Some major cities offer space on concrete litter receptacles at major commercial intersections.

Inflatibles

These are oversized versions of products or trade characters. They are real eyestoppers because of their size.

Paper-book Advertising

Bound-in inserts are available. Approximately 350-million pocket books are sold annually. The audience can be pinpointed by book title.

Shopping Bags

Bags are offered to grocery chains on a regionally exclusive basis. A shopper's checklist is printed on both sides, and advertisers can have their names printed on the list next to or in place of the category designation.

Taxicab Advertising

The back panel of front seats, the outside rear, and displays built on the roof provide day and night exposure. Rear-screen slide projectors facing riders are also available in some major markets.

Theater-screen Advertising

Commercials ranging from 30 seconds to 2½ minutes are screened at performances in most indoor and drive-in theaters. The average national movie audience consists of approximately 500 million people per week, with women and younger people dominant.

Laboratory Applications

1. What other off-the-wall media can you think of that might help pull customers off the fence?

2. How effective do you think the off-the-wall media described here are for advertisers?

Characteristics of media audiences

When we speak of a medium's *audience,* we are referring to the total number of people who are reached by that medium. The media planner needs to know how many people are reached by a station or a publication in order to make a realistic judgment of that medium's potential effectiveness. Data on the size and characteristics of media audiences are readily available from a wide variety of media research organizations.

In addition, the planner will want to know (1) the degree of interest people have in the publication or program and (2) how closely the characteristics of the medium's audience match the profile of the target market.

TV-Q and Simmons Market Research Bureau measure the degree of audience interest and attentiveness in television programs. For print media, reader interest may be inferred from the trend of circulation. A consistently growing circulation may indicate greater reader interest, whereas a dwindling circulation may point to declining reader interest. Another way to assess this is to check the percentage of subscription renewals over the past several years.

Readership and audience studies conducted by various media have yielded information of special importance to media planners about the characteristics of their audience. These data enable the media planner to determine how closely the audience characteristics match the profile of the target market prospects.

For example, if the product is intended for tennis enthusiasts, it is essential that the medium selected is the one that reaches tennis players most efficiently. This information is available from various media research organizations. Research data from the W. R. Simmons Company, for example, includes the age, income, occupational status, and other factors of a wide range of magazine readers. Simmons also publishes demographic and psychographic data on product usage among a varied group of consumers.

The *content* of a medium will also reflect the type of people in its audience. For instance, some radio stations emphasize in-depth news or sports, others jazz or rock, and still others symphonic music or operas. Each type of programming attracts a different audience, the character of which can be determined by analysis. Figure 12–11 gives Simmons data on the appeal of various radio formats to different age groups.

Geographic coverage

There is no point in advertising to people who don't live in an area where the product or service is sold. Therefore the geographic coverage of a medium is often the determining factor in selection.

Many national brands face tougher competition in certain regions than in others. Often extra advertising dollars are concentrated in areas where competition is stiffer. Airlines select media that cover the cities they serve and omit media that are circulated in other areas.

Geographic considerations have given rise to the popularity of regional editions of magazines, the use of spot TV instead of network TV, and the use of local media instead of national media for national advertisers.

FIGURE 12–11   Average quarter-hour audiences by formats

Total adults in U.S. 6 A.M.–midnight, Monday–Friday	U.S. total	Total radio	Adult contemporary	All news	Beautiful music	Black	Classical/ semiclassical	Country	Golden oldies	Middle of the road	Progressive	Soft contemporary	Standard	Talk	Top 40
18 to 24															
Percent of composite	18.3	21.7	38.8	6.6	5.7	37.0	9.1	11.8	49.8	14.9	39.0	41.1	9.3	5.0	39.1
Index	100	119	212	36	31	202	50	64	272	81	213	225	51	27	214
25 to 34															
Percent of composite	22.0	24.4	30.7	14.6	15.2	30.8	12.4	21.2	29.8	28.5	43.9	36.8	13.8	8.0	30.7
Index	100	111	140	66	69	140	56	96	135	130	200	167	63	36	140
35 to 44															
Percent of composite	15.6	17.4	10.5	13.3	23.1	18.6	28.6	27.8	11.9	18.3	8.1	6.5	21.3	14.1	14.9
Index	100	112	67	85	148	119	183	178	76	117	52	42	137	90	96
45 to 54															
Percent of composite	15.7	15.4	8.0	24.3	22.8	10.9	33.2	15.9	3.1	19.6	6.1	6.5	23.3	26.8	8.3
Index	100	98	51	155	145	69	211	101	20	125	45	41	148	171	53
55 to 64															
Percent of composite	13.6	12.0	6.9	19.0	20.3	1.6	11.2	15.2	2.8	10.6	2.3	6.9	16.6	21.1	3.9
Index	100	88	51	140	149	12	82	112	21	78	15	51	122	155	29
65 or over															
Percent of composite	14.8	9.1	5.1	22.2	12.8	1.2	5.4	8.2	2.3	8.2	0.7	2.6	15.7	25.3	3.2
Index	100	61	34	150	86	8	36	55	16	55	5	18	106	171	22
18 to 49															
Percent of composite	63.0	69.8	83.0	46.0	54.1	92.4	57.7	69.8	93.7	70.2	91.7	87.8	53.8	36.0	87.6
Index	100	111	132	73	86	147	92	111	149	111	146	139	85	57	139
35 to 49															
Percent of composite	22.7	23.7	13.6	24.8	33.2	24.7	36.1	36.8	14.1	26.8	8.8	9.8	30.7	22.9	17.9
Index	100	104	60	109	146	109	159	162	62	118	39	43	135	101	79

Exposure, attention, and motivational value

As we pointed out earlier, the goal of the media planner is to match the right media with the target audience so that the advertisements not only achieve the desired *exposure* but also attract *attention* and *motivate* prospective customers to act. This is the true art of media planning. But it is very difficult since little reliable data has ever been developed to measure the relative strength of one medium over another in terms of exposure, attention, or motivation values. However, these are still important issues that experienced media planners must consider every day.

Exposure To understand the concept of exposure, think in terms of how many people your ad sees rather than the other way around. If you place an advertisement in a magazine with 3 million readers, how many of those 3 million will your ad actually see? If a given television program has an audience of 10 million viewers, how many people will your commercial actually see?

The numbers are usually considerably less than the total audience or readership. Some people read only one article in a magazine, set it aside, and never pick it up again. Others thumb through every page with as much interest in the ads as in the articles. Many people watch television until the commercial, then jump up and change the channel or go to another room to get a snack. Other programs may keep people glued to their chairs but still have to contend with conversation about the show during the commercial break.

Thus, assessing the exposure value of one publication, radio station, or TV program over another is a difficult task. And without statistics, it is up to the media planner to use his or her best judgment—based on experience.

Attention The degree of attention paid to ads by those exposed to them is another consideration. If you are not interested in motorcycles or cosmetics, then you probably don't even notice ads for them when you do see them. On the other hand, if you are in the market for a new automobile, you probably notice every new-car ad you see.

Whereas exposure value relates only to the medium itself, attention value relates to the advertising message and copy just as much as to the medium (Figure 12–12). It is logical to assume that special-interest media, such as tennis magazines, offer good attention value to a tennis product. But what kind of attention value does the daily newspaper offer to a boating product? Will the boating enthusiast be thinking about a boat while reading the newspaper? There are no simple answers to these questions, and much research still needs to be done. But six factors have been found to positively affect the attention value of a medium:[3]

1. Audience involvement with editorial content or program material.
2. Specialization of audience interest or identification.
3. Number of competitive advertisers (the fewer, the better).
4. Audience familiarity with advertiser's campaign.
5. Quality of advertising reproduction.
6. Timeliness of advertising exposure.

Motivation These same factors affect a medium's motivation value. In some cases, though, they are a more important contributor to motivation than to attention, and vice versa. For instance, familiarity with the advertiser's campaign may affect attention significantly but motivation very little. On the other hand, good-quality reproduction and timeliness can be very motivating to someone interested in

FIGURE   12–12

Attention value for Porsche's well-known and well-produced campaign will be enhanced in publications where audience involvement with editorial content is high.

the product (Figure 12–13). Therefore, attention value and motivation value should be considered separately when assessing alternative media.

One method media planners use to analyze these values is to assign a specific numerical value to their subjective assessment of a medium's various strengths and weaknesses. Then, using either a simple or complex weighting formula, they basically just add them up. Similar weighting methods are used for evaluating other subjective considerations in media selection, such as the relative importance of audience age demographics against income characteristics.

Cost efficiency

The final step in determining what media to select is to analyze the cost efficiency of each medium available.

A common term used in media buying is *CPM*, or *cost-per-thousand*. The media compare their prices with those of other media by the cost of reaching 1,000 people in their audience. For example, if a daily newspaper has 300,000 subscribers and charges $5,000, then the cost-per-thousand would be calculated as:

$$CPM = \$5,000 \div 300 = \$16.67$$

PEOPLE IN ADVERTISING

Mark S. Oken

Senior Vice President and Media Director
The Bloom Agency

Media specialist Mark S. Oken is senior vice president and media director of The Bloom Agency, Dallas, one of the 10 fastest growing full-service advertising agencies in the United States.

A graduate of Northwestern University, where he received a B.S. in business administration (accounting) in 1956, Oken went on to obtain an M.B.A. in marketing at the University of Michigan.

He launched his career in advertising as a media buyer for Kenyon & Eckhardt. Four years later Oken joined Needham, Louis & Brorby as a time buyer. He moved to Foote, Cone & Belding in 1963 as manager of network facilities. Within four years Oken became media supervisor at Needham, Harper & Steers. In 1971 he was named senior vice president and media director of The Bloom Agency, whose clients include Mitsubishi Aircraft International, Pet, Inc., Six Flags, and Southwest Airlines. The agency, which has more than doubled in size during the past five years, today has nearly 300 employees and annual billings of over $61 million.

The growing success of The Bloom Agency, according to Oken, is due in part to the fact that it performs media planning and selection for its clients not on the traditional 15 percent commission

A weekly newspaper with a circulation of 250,000 that charges $3,000 for a full page would promote itself as less expensive because its cost per thousand would be considerably less:

$$CPM = \$3,000 \div 250 = \$12.00$$

However, media planners are normally more interested in the *cost efficiency* of reaching the target audience, not the cost of reaching the medium's total circulation.

The media planner must evaluate all the criteria discussed above to determine (1) how much of each medium's audience matches the target audience, (2) how each medium satisfies the needs of the campaign's objectives and strategy, and (3) how well each medium measures up in attention, exposure, and motivation value. At that point it might then be determined that, even with a higher cost-per-thousand circulation, the daily newspaper is still a better buy from a cost-efficiency standpoint and, therefore, the more attractive selection.

Selection approaches

In our analysis of media efficiency, we may discover that several media are attractive to use because each contains a segment of pros-

---

basis, as most agencies do, but on a fee basis. "This fee system," Oken reports, "has proven to make our media services for clients much more effective. It motivates better work," he explains, "and puts the emphasis in our work where the client wants it."

Oken also believes that the fee formula affords the agency greater flexibility in its approach to clients' media goals. For media people, he notes, the fee system "provides greater freedom to examine overall marketing objectives—and to offer useful suggestions for achieving them that might not otherwise be possible." These suggestions, says Oken, "might even recommend against media spending. We might urge heavier consumer or trade promotional activity instead." And where media use is indicated, Oken observes, "the fee system enables the agency to recommend certain unique types of media that might not be profitable for the agency were it compensated solely by media commissions."

Clients can help to make their agencies' media services even more effective, says Oken, by observing the following practices:

1. Formulate specific and realistic media objectives.

2. Share important data with your agency's media staff, including sales, budget, product development, and brand performance information.
3. Permit innovative media planning.
4. Be willing to look beyond "media numbers" to achieve more productive media plans.
5. Discuss and make media decisions with your agency rather than deviating from it or superseding it arbitrarily.
7. Avoid last-minute media buys or changes that can undermine the effectiveness of your media program.
8. Don't be drawn in by "bargain" buys that are not efficient.
9. Ask your agency to show you and your personnel how to understand and evaluate its media recommendations.

Oken is a frequent contributor to media trade publications and a member of the Newspaper Committee of the American Association of Advertising Agencies. He is active in numerous organizations and serves on the board of directors of the Advertisers Club, Chicago; the Association of Broadcast Executives of Texas; and the Dallas Advertising League.

pects for our product. So the question may arise as to how to reach the greatest number of prospects.

One consideration might be to use a *broadside approach*, sending an equal number of messages to each group and hoping for the best. Another approach, called *profile matching*, might be to split up the media schedule so that the messages are delivered to each segment in proportion to that segment's importance among all prospects. This would probably result in greater reach than the broadside approach. The third method would be to work the various market segments as a gold miner works several claims—start with the richest claim first. This method, called the *high-assay principle*, suggests starting with the medium that produces the best return and then moving to other media only when the first becomes unavailable or loses its effectiveness. According to Longman, unless prospects can be individually identified, this is the best method to maximize reach.[4]

When the rate of return (i.e., added new reach) of the one medium falls below what the rate of return would be from another, then it is time to switch or add other media.

These principles are very important for the media planner to understand. However, they are also highly theoretical and based on extremely simple hypothetical cases. In the real world many factors complicate the process. Cost factors must be considered. It is very difficult to weigh the actual sales potential of given market segments. And combination effects of media overlapping from the advertiser's media schedule produce distorted figures that make accurate measurement of results difficult. Other things being equal, though, if our objective is to reach the most prospects, we prefer the media with the largest audiences and the greatest number of prospects for concentrated scheduling.[5] If our objective is higher frequency, we prefer to select several media vehicles with smaller audiences.

FIGURE   12–13

If you're a camping enthusiast and summer is fast approaching, the motivation value of *Field and Stream* magazine will probably be very high for this beautifully produced Jeep ad.

ROWLETT'S
HAS ENOUGH
CANOES TO
SINK A SHIP.

Aluminum Canoes by Grumman.
Now $50-150 off.

ABS Canoes by Old Town, Mohawk,
and Mad River.
Prices start at $450.

Fiberglass Canoes by Mohawk,
Grumman, Mad River, and Old Town.
Prices start at $295.

It's true. In fact, Rowlett's has
more canoes than anybody else in
Central Virginia.
Canoes by Grumman Old Town
Mohawk, Mad River, and Coleman.
Plus paddles, cushions, car racks,
and many other accessories.
Now when you're anxious to
get afloat, you know the best place
to get a canoe.
Rowlett's, at the corner of
Staples Mill and Broad. We're open
daily till 6, Fridays till 9, and
Saturdays till 5.

FIGURE   12–14

Virginians probably don't see this
ad in the depths of winter. But if
Rowlett's is smart, they'll spend a
lot to have it seen in the summer.
It's a fine example of graphic
design, illustration, and
copywriting.

Scheduling Criteria

After we have selected the media vehicles we wish to use, we must decide how many of each media vehicle's space or time units should be bought and over what period of time these units should be used.

As we mentioned earlier, reach and frequency objectives are normally considered for four-week periods. In other words, how many people do we want to reach and how many times do we want to reach them during a given four-week period? The next consideration, then, is how many four-week flights we want to use. Do we want to schedule a steady year-round campaign of 13 four-week flights achieving 120 gross rating points of reach and an average frequency of 3.5 during each month of the year? Or do we want to pulse our campaign, concentrating heavily at first for two months and then backing off and running only occasionally for the rest of the year?

Types of schedules

There are many kinds of schedules in use today. The following are the six basic types most commonly used:[6]

1. *Steady.* These are the easiest types of schedules to prepare: one ad per week for 52 weeks, or one ad per month for 12 months.
2. *Seasonal pulse.* Suntan oil is rarely advertised in the winter; snow tires rarely in the summer. Seasonal buying patterns dictate heavy media use during peak selling periods (Figure 12–14).
3. *Periodic pulse.* When media pulses are scheduled at regular intervals but are not related to the seasons of the year, we have what is called a periodic pulse pattern.
4. *Erratic pulse.* When the advertising is spaced at irregular intervals, the company may be trying to cause changes in typical purchase cycles, as we discussed in the section on media strategy.
5. *Start-up pulse.* This is a common pattern designed to start off a campaign with a bang. It is very common to see this every year when the new automobile models are introduced. It is almost always used to introduce a new product.
6. *Promotional pulse.* Often the media schedule must be designed to support some special promotion of the manufacturer, so buying will be heavier during the time of the promotion than at other times.

As we can see, pulsing (or flighting) of some form characterizes all but the simplest media schedules, and the degree of continuity (or pulsing) is a function of the media strategy. Therefore, at the time the media planner is preparing the actual schedule, it is wise to review the strategy section of the media plan to be sure the final schedule actually reflects what was originally intended.

Analyzing reach, frequency, and continuity

It is up to the media planner to determine the right combination of reach, frequency, and continuity. It is not uncommon for media people to simply say, "match the competition . . . and then some." But, of course, if everybody did that a vicious circle would ensue. It is a little more scientific for the media planner to remember the basic findings of research:

1. Continuity is important because advertising is often quickly forgotten when consumers are not continually exposed to it. In most cases it is a waste of money for advertisers to run ads one week, wait six weeks, and then run ads for another week. To achieve continuity requires committing dollars over some continuous period of time.

2. Repeated exposures are needed to impress a message on the memories of a large proportion of consumers. The advertiser who runs only four or five radio spots per week gives up so much frequency (usually for the sake of continuity) as to make the schedule almost worthless.

3. As the number of exposures increases, both the number of persons who remember it and the length of time they remember it increase. This is why so many media planners believe frequency is the most important media objective. It's the key to remembering.

4. An intensive "burst" of advertising is more likely to cause a large number of people to remember it, at least for a short time, than is spreading a schedule thinly over a 12-month period. This is the most common strategy for building frequency on a limited budget and the rationale behind pulsing advertising schedules.

5. Fewer exposures per prospect in a comparatively large group promote greater memory of the advertising than do more exposures per prospect in a smaller group. In other words, there's a point at which reach becomes more important than frequency in promoting memory.

6. As additional exposures per prospect are purchased, the dollar efficiency of advertising decreases. At some point, therefore, it is again more important to seek reach rather than additional frequency.

The media planner must decide how to weight reach, frequency, and continuity to maximize the impact and efficiency of the advertising dollar. Since no perfect scientific method has been devised to do that, this is part of the *art* of media planning.

Summary

The decisions made in media planning frequently involve as much creativity as the decisions made by art directors and copywriters. And like good art and copy ideas, media decisions should be based on sound marketing principles and research, not just on experience and intuition.

The media function involves two basic processes: media planning and media selection. Media planning begins by determining primary target audiences and then setting goals or objectives for communicating with those audiences. Media objectives may be expressed in terms of reach, frequency, impressions, gross rating points, and continuity.

In developing the appropriate media strategy, the planner must consider many variables. These include the scope of the market, the nature of the message, consumer purchase patterns, budget levels, the mechanical limitations of the media, competitive strategy, the merchandising needs of the advertiser, and the basic nature of the medium itself.

After the media strategy is developed, the tasks of selecting specific media vehicles begins. Numerous factors influence the selection process: (1) campaign objectives and strategy; (2) the size and characteristics of each medium's audience; (3) geographic coverage; (4) the attention, exposure, and motivation value of each medium; (5) cost efficiency; and (6) the intended selection approach.

Once the particular media vehicles have been selected, the problem arises as to how to schedule their use; that is, how many of each medium's space or time units should be bought over what period of time? There are many ways to schedule a media campaign, from steady, continuous advertising to erratic pulses of commercials. This decision is usually a function of the media strategy.

The final result must be a logical weighting of reach, frequency, and continuity to maximize the effectiveness of the campaign and the efficiency of dollars spent. This is referred to as the *art* of media planning.

Questions for review and discussion

1. What must the media planner take into consideration before media planning can begin?
2. What are the first two steps in media planning?
3. How are media objectives expressed? Describe.
4. What is the primary factor that determines the level of reach, frequency, and continuity?
5. What are the six basic types of media schedules? Give details on how each is used.
6. How important a consideration is competitive strategy to a media planner? Explain.
7. What are the major factors that influence the use of specific media vehicles? Justify the importance of each factor.
8. What method may be used to determine a medium's cost efficiency?
9. What is the difference among the following media selection approaches: (*a*) broadside approach, (*b*) profile matching, and (*c*) high-assay principle?
10. What is the best approach for maximizing frequency in a media schedule?

13

PRINT MEDIA

If records were kept for creating the most successful newspaper campaign in the least time and for the least money, a campaign for a Minneapolis haircutting salon, 7 South 8th for Hair, might well hold the world title.

"This was a very easy campaign to create, really painless," says Jarl Olsen, the copywriter at Fallon McElligott Rice. "The whole thing took less than a day to plan."

The campaign ran in local newspapers because of their ability to reach a large audience quickly at reasonable cost. Newspapers were also best for getting across the simple, straightforward message planned for the campaign.

"We wanted to generate some talk value, so we used something that everyone could laugh at." The instructions from the client were sparse; the only requirement was that the salon's name be on the ads. "We were all over the board," recalls Olsen, "and all of the ideas were weird."

Random scrawlings eventually led to the ad shown in Figure 13–1, which features the sorceress Medea and the caption reads "A bad haircut is a real can of worms." The rest of the campaign is the result of spinoffs of that original idea.

"We sat around trying to think of bad haircuts," Olsen recalls with a laugh. "We thought of several, but we could only think of a few copy lines that made any sense."

The ads, which consist of stock photos of famous bad haircuts, a witty line of copy, and the client's name and address, appeared all over Minneapolis newspapers and later in local magazines and posters. The campaign took the city by storm.

"These ads were everywhere," Olsen recalls, "and everyone was talking about them. Other shops were cutting the ads out and sticking their own logos on them. I called 7 South 8th to tell them about it," he continues. "They laughed and said they knew. They thought it was funny."[1]

USING NEWSPAPERS IN THE CREATIVE MIX

Advertising people are constantly looking for *creative* solutions to their clients' marketing problems, as we pointed out in Chapter 7. However, many factors besides advertising creativity are involved in sales: the product, value offered, price, availability, competitive pressures, timing, and even the weather, all have an impact on sales. Nevertheless, creative advertising can give the advertiser a chance to be heard, to present an offer. A fresh creative approach can do that superbly.

The printed page, in general, and the newspaper, in particular, provide a unique, flexible medium for the maker of advertising to express this creativity.

How Newspapers Assist Creativity

The newspaper provides all the basics. It is read by almost everybody who can reasonably be thought of as a consumer, and it is read almost daily. According to research, most people read the newspaper in a reasonably ordered way. In the course of their reading they open and look at 84 percent of the pages—giving the advertiser a good opportunity to gain their attention if the method used is creative enough to merit it.

The newspaper offers great flexibility, which assists creativity. There is little limitation on ad size; there is black and white, spot color, full color; and, through preprinted inserts, there is an endless variety of shapes, paper stocks, and printing methods. Finally, the advertiser's printed message lasts. It stands still for rereading and reconsideration, for clipping, and for sharing. The newspaper can be shopped from because it is really news about the marketplace.[2]

■ What Works Best in Newspapers?

Newspapers have inherent features that have traditionally set them apart from other media.[3] For example:

1. Newspapers are a *mass* medium, penetrating every segment of society.
2. Newspapers are a *local* medium, covering a specific geographic area, which is both a market and a community of people sharing common concerns and interests.
3. Newspapers are *comprehensive* in scope, covering an extraordinary variety of topics and interests.
4. Newspapers are read *selectively* as readers search for what is personally interesting and useful.
5. Newspapers are *timely* since they are primarily devoted to the news.

FIGURE 13–1

But great advertising can create the right bait.

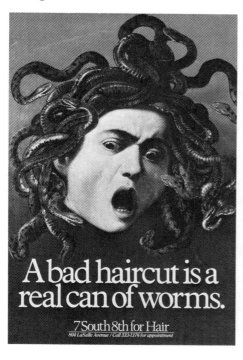

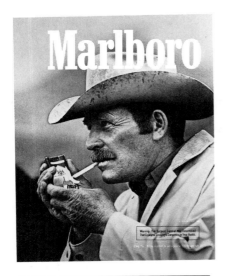

FIGURE   13–2

Marlboro illustrates the concept of creative continuity. Bill Campbell, executive vice president of Philip Morris, USA, comments on the creative content of the Marlboro newspaper ad. "The power lies in its utter simplicity—in the stark contrast a Marlboro ad in the newspaper has compared to other ads in the same issue." With no copy other than the name and the required "tar" information, the campaign is at a point, because of its consistency through the years, "where you can show a cowboy and not even say the name, and people will know it's a Marlboro ad."

6. Newspaper readership is *concentrated* in time. Virtually all the reading of a particular day's paper is done that day.

7. Newspapers represent a *permanent* record that people use actively. Ads and articles are often saved for permanent reference.

These features give rise to a number of special attributes of newspapers that offer clues to the ad maker who is seeking what will work best creatively:

1. Newspapers provide the opportunity for massive same-day exposure of an advertising message to a large cross-section of any market. That means very broad *reach*. For advertisers like Marlboro, newspapers are a valuable reminder medium for a campaign that has long been established in the consumer's mind (Figure 13–2).

2. Newspapers combine broad reach with highly *selective attention* from the very small number of active prospects who, on any given day, are interested in what the advertiser is trying to tell them or sell them.

3. Newspapers provide great creative flexibility to the advertiser. The ad's physical size and shape can be chosen and varied to give the degree of dominance or repetition that suits the advertiser's purpose. The advertiser can use black and white, color, Sunday magazines, or custom inserts. The newspaper, therefore, is almost a media mix by itself.

4. With newspapers the advertiser can go where the customers are. That may mean concentrating the messages in one market or spreading them out over a national schedule. It may mean running the ad in one part of the paper or in several sections. The advertiser can place ads on short notice, localize copy, and work with retailers by using co-op programs.

5. The newspaper is an active medium rather than a passive one.[4] Readers turn the pages, clip and save, write in the margins, and sort through the contents, screening out what they don't want from those things they want to concentrate on. This reader-involving quality of newspapers offers unlimited creative opportunities to advertisers. Coupon ads are an obvious example.

■ Some Drawbacks to Newspapers

While newspapers offer the many advantages and opportunities mentioned above, like all media they also have their drawbacks.

Newspapers enable advertisers to be *geographically selective*, but they do not isolate and cover specific socioeconomic groups. Instead, most newspapers reach broad, diverse groups of readers. The consumer desires and needs of these broad groups may not be compatible with the marketing segmentation objectives of the advertiser. For example, a newspaper sports section may be a good place to advertise general sports products or services, such as surfboards or football tickets, but it would be highly inefficient for advertising sports products to retail sporting goods dealers because of the tremendous waste of circulation.

The *life span* of a daily newspaper is usually only a few hours. Unless a reader clips and saves a newspaper ad or coupon, it may be lost forever. Almost nobody reads yesterday's paper.

Newspapers lack *production quality*; there is no time to use high quality reproduction techniques. And generally the coarse paper used for newspapers creates a finished product far less impressive than magazines with their slick, smooth paper stock.

Each ad *competes for notice* with every other ad on the same page or spread. So many advertisements appear in a single issue of a newspaper (64 percent of the average daily paper) that the potential for any one ad to capture major attention is minimized.

The advertiser has *little or no control over placement*. And yet, the position in which an advertisement is placed on a newspaper page can determine how many readers will see it and how much attention they will give it. Studies have found that ads placed above the horizontal fold of a newspaper are seen more frequently than those placed beneath the fold. Similarly, ads in the outside columns of a page are seen more frequently than those in the inside column.

Many areas are served by newspapers that have *overlapping circulation*; that is, some residents read not one, but two or more different newspapers. Thus, advertisers may be paying for circulation that their ads have already reached in a different newspaper.

Who Uses Newspapers?

Newspapers are the nation's dominant medium in terms of advertising volume. They receive nearly 30 percent of the dollars spent by the nation's advertisers. In 1984 newspapers derived an estimated $15.6 billion from advertising revenues.[5]

Consider these important facts:

1. The typical U.S. newspaper averages 72 pages for morning editions, 60 pages for evening editions, and 208 pages for Sunday editions. There are 2.13 weekday and 2.25 weekend readers per copy.
2. The printed matter averages 64 percent for advertising and 36 percent for editorial matter.
3. The average U.S. metropolitan daily newspaper obtains about 75 percent of its income from sales of advertising space. The bulk of the remaining income comes from subscriptions and vendor sales. Estimates are that, without advertising income, the *New York Times* would have to sell its Sunday edition for $7 a copy—just to break even.

In 1984 there were 1,711 daily newspapers in the United States with a total circulation of 62.4 million. The nation's more than 7,602 semiweekly and weekly newspapers have a combined circulation of more than 41 million.

The newspaper is the major community-serving medium for both news and advertising. With the huge growth of radio and television over the past 20 years, more and more national advertising has shifted to these electronic media. The result is that radio and television today carry most of the national advertising, while 85 percent of newspaper advertising revenue comes from local advertising. The major national advertisers in newspapers are automobile manufacturers, tobacco companies, food processors, and airlines (Figure 13–3).

Or buy a Volkswagen.

FIGURE 13–3

Classic Volkswagen advertising. This famous ad ran at the height of the energy crisis and demonstrated the immediacy of newspaper advertising. Charles Piccirillo, the art director at Doyle Dane Bernbach, was looking for a way to express the frustration everyone felt with the fuel shortage. "This was my first sketch, with a big fat magic marker. They ripped it off my pad and took it to the client, and it came back approved."

FIGURE 13–4

This ad for the Australian Newspaper Advertising Bureau hooked a number of advertising awards for its fresh approach to an old problem—how to sell the benefits of newspaper advertising.

How Newspapers Are Classified

Newspapers may be classified by their frequency of delivery, by the type of audience they reach, or by their physical size.

Frequency of delivery

The two basic types of newspapers are *dailies* and *weeklies*. Dailies are published at least five times a week, Monday through Friday. Some are published on Saturday and Sunday as well.

Dailies are produced as either morning or evening editions. Of the 1,711 dailies in the United States, 1,324 are evening papers, 357 are morning papers, and 30 are "all-day" newspapers. One recent study found that morning editions tend to have a broader geographic circulation and a larger male readership, while evening editions were read more by women. Despite these broad characteristics, each daily newspaper has its own circulation traits chiefly determined by the geographic region it serves and the demographic makeup of its readers (Figure 13–4).

The weekly newspaper characteristically serves readers in small urban or suburban areas or farm communities. One reason for the growth of readership among many weekly newspapers is their exclusive emphasis on local news and advertising. Weekly newspapers offer their readers relief from unsettling national and international crises in the form of familiar names, news of local personalities, and hometown sports, entertainment, and social coverage.

The weekly newspaper usually offers advertisers a high degree of readership but at a cost per thousand that is often higher than that of the daily paper. The rate may be justified since the weekly has a longer life than the daily and is often exposed to more readers per copy.

Size

The two basic newspaper formats are standard and tabloid. The *standard-size* newspaper is generally 22 inches deep and 14 inches wide. This type of newspaper is usually eight columns wide, although a recent trend has been toward a six-column layout and a slightly reduced page size.

The *tabloid* newspaper is generally about half the size of a standard-size newspaper, about 14 inches deep and 10 inches wide, though size varies from one tabloid to another. Tabloids are sold flat, without folding, and look like an unbound magazine. Most tabloid pages have five columns, each about two inches wide. Three national tabloid newspapers, all fighting with sensational news stories for single-copy sales through grocery supermarkets across the country, are the *National Enquirer, The Star,* and the *Midnight Globe.* Their combined circulation is 11 million a week.

In contrast, other tabloids emphasize "straight" news and features. The *New York Daily News,* for example, has the nation's largest daily and Sunday newspaper circulation—over 1.3 million readers daily and over 2.5 million on Sunday.

More than 1,400 newspapers representing more than 93 percent of total daily circulation use the *Standard Advertising Unit (SAU) System* which features 25 individual advertisement sizes that can be accepted by all standard-size newspapers without consideration of their precise format or page size. In addition, there are five alternative sizes for six-column papers. Within these sizes there are l6 units that can also meet the needs of tabloid newspapers. This system allows advertisers to prepare one advertisement in a particular size or SAU and place it in various newspapers, regardless of the format (Figure 13–5).

■ *Specialized audience*

Some dailies and weeklies are aimed at specific special-interest audiences, such as military, ethnic, social, or religious groups. Some are published by fraternal, labor union, or professional organizations. Their specialized news and features enable them to achieve high readership. They generally contain advertising oriented to their special audiences, and they may have unique advertising regulations.

Among these newspapers, for example, are those that specifically

FIGURE 13–5

Standard Advertising Units (SAUs).

NEWSPAPER STANDARD AD UNITS

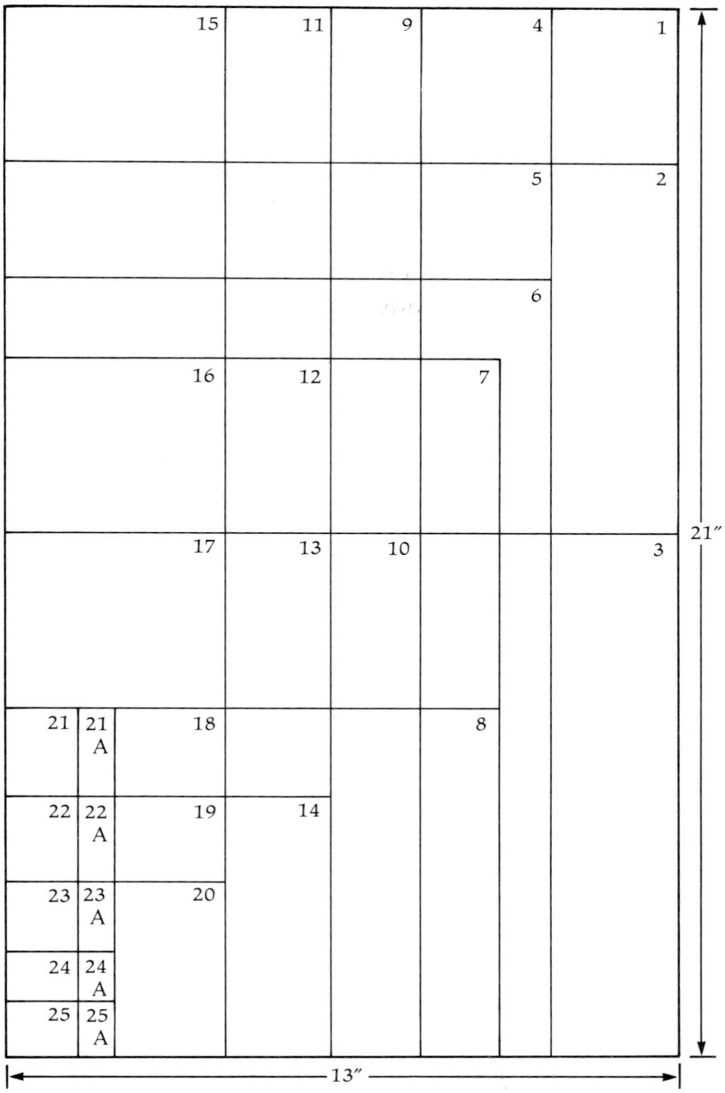

Size of standard advertising units

Standard advertising unit	Width in inches	Depth in inches	Fits tab	6 column format only
1	13" (Full)	21" Full		
2	13" (Full)	18"		
3	13" (Full)	10-7/16"		
4	10-5/8"	21" (Full)		
5	10-5/8"	18"		
6	10-5/8"	15-5/8"		
7	9-5/8" (Tab Full)	13-15/16" (Tab Full)	●	
8	9-5/8" (Tab Full)	6-15/16"	●	
9	8-1/16"	21" (Full)		
10	8-1/16"	10-7/16"	●	
11	6-5/16"	21" (Full)		
12	6-5/16"	13-15/16" (Tab Full)	●	
13	6-5/16"	10-7/16"	●	
14	6-5/16"	5-3/16"	●	
15	4-1/4"	21" (Full)		
16	4-1/4"	13-15/16" (Tab Full)	●	
17	4-1/4"	10-7/16"	●	
18	4-1/4"	6-15/16"	●	
19	4-1/4"	5-3/16"	●	
20	4-1/4"	3-7/16"	●	
21	1-3/8"	6-15/16"	●	
22	1-3/8"	5-3/16"	●	
23	1-3/8"	3-7/16"	●	
24	1-3/8"	2"	●	
25	1-3/8"	1"	●	
21A	2-1/16"	6-15/16"		●
22A	2-1/16"	5-3/16"		●
23A	2-1/16"	3-7/16"		●
24A	2-1/16"	2"		●
25A	2-1/16"	1"		●

serve black readers. Today 203 dailies and weeklies nationwide are oriented to blacks (e.g., the *Amsterdam News*). Still other specialized papers serve foreign-language ethnic groups, such as Spanish, German, Polish, Chinese, or Armenian readers. The United States has ethnic newspapers published in 43 languages other than English.

Specialized newspapers are also produced for business and financial audiences. *The Wall Street Journal* is the leading national business and financial daily, with a circulation of more than 2 million.

The leading U.S. military newspaper is *Stars and Stripes*. Its daily and Sunday European and Pacific editions are read by more than 1 million overseas armed services personnel.

Other types of newspapers

Some 720 of the nation's daily newspapers publish Sunday editions. The combined circulation of these Sunday papers is more than 54 million. Sunday newspapers generally combine standard news coverage with their own special functions. These functions include:

1. Much greater classified advertising volume.
2. Much greater advertising and news volume.

PEOPLE IN ADVERTISING

Rance Crain

President and Editorial Director
Crain Communications, Inc.

Publishers should stay "alert and aggressive—and not become smug or complacent," cautioned G. D. Crain, Jr., founder of Crain Communications, Inc. His son Rance listened. At 34, Rance Crain became president and editorial director of the Chicago-based firm that has produced some of the nation's leading trade publications for over half a century. One of them is prestigious *Advertising Age*, which Rance Crain heads today as editor-in-chief.

Crain, whose college-boy appearance belies his 45 years, pursued an early interest in publishing by attending Northwestern University's Medill School of Journalism, where he was graduated in 1960. He soon became a reporter for the Washington bureau of *Advertising Age* and later went on to its New York and Chicago offices. In 1965 he was named senior editor of *Advertising Age* and the first editor of *Business Insurance*. Crain advanced to editorial director of *Ad Age* in 1971. Two years later, after the death of his father, he became president and editorial director of Crain Communications, Inc.

Under Rance Crain's leadership, the company quickly embarked on an aggressive program of expansion. Within four years *Advertising Age* had nearly doubled its circulation. The firm started *Pensions & Investments* and acquired *Rubber & Plastics News* and *Modern Healthcare*. It expanded into the consumer market with *Autoweek* and other ti-

3. In-depth coverage of developments in the arts, business, sports, housing, entertainment, and travel.

4. Review and analysis of the past week's events.

Most Sunday newspapers also feature a newspaper-distributed magazine, or *Sunday supplement*. Some publish their own supplement, such as the *Los Angeles Times'* "Home" magazine. The remaining newspapers subscribe to a syndicated magazine supplement. These are compiled, edited, and printed by a central organization, then shipped to individual newspapers for insertion in their Sunday editions. Three examples of syndicated supplements are shown in Figure 13–6.

Sunday supplements are distinct from other sections of the newspaper since they are printed by rotogravure on smoother paper stock. This heavier, higher quality paper is more conducive to quality color printing. Therefore, it enables Sunday supplements to attract and feature higher quality national advertising.

Another type of newspaper is the independent shopping guide or free community newspaper. Sometimes called "pennysavers," newspapers (or shoppers) of this type carry little news and practically no

tles. In 1978 the company launched *Crain's Chicago Business* with Rance Crain as editor-in-chief and, two years later, *Crain's Cleveland Business* and *The Collector-Investor*. Today the firm publishes 22 titles, including *Automotive News* and *Business Marketing*. It also produces books, seminars, and a home-study course. The family-owned company is run by Crain, his brother, Keith, as secretary/treasurer and publisher of *Automotive News* and *Autoweek,* and their mother, Gertrude Crain, as chairman of the board.

Rance Crain continues to be the idea man of the organization. His modest corner office filled with memorabilia is a beehive of activity. Despite administrative demands, Crain spends more than half his time as editor-in-chief of *Advertising Age,* personally overseeing a myriad of editorial and production details.

Ad Age is the leading trade publication of the nation's advertising and marketing industries, a $25-million enterprise with 70 full-time reporters. Its international coverage is constantly expanding, and it now has 50 correspondents worldwide. Issued twice weekly, it is widely read by persons in publishing and other allied fields. It's a slick, attractive illustrated bi-weekly tabloid that reports the latest advertising and business news, including information on government actions that affect advertisers, agencies, media, and suppliers. Also

covered are advertising campaigns for new and established products, agency appointments, and personnel changes. *Ad Age* data on radio, television, newspapers, magazines, and other media, and its special issues each year filled with statistical media data are widely read throughout the advertising industry.

Explaining his success, Crain said, "Change and growth have become a way of life in our company. My brother and I pride ourselves on our ability and willingness to constantly build on that philosophy, avoid stagnation, and keep pace with a world which is changing faster than ever before. We intend to keep up with it, and—if possible—to even anticipate it."

That anticipation, he notes, has resulted in *Electronic Media,* a publication for the broadcast industry started a little over four years ago, and the 1984 acquisition of *Monthly Detroit,* a city magazine. The startup of *Crain's New York Business* began in 1984, and *Crain's Detroit Business* began in 1985.

Mr. Crain is a past president of the Chicago Business Publications Association and is currently on the board of directors. He is also a board member of the Chicago chapter of the International Advertising Association and the Better Business Bureau of Metropolitan Chicago, and was formerly on the board of Northwestern University's Alumni Association.

FIGURE   13–6   Syndicated Sunday supplements

Supplements	Number of papers	Circulation	Cost per page		Cost per thousand	
			Black and white	Color	Black and white	Color
Family Weekly	364	12,906,894	$112,255	$128,130	$8.68	$ 9.93
Parade	133	24,370,000	213,470	261,950	8.76	10.75
Sunday	54	23,392,022	192,163	235,332	8.21	10.06

features. Instead, they are distributed free and are filled with advertising aimed at essentially the same audience as the weekly newspapers—urban and suburban community readers.

Shoppers may be published weekly, biweekly, or monthly. Readership is generally high, and the publisher strives to achieve maximum saturation of the circulation area.

National newspapers like *USA Today* and the *Christian Science Monitor* have experienced tremendous growth in recent years. After only two years of being sold nationwide, *USA Today* achieved a circulation of 1.2 million, making it third only to *The Wall Street Journal* and the *New York Daily News* in national distribution.

Types of Newspaper Advertising

The major classifications of newspaper advertising are: display, classified, public notices, and preprinted inserts.

Display advertising

The size of display advertising runs from small boxes to one- and two-page ads. Display ads are generally featured in all areas of the newspaper except on page one, the editorial page, the obituary page, the first page of major sections, and the classified section.

The two principal types of display advertising are *local* and *general* (national). Most newspapers charge the local advertiser and the national advertiser different rates. The national rate averages 51 percent higher than the local rate. Newspapers attribute these higher national rates to the added costs they incur in serving national advertisers. For instance, they point out that this advertising is usually placed by an advertising agency to which the newspaper gives a 15 percent commission. Some newspapers serve these agencies through media representatives, to whom they must also pay a commission. If the advertising comes from another city or state, still other costs are involved. Therefore, publishers feel the higher national rates are justified.

This dual rate system has been controversial among advertisers. Many agencies and advertisers use every available means to qualify for the lower local rate. Some locally based agencies specialize in placing ads for national clients at the lower rate and then charge them a 3 to 4 percent commission for this money-saving service.

In 1984 about 85 percent of all newspaper display advertising was local. The largest source of newspaper display revenue is local retail merchants (Figure 13–7).

Display ads can be black and white, multicolored, or full-colored, with or without pictures. Most local display advertising is either black and white or some basic colors printed directly on the newspaper. In contrast, much national advertising is preprinted on magazine-supplement-type paper and fills an entire page. The opposite side of the page may then be left for the newspaper to use.

One common variation of the display ad is the *reading notice*. This type of ad looks like editorial matter. It is sometimes charged at a higher space rate than normal display advertising. To prevent readers

FIGURE 13–7

This *flex-form* ad for Southern Bank shows the versatility of newspaper advertising as well as the flexibility of the bank's auto loan program.

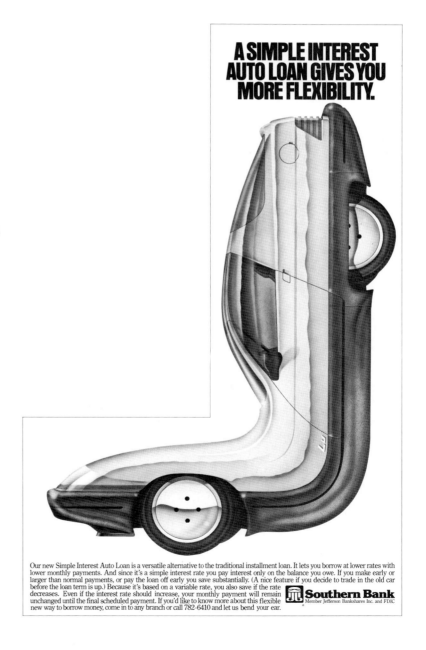

from mistaking it for editorial matter, the law requires that the word "advertisement" appear at the top of the reading notice. Many, but not all, newspapers accept reading notices.

Classified advertising

Classified advertisements are a unique and important feature of newspapers. They provide a community marketplace for goods, services, and opportunities of every type, from real estate and new-car sales to employment openings and business proposals of major magnitude. Such ads are usually arranged under subheads that describe the class of goods or the need that the ads seek to satisfy. For example, you would look for a job under the classification "Help Wanted" and for an employee in the listings headed "Situations Wanted." Classified rates are based on the amount of space purchased and how long the ad is to run. Most employment, housing, and automotive advertising run today is in the form of classified advertising.

Some newspapers also accept classified display advertising. Such ads are run in the classified section of the newspaper and are generally characterized by larger-size type, photos, art borders, abundant white space, and sometimes even color.

Public notices

For a nominal fee, newspapers will carry legal notices of changes in business and personal relationships, public governmental reports, notices by private citizens and organizations, and financial reports. These ads follow a preset format and thus require little creativity.

Preprinted inserts

Preprinted inserts are inserted into the fold of the newspaper and look like a separate, smaller section of the paper. The inserts are printed by the advertiser and then delivered to the newspaper plant to be inserted into a specific edition either by machine or by the newscarriers. Sizes range from a typical newspaper page to a piece no larger than a double postcard. Formats include catalogs, brochures, mail-back devices, and perforated coupons.

A number of large metropolitan dailies allow advertisers to distribute their inserts to specific circulation zones only. A store that wants to reach shoppers in its immediate area only can place an insert in the local-zone editions. Retail stores, auto dealers, large national advertisers, and others have found it less costly to distribute their circulars in this manner than by mailing them or delivering them door to door.

HOW TO BUY
NEWSPAPER SPACE

Newspapers serve different reader audiences in varying degrees. It is important that the media buyer and advertiser know the characteristics of a newspaper's readership—the median age, sex, occupation, income, educational level, and buying habits of the typical reader.

In single-newspaper cities, the demographic characteristics of readers are likely to reflect some cross-section of the population as a whole. In cities with two or more newspapers, however, these characteristics may vary widely. Los Angeles, for example, is served by the *Times,* noted for its moderate political outlook, and the *Herald-Examiner,* considered politically conservative. Each newspaper has a different readership.

Readership is also determined by the time of day a newspaper is published. An advertiser, for example, may have to decide between advertising a bedding sale in a morning newspaper that has a 70 percent male readership or an evening newspaper read by equal numbers of men and women. Each alternative has its advantage. The morning paper can advertise the sale that day and attract immediate shoppers, and the evening paper can be read by husband and wife together and motivate them to come to the sale the following day. The advertiser must decide about these and other factors to determine the optimum timing and placement for the ad.

■ Reading Rate Cards

Newspapers provide potential advertisers with a printed information form called a *rate card.* This card lists the advertising rates, mechanical and copy requirements, advertising deadlines, and other information the advertiser needs to know before placing an order. Some of the common terms used on rate cards are described here.

■ *Agate lines versus column inches*

Newspaper space has traditionally been sold by *agate lines* (a unit of measurement for depth) or by *column inches.* The agate line measures 1/14-inch deep by one standard column wide. A standard column is usually two inches wide, but many editors use different column widths to enhance their paper's layout. Buyers and sellers of newspaper space refer to agate lines as "linage."

AD LAB 13–A   How to compare newspaper rates

One way an advertiser can compare the rates of different newspapers is by computing the cost per thousand readers of each paper. A more common method of comparing newspapers is by computing their *milline rate,* which is the cost per line of space per million circulation.

Here is the formula:

$$\frac{1,000,000 \times \text{Rate per line}}{\text{Circulation}} = \text{Milline}$$

For example, the milline rate of a newspaper with 1 million circulation and a rate of $2 per line would be:

$$\frac{1,000,000 \times \$2.00}{1,000,000} = \$2.00$$

In comparison, the milline rate of a newspaper with 500,000 circulation and a rate of $1.50 per line would be:

$$\frac{1,000,000 \times \$1.50}{500,000} = \$3.00$$

Remember: The milline is a means for comparing rates and *not* a unit for buying space (Figure 13–11). Actual space is purchased by the inch.

Laboratory Application

Compare the milline rate of two newspapers in your area. Based on the milline rate, which is the best buy?

Most newspapers now sell advertising space by the column inch. A column inch is one inch deep by one column wide. It is equivalent to 14 agate lines. Can you compute how many agate lines an ad would be that is eight inches tall and four columns wide? (See Ad Lab 13–A.)

Retail versus general rates

National advertisers, as noted earlier, are usually charged a higher rate than local advertisers. Local advertisers can sometimes earn even lower rates by buying large or repeated amounts of space at *volume discounts*. Such incentives are not offered by all newspapers, however. Many national papers charge *flat rates*, which means they allow no discounts for large or repeated space buys. And some newspapers offer a single flat rate to both national and local advertisers.

Newspapers that offer the advertiser volume discounts have an *open rate*, which is their highest rate for one-time insertions, and *contract* or *earned* rates. Local advertisers can obtain discounts of up to 70 percent by signing a contract for frequent or bulk space purchases. These bulk discounts offer the advertiser decreasing line rates as the number of inches used increases. The contract is renewed annually. Frequency discounts may be earned when a given ad is run repeatedly during a specific period of time (Figure 13–8).

FIGURE   13–8

The *Newspaper Rates and Data* listing for the *Los Angeles Times*. Note the variety of rates available to advertisers depending on the volume of their linage.

Los Angeles Times
Times-Mirror Square, Los Angeles, CA 90053.
Phone 213-972-3000, TWX, 910-321-2460, 1-800-528-4637.

newsplan
DISCOUNTS FOR CONTINUITY
(ABC)

Media Code 1 105 4125 7.00   Mid 016171-000
MORNING AND SUNDAY.
Member: INAME; NAB, Inc.

1. PERSONNEL
Pub. & Chief Exec. Officer—W. Thomas Johnson.
Pres. Chief Operating Officer—Donald F. Wright.
Executive Vice-Pres. Mkt.—Vance L. Stickell.
Display Advertising Director—Donald J. Maldonado.
General Advertising Manager—Larry Letters.

2. REPRESENTATIVES and/or BRANCH OFFICES
BRANCH OFFICES
New York 10017—Dennis Schultz, Mgr., 711 Third Ave. Phone 212-697-6200.
Chicago 60611—Thomas C. Rupp, Mgr., 500 N. Michigan Ave. Phone 312-527-4410.
San Francisco 94111—100 Lee Kensil, Mgr., California St., Suite 870. Phone 415-421-6643.
REPRESENTATIVES
Times Mirror National Marketing.

3. COMMISSION AND CASH DISCOUNT
15% to agencies; no cash discount.

4. POLICY-ALL CLASSIFICATIONS
60-day notice given of any rate revision.
Alcoholic beverage advertising accepted.
Our liability for error shall not exceed cost of space occupied by the error. Credit allowed for first insertion only.
Notice of errors must be given in time for correction before second insertion, otherwise no credit for repetition shall be allowed.
Copy corrections after 1st revised proof, composition charge 26.30 per hour.
The publisher reserves the right to revise or reject, at its option, any advertisement which it deems objectionable in text or illustration or detrimental to its business.
All ads measured cut-off rule to cut-off rule.
ADVERTISING RATES
Effective February 1, 1985. (Card No. CG-4.)
Received December 10, 1984.

5. BLACK/WHITE RATES

	Daily	Sunday
SAU open, per inch	222.92	270.43
Full page, per inch	194.54	230.23

Inches charged full depth: col. 21.5; pg. 129; dbl truck 268.75.

BULK INCH CONTRACT RATES

Within 1 year:	Daily	Sunday
135"	202.06	239.26
270"	197.55	234.96
540"	189.81	230.44
805"	188.31	225.28
1,075"	185.30	220.34
1,345"	183.58	217.97
1,880"	180.99	215.82
2,685"	178.85	214.10
4,030"	176.48	211.10
5,375"	174.13	209.38
8,065"	166.38	203.79
10,750"	162.51	199.48
13,440"	160.14	194.34
16,125"	157.57	191.96
18,810"	155.42	189.39
21,500"	153.06	187.45
26,875"	150.69	184.65
32,250"	148.12	183.37
37,625"	145.53	180.14
43,000"	143.38	178.00
48,375"	138.22	175.40
53,750"	136.72	173.47

FULL PAGE CONTRACT
— Per inch —

Pages	Daily	Sunday
10	178.85	214.10
15	174.13	209.38
20	169.39	203.79
30	164.88	199.48
40	162.51	196.48
50	160.14	194.34

Less than full pagae (129 inches) units will take the applicable bulk rate. Full page space will also be included in computing the earned bulk rate. If both full page and fractional units are to be used, a bulk rate contract and a full page contract must be signed in advance.

NEWSPLAN—SAU

Pages	% Disc.	Morn.	% Disc.	Sun.	Inches
6	14.85	189.81	14.79	230.44	540
13	17.64	183.58	19.40	217.97	1,345
26	19.77	178.85	20.83	214.10	2,685
52	21.89	174.13	22.58	209.38	5,375
65	25.36	166.38	24.64	203.79	8,065
78	27.10	166.38	26.23	203.79	8,065
91	28.16	162.51	28.14	199.48	10,750
104	28.13	162.51	28.14	199.48	10,750

See Newsplan Contract and Copy Regulations—items 4, 5, 6, 7, 9, 11, 13, 14, 19, 21, 22, 26, 30, 31.

7. COLOR RATES AND DATA
Available: B/w 1 c Monday thru Sunday. Extra charge for special color ink and 14 day lead time is required. No leeway available. All color booked firmly.
Use b/w rate plus the following applicable costs:

55 inches minimum to 1 page:	b/w 1 c
Daily, extra	4,356.00
Sunday, extra	5,253.00

Closing dates: 2 days before publication date; 4 days for Thursday Food Section.

9. SPLIT RUN
Non-commissionable mechanical charge of 273.00 for black and white and 546.00 mechanical charge plus color premium for black and 1 color. Ads must be of same size dimension and products.
Established rate prevail with minimum 25 inches. Both ads must be same size, dimensions and product.

11. SPECIAL DAYS/PAGES/FEATURES
Best Food Day: Thursday.

12. R.O.P. DEPTH REQUIREMENTS
Ads over 18 inches deep charged full col.

13. CONTRACT AND COPY REGULATIONS
See Contents page for location of regulations—items 1, 4, 9, 10, 11, 12, 13, 14, 18, 23, 31, 32, 34, 39.

14. CLOSING TIMES
Sunday deadlines: Calendar. View, Travel and Real Estate copy due Tuesday p.m. before publication; reservations by 9:00 a.m., Main News, Financial, Sports 6:00 p.m., Wednesday.
Daily: Monday 9:00 a.m., Friday before; Thursday Food Section, 10:00 a.m. Monday. Other daily editions 2 days before publication.

15. MECHANICAL MEASUREMENTS
For complete, detailed production information, see SRDS Print Media Production Data.
PRINTING PROCESS: Photo Composition & Offset.
6/12-5/9—6 cols/ea 12 picas-5 pts/9 pts betw col.
Inches charged full depth: col. 21.5; pg. 129; dbl truck 268.75.

17. CLASSIFIED RATES
For complete data refer to classified rate section.

18. COMICS
Effective February 1, 1985. (Card No. CG-4.)
Received December 10, 1984.

COLOR RATES AND DATA
3 colors & black:

1 page	27,627.00	1/3 page	10,817.00
2/3 page	21,634.00	1/6 page	5,409.00
1/2 page	16,226.00		

CLOSING TIMES
Reservations, 5 weeks; 4 weeks, materials.
MECHANICAL MEASUREMENTS
Page size 13" wide x 20" deep.

19. MAGAZINES
Calendar
SUNDAY.
POLICY—ALL CLASSIFICATIONS
Medical copy accepted only upon approval.
Effective February 1, 1985. (CG-4.)
Received December 10, 1984.
BLACK/WHITE RATES
Per inch 270.43
R.O.P. Bulk Discounts apply.
COLOR RATES AND DATA
Minimum full page.
B/w rate plus 5,253.00 extra charge.
CLOSING TIMES
9:00 a.m. Tuesday, Black & White copy, noon Wednesday prior to publication.
Color: 11 days prior to publication.
MECHANICAL MEASUREMENTS
PRINTED PROCESS: Offset.
Page size 5 cols x 13 inches.
Book Review
Effective February 1, 1985. (CG-4.)
Received December 10, 1984.
BLACK/WHITE RATES
Per inch 270.43
R.O.P. Bulk Discounts apply.
CLOSING TIMES
9:00 a.m. Tuesday, Black & white copy noon Wednesday prior to publication.
Color: 11 days prior to publicaton.
MECHANICAL MEASUREMENTS
PRINTING PROCESS: Offset.
Page size 5 cols. x 13 inches.

Short rate

If an advertiser contracts to buy a specific amount of space during a one-year period at a discount rate and then fails to buy this amount of space, he or she is charged a *short rate*. This is computed by determining the difference between the standard rate for the lines run and the discount rate contracted. Conversely, an advertiser who buys more lines than the number contracted may be entitled to a rebate.

Combination rates

Combination rates are offered for placing a given ad in (1) morning and evening editions of the same newspaper; (2) two or more newspapers owned by the same publisher; and (3) in some cases, two or more newspapers affiliated in a syndicate or newspaper group. Combination rates are sometimes also offered for placing a given ad in consecutive Saturday and Sunday editions of the same newspaper. At one time, some newspapers were requiring advertisers to buy combinations. Courts have declared this practice illegal, and combinations are now optional.

Run of paper (R.O.P.)

R.O.P. advertising rates entitle a newspaper to place a given ad on any newspaper page or in any position it desires—in other words, where space permits (Figure 13–9). Most newspapers, however, make an effort to place an ad in the position requested by the advertiser.

FIGURE 13–9 Newspapers: Circulation and rates

Newspaper	Circulation	Open line rate	Milline rate
The Wall Street Journal	2,081,995	$37.65	$18.08
New York Daily News	1,374,858	18.48	13.43
USA Today	1,284,613	14.50	11.29
Los Angeles Times	1,057,536	14.61	13.81
New York Times	970,051	16.47	16.98
New York Post	963,069	16.07	16.69
Philadelphia Inquirer/News	828,236	13.82	16.69
Chicago Tribune	779,259	13.05	16.75
Washington Post	768,288	13.78	17.94
San Francisco Chronicle/Examiner	691,771	12.25	17.71
Chicago Sun-Times	663,693	10.53	15.87
Detroit News	657,015	14.18	21.58
Detroit Free Press	645,623	12.83	19.87
Long Island Newsday	533,384	7.81	14.64
Kansas City Times/Star	528,777	5.17	9.78
Miami Herald/News	514,702	11.08	21.53
Cleveland Plain Dealer	492,002	6.58	13.37
Milwaukee Journal	486,426	8.77	18.03
Houston Chronicle	443,592	6.03	13.59
Baltimore Sun	349,182	6.77	19.39

Color rates

Color advertising is available in many newspapers on an R.O.P. basis. Since newspapers are not noted for their high-quality color printing because of high-speed presses and porous paper stock, advertisers frequently preprint ads using processes known as HiFi color and Spectacolor. The advertisement is printed on a roll, and the roll is fed into the press by the newspaper, which prints its own material on the blank side.

Preferred position

An advertiser can assure a choice position for an ad by paying a higher *preferred position* rate. For example, a dictating machine manufacturer must pay this rate if it wants to assure that its ad will be on the business or financial page. And a jeweler may do the same to assure a position in the women's pages.

There also are preferred positions on the newspaper page itself (Figure 13–10). The preferred position near the top of a page or on the top of a column next to reading matter is called *full position*. It is usually surrounded by reading matter and costs the advertiser 25 to 50 percent more in many newspapers. Slightly less good, but also a preferred position, is placement "next to reading matter" (N.R.), which generally costs the advertiser 10 to 20 percent more.

FIGURE   13–11   Newspaper readership by editorial content

Editoral content	Percent of readers opening average page	
	Males	Females
Sports	85	69
Amusements	84	90
Radio, TV	83	69
General news	82	88
Society	81	94
Business, finance	77	69
Food, fashion	73	88
All other	80	85

Rate differentials

Newspapers charge different rates for different types of advertising. For example, by law, newspapers—and other media—are required to charge political advertisers no more than the rate offered to any other advertiser for comparable use of space. Some newspapers charge another rate for advertising in the theater or entertainment section. This rate is generally lower than that for general display ads. And some newspapers offer special low rates or other incentives for "In Memoriam" advertisements and religious announcements.

Split runs

Many newspapers (as well as magazines) offer *split runs*. The advertiser runs two different ads of identical size for the same product or service in the same or different press runs on the same day. In this way the advertiser can test the pulling power of one ad against the other. Newspapers set a minimum space requirement and charge extra for this service.

Audience Segmentation by Section

In a sense, every reader of the newspaper reads a different newspaper, because every newspaper contains such a wide variety of material. This offers opportunities to the advertiser who wants to target advertising to specific groups. Traditional male-female readership figures by editorial content are shown in Figure 13–11. The sports section offers heavy male readership; society sections offer heavy female readership. Businesspeople, male and female, are normally interested in the business or finance section (Figure 13–12). And children love to read the comics.

FIGURE 13–12

The simplicity of excellence is demonstrated as well as touted by this ad for Westin Hotels. Created by Cole & Weber, Seattle, the ad won the coveted Best in the West Award as well as numerous national awards in the category of color newspaper campaigns.

Insertion Orders—Tear Sheets

An advertiser who is ready to run an advertisement submits an *insertion order* to the newspaper (Figure 13–13). This form states the date(s) on which the ad is to run, its size, the requested position, and the rate. It also states whether finished art, mechanicals, Velox prints, or mats will be furnished with the ad.

When advertising copy and art are created by the newspaper, the advertiser is provided a *proof copy* for checking purposes before the ad is run. In contrast, most national advertising is submitted with the art, copy, and layout in final form. It is important that the agency or advertiser receive verification that the ad has run. Therefore, the newspaper tears out the page on which the ad appeared and sends it to the agency or advertiser. Today most *tear sheets* are forwarded through a private central office, the Advertising Checking Bureau.

When a tear sheet arrives, it is examined to make certain that the advertisement ran according to the instructions of the agency or advertiser—particularly with regard to the section of the paper in which it ran, its page position, and its reproduction. If the advertisement did *not* run as instructed, the agency or advertiser may be entitled to an adjustment. This may be a free rerun of the ad.

FIGURE 13–13

This insertion order of an advertising agency, Fallon McElligott Rice, gives directions for the placement of an ad for U.S. West.

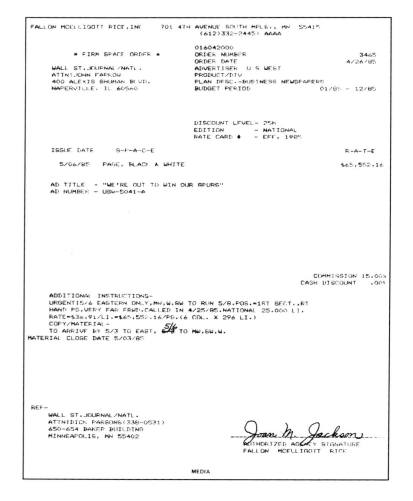

USING MAGAZINES IN THE CREATIVE MIX

What would you do to make a complex, abstract message—scientific findings and technical achievements—fun, human, and enjoyable to understand? That was the challenge facing Widen and Kennedy, the Portland, Oregon, advertising agency for Nike athletic shoes.

The high-tech fervor with which Nike approaches its research and development is reflected in the charts and graphs in its magazine ads. All is not hard facts and figures, however; each ad also contains a visual that puts all of the data into human perspective.

An example is an ad that features a new series of lasts, the forms over which the shoes are finally assembled (Figure 13–14). The ad discusses three lasts that were developed to meet the needs of runners with different running styles. It also provides the model names of shoes that were made from each type of last.

"At first," recalls David Kennedy, art director and partner at the agency, "Nike wanted to use quarter-page ads to introduce the new shoes. But other manufacturers use that format, so quarter-page ads wouldn't have the same impact as spreads would."

"The spreads had another advantage," adds Dan Wieden, copywriter and other agency partner. "They allowed us to use a single issue of a magazine to focus on a particular shoe. For instance, we ran a spread on the new lasts and then followed through with a full-page ad for a shoe mentioned in the spread."

A measure of the campaign's success can be found in the response to the final ad. It mentioned a free booklet, *How to Tell Your Children the Facts of Running*. The week after the ad broke, Nike was receiving 400 to 600 responses a day.[6]

FIGURE   13–14

Nike finds a way to make a complex, abstract message fun, human, and enjoyable to understand. The physical dimensions and reproduction quality of magazines facilitates the task.

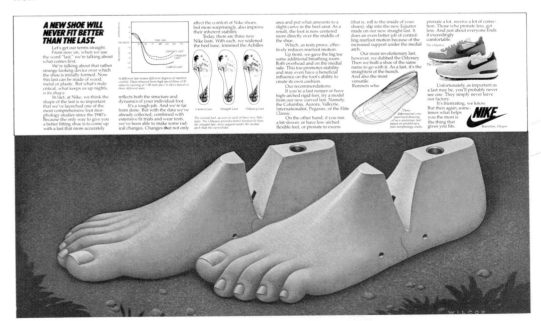

What Works Best in Magazines?

The Nike campaign illustrates the best use of magazines as an element of the creative mix. Flexible design, the availability of color, excellent reproduction quality, believability and authority, permanence, prestige, and, most of all, excellent audience selectivity at an efficient cost characterize the opportunities magazines offer advertisers.

1. Magazines are the most *selective* of all media except for direct mail. The predictable editorial environment selects the audience and enables advertisers to pinpoint their sales campaign. Most magazines are written for special-interest groups. *Golf Digest* helps a golf club manufacturer reach golfers; *Business Week* reaches businesspeople; *Seventeen* reaches teenage girls; and *Ebony*, a black-oriented magazine, helps advertisers reach the black market (Figure 13–15).

2. Magazines offer *flexibility* in both readership and advertising. They cover the full range of prospects—with a wide choice of regional editions as well as national coverage. Each magazine lends itself to a variety of lengths, approaches, and editorial tones. The advertiser, therefore, has the choice of using long copy, black and white, editorial ads, or short copy, colorful poster ads, or humorous cartoons, or any of an infinite variety of approaches.

3. Magazine *color* spreads a spectrum of exciting visual pleasure before the reader. Nowhere can better color reproduction be seen than in the slick magazines. Color in such publications as *National Geographic* enhances image and identifies the package. In short, color sells.

4. If the advertiser wants to speak with *authority* and *believability*, magazines can enhance the message. People believe what magazines say. Their influence affects people's ideas, opinions, and desires. This enables magazines to counsel people on child-rearing

FIGURE 13–15

Magazines offer selectivity by targeting various specific groups including religious, ethnic, or simply special-interest groups.

Louis Vuitton. The art of travel.

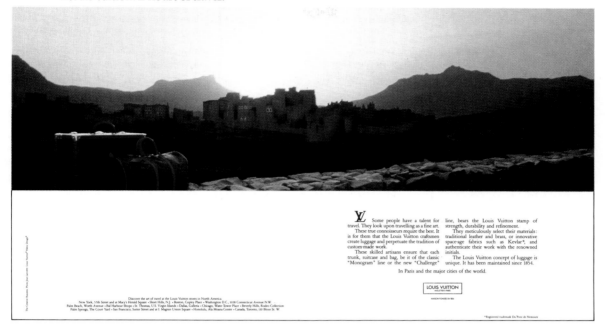

FIGURE 13–16

The efficiency of magazines in selecting target markets, as well as the prestige and fine quality reproduction, serves fashion-conscious advertisers like Louis Vuitton better than any other medium.

(*Parents*), financial difficulties (*Money*), marital problems (*McCall's*), and advertising (*Advertising Age*).

5. Magazines offer *permanence*. For the advertiser who wants to communicate lasting information and enjoyment, magazines give the reader more opportunity to appraise ads in considerable detail. Advertisements can deliver a more complete educational/sales message and can effectively communicate the total corporate personality. Magazines also enable advertisers to generate reprints and materials, which further promote and merchandise their corporate advertising campaigns.

6. Advertising a product in such magazines as *Sports Illustrated, Time,* and *House Beautiful* provides the advertiser with *prestige* for the product. The professionalism that publishers strive to maintain can be a great asset in building prestige through institutional advertising.

7. Magazines can be very *cost efficient*. By selecting the specific magazines and editions that reach prospects, the advertiser can keep wasted circulation to a minimum. The selling power of magazines has been proved and results are measurable, so they are the growing choice of many leading advertisers (Figure 13–16).

There are also other advantages. Magazines have extensive "pass-along" or secondary readership. They generate loyalty among readers that sometimes borders on fanaticism. Magazines also may reach prospects that salespeople can't because of geographic or other reasons. Hard-to-reach occupational groups, such as doctors and entertainment personalities, are nearly all reached readily by magazines. (See the Checklist of what works best in print.)

■ Drawbacks to Magazines

Although magazines offer excellent creative capabilities for advertisers in a print medium, they do have drawbacks. The immediacy of newspapers, for example, is lost in magazines. Likewise, magazines don't offer the depth of geographic coverage or the local reach of newspapers. Nor do they offer the national reach of the broadcast

---

 Checklist of what works best in print

☐ Use simple layouts. One big picture works better than several small pictures. Avoid cluttered pages. (Layouts that resemble the magazine's editorial format are well read.)

☐ Always put a caption under a photograph. Readership of picture captions is generally twice as great as of body copy. The picture caption can be an advertisement by itself.

☐ Don't be afraid of long copy. The people who read beyond the headline are *prospects for your product or your service.* If your product is expensive—like a car, a vacation, or an industrial product—prospects are hungry for the information long copy gives them. Consider long copy if you have a complex story to tell, many different product points to make, or an expensive product or service to sell.

☐ Avoid negative headlines. People are literal-minded and may remember only the negatives. Sell the positive benefits in your product—not that it won't harm or that some defect has been solved. Look for emotional words that attract and motivate, like *free* and *new* and *love.*

☐ Don't be afraid of long headlines. Research shows that on the average long headlines sell more merchandise than short ones.

☐ Look for *story appeal.* Next to the headline, an illustration is the most effective way to get a reader's attention. Try for story appeal—the kind of illustration that makes the reader ask: "What's going on here?"

☐ Photographs are better than drawings. Research says that photography increases recall an average of 26 percent over artwork.

☐ Look at your advertisement in its editorial environment. Ask to see your advertisement pasted into the magazine in which it will appear. Or, for newspapers, photostated in the same tone as the newspaper page. Beautifully mounted layouts are deceptive. The reader will never see your advertisement printed on high-gloss paper, with a big white border, mounted on a board. It is *misleading* for you to look at it this way.

☐ Develop a single advertising format. An overall format for all print advertising can double recognition. This rule holds special meaning for industrial advertisers. One format will help readers see your advertisements as coming from one large corporation, rather than several small companies.

☐ Before-and-after photographs make a point better than words. If you can, show a visual contrast—a change in the consumer, or a demonstration of product superiority.

☐ Do not print copy in reverse type. It may look attractive, but it reduces readership. For the same reason, don't surprint copy on the illustration of your advertisement.

☐ Make each advertisement a complete sale. Your message must be contained in the headline. React to the overall impression, as the reader will. Only the advertiser reads all his advertisements. Any advertisement in a series must stand on its own. *Every one* must make a complete sale. Assume it will be the only advertisement for your product a reader will ever see.

media. They also suffer from the inability to deliver high frequency figures or mass audiences at a low price. The disadvantages of magazines, therefore, are several.

1. Advertising in magazines requires long *lead time*. Space must be purchased and the advertisement prepared well in advance of the date of publication—sometimes as long as three months. Weekly magazines, particularly those that run color advertisements, often require that advertising materials be in their hands weeks in advance of the publication date. And once the closing date has been reached, no changes in copy or art can be allowed.

2. Magazines have problems offering *reach* and *frequency*. It's interesting to note that magazines were the first national medium, yet today their coverage is generally lower (on an individual basis) than that of other media. Where selectivity is not a major marketing consideration, using selective magazines is very costly for reaching broad masses of people. Frequency can actually be built faster than reach by adding numerous smaller audience magazines to the schedule. However, most magazines are issued only monthly, or at best weekly, so building frequency in one publication is very difficult.

3. Magazines that are popular have the problem of heavy *advertising competition*. This can deter other advertisers. Of the 52 magazines that account for 66 percent of total magazine circulation, the average relationship of advertising to editorial linage is 52.4 percent advertising to 47.6 percent editorial matter. Because each advertisement is in so much competition with others, advertisers use a variety of techniques to gain attention, including those discussed in the next section.

4. The *cost* of advertising in magazines can be very high. While national magazines offer an average black-and-white cost per thousand that ranges from $3 to $12 or more, some trade publications with highly selective audiences have a cost per thousand of over $20 for a black-and-white page.

The advertiser naturally must weigh these disadvantages against the advantages mentioned above when determining the appropriate creative mix. Studies have determined that many of these disadvantages can be overcome and campaign effectiveness greatly enhanced by including magazines as part of the mix of media used to communicate the advertiser's message. Then the low-cost reach and frequency of other media can be supported by the permanence, prestige, and selectivity attributes of magazines.

■ Special Possibilities with Magazines

Magazines offer advertisers a wide variety of creative possibilities through various technical or mechanical elements. These include bleed pages, cover positions, inserts and gatefolds, and special-size ads such as junior pages and island halves.

When the dark or colored background of the advertisement extends to the edge of the page, it is said to "bleed" off the page. Most magazines offer *bleed pages,* but advertisers usually have to pay a 10 to 15 percent premium for them. By buying a bleed page, though, the artist has greater flexibility in expressing the advertising idea, the printing space is slightly larger, and the ad can be more dramatic than with a white border. The front cover of American magazines is commonly referred to as the "first cover." It is almost never sold. The inside front, inside back, and outside back covers are almost always sold at a premium. They are called the second, third, and fourth covers, respectively.

When you turn a page in a magazine and find it extended and

AD LAB 13–B   Innovations in magazine advertising

Microfragrance (microencapsulation)

A *perfumed* advertisement such as "Scratch 'n Sniff" strips use the 3M microencapsulation technique for emitting the odor of perfume, soap, men's cologne, and liquor.

3D illusion printing

Originally introduced by *Look* magazine, Xograph 3D is a process of using a three-dimensional insert in a magazine. Many manufacturers have used this process since its debut, including Pfizer Laboratories, International Harvester, British Overseas Airways, and American Express.

Metallic ink

An ink that shines brightly creates a striking visual effect.

Pop-ups

Illustrated pop-ups have been used by Wm. Wrigley Jr. Company to feature Wrigley zoo animal stars in children's magazines. A manufacturing company ran a three-dimensional pop-up of a prefabricated building in *Nation's Business* and *Better Buildings*.

Recordings

Remington's theme of music-to-shave-by was recorded on vinyl plastic and inserted in magazines. Eva-Tone Soundsheets can be bound into most business and consumer publications.

Invisible ink

Ebonite used invisible ink in a four-color spread promoting its bowling balls. The ad carried a coupon of which 5,000 were surprinted with a fluorescent ink. When the special card was presented with the invisible ink, the dealer gave recipients a free bowling ball.

Product samples

Johnson & Johnson's Band-Aids, Scott Towels, Curtis candies, and Vanity Fair Lanolin Facial Tissue have all appeared in magazine advertisements—with samples of the product.

Talking magazines

The printed page may talk. *Time* magazine, for example, is working with Microsonics to perfect the technology by which record grooves can be imprinted on a printed page. With the use of a microphonograph, the reader will be able to pass across the page and actually hear the voice of the person whose quotation he or she is reading.

Laboratory Application

Pick one of the above innovations. What applications can you suggest in addition to those given? What are the implications for advertisers?

folded over to fit into the magazine, this is called a *gatefold*. The gatefold may be a fraction of a page or two or more pages. It may occupy the cover position or the centerfold. Gatefolds, also called *dutch doors*, are useful in making spectacular and impressive announcements. Not all magazines provide gatefolds, and they are always sold at a premium.

Often an advertiser will have an ad printed on a special paper stock to add weight and drama to the message. This can then be *inserted* into the magazine at a special price. The same is true for special effects such as *encapsulations* of scents. These ads are normally printed in advance and then inserted. (See Ad Lab 13–B.)

One publisher of a large-sized magazine discovered he could generate business with a simple strategy. He accepted the plates for the standard-size magazine page even though the advertisement covered only 60 percent of the page. Then he surrounded it with editorial matter. This saved the advertiser the cost of new plates, which can be considerable. A special flat rate was set for this unit of space, called a *junior* unit or page. The junior unit is usually found on a page with no other advertising. It is an inexpensive method of dominating a page, but not all magazines accept it.

Similar to junior units are *island half-pages*, except that there is more editorial matter surrounding them. The island sometimes costs more than a regular half-page, but, since it dominates the page, many advertisers consider the premium a small price to pay (Figure 13–17).

How Magazines Are Classified

Although there are many ways to classify magazines, the most common methods are by content, geography, and size.

Content

One of the most dramatic developments in publishing during the last three decades has been the emergence of magazines with specialized appeal and content. Although specialization has been no guaran-

FIGURE 13–17

Magazine space combinations that can create big impact.

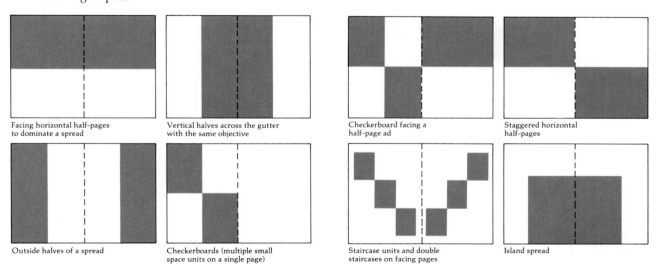

Facing horizontal half-pages to dominate a spread

Vertical halves across the gutter with the same objective

Checkerboard facing a half-page ad

Staggered horizontal half-pages

Outside halves of a spread

Checkerboards (multiple small space units on a single page)

Staircase units and double staircases on facing pages

Island spread

tee of success, it has given many publications good prospects for long-term growth.

The broadest classifications of content are consumer magazines, farm magazines, and business magazines. Each of these, though, may be broken down into hundreds of categories.

Consumer magazines are purchased for entertainment, information, or both and are edited for people who buy products for their own consumption.

The *farm publications* are magazines directed to farmers and their families or to companies that manufacture or sell agricultural equipment, supplies, and services. These magazines include those devoted to dairy and dairy breeds, farm education and vocations, cooperatives and farm organizations, and other specialized agricultural areas. The most widely circulated farm publications are the *Farm Journal, Progressive Farmer, Prairie Farmer,* and *Successful Farming.*

Business magazines are directed to business readers (Figure 13–18). They can be classified in the following ways: (1) trade papers (aimed at retailers, wholesalers, and other distributors); (2) industrial magazines (aimed at businesspeople involved in manufacturing); and (3) professional magazines (aimed at lawyers, physicians, dentists, architects, teachers, and other professional people).

Magazines may also be classified by the amount of geography they attempt to cover.

Local magazines have become popular, and now most major American cities have magazines named after them: *San Diego Magazine, New York, Los Angeles, Chicago, Philadelphia, Palm Springs Life,* and *Crain's Chicago Business,* to name a few. Their readership is usually upscale, professional people interested in the arts, fashion, culture, and business. A few are owned by local Chambers of Commerce, but most are the products of individual entrepreneurs.

Magazines are not limited by geography like newspapers or broad-

FIGURE   13–18

Industrial and other business-to-business advertisers find the cost-efficiency of magazines advantageous over most other media. The production quality required for this Honeywell ad could only have been accomplished in magazines or direct mail.

There's a little bit of chicken in all of us.

One big trouble with being chicken is that you can wind up with nothing much to crow about.

Consider, for example, the job of picking a computer. If you back off from the computer you honestly think is best and pick another one just because it's "safe", you're not doing yourself (or us) any good.

So get plenty of facts, then base your decision on them. Find out which new-generation computers have been selling and why . . . and if you now have an older computer, which new models make conversion easiest. Find out who has the best record for delivering both software and hardware on time.

Find out who has the widest choice of rental and purchase plans, and how this can save you money.

Find out who is best equipped to provide computer speed and capacity for both today's needs . . . and tomorrow's.

Get all the facts, then be hard-nosed about your decision. Don't be chicken . . . be right.

Honeywell
ELECTRONIC DATA PROCESSING

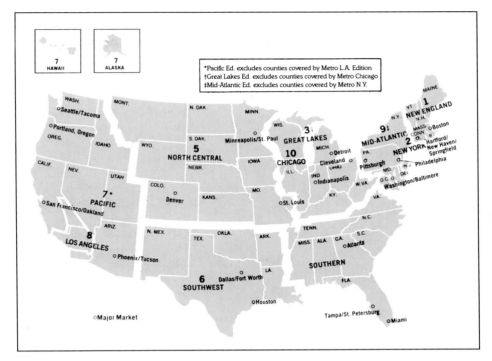

FIGURE 13–19

Reader's Digest promotes its numerous geographic editions in its advertising rate card.

cast stations. However, it may be more profitable to limit circulation to a certain *regional* area. *Sunset* magazine, for example, took editorial techniques from *Better Homes and Gardens* to build up an audience only on the West Coast. Such restrictions are by choice, not necessity.

National magazines sometimes offer advertisers special market runs that allow the selection of specific geographic regions. Many regional editions have been developed largely to substitute audience selectivity for size in the face of spot television competition. *Time, U.S. News & World Report, Newsweek, Woman's Day,* and *Sports Illustrated* have developed their coverage to such an extent that an advertiser wishing to buy a single major market can do so. Almost 20 percent of all magazine advertising is now regional in nature (Figure 13–19).

Typically, *national magazines* have reached across the country with varying levels of circulation. The best-known national magazines have large circulations. *TV Guide,* which in 1985 had a circulation of over 17,345,000, is outdistanced only by *Reader's Digest,* with a national circulation of 17,900,000 in the United States.

There are thousands of lesser-known national magazines with circulations of 100,000 or less. These publications are more often than not trade, industrial, professional, or farm magazines.

Size

It doesn't take a genius to figure out that magazines come in different shapes and sizes, but sometimes it takes one to figure out how to get the same advertisement to run in different sized magazines and still look the same. Magazine sizes run the gamut from very large to very small, which makes efforts at production standardization an occasional nightmare. The most common magazine sizes might be grouped as follows:

Classification	Magazine	Approximate size of full-page ad
Large	Life	4 col. × 170 lines (9⅜ × 12⅛ inches)
Flat	Time, Newsweek	3 col. × 140 lines (7 × 10 inches)
Standard	National Geographic	2 col. × 119 lines (6 × 8½ inches)
Small or	Reader's Digest, TV	
pocket	Guide	2 col. × 91 lines (4½ × 6½ inches)

At one time most magazines appeared in the standard format, but today few use it. Most magazines now are in the flat format size.

HOW TO BUY MAGAZINE SPACE

The effective media buyer considers the selection of magazines on the basis of circulation, readership (who reads them), and cost and mechanical requirements. The buyer must understand the magazine's circulation statistics and rate card information.

■ Understanding Magazine Circulation

A magazine's audience may be determined by several factors: its primary and secondary readership, the number of subscription and vendor sales, and the number of copies that are guaranteed versus those that are actually delivered.

Primary and secondary readership

The Audit Bureau of Circulations or other verified report tells the media buyer what the magazine's total circulation is. This is *primary circulation,* and it represents the number of households that receive the publication. They may purchase it on newsstands or through a regular subscription. *Secondary* (or pass-along) readership is exactly what the name suggests. After the first reader is finished, he or she may give it to others to read. Pass-along readership can be very important to some magazines since some publications may be read by more than six different people. Multiply that by a million subscribers, and the magazine can boast very substantial readership.

Vertical and horizontal publications

There are two classifications of business publications: vertical and horizontal. A choice of one or the other depends on how deeply an advertiser wishes to penetrate a particular industry or how widely the advertiser wishes to spread the message.

Vertical publications cover a specific industry, such as *Retail Baking Today* aimed only at those people interested in selling baked goods on the retail level. They are read by individuals interested in a specific area of study. *Horizontal* publications deal with a particular job function that cuts across industry lines, such as *Electronic Design* and *Purchasing.*

Subscription and vendor sales

Since World War II the ratio of subscription to newsstand sales has increased, and today subscriptions account for the majority of sales for most magazines. Newsstands are still a major outlet for sales of single copies, but no newsstand can possibly handle more than a fraction of the magazines available. Display space is limited, and vendors sometimes complain that distributors make them take publications they do not want in order to get others they do want.

From the advertiser's point of view, newsstand sales are impressive because they indicate that the purchaser really wanted the magazine and was not merely taking a subscription out of habit. Single-copy sales in 1985 accounted for an average of 33 percent of all sales, according to the Magazine Publishers Association. Some publications are sold entirely through newsstand sales. Others, such as most trade publications, are sold entirely through subscription.

Paid and controlled circulation

Business publications are published on a *paid* basis or a *controlled* basis. If the publication is available on a paid basis, the recipient must pay the subscription price in order to receive it. Circulation that is free (controlled) means it is mailed to a selected list of individuals whom the publisher feels are in a unique position to influence sales. In order to get the publication they must indicate in writing a desire to receive it and their professional designation or occupation. Ordinarily, to qualify for the subscription list they must also include information about their job title, function, and purchasing responsibilities.

Since advertising rates are based principally on circulation, controlled circulation magazines can characterize their readers as good prospects for the goods and services advertised in the publication's pages. Advertisers are not paying for subscribers who have little or no interest in what they are offering. Publishers of paid circulation magazines say that subscribers who pay are more likely to read the publication than are those who get controlled or free copies. On the other hand, publishers of controlled circulation publications state that giving the publication away without charge is the only way to get good coverage of the market and that there is little or no effect on readership.

In order to avoid confusing these terms, it should be pointed out that some paid circulation publications "control their circulation" in a sense by allowing persons to subscribe only if they represent the kind of circulation they want to build, even though they require the subscriber to pay for the subscription.

Guaranteed versus delivered circulation

A magazine's rate structure is based on its circulation. The advertiser who purchases space is assured of reaching a certain number of people. The *guaranteed* circulation figure is the number of copies of the magazine that the publisher expects will be sold. Since some of these copies are usually sold on newsstands, it is possible that the guaranteed circulation figure may not be reached. If this *delivered* figure is not reached, the publisher will have to give a refund. For that reason, most guaranteed circulation figures (which advertising rates are based on) are stated safely below the average actual delivered circulation.

Reading Rate Cards

Magazine rate cards, like newspaper rate cards, follow a standard format. This enables advertisers to readily determine the cost of advertising, any discount opportunities, the mechanical requirements of the publication, the issue and closing dates, special editions, and the additional amount required for features like color, inserts, bleed pages, or split runs.

Rates

One means of comparing magazines is to look at the one-time cost for a full-page black-and-white ad, multiplied by 1,000, and divided by the publication's total circulation:

$$\frac{\text{Page rate} \times 1,000}{\text{Circulation}} = \text{Cost per page per thousand (CPM)}$$

For example, in 1985 the page-rate for a one-time, black-and-white ad in *Flying* magazine was $11,975 on a rate base (guaranteed circulation) of 300,000. At the same time *Plane and Pilot* magazine offered a full-page, black-and-white ad for $2,346 on a rate base of 65,000. Can you tell which was the better buy from the standpoint of cost per thousand?

Each of these publications, by the way, claimed substantial pass-along readership, thereby giving *Flying* a total audience of 985,224 and *Plane and Pilot* a total of 253,668 readers. If you believed these readership figures, which magazine would then have the better cost per thousand?

As with newspapers, discounts are given based on frequency and volume. Frequency discounts are generally based on the number of insertions. Volume discounts are offered on the total space used during a specific period. Almost all magazines offer cash discounts—usually 2 percent.

Color, if it is available, normally costs 25 to 60 percent more than black and white. Some publications, like *Money,* even offer metallic and aluminum-based inks and the use of five colors by special arrangement.

Bleed pages add up to 20 percent to regular rates, although the typical increase is about 15 percent.

Typically second and third cover rates (the inside covers) are less than the rate for the fourth (back) cover. The cover rates usually include color, whether the ad is to be run in color or not. *U.S. News & World Report* charges $38,365 for the second and third covers and $48,965 for the fourth cover.

Magazines offer different rates for advertisements in issues that go to a particular market, either geographic or demographic. *Time* offers four-color ads in Portland, Oregon, for $2,720 (32,000 circulation); in Houston, Texas, for $3,110 (61,000 circulation); to college students for $17,580 (550,000 circulation), and to the 35 largest metropolitan markets for $53,130 (2,790,000 circulation).

■ *Issue and closing dates*

In buying magazine advertising there are three important dates:

Cover date—the date appearing on the cover.
On-sale date—the date the magazine is actually issued.
Closing date—the date when all ad material must be in the hands of
   the publisher for inclusion in a specific issue.

The closing date is sometimes the first thing the advertiser looks at.
After determining whether the advertising materials can be ready by
a certain date and which issue would be best, the space can be bought
according to the factors we have discussed.

■ *Merchandising services*

Like newspapers, magazines often provide special services to advertisers. These include mailings prepared for the advertiser to notify
dealers of the impending advertisement. Also, countercards for use
in stores stating "As advertised in" are sometimes forwarded to retailers. Other services provided by magazines include special promotions to stores; marketing services that help readers find local outlets
through a single phone number; aid in handling sales force, broker,
wholesaler, and retailer meetings; advance editions for the trade; and
research into brand preference, consumer attitudes, and market conditions.

SOURCES OF PRINT
MEDIA INFORMATION

There are many general sources of information about newspapers
and magazines; more specific, detailed information about the publication itself may be obtained through direct contact. Here are some of
the principal sources of information that are commonly analyzed by
media planners.

● **Audit Bureau of Circulations (ABC)** The ABC was formed in
1914 to verify circulation and other marketing data on magazines and
newspapers. Each publication submits a semiannual statement,
which is checked by specially trained ABC field auditors. They examine all records necessary to verify the figures the publisher reports
(Figure 13–20).

The information the publisher supplies includes paid circulation for
the period covered. This is broken down by subscription, single-copy
sales, and average paid circulation—by regional, metropolitan, and
demographic editions. It also analyzes new and renewal subscriptions by price, duration, channel of sales, and type of promotion.

● **Newspaper Advertising Bureau** Several industry organizations
and publications offer helpful aids for planning newspaper advertising. One of them is the Newspaper Advertising Bureau of the American Newspaper Publishers Association, the promotional arm of the
nation's newspaper industry. The bureau also provides its newspaper members market information by conducting field research and
collecting case histories.

FIGURE 13–20   Selected consumer magazines: Circulation, readership, and cost

Magazine	Total paid circulation	Percent Male	Percent Female	Readers per copy Men	Readers per copy Women	Percent in-home readers	Median age	Median income	Percent any college	Page costs (1 time) B&W	Page costs (1 time) Four-color
Better Homes & Gardens	8,000,000	22	78	1.21	3.23	62	41	$23,241	36	$61,030	$73,820
Business Week	845,000	72	28	4.85	2.10	37	39	30,884	68	23,120	35,140
Car & Driver	725,000	88	12	4.84	.53	41	31	25,982	45	15,450	23,795
Cosmopolitan	2,250,000	17	83	1.19	4.26	56	28	22,785	46	21,535	28,980
Ebony	1,250,000	42	58	2.60	3.48	62	33	16,505	29	16,200	21,886
Family Circle	7,450,000	13	87	.75	3.51	72	41	21,785	34	53,780	62,750
Field & Stream	2,000,000	79	21	5.38	1.79	49	34	24,337	29	22,240	33,760
Forbes	700,000	74	26	2.53	1.29	40	42	36,783	74	16,520	25,090
Fortune	670,000	71	29	4.01	1.96	29	40	35,204	72	10,760	30,040
Glamour	1,800,000	6	94	.49	4.52	49	27	21,828	44	17,250	24,340
Golf Digest	1,025,000	82	18	2.47	.99	59	43	32,949	54	17,750	26,625
Good Housekeeping	5,000,000	13	87	1.25	4.89	62	39	21,980	35	46,235	58,020
Harper's Bazaar	650,000	8	92	1.71	2.57	36	35	25,358	55	11,200	16,200
Hot Rod	850,000	78	22	6.12	1.33	49	27	23,056	24	12,750	20,400
House & Garden	1,000,000	19	81	2.78	7.72	47	41	23,726	39	17,290	25,430
House Beautiful	800,000	16	84	1.94	8.44	45	40	24,198	42	13,525	19,775
Ladies' Home Journal	5,000,000	12	88	.62	3.55	62	39	21,583	36	39,000	48,000
Mademoiselle	1,000,000	9	91	.53	4.04	48	29	23,660	50	11,130	16,280
McCalls	6,200,000	12	88	.55	3.19	62	40	20,690	32	48,670	59,830
Mechanix Illustrated	1,600,000	81	19	3.84	.89	51	38	22,568	38	17,500	24,815
Money	1,000,000	58	42	4.01	2.45	46	37	31,587	58	16,450	25,740
Motor Trend	750,000	84	16	5.18	.83	42	33	23,878	40	13,690	21,905
Ms.	450,000	16	84	.65	4.26	51	30	24,107	56	6,500	7,845
National Enquirer	4,637,000	40	60	1.57	2.90	68	36	19,969	24	21,000	26,500
National Geographic	8,400,000	55	45	1.86	1.65	64	42	26,294	51	73,520	95,575
National Lampoon	580,000	72	27	6.78	1.47	39	25	22,888	49	6,700	9,900
Newsweek	2,950,000	62	38	4.12	3.17	45	36	26,719	53	40,930	63,850
Outdoor Life	1,500,000	82	18	4.17	1.40	51	35	23,596	29	16,520	28,475
Parents Magazine	1,650,000	22	78	1.08	4.13	43	29	20,779	37	22,240	36,960
People	2,350,000	40	60	4.19	6.50	48	32	23,971	40	30,900	39,850
Playboy	5,000,000	78	22	3.25	.97	59	31	24,051	43	39,780	55,710
Playgirl	650,000	36	64	2.13	4.26	53	30	19,329	36	5,415	7,220
Popular Mechanics	1,600,000	81	19	5.81	1.65	50	38	25,474	36	18,966	26,932
Popular Science	1,800,000	80	20	3.97	1.15	49	37	26,542	44	18,910	26,820
Reader's Digest	17,900,000	44	56	1.38	1.75	75	46	21,802	34	81,399	97,700
Redbook	3,800,000	11	89	.66	3.26	61	35	22,794	35	32,270	42,675
Road & Track	630,000	89	11	6.06	.65	61	30	28,093	35	11,945	18,775
Rolling Stone	700,000	66	34	4.65	2.61	48	25	24,074	47	11,915	17,770
Scientific American	720,000	68	32	4.01	1.91	40	35	29,531	78	16,000	24,000
Seventeen	1,500,000	9	91	.84	3.98	51	29	21,251	33	13,325	19,250
Sports Illustrated	2,250,000	80	20	5.25	1.66	53	32	26,275	46	34,720	54,165
The Star	3,400,000	35	65	1.02	1.99	72	35	19,156	20	17,400	21,350
Time	4,400,000	56	44	2.92	2.29	52	36	26,908	53	55,045	85,870
True Story	1,400,000	18	82	.77	3.98	69	39	14,325	10	10,330	13,435
TV Guide	17,345,000	45	55	1.24	1.47	87	35	20,461	31	65,600	77,400
U.S. News & World Report	2,050,000	63	37	3.25	1.75	45	42	26,998	57	26,935	42,510
Vogue	950,000	11	89	.88	5.75	40	31	23,452	48	12,500	18,000
Woman's Day	7,125,000	8	92	.66	5.29	46	39	21,910	47	51,740	60,435

● **Magazine Publishers Association (MPA)** The MPA has a total membership of 113 publishers who represent 430 publications. This trade group makes available the combined circulation of all ABC member magazines (general and farm) from 1914 to date, with yearly figures related to population. It estimates the number of consumer magazine copies sold by year from 1943. It lists the 100 leading ABC magazines according to circulation and cost of magazine advertising according to circulation.

The association provides the industry with a sales, research, and promotion arm that attempts to stimulate greater and more effective use of magazine advertising.

● **Standard Rate and Data Service (SRDS)** SRDS publishes *Newspaper Rates and Data* and *Consumer Magazine and Publication Rates and Data, Business Publication Rates and Data,* and other monthly directories that eliminate the necessity for advertisers and their agencies to obtain rate cards for every publication. For the type of information provided, see Figures 13–10 and 13–21.

● **Audience studies provided by publications** Circulation figures are not enough. Newspapers and magazines also offer media planners many other types of statistical reports. The information contained in these reports details reader income, demographic profiles, percentages of different kinds of advertising carried, and much more.

Reader's Digest, for example, cites research which shows that "more

FIGURE 13–21

The *Consumer Magazine and Agri-Media Rates and Data* listing for *People Weekly.* Note the premium charged for cover position; also the lead time required for color ads as opposed to black and white.

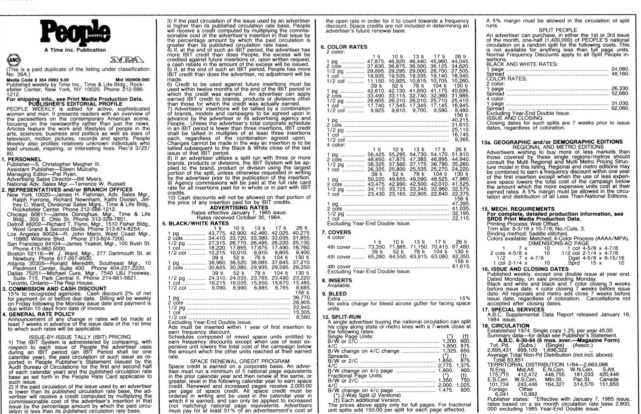

people spend more time with each issue of the *Reader's Digest* than with any other magazine.''

The magazine also promotes the quality of their readers. Research shows that 35.6 percent of their readers own two or more cars which were bought new, 36 percent bought a new dishwasher in the last year, 30 percent have passports, and 34 percent spend more than $60 per week on groceries.

These are interesting statistics to the advertiser selling automobiles, household appliances, travel, food, and associated products and services.

Similarly, *Time* magazine promotes its special business edition of *Time B* by citing statistics on its readers. Their average household income, for instance, exceeds $35,000; further, 87.5 percent attended college; and, most importantly, 100 percent are in professional or managerial positions. This underscores the magazine's claim that *Time B* is directed exclusively to businesspeople. And for advertisers of computer equipment, financial services, heavy machinery, or corporate aircraft, this is significant data.

Summary

The printed page in general and the newspaper in particular provide a unique, flexible medium for advertisers to express their creativity. The newspaper is a mass medium that is read by almost everybody. It offers great flexibility, which assists creativity, and its printed message lasts. However, newspapers also have their disadvantages. These include: lack of audience selectivity, short life span, poor production quality, heavy advertising competition, potentially poor ad placement, and overlapping circulation. Still, the newspaper is the major community-serving medium today for both news and advertising.

The newspaper's rates, mechanical requirements, and other pertinent information are printed on its rate card. This will also tell whether the newspaper's space is sold by the agate line or the column inch. The rates listed vary for local and national advertisers. Also listed are the newspaper's short rate policy, combination rates, frequency discounts, run of paper rates, and other data.

Magazines offer different advantages. They are the most selective of all media. They are flexible in both readership and advertising. They offer unsurpassed availability of color, excellent reproduction quality, believability and authority, permanence, and prestige at an efficient cost. However, they require long lead time, they have problems offering reach and frequency, and they are subject to heavy advertising competition. And the cost of advertising in some magazines is very high.

In selecting magazines for advertising, the media buyer must consider the publication's circulation, its readership, and its cost and mechanical requirements. A magazine's rates may be determined by several factors: its primary and secondary readership, the number of subscription and vendor sales, and the number of copies that are guaranteed versus those that are actually delivered.

Magazine rate cards, like newspaper rate cards, follow a standard format so advertisers can readily determine the cost of advertising. The rate card lists black-and-white rates, discounts, color rates, issue and closing dates, and mechanical requirements.

Questions for review and discussion

1. If you were working for a retailer, would you recommend the use of newspaper advertising? Why or why not?
2. In the same situation as above, what would be the basic types of newspaper advertising available to your company?
3. What advertising opportunities are presented by Sunday supplements?
4. How does a short rate affect advertisers?
5. What effect does primary and secondary readership have on the cost efficiency of newspaper advertising?
6. How do advertisers benefit from split runs?
7. If you worked in the advertising department of a bank, would you recommend magazine advertising? Why or why not?
8. Based on the information in Figure 13–20 does *Time* magazine or *Newsweek* have the higher cost per thousand?
9. What is the importance of the Audit Bureau of Circulation?
10. What is the advantage of magazine advertising to businesses that sell to other businesses?

14

ELECTRONIC MEDIA

By the age of 49, Tom Mabley had already been through a lot of advertising wars. Now he was senior vice president/creative director for Lord, Geller, Federico, Einstein, a J. Walter Thompson subsidiary with a list of classy clients including Steinway pianos, Hennessy cognac, and IBM.

Lord, Geller had already been handling IBM's corporate image advertising when they were asked to design a campaign for IBM's new, top secret personal computer. With the client, the agency's account team developed the basic advertising strategy.

The IBM PC would arrive on the scene just when such machines were beginning to win wide public acceptance.

IBM wanted to break down the widespread public fear of the computer, demonstrate its essential simplicity, and communicate the many ways it could be used. At the same time, IBM wanted to create a unique identity for its PC that would distinguish it from other IBM products and from the plethora of competitors like Radio Shack's TRS-80 and Apple.

In searching for the big idea for IBM, Mabley and art director Bob Tore came up with a variety of concepts. "We were talking about the problems of big computers and their unfriendliness," says Tore. "We had the idea of showing the history of the computer shrinking—a big white box in a white, sterile room that would get smaller and smaller. We wanted to have a person reacting to it, and with all that white background, we obviously needed a character in a black suit to stand out."

They decided they wanted a single, friendly person who would represent Everyman. Then they suddenly realized there really wasn't a need for on-camera dialog. That pointed to mime.

"We developed the criteria for who this mime should be," says Mabley, "and ended up with the conclusion that it could only be Charlie Chaplin's Little Tramp. After that we were on a roll, and everything began to work."

The finished commercial opens with a big white block representing a mysterious, intimidating machine. An off-camera announcer describes how the first computers were like closed doors to most people. Suddenly on the block appears a door, which the Chaplin character tries to penetrate only to have it slam in his face. Then the block begins to shrink until it reaches the dimensions of a medium-sized box.

Chaplin breaks open the box and takes out his new IBM personal computer. He quickly scans an instruction book and immediately sits down in his white designer chair, at a white table, ready to work on his white computer which will make him more productive and more creative.

As the narrator mentions creativity, Chaplin sniffs a red rose in a white vase on the table. The rose, a light touch subtly symbolizing creativity and individuality, becomes a regular feature of the campaign along with the Chaplin character himself (Figure 14–1).

With Lord, Geller's "Little Tramp" character and some $30 million in television time, IBM rapidly carved out a 28 percent share of the personal computer market in two short years. By 1984, they were selling at a clip of a half million a year and still rising. A great idea with great execution, backed by a solid product, had paid off.[1]

USING TELEVISION IN THE CREATIVE MIX

Although advertising on television seems to come under severe attack on a somewhat regular basis, no one ever denies the creative potential of the television medium. In fact, it is television's very potential for creativity and impact that has fueled so much criticism. As a means of reaching a mass audience, no other medium today has the unique creative abilities of television: the combination of sight, sound, and movement; the opportunity to demonstrate the product; the potential to use special effects; the believability of seeing it happen right before your eyes; and the empathy of the viewer.

In this chapter we want to understand the electronic media—television and radio—from the standpoint of their roles in the creative mix. We will give a general overview of both media and then look specifically at how advertisers evaluate and buy television and radio time.

■ What Works Best in Television?

Television has grown faster than any other advertising medium in history. From its beginnings after World War II, it has emerged as the medium that attracts the largest volume of national advertising—totaling over $11 billion in 1984. Why is this? It is because of the unique advantages that contemporary television offers advertisers over competing media.

▪ *Mass coverage and low cost*

A substantial portion of television's national advertising revenue comes from the packaged goods industry (foods and drugs). Procter & Gamble, for instance, has led all other advertisers in spending since 1951. In their nationwide distribution of high-volume, low-profit products in supermarkets, they use television to reach a mass audience and presell their brand names at a very low cost per thousand.

FIGURE 14–1

ANNCR V.O.: If you run a small business, profits can get squeezed when inventory doesn't match up with production. What you need is a tool for modern times.

The IBM Personal Computer. Not only can it help you plan ahead, it'll balance your books and give you more time to make dough.

And the cost? That's the icing on the cake. Your own IBM Personal Computer. Try it at a store near you.

FIGURE   14–2

(Joan Collins uses her sexy bad-girl image to promote the "fire" of Scoundrel perfume.)

JOAN COLLINS: It takes . . . something black.
Something brilliant.
Something cool.
Something hot.
Something Scoundrel. My favorite fragrance.
It's sophisticated and elegant. And there's something sexy about it, too.
Then, when something happens, and it will, you can always say: "It wasn't me. It was my Scoundrel."

ANNCR V.O.: Scoundrel. From Revlon.

MAN: Somebody here report a fire?

In 1984, 98 percent of all American homes had a TV set, and most had more than one. The average is 1.67 sets per household, and over 86 percent of these are color sets.[2] The overwhelming odds are that at least one person in your family will be watching TV on any given day. This is a safe assumption because, of the homes that own TV sets (television households), 92 percent view TV at least once during the average day. More than 98 percent of television households tune in during an average week.

Typical network nighttime programs reach 15 percent of all television households. The more popular shows and special attractions reach 25 percent and more. For example, over 40 percent are usually reached by a Super Bowl game.

Television, therefore, has historically been a mass medium for mass-consumption products. Despite the often huge initial outlays for commercial production and advertising time, television's equally huge audiences bring the per-exposure cost for each commercial down to a comparatively low level.

Viewer empathy

TV advertising can depict people more realistically than any other medium. The subjects are seen to worry over the same problems and cope with the same hardships that the viewer does. As the solutions to these problems occur in the privacy of the home, television becomes a highly personal medium (Figure 14–2).

Selectivity

In spite of the fact that television audiences are mass audiences, they can vary a great deal depending on the time of day and the day of the week. This permits the advertiser to present the message when this potential audience is best. Also, some segments of the population, such as those living in the suburbs, are more easily reached by TV than by other media.

The U.S. distributor of the prestigious Omega watch line had always used print media to reach its rather limited, upper income market. After testing television in three different geographic markets, it rapidly switched its print dollars to television and spread its campaign to 30 markets. But it still bought very selectively around the "adult" shows: "Today," "Tonight," various news shows, and serious programming like "Meet the Press." Sales increased 70 percent over the next two years.

Now, with the sudden growth of cable programming, a wide variety of opportunities exist for "narrowcasting" to select local target markets and for broadcasting to traditional mass audiences.

Impact

The ability to bring a moving picture with sound into the living rooms of America is practically tantamount to having an army of door-to-door sellers. The sales impact of television was measured by the NBC-Hofstra Study of low-cost, high-volume brands. This study showed that products advertised on TV had an average 30.1 percent sales *increase*, whereas products advertised but not on TV had an average 19.1 sales *loss* among TV viewers. Similar sales differences were found for durable goods.

Creativity

Television's creative potential is limited only by the commercial creator's talents. The various facets of the television commercial—sight, sound, motion, and color—all permit an infinite number of original and imaginative appeals. For some interesting facts on how to create effective TV commercials, see the Checklist of what works best in television.

Prestige

Hallmark, Xerox, Beatrice Foods, and IBM have all experienced an increase in prestige and corporate awareness by sponsoring dramatic presentations and other cultural highlights. Potential distributors, the company's sales force, and customers are impressed by a product's association with quality programming.

Social dominance

Television has exhibited a power that goes beyond impact and prestige. The entire nation has been emotionally stirred by TV screenings of the Olympic Games, space travel, assassinations, wars, and political scandals. The *New York Times* has said of television, "Its impact on leisure, politics, reading, and culture [is] unparalleled since the advent of the auto."

The real relationship between the power of television and the sale of an advertiser's product is difficult to gauge. However, we can probably safely assume that the magnetic attraction of television events gives this medium a potential for advertising unlike any other.

Drawbacks to Television

Although television's power as a creative tool may be unmatched, the medium still has many drawbacks that keep it from being used by most advertisers. Television advertising involves several unique problems. In many instances, television just doesn't "fit" in the creative mix. This may be because of cost, lack of audience selectivity, its inherent brevity, or the clutter of competitive messages.

Cost

Television suffers its greatest handicap from the high cost of producing commercials and buying airtime. The production costs for a TV spot vary with how the advertiser chooses to present the product. Most national advertisers film their commercials and usually pay $50,000 or more for each. In Chapter 11, we discussed how Levi's spent $250,000 to produce its highly effective animated commercials.

The cost of professional talent has also become a major expense. Singer Julio Iglesias enjoyed a $1 million commercial contract with Coca-Cola. And Michael Jackson signed for $5.5 million with Pepsi-Cola. While most professional actors and actresses earn far less, as a group they receive a total of more than $100 million yearly from their work in TV commercials.

The second major area of expense is network time. A single 30-second commercial during prime time may cost $100,000 (Figure 14–3). Special attractions can cost much more. A minute of commercial time during the 1984 Olympic Games cost $250,000, for example.

FIGURE   14–3   Network TV cost estimates*

	Prime time	Day time	Early evening news (M–F)	Late fringe
Cost per 30 seconds	$80,900	$12,100	$42,600	$17,200
Average rating	17.7	6.5	13.7	5.5
Homes (000)	14,030	4,860	9,250	5,780
Cost per rating point	$4,570	$1,862	$3,109	$3,127

*Costs reflect an average of all three networks with complete quarterly activity.

For the large advertiser, television can be relatively efficient, with the cost per thousand viewers running from $3 to $7. But the cost of large coverage, even at relatively low rates, usually prices the small and medium-sized advertisers out of the market.

Checklist of what works best in television

☐ The picture must tell the story. Forget every other rule in this chapter, and you will still be ahead of the game. It's the most important rule of all! Television is a *visual* medium. That's why the people in front of a set are called *viewers*. They remember what they *see*, not what they hear. Try this trick for looking at a storyboard. *Cover the words.* What is the message of the commercial with the sound turned off? Is there a message at all?

☐ Look for a "key visual." Here's another test to apply to the storyboard. Can you pick out *one* frame that visually sums up the whole message? Most good commercials can be reduced to this single "key visual." A commercial with many different scenes may look interesting in storyboard form but can turn out to be an overcomplicated piece of film. Busy, crowded, fast-moving commercials are hard to understand. The small television screen is not a movie theater. A *simple* storyboard can fool you. It may look hopelessly dull on paper. But film thrives on simplicity.

☐ Grab the viewer's attention. The *first five seconds* of a commercial are crucial. Analysis of audience reaction shows either a sharp drop or a sharp rise in interest during this time. *Commercial attention does not build.* Your audience can only become less interested, never more. The level you reach in the first five seconds is the highest you will get, so don't save your punches. Offer the viewer something right off the bat. *News.* A *problem* to which you have the solution. A *conflict* that is involving.

☐ Be single-minded. A good commercial is uncomplicated. Direct. It never makes the viewer do a lot of mental work. The basic commercial length in U.S. television is 30 seconds. The content possible in that time is outlined in the phrase: "name-claim-demonstration." The name of your product, your consumer benefit, and the reason the consumer should believe it. Longer commercials *should not add copy points.* A 60-second commercial tells the same story as the 30-second one, with more leisure and detail. Or—best of all—*repetition.* The 60-second allows time for a mood to be created; the 30-second generally does not. The 20-second and 10-second commercials are one-point messages. The 10-second registers the brand name

Lack of selectivity

Many advertisers are seeking a very specific, small audience. In these cases television is not cost effective and is therefore at a disadvantage. This situation is changing, however. Television seems destined to follow magazines and radio. With the ever-increasing influx of UHF, public, and cable channels, the viewer is offered a larger variety of programming from which to choose. And small advertisers are being offered more selective television alternatives.

Brevity

A television advertising message is brief, usually lasting only 30 seconds. The objective is to get enough viewers' attention and to leave them with a favorable attitude toward the product (or at least make them remember it). But in 30 seconds, that's a tall task.

Clutter

One major drawback to television advertising is that a commercial is seldom seen in an isolated position. It is usually surrounded by

---

and promise. The 20-second makes the promise more explicit. Both these lengths are usually *reminder* messages, run in a media schedule with longer commercial lengths. If your campaign plans include both :60s and :30s, look at the :30s *first.* If the message cannot be delivered in 30 seconds, you are not being single-minded.

☐ Register the name of your product. Too often, a viewer will remember the commercial but not the name of your brand. This is a problem particularly troublesome with new products. Showing the package on screen and mouthing the name is not enough. Take extra pains to implant your product name in the viewer's mind.

☐ The tone of your advertising must reflect your product personality. If you are fortunate enough to have a product with an established brand image, your advertising *must* reflect that image. It takes dedication on the part of advertiser and agency to build a brand personality. Discipline yourself to reject advertising that conflicts with it. (It helps to have a written "personality statement" of your product; if it

were a person, what sort of person would it be?) When you launch a new product, the very *tone* of your announcement commercial tells viewers what to expect. From that moment on, it is hard to change their minds. Once you have decided on a personality for your product, sustain it in every commercial. Change campaigns when you must, but retain the same tone of voice.

☐ Avoid "talky" commercials. Look for the simplest, and most memorable, set of words to get across your consumer benefit. Every word must work hard. A 30-second commercial usually allows you *no more* than 65 words, a 60-second commercial twice that amount. Be specific. Pounce upon clichés, flabbiness, and superlatives. Try this discipline. When you ask for 10 words to be added to a commercial, decide which 10 you would *delete* to make room for them.

station-break announcements, credits, public-service announcements, and "billboards" (just the name or slogan of a product), not to mention six or seven other commercials. With all these messages competing for attention, the viewer often comes away annoyed and confused, and with a high rate of product misidentification.

In 1985, the networks announced that for the first time they would accept 15 second commercials. Looking to the future, the J. Walter Thompson advertising agency has already screened one- and three-second television commercials, predicting they may be commonplace by the 1990s. In a one-second commercial, we might hear a phone ring over a flash of a service company logo followed by a flash of a repairman arriving at a door. Consumers of the future are expected to have faster comprehension. But the effect these new commercial formats will have on the clutter problem is cause for concern.

OVERVIEW OF THE TELEVISION MEDIUM

In 1947 five television stations began broadcasting. By 1984 the number had grown to more than 750 commercial stations. Of these, more than 500 were VHF (very high frequency—channels 2 through 13), and more than 250 were UHF (ultra-high frequency—channels 14 through 83).

Until 1952 all stations were VHF. Then the Federal Communications Commission (FCC) authorized 70 more channels (14 through 83) and referred to them as UHF. To equalize coverage, a law was passed in 1965 requiring all new TV sets to be designed to receive UHF broadcasts. This, along with the tremendous growth of cable networks in the late 70s, brought many more UHF stations into existence (Figure 14–4).

Today there are two additional types of special stations: *satellite* stations like Ted Turner's WTBS (see Chapter 3), which duplicate a major portion of the broadcasts of a parent station and originate some minor programming of their own; and *translator* stations, which rebroadcast regular stations to fringe areas using the higher UHF frequencies but are usually incapable of originating local programming.

■ Audience Trends

Middle-income, high school-educated viewers and their families are the heaviest viewers of television. There are two possible reasons for this. First, most television programming is directed at this group. Second, people with considerably higher income and education usually have a more diversified range of interests and entertainment options.

The average number of viewing hours has steadily increased since television was introduced. Children under 12 view an average of 26 hours per week; middle-aged men, 27.3; and middle-aged women, 33.3. By age 18, the average child has watched around 26,000 hours (three years) of TV. In 1985 the average household TV usage was about seven hours a day. Older women viewed the most, teenage females the least.

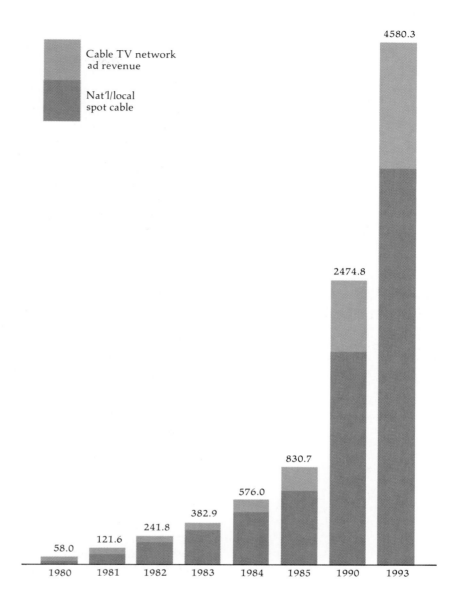

FIGURE 14–4

Advertising revenue growth estimates.

Individual program audiences vary a great deal. A sporting event, for example, attracts proportionately more men in the 18–34 age category than any other group. Adults over 50 have traditionally shown a marked tendency toward westerns, and children rate adventure and situation comedy highest. Look at the audience composition statistics in Figure 14–5. How would you describe the primary viewers of network movies?

The amount of television viewing time varies according to the season and the time of day. The number of viewers rises slowly in the morning, levels off during the afternoon, and increases dramatically in the evening. The audience is approximately two or three times larger in prime time than in the morning. The number of homes viewing TV is highest in the winter and averages 20 to 30 percent less in the summer.

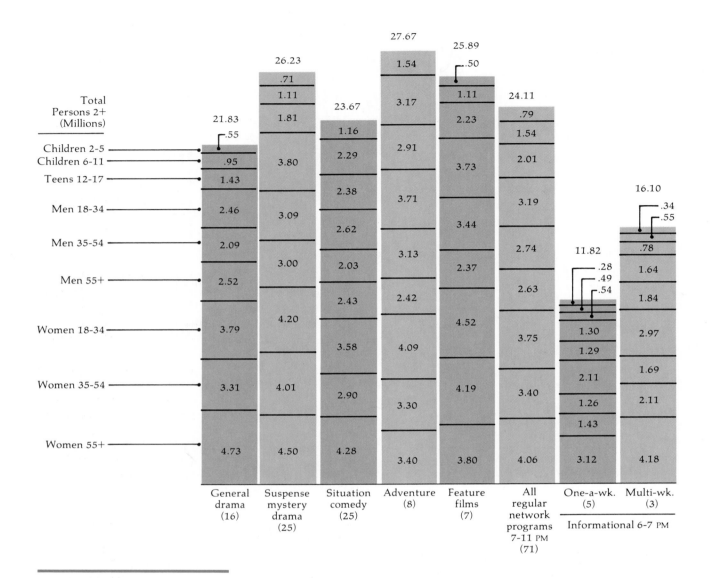

FIGURE   14–5

The Nielsen Report on Television shows the disproportionate distribution of audience composition by selected program type of regularly scheduled network programs during prime time. For example, women 55 and over are the largest segment of viewers of general drama, while women 18 to 34 comprise the largest segment of viewers of feature films.

 Growth of Television Advertising

As television viewing has increased over the years, so have the number of advertisers and the amounts they spend. In 1950 only 3 percent of total advertising volume was placed on television. That amounted to $171 million. By 1984 that figure had grown to over $15 billion and accounted for more than 22 percent of all ad spending. Over half of that $15 billion dollars was spent by just the top 100 advertisers.

BUYING TELEVISION
TIME

To buy television time the advertiser must first understand the various commercial opportunities available. Second, a knowledge of audience measurement techniques and terminology is important in order to evaluate the available commercial time. And, finally, the advertiser needs to know the proper procedures for "making the buy." We will discuss each of these areas in this section.

■ Commercial Opportunities in TV

There are three ways advertisers can buy advertising time on television. They may sponsor an entire program, participate in a program, or use spot announcements between programs.

▪ Network sponsorships

One way to advertise is to purchase airtime from one of the three national networks: Columbia Broadcasting Company (CBS), National Broadcasting Company (NBC), or American Broadcasting Company (ABC). Networks offer the large advertiser convenience and efficiency because the message can be broadcast simultaneously throughout the country.

When an advertiser undertakes to present a program alone, it is called a *sponsorship*. The advertiser is responsible for the program content and the cost of production as well as the advertising. This is generally so costly that single sponsorships are usually limited to specials (Figure 14–6).

For companies that decide on this method (AT&T, Xerox, and Hallmark, for example), there are two important advantages. The first is that the public more readily identifies with the product(s), and the

FIGURE   14–6

(AT&T sponsors human interest programs with highly human commercials.)

BOY #1: Bet you're glad your brother finally went away to school.

BOY #2: Yeah.

BOY #1: You get his room, his bike, and everything. What a deal.

BOY #2: Yeah.

BOY #1: And just think . . . no one to call you Peeper anymore.

BOY #2: Yeah.

MOTHER: David, your brother's on the phone. He wants to talk to you.

BOY #2: Brian? For me? Oh boy!

OLDER BROTHER: Hey, Peeper! How ya doin' kid?

MUSIC AND SINGERS: Reach out, reach out and touch someone.

company gains from the prestige attached to sponsoring first-rate entertainment. The second is that the sponsor has control over the placement and content of the commercials. The commercials can be fit to the program and run any length desired as long as they are within network or station regulations. Some major car manufacturers, for example, sponsor an hour-long program in the fall and run a single five-minute commercial that introduces the new line of cars.

The centralization offered by networks also simplifies bookkeeping as the advertiser gets only one bill. The total cost per thousand is low—lower even than time purchased on a spot basis (discussed later).

The high cost of sponsoring a program has encouraged many advertisers to cooperate. This permits them to realize some of the advantages of sponsorship but at lower cost and risk. They often sponsor on alternate weeks or divide the program into segments. Most sporting events, for instance, are sold as multiple sponsorships.

Participations

Most network television advertising is sold on the *participating* basis with several advertisers buying 30- or 60-second segments within the program. Advertisers can participate in a program once or several times on a regular or irregular basis. This allows the advertiser to spread out the budget and makes it easier to get in and out of a program without a long-term commitment. It also enables the small

---

PEOPLE IN ADVERTISING

Ed McCabe

President
Scali, McCabe, Sloves

Ed McCabe, writer of some of the world's simplest—and most successful—TV commercials, is a founder, president, and worldwide creative director of Scali, McCabe, Sloves. Now in its 17th year, SMS has an annual billing of $250 million and offices in New York, Toronto, Montreal, Mexico City, Melbourne, London, and Dusseldorf.

Even in an industry that sometimes places a premium on youth, McCabe's age on landing his first agency job was surprising. He joined McCann-Erickson in Chicago when only 15. Then he moved to New York, where he wrote for Young & Rubicam, Benton & Bowles, Marschalk, and Carl Ally before cofounding SMS in 1967.

Seven years later, at 35, McCabe became the youngest person ever to be elected to the Copywriter's Hall of Fame.

Known for his crisp, concise copy, McCabe has written on everything from automats to autos, noise pollution to hi-fi. But his TV commercials for Perdue Farms chickens stand out. In 1971, Frank Perdue awarded his advertising account to SMS after personally interviewing 26 other agencies. What McCabe did was turn Perdue's chickens (see Chapter 3) into America's first brand-name chickens, with a TV campaign built around the line, "It

advertiser to buy a limited amount of time and still have nationwide coverage.

Network advertising also has its disadvantages. An advertiser who desires to buy fewer stations than the full network lineup often finds that preference is given to those willing to buy more. The advertiser who seeks to advertise to a limited market usually finds that the network lineup does not coincide with that need.

Spot announcements

Other than sponsorships and participations, *spot announcements* are the only other means of presenting a commercial on television. National spot advertising offers the advertiser greater flexibility since commercials can be concentrated on the markets most likely to pay off, and they are less expensive than participations because they are run in clusters between programs. Spots may also be used to introduce a new product into one area at a time. Advertisers with limited distribution and budgets find this advantageous.

Spots may be sold either nationally or locally and can be purchased in segments of 10, 20, 30, or 60 seconds. The most common length by far is 30 seconds, and 20-second commercials have virtually disappeared.

Spot advertising is more difficult to purchase than network advertising. It involves contacting each station directly. And the complex bookkeeping can become a headache.

Takes a Tough Man to Make a Tender Chicken." As a result of that campaign, sales of Perdue's premium-priced chickens have soared sevenfold.

Like his copy, McCabe is to the point: "Really great TV commercials are simple. If you strip away the nonsense and if you present them with a little bit of a twist, that's when they appear to be magic."

And for all his outstanding writing credits, McCabe does not downplay the value of the visual. "We are talking about a total piece of communication—the look of something is part of it. I am very concerned with who can deliver what kind of look, whether it's appropriate, and how it meets what I have in mind. I search for a look that will separate my client from others—someone who can understand what I'm trying to do and can help bring it off."

In doing so, McCabe focuses on using new talent and fresh approaches. "We've probably never used the same director or production company twice."

McCabe feels that image is becoming increasingly important, perhaps all-important. "The new direction we are heading in is simple, striking visual communication. If you can say something in a picture which expresses a memorable idea about your product, it's the most relevant form of communication for today."

And what about tomorrow? "The time is coming when the most powerful presentation will be with the fewest possible words." McCabe has already mapped his strategy for this coming challenge. "As soon as everyone is doing it with all pictures," he smiles, "I'm going to come out with all words."

And McCabe's words are perhaps the best way to sum up his candid philosophy:

On corporate advertising: "There's no such thing. Anyone who wants to do corporate advertising *has* to advertise a product or a service in order to make a corporate statement."

On maintaining a high level of quality." "We're not concerned with beating other agencies, but with beating ourselves."

On hard-sell advertising: "All advertising that is worth a damn is hard-sell advertising."

On good copy: "Show me something great, and I'll show you a bunch of monosyllables."

McCabe frequently speaks to advertising groups in countries where English is a second language. Communication hasn't been a problem, however. They all seem to understand his monosyllables.

Another drawback is that spot advertising during network programming is available only at station breaks and when network advertisers have purchased less than the full lineup. In such cases, the station sells a spot and fits it between network and local ads. Most advertising time of network affiliates is sold in this way.

Local

Retailers, often in cooperation with nationally known manufacturers, may buy time from local stations. As a rule, local airtime is sold as spot announcements, but sometimes programs are developed and sponsored by local advertisers. Or local firms can buy the rights to a syndicated film series and sponsor it in their own market.

Audience Measurement

Assume you are the director of corporate advertising for a major international corporation whose stock is traded on the New York Stock Exchange. A study you have commissioned reveals that your company, as large as it is, is suffering from an "identity void"; that is, nobody hates you, nobody loves you, nobody knows you. Furthermore, because of this identity void, your company's stock is rarely recommended by financial analysts, and even your current shareholders are dissatisfied with your stock's performance.

You decide you need to advertise—to inform financial decision makers (analysts, pension fund managers, bank portfolio managers, investment bankers, stockbrokers, and corporate executives) about your company, its activities, its growth, and its future. Would you use television as the mainstay in your creative mix?

A company called TRW did. But first they had to be sure they could reach their target audience efficiently with that medium. That meant studying the audiences of various programs and analyzing the programs' impact and cost-effectiveness against those of other media vehicles. To do that, of course, requires an understanding of audience measurement techniques and the terminology used for television advertising.

Rating services: "The book"

A number of rating services measure the program audiences of TV and radio stations for advertisers and broadcasters. They pick a representative sample of the market and, through various techniques, furnish data on the size and characteristics of the audiences that view or listen to the programs.

Several of these research organizations gather the data at their own expense and publish it. Companies interested in their findings subscribe to the service and use it as a basis in making media plans for advertising.

The most commonly used services for TV are *Arbitron* (ARB) and the *A. C. Nielsen Station Index* (NSI). For demographic studies of TV audiences, advertisers also commonly use the *Simmons Reports.*

These services publish their findings two or more times per year, depending on the size of the market, in a publication generally referred to as *The Book.* (See Ad Lab 14–A.) The book reports a wide array of statistics on how many people, in what age groups, and of

AD LAB 14–A   Where do those infamous television ratings come from?

Nielsen Ratings

The A. C. Nielsen Company uses 50,000 diaries to sample the viewing habits of households in more than 200 markets in order to report ratings in its Nielsen Station Index (NSI) for local television.

The Audimeter, a complex electronic instrument attached to TV sets in 1,200 scientifically selected homes, is used to prepare national estimates of network television audiences for its Nielsen Television Index (NTI). The instrument reports time of day, set usage, and station tuning and transmits this information to a central computer.

Nielsen provides media buyers with information about home audience size and other demographic data, which are used as a basis for determining the time and placement of television commercials for network buyers.

Arbitron Ratings

The Arbitron Company gathers information on local television audiences by using diaries in which families record the television viewing habits for each television set in the home. The end result is a viewing report broken down by stations, programs, time periods, and demographics.

Arbitron also uses an electronic meter for audience measurement in the four largest markets, New York, Chicago, Los Angeles, and San Francisco. Data are fed to a computer which produces instantaneous reports ("overnights").

Arbitron (as well as A. C. Nielsen) reports are used for making spot buying decisions.

A fieldperson installing an instantaneous Audimeter in a Nielsen household.

Sample material from the Nielsen Television Index for San Francisco/Oakland.

A sample page from Arbitron's television rating book for Detroit.

Laboratory Applications

1. What are the advantages and disadvantages of the television audience measurement methods?

2. Which audience rating method do you consider the best? Why?

what sex are watching TV at various times of the day within a specific market area.

Television markets

Newspaper and magazine publishers generally report their circulations by state. Television rating services use a more precise definition of their markets to minimize the problem of overlapping TV signals.

Areas of dominant influence (ADI)   Arbitron introduced the concept calling its TV markets *areas of dominant influence (ADI)*. An ADI is defined as "an exclusive geographic area consisting of all counties in which the Home Market stations receive a preponderance of total viewing hours." Thus, the Charlotte ADI is all counties in which the Charlotte TV stations are the most watched.

Designated market areas (DMA)   The Nielsen station index uses a similar method known as *designated market areas (DMA)*. When TRW decided to try television advertising as a means to fill up its identity void, the company discovered that approximately half of all its shareholders were in the top 10 DMAs, which include the nation's largest cities from New York to Pittsburgh. Therefore, the company's first ads were scheduled in these top 10 markets with one exception: Houston was substituted for Pittsburgh because of the number of TRW customers in that area.

Dayparts

The next questions for TRW were when to air its commercials and on what programs. Unlike radio, there is little or no station loyalty in television. Viewer loyalty is to programs, and programs continue to run or are canceled depending on the size of their ratings (percentage of the population watching). Ratings also depend on what time of day a program runs.

Television time is divided into *dayparts* as follows:

	Daytime:	9 A.M.–4 P.M. (EST)
	Early fringe:	4–5:30 P.M. (EST)
Combine as early fringe	Early news:	5 or 5:30–7:30 P.M. (EST)
	Prime access:	7:30–8 P.M. (EST)
	Prime:	8–11 P.M. (EST)
Combine as late fringe	Late news:	11–11:30 P.M. (EST)
	Late fringe:	11:30 P.M.–1 A.M. (EST)

There are different levels of viewing during each daypart. The highest viewing level, of course, is in prime time (7:30–11 p.m.). Late fringe time also ranks fairly high in most markets among adults. Daytime and early fringe tend to be viewed most heavily by women.

To reach the greatest percentage of the advertiser's target audience with maximum frequency, all within budget, the media planner determines a *daypart mix* based on the TV usage levels reported by the rating services.

In TRW's initial studies of its target group, it learned that its market watched television for entertainment and information, principally

FIGURE 14–7

Did you ever notice that just when you think you see the whole picture, the picture changes. Technology from a company called TRW lets us look at our world in fresh ways. Because there's more to everything than meets the eye. Tomorrow is taking shape at a company called TRW.

during prime time and late evening news; they listened to the radio on the way to work; and they read trade publications related to their work. When TRW scheduled its first TV ads, then, it bought enough late evening news from the two top-rated stations in each market to achieve a balance of good reach and frequency totaling a minimum of 50 gross rating points per week. This TV schedule was then supported with additional ads on morning radio and in major business publications (Figure 14–7).

Audience measures

There are numerous other terms that rating services and media planners use to define a television station's audience, penetration, and efficiency. We will discuss a few more of these before examining the procedures used to buy television time.

TV households (TVHH) refers to the number of households that own television sets. In the United States approximately 70 million households (over 98 percent of all households) own television sets. By looking at the number of households that own TVs in a particular market, we can gain a sense of the size of that market. Likewise, by looking at the number of TV households tuned in to a particular program, we can get a sense of how popular the program is and how many people our commercial is likely to reach.

The percentage of homes in a given area that have one or more TV sets turned on at any particular time is expressed as *households using TV*. If there are 1,000 TV sets in the survey area and 500 are turned on, the HUT figure is 50 percent.

We're all familiar with TV shows that have been canceled because their ratings slipped. What does that really mean? The percentage of TV households in an area that are tuned in to a specific program is called the *program rating.*

$$\text{Rating} = \frac{\text{Number tuned to specific station}}{\text{TVHH}}$$

The networks are interested in high ratings because that is a measure of a show's popularity. If a show is not popular, advertisers will not want to advertise on it, and a network's revenue will fall. Similarly, local stations often make changes in their local news shows in order to increase their popularity and, thereby, their ratings.

The percentage of homes that have sets in use (HUT) tuned in to a specific program is called the program's *share of audience.* A program with only five viewers could have a 50 share if only 10 sets are turned on. For that reason the program rating figures are important because they measure the audience as a percentage of all TV households in the area, regardless of whether the TV set is on or off.

The total number of homes reached by some portion of a program is referred to as *total audience.* This figure is normally broken down to determine *audience composition* (the distribution of audience into demographic categories).

Gross rating points

In television, *gross rating points* are the total weight of a media schedule against TV households. For example, a weekly schedule of five commercials with an average household rating of 20 would yield

100 GRPs, or a total audience equivalent to the total number of TV households in the area.

TRW determined that a schedule of 50 GRPs per week would be sufficient at the beginning of its television campaign. This might have been accomplished by buying 10 spots with an average rating of 5 or only 2 spots with an average rating of 25.

The latter might have been feasible by using a highly rated prime-time program, but then the frequency would have been very low. So TRW opted to use the late evening newscasts, which had lower ratings against total TV households but higher shares of those adults watching; it also afforded the company the ability to gain frequency.

The results of TRW's decision demonstrated the wisdom of its choice. In key markets where the commercials ran, surveys were taken, and the number of respondents who looked on TRW as an attractive investment alternative increased 20 percent—to more than 60 percent total. In control markets where the TRW commercials did not air, the company's image remained virtually unchanged.

■ Television Buying Procedures

The process of buying TV time can be rather lengthy as advertisers determine what programs are available to them at what cost, analyze the various programs for efficiency, negotiate with stations or reps on price, determine what reach and frequency they are achieving, eventually sign the broadcast contracts, and then finally review the affidavits of performance to be sure the commercials ran as agreed. The buying procedures for television are so complex that most large advertisers seek the assistance of professional advertising agencies or media buying services. For the local advertiser, the assistance of station reps also proves invaluable in determining the best buys for the money.

■ *Requesting avails*

To find out what programs are available to them, media buyers contact the sales representatives for the stations they are considering. These may be local station salespeople, national media rep organizations that sell for one station in each market, or network reps. The media buyer gives the rep information about the advertiser's media objectives and target audiences and asks the rep to supply a list of available time slots along with their prices and estimated ratings (Figure 14–8). The information supplied by the media buyer includes:

Name of advertiser.
Desired dates of schedule.
Desired daypart mix (e.g., 60 percent prime, 30 percent news, 10 percent late fringe).
Total household GRP goals (e.g., 100 points per week for four weeks).
Demographic target audience. (Primary: Adults 25 to 34. Secondary: Young adults 18 to 25.)

The information requested from the rep on all the available programs includes:

ADI household ratings.
Total households (in thousands).
Total persons in target audience (in thousands).
ADI HUT (percentage of homes using TV).
Prices for each available program.

The avails submitted by the rep should include all the data requested based on the most recent Nielsen or Arbitron book. Many media buyers ask for the information based on the last two or three books in order to see whether a show's ratings are consistent or have an upward or downward trend.

Selecting programs for buys

To determine which shows to buy, the media buyer must select the most efficient ones in relation to the target audience. To do this, a simple computation is made of the cost per rating point (CPP) and the cost per thousand (CPM) for each program, as follows:

$$\frac{\text{Cost}}{\text{Rating}} = \text{CPP} \qquad \frac{\text{Cost}}{\text{Thousands of people}} = \text{CPM}$$

For example assume "Family Feud" has a rating of 25, reaches 200,000 people in the primary target audience, and costs $2,000 for a 30-second spot on station WXYZ in Everittown, U.S.A. Then,

$$\frac{\$2,000}{25} = \$80 \text{ CPP} \qquad \frac{\$2,000}{200} = \$10 \text{ CPM}$$

Obviously, the lower the cost per thousand, the more efficient the show is against the target audience. The media buyer's task, therefore, is to compare the packages of each station, substituting stronger programs for less efficient ones. For example, prime time may be very

---

FIGURE 14–8

The *Spot Television Rates and Data* listing for WALB–TV in Albany, Georgia, shows the rate charged on its grid plan for various time slots during the week. The grid used will depend on program audience estimates at the time.

WALB-TV
(Airdate April 15, 1954)
ALBANY

 GRAY COMMUNICATIONS SYSTEMS INC.

 **NBC Television Network**

ndb   TvB

Gray Communications Systems, Inc.
Media Code 6 211 0050 2.00   Mid 007346-000
WALB-TV
1709 Stuart Ave., Albany, GA 31707. Phone 912-883-0154, TWX, 810-781-5104.
Mailing Address: Box 3130, Albany, GA 31708.

1. PERSONNEL
Vice-Pres. & Gen'l Mgr.—Raymond E. Carow.
Vice-President Sales—R. Douglas Oliver.
General Sales Manager—Jerry Smithwick.
Chief Engineer—William N. Williams.
Traffic Manager—Susan Seiy.

2. REPRESENTATIVES
Katz Television, Continental.

3. FACILITIES
Video 316,000 w., audio 43,900 w.; ch 10.
Antenna ht.: 958 ft. above average terrain.
Operating schedule: 6:45-2 am Mon thru Fri; 7-1 am Sat; 7-1 am Sun. EST.

4. AGENCY COMMISSION
15% to recognized agencies: no cash discount.

---

5. GENERAL ADVERTISING See coded regulations
General: 2b, 3a, 3b, 3c, 3d, 4a, 5, 6a, 7b, 8.
Rate Protection: 10h, 11h, 12h, 13h, 14h.
Contracts: 20a, 21, 22a, 22c, 23, 26, 28, 29, 30, 31a, 31b, 31c, 32d, 34.
Basic Rates: 40b, 41a, 41b, 41c, 41d, 42, 45a, 47a, 51, 52, 52a.
Cancellation: 70a, 70b, 70g, 72, 73a, 73b.
Prod. Services: 80, 81, 82, 83, 84, 85, 86, 87a, 87b, 87c.
    Medicinal Accounts
Acceptable upon approval of management.
    Premium Offers
Premium mail will be sent to advertisers Post Office Box.
Affiliated with NBC Television Network.

6. TIME RATES
   No. A5 Ann rates eff 10/1/84—Rec'd 10/29/84.
   No. P2 Prog. rates eff 7/20/84—Rec'd 8/14/84.

7. SPOT ANNOUNCEMENTS
30 SECONDS-DAYTIME & FRINGE

	F	I1	I2	I3
MON THRU FRI, AM:				
6-6:30, Sunrise	60	55	45	35
6:30-7, Today In Georgia	80	70	60	55
7-9, Today Show	100	85	75	70
9-10, Hour Magazine	85	70	55	45
10-noon, NBC Rotation	110	90	70	60
PM:				
Noon-12:30, Town & Country	100	85	80	70
12:30-4, NBC Afternoon Rotation	140	130	120	110
4-4:30, Heathcliff	120	100	85	75
4:30-5, happy Days	120	100	95	90
5-5:30, People's Court	140	120	110	100
5:30-6, Three's Company	160	140	120	110
6-7, NewsCenter 10	350	300	275	250
7:30-8, Barney Miller	400	350	275	250
11-11:30 Mon thru Sun, NewsCenter 10	300	250	225	200
11:30 pm-12:30 am, Tonight Show	80	65	55	50
12:30-1:30 am Mon thru Thurs, Late Night w/Letterman	65	50	35	30
12:30 am-concl, Friday Night Videos	65	50	35	25

WEEKEND

SAT, AM:				
7-7:30, Georgia Farm Monitor	100	85	70	40
7:30 am-1 pm, Kid's Rotation	120	100	95	85
PM:				
1-7, Various	120	100	95	85
6-6:30, NewsCenter 10	300	250	225	200
7-8, Hee Haw	350	300	275	250
11:30 pm-12:30 am, Solid Gold	130	110	90	75
12:30 am-concl, Saturday Night Live	90	75	60	50
SUN, AM:				
7-8, Gospel Singing Jubilee	75	60	50	40
8-noon, Religious/Various	70	55	45	40
PM:				
Noon-7, Various	120	100	85	75
6-6:30, NewsCenter 10	300	250	225	200
11:30-concl, Barnaby Jones/Love Boat	65	50	45	40

PRIME TIME

	F	I1	I2	I3	I4
8-11 Mon thru Sat; 7-11 Sun	900	800	700	600	500

60 sec: double the 30 sec.
10 sec: 50% of 30 sec rounded to next dollar.
No 10 seconds within NewsCenter 10.
F—Fixed.
I—Immediately preemptible.

10. PROGRAM TIME RATES

Daily:	1 hr	1/2 hr	1/4 hr	10 min	5 min
8-11 pm	2500	1800	1500	1400	1200
6-8 pm	1500	1200	1100	1050	1000
Noon-6 pm & 11-11:30 pm	1000	600	500	450	400
Sign-on-noon & 11:30 pm-sign-off	600	400	300	250	225

11. SPECIAL FEATURES
    COLOR
Schedules network color, film, slides, tape and live.
Equipped with high and low band VTR.

13. CLOSING TIME
48 hours prior telecast; Sat & Sun material closes at 5 pm Thurs.

strong on one station but news time very weak. The media buyer tries to use the best areas each station has to offer to construct suitable packages. Then the bottom line (cost per thousand) for each station is compared for each daypart considered.

	WAAA		WBBB		WCCC	
	GRPs	CPM	GRPs	CPM	GRPs	CPM
Prime	50	$10.00	55	$9.00	40	$8.50
Fringe	50	5.00	45	6.00	60	4.75

In this situation, WBBB is the first choice for prime time because it is efficient and offers the best audience delivery. WAAA delivers less and costs more. WCCC costs less but doesn't deliver as much. For fringe time, WCCC offers the greatest delivery at the lowest cost. To use two stations' packages for prime and/or fringe, the media buyer tries to negotiate prices to bring the two stations' CPMs into line.

Estimating reach and frequency

As we discussed in Chapter 12 on media planning, the objectives of reach and frequency are very important to the media planner. Therefore, once the package has been determined, the media buyer may ask the rep to do a computer run on the schedule to get an estimate of the expected reach and frequency. To do this, the media rep needs to know the total target audience in each of the dayparts as well as the total GRPs and the number of spots per daypart in the schedule.

Large advertising agencies prepare their own reach and frequency estimates based on their own statistical tables or computer programs. These are too sophisticated for us to consider here. But it is important to realize that, although figures imply preciseness, they are really only estimates based on current state-of-the-art media research principles. Like all statistics, they may vary greatly depending on immeasurable and uncontrollable factors.

Negotiating prices and contracts

While print media normally stick to rate cards because of their guaranteed circulation, broadcast stations are willing to negotiate prices since their audiences are, at best, estimated.

The purpose of price negotiation from the advertiser's standpoint is to get the best schedule possible within the budget. The media buyer contacts the rep and explains what efficiency the advertiser needs, in terms of delivery and CPM, to make the buy. The media buyer rarely discloses other stations' prices but uses CPMs as a negotiating tool in an effort to get the most GRPs within the budget.

Each station contract is a legal document. As such, it is imperative that the media buyer catch any discrepancies before signing it. The contract indicates the dates, times, and programs on which the advertiser's commercials will run, the length of the spots, the rate per spot, and the total amount. The reverse side of the contract defines in small print the various obligations and responsibilities of the advertiser, the agency, and the station, and the terms of payment.

After the spots run, the station returns a form to the advertiser or agency, signed and notarized, indicating when spots aired and what *make-goods* run to compensate for spots the station missed or ran incorrectly. This *affidavit of performance* is the station's legal proof that the advertiser got what was paid for.

USING RADIO IN THE CREATIVE MIX

Everybody knows what a newspaper coupon is. You clip it, take it to the store, and save 15 or 20 cents on a roll of bathroom tissue or a can of dog food. Advertisers invest big budgets in print coupons, but *Advertising Age* reports that only about 4.5 percent of the coupons printed are ever redeemed by shoppers.

McDonald's advertising agency had an idea to use coupons to help promote Big Mac sales. But they gave this idea a creative twist. They introduced radio coupons and used the voices of kids to explain the promotion.

When the campaign broke, the general manager of the agency stated that "if successful, the idea would have long-reaching implications for testing the effectiveness of radio for couponing."

After the campaign, Dale Smith, manager of McDonald's 96-store co-op, reported that the stores had received thousands of coupons (like those shown in Figure 14–9). In most promotions a 10 percent sales increase is considered good. But in this one Big Mac sales increased 15 to 17 percent. And the cost of this promotion against the sales generated was excellent. As a result McDonald's decided to use the coupon promotion with other products.

FIGURE 14–9

CLARA: What are you doing, Glen?

GLEN: Making McDonald's radio coupons.

CLARA: Radio coupons?

GLEN: Don't you listen to the radio, Clara? Place a dollar bill on a piece of paper and draw a dotted line around it.

CLARA: Then what?

GLEN: Than take a pencil, crayons, whatever, and draw a picture of a Big Mac on it.

CLARA: Why, Glen?

GLEN: 'Cause every time you buy a Big Mac, you can turn in your homemade coupon—and get a free regular-size soft drink.

CLARA: Why so many coupons, Glen?

GLEN: 'Cause I love Big Macs— and I love soft drinks.

CLARA: A free soft drink at McDonald's is great but . . .

GLEN: Yeah?

CLARA: Glen, your drawings are silly.

GLEN: They're impressionistic, Clara.

CLARA: Glen, you're a bad artist.

GLEN: I'm paid well.

CLARA: Glen, you're clipping McDonald's.

GLEN: That's the whole idea, Clara.

CLARA: Cut it out, Glen!

GLEN: OK, Clara.

ANNCR: You heard it on radio, folks! Make your own dollar-bill-sized coupon. Draw a Big Mac on it—pencil, ballpoint, colors— whatever. When you buy a Big Mac, turn in your coupons for a free regular-size soft drink. Get cuttin', Washington. Offer ends September 17th.

SINGERS: [*music up*] At McDonald's . . .

GLEN: [*clip-clip-clip*] Clara, that's a beautiful coupon!

SINGERS: *We do it all for you.*

(Two examples of hand-drawn *radio* coupons turned in at McDonald's stores . . . one from a six-year-old, the other from a 25-year-old.)

Since that time, the radio coupon has received wide attention by supermarkets, discount chains, sporting goods dealers, and many other fast-food chains. As a promotional device, radio coupons are just one of the many advantages of using radio in the creative mix. Radio can be fun—it's flexible, it's involving, it's fast, and it can be very inexpensive.

 What Works Best in Radio?

Radio is an integral part of our daily lives. We rely on clock radios to wake us in the morning. At breakfast we tune in the morning news. Radio entertains us while we drive to work or school or do household chores. And chances are good that if you work in an office or plant, you enjoy background music supplied by a local radio station. With its unique ability to relax, inform, and entertain, radio has become the daily companion of millions at work, at play, and on the highway.

In short, radio is a popular medium. In fact, in 1984 people spent more money buying radios than they did buying stereos and phonographs, records, movies, spectator sports, musical instruments, or film developing.

In an average week 95.9 percent of all the people in the United States listen to the radio—over 83 percent on an average day. The average adult spends 3 hours and 28 minutes per day listening to the radio. In fact, radio leads all other media in both daily and weekly reach. This has tremendous implications for advertisers, and, as a result, radio's advertising revenues have grown steadily (Figure 14–10).

The largest national advertisers are food producers, auto manufacturers, travel companies, breweries, wineries, consumer services, drug producers, and cosmetics. But radio's biggest source of revenue

FIGURE   14–10

Daily and weekly reach of major media.

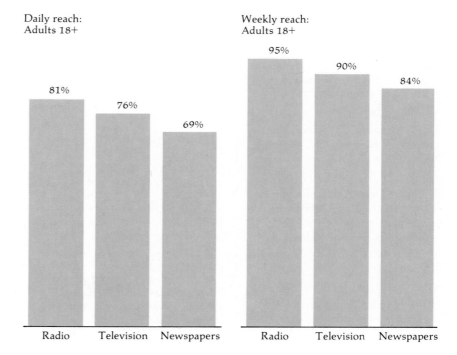

is composed of the many thousands of local neighborhood businesses that use the medium to reach out and talk to their local customers. Of the almost $4.7 billion spent in radio in 1984, over $3.5 billion came from local advertisers. Why is that?

■ Reach and frequency

Radio offers an excellent combination of reach and frequency. With the average adult listening more than three hours a day, radio builds a large audience quickly; and a normal advertising schedule easily allows repeated impact on the listener. The ability to quickly expose the people a sufficient number of times to motivate them to buy makes radio very attractive to local merchants.

■ Selectivity

The wide variety of specialized radio formats available, with their prescribed audiences and coverage areas, enables advertisers to select just the market they want to reach. Commercials can be aimed at listeners of a specific sex, age group, ethnic or religious background, income group, employment category, educational level, or special interest. Whether commercials are intended for middle-aged homemakers or pro football fans, an advertiser is bound to find a station with just the programming to reach these people.

■ Efficiency

Radio's strong appeal to advertisers is large ′ its economy. Radio has the ability to offer its reach, frequency, ar ᵢ selectivity at one of the lowest costs per thousand. Thus, the budget needed for an effective radio schedule is often less than that needed for newspapers, magazines, or television.

In 1984, for example, the cost of buying 25 GRPs on network radio was only $1.70 per thousand. This compares favorably with the cost of daytime network TV, whereas prime-time TV in 1984 cost an average of $3.77 per thousand, national magazines $8.05 per thousand, and newspapers $12 per thousand. In fact, only outdoor consistently offers a lower CPM at $0.51 per thousand impressions.

Radio production is also relatively inexpensive. National spots can usually be produced for 1/10 of the cost of a TV commercial. And in some cases there are no production costs at all since local radio stations frequently produce commercials free for their local advertisers.

■ Drawbacks to Radio

In spite of its great advantages, radio has traditionally suffered from certain limitations: it is only an aural medium; its audience is highly segmented; the advertiser's commercials are short-lived, and often they are only half-heard; or the listener is interrupted causing the advertisers to be heard sporadically or out of context.

■ Limitations of sound

Radio is heard but not seen. This fact can limit the effectiveness of commercials for products that need to be seen to be understood. Advertising agencies often prefer the freedom of creating with sight, sound, color, and motion, as in television. Some see radio as restricting their creative options.

Checklist of what works best in radio

☐ Stretch the listener's imagination. Voices and sounds can evoke pictures.

☐ Listen for a memorable sound. What will make your commercial stand out from the clutter? A distinctive voice, a memorable jingle, a solution to the listener's problem.

☐ Present one idea. It is difficult to communicate more than one idea in a television commercial. In radio, which is subject to more distractions, it is nearly impossible. Be direct and clear.

☐ Select your audience quickly. It pays to flag your segment of the audience at the beginning of the commercial—before they can switch to another station.

☐ Mention your brand name and your promise early. Commercials that do so get higher awareness. It heightens awareness if you mention the brand name and promise *more than once*.

☐ Capitalize on events. Exploit the flexibility of radio to tie in with fads, fashions, news events, or the weather.

☐ Use radio to reach teenagers. Teenagers don't watch much television. They do listen to a lot of radio. Media experts say it's the best way to reach teens. Some say it's the *only* way.

☐ Music can help. It is particularly effective in reaching teenagers who prefer the "now sounds" offered by music stations. You can give your campaign infinite variety with the same lyrics arranged in different ways and sung by different people.

☐ Ask listeners to take action. People respond to radio requests for action. They call the station to exchange views with the disc jockey or ask for certain music. Don't be afraid to ask listeners to call now, or write in, or send money.

Notwithstanding, many brilliant creative efforts have been achieved with radio through the use of "theater of the mind" techniques. Pittsburgh Paints, for example, used a campaign that actually capitalized on radio's aural limitation. "Imagine yellow . . ." the announcer said, and soft music swelled in the background. The campaign, which used the same concept to describe other colors with music, proved to be highly effective. (See the Checklist of what works best in radio.)

Segmented audiences

Radio's ability to deliver highly selective audiences can also be a handicap to some advertisers. The large number of radio stations competing for the same audience may make the purchase of effective airtime very difficult for the advertiser. For example, while one city may have only three television stations, it may have 20 radio stations competing for a market of, say, 1.5 million people. Each of these stations is distinctive in format and programming, ranging from all news and sports to hard rock to country-western music. Clearly, the advertiser who is seeking to blanket this market will have to buy multiple stations; and this may not be cost-effective.

Short-lived and half-heard commercials

A radio commercial is brief and fleeting. You can't keep it like a newspaper or a magazine ad. It lasts only moments, and then it's gone.

For many listeners, radio provides only a pleasant background sound while they are driving to work, reading, studying, or entertaining. Thus, radio must compete with other activities for their attention, and it does not always succeed. As a result some advertisers are skeptical of radio's ability to work for them.

It is for these very reasons that creativity is so important to the success of radio advertising. Monotonous or boring radio commercials simply go in one ear and out the other. The astute advertiser, though, will use radio's unique theater-of-the-mind ability to penetrate the listener's consciousness.

OVERVIEW OF THE
RADIO MEDIUM

Radio is the most subjective of all mass media. It offers a wide variety of program formats like rock, easy listening, all news, middle of the road (MOR), sports, and classical music. Within each format, there is a variety of entertainment and information for the station's audience.

Unlike TV or newspaper, though, radio listening is usually done by one person alone. It is a personal, one-on-one medium. And it is mobile. Radio can entertain a person while driving, while walking, and while at home or away from home. Where commuting is done by automobile, radio is an extremely strong medium. In markets like New York, though, where most commuting is done by train, bus, or subway, newspaper is the stronger "drive time" medium.

Radio is also adaptable to moods. In the morning some people may want to hear the news, upbeat music, or interesting chatter from a disc jockey to help them wake up. In the afternoon the same people may want to unwind with classical or easy-listening music. As a result, most people consistently listen to three or four different radio stations representing different types of programming (Figure 14–11).

For the advertiser, therefore, an appropriate mix of dayparts and formats is important to developing a good radio schedule.

FIGURE   14–11

The Radio Advertising Bureau helps its member-stations by advertising heavily to prospective radio advertisers. Here the bureau promises to deliver "the impact of television at a fraction of the cost"—a take-off on the slogan for Western Union's Mailgram—which, at that time, was handled by the same agency, Trout & Ries.

FIGURE   14–12   Radio's cumulative audience among a range of demographic groups

Audience	Average daily cume			Weekly cume (Mon.–Sun.)			Average hours listening daily		
	Total	Men	Women	Total	Men	Women	Total	Men	Women
Persons 12+	81.4%			95.3%			3:24		
Teens 12–17	91.1			99.9			3:01		
Adults:									
18+		81.9%	78.2%		95.8%	93.6%		3:26	3:28
18–24		88.7	87.1		99.9	98.7		3:58	3:47
25–34		86.7	81.8		99.0	97.0		3:49	3:36
35–49		83.0	80.2		97.2	96.1		3:18	3:41
50+		74.2	70.7		90.4	87.8		2:59	3:06
Household income:									
$25,000+		86.4	85.1		99.8	99.9		3:28	3:39
$20,000–24,999		85.3	81.3		98.1	96.0		3:42	3:34
$15,000–19,999		85.2	81.1		97.7	95.0		3:45	3:42
Under $15,000		73.5	71.6		89.1	88.1		3:07	3:14
College educated		85.8	82.6		97.8	96.5		3:22	3:32

■ Who Uses Radio?

In increasing number, national advertisers are discovering the reach and frequency potential of radio (Figure 14–12). Maxwell House coffee advertised only on television for many years until discovering that coffee consumption declined continually throughout the day. While television reaches most coffee drinkers, it does not do so at the time they are most likely to be drinking coffee. Radio listenership, on the other hand, almost perfectly fits coffee consumption. Also, with radio, Maxwell House could extend its reach from 90 percent to 95 percent, and the cost per thousand was almost a full dollar less than for television.

Office product companies have discovered the same thing. With radio they can reach corporate decision makers more precisely and effectively during drive time while work is still on their minds (Figure 14–13).

Local retailers also like the medium because they can tailor it to their immediate needs, because it offers defined audiences, and because they can create an identity for themselves by doing their own ads.

In Forest City, North Carolina, Henry Bruegge, the owner of House of Gems, devotes 80 percent of his advertising budget to radio. He gets immediate response, and it gives him a chance to tell about his other services (like watch repair), which are an important part of his business. Using two radio stations, he runs an average of 30 to 35 spots a week. For special promotions, the radio stations broadcast from his store. These "remotes" are very successful in drawing traffic and creating an image of activity.

Radio Programming and Audiences

Stations plan their programming carefully in order to reach specific markets and capture as many listeners as possible. The larger its audience, the more a station can charge advertisers for commercial time. Therefore, extensive planning and research go into programming and program changes. When low ratings occur, they can sometimes be reversed by a sharp change in programming. Other times stations may test new program concepts to determine the ones that will attract new listeners.

Most stations maintain the same general type of programming throughout the broadcast week to keep their specific audience. However, they may add special features, such as local sporting events or contests in which prizes or free tickets are awarded, to boost their audience figures.

The most common radio formats have traditionally been progressive rock, contemporary top 40, middle of the road (MOR), "good" music, classical and semiclassical, country-western, all news, and talk.

The perennial favorite of young men and women 18 to 34, progressive rock stations (also called album-oriented rock) base their programming on current big sounds from well-known groups. Often the trendsetters in musical style, the progressive musicians and DJs usually relate closely to their audiences in social, political, and cultural attitudes as well as music (Figure 14–14).

Contemporary top 40 music stations base their programming on current record and album sales. They air the top-selling "hits" throughout the program day. Some feature colorful disc jockeys, with names like Murray the K and Wolfman Jack. Their listeners are chiefly avid, young, black and white teenagers, and their music is described in the trade as having a more "bubblegum" sound. These stations naturally do very well with soft drink advertisers, fast-food outlets, movies, and clothing retailers.

FIGURE 14–13

(The Bloom Agency set a new standard for *chutzpah* in this comparative ad for New York Air.)

SFX: *Meeting noises, conversation.*

ANNCR V.O.: Recently the folks at New York Air made a very intelligent decision.

1ST MAN: Listen, we want people to compare our Boston/La Guardia shuttle with Eastern's, right? So let's give them a free ride on Eastern!

2ND MAN: You mean pay them to fly the competition?

1ST MAN: Exactly!

WOMAN: Great idea!

2ND MAN: Sounds dumb to me!

1ST MAN: It's simple. They fly one way on New York Air, at the $45 peak fare, then we pay them to fly back on Eastern.

SFX: *All meeting members agree.*

2ND MAN: But that's like giving money away.

1ST MAN: No, it's an investment! Once they enjoy all the extras we give them, like a *New York Times* in the morning.

WOMAN: And drinks, wine and snacks all day.

2ND MAN: But—

WOMAN: Even though we don't have back-up sections, we do have seat selection and extra leg room!

2ND MAN: But what if—

1ST MAN: And compared to that Eastern hassle, we. . . .

2ND MAN: (*Speaking over the others*) But what if they like Eastern?

SFX: *Pregnant pause, then hysterical laughter by all. Music up.*

ANNCR V.O.: And so, June 12 is Compare Day on New York Air. To get you to fly us, we'll pay you to fly them. Just call us for details. New York Air, the intelligent shuttle between Boston and La Guardia.

SFX: *Singers and music up.*

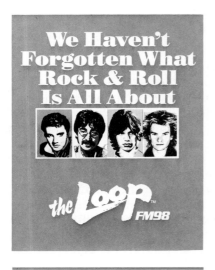

FIGURE 14–14

Chicago's LOOP features popular rock albums for their audience.

Middle of the road (MOR) stations are similar to rock stations in that they play popular current hits. However, they avoid the harsh rhythm and strident sounds that characterize hard rock. Instead they feature popular music, past and present, and subdued rock and roll, and their audiences tend to be somewhat older (25 to 49) and have proportionately higher incomes.

"Good" music stations tend to have older and more mature listeners. They play chiefly instrumental music and some ballads.

Classical/semiclassical offer contemporary classics and music of the "masters" as well as chamber music, opera, and other selections that have passed the test of time. Many such stations lean toward the fuller "concert" sounds. Classical audiences tend to be considerably older (over 35), have substantially higher incomes, be white or Hispanic, and live in the West.

Country and western stations usually feature the "Nashville sounds": ballads, folk, and folk-rock music performed in basic rhythms. There are several types of stations within this category. Some air easy-listening, pop western music. Others tend toward repetitive down-home country ballads. The largest country audiences are in the Midwest, South, and Southwest. They tend to earn less money, be over 35 years old, and be predominantly white.

Unlike most stations, which offer a brief summary of the news every hour or half-hour, all-news stations broadcast continuous news throughout the day. Programs are divided into segments devoted to national, international, regional, and local news. Advertisers tend to favor all-news formats to reach the older, upscale, mature men and women who are interested in business and civic affairs.

"Talk" stations invite listeners to participate in programming by expressing their views and ideas on the air. Typically a personable announcer encourages listeners to air their views by phoning the station and talking with the announcer or with a featured guest. Such programs tend to emphasize lively and controversial issues, bizarre subjects, and sex. Most have a loyal listenership of older men and women at the lower end of the income scale.

In addition to the formats presented above, there are seemingly limitless variations like soft rock, oldies but goodies, disco, and ethnic formats (Spanish, black/soul, etc.), which cater to smaller or more specialized market segments.

BUYING RADIO TIME

As in television buying, advertisers need to have a basic knowledge in order to buy radio effectively. First, it's important to be aware of the types of radio advertising available for commercial use. Second, a basic understanding of radio terminology is necessary. And finally, the advertiser needs to know the steps in preparing a radio schedule.

Types of Radio Advertising

Radio time may be purchased by an advertiser in one of three forms: local, spot, or network. Local purchases account for 75 percent of all radio time sold. Spot radio represents another 20 percent and network 5 percent.

Networks

Advertisers may use one of the national radio networks (ABC, CBS, NBC, Mutual, etc.) to carry their messages to the entire national market simultaneously via the networks' affiliated stations. However, radio networks generally provide much less programming than the TV networks. Most is in the form of hourly newscasts and special news or sports events (Figure 14–15).

In addition, there are more than 100 regional radio networks in the United States which operate as state news and farm networks with information oriented toward specific geographic markets.

The use of networks provides national and regional advertisers with simple administration and low effective net cost per station. The amount of paperwork and clerical time is greatly reduced, and the cost per station is usually lower than if comparable times were bought on individual stations. However, the disadvantage lies in the lack of flexibility in choosing the affiliated stations, the limitation of the number of stations on the network's roster, and the long lead time required to book time.

FIGURE 14–15 Network radio costs

	Radio network	Number of stations	Average 60-second cost	Average 30-second cost
ABC	Information Network	589	$3,560	$1,780
	Entertainment Network	474	$3,560	$1,780
	Contemporary Network	351	$4,900	$2,450
	FM Network	145	$4,000	$2,000
	Rock Radio Network	56	$3,000	$1,500
	Directions Network	97	$1,900	$ 950
CBS	Radio Network	430	$3,600	$1,800
	Drama Network	286	$2,000	$1,000
	Radio Radio	100	$2,300	$1,150
Mutual Broadcasting System		902	$2,100	$1,050
National Black Network		92	$1,000	$ 650
American Black Information Network		50	$ 600	$ 400
NBC	Radio Network	382	$2,600	$1,300
	The Source	190	$4,500	$3,000
RKO	Radio Network I	250	$4,400	$2,200
	Radio Network II	220	$4,400	$2,200
	Radio Network III	225	$6,000	$3,000
Sheridan Broadcasting Network		122	$1,600	$ 800

AD LAB   14–B   The book that makes or breaks radio stations

Two major audience rating services are offered to broadcasters and advertisers. Media buyers use the data obtained by these services as a basis for comparing programs and stations in order to make the right choices.

Arbitron diary

The Arbitron rating service chooses a group of representative listeners and provides them with a diary, which they are instructed to carry with them throughout the day. They are asked to record all the time spent listening to a radio. The diary is returned to Arbitron at the end of the week for tabulation, and a new diary is distributed. The service is available to clients on a subscription basis.

RADAR reports

RADAR (Radio's All-Dimension Audience Research) audience estimates are based on daily telephone interviews that cover seven days of radio listening behavior. The measurements are conducted during four weeks in the spring and four weeks in the fall of each year. The service provides estimates of the audiences of all AM and FM radio stations in total and of several segments of radio use and of the population.

The RADAR studies are jointly sponsored by ABC, CBS, NBC, and the Mutual Broadcasting Company and are available to stations, advertisers, and agencies by subscription.

These rating reports are important not only to advertisers in determining the listenership of a particular station, but to stations as well who may fine tune or completely change their format as a result of the reports.

Laboratory Applications

1. What do you think might be the advantages and disadvantages of the two radio audience measurement methods?

2. Which audience rating method would you consider better? Why?

Spot radio

When national advertisers buy airtime on individual stations, it is referred to as *spot* advertising. Spot advertising should not be confused with spot *announcements,* which is merely another term for individual commercial messages.

Buying spot radio affords advertisers great flexibility in their choice of markets, stations, airtime, and copy. The advertiser can choose as long or as short a flight as is required. In addition, spot advertising enables the message to be presented to listeners at the most favorable times.

By purchasing radio time in this way, commercials can be tailored to the local market. And they can be put on the air quickly. Some stations are willing to run a commercial with just 20 minutes lead time.

Spot advertising also enables advertisers to build local listener acceptance of their product or service by using local personalities or by purchasing airtime on locally produced programs.

Local radio

Local time denotes radio spots purchased by a local advertiser. It involves the same procedure as national spots. The sole difference is the location of the advertiser.

Radio advertising also can be classified as live, taped, or transcribed (a form of record). In recent years there has been a trend toward recorded shows with live news in between. Nearly all radio commercials today are recorded to reduce costs and maintain broadcast quality.

■ Radio Terminology

Buying radio time requires a basic understanding of radio terminology. Naturally, much of the language used for radio advertising is the same as that used for other media. But radio also has numerous terms that are either peculiar to it or have a special meaning when applied to radio advertising.

The most common of these are the concepts of dayparts, average quarter-hour audiences, and cumes (cumulative audiences). Our purpose here is simply to define these terms and their importance to the advertiser. The student of advertising should know, however, that volumes have been written on these subjects in the specialized literature of media planning and radio buying.

■ Dayparts

The radio day is divided into five basic dayparts:

6 a.m.–10 a.m.	Morning drive
10 a.m.–3 p.m.	Daytime
3 p.m.–7 p.m.	Afternoon (or evening) drive
7 p.m.–12 a.m.	Nighttime
12 a.m.–6 a.m.	All night

The rating services (namely, Arbitron and Burke) measure the audiences for only the first four of these dayparts, because all-night listening is very limited and not highly competitive. (See Ad Lab 14–B.)

The heaviest radio use occurs during drive times (6–10 a.m. and 3–7 p.m.) during the week (Monday–Friday). One exception to this is that easy listening (or "good" music) stations traditionally have their heaviest use during daytime (10 a.m.–3 p.m.). Otherwise, drive time is radio's prime time.

This is important to advertisers because, as we mentioned in the case of Maxwell House Coffee, usage and consumption vary for different products. Television advertising in prime time, for example, is seen when viewers are least likely to consume coffee. On the other hand, radio's morning drive time coincides perfectly with most people's desire for a steaming, fresh cup of coffee.

Radio stations base their rates on the time of day the advertiser wants commercials aired. To achieve the lowest rate, an advertiser can order spots on a *run of station* (ROS) basis, similar to ROP in newspaper advertising. However, this leaves total control of spot placement up to the station. Most stations, therefore, offer a *total audience plan* (TAP) package rate, which guarantees a certain percentage of spots in the better dayparts if the advertiser buys the total package of time (Figure 14–16).

Naturally, the subject of daypart advantages can be exhausting for the sophisticated advertiser who has the time, resources, and facilities to study it in depth.

FIGURE 14–16

The *Spot Radio Rates and Data* listing for WNEW–FM radio in New York City shows that spot announcement rates vary from a high of $350 to a low of $75 per minute, depending on the number bought and the dayparts used.

Average quarter-hour

This term is used to identify the average number of people who are listening to a specific station during any 15-minute period of any given daypart. Following is an example of an average quarter-hour listening estimate:

Station	Average ¼ hour; Mon.–Sun., 6 A.M.–midnight; Persons over 12 years old
KAKZ	4,200

This means that any day Monday–Sunday, during any 15-minute period between 6 a.m. and midnight, it is probable (more than likely) that 4,200 people over 12 years old are tuned in to radio station KAKZ (Figure 14–17).

This same idea can be expressed in terms of "share" if the station's audience is shown as a percentage of the total listening audience in the area. For example, in our illustration the total average quarter-hour listening audience for all stations is 48,900. Therefore, the average quarter-hour audience of radio station KAKZ could be expressed as an average quarter-hour "share" of 8.6:

$$\frac{42}{489} = .086 \text{ or } 8.6 \text{ percent}$$

Rating points

By extending our computations a little further, this same audience could be expressed in terms of rating points if we showed it as a percentage of the population. For example, if radio station KAKZ were located in a city of 100,000 people, then its average quarter-hour audience could be expressed as an average quarter-hour "rating" of 4.2:

$$\frac{4,200}{100,000} = .042 \text{ or } 4.2 \text{ percent}$$

FIGURE   14–17

Average quarter-hour listening estimates.

MONDAY–SUNDAY
6:00AM–MIDNIGHT

AVERAGE PERSONS—METRO SURVEY AREA, IN HUNDREDS

STATION CALL LETTERS	TOT. PERS. 12+	MEN 18-24	25-34	35-44	45-54	55-64	WOMEN 18-24	25-34	35-44	45-54	55-64	TNS. 12-17
KAKZ	42	2	6	6	2	1	2	6	6	1		2
KARD	35	1	6	1	4			6	7	3	3	2
KBRA	36		4	1	4	4	1	2	3	3	6	
KEYN	55	13	7	2			8	7	3			15
KFDI	51		2	6	7	3	1	2	8	6	7	
KFDI FM	45	7	2	5	2	2	4	5	8	5	2	1
KFH	58		2	7	4	3	1	5	2	6	3	1
KGCS	15	2	1	2				2	3	1	3	1
KICT	71	23	5	1			13	3				26
KQAM	17	1	5	1		1	3	4		1		1
*KSGL	6				1		1	1	1		1	
KWKN	26	2	7			1	3	8	1	1		1
*KJRG	2									1	1	
KOEZ	7									5	1	
KSKU	3	1						1				1
	489	53	49	33	27	16	45	54	39	37	30	51

TOTAL LISTENING IN METRO SURVEY AREA

SHARES—METRO SURVEY AREA

STATION CALL LETTERS	TOT. PERS. 12+ %	MEN 18-24 %	25-34 %	35-44 %	45-54 %	55-64 %	WOMEN 18-24 %	25-34 %	35-44 %	45-54 %	55-64 %	TNS. 12-17 %
KAKZ	8.6	3.8	12.2	18.2	7.4	6.3	4.4	11.1	15.4	2.7	10.0	3.9
KARD	7.2	1.9	12.2	3.0	14.8		13.3	13.0	7.7	8.1	6.7	3.9
KBRA	7.4		8.2	3.0	14.8	25.0	2.2	3.7	7.7	8.1	20.0	
KEYN	11.2	24.5	14.3	6.1			17.8	13.0	7.7			29.4
KFDI	10.4		4.1	18.2	25.9	18.8	2.2	3.7	20.5	16.2	23.3	
KFDI FM	9.2	13.2	4.1	15.2	7.4	12.5	8.9	9.3	20.5	13.5	6.7	2.0
KFH	11.9		4.1	21.2	14.8	18.8	2.2	9.3	5.1	16.2	10.0	2.0
KGCS	3.1	3.8	2.0	6.1				3.7	7.7	2.7	10.0	2.0
KICT	14.5	43.4	10.2	3.0			28.9	5.6				51.0
KQAM	3.5	1.9	10.2	3.0		6.3	6.7	7.4		2.7		2.0
*KSGL	1.2				3.7		2.2	1.9	2.6		3.3	
KWKN	5.3	3.8	14.3			6.3	6.7	14.8	2.6	2.7		2.0
*KJRG	.4									2.7	3.3	
KOEZ	1.4									13.5	3.3	
KSKU	.6	1.9								2.2		2.0

Determining the gross rating points of a radio schedule, therefore, simply requires multiplying the average quarter-hour rating by the number of spots. For example,

$$4.2 \text{ (rating points)} \times 12 \text{ (number of spots)} = 50.4 \text{ (GRP)}$$

Likewise, the GRPs could also be determined by multiplying the average quarter-hour audience by the number of spots and dividing by the population. For example,

$$\begin{array}{ccc} 4{,}200 & \times \quad 12 \quad = & 50{,}400 \\ \text{(average quarter-} & \text{(number} & \text{(gross} \\ \text{hour audience)} & \text{of spots)} & \text{impressions)} \end{array}$$

Therefore:

$$\frac{50{,}400}{100{,}000} = .504 \text{ or } 50.4 \text{ GRPs}$$

Cume audience

This capsule term for "cumulative audience" describes the total number of *different* people listening to a radio station for at least one 15-minute segment over the course of a given week, day, or daypart (Figure 14–18).

In the example above, we generated 50,400 gross impressions with our schedule on station KAKZ. But that does *not* mean that 50,400 *different* people heard our commercials. Many people might have heard our commercial three, four, or five times, depending on how long they stayed tuned to KAKZ.

By measuring the cumulative number of *different* people listening to KAKZ, the rating services give us an idea of the reach *potential* of our radio schedule.

Thus, *cume* and *average quarter-hour* are important concepts. A high cume figure means that a lot of different people are tuning in to the station for at least 15 minutes. A high average quarter-hour figure usually means that people are listening and staying tuned in.

FIGURE 14–18

Cume listening estimates.

WICHITA, KS

MONDAY-SATURDAY 6:00 AM-10:00 AM

STATION CALL LETTERS	TOTAL PERS. 12+	MEN 18-24	25-34	35-44	45-54	55-64	WOMEN 18-24	25-34	35-44	45-54	55-64	TNS. 12-17
KAKZ	569	28	96	65	28	27	38	79	67	19	25	44
KARD	354	10	78	11	20	9	78	52	38	14	14	25
KBRA	313		36	16	25	31	8	23	33	40	39	6
KEYN	549	101	79	27	5		78	61	44	4	4	147
KFDI	467		18	71	43	58	15	28	57	36	47	13
KFDI FM	332	36	36	27	20	13	31	42	38	37	14	19
KFH	648	10	24	60	62	58	15	65	34	55	54	6
KGCS	137	18	12	22	10		9	34	15	11		6
KICT	428	138	36		5		46	24	14			165
KQAM	254	27	48	21		13	31	65		10	7	32
KSGL	82		6	11	14		15	14	9		4	
KWKN	413	55	66	21	18	4	38	71	28	11	14	19
KJRG	23			5						6	7	
KOEZ	57			11	4				21	7		
KSKU	35	18					5		6			6
METRO TOTALS	2867	257	323	218	174	141	224	309	230	183	161	353

MONDAY-SATURDAY 10:00 AM-3:00 PM

STATION CALL LETTERS	TOT. PERS. 12+	MEN 18-24	25-34	35-44	45-54	55-64	WOMEN 18-24	25-34	35-44	45-54	55-64	TNS. 12-17
KAKZ	361	9	65	21	14	13	23	56	58	8	14	18
KARD	200		36	5	16		31	52	28	6	7	19
KBRA	300		24	11	19	22	15	14	14	40	47	
KEYN	413	55	78	11			32	65	29	4		139
KFDI	426	9	18	43	44	44	23	14	57	25	57	6
KFDI FM	305	54	30	32	14	9	38	28	43	8	11	19
KFH	435	9	24	33	36	44	23	33	24	27	39	6
KGCS	133	18	12	21	9			14	24	11	7	12
KICT	404	147	42	11			70	28	9			101
KQAM	174	9	30	11		4	31	52	9	4	7	12
KSGL	68				14		15	9	9			7
KWKN	321	9	55	11	4	4	48	72	19	6	7	38
KJRG	41			9	4			9	6	4		
KOEZ	85			14	4		8		5	29	11	
KSKU	47	9	12				15	5				6
METRO TOTALS	2407	210	246	152	137	115	232	277	206	137	136	284

For the beginning advertising student, it is important to remember one basic concept about these radio audience measurements. They are derived from the manipulation of statistical data, which involves a complex weighting of various members of the station's surveyed audience. These manipulations produce an important result: Generating the average quarter-hour audience figure is dependent on the *length of listening*. The longer the survey respondent listens, the larger the average quarter-hour audience will be. The cumulative audience is dependent on numerous *different* people tuning in to the radio station. The more respondents that tune in, the higher the cume will be.

Thus, the most stable (accurate) number for estimating the size, scope, and depth of a radio station is the cume. This is because, in the rating service's survey, the cume number is based on a larger sample size!

■ How to Prepare a Radio Schedule

A procedure similar to that discussed in the television section is used by advertisers to prepare their radio schedules. The steps are as follows:

1. Identify those stations with the greatest concentration (cume) of the advertiser's target audience by demographics (e.g., men 25 to 34). As we pointed out previously, the cume figure gives us the best idea of the reach potential of our radio schedule.
2. Identify those stations by format type (e.g., hard rock, MOR) that typically offer the highest concentration of potential buyers. We may know, for instance, that while many men and women between the ages of 35 and 49 may listen to a beautiful music station, the best format for potential tire purchasers in that age group is an all-news or sports format.
3. Determine what time periods (dayparts) on those stations offer the greatest number (average quarter-hour) of potential buyers. Here again, it is more likely that our prospective tire buyers will be concentrated in drive time rather than midday.
4. Using the stations' rate cards for guidance, construct a schedule with a strong mix of these best time periods. An average weekly spot load per station may be anywhere from 12 to 30 announcements depending on the advertiser's budget. At this point, it is often wise to contact the station reps, give them a breakdown of your media objectives, suggest a possible budget for their station, and ask what they can give you for that budget. This gives the media buyer a starting point for analyzing costs and negotiating the buy.
5. Determine the cost for each 1,000 *target* people each station delivers. The operational word here is "target." We are not interested in the station's total audience.
6. Negotiate and place the buy.
7. Assess the buy (with the help of the agency's or radio station's computer) in terms of reach and frequency.

While these steps are far from all-inclusive, they demonstrate some of the complexity media planners and buyers deal with daily in their efforts to match the advertiser's message with a target audience on radio.

Summary

As a means of reaching the masses, no other medium today has the unique creative ability of television. It offers the combination of sight and sound and movement, the opportunity to demonstrate the product, the believability of seeing it happen right before your eyes, and the empathy of the viewer.

Television has grown faster than any other advertising medium in history because of the unique advantages it offers advertisers: mass coverage at low cost, audience selectivity, impact, prestige, and social dominance.

While television's power as a creative tool may be unmatched, the medium still has many drawbacks. These include cost, brevity, clutter, and lack of selectivity.

The heaviest viewers of television are middle-income, high school-educated people and their families. Over the years television viewing has steadily increased. By 1985 the average household TV usage reached nearly seven hours daily.

There are three forms of television advertising: network, spot, and local. Within these classifications, there are many commercial opportunities for advertisers. These are generally grouped as sponsorships, participations, and spot announcements.

To determine which shows to buy, the media buyer must select the most efficient ones against the target audience. The task, therefore, is to compare the packages of each station, substituting stronger programs for less efficient ones, and negotiating prices to get the best buy.

Radio is also recognized as a highly creative medium. However, its greatest attribute is probably its ability to offer the combination of excellent reach and frequency to selective audiences at a very efficient price. Its drawbacks relate to the limitations of sound, the fact that radio audiences are very segmented, and the nature of short-lived and half-heard commercials.

Radio stations are normally classified by the programming they offer and the audiences they serve. The most common radio formats are progressive rock, contemporary top 40, middle of the road, "good" music, classical, country-western, all news, and talk.

Radio time may be purchased by an advertiser in one of three forms: local, spot, or network.

Buying radio time requires a basic understanding of radio terminology. The most common terms are dayparts, average quarter-hour, and cumulative audiences.

Questions for review and discussion

1. What are the advantages of television advertising for a convenience good manufacturer?
2. Of the various kinds of commercial opportunities available on television, what do you think is the best? Why?
3. What does the term "spot" mean?
4. What is the difference to a media planner between TVHH and HUT and between program rating and share of audience?
5. What would you do to purchase time from a local television station? Outline the procedure you would follow.
6. What would you do if you noticed that your company's TV spot didn't run correctly on a local station?
7. Why do you suppose some advertisers don't believe in the effectiveness of radio advertising?
8. What is the format of the radio station you listen to most? How would you describe the demographics of its target audience?
9. What is the difference between average quarter-hour and cume audiences? Which is the better measure for media planners?
10. What is the importance of dayparts to advertisers?

15

DIRECT MAIL AND OUT-OF-HOME MEDIA

B ecause its publications are not sold on newsstands or in bookstores, the National Geographic Society has learned how to use direct mail effectively to market to its membership its monthly yellow-bordered journal and many special books. *Journey into China*, a recently published 518-page book with 400 full-color illustrations, was the beneficiary of this long experience.

The Society had set aside $1.8 million to sell 380,000 copies of the new book to its members and subscribers. The offer included a separate wall map of China.

Before putting all $1.8 million into a mass mailing, the Society conducted a test mailing. One thing it wanted to find out was which of three prices to sell the book for: $19.95, $22.95, or $24.95. In addition, for the first time it offered the option of buying a more expensive deluxe edition for an extra $10.

The test also sought to determine which of two brochure covers would work best. One displayed a photograph of a person carrying two baskets through a deep-green rice paddy, bannered with the caption "Take a spectacular tour of today's China." The other cover was red with a small color photograph of a pagoda and a waterfall; its caption read "Take a family tour of China for only (book's price)."

The brochure was accompanied by a perforated order card and a blue and black two-tone photograph of the Forbidden City in Peking. A four-page sales letter on National Geographic Society letterhead used the blue and black ink for alternating paragraphs. The package was completed with a half-page letter from the publisher folded inside a small map of China.

The version with the photograph of the rice paddy achieved the best response in the test, so it was chosen for the mass mailing. And the most profitable price turned out to be $19.95.

The results were stunning. It was the second most successful direct-mail campaign for a single book in the Society's history. The original mailing to Society members produced sales of more than 410,000 (a 4.28 percent response), well above the goal of 380,000. Moreover, 30 percent requested the deluxe edition. Since only 420,000 copies were printed in the first run, two additional press runs of 50,000 were required that year to fill later orders resulting from an insert card sent out with bills and from the Society's Christmas catalog (Figure 15–1).[1]

DIRECT MAIL AS A MEDIUM

Direct-mail advertising is the term given to all forms of advertising sent direct to prospects through the U.S. Postal Service or private services. In dollars spent, direct mail is the third-ranked advertising medium today, surpassed only by newspapers and television.

No matter how large or small a company may be, direct mail is nearly always used in its advertising program. When a firm starts in business, its first medium of advertising is generally direct mail. And as it grows, it usually continues to use direct mail. The reason is clear. The shortest distance between two points is a straight line. And of all the media, direct mail offers the "straightest" line to the desired prospect.

■ Direct Mail versus Direct Marketing

Several popular terms are frequently confused with *direct mail*. These include *direct marketing, direct response advertising, direct advertising,* and *mail-order advertising.* How are these terms similar, and how do they differ?

Direct marketing is a marketing system in which the advertiser uses the media to build a database of customers. The choice of media can be direct mail, newspapers, magazines, radio, or television used singly or in combination. The objective of direct marketing is to get inquiries, to sell merchandise or services direct, to get contributions, or to get people to visit stores. Underlying all direct marketing success is the ability to trigger a direct, measurable action that is cost-effective. This can be achieved by using any of these selling methods: (*a*) buyer seeks out seller through a retailer or exhibit, (*b*) seller seeks out buyer through personal selling, or (*c*) buyer seeks out seller by mail or phone in order to obtain a mail order.[2]

Direct response advertising is a message that asks the reader, listener, or viewer for an immediate response. A newspaper ad, for example, may ask the reader to fill in and mail a featured coupon to obtain free information about mutual funds or other financial products (Figure 15–2). Direct response advertising can take the form of direct mail, or it can use a wide range of other media, from matchbook covers or magazines to radio or TV.

Mail-order advertising is both a form of direct response advertising and a method of selling in which the product or service is promoted through advertising and the prospect orders it *through the mail* (Figure 15–3). It involves no intermediate salespeople. As it is practiced today, mail-order advertising may be received in any of three distinct forms: mail-order catalogs (like Sears or Spiegel); advertisements in a wide variety of print and electronic media; and direct-mail advertising.

Direct advertising is any form of advertising issued direct to the prospect through the use of the mails, salespeople, dealers, or other

FIGURE   15–1

National Geographic's direct-mail package included a four-page sales letter, a brochure, a duotone photograph of the Forbidden City, a half-page letter from the publisher folded inside a map of China, and a perforated order card, all to promote its book *Journey into China.*

FIGURE 15–2

The Bank of Boston may not want to tell you what they're about, but they do want you to send in the coupon. Actually, the great amount of gratis white space has the effect of directing the reader's eye directly to the action device. Their hope, in this case, is that that's all they need to get the inquiry.

means. It does not involve the traditional mass media. Such advertising may take the form of door-to-door circulars, telephone solicitations, handbills, or direct mail.

Direct mail is any form of direct advertising that is sent through the mail. It is perhaps the most popular form of direct advertising today. A brochure sent to a prospect by mail is direct-mail advertising. But if the same brochure is distributed door to door, it is not direct mail. (It is still direct advertising.) The difference, then, is the method of distribution.

◼ Growth of Direct Mail

Direct mail is successful because it uniquely meets the needs of today's changing lifestyles. Whereas consumers and businesspeople once shopped at local stores, rising fuel costs and parking inconve-

FIGURE 15–3   Top 10 mail-order product categories

Rank	Category	Sales ($ millions)	Rank	Category	Sales ($ millions)
1	Insurance	4,000	6	Collectibles	920
2	General merchandising/home furnishings/housewares/gifts	2,700	7	Sporting goods	780
			8	Crafts	550
3	Magazine subscriptions	1,900	9	Foods	500
4	Books	1,388	10	Records and tapes	478
5	Ready-to-wear	1,340			

FIGURE   15–4   Attitudes toward consumer response advertising

I would buy more via direct response if:	Percent of all adults	I would buy more via direct response if:	Percent of all adults
I could be sure I would get what I expected.	79	It were easier to get problems straightened out.	69
Offers were from companies I could trust.	78	Offers were from well-known company.	64
They offered things I couldn't buy near me.	77	I were offered a free-trial period to examine order.	61
It were easier to return merchandise.	77	I were billed after order is received.	59
They gave me a money-back guarantee.	75	I could pay over a period of time	43
Prices were lower.	74	I could use my credit card.	40
They offered things that interest me.	71	They gave me a charge account.	28
They sent me receipt or confirmation of order.	70		

nience have made at-home and in-office shopping increasingly appealing. Also, shoppers can get more detailed product information through direct mail. Added to this, all product claims made "in writing" make the seller liable for their accuracy (Figure 15–4).

The entry of mass marketers into direct-mail advertising has greatly spurred its growth. Food and detergent industries mail cents-off coupons by the millions. Product makers combine their offers in big "package" mailings. More recent has been the debut of free direct-mail "homemaker" magazines that combine interesting recipes and household hints with coupons and premium offers by multiple "co-op" advertisers.

Direct-mail advertising also has boomed as a result of the consumer credit card explosion. Credit-based mass marketers have expanded their profits by stuffing monthly customer statements with tempting mail-order product offers from small personal items to major appliances. And the increased availability of credit has enabled them to sell high-priced items to consumers. Products that are innovative, can be shipped fairly easily, and are not readily available through other distribution channels are the most likely candidates for direct-mail selling.

Another reason for the success of direct mail is that it gets into your home when a salesperson cannot. And it gets your attention. In effect, mail is the most important person-to-person medium.

Direct-mail advertising is being used by most companies across America, from the neighborhood garage to giant industrial leaders like U.S. Steel and Xerox. More than 250,000 firms have third-class mailing permits. And the growing use of direct-mail advertising has spawned scores of private postal services that operate chiefly to deliver advertising mail.

USING DIRECT MAIL
IN THE CREATIVE MIX

Direct mail is an efficient, effective—and economical—medium for sales and business promotion. Thus, it is used by a wide variety of retail, commercial, and industrial companies, charity and service organizations, and individuals. Direct mail can also increase the effectiveness of advertising in other media if carefully coordinated. The *Reader's Digest*, for example, uses TV spots in conjunction with its direct-mail campaigns to alert viewers to the coming arrival of their direct-mail contest promotions (Figure 15–5).

What Works Best in Direct Mail?

Next to the personal sales call, direct mail is the most effective medium an advertiser can use to put a message in front of a prospect. However, it is also the most expensive on a cost per exposure basis.

As a medium competing for advertisers' dollars, direct mail traditionally offers several key advantages over its competition.

Selectivity

Direct mail enables the advertiser to select only the prospects he or she wants to reach. By mailing only to these prime prospects—the ones most likely to buy the product or service—the advertiser can reduce sales costs and increase profits.

For example, if you wanted to advertise a 10-gallon paint compressor to professional painters, you wouldn't want to use TV. TV's reach is too broad, and you would have to pay for the total audience. But by acquiring a list of professional painters and mailing your message directly to them, you could reach your desired audience more effi-

FIGURE 15–5

Banana Republic achieved smashing success in a very short time by widely distributing its direct-mail catalog through the mail and as an insert in daily papers. This effort was supported by a highly graphic newspaper ad campaign using exactly the same illustrations as the catalog. The result: lines of customers ready to buy their Army-surplus-like safari clothes while other stores in the same area are vacant.

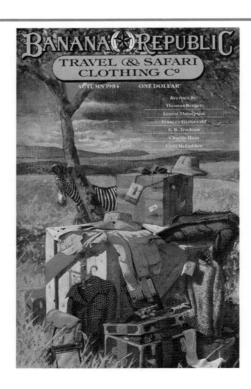

ciently, at a lower cost, and with greater results. Today the availability of computerized mailing lists enables advertisers to obtain the names of a variety of occupational groups in specific regions or states and in given age groups, income categories, and other classifications. (See Ad Lab 15–A.)

AD LAB 15–A   College grad gets job through mail

A 21-year-old college graduate of Glassboro State College (B.A. in communications/liberal arts) skillfully used his education in direct response marketing to get a job.

He sought to test a direct-mail package and personal sales presentation in the Philadelphia area before proceeding to New York, to meet industry leaders, to secure at least 10 interviews at direct response marketing agencies in New York City, and to obtain two job offers.

His marketing plan included a direct-mail package, a mailing envelope, a letter to get interest, a folder to explain the product, and a reply card to make responding easier. Two weeks following the mail drop, he initiated a telephone call to each nonrespondent. The purpose was to confirm receipt of the direct-mail package and to ask for a personal interview.

Chief executive officers or presidents of direct response marketing agencies, or of direct response divisions of advertising agencies were contacted. The test market was composed of medium to large size advertising agencies in the Philadelphia area who listed direct-mail or direct response advertising as part of their media breakdown.

The Philadelphia list was compiled from an area business publication, *Focus Magazine*, which annually devotes one issue to Philadelphia's advertising agencies. The information listed is basically the same as the Redbook.

The initial mailing consisted of 43 pieces to Philadelphia mailed the first week of June and later 24 pieces to New York, mailed the first week of July. The total allocated budget for this program was $723.

The result of this campaign was that the graduate secured nine interviews in New York City and received two job offers in New York City.

Laboratory Application

If you were to prepare a job-hunting direct-mail advertising campaign for yourself, what reader benefits would you include? (See Chapter 8 on copywriting.)

Figure 15–6

Flexibility and control of size, design, color, and budget are two of the most appealing features of direct-mail advertising.

Intensive coverage and extensive reach

Most of the mass media are limited in the number of readers, viewers, or listeners they can reach. Not all viewers, for example, have their TV sets tuned to the same channel at the same time to see a given commercial. Not everyone in a community subscribes to and reads the local newspaper on the day a given ad is run. But virtually everyone has a mailbox and, by using direct mail, an advertiser can achieve 100 percent coverage of the homes in a given area. Direct mail literally reaches out and touches everyone you select.

Flexibility

There are few limitations on direct-mail format, style, or capacity. In addition, the wide variety of materials and processes available enable direct-mail advertising to be uniquely creative and novel, limited only by the ingenuity of the advertiser, by the size of the advertising budget, and by the regulations of the U.S. Postal Service (Figure 15–6).

The direct-mail piece may be a simple postcard or letter, or it may be a large folded broadside, multipage brochure, or even a box. The advertiser can tell the prospect a little bit or include all the details necessary to understand a complex product (Figure 15–7).

Moreover, the advertiser can usually produce a direct-mail piece and distribute it in considerably less time than it would take with most other mass media. So when speed is important, direct mail is usually considered.

Control

Direct-mail advertisers have a high degree of control over the circulation and the quality of the message. They can choose the exact audience they want as well as the number of recipients and their locations, ages, gender, and other factors.

Preprinted direct-mail pieces enable a large advertiser, such as a department store chain, to control the quality of advertising reproduction for all its outlets. In contrast, a retail organization conducting a chainwide advertising campaign in 16 different newspapers is likely to find significant differences in their quality of printing, page placement, position, and reader responses.

Personal impact

Direct mail can be conceived and personalized to the needs, wants, and whims of specific audiences. The privacy of direct mail also allows the advertiser to make special offers to a specific group without offending other prospects or customers. And a customer acquired by mail often remains a mail-oriented customer and can be sold again and again, often without expensive sales calls, by using highly-targeted direct-mail promotions (Figure 15–8).

These factors, however, can also cause occasional problems for unwary advertisers. One major airline invited company executives to bring their wives along on their next flight and then sent a cordial thank-you note to each "wife." Unfortunately, some of the wives who received these notes hadn't gone on the flights after all. The airline's gracious effort not only unsettled a number of households, but also lost at least a few executive customers—perhaps perma-

Figure 15–7

Federal Express used a direct-mail solicitation and an offer of a telephone as a premium to promote its new Saturday service.

nently. The personal nature of direct mail requires more caution—and discretion—by the advertiser than most other media. (See the Checklist of what works best in direct mail.)

Exclusivity

When the prospect opens the mailbox and takes out a piece of direct-mail advertising, competitive distractions are at a minimum. In contrast, a magazine contains many eye-catching ads as well as articles, stories, and illustrations. These distractions reduce the attention that the reader is likely to give to a single ad.

Response

Direct mail normally achieves the highest percentage of response per thousand people reached than any other advertising medium. And with direct mail, it's easy to measure the results. In addition, direct mail is unique in its ability to measure the performance of a campaign strategy. As a rule of thumb, the direct-mail advertiser receives 15 percent of the responses within the first week of a mailing and therefore knows almost immediately if the campaign is going to be successful.

This relatively short-term measurement affords the advertiser still another advantage. The early stages of a campaign can be used to test product acceptability, pricing, audiences, offers, copy approaches, sales literature, and so on to analyze prospect reactions. Like the National Geographic Society, direct-mail advertisers often test two or more different approaches to a campaign before deciding on the final format and contents. Direct mail also can be used to determine the most effective appeals for other media.

Drawbacks to Direct Mail

Although direct mail's advantages are many and unique, it also offers certain disadvantages over other media forms.

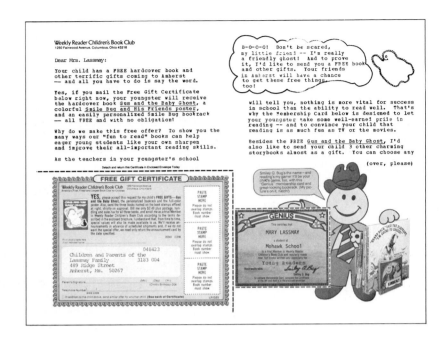

FIGURE   15–8

This personalized direct-mail piece invites a young girl and her parents to join a children's book club.

High cost per exposure

Direct mail has the highest cost per thousand prospects of any of the major media—about 14 times as much per thousand readers as most magazine and newspaper advertising. The reasons for this are apparent. Postal rates have soared in recent years and are continuing to climb. Paper costs also have risen sharply. Production and printing costs, particularly for full-color mailers, are at an all-time high. Even a one-page sales letter cannot be produced and printed and prepared for mailing for much less than $85 per thousand, and that doesn't include postage (Figure 15–9).

Delivery delays

A newspaper offers subscribers precise delivery times. The Sunday morning paper, for example, is home-delivered on Sunday mornings. Similarly, radio and TV shows are nearly always aired at the exact time scheduled. However, the U.S. Postal Service makes no delivery commitments on third-class mail. This may pose problems, particularly for "dated" mailers. Large retail stores generally allow 48 to 72 hours for the mail delivery of special "sale" announcements. In some cases, however, "sale" mailers have arrived four to six days after a sale ended.

Lack of content support

Magazine advertising usually owes its readership to the articles, stories, and illustrations that surround it. Direct mail, on the other hand, has to stand alone; it must capture and hold the reader's attention without assistance. For this reason, direct-mail advertising must be conceived, written and produced very carefully. To be successful, it must combine strong verbal and non-verbal appeals in an attractively laid out and well-produced format.

Checklist of what works best in direct mail

☐ Make sure your offer is right. More than any other element, what you offer the consumer—in terms of product, price, or premium—will make the difference. Consider combinations instead of single units, optional extras, different opening offers, and commitment periods. *Free* is the most powerful offer you can make, but beware of its attracting lookers instead of buyers.

☐ Demonstrate your product. Offer a free sample, or enclose a sample if you can. Sampling is the most expensive promotion in absolute cost, but is often so effective that the investment is quickly paid back with a larger business base. If you measure response on a profit per piece mailed, it sometimes pays to spend a few more cents.

☐ Use the envelope to telegraph your message. Direct mail must work fast. Your envelope has only seconds to interest the prospect, or go unopened into the wastebasket.

☐ Have a copy strategy. Like any other advertising medium, direct mail will be more productive if you decide *in advance* the important issues of target audience, consumer benefit, and support, tone, and personality. While your promise should relate specifically to your product, experts say the most potent appeals in direct mail are how to make money, save money, save time, or avoid effort.

☐ Grab the reader's attention. Every beginning copywriter in direct mail learns the AIDA formula. The letters stand for the ideal structure of a sales letter: Attention, Interest, Desire, Action. Look for a dramatic opening, one that speaks to the reader in a very *personal* way.

☐ Don't be afraid of long copy. The more you tell, the more you sell—particularly if you're asking the reader to spend much money or invest time. The Mercedes-Benz Diesel car letter was five pages long. A Cunard Line letter for ocean cruises was eight pages long. The key to long copy is *facts*. Be specific, not general. Make the letter visually appealing. Break up the copy into smaller paragraphs and emphasize important points with underlines or handwritten notes. Including several pieces in a direct-mail package often improves response.

☐ Don't let the reader off the hook. Leave your readers with something to do, so that they won't procrastinate. It's too easy to put off a decision. Use action devices like a yes/no token to be stuck on a reply card. *Involvement* is important. Prod them to act *now*. Set a fixed period of time, like 10 days. Or make only a limited supply available. Make it extremely easy for the reader to respond to your offer. But always ask for the order.

☐ Pretest your promises and headlines. Don't guess at what will appeal to the reader. There are many ways to sell your product benefits, and as many inexpensive testing methods. Avoid humor, tricks, or gimmicks. It pays to be serious and helpful.

Selectivity problems

If the advertiser incorrectly indentifies the prime audience for the mailing or does not obtain a good list of prospects, the mailing may fail.

Some groups of prospects have been saturated by volumes of mail and are therefore less responsive than others to direct-mail advertising (Figure 15–10). Physicians, for example, are the target of many financial, real estate, and insurance advertisers because of their favorable income image. The result is that the response rate among physicians is lower than that among most other professional groups.

WORKSHEET FOR PLANNING PROFITABLE MAILINGS

Date: June 27, 1985

PROPOSITION   Underwater Watch   KEY   64

1. Price of Merchandise or Service.. | **$25.00**

2. Cost of Filling the Order

    a) Merchandise or Service.. | $5.00
    b) Royalty... | —
    c) Handling Expense... | .75
    d) Postage and Shipping Expense............................. | .60
    e) Premium Including Handling and Postage............... | .30
    f) Use Tax, if any (1 × 15%)................................... | .75
    TOTAL COST OF FILLING THE ORDER...................... | | 7.40

3. Administrative Overhead

    a) Rent, Light, Heat, Maintenance, Credit Checking, Collections, etc. (10% of #1)...... | 2.50
    TOTAL ADMINISTRATION COST................................ | | 2.50

4. Estimated Percentage of Returns, Refunds or Cancellations.......................... | 10%

5. Expense of Handling Returns

    a) Return Postage and Handling (2c plus 2d)............ | 1.35
    b) Refurbishing Returned Merchandise (10% of #2a)... | .50
    TOTAL COST OF HANDLING RETURNS..................... | 1.85

6. Chargeable Cost of Returns (10% of $1.85)................................ | | .19
7. Estimated Bad Debt Percentage... | 10%
8. Chargeable Cost of Bad Debts (#1 × #7).................................. | | 2.50
9. Total Variable Costs (#2 plus #3, #6, and #8)........................... | | 12.59
10. Unit Profit after Deducting Variable Costs (#1 less #9)............... | | 12.41
11. Return Factor (100% less #4)... | 90%
12. Unit Profit Per Order (#10 × #11)....................................... | | 11.17
13. Loss Per Unit Profit Due to Returned Merchandise (10% of #2a)...... | | .50
14. Net Profit Per Order (#12 less #13)..................................... | | 10.67
15. Cost of Mailing Per 1,000... | 96.03
16. NUMBER OF ORDERS PER 1,000 NEEDED TO BREAK EVEN.......... | | 9.0

FIGURE   15–9

Projection of costs and profits is essential in planning a successful direct-mail campaign.

 Types of Direct Mail

Direct-mail advertising has many forms. These include sales letters, brochures, and even handwritten postcards. The message can be as short as one sentence or dozens of pages long. And within each format—from tiny coupon to giant 100-page catalog—there can be almost infinite variety.

Sales letters are the most common form of direct mail. They can be typewritten, typeset and printed, printed with a computer insert (such as your name), or fully computer-typed. They are often mailed with brochures, price lists, or reply cards and envelopes.

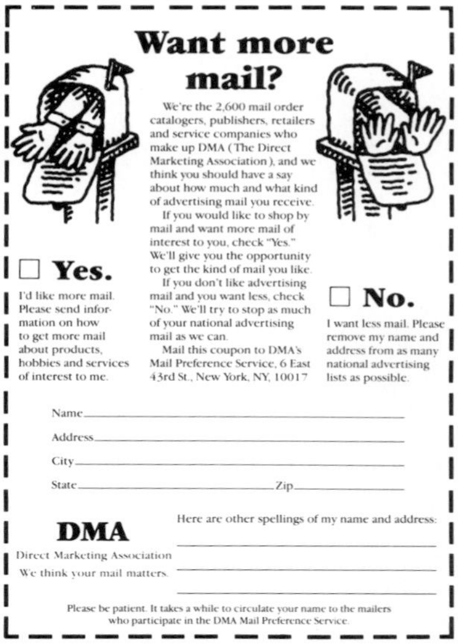

Want more mail?

We're the 2,600 mail order catalogers, publishers, retailers and service companies who make up DMA (The Direct Marketing Association), and we think you should have a say about how much and what kind of advertising mail you receive.
If you would like to shop by mail and want more mail of interest to you, check "Yes."
We'll give you the opportunity to get the kind of mail you like.
If you don't like advertising mail and you want less, check "No." We'll try to stop as much of your national advertising mail as we can.
Mail this coupon to DMA's Mail Preference Service, 6 East 43rd St., New York, NY, 10017.

☐ **Yes.**
I'd like more mail. Please send information on how to get more mail about products, hobbies and services of interest to me.

☐ **No.**
I want less mail. Please remove my name and address from as many national advertising lists as possible.

Name_____
Address_____
City_____
State_____ Zip_____

DMA
Direct Marketing Association
We think your mail matters.

Here are other spellings of my name and address:
_____
_____

Please be patient. It takes a while to circulate your name to the mailers who participate in the DMA Mail Preference Service.

FIGURE 15–10

Direct mail is just too expensive to waste on people who don't want it. For those who want to reduce the amount of direct mail they receive, the DMA offers a unique service. It has informed more than 30 million readers that they could obtain a name-removal form from the DMA Mail Preference Service. This form, the ad explains, will enable them to remove their name from advertiser mailing lists. The names and addresses on these forms are recorded on magnetic tape and made available to mailing-list brokers and advertisers. The same campaign also offers readers a chance to receive more direct mail if they want it—particularly in their specialized areas of interest. Of all the responses received, over 35 percent have been requests from people who want it. DMA also offers a telephone preference service for consumers who wish to have their names removed from national commercial calling lists.

Postcards are generally used to announce sales, offer discounts, or otherwise generate customer traffic. Postcards may travel by first- or third-class mail. The first-class postcard may feature a handwritten message. Third-class postcards, however, must be printed and may not contain any handwritten material.

Some advertisers use a double postcard. This enables them to send both an advertising message and a perforated reply card. A recipient who wants the product or service advertised simply tears off the reply card and mails it back to the advertiser. To encourage this, some advertisers use a postpaid reply card. This requires having a first-class postal permit, which is available for a nominal fee from the local postmaster.

Leaflets or *flyers* are generally a single, standard-size (8-1/2 by 11 inch) page printed on one or both sides and folded one or more times. They usually accompany a sales letter and are used to supplement or expand the information it contains.

Folders are larger than leaflets in most cases and are printed on heavier paper stock. Their weight and size enable them to "take" a printed visual image well. They are often designed with photos or other illustrations, usually in full color. Folders can accommodate a longer, more detailed sales message than most leaflets. Often they are folded and sent as self-mailers, without envelopes, for increased economy.

Broadsides are larger than folders. Though sometimes used as window displays or wall posters in stores, they can be folded to a compact size that will fit into a mail bag.

Self-mailers are any form of direct mail (postcards, leaflets, folders, broadsides, brochures, catalogs, house organs, magazines) that can travel by mail without an envelope. Such mailers are usually folded and secured by a staple or seal. They have a special blank space on which the prospect's name and address can be written, stenciled, or labeled.

Reprints are direct-mail enclosures that are frequently sent by public relations agencies or departments. They are duplications of publication articles that show the company or its products in a favorable light.

Statement stuffers are advertisements that are enclosed in the monthly customer statements mailed by department stores, banks, or oil companies. A wide variety of products—from camping equipment to stereo systems—is sold in this way. To order, all the customer needs to do is write the credit card number on the reply card.

House organs are publications produced by business organizations. They take many forms, including stockholder reports, newsletters, consumer magazines, and dealer publications. Most are produced by the company's advertising or public relations department, or by its agency. Today an estimated 10,000 different house organ publications are mailed in the United States each year and read by more than 3.5 million people.

Catalogs are reference books that list, describe, and often picture the products sold by a manufacturer, wholesaler, jobber, or retailer. Nearly everyone is familiar with the Sears, Roebuck and Montgomery Ward catalogs, but similar catalogs are mailed by the millions each year by industrial, mail-order, and retail firms (Figure 15–11).

FIGURE 15–11

Catalog cover for Esprit sportswear.

Manufacturer's catalogs often have looseleaf formats. This enables the easy insertion or removal of pages as products are added to or withdrawn from the company line. The use of looseleaf catalog sheets also enables the manufacturer to mail them individually as sales literature.

BUYING DIRECT MAIL

Direct-mail advertising entails three basic costs: (1) list rental or purchase; (2) conception, production, and handling of the direct mailer; and (3) distribution.

Direct-Mail Lists

Bob Stone speaks of mailing lists as being the "heart" of every direct-mail operation. Each list, he points out, actually defines a market segment. These may be grouped as house lists, mail response lists, and compiled lists.[3]

1. *House lists.* A company's customers are its most important asset. It stands to reason, therefore, that the list of names of customers and prospects compiled by the company over a long time is also its most important and valuable direct-mail list. These lists may contain current customers, recent customers, and long past customers or future prospects. They may be further broken down by other demographic or behavioristic characteristics such as size of purchases. Or perhaps they may be segmented by the promotional strategy initially used to

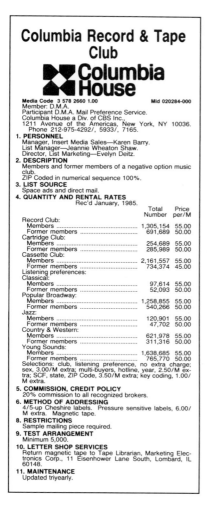

Columbia Record & Tape Club

Columbia House

Media Code 3 578 2660 1.00   Mid 020284-000
Member: D.M.A.
Participant D.M.A. Mail Preference Service.
Columbia House a Div. of CBS Inc.,
1211 Avenue of the Americas, New York, NY 10036.
Phone 212-975-4292/, 5933/, 7165.
1. PERSONNEL
Manager, Insert Media Sales—Karen Barry.
List Manager—Jeannie Wheaton Shaw.
Director, List Marketing—Evelyn Deitz.
2. DESCRIPTION
Members and former members of a negative option music club.
ZIP Coded in numerical sequence 100%.
3. LIST SOURCE
Space ads and direct mail.
4. QUANTITY AND RENTAL RATES
Rec'd January, 1985.

	Total Number	Price per/M
Record Club:		
Members	1,305,154	55.00
Former members	691,689	50.00
Cartridge Club:		
Members	254,689	55.00
Former members	285,989	50.00
Cassette Club:		
Members	2,161,557	55.00
Former members	734,374	45.00
Listening preferences:		
Classical:		
Members	97,614	55.00
Former members	52,093	50.00
Popular Broadway:		
Members	1,258,855	55.00
Former members	540,266	50.00
Jazz:		
Members	120,901	55.00
Former members	47,702	50.00
Country & Western:		
Members	621,978	55.00
Former members	311,316	50.00
Young Sounds:		
Members	1,638,685	55.00
Former members	765,770	50.00

Selections: club, listening preference, no extra charge; sex, 3.00/M extra; multi-buyers, hotline, year, 2.50/M extra; SCF, state, ZIP Code, 3.50/M extra; key coding, 1.00/M extra.
5. COMMISSION, CREDIT POLICY
20% commission to all recognized brokers.
6. METHOD OF ADDRESSING
4/5-up Cheshire labels. Pressure sensitive labels, 6.00/M extra. Magnetic tape.
8. RESTRICTIONS
Sample mailing piece required.
9. TEST ARRANGEMENT
Minimum 5,000.
10. LETTER SHOP SERVICES
Return magnetic tape to Tape Librarian, Marketing Electronics Corp., 11 Eisenhower Lane South, Lombard, IL 60148.
11. MAINTENANCE
Updated triyearly.

FIGURE   15–12

A typical listing from Standard Rate and Data Service, *Direct Mail List Rates and Data (Consumer Lists).*

attract them: direct mail, TV advertising, newspaper coupon, and so forth.

2. *Mail-response lists.* Second in importance are those who have responded to the direct mail solicitations of other companies, especially those whose efforts are complementary to the advertiser's. For example, if you plan to advertise wool scarves and sports car caps, you might find the most attractive response list to be held by the company that markets driving gloves. Thousands of such response lists are available from an array of firms. They are simply the house lists of other direct-mail advertisers, and they are usually available for rental with a wide variety of demographic breakdowns.

3. *Compiled lists.* The third kind of list is the most readily available in volume but offers the lowest expectation. It is simply a list that has been compiled for one reason or another by a source. These may include lists of automobile owners, new-house purchasers, city business owners, Chamber of Commerce presidents, union members, or what have you. Compiled lists are often computer merged with mail response and house lists. This "merge and purge" process involves merging all names and purging all duplicates so that no more than one piece of mail is sent to one name.

Direct-mail lists can be purchased or rented. They can be brokered or exchanged with list houses or other noncompetitive companies.

The variety of lists available today is virtually unlimited. The SRDS *Direct Mail List Rates and Data* comes in two volumes: Volume I, *Consumer Lists,* and Volume II, *Business Lists.* There are over 50,000 list selections in hundreds of different classifications (Figure 15–12).

The average mailing list changes more than 28 percent a year. One reason for this is that some 22 percent of the nation's population relocates to a new address each year. Large numbers of people also make job changes, get married, or die. Therefore, mailing lists must be continually updated. This "cleaning," as it is called, assures that the list is current and correct.

One way for the advertiser to keep a house list up to date is to print or stamp "Address Correction Requested" on the face of the mailer. For a fee, the U.S. Postal Service will enter the new, correct address of the relocated prospect on the mailer and return it to the advertiser.

The prices of mailing lists vary according to their quality. Rental rates average about $28 per thousand, but lists can be secured for as little as $15 per thousand or as much as $300 per thousand. The more stringent the advertiser's selection criteria, the more expensive the list. Spending an extra $10 per thousand is often well worth the savings in wasted mailers and postage that result from using a less precise list.

With the computer, an advertiser can also test the validity and accuracy of a given list. This is done by renting or buying every nth name and sending a mailer to that person. If the results are favorable, additional names can be purchased, usually in lots of 1,000.

Mailing lists are usually rented for one use only. This means the advertiser agrees to use the list for a single mailing. Most list owners require the advertiser to submit a sample mailer in advance. This enables them to be sure that the advertiser will not mail anything that reflects poorly on them or that conflicts with their own products or services.

Many lists are handled by list brokers. A list owner who does not want to be bothered with the details of renting it can retain a broker to handle it. For this service, brokers are paid a commission (usually 20 percent) by the list owner. The advertiser also gains by getting the broker's direct-mail knowledge and expertise without paying more than the rental cost of the list.

■ Production and Handling

The advertiser can create a direct-mail package or retain the services of an advertising agency or free-lance designer and writer. Some agencies specialize in direct mail.

Once the mailing package is conceived and designed, it is ready for printing. The size and shape of the mailing pieces as well as the specified type, illustrations, and colors all influence the printing cost. Special features like simulated blue-ink signatures, cardboard pop-ups, and die cutting (the cutting of paper stock into an unusual shape) add to the cost. The larger the printing volume, or "run," however, the lower the printing cost per unit.

The remaining production tasks can be handled by a local *letter shop* unless the advertiser prefers to do them internally. On a cost-per-thousand basis, such firms stuff and seal envelopes, affix labels, calculate postage, and sort, tie, and stack the mailers. Some also offer creative services. If the advertiser plans to use third-class bulk mail, the mailers must be separated by ZIP Code and tied into bundles to

PEOPLE IN ADVERTISING

René Gnam

Chairman
René Gnam Consultation Corporation

René Gnam is a leading authority on the science of direct-mail testing and the art of structuring persuasive pieces for business and consumer markets.

"When advertising newcomers look at direct mail, their first thought is consumer advertising," Gnam says, "because they're accustomed to seeing lavish promotions at home. But the biggest growth area in direct mail is business-to-business marketing."

Many people have the wrong idea about direct mail marketing. As Gnam says, it is the exclusive prince of neither kitchen-table operators hoping to make a fortune opening envelopes nor of the world's largest and savviest corporations. "You may think your company is too small to compete with the giant like Exxon or U.S. Steel," he says. Direct mail lets the little guy tackle Goliath.

Gnam offers this case history: Norelco Lighting Supply Company is one small division of the giant Norelco known for coffee makers, hair dryers, and shavers. In May 1979, Norelco Lighting had just one salesperson in the United States and a marketing manager who came to Gnam to give Norelco Lighting a better share of the U.S. market.

qualify for low bulk rates. When these tasks are finished, the lettershop delivers the mailers to the post office.

■ Distribution

Distribution costs are chiefly based on the weight of the mailer and the method of delivery. The advertiser can choose among several such methods including the U.S. Postal Service, United Parcel, air freight, and private postal services.

Direct mail has been found to be most effective when it arrives on Tuesdays, Wednesdays, and Thursdays. This may be because some people are affected by Monday back-to-work blues and Friday can't-wait-for-the-weekend elation, or because the growing acceptance of the four-day work week and expanded weekends means fewer people are "in town" from Friday through Monday.

The most common means of delivery is the U.S. Postal Service. It offers the advertiser a choice of several types of mail delivery.

1. *First-class mail.* Contrary to popular belief, a large amount of direct-mail advertising is sent first class. The reasons are that first class assures fast delivery, returns any mail that is undeliverable, and forwards mail (without additional charge) if the addressee has moved and filed a forwarding address.
2. *Business reply mail.* This type of mail enables the recipient to respond without paying postage. The advertiser must first obtain a

---

Gnam suggested three mailings. Mailing 1, to businesses in North Carolina, was just a test. It produced only 39 leads from 16,000 pieces mailed, but 20 of those leads became customers. And each sale was worth $800 to $4,000 revenue per year.

Mailing 2, to Michigan, produced 48 customers, with similar revenue-producing sales.

Nine months later, in February 1980, management hired a national sales manager, salespeople in two cities, and a staff copywriter to create more mailings. Mailing 3 went to eight states and expansion plans were then made for 30 states.

By June 1980, within just 12 months of the first mailing, Norelco Lighting had become a multimillion-dollar nationwide business.

A founding director of the Association of Direct Marketing Agencies, Gnam frequently appears as keynote speaker and seminar leader for association and corporate conventions and sales meetings in North America and Europe. He conducts private consulting workshops and seminars in several cities and has trained over 12,000 ad executives at his public presentations.

Author of *1,001 Direct Response Techniques, The Business of Direct Mail* and numerous articles for such leading industry publications as *Direct Marketing, ZIP, Folio,* and SRDS' *Direct Mail List Bulletin,* Gnam also is consulting editor for *Mail Order Connection, Personal Communications,* and *The Catalog Marketer.*

Gnam wrote and presented America's first TV series on direct mail for Kentucky Educational Television, a PBS affiliate.

"Direct mail," Gnam says from long experience, "is a reliable source of revenue if your customer base has been clearly identified and you have proven offers to make to that base."

Gnam stresses to direct-mail marketers that they seek professional help because "heightened competition in recent years, plus rapidly changing economic market conditions, mean that guesswork rarely succeeds. Use professionals in your area of specialization who have a track record of success."

special permit number, which is available from the postmaster. Then this number must be printed on the face of the return card or envelope. On receiving a response, the advertiser must pay postage plus a few cents handling fee. This "postage-free" incentive tends to increase the rate of response.

3. *Third-class mail.* There are four types of third-class mail: single piece, bulk, bound books or catalogs, and nonprofit organization mail. Most direct-mail advertising travels by third-class mail. It represents a significant savings over first-class rates.

4. *Fourth-class mail.* This class applies only to mail that weighs over 16 ounces.

OUT–OF–HOME MEDIA

In late 1984 Sharlene Wells was crowned Miss America for 1985 on a network television show with an audience of over 50 million viewers. In fact, it was one of the highest rated television specials of the year. Shortly thereafter Sharlene appeared on five more network television shows as well as dozens of local television and radio programs. The Sharlene Wells name and picture were also shown in hundreds of newspapers and a considerable number of national magazines.

In December 1984 a study sponsored by the Institute of Outdoor Advertising was conducted in two test markets by an independent research organization, Lee Cobb & Associates. One simple question was asked: "What is the name of Miss America for 1985?" In spite of all the national publicity, all the network TV shows, and all the newspaper and magazine photos, only 1.5 percent of the respondents could give the correct answer.

On January 15 the Institute sponsored a one-month coast-to-coast billboard campaign. Some 2,500 poster panels (billboards) carried a photograph of Miss Wells and the simple statement: "Sharlene Wells, Miss America 1985" (Figure 15–13). In the two test markets a 100 GRP showing was posted (approximately 60 billboards) for the month. When the Institute conducted a second wave of interviews in March

FIGURE   15–13

The outdoor advertising industry sponsored a nationwide posting of this billboard for its study on the effectiveness of outdoor advertising.

and April, 11.9 percent of those questioned knew who Miss America was—an eightfold increase in awareness. If those results could be projected nationally, that would mean that outdoor advertising had communicated a new and unusual name to more than 15 million adult Americans, about 1 in every 10.

■ What Works Best in Outdoor Advertising?

The advantages of outdoor advertising are numerous and distinct. They relate to the medium's reach, frequency, flexibility, and cost, as well as to its impact. (See Outdoor advertising: A 20th century art form.)

▨ Reach

Often an advertiser requires saturation of a market to accomplish objectives such as the introduction of a new product or feature or a change in package design. Outdoor advertising is a mass medium that makes broad coverage possible overnight.

For example, a 100 gross rating point showing (also called a number 100 showing) covers a market fully by reaching 9 out of 10 adults daily over a 30-day period. In a single day, therefore, with a 100 GRP showing, an advertising message can be given a total number of exposure opportunities equal to the entire population of a market.

If the advertiser desires even greater saturation, the number of posters can be increased to reach a 200 GRP showing or even 300 GRPs.

Even more important to most advertisers is the audience reached by outdoor. For the most part, outdoor's audience is a young, educated, affluent, and mobile population—very attractive to most national advertisers.

▨ Frequency

Outdoor offers frequency of impressions. According to a W. R. Simmons study, the 9 out of 10 people reached with a 100 GRP showing receive an average of 31 impressions each over a 30-day period (Figure 15–14). This frequency increases for groups that are better educated and have higher incomes—again, very attractive.

Data on frequency and reach for more than 8,000 markets is available from Audience Market by Market for Outdoor (AMMO), one of the services of the Institute for Outdoor Advertising.

▨ Flexibility

In addition, outdoor offers advertisers great flexibility. They can place their advertising geographically where they want it—in any of 9,000 markets across the country—nationally, regionally, or locally. An outdoor advertiser can buy just one city or even a small section of that city.

The flexibility can be demographic. Messages can be concentrated in areas frequented or traversed by young people, upper-income people, or people of specific ethnic backgrounds.

Outdoor can even be pinpointed by activity—travelers on their

OUTDOOR
ADVERTISING:
A 20TH CENTURY
ART FORM

A. The San Diego Zoo appeals to local residents to visit their own world-famous park more often with this clever billboard designed by their agency Phillips-Ramsey.

B. A Canadian billboard for Sunkist oranges. This advertiser consistently uses clever copy attached to excellent design to make outdoor work for them.

C. The feeling of performance and motion. Isn't that what Honda's selling? No need for words, here.

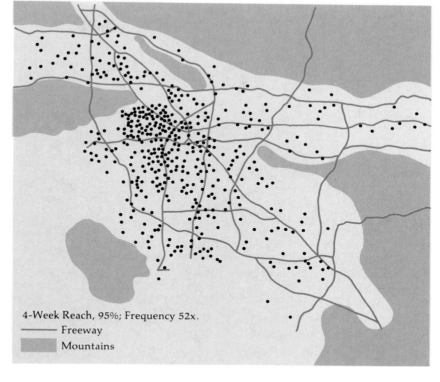

4-Week Reach, 95%; Frequency 52x.
——— Freeway
▓ Mountains

FIGURE 15-14

A freeway map of Southern California shows that for $141,669 an advertiser can obtain at least 100 GRPs each day for four weeks throughout Los Angeles and Orange counties. While that may sound like a lot of money, the reality is that an advertiser could never obtain that kind of intensity at that price on radio or TV.

Would the person responsible for this please contact Piper West Flight School

FIGURE 15-15

This very clever Australian billboard ran in Sydney for Piper West Flight School and shows the creative potential of outdoor for imaginative advertisers.

way to the airport, shoppers on their way to the store, businesspeople on their way to and from work (Figure 15–15).

▓ Cost

Outdoor advertising offers the lowest cost per message delivered of any major advertising medium. Rates vary depending on the size of the particular market and the intensity desired.

The industry uses the term *showing* to indicate the relative number of outdoor posters used during a contract period. Numbers have traditionally been used to indicate the intensity of market coverage. For example, a 100 showing provides an even and thorough coverage of the entire market. A less expensive 50 showing is half as many locations as a 100 showing, a 25 showing one fourth as many, and so forth.

Now the industry has largely changed over to the gross rating point (GRP) system similar to that used for TV. If a showing provides 750,000 total impression opportunities daily in a market with a population of 1 million, it is said to deliver 75 gross rating points daily. Over a period of 30 days, this showing would earn 2,250 gross rating points. The GRP system makes cost comparison possible from market to market (Figure 15–16).

Local and national advertisers are charged the same rates. These are quoted on a monthly basis for various GRP levels, and they vary considerably from market to market. Differences are due to variations in property rentals, labor costs, and market size. Higher rates are found in larger markets where traffic volume is high.

Detailed rate information may be found in the *Buyers Guide to Out-*

FIGURE   15–16   Outdoor advertising costs

Rank	Area	Number 25 showing			Number 50 showing			Number 100 showing		
		No. of panels	Average cost per panel per month	Total per month	No. of panels	Average cost per panel per month	Total per month	No. of panels	Average cost per panel per month	Total per month
1	New York	386	$213	$82,218	660	$225	$148,500	1,169	$218	$254,842
2	Los Angeles	157	237	37,209	300	241	72,300	583	243	141,669
3	Chicago	163	184	29,992	284	196	55,664	529	202	106,858
4	Philadelphia	221	215	47,515	367	219	80,373	655	214	140,170
5	San Francisco	79	225	17,775	145	233	33,785	277	236	65,372
6	Boston	132	172	22,704	223	183	40,809	413	188	77,644
7	Detroit	120	197	23,640	176	222	39,072	315	233	73,395
8	Washington, D.C.	78	124	9,672	102	135	13,770	180	134	24,120
9	Cleveland	144	158	22,752	224	177	39,648	416	184	76,544
10	Dallas–Ft. Worth	186	112	20,832	248	123	30,504	417	129	53,793

door Advertising. This is published twice a year by the Institute of Outdoor Advertising.

Impact

All this adds up to economical intensity of impressions for the advertiser—impact. With relatively low cost, the advertiser can build up GRPs very fast by hitting a large percentage of the market many times over a very short time. This, of course, is ideal for advertisers who have a short, simple, dogmatic message.

The inherent features of outdoor add impact to the advertiser's message. Outdoor offers the largest display of any medium (Figure 15–17). Plus, it offers the spectacular features of lights, animation, and brilliant color. (See the Checklist of what works best in outdoor.)

Finally, whereas other media carry the message to the prospect, outdoor catches people on their way to shop, work, or play, selling continuously day and night. This gives it additional impact for impulse products as well as hotels, motels, restaurants, tourist attractions, and auto-related services.

Drawbacks to Outdoor Advertising

Just as there are numerous advantages to outdoor, there are also numerous disadvantages. Posters are passed very quickly. To be effective, therefore, outdoor advertising must intrude. The design and legend must tell a story briefly and crisply, and they must sell.

Although outdoor advertising is fine for reaching a wide audience, it generally has limitations for reaching a narrow demographic group.

Printing and posting outdoor messages are very time-consuming, so outdoor campaigns must be planned far in advance. Usually a six- to eight-week lead time is required.

FIGURE 15-17

This outdoor spectacular bulletin for Chevrolet has motor-driven extensions that open in tandem to invite closer inspection of the Corvette. The full sequence repeats every six seconds.

The high initial preparation cost may sometimes discourage local use, although printing methods such as silk screening offer lower preparation costs.

Another disadvantage is the difficulty of physically inspecting each outdoor poster panel (as opposed to checking tear sheets of space advertising or monitoring commercials).

And, finally, the outdoor message is influenced somewhat by its environment. A billboard in a depressed or generally run-down area will certainly detract from the medium's ability to lend prestige to the product being advertised.

■ Standardization of the Outdoor Advertising Business

Most advertising that appears out of doors is not *standardized* outdoor advertising but rather on-premise signs that identify a place of business. This type of sign, though certainly helpful to a business,

Checklist of what works best in outdoor

□ Look for a big idea. This is no place for subtleties. Outdoor is a bold medium. You need a poster that registers the idea quickly and memorably. A "visual scandal" that shocks the viewer into awareness.

□ Keep it simple. Cut out all extraneous words and pictures, and concentrate on the essentials. Outdoor is the art of brevity. Use only one picture, and no more than seven words of copy—preferably less.

□ Personalize when you can. Personalized posters are practical, even for short runs. Mention a specific geographic area ("New in Chicago"), or the name of a local dealer.

□ Look for human, emotional content for memorability. It can be an entertainment medium for travelers who are hungry or bored.

□ Use color for readability. The most readable combination is black on yellow. Other combinations may gain more attention, but stay with primary colors—and *stay away from reverse*.

□ Use the location to your advantage. Many new housing developments capitalize on their convenient locations with a poster saying: "If you lived here, you'd be home now." Use outdoor to tell drivers that your restaurant is down the road, your department store is across the street. Don't ignore the ability of outdoor to reach ethnic neighborhoods. Tailor the language and the models to your consumer.

does not provide coverage of a market. On the other hand, standardized outdoor advertising locates its structures scientifically to deliver an advertiser's message to an entire market. Standardized outdoor advertising is a highly organized medium available to advertisers in more than 15,000 communities across the country. The structures on which the advertising appears are owned and maintained by individual outdoor advertising companies known as "plants." The structures are built on private land that the outdoor plant operators own or lease and are concentrated in commercial and business areas where they conform to all local building code requirements.

The industry consists of about 600 local and regional plant operators. They find suitable locations, lease or buy the property, erect the outdoor structures, contract with advertisers for poster rentals, and post the panels or paint the bulletins (Figure 15–18). They also have to maintain the outdoor structures so lights are working and torn sheets are replaced, and keep the areas surrounding the structures clean and attractive.

Although national advertising comprises the bulk of outdoor business, about one fourth of the business of a typical outdoor plant is from local advertisers. Usually, the smaller the market, the larger is the percentage of local advertisers. The outdoor firm may employ an art staff to perform creative services for local advertisers, but the creative work for national advertisers is usually handled by advertising agencies.

FIGURE 15–18

A. Printed poster sheets are collated, prepasted, and vacuum sealed in plastic bags. The glued sheets will remain moist for weeks. Each bag is identified and scheduled for posting routes. First, "blanking paper" is pasted down to form a border. Next, beginning from the bottom, the person doing the posting takes the prepasted sheets and applies the first section to the panel.

B. By starting at the bottom and working upward, each sheet overlaps the previous section. This forms a "rain-lap" and helps prevent flagging or tearing of the outdoor poster copy. Because the sheets have been prepasted, the person doing the posting is able to use a dry brush to make the paper adhere to the panel. Prepasting techniques eliminate glue streaks from dark backgrounds.

C. Since a poster is a series of sheets, a flexibility of sheet arrangement is possible. The advertiser can localize a campaign to an area, include a dealer's name, or change a package shown. Sheet by sheet, the giant paper mosaic is assembled to build the advertiser's message into a clean, colorful 25' by 12' display. This poster will be exposed to the mass public for at least 30 days.

Standardized Outdoor Structures

Standardized outdoor advertising structures have two basic forms: the poster panel and the bulletin. Each has its individual function, yet they work well together to provide coverage of a market and to reach large numbers of people economically in a short time with a high rate of frequency.

Posters

Posters ("billboards") are the basic form of outdoor advertising and the least costly per unit. A poster is a structure of blank panel with a standardized size and border. It is usually anchored in the ground, or it may be affixed to a wall or roof. Its advertising message is first printed at a lithography or silkscreen plant on large sheets of paper. These are then mounted by hand on the panel.

Posters sizes are referred to in terms of sheets. At one time, covering a structure 12 by 25 feet required 24 of the largest sheets a printing press could hold. The designation "24-sheet" is still used even though press sizes have changed and most poster sizes are larger. The poster is still mounted on a board with a total surface of 12 by 25 feet, but today there are two basic sizes of posters:

1. 30-sheet poster—with a 9'7" by 21'7" printed area surrounded by a margin of blank paper. The 30-sheet provides 25 percent more copy area than the old 24-sheet size of 8'8" by 19'6".
2. Bleed poster—with a 10'5" by 22'8" printed area extending all the way to the frame. The bleed poster is about 40 percent larger than the old 24-sheet.

One way some local advertisers get high-quality outdoor advertising at lower than usual cost is to use ready-made 30-sheet posters. These stock posters are available in any quantity. They often feature the work of first-class artists and lithographers. Local advertisers simply order as many as they need and have their name placed in the appropriate spot. These ready-made posters are particularly suitable for such local firms as florists, dairies, banks, bakeries, and others that have sales stories similar to those of their competitors.

Advertisers of grocery products and many local advertisers like to use smaller poster sizes, such as "junior panels." These are also referred to as 8-sheet posters and offer a 5' by 11' printing area on a panel surface 6' wide by 12' deep.

Painted displays

These are meant for long use and are usually placed in only the best locations where traffic is heavy and visibility is good. They fall into two general categories: bulletins and walls. Painted bulletins may be painted in sections in the plant's shop and then transported to the site where they are assembled and hung on the billboard structure. Painted walls obviously must be painted at the site.

Although usually standardized in width and height, actual sizes depend on the available location, the advertiser's budget, and the character of the message. Bulletins are more custom-made than posters, generally larger, and usually longer. Typical sizes are 14' by 48'; however, some even extend to 18' by 62'10".

Painted displays are normally illuminated and repainted several

FIGURE 15–19

Chiat-Day's novel billboard campaign for Nike has almost become an art form itself. The commercial message is seemingly nonexistent. But, in reality, the space is used to a maximum degree to create a feeling or tone for the product—a Nike mystique—that says more nonverbally than any words could ever say.

times each year to keep them looking fresh. Some are three-dimensional and embellished by cutouts that extend beyond the frames (Figure 15–19). Variations include the use of cutout letters, plastic facing, back-lighting, moving messages, clocks, thermometers, electric time and temperature units called "jump clocks," and novel treatment of light and color. (See Ad Lab 15–B.)

Some advertisers overcome the higher expense of painted bulletins by using a *rotary plan.* The bulletins are rotated to different choice locations in the market every 30, 60, or 90 days, giving the impression of wide coverage over time.

Backlights

Backlights have been available in Canada's top markets for more than 10 years, and they are now becoming increasingly available in the U.S. Words and pictures are reproduced on polyvinyl chloride, mounted on a special frame, and backlit 24 hours a day. The lighting provides a beacon-like visibility at night, despite rain or fog. Even by day, colors are brilliant, and shadows are eliminated. It's the most stunning outdoor display available. These signs are like a giant, lighted 35mm slide.

AD LAB   15–B   How to use color in outdoor advertising

Color contrast and value

The availability of a full range of colors, vividly and faithfully reproduced, is one of the outstanding advantages of outdoor advertising. A huge poster or bulletin alive with brilliant reds and greens and yellows and blues can produce an effect approached by no other medium.

In choosing colors for outdoor, the designer should seek out those with high contrast in both hue (the identity of the color, such as red, green, yellow) and value (the measure of the color's lightness or darkness). Contrasting colors work well at outdoor-viewing distances, while colors without contrast blend together and obscure the message.

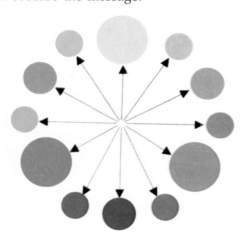

The color wheel illustrates the need for contrast in both hue and value. For example, green and red are opposite each other on the wheel and are therefore complementary colors. They represent a good contrast in *hues*, but in *values* they are very similar. As a result, they set up an annoying vibration. The same is true of blue and orange.

Blue and green and orange and red are especially poor combinations because they are similar in both hue *and* value.

On the other hand, yellow and purple—*dis*similar in both hue and value—provide a strong and effective contrast for outdoor. Of course, white goes well with any dark-value color, while black is good with colors of light value.

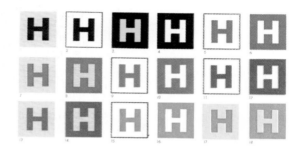

Color impact

Among the color combinations shown, legibility ranges from best in combination 1 to poorest in combination 18.

Color combinations

Color combinations illustrate need for contrast in hue and value. Blue and green do *not* work well together; yellow and purple *do* work well.

Laboratory Applications

1. Which outdoor advertisements in this chapter use color the most effectively?

2. What examples of outdoor advertising have you seen that use color effectively?

TRANSIT ADVERTISING

In 1910 Wrigley's Gum decided to undertake a new test campaign in Buffalo, New York, because gum had been so difficult to sell there. Wrigley's contacted the Collier Service Company in New York City, which had been established to provide copy and illustration service as well as to sell transit (bus) advertising. At the time, Collier employed some of the best writers in America, including F. Scott Fitzgerald and Ogden Nash. Collier's organization developed the famed "spear man," which subsequently became the symbol of chewing gum for generations of Americans.

Wrigley's spear man was then printed on cards and carried on buses throughout Buffalo. The Buffalo program was so successful that it was repeated in city after city across the nation.

It was around the same time that the Campbell Soup company began to think of using advertising to sell its products. Spending its first $5,000 on car card advertising, Campbell contracted to place its advertisements on one third of the surface buses in New York City for one year. After only six months the campaign was so obviously successful that the contract was enlarged to include all surface vehicles in New York City. This produced a 100 percent increase in business, and for 12 years transit advertising was the sole medium used by the company (Figure 15–20).

■ Types of Transit Advertising

Transit advertising, like standardized outdoor advertising, is referred to as an out-of-home medium. Transit advertising depends on the millions of people who ride on commercial transportation facilities (buses, subways, elevated trains, commuter trains, trolleys, and airlines) plus pedestrians and auto passengers who see the advertising (Figure 15–21).

Transit advertising actually includes three separate media forms: inside cards; outside posters; and station, platform, and terminal posters.

■ *Inside cards*

The standard size of the inside card, placed in a wall rack above the windows, is 11" by 28". Four other widths are available in multiples of 14 inches (11" by 14", 11" by 42", 11" by 56", and 11" by 84"). Cost-conscious advertisers print both sides of the card so it can simply be reversed to change the message, thus saving on paper and shipping charges.

Inside car end posters (in "bulkhead" positions) are usually larger and of varying sizes. One common size is 22" by 21". Some top-end or over-door cards are 16" by 39" or 16" by 44". The end and side positions carry a premium rate.

■ *Outside posters*

Printed on high-grade cardboard and often varnished to be weather resistant, the most widely used exterior units are these: (1) side of bus—king size (30" by 144"), queen size (30" by 88"), and traveling display (21" by 72"); (2) rear of bus—taillight spectacular (21" by 44"); and (3) front of bus—headlights (17" by 21" and 21" by 44").

FIGURE 15–20

Campbell Soup Company started using transit advertising in the early 1900s, and they're still using it 80 years later as shown by this inside card for Campbell's vegetable soup in a subway car.

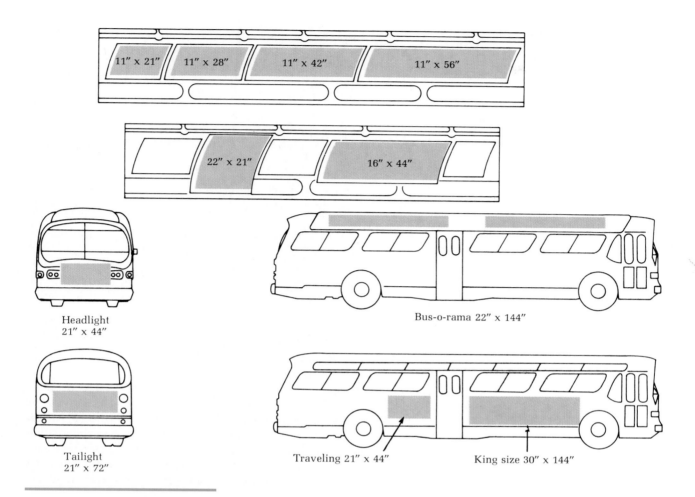

FIGURE 15–21

Illustrated are the common sizes for inside cards and outside posters available in transit advertising.

 Station, platform, and terminal posters

In many bus, subway, and commuter train stations, space is sold for one-sheet, two-sheet, and three-sheet posters. Also, major train and airline terminals offer a variety of special advertising forms that might be compared to outdoor spectaculars. These are usually custom designed and include such attention-getters as floor displays, island showcases, illuminated signs, dioramas (three-dimensional scenes), and clocks with special lighting and moving messages.

Why Transit Advertising Works

Why was Campbell's campaign on bus cards so successful? What was it about transit that helped Wrigley become a household name? The answers to these questions are numerous, and they define the many advantages of transit advertising: high reach, frequency, exposure, and attention values at very low cost.

Transit advertising gives long exposure to the advertiser's message because the average ride is about 25 minutes. It has repetitive value; many people take the same routes day after day. The messages are eagerly read by riders attempting to escape from boredom. Surveys show that readership is high.

The cost is low. This is partly because capital costs are paid for by the fares, with no huge capital investment needed for equipment. The dollar outlay is generally less than for any other medium.

Many riders are on their way to shop downtown and therefore are susceptible to advertising suggestions. Transit cards offer unexcelled color reproduction at relatively low cost. Small advertisers are not overshadowed by large ones.

Transit advertising also reaches mass audiences. It offers geographic flexibility and can reach various ethnic or neighborhood groups.

It is a good major market media form that can be used to magnify the total frequency. It permits special constructions and color effects.

While outdoor advertising has been a target of the environmental movement, transit advertising has been one of its beneficiaries. Energy problems have increased social pressure to use public transportation instead of private autos. At the same time, federal subsidies for the transit industry have resulted in larger and better transit systems as well as some new ones.

As the industry has progressed, it has developed more efficient standardization, better research, additional statistical data, and measured circulation, thus making it easier for national advertisers to include transit advertising in their schedules.

National advertisers who have used the medium in recent years have included food and beverage producers, tobacco companies, oil companies, financial institutions (Figure 15–22), proprietary medicines, and, of course, chewing gum. The medium is especially suitable for reaching middle- to lower-income, urban consumers, providing supplemental coverage to these groups. Several national advertisers besides Campbell and Wrigley's have used transit advertising for more than 50 years.

Transit advertising is about equally popular with local advertisers. Such advertisers as theaters, restaurants, and retailers find it a productive medium for reminders and special announcements.

Figure   15–22

Wells Fargo Bank used side-of-bus posters as a moving billboard for its Old American West ad campaign.

FIGURE 15–23

When Bon Jour jeans purchased a full showing, they bought space ads that stated "Bon Jour buses dominate New York."

Disadvantages of Transit Advertising

Among the weaknesses of transit advertising are its general lack of coverage of some segments of society, such as suburbanites who drive their own cars, rural dwellers, and business and professional people who seldom use mass transportation. Other disadvantages follow:

It lacks the status of an important advertising medium.

Its rush-hour crowds limit the opportunity and ease of reading.

It reaches a nonselective audience, which may not meet the needs of some advertisers.

Cards are so numerous and look so similar that they may be confusing.

The transit vehicle environment, which may be crowded and dirty, may not lend prestige to the product.

The trend to outlying shopping centers means fewer shoppers make trips downtown.

Although transit cards may carry longer messages than billboards, copy is still somewhat limited.

Buying Transit Advertising

One of the most often cited advantages of transit advertising is the cost per exposure: approximately 13.7 cents per thousand in the nation's "A" markets (the 22 largest metropolitan areas in the United States). In fact, outside transit ad costs can be as low as 6 cents per thousand exposures.

The unit of purchase is a showing, also known as a run or service. In transit advertising, a full showing (or No. 100 showing) means that one card will appear in each vehicle in the system. Space may also be purchased as a one-half (or No. 50) showing or a one-quarter (or No. 25) showing. Exterior displays are purchased on a showing basis (Figure 15–23).

Rates are usually quoted for 30-day showings—with discounts for 3-, 6-, 9-, and 12-month contracts. The advertisers must supply the cards at their own expense.

Cost depends on (1) the length of the showing, (2) the saturation of the showing, and (3) the size of the space. Rates vary extensively, depending primarily on the size of the system.

Rates for specific markets may be obtained from the local transit company and from Transit Advertising Association's *TAA Rate Directory of Transit Advertising* (the industry's rate book).

Special inside buys

In some cities advertisers may buy all the inside space on a group of buses, thereby gaining complete domination. This buy is called the *basic bus*. In addition, pads of business reply cards or coupons (called *take ones*) may be affixed to interior advertisements for an extra charge. This allows passengers to request more detailed information, send in application blanks, or receive some other advertised product benefit.

▨ *Special outside buys*

Some transit companies offer *bus-o-rama signs*. This is a jumbo roof sign, which is actually a full-color transparency backlighted by fluorescent tubes, running the length of the bus. Two bus-o-rama positions are on each side of the bus.

A single advertiser may also buy a *total bus*—all the exterior space on a bus including the front, rear, sides, and top. This gives the product message powerful exclusivity.

Some transit companies offer other unique capabilities. With the introduction of new advance-design buses in Houston, for instance, the TDI transit advertising company offered advertisers up to 20 feet of sign space along the street side of the bus. The new, futuristic buses provided a smooth outer surface to which TDI was able to directly apply pressure-sensitive vinyl. Available in several reflective colors and textures, the 30″ by 240″ vinyl signs offered a versatile alternative to Houston advertisers. In addition, they could be die-cut to any shape within the sign area, so anything from soft drink bottles to carpenter's pencils could travel the streets daily.

To keep advertisers informed of opportunities in transit advertising, the industry has two organizations—the Transit Advertising Association and the American Public Transit Association. The TAA is the main source of information—it performs research and supplies industry data on the number of vehicles, trends, and rider demographics. The TAA is the national trade organization and promotion arm of the industry. Its members represent 80 percent of the transit advertising volume in the United States and Canada.

Summary

Direct-mail advertising includes all forms of advertising sent direct to prospects through the mail. As an advertising medium, it ranks third in dollars spent, surpassed only by newspapers and television.

Next to the personal sales call, direct mail is the most effective way an advertiser can put a message in front of a prospect. It is also the most expensive on a cost per exposure basis. As an advertising medium, it offers several advantages. These include selectivity, intensive coverage, flexibility, control, personal impact, exclusivity, and performance.

The drawbacks to direct mail include the high cost per exposure, the delays often experienced in delivery, the lack of other content support for the advertising message, and certain problems with selectivity.

Direct-mail advertising comes in many forms: sales letters, brochures, and even handwritten postcards all qualify as direct-mail advertising. The message can be as short as one sentence or dozens of pages long.

The direct-mail list is the heart of the medium because each list actually defines a market segment. There are three types of direct-mail lists: house lists, mail response lists, and compiled lists. Their prices vary according to their quality.

Of the major advertising media, outdoor advertising offers the lowest cost per message delivered. In addition, the medium offers other attractive features. These include instant broad coverage (reach), very high frequency, great flexibility, and impact. Drawbacks include the necessity for brief messages, the limitations for reaching narrow demographic groups, and the lead time required. In addition, the high initial preparation costs and difficulty of physically inspecting each billboard discourage some advertisers.

The standardized outdoor advertising industry consists of about 600 local and regional plant operators. National advertising comprises the bulk of outdoor business.

The two most common forms of standard outdoor advertising structures are the poster panel and the bulletin. The poster panel is the basic form, the least costly per unit, and available in a variety of sizes. Painted bulletins are meant for long use and are usually placed in the best locations where traffic is heavy and visibility is good. Some advertisers overcome the relative higher expense of painted bulletins by using a rotary plan.

Transit advertising offers the features of high reach, frequency, exposure, and attention values at very low cost. It furthermore gives long exposure to the advertiser's message and offers repetitive value and good geographic flexibility. In addition, advertisers have a wide choice in the size of space used.

Its disadvantages, of course, are numerous. It does not cover some segments of society, it reaches a nonselective audience, it lacks prestige, and copy is still somewhat limited.

Questions for review and discussion

1. What advantages does direct mail offer the National Geographic Society as compared to other forms of advertising it might use?
2. What is the difference between direct-mail and direct response advertising?
3. Although direct mail offers the advantage of selectivity, what are the associated problems?
4. What are the three types of mailing lists? Which is the best? Why?
5. What costs are advertisers likely to incur in a direct-mail campaign?
6. What advertising objectives are the outdoor media mostly suitable for?
7. Do you feel outdoor would be an effective advertising medium for a politician? Why?
8. What is the difference between a poster panel and a painted bulletin?
9. Why is transit advertising considered three separate media forms?
10. What characteristics of transit advertising benefit advertisers the most?

16

SALES PROMOTION
AND
SUPPLEMENTARY
MEDIA

T he airline business is plagued with season-long stretches of greatly reduced traffic—and hence a lot of empty seats. United Airlines, faced with the prospect of another of these recurring slumps, decided to do something about it.

The strategy devised by the airline in a recent campaign was to distribute scratch-off, instant-winner game cards to all its passengers and to offer free game cards to people who wrote in for them. The original 10,000 winning tickets entitled the bearers to a travel certificate good for a round-trip ticket to any United Airlines destination in the country, including Hawaii, between June 1 and December 15. Part of the plan was to extend the promotion for an extra 10 days and to offer an additional 5,000 trips.

The $2.5 million budget for the promotion was spent on the game cards as well as on TV, radio, and newspaper (ROP) ads announcing the contest (Figure 16–1).

Was the promotion a success? Besides all the game cards distributed on board United flights, the airline sent out an additional 4 million cards in response to written requests. The 15,000 winners not only found out about all the routes flown by United and got the chance to fly first-class, they also, in most cases, brought along a paying friend. After all, who wants to go off alone on a free trip to Hawaii—or anywhere else?

The first in-flight sweepstakes conducted in airline history thus reached its objectives and then some. It did indeed fill seats during United's off season and undoubtedly laid the groundwork for future business, some of it from new-found friends of first-class flight.[1]

ROLE OF SALES

PROMOTION

What would United's ticket sales have been without the promotion—if United had simply advertised? The answer to this question is the key to understanding what sales promotion is and how it works.

The purpose of all marketing tools such as advertising, public relations, and sales promotion is to help the company achieve its marketing objectives (see Chapter 4). Specific marketing objectives may include the following:

1. To introduce new products.
2. To induce present customers to buy more.
3. To attract new customers.
4. To combat competition.
5. To maintain sales in off seasons.
6. To increase retail inventories so more goods may be sold.

As we know, the marketing strategy the company uses to achieve these objectives may include a high degree of personal selling. It may also include nonpersonal selling activities such as advertising the company's products in the national media or in trade journals read by its dealers. It may include public relations activities such as feature stories and magazine interviews. Or it may include a major sales promotion campaign like United's.

Sales promotion is used to help produce and increase sales. It is sometimes referred to as *supplementary* to advertising and personal selling because it binds the two together, making both more effective. In reality, however, it is far more than supplementary since it may now represent as much as 60 percent of the typical marketing budget versus 40 percent for advertising.

By definition, *sales promotion is a direct inducement offering extra incentive all along the marketing route—from manufacturers through distribution channels to consumers—to accelerate the movement of the product from the producer to the consumer.* Therefore, there are three important things to remember about sales promotion.

1. It is an *acceleration tool* designed to speed up the selling process.
2. It normally involves a *direct inducement* (such as money, prizes, extra products, gifts, or specialized information), which provides *extra incentive* to buy, visit the store, request literature, or take some other action.
3. It may be used *anywhere along the marketing route:* from the manufacturer to the dealer, from dealer to consumer, or from manufacturer to consumer.

Sales promotion is used to *maximize* sales volume. It does this, in some cases, by motivating consumers who have been unmoved by other advertising efforts or, in other cases, by motivating particular brand selection when all brands are considered more or less equal. In short, sales promotion ideally generates sales that would not otherwise be achieved.

Studying the United example, can you tell what marketing objectives the company wished to achieve? How well did the United Airlines program satisfy the definition of sales promotion?

FIGURE   16–1

United Airlines used newspaper advertisements to announce the first in-flight sweepstakes in airline history and to offer game cards to anyone who wanted to participate.

SALES PROMOTION:

THE SALES

ACCELERATOR

S. C. Johnson & Son, manufacturers of Johnson's Wax, has been a leader in the car, floor, and furniture wax business since its beginning many years ago. When that market appeared to level off, Johnson decided to turn to the health and beauty aids market for additional business. It successfully introduced Edge Shaving Creme in the late 60s, but that was followed by a number of dismal failures over the succeeding years.

Finally, the company developed a superior hair creme rinse, Agree, with an extra benefit that "helps stop the greasies" (Figure 16–2). It was priced competitively against the market leader, Revlon's Flex, Balsam & Protein.

However, the company was aware that its Johnson's Wax sales force had little experience with this highly competitive, fast-turning, dog-eat-dog product category. And retailers, who had witnessed Johnson's other product failures, would not be inclined to give much shelf space to a new Johnson entry.

Johnson's introductory objectives for Agree, therefore, were rather heady: to rapidly promote enough sales of the new product to (1) achieve and maintain market leadership and (2) create a positive image for Johnson as a marketer of personal care products with its trade customers as well as with consumers. To succeed, Johnson had to develop a sales promotion strategy for Agree that would *push* the

FIGURE 16–2

S. C. Johnson & Son put $17 million into marketing its new Agree hair creme rinse and conditioner. This effectively catapulted the product into a leadership position. The power of its campaign was as much in its trade promotion as in its consumer promotion.

product into the dealer pipeline and also induce consumers to try the product, thereby *pulling* it through the pipe. After testing the product's acceptance with consumers and testing possible sampling techniques, Johnson prepared to launch Agree.

Prepacked floor displays, which together would hold over 7 million 29-cent, two-ounce, trial-size bottles, were constructed and shipped to retailers. The dealers were offered introductory price allowances, distribution allowances, and advertising dollar allowances just to stock the product and set up the prepacked displays.

Then samples were distributed to consumers—31 million samples— and 41 million coupons allowing 15 cents off on the purchase of the product. This alone catapulted Agree into a leadership position by generating rapid awareness and trial among its target group of women aged 14 to 30. And to top it all off, the company ran 300 prime-time network TV commercials, ads in 26 leading magazines, and the heaviest creme rinse radio campaign in history.

In all, the company spent over $17 million to introduce Agree. Within five months the product grabbed a 20 percent share of market and was running neck and neck against Revlon's Flex. A consumer attitude study revealed that awareness of Agree was at a whopping 77 percent, with trial of the product at 38 percent and repurchase intent estimated at 78 percent.

As a result, Johnson not only achieved its leadership position with Agree, but it also earned its spurs with the trade, which should make its next product entry infinitely easier.[2]

Balancing Push and Pull Strategy

How does a company go from 0 to 20 percent share of market in creme rinse conditioners in only five months? Simply by spending lots of money? Hardly.

Johnson started with a superior product. Then they tested it along with the levels of advertising and sales promotion that would make it go. They developed a national strategy based on their test results. This strategy would ensure that consumers who sought the product would be able to find it in the stores. And it ensured that dealers who bought the product would have customers wanting to try it.

Then, and only then, did Johnson commit the very big dollars—$6 million in advertising, over $6 million in sampling, and another $5 million in trade promotion—to its assault on the market.

What do you suppose would have been the result if Johnson had not spent money on the trade promotion? On the sampling? On the advertising? How vital was each of these individual elements to accomplishing Agree's success? Do you think any of them could have been left out?

Push Strategy Techniques

The success of Agree was dependent to a great extent on the cooperation of retail dealers. To get this cooperation, though, S. C. Johnson had to offer substantial inducements in the form of introductory price allowances, other dollar-saving devices, and usable product displays.

Any manufacturer who markets through normal channels must secure the cooperation of retailers. This sometimes is easier said than done because the retailers, in turn, have specific problems of their own. In today's crowded supermarkets, shelf space and floor space are hard to come by. Department stores, in order to maintain their own images, have been forced to set standards for manufacturers' displays. This means that retailers are often unable to use the special racks, sales aids, and promotional literature supplied by the manufacturers. As a consequence, substantial waste occurs as material is thrown away or left unused in a stockroom. Many retailers are pressed for time and lack the personnel to effectively use the flood of manufacturers' sales promotion material. So packages of promotion literature remain unopened, and displays remain unassembled.

Retailers often say their needs are "different," the material does not fit their market, they lack the space for displays and the time to assemble them, and other reasons. True or not, such contentions reveal a need for promotion people to spend time in the field and for distributors' and manufacturers' salespeople to report their findings thoroughly to headquarters.

PEOPLE IN ADVERTISING

William A. Robinson

President
William A. Robinson, Inc.

Sales promotion specialist William A. Robinson is founder and president of William A. Robinson, Inc., Chicago, one of the nation's leading marketing services agencies. Since its inception in 1961, the Robinson agency has developed successful promotional programs for clients like AT&T, Amtrak, Sunkist, Apple Computer, AVCO Financial Services, McDonald's, Procter & Gamble, Heublein, Zenith, Colgate-Palmolive, Lipton, Sara Lee, Borden, and Frito-Lay.

"Our goal is to move products and purchasers closer together," said Robinson. "We begin by examining the client's brand—its marketing strategy, selling proposition, and promotional stance. Next, we look at the brand's objectives—its sales and share projections, distribution, and communications goals." Armed with this, he said, "We determine how to sell *more* of the product."

Yet sales promotion doesn't always work, Robinson warned. "If a product is unacceptable to consumers," he said, "promotion won't change that. If an established product is experiencing declining sales, promotion won't turn it around. Promotion can't create an 'image' for a brand. And a single promotion won't motivate consumers to buy a product over a long period of time."

What promotion *can* do, Robinson explained, is offer consumers an immediate inducement to buy. It can also prompt a consumer who knows nothing about a product to try it—and to buy it again. Promotion can make current users buy more of a

Despite these problems, many manufacturers do an excellent job of implementing push strategy in sales promotion. This is accomplished by using a wide range of promotional programs closely keyed to retailer needs (Figure 16–3). One example of this is the dealer plan book used in the automotive industry. Its many color pages present a well-organized and complete selection of advertising and promotion tools—from window and showroom display materials to catalogs, ad kits, wall plaques, and color charts—all designed to make the dealer's job easier.

Another example of a far-sighted program was that of an appliance manufacturer. Dealers and distributors complained to the manufacturer that they were under a constant barrage of separate and unrelated bulletins and letters from different factory departments concerning new products, display material, promotion booklets, service problems, policy, ad mats, and countless other topics. The manufacturer solved this problem by incorporating all such necessary information into one compact monthly newsletter, a newsy publication that the dealers and distributors actually looked forward to receiving each month.

brand or buy larger sizes. And it can motivate salespeople, wholesalers, and retailers to get squarely behind a product.

"Consumers today are exposed to more advertising than ever before," said Robinson. "Thus, it takes more impact to get their attention in the marketplace."

To determine what type of sales promotion works best for a product, the Robinson agency tests the value of various promotion techniques from their inception, using focus groups, interviews, and field surveys. "We set measurable goals and assign specific responsibilities for their accomplishment," said Robinson, citing the 10 promotion techniques most often used.

"*Samplings* and *coupons* are best for inducing consumers to try a product. *Price-off* packings can prompt current users to buy more. *Refund offers* reinforce brand loyalty. *Value packs* can convert triers to users. *Trade allowances* in combination with *trade communication programs* can increase distribution. *Contests* and *sweepstakes* can enhance brand image. *Premiums* can be used in various ways," Robinson said. "On or near the package, they can attract new triers. Free in the mail, they often increase purchases. When self-liquidated, they can enable low-cost store displays. And *continuity programs* can create differences among parity products and develop loyal users. Special events can enhance brand image."

"Every promotion technique has well-defined strengths and weaknesses," Robinson observed. "By maneuvering these techniques, alone or in combination, we determine the most effective strategy."

Author of the column "Robinson on Sales Promotion" featured in *Advertising Age,* Robinson also created the "Best Promotions" program with *Ad Age* that has been shown throughout the United States and abroad since 1972. Five volumes of his annual review of the outstanding work in the field, *Best Sales Promotion,* are now in print. He is coauthor, with Don E. Schultz, of two definitive texts on the industry, *Sales Promotion Essentials* and *Sales Promotion Management* and is a major contributor to the new *Professional Development Program on Sales Promotion* published by Crain Books.

He has participated in Creativity and Promotion Workshops sponsored by *Advertising Age,* the American Marketing Association Spring Seminar, the APAA Annual Show, the National Conference of the American Academy of Advertising, and Boston Ad Club programs. Robinson has also presented numerous seminars for a host of companies on the trends and future of sales promotion.

Mr. Robinson has taught sales promotion courses at the undergraduate and graduate school levels at several leading universities, including the University of Florida, Michigan State University, and Northwestern University.

FIGURE   16–3

Alaska has used the imagery of its magnificent scenery in a variety of consumer and trade media to promote itself as a tourist destination to travel agents and travelers alike.

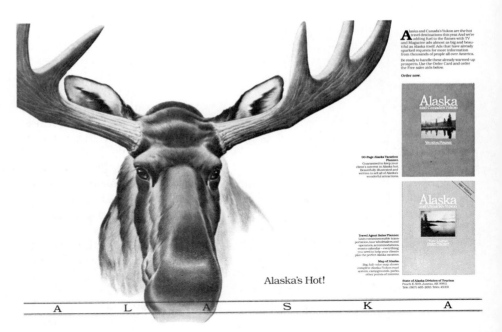

Alaska's Hot!

A   L   A   S   K   A

Manufacturers use many sales promotion techniques to offer dealers extra incentives to purchase, stock, and display their products. Among the more common are the following.

Dealer displays Also referred to as point-of-purchase advertising, these in-store displays, counter stands, and special racks are designed to provide the retailer with ready-made, professionally designed vehicles for selling more of the featured products. A well-designed dealer display can induce dealers to stock more of the product than they normally would.

Deals Trade deals offer limited discounts on the cost of the product, special displays at reduced charges, or other dollar inducements to sell the product. Trade deals must comply with the Robinson-Patman Act by being offered on an equal basis to all dealers.

Dealer premiums Prizes and gifts are often used to get retail dealers and salespeople to reach specific sales goals or to stock or display a certain product.

Cooperative advertising Local advertising expenses are often shared by the retailer, distributor, and manufacturer through cooperative advertising plans. The manufacturer may repay 50 or 100 percent of the dealer's advertising costs or some other amount based on sales. Under the Robinson-Patman Act, the same terms must be extended to all distributors and dealers (Figure 16–4).

Sometimes special cooperative allowances are made to introduce new lines, advertise certain products, or combat competitive activity.

Advertising materials In addition to sharing the cost of advertis-

st.John for *Marshall Field's*

FIGURE 16–4

St. John provides beautifully produced advertising materials to its retail dealers as part of its nationwide co-op program. All the dealer has to do is insert the store name at the bottom of the ad.

ing, many manufacturers provide extensive prepared advertising materials: ad mats, slicks, glossy photos, sample radio commercials, preprinted inserts, and others. Most appliance manufacturers, for instance, supply the material and insist that it be used for their dealers to qualify for co-op advertising money.

Push money Retail salespeople are encouraged in many ways to push the sale of particular products. One of these inducements is PM (push money), also called "spiffs." For example, when you buy a pair of shoes, frequently the salesperson will push special cushioned insoles or shoe polish or some other high-profit "extra." For each bottle of shoe polish sold, the salesperson may receive a 25- to 50-cent spiff, depending on the product.

Collateral material In industrial sales and high-ticket consumer product sales, it is usually difficult to get a purchase decision from the buyer without giving considerable data on every aspect of the product. For this reason, dealers request catalogs, manuals, technical specification sheets, brochures, presentation charts, films, audiovisual materials, or other sales aids available from the manufacturer. As a category these are all referred to as collateral sales material.

Company conventions and dealer meetings To introduce new products, sales promotion programs, or advertising campaigns, dealer meetings are held by most major manufacturers. These are also opportune times to conduct sales and service training sessions. Meetings are frequently promoted as opportunities to learn and also share in camaraderie with other company salespeople and executives. As such, they may be used as a dynamic sales promotion tool by the manufacturer.

Much of the advertising created and placed by companies today is invisible to the consumer because it appears only in trade journals read by particular businesspeople. Likewise, the push techniques of sales promotion are usually invisible. These techniques are used to help accelerate sales by offering inducements to dealers, retailers, and salespeople. If the inducements are successful, the product will be given more shelf space, special display, or extra interest and enthusiasm by salespeople. The difference between no interest and extra interest can spell the difference between product failure and success in today's competitive marketplace.

■ Pull Strategy Techniques

The most visible forms of sales promotion are those aimed at the ultimate purchaser of the product. In the case of Agree, 31 million free samples of the product were distributed. That is a very strong, albeit expensive, inducement to try a new product. In addition, 41 million cents-off coupons were distributed—another strong inducement to try the product.

The list of pull techniques used to accelerate the sales of products is long and constantly growing as new ones are always being devised. Some of the most common and successful include the following.

FIGURE   16–5

Advertisers like Borden's use coupons to stimulate product trial, or repurchase, or to manipulate their pricing strategy in order to compete for share points with other manufacturers.

Sampling   As in the case of Agree, the success of a sampling campaign depends heavily on the merits of the product. This is the most costly of all sales promotions. It offers consumers a free trial, hoping to convert them to habitual use. To be successful, sampling must deal with a product that is available in small sizes and purchased frequently. Also, the sampling effort should be supported by advertising.

Samples may be distributed by mail, door to door, or via coupon advertising. They may be given free or for a small charge.

Sampling in stores is sometimes less expensive than distribution by mail. But retailers normally are not aggressive in their promotion. Sometimes samples are distributed with related items, but then their distribution is restricted to those who buy the other product.

Many times samples are distributed to specific markets, such as cosmetics to college coeds, new drugs to physicians (push), or shampoo to beauty shop operators (push).

Several firms provide specialized sample distribution services, including Welcome Wagon, Gift Pax, and Reuben H. Donnelley Corporation.

Cents-off promotions   A common offer is that made by Campbell Soup when it gives 10 cents off on a can of soup. A variation used by cigarette companies is a $3 refund for proof of purchase of a carton. Companies must be careful to specify that price reductions are for a limited time only, or they may find it difficult to raise the price later. Cents-off promotions take different forms including basic cents-off packages, one-cent sales, free offers, and boxtop refunds.

Special problems may be created by cents-off packages where the retailer already has merchandise in stock marked at a higher price or does not want to lower the price.

Cents-off coupons   A coupon is a certificate with a stated value that is presented to the retail store for a price reduction on a specified item (Figure 16–5). More than 130 billion coupons, worth about $30 billion, were distributed in 1985. Only about 6 billion coupons were actually presented at the checkout counter.[3] Coupons may be distributed in newspapers, magazines, door to door, on packages, and by direct mail. The retailer sorts the coupons, submits them to the manufacturer or a coupon clearinghouse, and is then reimbursed for the coupon's face value plus a handling charge (Figure 16–6).

Fraudulent submission of coupons is now costing the industry some $100 million annually. Coupon fraud comes in a variety of forms, including counterfeiting and submitting coupons for products that were never purchased. The cost of this fraud is borne by the manufacturers at first but ultimately by the consumer in the price paid for products.

Combination offers   Food and drug marketers have successfully used combination offers, such as a razor and a package of blades or a toothbrush with a tube of toothpaste at a reduced price for the two. For best results the items should be related. Sometimes a combination offer may be used to introduce a new product by tying its purchase to an established product at a special price.

FIGURE 16–6

Clearinghouses like Coupon Clearing Service in Newport Beach count and sort millions upon millions of coupons every month—all by hand. The coupons are sent to them from supermarkets and grocery stores around the country, and the stores don't get their money for the coupons until either the clearinghouse or the manufacturer sends it to them. For many retailers, much of their profit is tied up in these coupons, which they redeem as a courtesy to their customers.

Premiums A premium is an item that is offered free or at a bargain price to encourage the consumer to buy an advertised product. Premiums are intended to produce quick sales.

A good premium should have strong appeal and value and be useful or unusual. Also, it should be easily handled and mailed. It may be mailed free, or for a certain amount of money, on receipt of proof of purchase (boxtop or label). Or it may be given with the product at the time of purchase.

Usually the consumer pays the cost of the premium plus handling charges. This is known as a *self-liquidating premium.* The seller does not attempt to make a profit on such a premium but only tries to break even.

A variation of the self-liquidating premium is one distributed by the retailer. It may be a traffic-building or continuity premium given weekly to customers who return to the store to complete their sets of dinnerware or encyclopedias, for example.

In-pack premiums, such as plastic toys for children, are popular in the food field, especially cereals. *On-pack premiums* (those attached to the outside of the package) have good impulse value, but they may encourage pilferage. Another drawback is that they sometimes make it difficult for the grocer to stack the product on the shelves. (See Ad Lab 16–A.)

Coupon premiums, which require customers to save and collect in-pack coupons for later redemption of valuable premiums, can create great consumer loyalty. For instance, one long-time user of this device, Brown & Williamson Tobacco Corporation, consistently receives as many as 2 million Raleigh coupons daily from repeat cigarette customers who send for more than $10 million worth of premiums annually.

Numerous federal and state laws govern premiums. Most important, these laws restrict the use of the word *free*. A free offer must be absolutely that—with no extra cost. Nor can the price of the offering product be increased to cover the cost of the premium. This must be done at the outset—in conjunction with the word *free*.

Food and Drug Administration regulations govern in-pack premiums, and Federal Trade Commission rules apply to in-pack coupons. Other legal factors to be reckoned with are postal laws, sales taxes, misrepresentation of premiums, and lottery regulations.

AD LAB   16–A   The 10 commandments of creative promotion

Spelling out the commandments may help you see why creativity isn't—and shouldn't be—the exclusive jurisdiction of creative directors, writers, and art directors. You'll also find it handy for developing promotions and reviewing them.

1. Thou shalt set specific objectives. Undisciplined or undirected creative work is a frivolous waste. The first step in developing a promotion is to exercise your creativity by setting meaningful goals. And this is the place where brand managers, account executives, and researchers can get into the creative act. Lack of creativity at this stage results in vague and useless directions—and wasted time. You've got to focus. Do you want trial, or to increase brand awareness, off-shelf merchandise displays, build up trade inventories, etc.? Setting realistic, specific objectives is a quarter of the creative battle.

2. Thou shalt know how basic promotion techniques work. Knowing what a promotion technique can and can't do is another quarter of the creative battle. And this is knowledge that clients and account executives should have as well as creatives. You don't use a sweepstakes to encourage multiple purchases or a refund offer to get new users. A price-off deal cannot reverse a brand's downward sales trend. A sweepstakes can increase brand awareness. A refund can get off-shelf merchandise at modest costs.

3. Thou shalt have simple, attention-getting copy. This is on the head of the copy-

writer, usually. I say usually because there are times where promotional concepts become so complex it's impossible to write a simple or even understandable headline. It's directly on the writer's head when she or he takes a powerful offer such as "Save 75¢" and tries to get cute, burying the selling proposition in the process.

4. Thou shalt lay out contemporary, easy-to-track graphics. This is on the head of the art director, except when he or she gets 500 words of text and 20 items to illustrate on a quarter-page of a free-standing insert.

5. Thou shalt clearly communicate your concept. This could be a repetition of the third and fourth commandments, but there are times when promotion objectives are contradictory, or when a promotional ad is trying to carry a product advertising message plus promotional messages, and things get hairy. In this case, creative failure may not be blamed solely on the "creatives."

6. Thou shalt reinforce your brand's advertising message. When a brand has a big budget, long-term ad campaign it seems sort of dumb not to try to tie a promotion to it. For example, Smirnoff vodka has been running an ad campaign showing unusual party situations—a cookout in the snow with the line "Cookout—Smirnoff Style." Originally, Smirnoff ran a $25,000 contest called "Contest—Smirnoff Style" and required entries to have a snapshot of an unusual party and a title for it. It takes an extra shot of creativity on

Contests and sweepstakes A *contest* offers prizes based on the skill of the entrants. A *sweepstakes* offers prizes based on a chance drawing of entrants' names. A *game* has the chance element of a sweepstakes but is conducted over a longer time. Games include local bingo-type games designed to build store traffic. Their big marketing advantage is that customers must make repeat visits to the dealer to continue playing.

Both contests and sweepstakes have the common purpose of encouraging consumption of the product by creating consumer involve-

---

everyone's part to tie a prize or premium in with advertising, but it sure makes your marketing bucks work harder.

7. Thou shalt support the brand's positioning and image. What would you think about Kraft offering a recipe book of potent drink recipes or Marlboro offering pantyhose free in the mail? Especially for image-sensitive brands and categories—a family-oriented Kraft, a rugged Marlboro, or ultrapremium Chivas Regal—it's important to get creative about supporting positioning and image. You would not, for example, select a pantyhose premium for Marlboro because your purchasing agent located a warehouse full of hose offered at discount prices.

8. Thou shalt coordinate your promotional efforts with other marketing plans. Responsibility for this falls on a lot more people than creatives. I'm talking about things like timing a consumer promotion to break simultaneously with a big trade allowance, or using a promotion to get trial for a product improvement or line extension that's being introduced with a big new ad campaign. Don't schedule a promotion that requires a lengthy sell-in pitch to the trade when your salespeople are scheduled to go to a national sales convention for a week. Let the right hand know what the left hand is doing, and be creative about scheduling and planning.

9. Thou shall know the media you work through. Here we're talking about media directors, brand managers, account executives, and the creatives all getting into the act. Should you run a promotion with only magazine or newspaper ad support, or should you carry the whole thing through point-of-sale display? Or both? Maybe delivering samples through point-of-sale displays—as salable samples—is more effective and efficient than door-to-door distribution. If you're going with point-of-sale material, what's the strongest type of display for your objectives? Motion? Shelf-talkers? In print, what's the best publication to reach your target audience? There are a lot of creative judgments to be made by a lot more than creatives.

10. Thou shalt know when to break the other nine commandments. This is the ultimate creative exercise. It takes a confidently creative person to know when breaking any of the above rules is really the smartest way to go. It will increase redemption rates and sales. Creatively applying a technique or combination of techniques to meet stated objectives is critical to a successful promotion.

Laboratory Application

Thou shalt discuss these 10 commandments with specific reference to the Agree story presented earlier in the chapter.

ment. These devices are highly popular and pull millions of entries. Usually contest entrants are required to send in some proof of purchase, such as a boxtop or label. For more expensive products, the contestant may only have to visit the dealer to pick up an entry blank. (See Ad Lab 16–B).

In recent years sweepstakes and games have become more popular than contests. They are much easier to enter and take less time than contests and, therefore, have greater appeal for the average person.

AD LAB 16–B   The syrup with something extra

The "Dress-Up Mrs. Butterworth's" bottle-decorating contest was launched. Designed to boost product awareness, the promotion was supported by magazine ads (in such books as *McCall's*, *Redbook*, *Better Homes & Gardens*, and *Southern Living*) and by in-store promotion (created in-house). Consumers were asked to decorate the bottle using common craft items. They they submitted a photo or sketch of the bottle. Lever selected 200 finalists in each of two age categories (children under 14 and adults).

Prizes included family "dream" vacations to such resorts as Acapulco and Aruba. And consumer response was better than expected. Mrs. Butterworth's bottles were transformed into geishas, spacewomen, and nuns with such materials as paint, yarn, bread dough, seashells, and modeling clay.

At the beginning of this decade Mrs. Butterworth's edged out Aunt Jemima to become the second largest selling syrup in the country.

Laboratory Applications

1. Do you consider the creative packaging by Mrs. Butterworth's an effective sales promotion technique?
2. What package-related promotions might be created for other products to stimulate awareness of the products or their existing packages?

FIGURE 16–7

A display stand for a Yamaha keyboard offers a graphic point-of-purchase promotion for the product as well as facilitating trial of the product.

Sweepstakes require careful planning. No purchase can be required as a condition for entry, or else the sweepstakes becomes a lottery and therefore illegal. All postal laws must be obeyed in planning contests and sweepstakes.

To encourage a large number of entries, sponsors try to keep their contests as simple as possible. The prize structure must be clearly stated and rules clearly defined. National contests and sweepstakes are handled and judged by independent, professional contest firms.

Contests and sweepstakes must be promoted and advertised in order to be successful. An important element of this promotion is dealer support. To assure dealer cooperation, many contests and sweepstakes require the entrant to give the name of the particular product's local dealer. In these cases, prizes may also be awarded to the dealer who made the sale.

Point-of-purchase advertising (P-O-P) As a push technique, good dealer displays may induce a retailer to carry a certain line or promote a new product. However, P-O-P is primarily a pull technique consisting of advertising or display materials at the retail location to build traffic, advertise the product, and promote impulse buying. These materials may include window displays, counter displays, floor and wall displays to hold the merchandise, streamers, and posters. Often the product's shipping cartons are designed to double as display units. At times, a complete ''information center'' provides literature, samples, and product photos.

Such material has increased in importance with the trend toward self-service retailing. Even in stores that have clerks, display material can offer extra selling information and make the product stand out from the competition (Figure 16–7).

Trading stamps This promotion device was introduced by the Sperry & Hutchinson Company in 1896. For years the popularity of S&H Green Stamps in department stores, supermarkets, and service stations fluctuated. Finally, as discount stores and suburban shopping centers grew and the energy crisis affected service stations, interest in trading stamps began to wane. Today the several brands of trading stamps have largely given way to other forms of retail promotion such as games.

Miscellaneous The above is only a partial listing of the bewildering array of sales promotion tools. The choice of which to use in any given instance depends on a combination of factors. Timing is important. Fads and fashions come and go in sales promotion as in anything else. To be successful, sales promotions must take advantage of current consumer preferences.

A promotion needs to be unique to attract attention but time-tested to ensure probable success. For instance, certain types of sales promotion are known to work well for new products—namely, sampling, couponing, and money-refund offers. Other types have proven helpful in increasing the use of established products, such as premiums, price-off promotions, and contests and sweepstakes. (See Ad Lab 16–C.)

AD LAB   16–C   Smell: Powerful armament in retailer's arsenal

You are strolling past the bakery in your local shopping mall. Isn't that the irresistible odor of fresh-baked chocolate-chip cookies wafting from the ovens?

Maybe not.

International Flavors & Fragrances Inc., has succeeded in synthesizing the mouth-watering aroma not only of chocolate-chip cookies but also of hot apple pie, fresh pizza, baking ham, and even nongreasy French fries.

IF&F packages the artificial odors in aerosol cans and markets them along with $25 to $30 timed-release devices that periodically fire a burst of scent out into the shopping mall to tempt customers. The sprays are selling briskly, says Ernest Kmites, IF&F's manager of sales services, and cost the owners just "pennies a day."

That surely makes it one of the least expensive tricks in retailing, and doubtless one of the simplest. One favorite of used-car dealers is to rejuvenate an old clunker with a "new-car scent." One popular brand is something called Velvet Touch, made by a company in Wayland, Mass.

Marvin Ivy, president of the National Independent Automobile Dealers Association, a trade group, says he has heard of such a product but disapproves of its use. "I think you shouldn't," Mr. Ivy says. 'I think you'll deceive the public. That car could have 60,000 miles on it and smell like hell."

But Joseph Eikenberg, owner of Aero Motors in Baltimore, suggests that the scents may have a legitimate use in used cars, such as when the autos arrive with lingering smells left by dogs or smokers.

Laboratory Application

Do you believe using canned, artificial odors is a legitimate sales promotion technique?

SUPPLEMENTARY

MEDIA

Many miscellaneous promotional media are difficult to classify because they are tailored to individual needs and do not necessarily fall into any major category. They include the following.

 ### Specialty Advertising

Today nearly every business uses advertising specialties to some degree. These include everything from key chains, ballpoint pens, and calendars to matchbooks, thermometers, and billfolds (Figure 16–8). They are used by national advertisers, local merchants, banks and insurance companies, industrial firms, and service stations, to name just a few. There are said to be more than 10,000 different items sold, representing an annual volume of more than $5 billion.

While companies often spend substantial sums for these goodwill items, they must also exercise care. It is the one business in the advertising field where industry practice dictates that the advertiser pay for any production overage incurred, up to an agreed-on limit.

An advertising specialty is different from a premium. The recipient of a premium must give some consideration to the advertiser—buy a product, send in a coupon, witness a demonstration, or perform some other action of advantage to the advertiser. A premium may be an expensive item; therefore, it frequently bears no advertising message.

An advertising specialty is given free. It is an inexpensive, but useful, goodwill gift—a reminder that carries the company or product name or logo. It may feature a new product, a new plant, or some special event or promotion. Some may be kept for years and thereby serve as continuous, friendly reminders of the advertiser's business.

Catalog Houses

These include general merchandise houses such as Spiegel and Aldens, plus a growing number of specialty and gift houses such as Spencer Gifts, Sunset House, and Miles Kimball. These last three have more than 13 million customers who browse through their catalog pages to shop for gifts or other products they want or need.

Trade Shows and Exhibits

Every major industry sponsors annual trade shows and exhibitions where manufacturers, dealers, and buyers of the industry's products can get together for demonstrations and discussion. These occasions can be most productive to exhibitors. They have the opportunity of exposing their new products, literature, and samples to new customers as well as old. At the same time they can meet potential new dealers for their products (Figure 16–9).

As a result the construction of booths and exhibits has become a major factor in sales promotion plans. To stop traffic, booths must be simple in design and attractive, with good lighting. The exhibit should also provide a comfortable atmosphere to promote conversation between salespeople and prospects.

In the planning of exhibits or trade show booths, advertisers need to consider the following factors:

1. Size and location of space.
2. Desired image or impression of the exhibit.
3. Complexities of shipping, installation, and dismantling.
4. The number of products to be displayed.
5. The need for storage and distribution of literature.
6. The use of pre-show advertising and promotion.
7. The cost of all of the above.

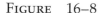

FIGURE 16–8

Radio is commonly referred to as a hot medium, and WLUM promotes itself as Milwaukee's hot FM station.

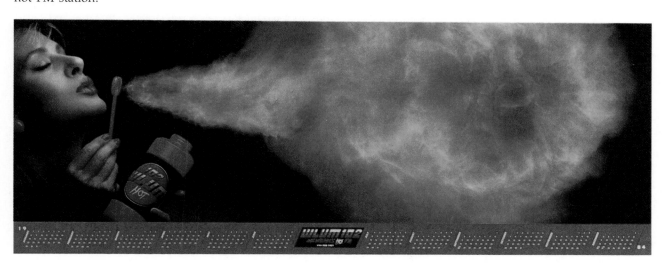

FIGURE   16–9

If you're a competitor, duck! Code-a-phone is taking aim at your share of the business. That, as least, is the implication in this trade ad for their exhibit at an upcoming trade show.

Audiovisual Systems

Audiovisual equipment has now become virtually synonymous with sales training and demonstrations. A wide variety of equipment is available including portable sound-slide filmstrip projectors, videotape monitors, and complex multi-screen equipment.

Directories and Yellow Pages

Literally thousands of directories are published—by trade associations, industrial groups, and others. While serving mainly as locators, buying guides, and mailing lists, they may also carry advertising aimed at specialized fields.

In the U.S. there are approximately 6,000 local telephone directories with a combined circulation of 286 million. They reach 85% of the households and every business. Directories are also widely used by local firms. National advertisers may seek help from the National Yellow Pages Service Association for rates, data, creative aid, and one-order placement. Such advertising is commissionable to advertising agencies.

Motion Picture Advertising

Advertising films fall into two classes. *Theatrical films,* usually ten minutes or shorter, are shown in about 12,000 movie houses in the United States. They should be entertaining, of high quality, and without obvious "commercials." Such movies are made for advertisers by professional producers. Distribution is handled by film distributors through the film exchanges that supply movie houses. *Sponsored films* should be both entertaining and educational. The advertiser engages a film distributing house to arrange bookings for clubs, churches, schools, fraternal societies, airport lounges, resorts, and even TV stations.

Summary

Sales promotion supplements advertising and personal selling for the purpose of stimulating or accelerating sales. It includes widely varied types of promotional activities with unlimited applications aimed at salespeople, distributors, retailers, and consumers. By offering direct inducements, such as money, prizes, gifts, or other opportunities, it provides extra incentive to buy a product, to visit a store, to request literature, or to take other action.

Sales promotion techniques are used in the trade to *push* products through the distribution channels or, with the ultimate customer, to *pull* them through the channel. Manufacturers use a variety of sales promotion techniques to offer dealers extra incentive to purchase, stock, and display their products. These include dealer displays, deals, dealer premiums, cooperative advertising, advertising materials, push money, collateral material, and company conventions and dealer meetings.

The most visible forms of sales promotion aimed at the ultimate purchaser of the product are sampling, cents-off promotions, cents-off coupons, combination offers, premiums, in-pack premiums, contests and sweepstakes, point-of-purchase advertising, and trading stamps.

Supplementary media are so diversified that they defy classification. One type is specialty advertising. There are more than 10,000 different items used as specialties. This includes everything from key chains, ballpoint pens, and calendars to matchbooks, thermometers, and billfolds. Other types are trade shows and exhibits, audiovisual systems, directories and Yellow Pages, and motion picture advertising.

Questions for review and discussion

1. How does the definition of sales promotion differ from the definition of advertising?
2. What is the relationship between sales promotion and advertising?
3. What examples can you give of push and pull sales promotion strategies?
4. Select three common push strategy techniques? What is your evaluation of them?
5. Select three common pull strategy techniques? What is your evaluation of them?
6. What is the difference between an advertising specialty and a premium?
7. What are trade shows and exhibitions? How do they aid advertisers?
8. What usefulness do audiovisual systems offer advertisers?
9. Should advertisers be interested in using directories and the Yellow Pages? Why?
10. What is the difference between theatrical films and sponsored films?

PART V

SPECIAL TYPES OF ADVERTISING

17

LOCAL
ADVERTISING

A few years ago, Ray Lemke was a barber in the little town of Papillion, Nebraska. His young wife, Gwen, stayed at home caring for their three small children. But she was bored doing the same thing every day.

That year a survey was published which predicted that by the mid-1980s Papillion would be in the center of the growing metropolitan area around Omaha. The Lemkes decided to go into real estate. They rented a little store-front office next to the barber shop and started listing homes and selling insurance, too. Gwen jumped in with both feet, answering the phone, helping with the contracts, and getting involved in the advertising and the sales. Soon Ray was forced to make a choice. With some trepidation, he sold the barber shop and moved into the real estate business full time.

They called this business Action Realty. It signified movement and gave them the first position in the phone book. They designed a dynamic "Action" logo to use on signs and in their newspaper ads. They created a standard ad layout which very quickly became recognizable as the Action format: large space, heavy borders, dominant logo, numerous listings of property, and bold type (Figure 17–1). They ran their ads in the local newspaper every week without fail.

They both got involved in local community activities—service clubs, charities, trade associations. They affiliated with a nationwide realty network, Home for Living, and participated in the programs that organization sponsored. They concentrated on developing training programs for their staff and exciting incentives, like vacation trips, for their top producers.

They encouraged their employees to be active in community affairs, and they publicized their successful employees with news releases and ads in the local press. They constantly tested new ideas.

Action Real Estate rapidly became the fastest growing real estate firm in Sarpy County. Within 10 years the company was operating six offices, had a sales staff of over 75 people, 20 secretaries, and an annual gross sales volume of over $40 million.

By this time Gwen had become president of the firm and Ray had retired from active participation so he could pursue his ambition of becoming a personal counselor and motivational speaker. They had both witnessed the potential of consistent, strong local advertising. And they had kept the promise made by their advertising—Action.

LOCAL ADVERTISING: WHERE THE ACTION IS

Local advertising, as opposed to regional or national advertising, refers to advertising by businesses within a particular city or county to customers within the same geographic area. In 1985, 44 percent of all dollars spent on advertising were for local advertising as opposed to national advertising.

Quite often local advertising is referred to as "retail" advertising because it is commonly performed by retail stores. However, retail advertising is often not local, but regional or national in scope, as witnessed by the volume of commercials run by national fast-food chains, department stores, or jewelry retailers, to mention just a few. Moreover, local advertising is also commonly done by insurance agents, real estate brokers, banks, investment houses, professional services, auto mechanics, plumbers, local manufacturers, and many other businesses that are not usually thought of as retail stores.

Local advertising is important because of the arena in which it is performed. Most sales are made or lost locally. A national auto manufacturer may spend millions advertising new cars. Local auto dealers as a group spend just as much or more to bring customers into their showrooms to buy the cars. In fact, if they don't make a strong effort on the local level, the efforts of the national advertisers may frequently be wasted. So when it comes to consummating the sale, local advertising is where the action is.

While the basic principles used by national advertisers are applicable to local advertising, local advertisers have special problems which this chapter examines. These problems stem from the simple, practical realities of marketing in a local area. There are many differences between local and national advertisers, including basic objectives and strategies, needs of the marketplace, amount of money available to spend on advertising, heavy emphasis by local advertisers on newspaper advertising, use of price as a buying inducement, and the sources of specialized help in preparing advertisements.

■ Types of Local Advertising

There are two major types of local advertising: product and institutional. *Product advertising* is designed to sell a specific product or service. It also hopes to get immediate action. *Institutional advertising* at-

FIGURE   17–1

The Action ad format may not be very pretty with its extensive use of heavy type and bold reverses. However, it has been very effective in creating a consistent presence for Action Realty and has lent credence to the promise inherent in their name.

tempts to obtain favorable attention for the business as a whole, not for a specific product or service that the store or business sells. The effects of institutional advertising are intended to be long rather than short range.

Product advertising

For most local advertisers, product advertising constitutes the greatest portion of their advertising efforts. Product advertising can be further subdivided into the following types.

Regular price-line advertising The purpose of this type of advertising is to inform consumers about the services available or the wide selection and quality of merchandise offered at regular prices (Figure 17–2).

Sale advertising In order to stimulate the movement of particular merchandise or generally increase store traffic, local merchants advertise items on sale (Figure 17–3). This type of advertising places the emphasis on special reduced prices.

Clearance advertising To make room for new product lines or new models, or to rid themselves of slow-moving product lines, floor samples, broken or distressed merchandise, or items that are no longer in season, local advertisers may do clearance advertising.

Institutional advertising

Institutional advertising involves selling an idea about the company. The purpose of such advertising is usually to make the public aware of the company and to build a solid reputation of service and good citizenship. An advertisement might stress longer hours of operation, a new credit policy, or store expansion. This type of advertis-

---

FIGURE 17–2

The Workout Loft suggests that its regular $6 price for a workout is a paltry sum for people who are dying to get into shape.

We'll kill you for $6.

We offer the most intense workout in Boston. So at a paltry $6 for a 90-minute class it's the best pain-per-dollar deal around. Plus there are no membership fees. No women-only policy. And no advance sign-up requirement. In fact, the only thing that's a pain in the ass about The Workout Loft is the exercise we do to keep your tail trim. Give us a call at 437-7131. But only if you're just dying to be in great shape

The Workout Loft 811 Boylston St.

A E R O B I C S ◇ S T R E T C H I N G ◇ S T R E N G T H E N I N G ◇ S P O T T O N I N G

FIGURE 17–3

To celebrate fall, Harold announces its annual fall in prices.

In the great annual tradition of Minnesota's thermometer, when the temperature drops so do our prices.

Our Annual Coat Sale
October 10-15
6 days only. For best selection, put the wraps on your new coat early.

HƎROLD
818 Nicollet Mall

ing is expected to reap long-term rather than short-term benefits because such advertisements frequently announce the store's concern for the community, local charitable causes, product and service quality, and the customer in particular.

Readership of institutional advertising may sometimes be lower than that of product advertising. But, if done effectively, institutional ads can be very helpful in building a favorable image for the business, in attracting new patronage, and in developing loyalty from existing customers (Figure 17–4).

■ Objectives of Local Advertising

Gerry Smith was a field technical representative for Motorola. He had lived in Mount Holly for many years and had become a local history buff. When the town fathers decided to celebrate the city's 100th birthday they turned to Gerry for help. They thought a centennial celebration might be a good stimulus for local business, but they weren't sure who would be interested in visiting this little community in North Carolina 100 miles west of Winston-Salem. They discovered that Gerry Smith was a born promoter.

When he presented his plan to them, they saw that his program would satisfy all the accepted objectives of local advertising:

FIGURE   17–4

Another great ad from the Midwest's hot shop, Fallon McElligott Rice, this long-copy, story-line ad for Winfield Potter's makes the reader anxious to try the restaurant's mesquite-charcoaled fresh seafood and aged meats. Institutional ads like this build lasting goodwill and reputation—as long as the advertiser backs up the promise by delivering the goods.

1. Introduce new customers to Mount Holly's products and services.
2. Build awareness of the town and its business.
3. Help keep old customers from shopping someplace else.
4. Increase the frequency of visits by regular customers.
5. Reduce the normal cost of selling to large numbers of customers.
6. Help curtail the seasonal dip in business.
7. Accelerate the turnover of retail inventory.

Not only all that, but his plan would cost the city virtually nothing, since he designed it to pay for itself.

First he contacted the local newspaper and arranged for extensive news coverage of the event scheduled for July 14. He also showed them how they would sell much more advertising that week than ever before (Figure 17–5). Next he contacted Freightliner Truck Corporation, which had just finished building a new plant in Mount Holly. They agreed to participate by holding a giant open house, running supportive ads in the newspaper, and contributing their largest show vehicles to the centennial parade.

When Smith approached the retailers, they were eager to get involved. They agreed to decorate their stores, run large centennial ads, wear costumes, offer prizes, and help sell centennial souvenirs. Meanwhile he arranged to have a monument erected to honor the founding families of Mount Holly. He had a commemorative bronze coin struck, bumper stickers printed, and even souvenir license plates made. These were put on sale at reasonable prices throughout the retail business district.

To publicize the event, he sent news releases to the community newspapers of all the surrounding towns and followed up with personal calls. Then he called the television station in Winston-Salem, and it arranged to have the unique event covered by CBS News.

When July 14 came, it was indeed a day of celebration in Mount

FIGURE 17–5

The Mount Holly centennial was a gala event for the local citizenry. Full-page newspaper ads promoted the fun, while souvenir license plates and bumper stickers were used to promote personal involvement.

Holly. A parade led by Freightliner's show trucks kicked off the event. Ending the parade were the town's youngsters on their bicycles, and a prize was given to the best decorated bicycle. Afterward local dignitaries unveiled the monument. An old-fashioned fair with contests, bazaar booths, and cotton candy was held all afternoon in the park. Freightliner opened its doors to the public and offered tours, truck rides, balloons, and refreshments. That evening a street dance was held downtown with live bands, and finally the whole event culminated with a brilliant fireworks show after dark.

Folks came from miles around to join in the fun. Those who couldn't come heard about it on radio and television. The merchants made money, the newspaper made money, the town gained some notoriety, Freightliner earned tremendous goodwill from its new neighbors, and Gerry Smith became a local hero.

The objectives of local advertising differ from the objectives of national advertising in emphasis and time. National manufacturers tend to emphasize long-term objectives of awareness, image, and credibility. On the local, retail level, the advertiser's needs tend to be more immediate. The emphasis is on making the cash register ring—increasing traffic, turning over inventory, and bringing in new customers. (See the Checklist of local advertising objectives.)

As a result, on the local level there are constant promotions, sales, and clearances, all designed to create immediate activity. The trade-off, of course, is that the day after the promotion or sale the traffic may stop. So to increase traffic again, the merchant may plan another sale or another promotion. Then another and another. What sometimes results is a cycle of sporadic bursts of activity followed by inactivity, sharp peaks and valleys in sales and a distasteful image of a business that should be visited only during a sale.

Long-term and short-term objectives work against each other when one is sought at the expense of the other. Successful local advertisers, therefore, think of long-term objectives first and then develop short-term goals in keeping with their long-term objectives. This usually increases the emphasis on institutional and regular price-line advertising and reduces the reliance on sales and clearances for creating traffic.

PLANNING THE ADVERTISING EFFORT

The key to success in any advertising program, local or national, is adequate planning. Planning is not a one-time occurrence, however. It is a continuous process of research, evaluation, decision, execution, and review. On the local level more advertising dollars are no doubt wasted because of inadequate planning than for any other reason.

Mount Holly's one-day centennial celebration was a success because Gerry Smith planned that promotion in detail. Action Realty's 10-year success was due to the fact that Gwen and Ray Lemke made planning a continuous, flexible process, which allowed for change, improvement, new facts, and new ideas.

Several steps are involved in planning the local advertising effort:

Checklist of local advertising objectives

☐ To introduce new customers. Every year many old customers are lost due to relocation, death, inconvenience, or dissatisfaction. To thrive, a business must continually seek new customers. Advertising is the best method to use.

☐ To build awareness and image. Many local businesses provide essentially the same services. To distinguish themselves from one another, stores can use advertising techniques to increase awareness and build a unique image.

☐ To help retain old customers and increase their frequency of visits. More customers are lost because of inattention than any other single reason. In addition, a barrage of advertising from competitors may lure customers away. A steady, consistent program of advertising can keep present customers informed and reinforce their desire to remain customers and visit your business more often.

☐ To reduce sales expense. By preselling many customers, advertising lightens the load on sales personnel. By increasing traffic, it allows salespeople to make more sales in a shorter time. These contribute to reducing the cost of sales.

☐ To curtail seasonal peaks. Each year there are dips and swings in the business cycle. One way to level off the peaks and valleys is to advertise consistently.

☐ To accelerate inventory turnover. Some businesses sell all the merchandise in a store four or five times a year. Others turn over the inventory 15 to 20 times. The more times inventory is turned, the more profit can be made. By turning inventory more rapidly, prices can also be kept down. In this way advertising contributes to lower customer prices.

analyzing the local market, analyzing the competition, conducting adequate research, determining objectives and strategy, establishing a realistic budget, planning media strategy, and determining creative direction.

Analyzing the Local Market and Competition

Through careful research, the type of local market in which the business is located must be identified. Whenever possible, local advertising should reflect the needs of the immediate area. Items to consider, therefore, are whether the area is rural or urban, conservative or progressive, high- or low-income, white-collar or blue-collar. A thorough knowledge of the local market and potential customers influences the goods and services the business offers, the prices established, and the design and style of advertising. Accurate analysis at this point prevents advertising misfires later on.

Similarly, a careful study should be made of all the competitors in the local area. What merchandise and services do they offer? What is their pricing strategy? Where are they located? How large are they? What is their advertising strategy? What media do they use? How much do they spend? Do their places of business invite customers or repel them?

Constant competitive research alerts the advertiser to new ideas, advantages and disadvantages, new merchandising techniques, and new material for advertising campaigns.

FIGURE   17–6

Research helps advertisers find the right appeal for their customers. People who live in Santa Barbara, for instance, were found to be very community minded and proud of their hometown. The appeal in this ad reflects that finding: "keep your money at home in a hometown bank where it can help the community."

■ Conducting Adequate Research

The local advertiser usually cannot afford to hire a specialized firm to conduct formal market research programs. However, because of its proximity to the marketplace, a local store or business should be well attuned to the attitudes of customers and be able to conduct informal research to measure customer reaction to merchandise and advertising campaigns. A good local advertising agency might assist in this regard.

Chapter 6 contained a thorough discussion of the field of advertising and marketing research. In this chapter we only want to examine those aspects of research that are unique to the local advertiser. As discussed in Chapter 6, there are two types of research. Primary research is data collected firsthand. Secondary research is data accumulated by others that can be adapted to the needs of the advertiser.

■ Primary research

To be successful, a local advertiser must have the answers to many important questions. Who are our present customers? Who are our potential customers? How many are there? Where are they located? How can our company best appeal to them? Where do they now buy the merchandise or services that I want to sell to them? Can I offer them anything they are not getting at the present time? If so, what? How can I convince them they should do business with me? (Figure 17–6.) To answer these questions, primary research should be conducted in the following areas.

Customer and sales analysis It is important to keep close track of customers—both charge and cash customers—so that their addresses can be correlated to census tract information. Census information includes such data as average income, family size, education, vehicle and home ownership, and age.

In retail stores, sales should be tabulated by merchandise classification. Careful analysis of this information helps identify changes in consumer buying patterns, which in turn affects the merchandise or services that will be bought and advertised in the future.

A comparison should be made of a company's sales by merchandise lines in relation to those of other companies in the area. Information about other companies' market share can be obtained from several sources mentioned later in this section.

Customer attitudes and satisfaction Feedback from sales personnel can provide valuable information about customers. In addition, having salespeople solicit information about customers can forestall problems by locating areas of customer satisfaction and dissatisfaction at an early stage. Customers will also feel that the store cares if it actively seeks information from them.

Advertising testing Because of the vast number of ads prepared by most local advertisers, it's unusual to test advertisements in advance of their placement. However, posttesting should be conducted to determine the advertising campaign's effect on sales, if any.

Determining the best medium in which to advertise, finding the best mailing lists, determining whether "hard" or "soft" sell works best, and testing music or slogans for broadcast commercials are very worthwhile (Figure 17–7).

Secondary research

Local advertisers should be aware of the many secondary sources of information that are available and can be adapted to their particular needs. These sources include manufacturers and suppliers, trade publications and associations, local advertising media, and various government organizations.

Manufacturers and suppliers Manufacturers and suppliers want their dealers to succeed. Their dealer-aid programs usually include valuable research on the retail market for their products. Dealer seminars are often conducted in which research results are explained.

Retail trade publications and associations Trade publications are excellent sources of information for a local advertiser's business. These publications contain important articles about trends in the business, new technology, and research studies that apply to the particular category of business to which the publication is directed.

Just a few of hundreds of such publications are *Stores, The Merchandiser, Progressive Grocer, Automotive News, Farm Supplier, Hotel & Motel Management, Modern Jeweler,* and *Shopping Center World.* A complete list of publications is available in *The Standard Periodical Directory* or *Ulrich's International Periodicals Directory.*

PEOPLE IN ADVERTISING

Jane Trahey

President
Trahey Advertising, Inc.

Popular author, screenwriter, columnist, playwright, and talk show guest Jane Trahey has made her major mark in the advertising world as founder and president of Trahey Advertising, Inc., New York and Chicago, an agency widely known for its retail campaigns.

Jane Trahey has twice been heralded as Ad Woman of the Year. She has been selected among the 100 Most Accomplished Women by *Harper's Bazaar.* Her distinctive copy has won a number of awards. Observed one writer, "Jane Trahey's talent and her independence are her trademark." Both have sparked her rapid rise to success.

Born in Chicago, Trahey received a B.A. from Mundelein College. After graduate studies at the University of Wisconsin, she went to work for the *Chicago Tribune.* Her interest in retail advertising led her to join Carson Pirie Scott, a Chicago department store. She went on to Neiman-Marcus, Dallas, where she became advertising and sales promotion director. Trahey was then named advertising director of a New York manufacturing firm, where she founded and led an in-house advertising agency. Two years later she decided to

ERNEST HEMINGWAY NEVER SLEPT HERE.

Only 18 rooms, 84 steps to the beach
Suites with fireplaces, garden courtyard with pool and spa
An Inn at 15 Chapala Street, Santa Barbara CA 93101 (805) 966-0851
Villa Rosa

FIGURE 17–7

Villa Rosa's unique rationale is part of an attractive, amusing campaign of similar highly graphic, tongue-in-cheek ads aimed at getting the reader's attention and creating awareness for a small, little-known hotel in Santa Barbara with convenient amenities—like 84 steps to the beach.

Advertising is frequently a topic in other publications, too. A glance under "Advertising" in the *Business Periodicals Index* shows the publication source for the various aspects of advertising a local advertiser may be concerned with.

The most important publication in the advertising field is *Advertising Age*. A weekly publication, it contains articles on all types of advertising written by experts in various fields, important data on advertising expenditures, stories on advertising agencies and their clients, and updates on government and its relationship to advertising. Many articles are of a how-to variety—practical, down-to-earth material that can be used by any advertiser whether the budget is large or small (Figure 17–8).

A glance at the *Encyclopedia of Associations*, available at most libraries, indicates the associations pertinent to a particular area of interest. A short letter will bring membership information as well as research data that may be available with little or no charge.

The National Retail Merchants Association (100 W. 31st Street, New York, NY 10001) publishes an extensive list of materials on research topics of interest to retailers. Also the Mass Retailing Institute's study of shoppers' behavior is available at reasonable cost (579 7th Avenue, New York, NY 10018).

Typical of the many associations that are good sources of research information are the National Office Products Association, National Association of Drug Stores, Menswear Retailers of America, United States Savings and Loan League, National Sporting Goods Association, and the American Society of Travel Agents.

launch her own agency, and Trahey Advertising, Inc., was born.

Since then Jane Trahey has become a leading name in fashion advertising, serving clients ranging from Elizabeth Arden, Bill Blass, Pauline Trigere, and Adele Simpson to major retailers like B. Altman, Neiman-Marcus, Bergdorf's, and Harzfeld's. She has also created ad campaigns for Lanvin, Charles of the Ritz, Dorsay, and Borghese. Other key accounts have included Union Carbide, Kayser Hosiery, and Olivetti.

In the interim Jane Trahey has continued her education, obtaining an M.A. from Columbia University and a Doctorate in Humane Letters from Mundelein College. She has written 11 books, two movies, a play, a monthly magazine column, and a score of newspaper and magazine articles. She has also appeared on virtually every major TV talk show in the nation.

Year after year her agency's campaigns for retail clients have scored impressive success. To achieve this, Jane Trahey first focuses on learning what is unique about the store. "Try to find a uniqueness," she urges, "or help to create one. If a retail account lets you create such a uniqueness," adds Trahey, "chances are it has one."

The next step, says Trahey, is to convey this uniqueness in advertising. "Ads should reflect the heart of the store," she emphasizes. "Ads should tell me what these institutions are—what they mean in their communities—what contributions they make to my life." Do most retail ads do this? No, says Trahey. "I can count on one hand the stores that have that extra readability in their ads that holds me for more than the flip of the page." Defining this "extra readability," Trahey makes clear, "It doesn't matter a lot about the art. It's what the ad *says* that sells the store—and sells the merchandise." Trahey reflects, "You should do the *best* you can for the client. The client trusts you. You want to be worth that trust."

Despite her demanding role as agency president, Jane Trahey still devotes time to her wide-ranging interests. She serves as a member of the Advisory Board of The Sisters of Providence at St. Mary of the Woods.

FIGURE 17–8

Advertising Age is the leading trade publication for marketing and advertising practitioners.

Advertising media and media associations The amount of research data that will be provided by local media depends on the size of the community. In large cities, the newspaper and broadcast stations provide in-depth market data about the communities they serve.

Even if a local advertiser lives in a community so small that the media are unable to provide any research data, the newspaper and broadcasters probably belong to national associations that conduct extensive research. Organizations of particular interest are the Direct-Mail Advertising Association, Newspaper Advertising Bureau, Radio Advertising Bureau, Magazine Publishers Associations, Television Bureau of Advertising, and Institute of Outdoor Advertising.

Government organizations Various government bureaus can provide a wealth of useful information to the local advertiser, including data on population projections, birth and death information, marriage license statistics, road construction plans, sewer and water-line extension plans, building permits, zoning and building code changes, and other items that might affect local business.

In every state government, departments in charge of commerce, taxation, labor, highways, and justice provide reports and statistical information. These materials can be useful in measuring local markets and making projections. Many states have bureaus in charge of getting new businesses to enter the state and in charge of economic development.

Of particular interest to most local advertisers is the Small Business Administration (SBA). It publishes a wealth of information, most of it free or available for only a nominal charge.

The Department of Commerce in the U.S. government also has pertinent materials, including: *Retail Data Sources for Market Analysis, Business Service Checklist* (a weekly guide to Department of Commerce reports, books, and news releases), *Bureau of Census Catalog, Census Track Studies,* the annual edition of the *U.S. Industrial Outlook, Current Retail Trade, Survey of Current Business, Monthly Department Store Sales, County Business Patterns,* the annual edition of the *Statistical Abstract of the United States,* and the *County and City Data Book.* Many of these publications are available at local libraries.

■ Determining Objectives and Strategy

In Chapter 7, "Marketing and Advertising Planning," the importance of establishing specific marketing and advertising objectives was discussed. The same holds true for local advertising.

When Gerry Smith presented his promotional plan to the city council of Mount Holly, he had very specific objectives in mind. The stated objectives of any marketing and advertising program, local or national, determine the particular marketing mix or strategy to be used. A local advertiser has the same options as a national advertiser when it comes to developing strategy: product, price, place, promotion.

■ Product

What merchandise should be sold? What services should be offered? Should some lines be expanded or dropped? How wide a selection should be offered? If a store intends to be a discount house, it

Davanni's hot hoagies blow subs right out of the water.

You may have heard submarine sandwiches are unbeatable, but one bite of a Davanni's hot hoagy will sink your opinion of them.

DAVANNI'S
PIZZA & HOT HOAGIES

Bloomington—97th & Lyndale 888-8232 • Minneapolis—2500 Riverside 332-5551 • Minneapolis—Hennepin & Lake 822-3111
St. Paul—Cleveland & Grand 690-4848 • Minnetonka—15200 Highway 7 938-4243 • Roseville—1905 West Perimeter Drive 636-3411
Brooklyn Center—Summit & Earle Brown 566-8220 • Richfield—66th & Penn 866-3324

FIGURE 17–9

Davanni's product concept is to specialize and offer the best sandwiches around—hot hoagies—in order to torpedo the competition.

may want to carry a broad line. If it wants to be a specialty shop, it may opt to carry only selected lines. In short, what is the store's product/service concept? (Figure 17–9.)

■ Price

What will the local market support? Should prices be high, low, or moderate? What should be included in the price? What about terms and warranties? Charge cards? What policy should be established on refunds? Are all these policies in keeping with the desired image?

■ Place

Where should the business be located? What is the trading area? For a bank, how many branches can be established? What kind of areas should we serve? What's the cost of doing business in different areas? Should we limit ourselves to only one location? How large should our facilities be?

■ Promotion

Should the business be highly promotional, semipromotional, or nonpromotional? Should we use regular price-line advertising? Sales? Clearances? Or merely institutional advertising and public relations? What is the impact of advertising activities on this type of business? Can we attain our objectives by advertising? How much advertising in what media?

Determining the objectives and strategies of any business—local, regional, or national—is the most important policy decision management ever makes. The decision as to objectives and strategies determines the whole complexion of the business in the years that follow. It gives direction to the enterprise, continuity to its various promotional efforts, and an understanding of the company in the marketplace. For that reason, the decisions regarding objectives and strategies should be highly specific and should be written down. Then they should be reviewed frequently and updated or revised on a regular basis as the business situation warrants. (See Ad Lab 17–A.)

■ Establishing the Budget

How much should a local business invest in advertising? New businesses usually require greater advertising expenditures than established ones. After the public becomes familiar with a company's goods or services, advertising costs should settle at a natural profitable level. But an advertising budget must be precisely designed for a particular business. Figure 17–10 illustrates, by type of establishment, the average percentage of sales invested in advertising. Since these figures are national averages, it is important to remember that they do not reflect the tremendous variety of factors that can affect the budget. The most important of these factors are the policies established when the company's objectives and strategies are determined.

Other influences are the following:

1. Location of the store.
2. Age and character of the firm.
3. Size of the store.
4. Type of product or service sold.

AD LAB 17–A   Mistakes commonly made by local advertisers

Even the best laid plans for local advertisers may go awry. However, chances of success are much greater if certain potential pitfalls are avoided.

Inattention to the advertising effort Advertising is sometimes not given the attention it deserves. This sometimes occurs because of distractions, lack of time on the part of the local advertiser, or lack of skill or interest in this aspect of the business.

Ego involvement Local advertisers sometimes succumb to the temptation to be a local celebrity by appearing in their own television commercials or placing a photograph of themselves (or the family) in the advertisement. This is dangerous. Most local advertisers are not effective spokespersons.

Inadequate supply of merchandise If there is an insufficient supply of merchandise to meet the demand generated by the advertising, the local advertiser loses because potential sales revenue is lost forever, the money spent on the advertising is wasted, and harm is done to customer goodwill.

Unqualified individuals handling the advertising Successful advertising requires competent individuals to plan, produce, and implement it. The smaller the establishment, the greater the chance that the person who handles the advertising will be unqualified to do so. Large stores have the advantage of being able to afford an advertising manager.

Compensating for mistakes by advertising Even the best advertising efforts cannot compensate for a bad location, poor selection of merchandise, untrained personnel, unreasonable high prices, or a host of other difficulties. A good advertising campaign only speeds up the failure of a poorly run business.

Lack of knowledge about what to advertise One of the most important decisions involves what to advertise. If an advertisement is to be successful, it must contain merchandise or services in which people have some interest. A good rule of thumb is to advertise items that are selling well already. Promote items that build traffic, and feature items in advertisements that are nationally advertised brands. These get attention because of the identifiable name, they take less explanation because of national promotion by manufacturers, and they help the local advertiser build a good reputation by association with a well-known name.

Wasting money on charity advertising There are always a host of charitable causes waiting for contributors. Particularly difficult to turn down are requests for advertising in high school yearbooks, church bulletins, athletic programs, and fraternal organizations. Rarely do these publications prove cost effective, however. They are very expensive on a cost per thousand basis. If contributions are made by placing advertisements, the advertising expense should be charged to "contributions to charitable organizations" rather than calling it an advertising expense.

Lack of coordination Advertising must be coordinated with the buying of the merchandise. Employees should be informed about the advertising so they can answer customers' questions. Merchandise must be properly priced and marked. Displays need to be in position. And local advertising should be coordinated with national advertising by manufacturers so that the advertising efforts reinforce one another.

Laboratory Applications

1. As an observer of local advertisers, identify and describe mistakes you feel they make in addition to those given above.
2. What should they do to correct their mistakes?

5. Size of the trading area.
6. Amount and kind of advertising done by the store's competitors.
7. Media available for advertising, their degree of coverage of the trading area of the store, and the costs of these media.
8. Results obtained from previous advertising.

If an advertiser's spending is much above or below the averages for that business shown in Figure 17–10, the reasons for this variance can usually be determined by checking the influencing factors listed above.

The local advertiser continually seeks to develop a budget in which the optimum amount of money is spent. If more is spent on advertising than necessary, the advertiser is wasting money. On the other hand, if the advertiser doesn't spend enough money and sales are not generated, then even more money is wasted. Therefore, it is easier to waste money by not spending enough than by spending too much.

■ *Budgeting strategy*

Advertising programs should be continuous. One-shot ads that are not part of a well-planned program are most often ineffective. Also,

---

FIGURE   17–10   Average advertising investments of retail business

Commodity or class of business	Average percent of sales	Commodity or class of business	Average percent of sales
Appliance, radio, TV dealers	2.3	Insurance agents, brokers	1.8
Auto accessory and parts stores	0.9	Jewelry stores	4.4
Auto dealers	0.8	Laundromats (under $35,000 in sales)	1.3
Bakeries	0.7	Liquor stores (under $50,000 in sales)	0.7
Banks	1.3	Lumber and building materials dealers	0.5
Beauty shops	2.0	Meat markets	0.6
Book stores	1.7	Men's wear stores (under $300,000)	2.4
Camera stores (under $100,000 in sales)	0.8	Motels	3.7
Children's and infants' wear stores	1.4	Motion picture theaters	5.5
Cocktail lounges	0.9	Music stores ($25,000 to $50,000)	1.8
Credit agencies (personal)	2.4	Office supplies dealers (under	
Department stores ($1–$2 million)	2.5	$100,000)	1.0
Discount stores	2.4	Paint, glass, and wallpaper stores	1.3
Drugstores (independent, under $70,000		Photographic studios and supply shops	2.4
in sales)	1.1	Real estate (except lessors of buildings)	0.6
Dry cleaning shops (under $50,000 in		Restaurants (under $50,000)	0.6
sales)	1.7	Savings and loan associations	1.5
Florists	2.1	Shoe stores	1.9
Food chains	1.1	Specialty stores ($1 million and over)	3.0
Furniture stores	5.0	Sporting goods stores	3.5
Gift and novelty stores	1.4	Taverns (under $50,000)	0.7
Hardware stores	1.6	Tire dealers	2.2
Home centers	1.3	Travel agents	5.0
Hotels (under 300 rooms)	6.7	Variety stores	1.5

advertising money should be spent when prospects are most receptive to buying a local advertiser's goods or services. In practice, this requires that advertising dollars be allocated in relation to sales volume month by month or even week by week. To achieve the objective of selling more merchandise at lower unit cost, well-timed advertising should be run to create month-by-month sales and advertising patterns like those illustrated in Figures 17–11 and 17–12.

There are several strategies or methods that local advertisers use to budget their advertising expenditures. Some of these were discussed in Chapter 7. However, most advertisers still use the percent of sales method, since it is the simplest to calculate and the easiest to defend with company bookkeepers and accountants.

For Action Realty, discussed at the beginning of this chapter, advertising has become such a large and complicated activity that Gwen Lemke now uses a computer to determine the advertising budget. The computer analyzes last year's sales along with various influencing factors to determine a budget based on anticipated sales this year. What results is an advertising expenditure curve that month by month slightly precedes the sales curve, as illustrated in Figure 17–12.

Developing the annual sales and advertising plan

Not all local advertisers have a computer at their disposal to forecast sales for the coming year. However, by doing some research, a fairly accurate sales forecast can be determined. Some basic questions a local merchant needs to have answered might be: (1) What is the anticipated increase in population for the local area during the next year? (2) What is the anticipated increase or decrease in overall retail sales? (3) What is the outlook for the local employment rate? (4) How are similar businesses doing?

FIGURE   17–11

Total retail sales by types of stores; percentage of the year's total sales made each month. These tables show how important each month is to the sale of a variety of products and services. These patterns illustrate when customers are most interested in buying. For example, May, which contributes approximately 9.9 percent of the year's sales of hardware stores, should logically get about this percentage of the year's advertising budget.

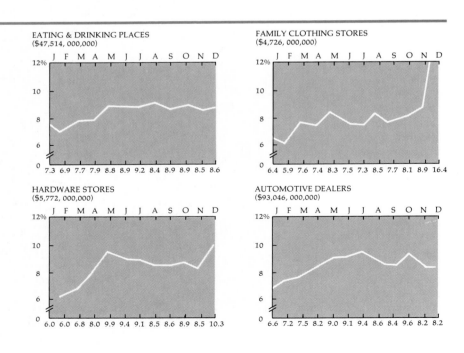

FIGURE 17–12

Advertising expenditure curves.

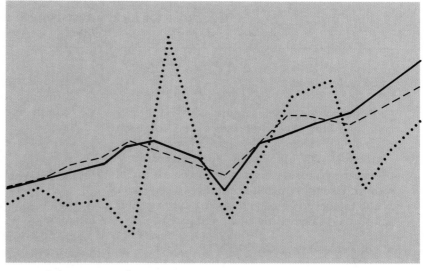

——— Sales ▪▪▪▪ Advertising

If you want well-timed advertising to sell more merchandise at lower unit costs, you want a sales and advertising pattern which month by month looks like this ▬ ▬ ▬ ▬ not this ▪▪▪▪▪▪

Local accountants, bankers, trade associations, Chambers of Commerce, and media representatives can be very helpful in answering these questions. After all the factors that affect finance, production, and marketing have been considered, a realistic sales plan for the year, month by month and even week by week, should be developed. From that sales plan an advertising expense plan can be formulated.

Advertising should precede sales. In other words, the most advertising dollars should be spent just before the time when customers are most likely to respond. To determine this, compute the percentage of yearly sales that are anticipated for each month (or, better yet, each week) of the year. Plot this on a graph. Next plot an advertising curve that slightly precedes the sales curve, as in Figure 17–12. (Note that the advertising peaks are slightly lower than the sales peaks but the valleys are slightly higher.) The advertising curve indicates what percentage of the annual advertising expenditure should be spent each month.

This concept of plotting anticipated sales patterns enables business owners to allot a percentage of the total yearly advertising to each month. By plotting actual sales as the year progresses, the advertiser can compare weekly and monthly expenses to weekly and monthly sales goals. If the business has several departments or services, the same method can be used to allot advertising dollars to each.

A simple device that is commonly used by local advertisers is a monthly promotional calendar. The calendar should be large enough to accommodate information about media schedules, costs, in-house promotions, sales, and special events. The calendar then enables the advertiser to tell at a glance the shape and direction of the advertising program.

To establish such a calendar, the advertiser should enter all the holidays as well as traditional community events like "Washington's

Checklist for local advertising budgets

Set a Sales Goal

☐ Write down the sales figures for next month last year—for the whole store and for each department. Then in view of this performance and your own knowledge and judgment of this year's picture, rough in sales goals for next month. Use these profit pointers as a reminder of the factors to be considered in making your sales goal realistic but challenging:

● Your sales last year.

● Population, income, employment levels.

● New and expanded departments.

● Tie-ins with merchandising events.

● What competitors are doing, getting.

● More aggressive selling and advertising.

Decide How Much Advertising

☐ Write down how much advertising you used next month last year. Then considering your planned sales goal and what your competition is likely to do, write in your planned advertising budget for the coming month. Your budget as a percent of sales can be checked against the expenditure of other stores in your classification. The profit pointers can be used to double check your own thinking on the advertising budget you can afford and need to do the job:

● Stores in less favorable locations advertise more.

● So do those that are new and expanding.

● Strong competition raises the size of the budget needed.

● Stores stressing price appeal usually promote more.

● Special dates and events offer additional sales opportunities.

● Added sales produced by increased expenditure are more profitable . . . more money can be spent to get them.

● Co-op support.

Decide What to Promote

☐ Let your business experience guide you in weighing the advertising you will invest in each of your departments. For instance, if the sales goal of department A is 9 percent of the total store sales objective this month, then earmark for it something like 9 percent of the month's planned advertising space. Your list shouldn't be a straitjacket, but a basic outline.

☐ Check month's heavy traffic pullers.

☐ Look for departments whose seasonal curve drops next month . . . must be cleared now.

☐ Dig for "sleepers," currently hot, but which don't show up in last year's figures.

☐ Promote newly expanded departments harder.

☐ Calculate co-op support available for each line of merchandise.

Fill in a Day-by-Day Schedule to Take Full Advantage of:

☐ Payroll days of important firms.

☐ Days of the week traffic is heaviest.

☐ National and local merchandising events offering tie-in possibilities.

☐ New or expanded departments.

☐ Current prices and your stock on hand . . . jot down items, prices, and ad sizes for each day.

FIGURE 17–13

A typical *Pennysaver* cover. Each edition covers a relatively small community of 9,000 to 12,000 homes so that local advertisers may target their messages to those customers within their immediate trading area. Rate discounts on neighboring editions allow larger advertisers to increase their circulation at a nominal cost.

Birthday Specials.'' The local media, trade associations, and trade publications can be especially helpful in supplying this information. (See the Checklist for local advertising budgets.)

■ Planning Media Strategy

A few years ago Herb Sutton was an advertising sales representative for the *Los Angeles Times*. He had been with the *Times* for 15 years and had become the company's top salesman. Calling on retail merchants every day in the Orange County area, Herb ran into competitive media salespeople regularly. One day he encountered a man who had recently started a new direct-mail advertising publication called the *Pennysaver*. He explained to Herb the benefits the *Pennysaver* offered the local advertiser:

1. Total weekly coverage of local geographic areas.
2. Direct mail into the home once a week, rather than dropped outside on the driveway every day.
3. Low total cost due to limited circulation.
4. Optional coverage of neighboring locales for minimal ''pick-up'' rates.
5. High reader interest created by classified-type ''reader ads.''
6. No competition with editorial readership since the publication is devoted entirely to advertising.

After several meetings Herb decided to accept the offer of his new acquaintance to become partners. He quit his secure job with the *Times* to take over the sales and management of the *Pennysaver* in southern Orange County and northern San Diego County.

He established three publications to start with, covering the communities of Laguna Beach, San Clemente, and Oceanside. For several years he struggled, selling ads all day and supervising art, production, printing, and delivery to the post office at night. At times he and the young advertising salespeople he hired were forced to scurry around to the local merchants to collect enough money to make the Friday payroll.

But as the local communities grew, so did the *Pennysaver* (Figure 17–13). Herb established new publications to cover Laguna Hills, Laguna Niguel, San Juan Capistrano, Capistrano Beach, Vista, Carlsbad, and Escondido. Within five years he had more than 10 *Pennysaver* publications, a new company headquarters and printing plant, over 30 employees, and a frighteningly huge overhead. But with his employees' help, he bought out his partner and forged ahead.

Today Sutton has over 40 publications, more than 150 employees, another new company headquarters, several company airplanes, and a personal net worth of several million dollars. The *Pennysaver* was more than just successful; it made publishing history. And the reason was simple. As Herb's salespeople were always quick to point out to local advertisers, the *Pennysaver* ''pulled.''

Choosing the right local advertising media is very important for two reasons: (1) most local advertisers have advertising budgets so limited that they can't use all media that might be appropriate, and (2)

FIGURE 17–14

(The newspaper uses television to advertise its classified advertising section.)

ANNCR: Now the *Chicago Tribune* gives you a new way to advertise. Target Classified.

SFX: (Arrow hitting man's head)

MAN: Honey, did you see . . .

WOMAN: The Chippendale . . .

ANNCR: You can advertise in one zone, all six or any combination. And reach people, for less, where it will do you the most good.

MAN: Hi, we came about the Chippendale

WOMAN: Dining room set?

SELLER: Sure.

SELLER: Sure

ANNCR: Tribune Target Classified.

certain media are more effective for some businesses than others because the business is restricted either geographically or by type of customer.

Just like national advertisers, local advertisers select media depending on the type of customers the business is attempting to reach, the type of store or business doing the advertising, its location, trading area, competition, size of budget, and the nature of the message to be delivered.

Newspapers

For local advertisers, newspapers receive the greatest emphasis for the following reasons (Figure 17–14):

1. Most newspapers are oriented to the local community. This makes it possible for the local advertiser to reach the desired audience with a minimum of wasted circulation.
2. The cost is low considering the large number of prospects reached— so low, in fact, that it is affordable for most businesses. Also, most newspapers have a special rate for local or retail advertisers that is considerably lower than their national rates.
3. Advertising can be placed in the newspaper on very short notice.
4. Some selectivity is possible by advertising in special-interest sections of the newspaper, such as sports or business news. For advertisers with very limited budgets, the classified section can even be an appropriate place to advertise.

Drawbacks to newspapers include their limited selectivity and their poor reproduction due to the paper quality.

Newspapers have both display and classified advertising departments. These departments are usually equipped to help advertisers prepare the complete advertisement including copy, art, typesetting, and layout/design. Often the service is given without charge. Large papers even have personnel who will visit an advertiser's place of business to do artwork (clothing is a good example) for advertisements.

For more details on newspapers, review Chapter 13.

Independent shopping guides

A growing number of cities have publications like the *Pennysaver*, which are published as a forum for local advertisers. Some use the mail to distribute their publications and offer total circulation of a given area. This can be ideal for a local advertiser seeking distribution to the immediate trading area.

Shoppers (as they are called) are normally distributed free of charge, so the local advertiser should be careful to analyze the readership of the publication.

Magazines

The growth of local, slick, special-interest magazines has given local advertisers the opportunity to communicate with upper-income prospects through a prestigious medium. Publications such as *Palm Springs Life, Dallas Home and Garden,* and *Los Angeles Magazine* offer excellent photographic reproduction as well. Local advertisers who seek even greater prestige and selectivity can now use special city editions of major national publications such as *Time, Newsweek,* and *Sports Illustrated* through an organization called Media Networks Inc.

The attractiveness of magazine advertising may be limited because of cost or because a store's trading area may be much smaller than the market reached by the magazine. In addition, magazines require that advertising be submitted weeks before the publication date.

Review Chapter 13 for further information about magazines.

Radio and television

Advertising on local radio and TV stations is used increasingly by local advertisers because it usually reaches a strictly local audience, offers high impact, and actually has a very low cost per thousand. Since it offers so many exposures, though, the total cost may be considered high by some advertisers.

Broadcast commercial time is highly selective, since time slots can be purchased next to the most suitable programs for the product or service being offered. Top-40 radio stations, for example, are ideal advertising media for record dealers.

Immediacy and believability are additional benefits of broadcast media (Figure 17–15), since local personalities, or the advertisers themselves, can present the commercial message personally.

Most radio and television stations gladly offer assistance in the writing and production of commercials for local advertisers. Normally this assistance is provided at a nominal charge for studio time plus additional fees for talent, special set designs, and tape dubbing.

For additional information on radio, television, and broadcast production, review Chapters 11 and 14.

Signs

The most direct method for merchants to invite customers into their stores is through the use of signs. Three types of signs are used by local advertisers: store signs, outdoor advertising, and transit advertising. Signs offer mass exposure with color, potentially large size, and very low cost per viewer. A disadvantage is the inability to make frequent changes, which limits their use for promotion of many types of merchandise. When signs are used for specific products, it is usu-

FIGURE 17–15

ANNCR: This year, billions of bugs will lose their lives on the nation's highways. Chances are, a lot of them will end up on the front of your car. And if you don't get them off, they'll come back to haunt you.

SFX: *Music and sound effects under.*

ANNCR: You see, as bugs decompose, they give off a strong acid that actually eats away at your car's chrome and paint . . . making it dull. The hotter the weather, the faster the acid is made.

But there is a brighter side to all of this: come to Hot Springs Auto Wash. We've developed a way to completely remove bugs before they kill your car's finish.

In fact, Hot Springs is the only car wash to make this guarantee:

If you find as much as one single little mosquito on your car after we've washed and dried it, we'll give you your two dollars and ninety cents back.

SFX: *Music and SFX out.*

ANNCR: Next time, we'll talk to you about the problem with birds.

SFX: *Birds chirping.*

ally for items that have continuous appeal such as automobiles or fast-food restaurant items (Figure 17–16).

Sign companies offer copy and art service. Their local representatives frequently provide this service without charge. However, producing signs is usually quite expensive and should be investigated thoroughly.

Chapter 15 gives more complete information on the use of outdoor and transit advertising.

Classified directories

Because the telephone book stays in the home or office as a ready source of information, it is widely used by local advertisers. For some businesses, it is their sole means of advertising. Every business that has a telephone qualifies for a one-line insertion in the classified section without charge. Additional advertising must be paid for.

For local communities in large urban areas and for military bases, there are usually privately published classified telephone directories, which are less expensive to use than the large telephone company directories. These private directories cater to the special interests of the immediate locale and therefore offer excellent support to the small retail merchant or local professional service.

Handbills

Because of their low cost and their effectiveness, handbills can be an important medium for local advertisers. They are especially useful for making grand opening announcements, advertising sales, and periodically reminding people of the merchandise or service offered.

Handbills should be very carefully planned to create a good appearance. Attention should also be given to the message so that effective appeals are built into the headline and body copy.

Although the printer should not be relied on for advice about the copy, a good printer can provide sound advice about the quality of paper to use, colors, size, cost, and general appearance.

Direct mail

Although it can be used to reach mass markets, the superior advantage of direct-mail advertising is its ability to reach specific market segments. The greatest use of direct mail is envelope stuffers, which accompany monthly bills mailed to charge-account customers.

FIGURE   17–16

This billboard for a Portland restaurant utilizes the potential of outdoor signs for creative impact for local advertisers. This sign offers the appeals of fun and low price, and is aimed right at the youth segment.

If you're 60 or over and like to travel, send us a sign.

Our Carefree Banking customers can take advantage of daytrips, cruises, overseas vacations and a lot more—all at special group rates. Find out more and you'll know why it's worth making the change to Bank of Virginia.

Bank of Virginia

Name_____ Address_____

City_____ State_____ Zip_____

MAIL TO Bank of Virginia, Carefree Coordinator, P.O. Box 25970, Richmond, Virginia 23260

Member FDIC

FIGURE 17–17

Bank of Virginia offers discount travel opportunities for senior customers in this clever coupon ad.

Direct mail is likely to get the reader's undivided attention because it has no competition from other advertisers at the same time. Local advertisers with limited budgets can use direct mail to great advantage. The number of pieces mailed and the printing costs are simply adjusted to the budget. Unlimited graphic possibilities can be used to meet the requirements for most any product or service. Most local direct-mail houses can offer copy, art, and printing as well as mailing service.

■ Sales promotion

Many sales promotion methods discussed in Chapter 16 can be uniquely effective for local advertisers.

Sampling Giving the customer a small sample of the product is always effective. Products that lend themselves to this approach are ice cream stores, delicatessens, fabric stores, butcher stores, and bakery shops.

Specialties Specialties, including calendars, rulers, shoehorns, and pens, are inexpensive for the store but can be valuable to the customer. These items generally contain the store name, address, telephone number, and often a brief sales message.

Coupons Coupons provide a special inducement to the customer to make a purchase. Usually a reduction in price is given when the customer presents the coupon, which has been clipped from a newspaper ad or handbill or received in the mail. Coupons can be used to build store traffic, to encourage the use of a product for the first time, and to test the effectiveness of a particular advertisement (Figure 17–17).

Telephone selling This technique can be used to reach both customers and potential customers. Charge-account customers can be called about a sale, and inactive accounts can be revived by asking the individuals to return to the store once again. New accounts can also be developed with this method.

Demonstrations Local advertisers can develop their own demonstrations according to their product line and their market. Bridal shops can give sessions on how to plan for a wedding, and sporting goods stores can hire a golf pro to give lessons.

Shows Probably the most common type of local shows are the fashion shows given by clothing retailers. Other types include building and home shows given by hardware stores and new-car shows given by local car dealers.

Free publicity The media are always on the lookout for unusual items that may be of interest to their readers or listeners. Stores that hold major grand openings, have important personnel changes, or have new and unusual lines of merchandise are newsworthy and might be covered by the local media. Moreover, publicity is often more cost-effective than advertising and offers greater credibility.

Community involvement This is an effective method of enhancing the image of a business. It can involve sponsoring a local activity such as a baseball team, a summer camp for needy youngsters, or a scholarship. Another way of becoming involved with the community is allowing store facilities to be used for social of civic organizations for fund-raisers or meetings. Many businesses such as banks and savings associations have rooms specifically designed for community use.

■ Determining Creative Direction

One of the most competitive businesses in any local market is the grocery business. Characterized by high overhead, low profit, heavy discounting, constant promotion, and massive doses of food-day advertising, food retailing is a difficult business at best.

The Tom Thumb Page stores in Dallas had an additional problem. They had elected to avoid price competition whenever possible and instead to compete on the basis of quality and service. This policy made it potentially difficult to attract new customers and create store traffic, since grocery customers tend to be very price oriented.

The Tom Thumb chain had been doing what might best be described as "maintenance advertising" in routine food-day newspaper sections for about four years. When they hired their new advertising agency, KCBN, Inc., the chain's owners, Bob and Charles Cullum, explained their situation and their objectives. They asked the agency to develop a campaign that would show that Tom Thumb was, in fact, very competitive in giving top value even though the prices might be slightly higher.

Barbara Harwell and Chuck Bua, the agency's creative directors, responded by developing a local institutional campaign that made grocery advertising history. They suggested opening the campaign with a television promotion for Thanksgiving turkeys. They convinced the Cullums and Tom Hairston, the chain's president, that to present a truly quality image they would have to create an absolutely outstanding commercial in terms of production quality. (The problems they encountered producing this commercial were discussed in Chapter 11.) Furthermore, to communicate that Tom Thumb's policies truly warranted higher prices, they persuaded them to make such a bold, risky statement that it would actually impress the viewing public. Hairston and the Cullums agreed. Two weeks before Thanksgiving the campaign began.

The commercial opened with a tight closeup of a live turkey. As the off-camera announcer spoke, the camera pulled slowly back, and the turkey reacted to the copy with an occasional "Gobble."

The announcer said:

> At Tom Thumb we stand behind everything we sell . . . and that's a promise. It's always been that way. Even when we started, Mr. Cullum said, "We want our customers to be happy with everything they buy in this store. If a woman buys a turkey from us and comes back the day after Thanksgiving with a bag of bones and says she didn't like it, we'll give her her money back . . . or give her another turkey."

The moment he said that, the turkey reacted with a big "gobble" and

FIGURE 17–18

Tom Thumb stores talked turkey with customers by promising to stand behind everything they sell.

ran off-camera. The commercial closed on the company logo with the announcer saying, "That's the way we do business at Tom Thumb . . . we stand behind everything we sell, and that's a promise" (Figure 17–18).

The company merchandised the campaign by printing the slogan "We stand behind everything we sell . . . and that's a promise" on grocery sacks, on red lapel buttons for employees, and on outdoor billboards. The audio portions of the commercials were aired as radio spots. Most important, employee orientation meetings were held to explain the concepts to the company's personnel and to make absolutely sure that any customers returning merchandise received a friendly, cordial smile.

The reaction to the campaign was astounding. First it became the topic of local conversation. Then people began to wonder how many turkeys might be returned for the money. Local newspeople began talking about the campaign and showing the commercial in their newscasts. Finally the top disc jockey in Dallas started a contest inviting listeners to guess how many turkeys would be returned to Tom Thumb. The day after Thanksgiving the local television film crews were waiting at the stores to count and interview people carrying bags of bones.

One woman said she returned a turkey and got her money back with no questions asked. Another said she was given her money immediately but that she then gave the money back. She had just wanted to test them to see whether they were telling the truth.

The final score was 30,000 turkeys sold and only 18 returned, a fantastic marketing, advertising, and publicity success. Since that time the story has been reported in numerous grocery and advertising trade journals, and Tom Thumb Page Stores has successfully continued the "We stand behind everything we sell" advertising campaign theme.

In planning the local advertising effort, the last step is the determination of creative direction. (See the Checklist for creating local advertising.) Certain elements of the creative direction will have already been determined in the planning process. The local advertiser and its agency will have already decided, for example, who the primary audience is, what the competitive advertising environment is, what policies to follow regarding price competition, what strategies to use to achieve the company's objectives, how much to spend in the advertising effort, and what media are available to use.

Tom Thumb and KCBN had already determined these things before the creative process began. What remained was to determine how to say what they wanted to say and who could help them say it. In the case of Tom Thumb, KCBN provided the answer to both questions. For other local advertisers, the solution might have been considerably different depending on the creative direction and talent used.

Seeking creative assistance

Advertisers have a number of sources to whom they can turn for help, including (1) advertising agencies, (2) the local media (3) free lancers and consultants, (4) creative boutiques, (5) syndicated art services, and (6) wholesalers and manufacturers.

Advertising agencies Because they are usually not equipped to do their own advertising work, local advertisers increasingly turn to agencies for help. One misconception is that all agencies are large and handle only sizable accounts. In many communities there are small agencies that assist local advertisers. Local advertisers find they need help in locating markets, determining media mixes, developing better ads, and following up their advertising with effective evaluation (Figure 17–19). Of course, the quality of agencies varies tremendously, and only the competent agency can be a real aid to an advertiser. Specifically, an agency can help a local advertiser in the following ways:

Checklist for creating local advertising

☐ Make your ads easily recognizable. Studies have shown that advertisements which are distinctive in their use of art, layout techniques, and typefaces usually enjoy a higher readership than run-of-the-mill advertising. Try to make your ads distinctively different in appearance from the advertising of your competitors—and then keep your ads appearance consistent. This way, readers will recognize your ads even before they read them.

☐ Use a simple layout. Ads should not be crossword puzzles. The layout should carry the reader's eye through the message easily and in proper sequence: from headline to illustration to explanatory copy to price to your store's name. Avoid the use of too many different typefaces, overly decorative borders, and reverse plates.

☐ Use a dominant element—a large picture or headline—to insure quick visibility. Photographs and realistic drawings have about equal attention-getting value, but photographs of real people win more readership. So do action pictures. Photographs of local people or places also have high attention value. Color increases the number of readers.

☐ Use a prominent benefit headline. The first question a reader asks of an ad is: "What's in it for me?" Select the main benefit which your merchandise offers and feature it in a compel-

ling headline. Amplify this message in subheads. Avoid generalized quality claims. Your headline will be easier to read if it is black on white and is not surprinted on part of the illustration.

☐ Let your white space work for you. Don't overcrowd your ad. White space is an important layout element in newspaper advertising because the average page is so heavy with small type. White space focuses the reader's attention on your ad and will make your headline and illustration stand out. When a "crowded" ad is necessary, such as for a sale, departmentalize your items so that the reader can find his way through them easily.

☐ Make your copy complete. Know all there is to know about the merchandise you sell and select the benefits most appealing to your customers. These benefits might have to do with fashion, design, performance, or the construction of your merchandise. Sizes and colors available are important, pertinent information.

☐ State price or range of prices. Dollar figures have good attention value. Don't be afraid to quote your price, even if it's high. Readers often will overestimate omitted prices. If the advertised price is high, explain why the item represents a good value—perhaps because of superior materials or workmanship, or extra luxury features. Point out the actual saving to

1. Analyzing the local advertiser's business and the product or service being sold; evaluating the markets for the business including channels of distribution.
2. Evaluating the advertiser's competitive position in the marketplace.
3. Determining the best advertising media and providing advice on the costs and effectiveness of each.
4. Devising an advertising plan and, once approved, implementing it by preparing the advertisements and placing them.
5. Simplifying the advertiser's administrative workload by taking over media interviewing, analysis, checking, and bookkeeping.

---

the reader and spell out your credit and lay-away plans.

□ Specify branded merchandise. If the item is a known brand, say so in your advertising. Manufacturers spend large sums to sell their goods, and you can capitalize on their advertising while enhancing the reputation of your store by featuring branded items.

□ Include related items. Make two sales instead of one by offering related items along with a featured one. For instance, when a dishwasher is advertised, also show a disposer.

□ Urge your readers to buy now. Ask for the sale. You can stimulate prompt action by using such phrases as "limited supply" or "this week only." If mail-order coupons are included in your ads, provide spaces large enough for customers to fill them in easily.

□ Don't forget your store name and address. Check every ad to be certain you have included your store name, address, telephone number, and store hours. Even if yours is a long-established store, this is important. Don't overemphasize your signature, but make it plain. In a large ad, mention the store name several times in the copy.

□ Don't be too clever. Many people distrust cleverness in advertising, just as they distrust salespeople who are too glib. Headlines and copy generally are far more effective when they are straightforward than when they are tricky. Clever or tricky headlines and copy often are misunderstood.

□ Don't use unusual or difficult words. Many of your customers may not understand words which are familiar to you. Words like "couturier," "gourmet," "coiffure," as well as trade and technical terms, may be confusing and misunderstood. Everybody understands simple language. Nobody resents it. Use it.

□ Don't generalize. Be specific at all times. Shoppers want all the facts before they buy. Facts sell more.

□ Don't make excessive claims. The surest way to lose customers is to make claims in your advertising that you can't back up in your store. Go easy with superlatives and unbelievable values. Remember: if you claim your prices are unbelievable, your readers are likely to agree.

□ Ad attention increases with the size of the ad.

□ People note more ads directed at their own sex.

□ Tie-ins with local and/or special news events are effective in attracting readership.

FIGURE   17–19

An agency-produced ad for a local advertiser. The creativity available from professional advertising people is often worth the extra expense, as this award-winner shows.

6. Assisting in other aspects of the advertising and promotion effort by helping with sales contests, publicity, grand openings, and other activities.

Advertising agencies tend to be used less extensively with local advertisers than with national advertisers. A major reason for this is that most media, including newspapers, have two sets of advertising rates—one for national advertisers and another for retail or local advertisers. The local rate is lower, and it is not commissionable. Because the vast majority of local advertising is placed directly by the local advertiser rather than through an advertising agency, the advantage is a lower cost to the retailer for advertising media. Also offered are frequency and quantity discounts that give additional savings to the local advertiser.

Many advertisers simply don't spend enough money on advertising to warrant the hiring of an advertising agency. And many advertising agencies do not accept local advertisers as clients because of low budgets.

For a complete discussion of advertising agencies, see Chapter 3.

Local media The advertising media, in addition to selling space or time, offer a multitude of advertising services to local advertisers. These services range from planning advertising campaigns to actually preparing the advertisement. Also the media employ research companies to determine the demographic makeup of their readers or listeners.

Free lancers and consultants Because some advertising people like to be their own bosses, they act as free agents who often work out of their homes preparing copy, art and layout, photography, or other services. Free lancers often specialize not only in the type of service they perform but also in the type of advertisers, such as car dealerships, clothing stores, or travel agencies.

Creative boutiques A boutique performs only the creative work. Employees of such shops specialize as copywriters, graphic designers, and illustrators. They charge a negotiated fee or a percentage of

FIGURE   17–20

The feeling created by the graphic designer for this Ottawa restaurant is definitely "swank."

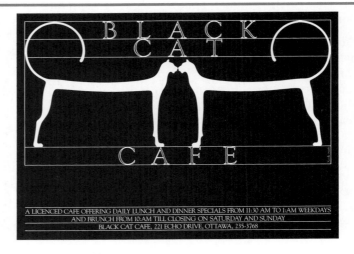

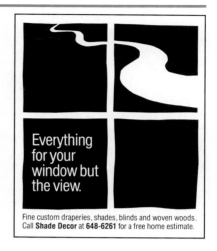

FIGURE 17–21

A series of ads created for drapery dealers and offered by the International Drapery Association.

the media expenditure. Local advertisers who want the best creative work but are not interested in any other services provided by a full-service agency frequently turn to this source for help (Figure 17–20).

Syndicated art services Syndicated art services can be useful to local advertisers by offering them a large book of artwork, called *clip art,* ready to be clipped and used in an advertisement. Clip art is available for various types of businesses and is often tied in to seasons, holidays, and other promotional angles. Clip art is available by direct subscription or through the advertising department of a local newspaper.

Wholesalers, manufacturers, and associations As a service to their distributors and dealers, wholesalers and manufacturers as well as some trade associations often provide ready-made advertising (Figure 17–21).

The most common type of help from manufacturers that local advertisers receive is called *vertical cooperative advertising.* The manufacturer normally provides the ad and a percentage of the cost of the advertising time or space (Figure 17–22). The local advertiser only has to have the local newspaper drop in the name and address of the business or have the radio and TV station add a tag line with the name, address, and telephone number of the firm. Because the manufacturer provides the ad, the manufacturer can be sure the ad puts forth the merchandise in the best possible light.

Horizontal cooperative advertising is a joint effort on the part of realtors, insurance agents, pharmacies, car dealers, or travel agents to pay for an institutional ad to create traffic for their type of business rather than for one particular business. Auto dealers in a central area of town often attempt to build traffic for all their business by pooling their advertising dollars and advertising the central area as the place to shop for cars. Shopping centers often do the same thing.

Creating the local advertising message

It was 1951 when Cal Worthington first started appearing on Los Angeles television stations to pitch his car dealership. Sponsoring third-rate movies on late-night and Saturday afternoon TV, Worthing-

FIGURE   17–22   Typical allowances for co-op advertising

Store	Co-op dollars as a percentage of total ad budget	Store	Co-op dollars as a percentage of total ad budget
Appliance dealers	80	Food stores	75
Clothing stores	35	Furniture stores	30
Department stores	50	Household goods	30
Discount stores	20	Jewelers	30
Drugstores	70	Shoe stores	50

FIGURE   17–23

Cal Worthington and his "dog" Spot prove that advertisers who do their own commercials can be highly successful.

ton appeared in a western outfit and cowboy hat and introduced a variety of hillbilly singers who were on hand all weekend to entertain customers looking at cars.

Thirty-four years later he was still at it, only the zaniness had increased. He now appears with any of a variety of domesticated wild animals (all of whom are introduced as "my dog Spot") and croons a tune promising to "stand upon his head" to make a deal on your new or used car. Or he offers 2,500 blue-chip stamps or a TV just to "come in and see me first."

Worthington has achieved far more than just sales success. He is ribbed by talk show host Johnny Carson in his monologues, and people stop him in airports to get his autograph. His fame, therefore, has spread well beyond the local market he serves (Figure 17–23).

The same thing has happened to local advertisers in St. Louis, New York, Des Moines, and around the country. *Dun's Review* refers to these pitchmen as the "Kings of the Tacky Commercials," calling them a "jarring, growing phenomenon on local TV."[1] Some of these low-budget, do-it-yourself advertisers have been so successful that they have engendered a near-cult following of viewers and imitators.

On the other hand, many who have tried the same approach of producing an assortment of low-budget, in-house commercials for viewing on late-night TV have failed miserably and eventually quit trying. Lee Shapiro, owner of Lee's Bars 'n Stools, appeared on Los Angeles TV as many as 60 times a week with his plea "don't judge us by our commercials, folks," which many people obviously did anyway. He's no longer using the medium.

In print advertising many local advertisers have achieved remarkable success using what some professional advertising agency artists might refer to as a "schlock" approach. Heavy bold type, items crowded into advertising space, loud headlines, and unsophisticated graphic design contribute to the "schlock" look.

As in the case of Action Realty, one has to ask: What are they selling? Is the creative message honest, consistent, and effective? If the answer is yes, then many people say that's all that matters. Invariably the question comes down to whether or not the objectives of the company are being met. To direct and control the creative aspects of advertisements and commercials, the local advertiser should develop a checklist of creative do's and don'ts for his or her particular business and follow it. This will at least assure consistency.

Summary

Local advertising is placed by businesses within a particular city or county and aimed at customers in the same geographic area. Local advertising is important because it is in the local arena that most sales are made or lost. While the basic principles used by national advertisers are applicable to local advertisers, local advertisers have special problems that they must address. Local advertising appears in either product advertising or institutional advertising. Product advertising can be further subdivided into regular price-line advertising, sale advertising, and clearance advertising.

The objectives of local advertising differ from those of national advertising in terms of emphasis and time. The needs of local advertisers tend to be more immediate. Therefore advertising is usually intended to increase traffic, turn over inventory, or bring in new customers right away.

Successful local advertisers realize the importance of marketing and advertising planning. This includes analyzing the local market, analyzing the competition, conducting adequate research, determining objectives and strategy, establishing a realistic budget, planning media strategy, and determining creative direction.

Local businesses are often highly seasonal. By plotting anticipated sales patterns throughout the year, business owners can allot a percentage of their total yearly advertising to each month. In general, the most advertising dollars should be spent just before the time when customers are most likely to respond.

There are many media normally available to local advertisers. These include newspapers, individual shopping guides, local magazines, local radio and television, and outdoor advertising. In addition, many local advertisers use direct mail, classified directories, sales promotion, and free publicity.

Perhaps the biggest problem for local advertisers is determining creative direction. Fortunately, there are a number of sources to whom they can turn for help. These sources include local advertising agencies, the local media, free lancers and consultants, creative boutiques, syndicated art services, and wholesalers, manufacturers, and distributors.

Questions for review and discussion

1. What are the objectives of the various types of local advertising?
2. What does a local advertiser expect to learn by analyzing the local market?
3. How can analyzing the competition give local advertisers the competitive edge?
4. What kind of primary research could you conduct to find out what customers think of your retail business?
5. What sources of secondary research data could inform local advertisers about future retail trends?
6. What are the most important factors influencing the advertising budget of a shopping mall tenant?
7. What basic questions would a local merchant need to answer to formulate an annual advertising plan?
8. Which media usually receive the most emphasis by local advertisers? Explain why.
9. What sales promotional tools would be uniquely useful for local advertisers? Why?
10. If you were a local advertiser what sources would you turn to for creative assistance? Why?

18

CORPORATE ADVERTISING AND PUBLIC RELATIONS

J im Murray, the assistant public relations director at Johnson & Johnson, was performing a rather mundane task at the company's corporate headquarters in New Jersey when the call came in. He had been preparing a speech for one of the company's directors. But then at 9:30 a.m. the phone rang, and a reporter from the Chicago *Sun-Times* started asking for background data on the company's leading pain-reliever product. At first the call seemed innocuous enough, but then Murray became suspicious. "What's going on?" he thought. "Why's he asking all these questions?"

Murray decided he'd better call Elsie Behmer at Fort Washington, Pennsylvania. She was the director of communications for McNeil Consumer Products Company, the Johnson & Johnson subsidiary that manufactured and marketed the product, so she might know if something was afoot. In fact, she herself had just picked up a scanty report from an assistant to McNeil's medical director, Thomas Gates. Gates had just finished talking with the chief toxicologist of Cook County, Illinois, and he wanted her to meet with him in the company president's office immediately. She was just leaving when Murray's call came in. "Is this about that terrible thing in Chicago," she asked. They compared the sparse details they both had, and then she headed for the meeting with Gates and McNeil's president, Joseph Chiesa.

Murray meanwhile ran two doors down the hall and told his boss, J&J's public relations director Robert Kniffin. Kniffin immediately called Gates, who confirmed that his office had just received press inquiries about the first three Chicago deaths. Kniffin quickly alerted the vice president of public relations, Lawrence G. Foster, and an emergency strategy session of J&J's top management was hastily assembled in the president's office. Within an hour Kniffin and a group of J&J staffers were in a helicopter on their way to McNeil to help Behmer and Gates field the flood of calls and official inquiries that they knew would start pouring in from all over the country.

At noon, the Cook County coroner held a press conference in Chicago and officially confirmed the rumors that had been flying around the country. The headlines the next day would scream about an unprecedented disaster—the Tylenol terrorism.

Three people had already succumbed, and another was ill and dying. A madman had tampered with some bottles of Extra-Strength Tylenol capsules and laced them with cyanide (Figure 18–1).[1]

THE ROLE OF CORPORATE ADVERTISING AND PUBLIC RELATIONS

Public relations is a term that is widely misunderstood and misused to describe anything from sales to hostessing, when in fact it is a very specific communications process. Every company, organization, association, and government body has groups of people who are affected by what that organization does or says. These groups might be employees, customers, stockholders, competitors, or just the general population of consumers. Each of these groups may be referred to as one of the organization's "publics." To manage the organization's relationship with these publics, the process called public relations (PR) is used.

As soon as Tylenol was linked to the Chicago deaths, the small PR staffs at Johnson & Johnson and McNeil suddenly became responsible for handling the deluge of phone calls from the press and the public and for managing all of the companies' communications with the media. Simultaneously, other company departments had to deal with the police and numerous local, state, and federal government agencies, distributors and trade customers, and the community at large—not just in Chicago or New Brunswick, New Jersey, but anywhere in the world someone was touched by this horrible disaster. In addition, myriads of small special-interest groups suddenly popped into the spotlight demanding special attention and care: the Proprietary Association of other drug manufacturers, the Food and Drug Administration, both houses of Congress, local politicians, police groups, the financial community, stockholders, employees, the local press, national networks, and the families, friends and acquaintances of the victims, to mention just a few.

Companies and organizations have learned that they must consider the public impact of their actions and decisions because of the powerful effect of public opinion. This is especially true in times of crisis, emergency, or disaster. But it is just as true for major policy decisions concerning changes in business management, pricing policies, labor negotiations, introduction of new products, or changes in distribution methods. Each of these affects different groups of people in different ways. Conversely, effective administrators can use the power of these groups' opinions to effect positive changes.

In short, the purpose of everything that is labeled public relations is to influence public opinion. In one instance the effort might be to rally

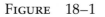

FIGURE 18–1

The front page of the *Chicago Tribune* announced the Tylenol poisonings.

public support, in another to obtain public understanding or neutral-
ity, or in still another to simply respond to inquiries.

Put yourself in the position of Lawrence G. Foster. As the public
relations vice president, he was in charge of overall corporate communications for J&J. Therefore he also had the primary communications responsibility for McNeil. What do you suppose would be the
major purpose of his staff's efforts in the days immediately following
the discovery of the Tylenol terrorism? What are some things they
might have been called on to do?

We will discuss these and other questions in this chapter. But first it
is important to understand the relationship between public relations
and advertising since they are so closely related but so often misunderstood.

Advertising versus Public Relations

Advertising is generally described as openly sponsored and paid for
media communications between sellers and buyers. Certainly, like
public relations, the purpose of advertising is to affect public opinion.
However, this is normally accomplished through the open attempt to
sell the company's products or services.

Public relations activities, like product advertising, may also involve media communications, but these are not normally openly
sponsored or paid for. Usually they appear through news articles,
editorial interviews, or feature stories. One means of relaying a public
relations message, though, is through corporate advertising, and we
will discuss that later in this chapter.

Advertising versus PR Practitioners

Another interesting difference between public relations and advertising is the orientation or perspective of professional practitioners in
the fields. Advertising professionals tend to be sales or marketing
oriented (the perspective of this text, for example). They view marketing as the umbrella process used by companies to determine what
products the market needs and what means will be required to distribute and sell the products to the market. To advertising professionals advertising and public relations are primarily tools
of marketing used to promote sales of the company's products and
services. As a rule, therefore, they tend to use advertising and
public relations as "good news" vehicles for the company and its
products.

Public relations professionals, on the other hand, consider public
relations as the umbrella process that companies should use to manage their continuing relationship with their various publics. From
their perspective, marketing and advertising are simply tools of public relations that should be used in the company's sales relationship
with customers and prospects. Other tools, though, such as program
sponsorships, publicity, house organs, newsletters, seminars, and
press conferences, are used for other publics, such as stockholders,
employees, or the financial community. The PR orientation tends to
be a "news" orientation, and, therefore, these various tools tend to be

used for giving open information and for "telling it like it is"—even if the company's news is bad news.

Very few companies are structured with a public relations orientation, but the perspective of the professional public relations person is important and interesting to understand. In times of crisis or emergency, it is normally considered the better perspective to adopt.

To achieve the greatest effectiveness, advertising and public relations efforts should be closely coordinated. As a result, many advertising agencies have public relations departments or perform public relations services. Many company advertising departments also supervise company public relations activities. And students of advertising are frequently interested in the public relations field. It is for these reasons that the topic of public relations is presented in this textbook along with its related counterpart, corporate advertising.

TYPES OF CORPORATE ADVERTISING

Advertising textbooks traditionally focus on the subject of product advertising, the primary process companies use to promote their various products and services. However, successful companies have found that people buy their products and services for a wide variety of reasons. Company reputation, familiarity, and overall impression are important, for example. Conversely, many people choose not to buy a particular company's products, service, or stock if the company is viewed negatively in the marketplace.

An obvious example of this is the airline industry. If a company has a poor safety record or a reputation for being reckless, how do you suppose ticket sales would be affected? Or company stock? A pharmaceutical company faces the same problem. Nothing like the Tylenol terrorism had ever happened before. Consumer confidence in Tylenol had resulted in $430 million in annual sales. But in the aftermath of the tampering, the company had to voluntarily withdraw the affected product from the market. One of Lawrence Foster's tasks, therefore, was to communicate that Johnson & Johnson was as concerned with product safety as it always had been and that the company would take every precaution to ensure against future tamperings.

To help manage their reputation in the marketplace, companies use public relations. As mentioned earlier, one of the basic tools of public relations is corporate advertising. However, there are several types of corporate advertising: public relations advertising, institutional advertising, corporate identity advertising, and recruitment advertising. Their use depends on the needs of the particular situation, the audience or public being addressed, and the message that needs to be communicated.

■ Public Relations Advertising

Immediately following the discovery of the Tylenol tamperings, J&J made a major effort through the national press to inform the Ameri-

FIGURE 18–2

An unusual public relations ad from Johnson & Johnson offering coupons to customers to replace their bottles of Extra-Strength Tylenol.

can public of the danger and to get people to immediately stop using the product. In fact, in Chicago, police used bullhorns on the streets to warn residents of the problem. As a result many customers threw their bottles of Tylenol capsules away instead of returning them to the store and exchanging them for unaffected Tylenol tablets. Others turned their bottles in to authorities for testing.

To many it looked like the end of the Tylenol brand. Stock analysts predicted a long and lingering effect on Johnson & Johnson stock, and adman Jerry Della Femina predicted the product would never make a comeback. But, in the days and weeks following the poisonings, there was a huge outpouring of support not only for the families of victims but for the company itself. J&J was gratified to learn through its public opinion surveys that people also viewed the company as a victim of the terrorist. Buoyed by this reaction, J&J felt it could indeed reintroduce the product, and the company moved to express its gratitude to its loyal customers. Throughout the country, in over 180 newspapers, Johnson & Johnson placed an unusual *public relations advertisement*. The ad expressed thanks to the American public for its confidence and offered product coupons good for a free replacement bottle of Tylenol (Figure 18–2).

Public relations advertising is often used when a company wishes to communicate directly with one of its important publics in an effort to express its feelings or enhance its point of view to that particular audience. Other public relations ads might be used for improving the company's relations with labor, government, customers, or suppliers.

Similarly, when companies sponsor programs on public television, they frequently place public relations ads in other media to promote the programs and their sponsorship. These ads are designed to enhance the company's general community citizenship and to create public goodwill (Figure 18–3).

Corporate/Institutional Advertising

In recent years the term *corporate advertising* has gained popularity to denote that broad area of nonproduct advertising used specifically to enhance the company's image and increase lagging awareness. The traditional or historic term for this is *institutional advertising*.

Institutional or corporate ad campaigns may be used for a variety of purposes—to report the company's record of accomplishment; to position the company competitively in the market; to avoid a communications problem with agents, dealers, or customers; to reflect a change in corporate personality; to shore up sagging stock prices; to improve employee morale; and so on.

Companies and even professional advertising people have historically questioned, or simply misunderstood, the effectiveness of corporate advertising. Retailers, in particular, have clung to the idea that institutional advertising may be pretty or nice but that it "doesn't make the cash register ring." However, a series of market research studies sponsored by *Time* magazine and conducted by the Yankelovich, Skelly & White research firm offered dramatic evidence to the contrary. In the first of these studies, 700 middle- and upper-management executives were interviewed in the top 25 U.S. markets. The researchers evaluated five companies who were currently doing corporate advertising and five who were not. They found that the companies that used corporate advertising registered significantly better awareness, familiarity, and overall impression than those that used only product advertising. In fact, the five corporate advertisers in the study drew higher ratings in *every* one of 16 characteristics measured, including being known for quality products, having competent management, and paying higher dividends.

Perhaps the most interesting aspect of the research was the fact that the five companies with no corporate advertising spent far more for total advertising than did the firms engaged in corporate advertising.[2] Subsequent to that study, two of the noncorporate advertisers have since instituted major corporate campaigns.

David Ogilvy, the founder and creative head of Ogilvy & Mather, has been an outspoken advocate of corporate advertising. But he has pointed out that most institutional advertising fails to produce measurable results because corporations fail to define the purpose of their campaigns. Good corporate advertising, he says, can hope to achieve one or more of only four objectives. It can build awareness of the company, make a good impression on the financial community, influence public opinion on specific issues, and motivate present employees as well as attract better recruits.[3] (See Ad Lab 18–A).

FIGURE 18–3

First Interstate Bank sponsors a hall of athletic fame near the site of the Los Angeles Olympics and invites visitors to share the glory of past achievements.

IN 1936, THE MAN WHO WORE THIS SHOE BROUGHT A NATION TO ITS FEET.

See it at the First Interstate Bank Athletic Foundation. Politics permeated the Berlin Olympics in 1936.
But an unassuming 22-year-old American named Jesse Owens shattered those overtones by shattering records.
Owens won gold medals in the 100-meter and 200-meter dashes, the long jump, and the 400-meter relay. He also won the hearts of 100,000 spectators, who jumped to their feet and chanted his name.
Today you can relive the excitement Jesse Owens generated nearly half a century ago. A shoe he wore has been preserved in

bronze to serve as a treasured memento of a truly legendary man. You'll find this shoe on display at the First Interstate Bank Athletic Foundation.
Reminders of the triumph of the human spirit. The Foundation, created in 1936 as the Helms

Athletic Foundation, is perhaps America's greatest sports museum. First Interstate is proud to sponsor this hall of fame and share with you the symbols that perpetuate the memory of athletic achievement.

You can see scores of keepsakes from modern Olympiads. Including medallions from 1896 and on. A jersey worn by two-time decathlon champ Bob Mathias. The shoes of decathlon champ Rafer Johnson.

Gold medals won by Frank Wykoff in anchoring relays in three Olympics, including Los Angeles in 1932. And medals won by shot put star Parry O'Brien and diving champion

Patricia McCormick. The Foundation also exhibits memorabilia from dozens of professional and amateur sports. You can see uniforms of baseball greats Babe

Ruth, Stan Musial, and Willie Mays. A bat used by Lou Gehrig when he hit 48 home runs. Red Grange's football jersey. Boxing gloves worn by Jim Jeffries, Jack Dempsey, and Joe Louis. Trophies of auto racing legends Ralph DePalma and Barney Oldfield. And basketballs from UCLA's 10 collegiate titles under coach John Wooden.
Just a short drive from the Coliseum. The Athletic Foundation is located in central Los Angeles off the Santa Monica Freeway in a 75-year-old Georgian mansion. To show its commitment to the city of Los Angeles, First Interstate Bank has restored the mansion and its grounds to their original magnificence in time for Olympic visitors to enjoy.
The Foundation is open Tuesday through Friday from 10 a.m. to 4 p.m. and Saturday from 9 a.m. to noon, holidays excepted. Admission is $2.
No other place evokes so many thrills from the achievements of so many lifetimes.

First Interstate Bank Athletic Foundation
2141 West Adams Blvd.
Los Angeles, California
Telephone: (213) 614-2995

First Interstate Bank Member FDIC

Look at the examples in the "Portfolio of corporate advertising". What do you feel are the objectives of these campaigns? How well are those objectives addressed?

 ## Corporate Identity Advertising

We previously discussed the pride that companies take in their logos and corporate signatures. In fact, the graphic designs that identify corporate names and products are considered valuable assets of the company, and great effort is expended to protect their individual-

---

AD LAB   18-A   Corporate advertising by David Ogilvy

I have had some experience with corporate advertising—for Shell, Sears, IBM, International Paper, Merrill Lynch, General Dynamics, Standard Oil of New Jersey, and other great corporations.

Big corporations are increasingly under attack—from consumer groups, from environmentalists, from governments, from antitrust prosecutors who try their cases in the newspapers. If a big corporation does not take the initiative in cultivating its reputation, its case goes by default.

If it were possible, it would be better for corporations to rely on public relations—i.e., favorable news stories and editorials—rather than paid advertising. But the media are too niggardly about disseminating favorable information about corporations. That is why an increasing number of public relations directors have come to use paid advertising as their main channel of communication. It is the only one they can control with respect to *content*, with respect to *timing*, and with respect to *noise level*. And it is the only one which enables them to *select their own battleground*.

So I guess that corporate advertising is here to stay. Why is most of it a *flop*?

First, because corporations fail to define the *purpose* of their corporate campaigns.

Second, because they don't *measure the results*. In a recent survey conducted by *The Gallagher Report*, only one in four of U.S. corporate advertisers said that it measured changes in

attitude brought about by its corporate campaigns. The majority fly blind.

Third, because so little is known about what works and what doesn't work in corporate advertising. The marketing departments and their agencies know a good deal about what works in *brand* advertising, but when it comes to *corporate* advertising they are amateurs. It isn't their bag.

Fourth, very few advertising agencies know much about corporate advertising. It is only a marginal part of their business. Their creative people know how to talk to housewives about toilet paper, and how to write chewing-gum jingles for kids, and how to sell beer to blue-collar workers. But corporate advertising requires copywriters who are at home in the world of big business. There aren't many of them.

I am appalled by the *humbug* in corporate advertising. The *pomposity*. The *vague generalities* and the *fatuous platitudes*.

Corporate advertising should not insult the intelligence of the public.

Unlike product advertising, a corporate campaign is the voice of the chief executive and his board of directors. It should not be delegated.

What can good corporate advertising hope to achieve? In my experience, one or more of four objectives:

1. It can build *awareness* of the company. Opinion Research Corporation states, "The

ity and ownership. What does a company do, though, when it decides to change its name, logos, trademarks, or corporate signatures? How does it communicate that change to the market it serves and to its other influential publics? This is the job of corporate identity advertising.

In a continuing effort to appear modern and up to date, companies traditionally change their corporate logos, graphics, and employee uniforms every few years to reflect current aesthetic tastes. But in 1984 Nissan Motor Corporation decided to change the name of its highly successful American company and product, Datsun—a very major

---

invisibility and remoteness of most companies is the main handicap. People who feel they know a company well are five times more likely to have a highly favorable opinion of the company than those who have little familiarity."

2. Corporate advertising can make a good impression on the financial community, thus enabling you to raise capital at lower cost—and make more acquisitions.

3. It can motivate your present employees and attract better recruits. Good public relations begin at home. If your employees understand your policies and feel proud of your company, they will be your best ambassadors.

4. Corporate advertising can influence public opinion on specific issues.

Abraham Lincoln said, "With public opinion against it, nothing can succeed. With public opinion on its side, nothing can fail."

Stop and Go—that is the typical pattern of corporate advertising. What a waste of money. It takes time, it takes *years,* for corporate advertising to do a job. It doesn't work overnight—even if you use television.

A few companies—a *very* few—have kept it going long enough to achieve measurable results.

U.S. Steel ran corporate advertising for 42 years. General Electric for 48 years. Du Pont for 43 years.

One man, George Cecil, wrote the A. T. & T. corporate advertising for 40 years.

Overwhelming requests have been made for Shell's "Answer" books because of the corporate advertising campaign by Ogilvy & Mather announcing their availability.

Laboratory Application

Discuss a corporate advertisement with which you are familiar that demonstrates what David Ogilvy refers to as "the humbug in corporate advertising, the pomposity, the vague generalities, and the fatuous platitudes."

and risky move. To effect the change, a corporate identity program was designed to gradually introduce the new corporate and product name on the car and in commercials. A series of advertisements in magazines, newspapers, and TV introduced the Nissan name and, over a period of time, gradually reduced the prominence of the Datsun name (Figure 18–4).

Other well-known examples of corporate identity programs are Exxon Corporation's consolidation of its various previous names (Standard Oil of New Jersey, Enco, Esso, Humble Oil, etc.) to the Exxon name, and the International Business Machines change to the simple, familiar IBM acronym.

In short, corporate identity advertising may be used when companies need to communicate a name or appearance change, an ownership change, or a change in corporate personality, or when the company is suffering from generally lagging awareness.

■ Recruitment Advertising

David Ogilvy pointed out that one of the prime objectives of corporate advertising is to motivate employees and attract better recruits. Certainly that objective is apparent in General Electric's well-known campaign (Figure 18–5).

However, when the sole objective is to attract employment applications, companies use recruitment advertising. These advertisements are most frequently found in the classified sections of daily newspapers and are typically the responsibility of the personnel department rather than the advertising department. Recruitment advertising has become such a large field, though, that many advertising agencies now have recruitment specialists on their staffs. In fact, some agencies specialize completely in recruitment advertising, and their clients are corporate personnel managers rather than advertising depart-

FIGURE   18–4

Nissan Motors announces the change in product name from the familiar Datsun to the corporate Nissan name.

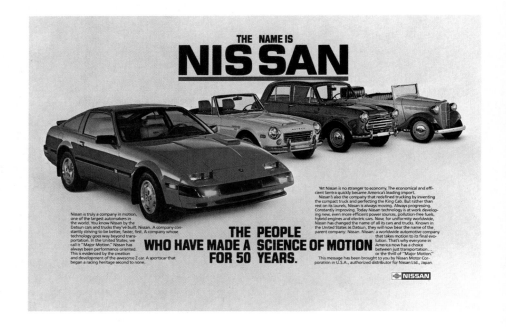

FIGURE 18–5

General Electric suggests that if you can dream it, you can do it. This type of corporate ad is instrumental in maintaining high employee morale and recruiting quality job applicants.

ment managers. These agencies create, write, and place classified advertisements in newspapers around the country and prepare recruitment display ads for specialized trade publications (Figure 18–6).

PUBLIC RELATIONS ACTIVITIES

Ironically, prior to the Tylenol tragedy, the company's public relations plan for the product had been rather low-key. Tylenol was originally introduced in the 1950s as a prescription-only children's elixir. The company promoted it through educational conferences for health care professionals. After the mid-70s, Tylenol was positioned as an over-the-counter adult product, and the promotion burden was carried exclusively by consumer advertising. So with that history, the product had no ongoing public relations program, and the firm had no emergency public information plan. That was the first thing that had to be prepared by Johnson & Johnson and McNeil's management strategists. Together they formulated three stages of action that had to be taken:

1. Identify the problem and take immediate corrective action. This meant getting information from the press, police, FDA, and FBI; identifying the geographic dimensions of the problem; correcting rumors; and withdrawing all affected products from the marketplace.
2. Cooperate with the authorities in the investigation to find the killer. (Rather than simply reacting to situations as they developed, Johnson & Johnson decided to get actively involved by helping the FBI and other law enforcement agencies in their efforts to generate leads and investigate security at the McNeil plants. The firm even offered a $100,000 reward for information leading to the arrest and conviction of the murderer.)

FIGURE 18–6

Typical recruitment ad for high-tech firm usually run as classified display in daily newspapers.

3. Rebuild the Tylenol name and capsule line including the Regular Strength capsules, which had been recalled along with the Extra-Strength.

The first job was to assure that the tampering had not occurred at McNeil. The company's two capsule production lines had to be shut down and dog teams brought in to search for evidence of cyanide. While everyone believed the problem was probably confined to the retail end of the chain, they had to be sure.

Simultaneously, the enormous appetite of the news media for background information and updates on the crisis, along with a flood of inquiries from anxious consumers, put the firms' public relations people under enormous pressure. Faced with a crisis of such severe proportions, a firm has little choice but to be open in handling inquiries. However, all communications between the media and the company had to be channeled through Foster's department. In addition, all customer communications, all trade communications, and all government communications had to be coordinated within the company. Only in this way could open, clear, consistent, *legal*, and credible communications be maintained. And only in this way could the potentially disastrous effects of rumor-mongering, political backbiting, and corporate defensiveness be minimized.

In the first 48 hours after the coroner's press conference, calls to Johnson & Johnson and McNeil were incessant. The moment one caller hung up, the telephone rang again. In the basement at McNeil, a bank of "800" phones, usually used for sales, was pressed into service and staffed by employees. But employees had to know what to say, what they were not allowed to say, and to whom unanswerable questions should be referred. That, of course, depended on who was calling and what they were asking.

At the same time, management and employees had to be notified, various authorities had to be contacted, and many others who were involved had to be reached. And all this had to be planned, coordinated, and supervised efficiently. That was suddenly the job of Lawrence Foster and his staff.

As unusual as disasters might be, they are the most important activities of PR professionals and public information officers in such highly sensitive organizations as airlines, police departments, military organizations, chemical and oil companies, and public utilities. These people are all employed in industries characterized by a constantly high demand for news and information. As a result, their activities are centered around planning, coordinating, and supervising the press relations of their organizations in a variety of pressure-cooker situations.

Most public relations professionals, however, are not occupied in these sensitive, high news-demand areas. Rather they are employed to *generate* news from basically low news-demand organizations, and the activities they are concerned with reflect that fact.

■ Publicity and Press Agentry

Publicity is the generation of news about a person, product, or service that appears in broadcast or print media and is usually thought of as being "free" because the medium has no publicity rate card. The media do not bill anyone for the publicity they run, and the media cannot be "bought" to run the publicity. The organization that seeks the publicity may go to considerable expense in an effort to get it, but there's no bill for the space or time received.

Press agentry refers to the planning of activities and the staging of events in order to attract attention and generate publicity that will be of interest to the media. Although celebrities, circuses, sports events, politicians, motion pictures, and rock stars come to mind as requiring press agentry, many public relations people use it to bring attention to new products or services or to put their company or organization in a favorable light. For example, if a company makes a donation to a charitable cause, press agentry can be used to bring the donation to the attention of the public.

The most common way to let the media know about an item worthy of publicity is through a news release, which is discussed in greater detail later in this chapter. Often news releases are accompanied by an appropriate photograph. Many stories in the business pages of a newspaper are either verbatim printings of news releases or stories based on publicity releases. In this case the public relations person acts as a reporter about a client or organization by releasing news that he or she wants published or broadcast. Opportunities for publicity include the introduction of a new product, awards, company sales and earnings, mergers, retirements, parades, and speeches by company executives.

For print media, the publicity person deals with editors and feature writers. For broadcast media, he or she deals with a program director, assignment editor, or news editor.

Just as an organization has an advertising program, it should also have a company publicity program. Like the advertising person, the professional public relations practitioner performs careful research, plans a publicity program, and then executes it. A complete program should be tentatively scheduled on a yearly basis and then incorporated into the budget.

Publicity material can have great promotional value. Organizations often reprint publicity received in newspapers or magazines and mail these reprints to appropriate audiences. Photographs of an organization's representative as seen on TV with a talk-show host or other celebrity can be sent along with an appropriate story written by the public relations practitioner. Sometimes these materials can even be used in point-of-purchase displays or sent to salespeople to be used in their portfolios as visual aids.

■ Public Affairs and Lobbying

Dealing with community officials and working with regulatory bodies and legislative groups are the tasks of *public affairs* people. Sometimes this work is handled by the public relations office, other times by specialists in public affairs. For example, Johnson & Johnson's director of federal affairs was Bertram Levine. During the crisis his office contacted all members of Congress on Capitol Hill to offer aid in answering constituents' questions. Then his office worked with various congressional committees to rapidly push through emergency legislation regarding tamper-resistant packaging.

Public affairs may involve many other activities, such as encouraging employees to vote or make political contributions, getting employees to participate in programs for the betterment of the community and the environment, and informing citizen groups of company objectives in order to enlist their support. Perhaps it can best be defined as *all activities related to the community citizenship of an organization.*

Because every organization is affected by the government, companies are doing an increasing amount of lobbying. Lobbying involves trying to inform and persuade government officials in the interests of the client to promote or thwart administrative action or legislation.

Promotion and Special Events Management

For profit-making organizations, promotion means using advertising and public relations techniques as a means of selling a product or service as well as enhancing the reputation of an organization. Promotion can be achieved through press parties, open houses, celebrations, issuing of press releases, sponsoring of contests, or a variety of other activities (Figure 18–7).

Special events can take the form of a grand opening of a new store, an autograph party for an author, the announcement of a new product, or the groundbreaking for a new public library. The list is almost endless. The public relations practitioner is responsible for conceiving

PEOPLE IN ADVERTISING

Dorothy E. Gregg

Corporate Vice President of Communications
Celanese Corporation

Dr. Dorothy E. Gregg, named one of America's top women business leaders by *Fortune* and *Business Week,* is corporate vice president of communications for Celanese Corporation. She was the first woman ever appointed to the corporate helm by Celanese.

From her handsome executive office, Dr. Gregg oversees all financial, corporate, government, public affairs, marketing, and employee communications for Celanese. She serves as secretary to the Public Responsibility Committee of the Board of Directors and to the Corporate Government Affairs Committee. She is also a member of the Corporate Contributions Committee.

Gregg came to Celanese from U.S. Steel Corporation, where she was assistant staff director of education services and then assistant director of public relations. Earlier she was a consultant to several corporations on management organization, recruitment, training, compensation, and incentive plans. Gregg served as an assistant professor of economics at Columbia University and the New School for Social Research. A graduate of the University of Texas with B.A. and M.A. degrees in economics, Gregg earned a Ph.D. in economics from Columbia University. She was awarded an honorary degree of humane letters by Salem Col-

FIGURE 18–7

Neiman-Marcus, as one of the events for their new Michigan Avenue store, hosted some cast members from "Dream Girls" to help publicize the Chicago opening of the musical.

ideas for special events as well as for planning and staging them. To capture the attention of the media and thereby to favorably impress the public is the responsibility of the public relations person.

lege and an honorary LLD by Northwood Institute.

Raised on a ranch in Tempe, Arizona, Gregg recalled, "Ranch life is vigorous. Everyone is a workaholic—you *have* to be to survive. As a child, I was encouraged to be independent, to be a leader. I was expected to take risks and to learn as much from failures as from success. I was always the first to jump from the highest haystack," she added. "If I got hurt, it taught me to make a better jump or to use better judgment next time."

Gregg was appointed by President Jimmy Carter to the President's Management Improvement Council. She has served on the Social Indicators Committee of the American Marketing Association, the UNESCO Committee to improve business education worldwide, and the White House Conference on Children.

President of the Foundation for Public Relations Research and Education, Gregg holds the Professional Chair in Public Relations of the New York Chapter, Women in Communications, Inc. She is a former executive officer of the New York chapter of the Public Relations Society of America, Women Executives in Public Relations, and the Advertising Women of New York.

The only woman on the Civilian Public Relations Advisory Committee of the U.S. Military Academy, Gregg also serves on the Secretary of the Navy's Advisory Board on Education and Training and the Committee on Long-Range Planning of the Public Relations Society of America. She is a member of the Public Relations Committee, Joint Council on Economic Education.

Recipient of the American Advertising Federation National Advertising Woman of the Year Award, Gregg was also one of the first to receive an Economic Equity Award from the Women's Equity Action League. That same year she was presented the Matrix Award in public relations by New York Women in Communications. Gregg is also the recipient of the Theta Sigma Phi Sound of Success Award and the Top Hat Award of the National Federation of Business and Professional Women's Clubs for her "significant contribution toward advancing the status of employed women."

Said Dr. Gregg, "My greatest reward came at an annual meeting of stockholders in Houston. A young woman, a Celanese chemical plant employee, introduced herself to me and said, 'Because of you, I know *anything* is possible.'"

Publications

Materials for which public relations persons are responsible often include company publications; news releases and media kits; booklets, leaflets, pamphlets, brochures, manuals, and books; letters, inserts, and enclosures; annual reports; posters, bulletin boards, and exhibits; audiovisual materials; and speeches and position papers. We will discuss these tools of communication in more detail later in this chapter.

 Research

Research is the process of obtaining reliable and valid information. Secondary sources of information are directories, the news media, professional journals, and government publications. One common form of public relations research is opinion sampling. During the Tylenol crisis, Johnson & Johnson performed continuous public opinion surveys so they could monitor the potential for reintroducing the product.

Because the purpose of all public relations activities is to influence public opinion, it is vital that the public relations person be concerned with measuring and analyzing changes in public attitude and sentiment.

 Fund Raising and Membership Drives

A public relations person may be responsible for soliciting money for the organization or for a cause the organization deems worthwhile, such as the United Way or a political action committee (PAC).

Charitable organizations, labor unions, professional societies, trade associations, and other groups rely on membership fees or contributions as a primary means of support. The public relations specialist must communicate to potential contributors or members the purposes and goals of the organization. The public relations specialist is often considered the chief communicator of the organization.

 Public Speaking

Because public relations practitioners frequently have to represent their employers at special events, it's essential that they be able to speak well. The ability to express oneself clearly reflects directly on the organization. Because organization spokespersons are often interviewed on TV or give speeches, organizations are now placing increased importance on the ability to communicate effectively.

 Planning and Execution

As pointed out at the beginning of this section on public relations activities, probably the most important role of a practitioner is to plan and execute the public relations program. To do this effectively, the practitioner must analyze the relationships between the organization and its publics, evaluate public attitudes and opinions toward the organization; assess the organization's policies, procedures, and actions as they relate to the organization's publics; and finally plan and execute a public relations program using any or all of the various PR activities described above.

PUBLIC RELATIONS
TOOLS

The tools of communication at the PR person's disposal are many and varied—from brochures to photographs to newsletters to audio-visual materials. We will discuss a few of these here because the same basic techniques of writing, art, layout, and production used in advertising are used in the production of public relations materials.

 ## News Releases and Media Kits

A news release is a typewritten sheet of information (usually 8 1/2 by 11 inches) issued to generate publicity or shed light on a subject of interest. A large variety of information is put in this form and sent to print and broadcast outlets. Subjects may include the announcement of a new product, promotion of an executive, establishment of a scholarship fund, or signing of a union contract, to name a few.

A media kit is used to gain publicity at staged events such as press conferences or open houses. It includes a basic fact sheet detailing the event, a program for the event or a schedule of the activities, a list of the participants with biographical data, brochures prepared for the event, a news story for the broadcast media, and news and feature stories for print media.

 ## Photography

As in advertising, a picture may be worth a thousand words. Photographs of events, products in use, new equipment, or newly promoted executives lend credence or interest to an otherwise dull news story.

Photography adds impact, realism, and believability to a news item. However, that impact can be negative as well as positive. On September 25, 1978, Hans Wendt, a staff photographer for the county of San Diego, was taking pictures for an upcoming hearing when he suddenly heard a boom over his head. Looking up, he saw a burning PSA airliner plummeting to earth. He pointed his camera and snapped the picture that subsequently appeared in every major newspaper and newsmagazine in the country (Figure 18–8).

How much negative PR do you feel that photograph might have created for the airline? Are questions of ethics involved when the media run sensational photographs like this?

 ## Booklets, Brochures, Pamphlets, and Books

Printed materials are used extensively in public relations. Materials are written to tell employees how they can aid the public relations program and how the organization started and grew, to teach employees how to go about doing their work, to explain the credit union and safety regulations, and a host of other things.

FIGURE 18–8

A startled Hans Wendt captured this picture during the tragic descent of Flight 182 on September 25, 1978. Since that day, the airline has discontinued the use of that flight number.

Frequently books are written on the company's history or as a biography of the company's founder. A common tool is a presentation booklet describing the organization to visitors, prospective employees, donors, students, and customers.

Letters, Inserts, and Enclosures

Letters may be written on behalf of the company and sent to customers, legislators, suppliers, retailers, or editors (letters to the editor often rebut a criticism of the company).

Inserts or enclosures may be used for public relations purposes. Inserts are often put in billings from oil or utility companies, for example, to explain rate increases or company views on political issues. These are the types of enclosures a public relations practitioner is responsible for. Who do you think would be responsible for the type of promotional inserts that offer merchandise at especially attractive prices?

Annual Reports

An annual report is a formal document issued yearly by a corporation to its stockholders. It is a reflection of a corporation's condition at the close of the business year. Annual reports contain an ever-expanding amount of information required by either generally accepted accounting principles or specific requirements. (For example,

FIGURE   18–9

Beautiful, contemporary graphic design utilizing multiple illustrations and photography in a grid format makes Potlatch Corporation's annual report readable and interesting.

FIGURE 18–10

House organ for World Typeface Center offers an article on Tin Can Typography—an almost-lost art form now experiencing revival.

Rule 14c-3, of the Securities Exchange Act of 1934 specifies that annual reports furnished to stockholders in connection with the annual meeting of stockholders include the following information: "certified" comparative financial statements, a five-year summary of operations, management's analysis of the summary operations, a brief description of the company's directors and executive officers and their principal occupations, and a statement of the market price range and dividends paid on voting securities for each quarterly period during the past two fiscal years.) Included in reports are financial statements. While the report is directed to the stockholders of the organization, it is also of interest to potential investors, unions, and legislators. Companies usually try to make their reports appealing, readable, and informative (Figure 18–9).

An annual report can be an important public relations tool because it is really management's justification for its performance. In addition, it can have a strong influence on potential investors who use it to discover the status and prospects of the business. It gives the organization the opportunity to answer questions about itself and to offer explanations for its actions. With the government delving into corporate affairs more and more, an annual report can help give agencies facts to overcome misconceptions they may have about operations.

Nonbusiness organizations also report to their members or trustees by using reports. These do not necessarily contain financial data, but they present progress on activities and plans for future programs. These reports are used as both internal and external public relations tools.

House Organs

A house organ (or house publication) is a company publication. Internal house publications are for employees only. External house publications may go to company-connected persons (customers, stockholders, and dealers) or to the public. They may take the form of a newsletter, a tabloid newspaper, or a magazine (Figure 18–10).

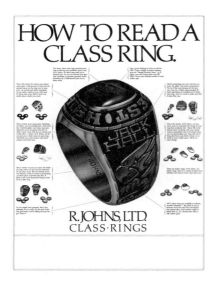

FIGURE 18–11

The company that makes class rings uses interesting, graphic posters to promote its product line.

Their purpose is to promote goodwill, increase sales, or mold public opinion. A well-produced house organ can do a great deal to get employees or customers to feel they know the people who make up a company. However, writing, printing, and distributing a house organ can be expensive.

Unfortunately, internal company newsletters often have the reputation of being gossip sheets or mouthpieces for management. When that is the case, they tend to go unread. Professional PR people have found that if the company openly talks about controversial issues and admits the negatives, readership of these publications increases and their effectiveness in building morale is strengthened.

 Speeches and Position Papers

Company executives give speeches before a great diversity of groups. Writing the speech often falls within the domain of the public relations person. Occasions for speeches may be congressional hearings, annual stockholders meetings, and important conferences and conventions. Practitioners may simply have to do the research for a speech, or they may prepare an outline or write the speech in its entirety for an executive of the company.

 Posters, Bulletin Boards, and Exhibits

Posters can be used internally to stress safety, security, reduction of waste, and courtesy, and externally to impart product information or other news of interest to the consumer (Figure 18–11).

Exhibits can give a history of the organization, present new products, show how products are made, or tell about future plans of the organization. Exhibits are often made at local fairs, colleges and universities, and trade shows.

Bulletin boards can announce new equipment, meetings, promotions, new products, construction plans, and recreation news to name just a few possibilities.

Audiovisual Materials, Films, and Closed-Circuit TV

These materials can take many forms, including slides, films, filmstrips, and video cassettes used for training, sales, or public relations.

"Nontheatrical" or "sponsored" films are films that are developed for public relations reasons. They are considered a form of corporate advertising. They are furnished without charge to movie theaters, organizations, and special groups, particularly schools and colleges. Examples of these films are *Why Man Creates*, produced for Kaiser Aluminum, and Mobil Oil Corporation's *A Fable*, starring the famous French mime Marcel Marceau.

Through the telephone company, a closed-circuit television system can be leased. It enables the broadcast of live pictures and sound from one point to another. Political parties use these systems for fund-raising dinners. Colleges use them to teach classes on different campuses. Companies use them for various types of meetings.

Open Houses, Plant Tours, and Other Staged Events

There are two kinds of public relations events: (1) those designed to create publicity and (2) those designed to improve public relations through personal contact. Often these two purposes overlap. For example, Macy's Thanksgiving Day parade in New York creates tremendous publicity but also a great deal of community goodwill because of personal contact. Also, an event designed to improve public relations among members of an association—the annual convention of the American Bar Association—can generate vast amounts of publicity.

Open houses and plant tours enable an organization to give the community a greater understanding of its inner workings. They can be instrumental in building goodwill. As part of a tour, companies often give away a sample of their product or a pamphlet about the organization. Organizations that typically give tours are newspapers and TV stations. The public relations person has to be able to plan the event or tour, control it, arrange for the location, devise the program and schedule speakers, send out invitations, and arrange for facilities.

Another type of event that is used as a public relations tool is the company-sponsored art, cultural, or sports event. The sponsorship enhances the identity of an organization. The cultural support creates goodwill in the community. For example, after cigarette companies were no longer able to advertise on radio or TV, they sponsored events such as golf and tennis tournaments in order to reach people via the airwaves.

THE PUBLIC RELATIONS PRACTITIONER

In times of corporate emergency, crisis, or disaster, the news media look to the company's public relations director for information. In military or other government organizations, the public relations person is frequently referred to as the public information officer. But the role is the same—to act as the primary communications link between the organization and its various publics.

 Government

How often do you read about actions by various government organizations—the IRS, SEC, FDA, the state attorney general, the local district attorney, and the police department? All these organizations have highly trained public relations people skilled at presenting their points of view or other information designed to stimulate the desired public opinion.

Many public relations people get their start working for some arm of the government or for political officeholders. The government is the largest user of public relations professionals in the country. And, for the most part, they are all in high news-demand positions, so it is excellent training ground.

PORTFOLIO OF
CORPORATE
ADVERTISING

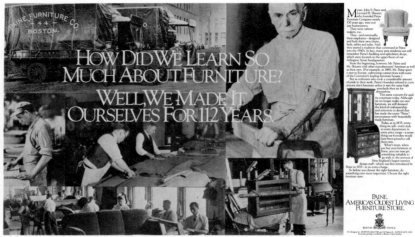

A. Paine Furniture uses local corporate advertising to maintain its high-end image as an old and reliable company.

B. Even the little children now know that when E. F. Hutton talks, people listen—probably one of the most effective corporate campaigns of the last decade.

C. How to keep your ideas on target? Bring them to Aerojet General. That's the objective of the corporate recruitment ad from this large defense contractor.

D. Much corporate advertising is aimed directly at the financial community as witnessed by this beautiful masterpiece from Greyhound Corporation. If you were considering an investment in Greyhound stock, how would this ad affect your thinking?

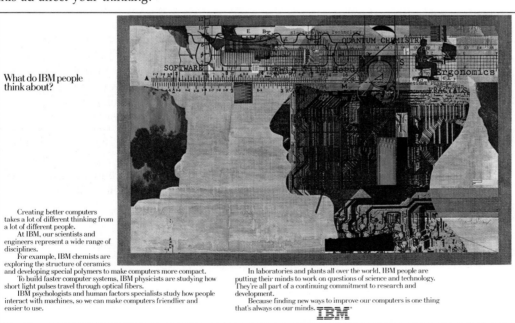

E. What IBM people think about is a very provocative question in this unusual corporate image ad for the computer company.

Business

The demand for news from business organizations is usually much lower except in those sensitive areas previously discussed. As a result, the role of the practitioner is oriented more to creating news that will positively influence public opinion and demonstrate the good citizenship of the particular business. In this regard, public relations is an important tool of marketing and it is in the interest of business to employ public relations people who also have a strong marketing background.

For example, in the late 70s, the baby food industry was under attack by consumers and the news media for the amount of sugar and salt added to their food products. Sales were declining, and consumer confidence was at a low ebb. Beech-Nut Corporation along with its PR firm, Daniel J. Edelman, Inc., launched an intensive public relations program centering around the company's introduction of reformulated products with no added salt and reduced added sugar. The program included press conferences, appearances on national news-talk shows, extensive articles in consumer magazines, consumer education in 50 top markets, and supportive reactions by leading consumer advocates.

After the initial announcement and the PR program were launched, advertising was placed to merchandise the idea of Beech-Nut's naturally good baby food. Continuing public relations and advertising kept the story alive for months, and within a year Beech-Nut's market share had increased several points while the competition had slipped.

 Nonprofit Organizations

As we shall discuss in Chapter 19, "Noncommercial and Political Advertising," the role of the professional practitioner in nonprofit organizations is to communicate the activities of the group in order to attract contributions as well as to build public awareness and understanding of the group's objectives. Therefore, PR professionals with an understanding of fund raising, direct mail, and advertising techniques are usually sought by these organizations.

 Career Opportunities

Because of the tremendous diversity in the demands made on a public relations practitioner, students should explore academic areas that will give them a wide variety of experiences. Newsom and Scott give nine areas of expertise that are desirable:[4]

1. Planning: ranges from aiding top management in other than PR problems to the details of the PR department's own organization and functioning. It incorporates the development of policy and procedure and communication of both to other departments.
2. Administration: goes beyond the administration of the PR department itself to interpreting top management to the entire organization, participating in association activities, coordinating all outside agencies and activities, accumulating information about the organization, and preparing and allocating the corporate PR budget.
3. Advising: implies doing the research necessary for authoritative

counsel and providing educational and informational materials to stockholders, lobbyists, and others.

4. Industry relations: working with personnel in improving employee relations, initiating communication systems with employees, helping to improve labor relations by participating in meetings and conferences with labor representatives, and working closely with labor negotiators in labor contracts and discussions.

5. Economic relations: involves relations with competitors, dealers, and distributors, and encompasses advertising and promotion, which often means working closely with marketing and merchandising.

6. Social relations: consists of both human relations, which includes preservation of personal dignity and employee protection (security), and social welfare, which incorporates recreational, medical, and civic activities.

7. Political activities: extend beyond the community's administrative, educational, and religious groups to legislative bodies and international contacts.

8. Communication: knowing how to communicate through both mass and specialized media by advertising and publicity.

9. Educational activities: encompasses working with employees, the general public, schools, company representatives such as salespeople and dealers, and consumer groups, and arranging appearances and writing speeches for corporate executives.

Inside firms

Internal public relations departments may consist of as few as one person or as many as several hundred persons. The greater the number, the more likely that work will be handled by specialists who are responsible for particular facets of public relations (Figure 18–12).

It is common for internal departments to retain the services of such outside suppliers as artists, printers, mailing houses, and clipping services for monitoring press coverage.

FIGURE 18–12 Ratings of functions by in-house public relations departments

Functions	Percent of importance	Functions	Percent of importance
News releases, media relations	99	Preparation of financial reports	41
Communications policy decisions	89	Advertising and identity programs	37
House publications	82	Marketing services	26
Contacting public officials	74	Fund-raising campaigns	21
Preparation of speeches, scripts	70	Financial-analyst meetings	20
Preparation of graphics or films	70	Competitive intelligence	19
Publicity of products, services	66	Recruiting personnel	19
Shows, exhibits, and special events	59	Membership drives	13
Training managers in PR/PA	55	Industrial relations (labor	
Representing employer at various		negotiations)	12
events	48		

There are many advantages of an internal department. An in-house practitioner is available on a moment's notice, and there is someone who can speak on behalf of the company when needed. It is sometimes less expensive to have someone on the payroll in-house than to hire an outside organization. However, the expertise of outside professionals may offset this minor savings. An in-house person has a more intimate knowledge of the organization than an outsider.

The disadvantages of an internal department include the fact that practitioners may lose their objectivity. It is sometimes difficult for them to step back as a member of the company team. In addition, it is difficult for them to obtain fresh viewpoints and an exposure to other companies' problems and solutions when they are tied to one company on a full-time basis.

Outside firms

Many advertising agencies offer public relations services. In addition, there are more than 1,600 firms that specialize in public relations exclusively. Many of these firms specialize in a particular area of public relations such as public affairs, financial public relations, or political public relations (Figure 18–13).

One advantage of an outside agency is the range of services available, which might be prohibitively expensive if maintained internally. A second advantage is objectivity. An outside specialist is above the daily operation of an organization. Third, many public relations firms are in New York City, the communications center of the United States. For some organizations it may be very important to have an outside agency located in the same area. Also, there's the prestige of having a well-known outside firm handle an organization's public relations.

FIGURE   18–13   Use of counseling firms and agencies by companies

Function	Percent of importance	Function	Percent of importance
Fact-finding:		Helping clients with their:	
Opinion research	73	Media contacts	95
Legislative intelligence	58	News releases	90
Competitive intelligence	49	Booklets, brochures, etc.	90
Counseling of:		Meetings, special events	87
Senior officials	93	PR/PA program proposals	86
PR department staff	73	Speeches and interviews	80
PA department staff	62	House publications	68
		Financial reports	68

Summary

Public relations is a process used to manage an organization's relationships with its various publics. These publics include the organization's employees, customers, stockholders, competitors, and the general populace. Many public relations activities involve media communications. However, unlike product advertising, these are not normally openly sponsored or paid for.

To help create a favorable reputation in the marketplace, companies use advertising. There are four types: public relations advertising, corporate (or institutional) advertising, corporate identity advertising, and recruitment advertising.

Corporate or institutional advertising is used to build awareness of the company, make a good impression on the financial community, influence public opinion, motivate present employees, or attract new talent.

Corporate identity advertising is used to communicate a name or appearance change, an ownership change, or a change in corporate personality, or to generate increased awareness.

Recruitment advertising has the sole objective of attracting employment applications. These advertisements are most frequently found in the classified section.

There are many types of public relations activities, including publicity and press agentry, public affairs and lobbying, promotion events management, publication preparation, research, fund raising and membership drives, and public speaking. However, the most important role of the practitioner is to plan and administer the public relations program.

The tools used in public relations are many and varied. These are news releases and media kits, photography, booklets, letters, annual reports, house organs, speeches and position papers, posters and exhibits, audiovisual materials, open houses, and staged events.

In times of emergency, crisis, or disaster, the news media look to the organization's public relations director for information. In government work, the public relations person is frequently referred to as a public information officer. Most government public relations people are in very high news-demand positions.

Except in sensitive areas, the demand for news from business organizations is usually much lower. As a result, the role of the public relations person is oriented more to creating news. In nonprofit organizations the practitioner's role is often to build public awareness and attract contributions.

There are many career opportunities in public relations inside organizations as well as outside in public relations agencies. Areas of expertise that are desirable in perspective employees include planning, administration, advising, industrial relations, economic relations, social relations, political affairs, communication, and education.

Questions for review and discussion

1. How does the definition of public relations differ from the definition of advertising?
2. How is the perspective of advertising practitioners different from that of PR professionals?
3. What are the various publics of a company? Discuss their importance to advertisers.
4. If you handled the public relations for a utility company, what activities do you think would be the most useful?
5. What do you think are the most important public relations tools for a major corporation? Why?
6. In what types of organizations are public relations practitioners usually found?
7. What is the purpose of recruitment advertising? Why is it under the domain of corporate advertising and public relations?
8. What are the various types of corporate advertising? Describe them.
9. What examples can you cite of corporate identity advertising? How effective were they?
10. What activities do you think would be best handled by outside public relations counsel? By an in-house department?

19

NONCOMMERCIAL AND POLITICAL ADVERTISING

"There are googols of little creatures squiggling and burrowing, flitting and squishing under the mud, through the swamps and over the sandy marshes. Sea squirts, copepods, lugworm larvae, and the babies of little fish. Each with a kind of brain, each with the breath of life. But their life is ebbing. And as they start to go—you do, too.

"You are standing on the threshold of time in as sacred a place as any in the world. It's where the life of the water and the life of the land converge in biological blur. These are the wetlands—the swamps and the mudflats that sometimes smell like rotten eggs. These are the marshes, clogged with weeds, swarming with bugs, teeming with beautiful life. This is where the moon moves the water in shallow ebbs and floods; where the sun pierces down to the ooze and the nutrients flow in a strange and marvelous way. Nowhere else except here in these sopping grounds is there so much life in so much concentration. But the life is dwindling. And as these lands start to go—you do, too.

"These squishy, mushy lands are where most of our fish are born, the fish that feed the fish that feed the fish that fill the sea. These narrow strips of estuarine land are where the birds come to rest and nest and feed; and they are tied inexorably to the life support for the raccoons and the bears and the deer a hundred miles away. And to you . . . ."

These are the first three paragraphs of an award-winning advertisement. What do you think is being advertised? A product? A service? Who do you think might have run this ad? A sporting goods store? An oil company? A boat manufacturer?

What do you think is the objective of this ad? To promote a new fishing area? To persuade people to invest in Florida land? To remind people to buy insect repellent?

Let's consider the last three paragraphs of the same ad.

"In California, most of the wetlands are already gone. In Florida, they're going fast. Once there were 127 million acres of interior and coastal wetlands. Now 40 percent are gone, the precious specks of life in these treasured lands exchanged for yacht clubs and marinas and industrial growth. As we dredge the bays and fill the marshes and cover the mud with asphalt; as we spray our poisons and scatter our waste and spew oil upon the waters—we destroy forever the great forces of life that began millennia ago.

"But now we have gone too far. Because this planet belongs not only to us, but to them as well. To the umpteen zillion other things that fly in the sky and roam on the land and swim in the sea and burrow beneath our feet.

"Now, especially now, if we will only stop to think—perhaps we will think to stop." (See Figure 19–1.)

In recent years the Sierra Club has been the nation's leading advocate for conservation. The club is a nonprofit organization whose primary objectives are to fight the destruction of our natural environment and to communicate the need for conservation to the public. The club has centered its interest on preserving parks and forests, fighting offshore oil drilling, protecting the nation's wild waters and wildlands, promoting energy conservation, and slowing the overdevelopment of urban areas. In the advertisement the club is attempting to communicate the importance of saving our rapidly disappearing marshes and swamplands.

But this advertisement also demonstrates the fine caliber of work often done by noncommercial advertisers. These organizations, which have no profit-making product or service to sell, are concerned only with promoting an idea, a philosophy, an attitude, a social cause, or a political issue. In many respects this is a far more difficult task than promoting the more tangible benefit of a new product or service.

This chapter deals with the difference between commercial and noncommercial advertising and describes the various types of advertising by nonprofit organizations to which we are exposed daily.

NONCOMMERCIAL ADVERTISING

What is the difference between the kind of advertising created for a commercial product or service and the kind we call noncommercial advertising? Is it the way the advertising is written or the media in which it is placed? Is it the type of artwork used or the mix of pictures and music we see on TV? What makes noncommercial advertising different?

The most obvious answer is that the thing being advertised is different; the product is different. Manufacturing companies advertise tangible products: cars, boats, food, soap, soft drinks, industrial equipment, machines, and so forth. Service companies advertise tangible services: restaurants, income tax services, plumbing, landscaping, etc. In contrast, we see advertisements daily for intangible hu-

FIGURE 19–1

The Sierra Club is one of the nation's leading advocates for conservation. In this advertisement the club attempts to communicate the importance of saving our rapidly disappearing marshes and swamplands.

4 out of 5 convicts were abused children.

In the United States, an average of 80% of our prisoners were abused children. That is why we are working so hard to help these children today, before

they develop into a threat to others tomorrow. With your support, we can have a full staff of trained people available 24 hours a day. Abused

children desperately need us. Please let us be there to help. Write for our free brochure, or send in your tax-deductible donation today.

San Francisco Child Abuse Council, Inc.
4093 24th Street, San Francisco, CA 94114

FIGURE   19–2

The cause of child abuse has been the recipient of a great deal of aid from the Advertising Council and other nonprofit organizations in recent years. Many of these ads are designed to simply promote awareness of the problem, while others invite readers to write for more information or to send money.

manitarian social causes (Red Cross), political ideas or issues (Sierra Club), philosophic or religious positions (Church of Latter Day Saints), or particular attitudes and viewpoints (labor unions). In most cases these advertisements are created and placed by nonprofit organizations. And the product they are advertising is their particular mission in life, be it politics, welfare, religion, conservation, health, happiness, or love.

There is a more subtle difference, however, and that relates to the specific objective of the advertisement. Commercial firms use advertising to stimulate sales by persuading people to buy. In noncommercial advertising the most similar objective would be to stimulate donations or persuade people to vote.

■ Objectives of Noncommercial Advertising

In Chapter 4 we learned that the general objective of all advertising is to inform, persuade, or remind people about the specific product being advertised. Likewise, in noncommercial advertising the general objective is to inform, persuade, or remind people about the particular idea, cause, or philosophy being advertised. The difference lies in the specific objectives being sought.

Whereas commercial advertisers may want to stimulate brand loyalty, the noncommercial objective might be to popularize a social cause (Figure 19–2). If a specific commercial objective for a new shampoo is to change people's *buying* habits, the related noncommercial objective for an energy conservation program might be to change people's *activity* habits, such as turning off the lights.

Figure 19–3 shows a variety of related specific objectives for commercial and noncommercial advertisers. Study the table and try to think of examples you may have seen of each objective. Can you think of any other possible specific objectives? Where did you see them? Are the noncommercial objectives usually different or always different?

What was the objective of the Sierra Club ad in Figure 19–1? To stimulate donations? To influence votes? To persuade people to like bugs? List all the possible objectives in their order of priority, from most important to least important.

■ Types of Noncommercial Advertising

The best way to categorize the various types of noncommercial advertising is by the organizations that use them. For instance, advertising is used by churches, schools, universities, hospitals, charitable organizations, and many other *nonbusiness institutions*. We also see advertising by *associations*, such as labor groups, professional organizations, and trade and civic associations. In addition, we witness millions of dollars worth of advertising placed by *government organizations*: the Army, Navy, Marine Corps, Postal Service, Social Security Administration, the Internal Revenue Service, and various state chambers of commerce.

Likewise, every year, as taxpayers and voters, we are forced to witness a massive barrage of advertising and propaganda by *political organizations*. In fact, political advertising has become such a contro-

FIGURE 19–3   Comparison of advertising objectives

Product advertising	Noncommercial advertising
Create store traffic	Stimulate inquiries for information
Stimulate brand loyalty	Popularize social cause
Change buying habits	Change activity habits
Increase product use	Decrease waste of resources
Communicate product features	Communicate political viewpoint
Improve product image	Improve public attitude
Inform public of new product	Inform public of new cure
Remind people to buy again	Remind people to give again

versial as well as interesting area that we have devoted the second half of this chapter to the subject.

Much of the advertising performed by the organizations mentioned above is referred to as public service advertising. However, the "advertising prepared in the public interest," which is performed by the Advertising Council, is unique, and we will discuss it here as a separate type of noncommercial advertising.

Advertising by nonbusiness institutions

"It's a matter of life and breath" is a familiar line to anyone who watches television. Every year the American Lung Association places an estimated $10 million worth of advertising on television and radio, in newspapers and magazines, and on outdoor and transit media. All this space and time are donated as a public service by the media involved. In its effort to educate the public about the damaging effects of smoking or the early warning signs of emphysema, lung cancer, and tuberculosis, the Lung Association joins a long list of nonbusiness institutions that use noncommercial advertising to achieve their objectives.

Not all nonbusiness institution advertising is donated, however. If you live in a large metropolitan area and want to place an ad for your favorite charitable organization, you will probably be charged a special nonprofit institution rate by your local city newspaper. Newspaper, radio, and TV advertising departments are besieged by requests from local churches, charity groups, hospital guilds, and other do-good social organizations to donate advertising space and time to these "favorite causes." As a result, out of self-defense, they are forced to charge for most local nonbusiness institution advertising.

The objectives of nonbusiness institution advertising are varied. The Foster Parents Plan uses massive doses of advertising to ask readers to adopt children from the country of their choice by spending $15 per month for their care and support. A similar organization, the Christian Children's Fund, enlists sponsors for starving orphans in underdeveloped countries around the world. Every year these two organizations raise millions of dollars for food, clothing, medicine, and shelter from Americans who care (Figure 19–4).

This fact, that Americans *do* care, is in great part the reason non-

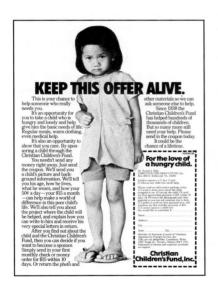

FIGURE 19–4

Ads like this one for the Christian Children's Fund are run free of charge by many of the nation's media. In the last 10 years, millions of dollars of media time and space have been donated to aid the less fortunate.

The taste that's made to order. And reorder.

The potatoes that most of your customers buy for themselves at home" are the ones they love to order when they're   dining out. That's why hearty, robust Idaho" potatoes are America's #1 best seller and the #1 way to guarantee that   your side orders really do get ordered. Again and again. For tasty new serving ideas, get your free Idaho Potato   Foodservice Kit. Write Gordon Randall, Idaho Potato Commission, P.O. Box 1068, Boise, Id. 83701 or call (208) 344-8545.

IDAHO

THE FIRST NAME IN POTATOES

FIGURE   19–5

The Idaho Potato Commission, a nonprofit organization, promotes consumption of potatoes for its members—farmers and others in the commercial potato-growing business.

profit charitable organizations have proliferated in this country. Another American who cared was Henry Bergh, who in the last century became the father of the humane movement in the United States. In April 1866 Bergh organized the American Society for the Prevention of Cruelty to Animals. Through a long and arduous advertising and publicity campaign, he persuaded state legislatures throughout the nation to pass laws to protect animals and raise the consciousness of Americans to the plight of these creatures.

Today the American Humane Association provides "unity and concert of action to promote the interests common to SPCAs and humane societies wherever found." In 1914 the association inaugurated its now-famous Be Kind to Animals Week. Every year literature is prepared, television and radio commercials are created, and publicity is released during May to remind Americans to take care of their animals and to suggest that they adopt one of the millions of lost pets given shelter every year by SPCAs and other humane societies.

Other familiar names in the long list of nonbusiness institutions that use noncommercial advertising are the United Way, Red Cross, American Cancer Society, American Heart Association, and the Boy Scouts of America, to mention just a few.

Advertising by nonprofit business associations

Attorneys have only recently been allowed to advertise their services. Bar associations, however, have used noncommercial advertising for years as an educational public service tool. Local and state bar associations ads are typical examples of how business, professional, trade, labor, farm, and civic associations use noncommercial advertising to achieve their individual objectives.

Frequently the purpose of advertising by nonprofit business associations is simply to create goodwill and a positive impression of the association's members by spotlighting the good works of individuals within the organization. Labor unions, for example, use advertising to inform the public how important union workers are to the nation's economy. By stimulating goodwill in this way they are potentially able to enlist more public support during labor disputes. Other associations use advertising for political impact to effect favorable legislative action.

So, even though the advertiser may be a nonprofit association, and even though the ads may be referred to as "public service announcements" or "noncommercial," the objective of these associations' advertising is often indirectly commercial. This is especially true of the advertising sponsored by trade, farm, and manufacturers' associations.

Look at the example of association advertising in Figure 19–5. What is the objective of the Idaho Potato Commission ad? Is this ad really noncommercial?

Advertising by government organizations

During World War II the poster of Uncle Sam pointing his finger and saying "Uncle Sam Needs You" became a famous and effective advertising tool for the Armed Forces. This same graphic theme is used today, 40 years later, in various configurations to remind people of the importance of patriotism.

Government bureaus and departments have been highly effective advertising and propaganda practitioners for years. In its effort to communicate with the voters, the government employs advertising agencies and public relations firms and maintains well-staffed, in-house graphics, communications, and press relations departments.

Much government advertising announces the availability of such valuable government services as consumer assistance, welfare aid, or career guidance. Similarly, great effort is given to instructing people on how to use government services correctly. The U.S. Postal Service, for example, has maintained a strong campaign for years to persuade and remind citizens to use ZIP Codes and also to mail early for Christmas.

Frequently government ads are carried free by the media as a public service. The Postal Service launched its first national paid advertising campaign in the 1970s, spending $4 million in some 370 newspapers to answer common consumer questions about the mail service. The Postal Service now spends more than $10 million annually to tell people how to use their services.

The 1970s also saw the Army, Navy, Air Force, and Marine Corps enter the paid advertising arena. With the end of the Selective Service draft came the need to recruit more volunteers, so the military pursued the most aggressive advertising techniques to draw young men and women to its ranks (Figure 19–6).

For the most part, government advertising is considered a public service. However, with the resources available to it, government can also use advertising techniques for propaganda purposes, and sometimes the dividing line is very thin. This has given rise to some controversy in the past. For example, at the beginning of every year the IRS places news releases about the new techniques it has developed to catch tax evaders. The objective of this massive annual "public

FIGURE 19–6

An ad for the U.S. Navy aimed at recruiting young men and women for Navy careers.

FIGURE 19–7

(Open on scenic footage of football games, concerts, sailing, and horseback riding. Music throughout.)

SINGER: *Start with the dawn of a new day! Exploring the wide open road. Follow the trail where it's leading you. And discover Ontario.*

You'll see the gleam on the water. You can feel the sun shining strong. You'll find the smile of a friendly face. That says this is where you belong.

See Ontario. See Ontario. Cause it's yours to discover.

And you're gonna love it. So come on everybody. Get up and discover Your Ontario.

SUPER: Ontario. Yours to discover.

relations'' campaign is obvious to many—to intimidate people into filling out their income tax forms correctly.

Many state governments use advertising to attract new businesses, tourists, or workers to aid their economy. Ohio advertises the availability of skilled workers and placement services for industrial concerns. Florida offers warm weather and entertainment. Ontario, Canada, invites you to explore the open road (Figure 19–7).

In totalitarian systems such as the Soviet Union, government often uses the media to communicate the official party view of world events in the guise of news. While the benefits of government advertising are many, the potential for abuses exists, and for that reason consumer and voter groups rightfully keep a watchful eye (Figure 19–8).

The Advertising Council

During the early months of World War II a group of prominent advertising industry figures formed a committee. They called themselves the War Advertising Council and volunteered to create and place advertising at the service of the government in the national interest.

In conjunction with the Office of War Information, the committee planned the council's first assignments of promoting the nation's conversion from peacetime to wartime industrial production. By the end of the war more than 100 public service advertising campaigns had been conducted to promote such things as war bonds, victory gardens, venereal disease prevention, and forest fire prevention. American business had donated more than $1 billion worth of advertising media time and space to these campaigns.

When the war ended, rather than disbanding, the committee changed its name to the Advertising Council and began working on the problems of conversion to peacetime. Among the programs continued were the Red Cross and forest fire prevention.

FIGURE 19–8

A public service ad created to support government legislation aimed at reducing crimes with guns.

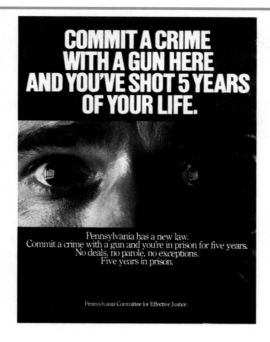

COMMIT A CRIME WITH A GUN HERE AND YOU'VE SHOT 5 YEARS OF YOUR LIFE.

Pennsylvania has a new law.
Commit a crime with a gun and you're in prison for five years.
No deals, no parole, no exceptions.
Five years in prison.

Pennsylvania Committee for Effective Justice.

Advertising Age reports that the council's policy today is basically the same as when it began: "Accept no subsidy from government and remain independent of it. Conduct campaigns of service to the nation at large, avoiding regional, sectarian, or special-interest drives of all kinds. Remain nonpartisan and nonpolitical. Conduct the Council on a voluntary basis. Accept no project that does not lend itself to the advertising method. Accept no campaign with a commercial interest unless the public interest is obviously overriding."

During America's bicentennial year the Advertising Council conducted 30 major public service campaigns, a record number in its 35-year history. In 1985 the value of donated time and space exceeded $500 million, and the total since 1942 exceeds $10 billion. Three of its earliest projects are still in continuous operation: forest fire prevention, U.S. savings bonds, and the American Red Cross.

Other familiar campaigns are for the United Negro College Fund ("A mind is a terrible thing to waste"), child abuse prevention ("Help destroy a family tradition"), the United Way ("It works for all of us"), and the U.S. Department of Transportation ("Drinking and driving can kill a friendship") (Figure 19–9).

POLITICAL ADVERTISING

It was a warm southern California morning just three weeks before the off-year elections. Seated in the living room of a state assemblyman who was running for reelection were the candidate and his wife, his administrative assistant, his advertising/PR man, and two men from Spencer/Roberts & Associates, the California Republican Party's professional campaign management firm. Stu Spencer and George Young had just flown in from Los Angeles for this urgent meeting

Figure   19–9

The picture tells the whole story in this Ad Council public service message for the Department of Transportation.

with the candidate and his staff. The conversation was intense, the air swollen with emotion.

Until two days before, the campaign had been flowing smoothly. It was a no-sweat contest. The Republican legislator represented a highly Democratic district, but he was immensely popular. With only three weeks left the latest polls showed him leading with more than 65 percent of the vote. There was ample money, an army of volunteers, and a track record built up over the years of conscientious representation of his constituents. He was the darling of the little old ladies, the quiet but highly principled spokesman for the conservative right, and also a sympathetic symbol for the struggling minorities in need of a leader. In short, he was a shoo-in.

Then out of a clear blue sky, lightning struck. The assemblyman and six other people who had served on the local city council four years before were suddenly, without warning, indicted by the county grand jury for bribery and conspiracy. They were charged with accepting campaign contributions four years before in exchange for their votes for a taxicab rate increase. The daily headlines and television networks were screaming the news. Bribery! Conspiracy! Indictments!

Despite his immediate protestations of innocence and no wrongdoing, the assemblyman's volunteer army quickly started deserting, the contributions stopped, and the polls immediately showed a complete reversal, with his popularity suddenly down to only 32 percent and still falling.

So this top-level meeting had been hastily called. The discussion had centered for over an hour on the situation—what had happened, how, why, was it true, and so on.

The conversation turned. "So what are we going to do?"

George Young, one of the men from Spencer/Roberts, had sat silently through most of this, just listening, analyzing, coolly evaluating. He was the epitome of objectivity. The candidate's wife finally turned to him and said, "You haven't said much, George. What do you think?" She was hardly prepared for his answer.

"Well," said George, as he prepared to present his plan to them. "It seems to me that what we have here is a marketing problem."

■ The Political Marketing Process

George Young was absolutely right. They did indeed have a marketing problem. With only three weeks left before the election, they had to create enough doubt in the voters' minds about the validity of the bribery charges that they would be willing to vote for this candidate in spite of the indictments.

They could not wait until after the trial. He would be found innocent two months after the election was held, but that was too late. In the three weeks that remained, they had to try to convince the voters that, in spite of everything, he was still the best-qualified candidate to serve the community's needs in the state legislature.

The old campaign was scrapped, and a new campaign was planned and launched. Flyers were distributed questioning the coincidentally late nature of the charges. Television and radio commercials were produced with local citizens proclaiming their trust. Rallies were

FIGURE 19–10

ANNCR (VO): In Japan last year, 48 people lost their lives to handguns.

In Great Britain . . . 8.

In Canada . . . 52.

And in the United States . . . 10,728.

God bless America.

held. Interviews were given. Money started pouring in again from party loyals all over the state. In three weeks a marketing blitz was conducted which showed the candidate as humble, sincere, hard-working, and most of all honest. The slogan, "We believe in you, Tom," was added to all his billboards.

On election day his support had risen to 46 percent. That was not enough to win, but it was a stunning showing nonetheless. Two months later he was found innocent in a court of law and vindicated of all the charges against him. Perhaps if the election had been held only one week later, he might also have been able to retain his seat.

George Young directed an excellent marketing and advertising campaign. He determined the needs of the marketplace and did his utmost to give them what they wanted. Yet this attitude that political advertising is just another marketing function, much like advertising for toothpaste and dog food, has incited unprecedented public outcry in recent years. Why? What's so different about political advertising that people should get so upset?

There are several things that differentiate political advertising from commercial advertising:

1. The product is a person or a philosophy rather than an item for sale or a service (Figure 19–10).
2. The time period for a political advertising campaign is often finite rather than ongoing.
3. The ethical question is larger due to the potentially far-reaching effects of misleading advertising claims.

This section will explore political advertising as a marketing process. In so doing, we will deal with these and other differences as well as the many similarities between political advertising and commercial advertising.

Political product versus commercial product

As we have discussed throughout this text, the first and most important element in any marketing mix is the product. The primary difference between commercial advertising and political advertising is that in politics the product is frequently a human being.

In commercial advertising the effort is to show how a product or service will satisfy a functional, social, or psychological consumer need. The consumer who perceives that the product will be beneficial may buy it. Similarly, in politics much time and effort are spent determining the needs of the marketplace. If a politician is to represent supporters faithfully, he or she must be tuned in to their desires, wants, and prejudices. The politician strives to communicate with, relate to, and empathize with the voters—to develop that special quality called charisma.

Political advertising, then, needs to communicate those attributes of the politician that relate to the constituents' needs. The candidate gains the voters' confidence—and their votes. In this way the political product is "packaged" much like a commercial product. The problem is that in commercial marketing, advertising may move the product off the shelf once, but only satisfied customers will buy it again. In politics, when advertising gets a candidate elected, the voters are stuck with their "purchase" for two to six years.

FIGURE   19–11

The Moral Majority jumped into the spotlight in 1980 with the election of many conservative congressmen and senators whom they had backed. They also came under fire from liberal groups. This ad outlined the group's position and offered a free copy of their newspaper, *The Moral Majority Report.*

Political campaigns are not the only places we see political advertising. And politicians are not the only type of political products. We are all exposed daily to forms of political advertising or propaganda that do not relate at all to political elections or campaigns. We see ads and hear speeches supporting myriad public issues. Special-interest groups print brochures or run ads condemning public policy on a certain issue (Figure 19–11).

During World War II, theaters ran anti-German and anti-Japanese war movies followed by short ads appealing to the citizenry to buy war bonds. The amount of money spent on political advertising during the Vietnam conflict, both pro and con, ran into the millions.

In short, we are confronted with political advertising daily. Much of it is so subtle that we are not even aware of its political nature. But just as in political campaign advertising, which is the primary subject of this chapter, these other forms of political advertising are similarly used to market ideas, attitudes, or political products.

Political market versus commercial market

In Chapter 4 we learned that a market is a group of people who share a common interest, need, or desire. Furthermore, we learned that for commercial products this group must be able to use the product to advantage, and they must be able to afford it.

In political campaigns, the market is likewise a group of people who share a common interest, need, or desire, which may be satisfied by the election of certain political candidates. However, unlike commercial products, people don't have to be able to afford the candidates—they only have to be able to vote for them. Therefore, the political market is composed of those people in the candidate's district of influence who are registered to vote. These people are called *constituents*.

Constituents may be segmented like commercial markets: by geography, age, sex, income, education, race, religion, or occupation. Furthermore, they may be classified by their political affiliation. In some states, when people register to vote, the party they belong to becomes public information.

This information is extremely useful to the political candidate in determining roughly the stance of the community on many important issues. It is also useful because the candidate can assess his or her potential strength by evaluating the number of party loyals in the community. Furthermore, the list of registered party members is the most logical source of both political contributions and campaign workers.

Due to the nature of campaigns and elections, as well as our history of self-government, the political market possesses other unique characteristics. For one thing interest is higher than it is for commercial products. Politics is news. We are confronted with political stories every day in all the mass media. In the United States about 65 percent of the electorate regularly votes in national elections. Most people want to know as soon as possible who won the election. Compare this with the interest expressed by people in what car is selling best or which brand of detergent cleans clothes the best.

Furthermore, politics generates an emotional level rarely reached in commercial marketing. People either love or hate their politicians;

FIGURE   19–12

The American Civil Liberties Union, a nonpartisan organization concerned with individual rights, responded to the Moral Majority's attempts to enact legislation based on its religious beliefs. In this ad they suggest that we're going to be in big trouble if the Moral Majority has its way.

they call them names, picket them. They may be enamored of a certain car or dislike another intensely, but we've never heard of a Cadillac being assassinated.

What this all means is that the political market is a potpourri of Republicans, Independents, and Democrats, hard-hats and white-collar workers, blacks, yellows, browns, and whites, men and women, old people and young people, rich people and welfare recipients, and many more, all of whom express varying degrees of emotion and interest in their political issues and candidates (Figure 19–12). From these groups the office seeker tries to select a target market that will generate enough votes to win on election day.

Political marketing problems

When George Young told the indicted assemblyman and his staff that they had a marketing problem, he knew what he was talking about. In political campaigns the marketing objective is almost always the same: gain a 50+ percent share of market by election day. But the marketing problems faced by political candidates are as varied as those faced by commercial marketers. Which issues appeal to which voters? How can we communicate with the greatest number of voters in the time available? Or, as in the case of the indicted assemblyman, how can I improve my image with the voters?

In general, most marketing problems faced by political candidates fall into one of four areas: the party affiliation of the constituency, the candidate's identity and image, the issues, and time and money.

Constituency The politics of the constituency, which is frequently reflected in the percentage breakdown of party membership in a district, is one of the most common as well as difficult problems politicians face. Imagine being a Republican candidate in a district that is 70 percent Democrat in registration, or vice versa. Or, worse yet, imagine being a Socialist Party candidate in virtually any district. Simply by reason of your party affiliation, you might have only a small chance of winning a political campaign.

With our two-party system most voters are born into either Republican or Democratic families. Many are raised in their party. As a result, they frequently have a tendency to vote the "straight ticket." They may cross over to vote for a major officeholder like the president, but if they are dyed-in-the-wool party members, they tend to return to the party line-up for the minor offices. To many people, changing parties is almost as serious as changing religions. Therefore, the minority-party candidate in a district has an uphill struggle to convince voters of the opposing party to cross over and vote for him or her.

The problem of the constituency's politics has become even more complex as the divergence of political viewpoints has increased. In fact, in 1984, registered Independents outnumbered registered Republicans. And politicians have to remind themselves that within both major parties there are both liberals and conservatives. Just paying attention to voter registration isn't enough any more.

Identity and image To some degree every candidate faces the problems of identity and image. *Identity*, or name I.D., as it may be called, means having one's name known by or at least familiar to voters. It is estimated that incumbents automatically pick up 10 percent of the vote because of the good name I.D. they already possess with the voters in the district.

On the other hand, *image* refers to what voters think or feel about a candidate, either rightly or wrongly. It is in this area that political challengers try to make up what they may have lost to the incumbent in identity.

The incumbent has a record of votes and actions to defend. The record may be good, or it may be bad. Either way the challenger attempts to use that record to discredit the incumbent. Therefore, while the incumbent tries to use the record to paint a self-portrait of a "good guy," the challenger is simultaneously using many of the same facts to paint a picture of the incumbent as the "bad guy."

Sometimes these roles get reversed. Instead of the challenger attacking the incumbent's record, the incumbent may attack the challenger's. The challenger may then be forced into a defensive position. If the incumbent is successful in changing the traditional focus in this way, repositioning the attacker as a defender, then the challenger faces a serious dilemma and may very likely lose.

In 1964 Senator Barry Goldwater attempted to discredit President

---

PEOPLE IN ADVERTISING

David Garth

**President and Chairman of the Board
Garth Associates, Inc.**

Political advertising mentor David Garth has guided more than 100 political campaigns to date, with a win record of 72 percent, the best in the industry. ". . . even more remarkable," observes *New Times*, ". . . all but 12 of his candidates started out as decided underdogs." Garth is president and chairman of the board of Garth Associates, Inc., a New York–based advertising and public relations firm that has handled some of the toughest fought campaigns in recent years.

Garth even looks like a fighter. His agency occupies offices on the 14th floor of a Fifth Avenue building across from the famed Plaza Hotel. Garth's private office, lined with Emmy citations and autographed photos of clients, contains a three-TV console and a fourth, larger TV set.

The reason for the sets is Garth's emphasis on TV commercials for fighting—and winning—campaigns. His crisp videotape spots usually have the candidate speak for himself. They are crammed with facts, both in the speech and on a printed "crawl" across the bottom of the screen. And they focus on just one issue in each spot. This emphasis on "hard information" sells his political clients, says Garth. The cost of Garth's services are $25,000 a month, plus expenses, plus a 15 percent commission on the extensive TV production he provides. Garth nets about $2 million a year.

Lyndon Johnson's handling of the Vietnam War. He tried to show Johnson as weak and incapable of satisfactorily ending the conflict and to show himself as strong, outspoken, and decisive. The roles got reversed, however, and Johnson was successful in discrediting Goldwater's image, painting him as a warmonger who might drop the atomic bomb on women and children. President Johnson meanwhile maintained the image of a man of peace, and he won by a landslide. Richard Nixon did the same thing to George McGovern by questioning his credibility and competency in 1972. McGovern lost. Jimmy Carter and Walter Mondale, on the other hand, both tried to reposition Reagan as a warmonger and failed. Reagan won both times (Figure 19–13).

Politicians may create images by the way they present themselves, by party affiliation, by the record, by the advertising, by sudden news events, or even by the opposition. The real image is actually the sum of these impressions as they are perceived in the minds of the electorate. In other words, their perception is the reality (to them).

However, the image that took years to create may be destroyed overnight. We saw in the introduction to this section how one politician's image was completely undone by a late-breaking news event. He was accused of having accepted a bribe. It made no difference that

Raised in a politically active Jewish home on Long Island, Garth was stricken with a severe mastoid infection at age eight and then with rheumatic fever. He spent much of his youth in bed. When Garth heard a doctor tell his parents he would not live past 15, he determined to get well. He did, but with exhausting effort. "You become terribly competitive," he said. "You are always testing your own existence." After college, Garth took graduate courses in psychology at Columbia. He was fascinated by the mechanisms of human motivation, tools that he would later put to work in political advertising.

Garth's first big assignment was John Lindsay's successful race for mayor of New York in 1965. Garth had Lindsay filmed strolling through the streets of New York, coat over his shoulder, shirtsleeves rolled up, tie askew. The energetic image invented by Garth was a "first" in the history of TV political advertising.

Along with commercials, Garth Associates does advance work, issues research, polling, speech writing, fund raising, press relations, and campaign management. Once David Garth decides to represent a candidate, his 21-member staff conducts extensive research and polling. Garth and the candidate then select the issues they will concentrate on in TV spots. From 15 to 35 spots are developed. Garth directs every one of them. When a campaign is on, Garth and his staff routinely work 15 to 18 hours a day, seven days a week. In his office Garth uses a 31-button computer phone directly linked to candidates, several governors, mayors, members of Congress, and key political reporters.

One of Garth's victories was for New York mayor Edward Koch, who was estimated to have less than 2 percent of the vote when the race began. Garth characteristically recommended exhaustive debating. Koch was drilled for two hours a day on the facts supporting his positions. He completed 62 debates—and emerged victorious.

Garth's other winners include Mayor Tom Bradley of Los Angeles and Senator Adlai Stevenson III (D-Ill.) He also participated in the 1980 U.S. presidential bid of Senator John Anderson (R-Ill.) and the 1984 U.S. presidential Democratic primary campaign of Walter Mondale.

Each year, on the average, more than 50 candidates seek out the services of Garth Associates. What Garth looks for, says *New Times*, "is the scrapper, the tough kid, smaller than the other guys . . ." And to those who think that sounds like David Garth himself, the same article concludes, ". . . this peculiar little man is one of the most powerful politicians in the country."

FIGURE   19–13

In spite of his opponents' efforts to reposition him, President Reagan promoted the idea that his leadership was working and that their leadership had failed. The voters agreed.

he was subsequently found completely innocent. He had already lost the election.

In the case of first-time or minor-office candidates, identity should normally be the primary objective. Many people are elected to school boards and water districts simply because they had more signs displaying their name than their opponent did.

For major-office candidates, image is more important. However, too many would-be officeholders strive for a glowing image without ascertaining first whether the voters even know who they are. What do you suppose is the usual result?

Campaign issues In a marketing sense, the candidate's positions on the various issues are the sales features. How politicians select issues and their record on past issues are major marketing problems. This is especially true on the national level or whenever there are major demographic differences within the candidate's voting district.

Unfortunately, the very nature of the politician—seeking approval from the voters—creates internal, psychological pressure to try to be all things to all people. Too many politicians lose sight of their marketing objective: 50 percent of the electorate plus one. In striving to please everybody, they fail to please the half they need.

Similarly, candidates frequently make the mistake of trying to take a major stand on every issue, even insignificant ones. As a result, they blend into the maze of politicians vying for support and fail to achieve any identity or image whatsoever. It is usually better, especially for first-time candidates with low identity, to take a strong stand on one major issue of vital importance to the electorate and hammer away at it. In this way the office seeker gains identity as "the person who stands for such and such." In addition, the candidate may even develop the image of someone who "speaks out" or "sticks to his guns," an important quality in elected representatives.

Time and money In 1976 Jimmy Carter might have lost the election to Gerald Ford if it had been held one week later. In 1980 he might have beaten Ronald Reagan if it had been held two weeks earlier. The time element is one of the major differences between political marketing and commercial marketing. And so is money.

In business, marketing is a never-ending effort continuously funded by the company. In politics everything is aimed at election day. You raise as much money through contributions as you can early in the campaign, and then you spend it all on advertising and other activities before a certain date. Timing is crucial. On election day you add up the votes and see who won. This is both the fun and the agony of political advertising (Figure 19–14).

But it is also one of the biggest problems. Certainly the greatest furor over political campaigns has centered on the subjects of campaign financing and last-minute tactics.

In 1972 a strict federal campaign spending bill went into effect limiting the amount of money federal office seekers may spend to 10 cents for each eligible voter. Of this, no more than 6 cents may be spent on broadcast media. Some local governments have even stricter laws. Many people have already been fined or jailed for violating these rules.

The power to shape
the future of our country
is at your fingertip.

On November 6, use your power of choice.
Register and vote.

FIGURE 19–14

Less is more in this full-page
newspaper ad urging people to
vote on election day.

In any campaign, advertising is the most expensive item. And advertising is as necessary as it is expensive. The candidate may be a fine person, but that doesn't help the voters if they don't find out.

The way the money is spent on advertising, then, is a major part of the campaign strategy. Most successful candidates design their strategies so that expenditures increase as the election draws nearer. The goal is for the candidate's identity, image, and popularity to all "peak" the day before the election. If they peak too soon or too late, the candidate may lose.

Some candidates keep a budget reserve for last-minute tactics. Inevitably, the weekend before the election the voters receive some bit of last-minute "news" about some candidate. This may be sponsored by the candidate or by the opponent. Usually the purpose is to either confuse the voter or smear the opponent when there is no time left for rebuttal.

What would you think if you were a registered Democrat and you received a letter the day before the election that read:

> Dear Fellow Democrat:
>
> We have become increasingly alarmed at the efforts of Senator Gluck to buy the upcoming election with illegal contributions from the big oil companies. While we want to support our Democratic Administration in the State Capital, we cannot stand idly by and watch this one Democrat make a mockery of our party and of our democratic system.
>
> As a result, on Tuesday, we urge you as loyal Democrats to write in the name of Admiral Barry Lipschitz on your ballot, so that Governor Weasel's policies may be carried out with honesty and dignity in the Legislature.
>
> We urge this in the name of democracy, in the name of Governor Weasel, and in the name of the Democratic Party.
> Yours very truly,
> Democrats for Honest Government

Who do you think might have sponsored this letter? Senator Gluck? His Republican opponent? Democrats for Honest Government? And who do you think the Democrats for Honest Government are? Are they really Democrats? And who is Admiral Lipschitz? Do you think he would be a good person to support Governor Weasel's policies?

Also, what do you think of this type of campaign tactic? Is it clever? Is it fair? What do you think Senator Gluck should do?

Political market research

It is vitally necessary to assess several important factors before formulating any specific strategies or advertising plans. This is accomplished through market research. Usually it is best to have an in-depth survey at the outset to discover the relative identity and image of the candidates and to determine the issues as well as the basic attitudes of the voters. From this information the campaign may be planned and budgeted. Toward the end of the campaign, most candidates engage in polling. Based on this information they may make last-minute decisions for major expenditures or strategy shifts.

More campaign money is wasted because of gut-level market research and seat-of-the-pants planning than any other way. In most

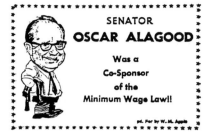

FIGURE   19–15

Notice the difference between these homegrown, nonagency advertisements for Oscar Alagood and the agency-produced ad for Whitney in Figure 19–16. The difference is not size, but quality. Which do you think succeeds in offering more appeal to the voters?

cases candidates are well advised to employ a professional market research firm at the outset before spending money on anything else. It is no fun to discover at the end of a campaign that you were on the wrong side of the most important issue.

Use of marketing professionals in politics

Many politicians employ professional campaign managers. These people usually have advertising or marketing backgrounds and have developed an expertise in people management and political strategy.

For a well-financed campaign, money for a skilled, professional manager is extremely well spent. Professional managers understand the importance of fact gathering, planning, organization, and direction, and they are usually instrumental in directing the emotion-ridden campaign coolly and objectively.

In addition to a professional manager, most candidates also find employing an advertising agency worthwhile. The agency is able to implement the strategy of the campaign with brochures, billboards, advertisements, or broadcast commercials. Likewise, if brought in at the beginning, the agency can be helpful in the early planning stages, recommending a reputable market research firm, helping to analyze statistics, and translating objectives into strategy and effective advertising vehicles (Figures 19–15 and 19–16). Forever on tight budgets, political candidates always welcome any friends in the advertising business who are willing to help.

Advertising Solutions to Political Marketing Problems

What an advertisement, brochure, or direct-mail piece says frequently has a great effect on the impression the voters get of a candidate. However, what the advertisement says is not merely a function of the words in the ad. Since voters, as people, receive all information subjectively, what an ad says is actually a function of many factors. Who is reading or viewing the advertisement? What words are used and how are they used? What does the ad look like? By what medium is the advertisement communicated? Does the ad ring true? Or does the ad simply smear the opposition candidate?

The political office seeker must ask all these questions of every advertisement before it is released to the media. In fact, these questions should be asked and answered before an ad ever goes into production.

Campaign strategy

The number of different campaign strategies that might be exercised is infinite. Frequently a candidate will mix two or more strategies depending on the particular circumstances of the campaign. Some of the strategies commonly used are:

Popularity (good for creating the bandwagon effect).
Appeal to authority (testimonials from well-known people).
Coat-tailing (using the popularity of a political ally).
Anti-establishment (or anti-special interest, anti-money, etc.).
Successful experience (most common for incumbents).

FIGURE 19–16

An appeal to change, as well as to the pocketbook, characterizes Fallon McElligott Rice's well-designed and cleverly worded advertisement for Whitney.

Appeal to sympathy (good for underdogs, minority candidates, war veterans, etc.).

Appeal to special interest (or special markets).

Appeal to fear or emotion.

Appeal to change.

Appeal to status quo.

Personality (only good for very charismatic candidates).

Bread and butter (jobs, taxes, etc.).

Attack strategy (may be used against incumbents or challengers).

Appeal to truth (or appeal to what people believe is the truth).

Orrin Hatch of Utah used an effective strategy of coat-tailing an improved economic and political climate to win reelection to his U.S. Senate seat. In order to pass needed school bonds, the Bond Election Support Team appealed to fear by pointing out the danger of sending children to school early in the morning (Figure 19–17).

One of the finest examples of an appeal to sympathy was former Cleveland mayor Carl Stokes's ad "Don't Vote for a Negro" (Figure 19–18). By stating the negative, he accentuated the positive in an extremely dynamic, logical manner. The result was to give voters a rational reason to vote for a candidate with whom they probably already sympathized.

The overall campaign strategy the candidate uses determines the mix of the various other campaign activities. It determines the stand on particular issues, the format of speeches, the type of printed materials, the nature of advertising activities, and the priorities for spending money in each area.

Creative strategy

As we have discussed, the creative strategy in advertising is determined by the mix of market, media, and message. In politics the

FIGURE 19–17

This ad for school bonds has won numerous awards. The message is so simple—and dramatic. The headline and black illustration tell the whole story.

FIGURE 19–18

A courageous ad run by Cleveland's black mayor Carl Stokes. He won.

Don't vote for a Negro.

Vote for a man.

Vote for ability. Vote for character.

Vote for experience and intelligence and dedication

Vote for an organizer. A man who can and will work with our industrial leaders, our bankers, our merchants, our labor leaders, our welfare people, our neighborhood group leaders, our religious leaders, our lawmakers.

Vote for a planner. A man who understands poverty, Cleveland slums, Cleveland's too quiet downtown, Cleveland's under-used seaport. Cleveland's over-used streets.

Vote for a leader. A man who can attack the problems and solve them. A man who can rally the people of Cleveland behind him.

Vote for a man.

A man who believes. Carl Stokes.

"It's time to believe in Cleveland"—Carl Stokes

importance of a well-defined creative strategy cannot be overemphasized. The voters are bombarded every election year with a plethora of appeals from many different candidates running for many different offices. If candidates do not have a clear, concise, well-defined strategy, they are seriously handicapped. It is probably in this area of strategy selection and implementation that professional managers and advertising agencies play their most important role.

Audience and geographic considerations In any advertising situation one of the first questions regarding creative strategy must be: Who is the intended audience of the advertisement? On the national level the question might be phrased: Where is this ad going to run?

A liberal candidate might not want to run an ad announcing sup-

**Fifty reasons
to
rePete duPont**

Count them.

FIGURE 19–19

Politicians should not be afraid of long-copy ads if they have something interesting and relevant to say. Pete du Pont found this to be true and easily won reelection.

port of forced busing in some geographic areas. On the other hand, a conservative politician might not wish to run an ad announcing opposition to busing in some other areas.

Ronald Reagan was accused of appealing to southern sectionalism during the 1984 campaign, but when the votes were tallied it was evident that he also must have had a western strategy, a northwestern strategy, a midwestern strategy, a north-central strategy, and a mid-Atlantic strategy.

Message and quality considerations The verbal and graphic presentations of the advertisement or brochure are the primary elements that determine what message is received by the audience. This is the one area where most candidates fall down in their efforts at political advertising.

Due to the extreme sensitivity politicians have about raising funds and spending money, the majority find the cost of advertising production distasteful and therefore repeat the same mistake election after election. Most political advertisements are so poorly presented from an aesthetic standpoint that it's a wonder many politicians ever get elected. Candidates who run clean, well-conceived, and well-created advertisements are so refreshing in their presentation that they automatically tend to gain prestige in the voters' eyes.

In product marketing, advertising has become such an important element that the quality of the ad is a factor in the quality of the product itself. The same holds true in political advertising. What is the public to think of a candidate whose newspaper advertisements are black, ugly, full of bold, reverse type, and laden with words that seem to scream, "Sale," "Bargain," or "Buy Me Cheap?" Yet, year after year, these political ads appear and reappear.

This is predominantly a problem in local elections where candidates frequently lack funds for professional creative talent. But the problem is not limited to local elections. Ads that lack taste in verbal and graphic presentation are common in statewide elections and sometimes even in national elections. One advertising agency in California became so dismayed by politicians' unprofessional use of advertising that it began sponsoring Annual Orchids & Onions Awards for the best and worst political ads every year.

On the other hand, some of the finest advertising is seen in the political arena. When Delaware governor Pierre du Pont was a congressman, he used an effective play on words to attract attention and simultaneously suggest direct action (Figure 19–19). Following the simple headline were four columns of copy describing in simple detail how Pete du Pont had worked and succeeded for Delaware and the country.

Contrast this with Hedberg's ads for the state senate, which say nothing, offer nothing, and use a hokey, unprofessional approach to gain attention (Figure 19–20). Which of these people would you want to represent you? Which do you think would be most effective as legislators?

In this area of creative presentation, the politician should use a professional advertising agency if at all possible. The American Association of Advertising Agencies publishes a booklet on political campaign advertising that every candidate should acquire. This brief but

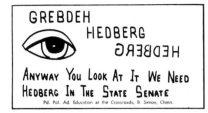

FIGURE   19–20

In an effort to be clever or cute, political candidates who are unsophisticated about contemporary advertising techniques can sometimes get into trouble by going overboard in their creative attempts.

invaluable guide to all the do's and don'ts is complete with pertinent suggestions on how to select and compensate an advertising agency for a political campaign.

Media selection   Media selection for political ads depends on the funds available, the strategy of the campaign, the message being communicated, and the audience desired.

Historically, direct mail has been the strongest medium a candidate can use. Most local candidates try to have at least two and preferably three mailings to their district during the campaign. Direct mail is also by far the most expensive medium on a cost-per-exposure basis. With direct mail, however, a candidate may target the message to a specific area or special-interest group. Direct mail can tell more of the story both graphically and verbally. And candidates will spend less money if the district is small than if they use mass media to reach the same audience.

To gain name I.D., outdoor is the most effective medium. From bumper stickers and small 2' by 2' quarter-cards placed on people's lawns to giant illuminated billboards, outdoor is a simple way to communicate the name of the candidate, the office sought, and perhaps one vital issue. Outdoor advertising with good graphic design may also be used to build credibility and show popular support for a candidate. This is especially true of bumper stickers and quarter-cards strategically positioned in residential areas. Some candidates believe that 100 bumper stickers can be as effective as one billboard.

Newspaper ads have always been important to the politician. The space available allows extensive verbal discussion as well as graphic presentation of the issues. The cost is usually far less than direct mail on a cost-per-thousand basis. And, like outdoor, popular support may be shown, in this case by listing influential supporters or picturing people in the community.

Radio and television advertising offers great opportunity to create image. For communicating to large numbers of people, they are by far the most economically efficient media to use. Radio lets the candidate experiment with sound, music, and words to stimulate the imagination of the audience. Television lends motion, color, and sound, all intermingled through professional, albeit expensive, production to create a lasting impression on the electorate.

■ Political Advertising as a Social Issue

The attitude that political advertising is just another marketing function with the same problems and complexities of product marketing is a recent one. The fact is that over the years little has really changed in political advertising except the media used and the skill of the people using them. (See Ad Lab 19–A.)

In 1952 Dwight D. Eisenhower became the first person to use television spots in a presidential campaign, and he was elected by an overwhelming majority. Suddenly the significance of this new, pervasive medium was realized, and we heard the first protests about packaging politicians like toothpaste and dog food. As the use of television has increased over the years, so have the protests. And so have the art and science of political campaign management and advertising.

There are, however, certain serious ethical problems that must be

AD LAB   19–A   Presidential candidate commercials: Deceptive or informative?

The candidates and their staffs spend millions of dollars creating and broadcasting commercials of 30 seconds, 60 seconds, and five minutes to sell themselves and their ideas to a potential 100 million voters. Sometimes they even buy half-hour programs, but the shortforms of 30 and 60 seconds are the real workhorses of campaigns.

Critics often attack the shortform commercials as dangerous to the democratic political process. Some have gone as far as advocating that they be banned from the air, even though such a ban would clearly violate the First Amendment.

Robert Spero, author of *The Duping of the American Voter: Dishonesty and Deception in Presidential Television Advertising*, dubbed political commercials "the principal medium of political deception." "Today," he wrote, "the use of commercials to camouflage candidates' inexperience is standard fare." Spero's cure for the political disease is free television time made available to all candidates.

Paid political commercials do not lack their defenders. One of them is political consultant John Deardourff who rejects the charge that the makers of political commercials fabricate images. "Good political advertising," he said, "has to bear a very close relationship to information the voters are receiving from other sources, because if it is at odds with the information people acquire on the news, then it will tend to be discounted."

"A candidate running for office is appealing to a mass of voters," he said, "usually in the hundreds of thousands or in the millions. The most effective means of reaching those masses is in prime-time television. Television audiences are accustomed to receiving information in short terms. Commercials are 30 to 60 seconds; news stories average about 90 seconds."

Marketplace reality
Harden H. Wiedemann, editor of *Campaigns and Elections*, says politics today "involves the use of many specialized fields—polling, statistical analysis, computers, media management, fund raising, voter targeting, telephone operations, organizational theory. The combination of new laws and increasing specialization has caused a radical change in political campaigns."

Baltimore advertising man, Robert Goodman, has emerged in the last few years as an influential and provocative figure in television political advertising. "Voting," proclaimed Goodman, "is an emotional experience, not an intellectual one. People tend to vote on honesty, competence, and charisma in that order. We try to show a candidate as sensitive, as attractive, and nice. The musical background is very important."

Goodman carefully oversees the personal habits of his clients. For men, "Polyester suits and loud ties are out," he said. "You have to worry about the hair. Can't be too short or too long. Slovenliness is not a virtue, but contrived casualness is."

"Feelings decide it all," said Goodman. "We must *like* this human being to vote for him or her. In most elections, the issue isn't foreign policy or inflation. The issue is really the human being."

"Honesty can't be invented in television commercials. Either it's there or it isn't there. The eyes, emotions, and body language reveal the person. But competence and charisma can't be dramatized."

The effect
After a study of news coverage and commercials, two Syracuse University political scientists, Thomas E. Patterson and Robert D. McClure, concluded that television commercials, "scorned by the intelligentsia as too short and too gimmicky to provide an honest basis for political choice," actually furnish voters with more serious information on the issues than all the regular network news programs put together. That opinion is still widely debated in political, news, and academic circles.

Laboratory Application

What is your view of political candidate commercials? Are they deceptive or informative? Base your reasoning on specific examples.

faced today and in the future by all those involved in political advertising. The first of these relates to campaign financing. As we mentioned earlier, strict laws have been enacted and are being enforced to govern the source and amount of contributions candidates may receive and the way in which these monies may be spent. However, as fast as new laws are created, new ways are discovered to avoid them. One of the strongest criticisms currently prevalent is that these laws enacted by incumbents tend to favor incumbents in future elections.

A second ethical question relates more directly to the style of advertising used in elections. Advertising tends to simplify the important issues at stake. Advertising may oversimplify the personality and the record of the politician. Advertising, the critics say, takes a multifaceted human being and makes him or her appear one-sided—all good. Likewise, well-financed proponents and antagonists of ballot propositions tend to oversimplify the often complex legislative initiatives offered to the voters. How are the voters to know which way to vote if they cannot get the whole story? Defenders of political advertising say that the press and the voters are responsible for investigating both sides of an issue.

A third ethical problem relates to what politicians say in their ads about one another. At what point does an attack on an opponent's record become libelous? What should a candidate be able to say, and when does this attack become slander? Many candidates feel they have been defeated by the mudslinging, distortions or outright lies of their opponents. And the fear of this keeps many potentially excellent office holders on the political sidelines.

Some of the largest and most respected advertising agencies in the country have declined to handle political advertising because of candidates' tendency to distort the truth about themselves or their opposition. Doyle Dane Bernbach was very embarrassed in 1971 by the disclosure of certain facts regarding President Lyndon Johnson's secret decisions before and after the 1964 election to increase U.S. military activity in Vietnam. They had been successful, as Johnson's agency, in picturing him as a man of peace and his opponent, Barry Goldwater, as the warmonger. Because of this embarrassment the agency decided not to handle any future political campaigns.

Similarly, J. Walter Thompson's creative director, George Edward Thompson, referred to political ads as the most virulent form of "subvertising"—advertising that subtracts from the total value of advertising.

Other agency executives, though, have suggested that more agencies should enter the political advertising arena to serve as a responsible, balancing force against the questionable practices of unscrupulous political advertising practitioners and the overwhelming power of the news media.

The point made by both these groups is the same. The professional advertising community does not want to be associated with dishonest, fraudulent, or misleading political advertising. The electorate is saying the same thing. And now finally more and more politicians are echoing the feeling.

Summary

The most obvious differences between commercial and noncommercial advertising are the sponsors and the things being advertised. Commercial firms usually advertise tangible goods and services, whereas noncommercial advertising usually stresses causes, ideas, attitudes, and viewpoints. A more subtle difference relates to the specific objectives of commercial and noncommercial advertising. One seeks to sell products or services, while the other seeks to change attitudes or popularize a social cause.

Noncommercial advertising may be categorized by its sponsors. These include nonbusiness institutions (churches, schools, universities, and charitable organizations), associations (labor groups, business and professional organizations, and civic associations), government organizations (Army, Postal Service, and state departments of tourism, for example), and political organizations.

To assist certain important causes in the public interest, members of the advertising profession formed the Advertising Council during World War II. During its 40 years of operation it has conducted up to 30 different campaigns a year for such projects as the American Red Cross, U.S. savings bonds, and the United Way. Over $10 billion worth of free advertising space and time has been donated by the media to the campaigns created by the council's volunteer advertising agencies.

Political advertising, like product advertising, is a marketing function. The political product, though, is a human being. Or, in the case of noncampaign advertising, it may be the particular ideology or viewpoint being promoted. Also, the time period for political advertising is limited rather than ongoing. Third, the ethical question is larger in political advertising.

The target market in politics is the candidate's constituency (the voters in the district), and the "product sales features" are the candidate's positions on the issues. The marketing objective is to achieve a 50+ percent share of market by election day. To do so requires overcoming marketing problems as diverse as those in product marketing.

Based on market research data, the campaign and advertising strategy is developed. The strategies used take into consideration the attitude of the constituency toward particular issues, the candidate's stand or record on those issues, the budget, and the various media available.

Once the strategy has been set, ads may be created. Just as in product marketing, the quality of the advertising reflects the quality of the product—in this case, the politician.

As a social issue, political advertising faces important ethical problems including campaign financing, oversimplification in ads, libelous claims, and truth in advertising.

Questions for review and discussion

1. What is the difference between noncommercial and commercial advertising?
2. What is the Advertising Council? Why is it considered an important organization?
3. What is the most important element in successful political marketing? How is this similar to product marketing? How is it different?
4. What is the difference between identity and image?
5. How does polling help political candidates? What other types of research may be used, and how do they differ?
6. What is the concept of peaking? How can this affect the outcome of an election?
7. What slogan can you cite that you believe was used effectively by a politician? Why?
8. What factors determine the quality of an advertisement? What bearing does that quality have on a candidate's campaign?
9. What is an appeal to authority? Cite one example of its use in politics today.
10. What are some ethical problems in political advertising? Discuss in detail and give your opinion.

20

INTERNATIONAL ADVERTISING

In this text we have discussed marketing and advertising planning, advertising creativity, and the advertising media. We have also offered some overall advertising perspectives and focused on certain special types of advertising. However, most of this discussion has been centered on advertising as it is practiced in the United States and Canada. The question arises, therefore, as to how applicable this discussion is to advertising in the rest of the world.

Companies advertising abroad face a variety of difficulties, which we will discuss in this chapter. But, to gain an understanding of these difficulties, consider the problems of advertising in Japan. The assistant to the president of Ogilvy & Mather once described the dilemma of the Western advertising person in Japan as "Tokyo Trauma." "The Japanese," he says, "seem bent on purging every ounce of precision, specificity, and clarity from communication."

Whereas in the United States we might use music in a commercial to create mood and arouse emotion, the Japanese accomplish this through the nuances of language. In the Japanese culture, images, feelings, and sensations can all be created through abstract word associations. To write a successful commercial in Japan, therefore, specific product features are not as important as the sensitivity of the wording, the actor's sense of intimacy, and a general good feeling.

Take the case of National Mini Refrigerators, a Japanese brand. If we planned to market this product to young, single, liberated women in the United States, we would probably take a very pragmatic approach, creating ads around the economical or space-saving characteristics of the product. Our advertisement might show the product in use and a very simple headline: "Save money. Buy a Mini."

Speaking to the same audience in Japan, though, the advertiser positioned the product in the background of the ad and, on the floor in the foreground, the mutilated photograph of a lost lover. The emotional copy, written in Japanese characters, reads: "There are nights when it's better to drink up rather than cry your eyes out. So set your heart at rest. Forget him. You have your Mini."

Japan is also a visually oriented society and as such has been in the forefront of what many Americans consider avant-garde graphic design. Consider the optical illusion in the ad for Suntory Whiskey in Figure 20–1.

More important than offering an interesting look at Japanese advertising, these examples illustrate the potential problems faced by all advertisers who contemplate entering a foreign market with a foreign culture, language, tastes, and a foreign system of values.

GROWTH AND STATUS OF INTERNATIONAL ADVERTISING

As U.S. companies entered world markets after World War II, consumption of American products grew tremendously. Today U.S. advertising expenditures account for over 50 percent of the world total. However, in the last 15 years expenditures by other countries have increased even more rapidly than American expenditures due to improved economic conditions and a desire to grow outward. As national economies have expanded and personal incomes have increased, so has the use of advertising.

For many years J. Walter Thompson was unchallenged as the largest agency in the world. But as the economies of previously underdeveloped countries have boomed, so has competition. By 1980 Dentsu Advertising, based in Tokyo, was the largest advertising agency in the world, with billings of over $3.2 billion.

Growth Trends in International Advertising

Advertising in one form or another is practiced in every country of the world. Actual figures are not available, but recent estimates of worldwide advertising expenditures outside the United States exceed $40 billion per year. The emphasis placed on advertising in individual countries, though, depends on the country's level of development and the national attitude toward promotion. Generally, advertising expenditures are higher in countries where personal income is higher. Moreover, advertising expenditures rise faster than income levels. However, a saturation point seems to be reached when advertising expenditures approach 3 percent of average national income; at that point they tend to plateau.

It is interesting to note the major deviations from this pattern—namely, France and Germany. This is probably caused by the aversion to promotion in some countries. In many societies "selling" has a very low status and is associated with hawkers in the streets. Also, in countries where there is no economic development, there is little pur-

FIGURE   20–1

Dentsu Advertising in Tokyo created this surrealistic, dreamlike ad for Suntory. The headline, which like so many in Japan almost defies translation, says: "FOREST BREATHING." Could you imagine such an ad for a liquor brand in the United States or Canada?

pose for advertising. Normally, though, as product lines and markets expand, distribution techniques become more complex and personal selling costs increase. Thus, the need for advertising grows.

 Changing Attitudes toward Advertising

Today advertising is used worldwide to sell ideas, policies, and attitudes as well as products. The Communist countries once con-

---

AD LAB 20–A   Advertising in the Soviet Union

Who ever would have thought that more than 100 advertising agencies would be plying their trade today in the Soviet Union? Certainly not Marx! According to traditional Marxist-Leninist doctrine, advertising is a tool of capitalistic exploitation. It siphons off the surplus value belonging to underpaid workers and puts it in the hands of overpaid white-collar workers who are nonproductively employed writing jingles.

Yet there has been an impressive growth of advertising agencies in the Soviet Union. The initial argument was that these agencies exist to develop advertising to support Soviet goods in export markets where it is necessary to compete against Western and other nations. But many advertisements also appear in print and broadcast media reaching Russian consumers. Another rationale was established at the 1957 Prague Conference of Advertising Workers of Socialist Countries, which made three points as to how advertising was to be used: (1) to educate people's tastes, develop their requirements, and thus actively form demand; (2) to help the consumer by providing information about the most rational means of consumption; and (3) to help to raise the culture of trade. Furthermore, Soviet advertising is to be ideological, truthful, concrete, and functional. The Soviets claim that their advertising does not indulge in devices used in the West. Their ads will not use celebrities—only experts will be used to promote a product. They will not use mood advertising. They will not create brand differentiation when none exists.

Experts think that the main use of Soviet advertising is to help industry move products that come into excess supply where the Soviets do not want to do the logical thing, cut prices.

Laboratory Application

How does the Pepsi-Cola advertisement illustrated succeed in satisfying Soviet policies on the use of advertising?

demned advertising as an evil of capitalism and still frequently express their theory of advertising as economic waste. But now even they are beginning to admit the benefits of advertising in developing planned economies. (See Ad Lab 20–A.) Most are even encouraging advertising in their trade and technical journals.

Certainly, as a communication form, international advertising is contributing to the shrinking of the world. And one benefit is increased understanding among people as foreign products, values, and ideas are introduced to new markets. The worldwide energy shortages of the 70s caused a flurry of advertising campaigns by governments and private business in every country, all working together to try to solve a single international problem.

As technology progresses, thereby improving communications in the less developed areas of the world, international advertising will continue to flourish. As a creative director for Ogilvy & Mather, Paris, said, "Nous n'avons pas mal de budgets." Loosely translated, "We're not hurting for business."

MANAGING INTERNATIONAL ADVERTISING

Imagine that you are the advertising manager of an American company planning to market its products abroad. You are aware of the potential problems—in the foreign market you may have to use a different creative strategy. You will be speaking to a new audience with a different system of values, a different environment, and probably a different language. Your foreign customers will probably have different purchasing abilities, different purchasing habits, and different motivations. The media you generally use may be unavailable or ineffective in a foreign market. As a result of these and other factors, your advertising may have to be different, too.

You also face another problem. How will the advertising be managed and physically produced? Will your in-house advertising department do it? Will your domestic advertising agency do it? Or will you have to set up a foreign advertising department or hire a foreign advertising agency?

To answer these questions, we need to ask two more: How does the company structure its foreign marketing operations? Within that structure, what are the most economical and effective means to conduct advertising activities?

▪ Foreign Marketing Structures

Just as in domestic situations, managing advertising in foreign markets depends to a great extent on the company's foreign marketing structure. Does the company intend to market its products internationally, multinationally, or globally? What is the difference?

The terms *international* and *multinational* are frequently used interchangeably, especially since the introduction of the newest term, *global*. However, the difference between all these terms relates to the degree of involvement in foreign markets.

International structure

Many firms get into international marketing simply by exporting the products they already produce. As companies get more involved, though, they may contract for manufacture, enter into joint ventures, or invest in some other foreign operations, such as sales offices, warehouses, and plants or manufacturing subsidiaries. However, these operations tend to be operated and viewed from headquarters as "foreign marketing divisions."

At first, foreign marketing activities are usually controlled and operated from the home office, but as the complexities of foreign operations expand, the pressure to decentralize also grows. For many years, the 3M Company operated internationally with virtually autonomous units in various countries around the world. Similarly, the foreign operations of many large retailers are also structured internationally with local management responsible for its own product lines, its own marketing operations, and its own profits and losses.

Multinational structure

As companies grow and prosper they may become true multinational corporations with direct investment in several countries and a view toward business based on choices available anywhere in the world.[1] Their essence, as Fayerweather says, is full and integrated participation in world markets. Foreign sales, a large part of the multinational's activities, usually grow faster than domestic sales.[2] Well-known American multinationals today include Eastman Kodak, Warner-Lambert, 3M, Ford, IBM, ITT, H.J. Heinz, and Gillette, all of whom earn over a third of their total sales abroad. There are also many well-known foreign-based multinationals such as Nestle's, Royal Dutch Shell, Nissan, Philips, and Unilever (Lever Bros.) (Figure 20–2).

A multinational's marketing activities are typically characterized by strong centralized control and coordination. Companies like Coca-Cola are called multinational organizations because they sell in many countries, they have strong direction and coordination from one central headquarters, and they have a standardized product line and a uniform marketing structure. The chairman of Coca-Cola called this strategy, "One sight, one sound, one sell" (Figure 20–3).

FIGURE   20–2

Gillette, a large multinational corporation, advertises its products around the world as this ad from Switzerland shows.

FIGURE 20–3

Trademarks for Coca-Cola used around the world. Notice the similarities of letterforms and style even when different alphabets are used.

■ *The global marketing debate*

According to Harvard marketing professor Theodore Levitt, Coca-Cola is actually the perfect example of a *global* marketer. Levitt envisions total worldwide product, marketing, and advertising standardization. In his book *The Marketing Imagination*, Levitt theorizes that companies that do not become true global marketers, with world brands like Coca-Cola, will surely perish on the rough seas of what he calls the "new global realities."

He argues that, thanks to cheap air travel and new telecommunications technology, the world is becoming a common marketplace in which people have the same tastes and desires and want the same products and lifestyles no matter where they live. This, he believes, allows for world-standardized products at low prices sold the same way around the world.[3]

Interestingly, his admittedly exaggerated theory stirred up a lot of dust on Madison Avenue. Several large multinationals dumped their multiple agency relationships in favor of one worldwide agency, and meanwhile the large international agencies raced to prove they were each best equipped to handle global brands. Suddenly, as more and more ads, brochures, and position papers on the subject appeared, "multinational" was out and "global" was in.

As the debate over the power of global marketing raged, Grey Advertising (which handled global campaigns for Revlon and BankAmerica Travelers Checks) suggested three questions companies should ask themselves before attempting a global strategy:

1. Has the market developed in the same way from country to country? (The continued popularity of clotheslines in Europe discouraged the demand for fabric softening products used in dryers.)
2. Are the consumer targets similar in different nations? (Canon found that, while Japanese consumers like sophisticated, high-tech products, consumers in the United States were fearful of complex, technological products.)

3. Do consumers share the same wants and needs around the world? (Tang was successfully positioned as an orange juice substitute in the United States. But in France, where people never drink orange juice at breakfast, Tang had to be repositioned as a daytime refreshment, as shown in Figure 20–4.)

Grey suggests that a negative answer to any one of these questions indicates that a global marketing attempt will probably fail.[4]

In reality, the direction a company takes depends on many variables, among them the breadth of its product line, the availability of qualified management, the ability to use similar marketing techniques, and the economic impact of particular marketing strategies. It goes without saying, though, that the decision to operate internationally, multinationally, or even globally has a strong influence on the advertising decisions that follow.

■ Agency Selection

To conduct foreign advertising activities, several types of agencies are available to advertisers. For example, when Mexico's oldest bank, Banamex (Banco Nacional de Mexico), wanted to promote an awareness of its bank to Americans, it selected a local California agency to handle its advertising in the border areas from California to Texas. Banamex already had an agency in Mexico City and another for its worldwide banking services in New York. But it knew that most of its potential American customers lived within a couple hundred miles of the border. So Banamex selected an agency that understood the local market and local media and could give local service.

Similarly, a wide choice is available to American companies based on their needs. They might use an international or global agency, a local foreign agency, an export agency, their normal domestic agency, or their house agency.

FIGURE   20–4

A youngster floating along listening to his Tang "radio" while the music plays "raspberry taste on the Tang frequency." The selling copy says Tang is "all ready, all new, and all good."

FIGURE 20–5   Comparison of top 10 agencies in U.S. versus non–U.S. income (gross income in millions)

Rank	Agency	U.S. income	Non–U.S. income
1	Young & Rubicam	$323	$157
2	Ogilvy & Math Intl.	270	151
3	Ted Bates Worldwide	263	161
4	BBDO International	235	105
5	J. Walter Thompson Co.	218	188
6	Foote, Cone & Belding	197	72
7	Leo Burnett Co.	163	91
8	Saatchi & Saatchi Compton	157	181
9	Grey Advertising	155	69
10	Doyle Dane Bernbach Intl.	154	64

International and global agencies

Even though Banco Nacional de Mexico selected a local foreign agency (from their perspective), many international advertisers find that only a large agency with offices or affiliates in many markets can do the job adequately.

As advertising has grown around the world, many of the larger American general agencies have established themselves in major foreign markets and shifted their focus from domestic advertising to international and even global marketing. As a matter of fact, foreign billings now account for over 37 percent of the total billings of the top 10 American agencies (Figure 20–5). Similarly many large foreign agencies have also taken the international challenge. In fact, with offices around the world, London-based Saatchi & Saatchi Compton Worldwide, one of the prime advocates of Levitt's global thesis, has attempted to position itself as *the* global agency (Figure 20–6).

Companies planning large multinational campaigns often deal with a large international agency. The agency's overseas offices are usually staffed with multilingual, multinational personnel in both creative and administrative positions. Each country in which they operate can be treated as a distinct market, or the campaign can be coordinated and controlled under one roof for a series of countries or markets.

People in other lands often have distinct attitudes, buying habits, business systems, and laws. Therefore it is seldom practical to simply translate American advertising into the other languages. A foreign-based staff of advertising specialists can transform and adapt basic concepts and strategies and add the verbal and visual elements that best appeal to local consumers (Figure 20–7).

Local foreign agencies

As Banamex did, American companies may also select local foreign agencies to coordinate their activities in particular markets. The for-

FIGURE   20–6

LONDON AIR TRAFFIC CONTROLLER: Roger, Manhattan, continue descent to F. L. eight 0. . . .

COPILOT: Roger, Heathrow, descending to F. L. eight 0. . . .

SFX: *Quiet, slightly spooky music, similar to "Close Encounters"*

LONDON AIR TRAFFIC CONTROLLER: Roger, Manhattan, continue to 2,000 feet. Reduce speed to one-seven-0 knots. . . .

STRAIGHT VO: Every year British

Airways fly more people to more countries than any other airline.

STRAIGHT VO: In fact, each year we fly more people across the Atlantic than the entire population of Manhattan.

eign agencies, of course, boast local talent who understand local attitudes and customers as well as the local media.

For many consumer products, a local agency in key markets might work out best. However, using a variety of local agencies in different markets can make it hard to coordinate a multinational advertising program.

Companies planning a multinational campaign with all activities centralized and coordinated from one location usually benefit by using one international advertising agency. On the other hand, if a company plans an international program that must promote differently to various markets, the company may be better off appointing local agencies who understand the needs of those particular markets. In selecting agencies, companies normally choose those that correspond in size to their service needs. In this way, clients don't pay for unnecessary services.

■ Export agencies

Some agencies specialize in creating ads for American companies engaged in international advertising. These *export agencies* may work in association with domestic agencies on particular accounts in addition to having clients of their own for whom they perform this same specialty.

Export agencies usually specialize in preparing ads for particular language groups or geographic areas and employ native-born writers in those languages and specialists familiar with the foreign media opportunities.

■ Domestic and house agencies

Many small companies exporting their products abroad simply ask their existing domestic agency to prepare their first ads for them. And, in fact, many domestic agencies handle the job quite adequately. Some domestic agencies are affiliated with foreign shops

FIGURE   20–7

Ogilvy & Mather/London
promotes itself as an international
agency that knows and
understands the differences in
people around the world. This
seems to fly in the face of the
"global" enthusiasts in the agency
business.

where they may receive media counsel, translation services, or production assistance. Other domestic agencies join international *agency
networks* to receive similar services in foreign markets as well as specialized services such as arranging local press conferences or trade
fairs. However, one of the problems with using a domestic agency is
that it may not have experience in international advertising; and advertising abroad, as we will see in the next section, can offer many
unique and difficult challenges.

Some companies, especially industrial firms, choose to use their
company advertising departments or house agencies for their foreign
advertising. While these may lack the creativity and objectivity of
outside agencies, in-house services have to please only one master
and can involve themselves completely in the company's projects.

Moreover, house agencies may possess greater technical knowledge of the subtle differences between certain industrial products and
may offer certain economies over outside professional help. Again,
though, they may lack expertise in the pitfalls of foreign advertising,
and that can prove far more costly in the long run.

CREATIVE STRATEGIES IN INTERNATIONAL ADVERTISING

As we have discussed throughout this text, advertising or creative
strategy is determined by the mix of product concept, target audience, communications media, and advertising message. The same is
true in international advertising, except that very often the creative
strategy used in foreign markets is different than the strategy used in
the United States. There are several reasons for this:

1. Influenced by their own particular environment, foreign markets
   reflect their local economy, social system, political structure, and
   degree of technological advancement. Therefore the *target audi-*

ences for advertising messages may be different, too.

2. The media used in domestic markets may not be available, or as effective, in foreign markets. Or they may simply be uneconomical. Therefore, the *media* strategy may also have to be different.

3. Consumers may not want to buy, or be able to buy, the same products (or product concepts) as here. Their motivations may be different, and there may be considerable differences in the way they buy. Therefore, the advertising *message*, and possibly even the product concept, may have to be altered.

In this section we will discuss these three Ms of advertising strategy—markets (audiences), media, and messages—to better understand their relationship to international advertising and the products marketed abroad.

PEOPLE IN ADVERTISING

Hideharu Tamaru

President
Dentsu, Inc.

A mild, affable former high school history teacher and avid reader of Japanese literature classics and eighth century poetry, Hideharu Tamaru hardly fits the image of his rigorous, demanding role today. Tamaru is President of Dentsu, Inc., the world's largest and one of the oldest advertising agencies, founded in 1901.

The genial academician exercises vigorously each morning to prepare himself physically and mentally for the ardous task of running the giant company, which is headquartered near Tokyo's Ginza district. A disciplinarian, Tamaru devotes himself totally to his work. He is among the first to arrive at the Dentsu building early each morning as well as one of the last to leave.

A promising young scholar, Tamaru attended Tokyo University, where he was graduated in 1938. Pursuing a long-time interest in history and literature, he soon became a high school teacher. Ten years later, however, Tamaru was personally offered a position in the field of advertising by the famed Hideo Yoshida, then president of Dentsu Advertising Ltd.

Tamaru accepted the challenge, and Yoshida quickly became his self-appointed mentor. He assigned Tamaru a series of difficult tasks that might have discouraged a less determined person. But Tamaru persevered and completed each one successfully.

What Yosida did, in effect, was to assure that the mild-mannered former schoolteacher received a thorough education in the fundamentals of advertising. In the years that followed, Tamaru worked in virtually every department at Dentsu, learning the agency business from the ground up. Tamaru

■ Market Considerations

What is the difference between the foreign market for a product and an American or Canadian market for the same product? The answer is simply environment. Any market is influenced by, and reflects, the market in which it exists. The environment in France is different from the environment in Japan. The environment in the United States is different from the environment in Mexico. And sometimes, as in the case of Canada, environments vary widely within a single country.

In Figure 20–8 we see two advertisements, one written in English and the other in French. However, both of these ads are promoting Toyotas in the same country—Canada. Many countries have more than one official language. Canada and Norway have two; Belgium,

---

proved to be a good student, and his perseverence ultimately paid off. Hideharu Tamaru was appointed president of Dentsu, Inc., in June 1977. Since then, Dentsu has continued forward as a progressive and future-minded company. Reflecting on his role at the helm, Tamaru said, "I am confident that my function as president is to set up a bridge to the 21st century. I propose three basic principles for Dentsu to follow in the coming century:

1. Make Every Aspect of Communication Dentsu's Sphere of Activities.

   Today we are engaged partly in communication activities through the advertising business. In the 21st century, however, the nature and extent of Dentsu's communication activities should be quite different from those of today as our earth becomes smaller through the further development of communications and transportation technologies and the communication media become more diversified through rapid changes and development brought about by advances in electronic technology.

   In line with these possible changes, we should embrace into our business all products, services, culture and human relations, and include every aspect of communication in our sphere of activities.

2. Positive Participation in the Discovery and Creation of New Cultural Values.

   The people are beginning to look for a "new affluence," which is the realization of a fulfilling life where the economic and cultural aspects are well-balanced and harmonized.

Up to now, Japan has made a substantial contribution to world development through economic activities, but now the world expects us to play a leading role in cultural activities too. We must rediscover the traditional cultural values of both Japan and the world to find the universal element in them and to create through integration a new culture for the future of the world.

In the field of culture in the 21st century, Dentsu should be the organizer, producer, and consultant by maintaining closer ties with the government, public enterprises, academic bodies, international organizations, and private corporations. And Dentsu should endeavor to broaden its sphere of activity in every field of culture, such as newspapers, broadcasting, publications, motion pictures, theater, music, fine arts, education, leisure activities, and sports.

3. Establishing Dentsu as a Global Communication Company.

   Dentsu must be fully prepared for globalization in the 21st century because the communication activities explained in (1) and the discovery and creation of new cultural values defined in (2) both have global contexts. Therefore, bases for Dentsu's activities should eventually be established in all principal cities of the world, and these bases should function as an organic unit.

   If we successfully take the initiative in this global scheme, I believe that it would contribute not only to the expansion of our business, but also to the expansion of economic and cultural interchange in the world."

FIGURE   20–8

What's the difference between these two Canadian ads for Toyota? Both ads use the same creative concept and say approximately the same thing. But one is not a literal translation of the other. The French headline translates "the Toyota Corolla is renowned for surpassing requirements." In French that headline works, but in English it's not good copy. The reworded English language headline, "A well-earned reputation for exceeding expectations," conveys approximately the same meaning and is effective copy.

Note the additional space required for the French copy. The layout has to be flexible to accommodate these linguistic differences.

three; and Switzerland, four. Canadians may be used to this situation, but this presents an immediate problem to the American advertiser.

To communicate with the foreign consumer, the environment that affects that consumer must be considered. And language is only one consideration. In fact several environments influence people's attitudes, tastes, and the way in which they think, speak, and feel. In addition to the social environments, of which language is a part, there are the economic environments, the technological environments, and the political environments. We will consider each of these briefly.

Social environments

In the United States and Canada, we live in a particular social environment based primarily on our family background, the language we speak, our education, religion, the friends with whom we associate, and the style of life we enjoy. Similarly, the social environments in Italy, Indonesia, and Upper Volta are based on language, culture, literacy rate, religion, and lifestyle.

In the United States, which is basically a Protestant culture, we are encouraged and coaxed (through advertising) to keep our mouths clean, our breath fresh, and our teeth healthy by brushing after every meal. Part of the Protestant ethic is that "cleanliness is next to godliness."

On the other hand, in many southern European countries, interfering with one's body by overindulging in toiletries and bathing has the opposite meaning. That type of behavior is considered vain, immoral, and improper.[5] So only one of three people brushes his or her teeth. If you are marketing a toothpaste brand, you might find it more acceptable to advertise your product as something modern and chic rather than as a cavity preventer.

Gillette International discovered that fact in the effort to market deodorants and ladies shavers in Europe. In the first case it found an inherited cultural resistance toward anything that impedes perspiration. People thought it unhealthy.[6] In the second case, Gillette learned that it didn't have to advertise women's razors because it could "personally give razors to all four Austrian women who wanted them."[7] Many European women do not shave their legs or under their arms.

Economic environments

The economic environment of a country usually refers to several things: the standard of living, the country's wealth and distribution of that wealth, the amount of business transacted, the principal occupations, and the possessions people have. In countries where people earn less money, there is naturally a lower demand for certain expensive products. For example, in some countries, the creative strategy for automobiles might be a target market approach to the relatively small group of wealthy, upper-class people. In another country with a large middle class, it might be a mass market approach positioning the car as a middle-class product.

Twenty-five years ago, Ernest Dichter divided the world into six groups of countries based on their attitudes toward automobile ownership. In Figure 20–9 we have adapted his chart to reflect those foreign attitudes characteristic of the 80s.

The country groups are based on the degree of social and economic development of a large middle class, which is the clue, Dichter feels, to appraising different cultures. Cultures range from the almost classless, contented Scandinavian countries to the primitive, underdeveloped countries. In the former, the automobile is viewed strictly as a functional vehicle, and luxury values are dismissed. In the latter, the automobile is a sign of wealth and position, and the few cars sold are usually driven by officials and bureaucrats.

Technological environments

The degree to which a country has developed its technology will, of course, have a bearing on that country's economic and social conditions. But it will also affect the market for certain products and services within that country. For example, countries that don't manufacture computers might not be good markets for certain peripheral products like disk drives and microprocessors. On the other hand, though, they might be very good markets for low-priced, imported computers.

Political environments

Some foreign governments exert far greater control over their citizens and businesses than does the U.S. government. For example, until fairly recently, there was virtually no market for American-made products in many of the Soviet bloc countries and China. They simply weren't allowed. The political environment, therefore, has a great effect on the potential market for certain products. Political control also extends to what products may or may not be advertised, what media may or may not be used, and what may or may not be said in commercials. In Scandinavia, for example, promoting a product as a sign of wealth and luxury is very risky. Due to the political environment of these socialist states, it is simply considered very bad taste.

FIGURE   20–9   World attitudes toward automobile ownership

Group number	Title	Characteristics/attitudes
Group I	The almost classless society, contented countries	Primarily the Scandinavian countries. The middle class takes up the whole scale with very few very rich or very poor people. Automobiles are strictly utilitarian. Reliability and economy most important. No special status value.
Group II	The affluent countries	Includes the United States, West Germany, Switzerland, Holland, Canada, Japan. Large middle class, but still room at the top for financial aristocracy. People want individuality in their products. However, they seek quiet elegance and reliability rather than cars for show-off.
Group III	Countries in transition	Spain, Portugal, Argentina, Brazil, South Africa. Working class still exists, but they are struggling to join the comfortable middle class. Upper classes still exist with maids and Rolls-Royces, but diminishing in size. Living standards are lower, but prestige still important. Cars are pampered extensions of one's personality. They represent major investments and for many people are living examples of their "success." Fluid, unstable markets. People hold onto their cars for 6 to 10 years. Style is important, though, and a desire for product adventure exists.
Group IV	Developing countries	Latin America, Middle East, India, China, Philippines, etc. Large groups of people emerging from extreme poverty. Large number of extremely rich people. Very small emerging middle class. Automobiles available to relatively small group. Expensive and considered a luxury. Taxed very highly. American cars considered the ideal. People show off with their cars. Small cars are a way to get started.
Group V	Primitive countries	Newly liberated countries of Africa and few remaining colonies. Very small group of wealthy businessmen, political leaders, and foreign advisors. Few cars sold are to government bureaucrats. No real car market yet.
Group VI	The new class society	Russia and satellite countries. Emerging class of bureaucrats who represent a new form of aristocracy. Everybody else in slow-moving, low middle class. Auto represents symbol of a new industrial society. Interest increasing in prestige cars. All the bourgeois symbols of capitalist countries are being copied—especially those of United States.

▓ The importance of marketing research

In the domestic market, one of the reasons we conduct marketing research is to help us understand our domestic environments so that we can make better advertising decisions. The same is true in international markets. However, for American or Canadian advertisers, new problems can arise when research activities are planned in some foreign countries.

The simple fact is that the research skills available in some developing countries are not comparable to those found in, say, the United

States, Canada, Western Europe, Australia, Japan, Mexico, and Brazil.[8] For example, while some secondary research statistics may be available, they may be out-of-date or invalid and, therefore, unreliable. When studying secondary data developed outside of the firm, managers should ask the following questions:

1. Who collected this data and why?
2. What research techniques were employed?
3. Would the source of the data have any reason to bias the data?
4. When was the data collected? How old is it?

The answers to all these questions are not always readily available, but the international advertising manager needs to exercise caution when presented with "facts" about foreign markets.[9]

Primary research conducted overseas is often more expensive than domestic research. But if a company is planning a worldwide or even Pan-European campaign, it is important to understand if the message will be viable in each of the individual markets. Companies that ignore an individual society's particular "design for living" risk the failure of their entire international marketing effort.[10]

Campbell Soup recently rediscovered this rule. After spending $2 million on an award-winning ad campaign, the company found out too late that they had failed to ask the housewife in Brazil what she wanted. She didn't consider herself an adequate homemaker if she did not make soups from scratch for her family.[11]

Marketers need more than just factual information about a particular country's culture. They need to develop an understanding and appreciation of the special nuances of different cultural traits and habits. This is difficult to achieve without living in a country and speaking its language. So the international marketer must depend on consultation with and cooperation of experienced, bilingual nationals with marketing backgrounds. And the marketer must be prepared to conduct primary research when necessary.

Performing original research, though, can be fraught with problems. First, it must be conducted in the language of the country being studied. But translating questionnaires can be very tricky. Secondly, as Fayerweather points out, customer information depends on people's willingness and ability to give researchers accurate information about their lives, opinions, and attitudes. This willingness is not always present. In many cultures, people view strangers with much greater suspicion and, correspondingly, have a greater desire to keep their personal life private.

Local conditions may further interfere with data collection. Tax evasion, for example, is common and tolerated in many Latin American countries. Under these conditions, an interviewer is not likely to get accurate information about income or even major appliance ownership. In fact, some interviewers have been suspected of being tax collectors in disguise and treated somewhat rudely.[12]

Regardless of all these problems marketers should realize the importance of continuous research to the success of their efforts. Competent research personnel are available in all the developed countries; and, in most of the developing nations, research assistance is available through local offices of major international research firms.

Media Considerations

It has been said that American advertising people can get used to the foreign styles of advertising faster than they can get used to foreign media. In the United States, if you want to promote a popular soft drink as a youthful, fun refresher, you use television. In several European countries, you are not able to. The same is true in many countries of Asia, South America, and Africa. Around the world, most broadcast media are owned and controlled by the government, and many governments do not allow commercials on radio or television.

In countries that do allow television advertising, you may have another problem. How many people own television sets, and who are they? In Europe the vast majority of the population now owns TVs. But in less developed nations TVs are found only among the upper-income groups. The result may be a different media mix in foreign markets than in the United States.

Types of media available

The same media we find here exist around the world. Virtually every country has radio, television, newspapers, magazines, outdoor, and direct mail. However, as we have pointed out, it may not always be legal to use all these media for advertising. In addition, cinema advertising is a very popular medium in many countries, as are some other selective specialty media that either do not exist here or are not widely used.

Generally the media available to the international advertiser can be categorized as either international media or foreign media, depending on the audience the particular medium serves.

International/global media Several large American publishers like Time, Inc., McGraw-Hill, and Scientific American circulate international editions of their magazines abroad. Likewise the *International Herald Tribune, The Wall Street Journal,* and London's *Financial Times* are circulated widely throughout Europe, the Middle East, and Asia. Usually written in English, these publications tend to be read by well-educated, upper-income consumers and are, therefore, the closest things to global media for reaching this audience. The *Reader's Digest,* which is no doubt the oldest global mass audience medium, is distributed to 170 foreign countries. However, it is printed in the local language and tailored to each country and, therefore, is sometimes viewed more as a local medium (Figure 20–10).

Recently there has been an increase in the number of international trade or specialty publications. *European Business* is published in Switzerland in English but is distributed throughout Europe. *Electronic Product News,* published in Belgium, is likewise printed in English and distributed throughout Europe.

In the past, international media have been limited primarily to newspapers and magazines. However, in 1985, Sky Channel, the new satellite-to-cable Pan-European TV channel, offered advertisers an opportunity to reach over 2 million viewers throughout Europe. With English language programming and advertising, it is being eyed as an experiment to see if global or pan-regional TV is a realistic possibility. For some years now, the Voice of America (VOA) and Radio Luxemburg have also served as examples of international broadcast media. In recent years, in an effort to correct the American trade deficit, the VOA has carried spots for American products on its broadcasts.

Foreign media Due to the scarcity of effective international media, international advertisers are usually obliged to use the local media of the countries in which they are marketing. Foreign media cater to their own local national audience. This, of course, requires advertisers to produce advertisements in the language or languages of each country. In some countries there is more than one official language. In Belgium, ads are prepared in both Dutch and French, and some magazines produce two separate versions.

Overspill media In addition to international and foreign media, a recent phenomenon is overspill media. This is actually foreign media aimed at a local national population that is inadvertently received by a substantial portion of the population of a neighboring country. In Europe, for example, where the major languages are French, German, and English, the key areas of overspill are Belgium, Switzerland, and Austria. There is also overspill into countries that are short on publications, particularly specialized ones, in their own native languages. English and German media have a large circulation in Scandinavian countries. French and English media are popular in Spain, Italy, North Africa, and various Middle Eastern countries. And a wide variety of foreign language media are spilling into the Eastern Bloc countries.

According to a study by the Foote, Cone & Belding advertising agency on overspill media in Europe, multinational advertisers are now faced with the danger that these media may carry both international and local campaigns for the same product or service. This may confuse potential buyers. As this media area develops, local subsidiaries or distributors must coordinate their programs to avoid confusion. However, overspill media offer the potential to save money by regionalizing campaigns.

Within the broad categories of international, foreign, and overspill media are the various types of media we are familiar with in the United States—namely, radio, magazines, television, newspapers, and so on. The difference lies not so much in the availability of the media as in the coverage offered and the economics of using one medium over another.

Media coverage

Whereas in the United States the broad middle class may be reached by any of innumerable media, this is not necessarily true in many foreign markets. For one thing, in some countries lower literacy rates and general education levels may restrict the coverage of mass press media. Furthermore, where income levels are low, ownership of televisions is similarly low. What occurs, therefore, is a natural segmentation of the market by the selective coverage of the various media.

In countries dominated by national newspapers, circulation may be primarily to upper-class, well-educated people. On the other hand, both Pepsi and Coca-Cola have reached the lower income markets successfully through the use of radio, which enjoys almost universal ownership. Moreover, in some developing countries, many stores and bars allow their radios to blare onto the street, making the sound available to any passersby. Auto manufacturers use television and magazines successfully to reach the upper class. And cinema advertising is used to reach whole urban populations where television ownership is low, since motion picture attendance there is still very high. However, there may be some selectivity by simply restricting the showing of commercials to upper-income areas or to lower-class

FIGURE   20–10   Global media

Title/publisher	Paid foreign circulation by region	Paid global circulation	Cost of worldwide full page B&W	Top worldwide advertisers
Dailies				
International Herald Tribune New York Times & Washington Post	Europe: 119,769 Middle East/Africa: 11,146 Asia/Pacific: 24,103 Other: 472	157,560	$ 26,500	AT&T ITT IBM Pan American Air France
Wall Street Journal Dow Jones & Co. New York	Asia: 27,727 Europe: 25,411	2,013,011	89,049	Hewlett-Packard AT&T Wang Laboratories Citibank Bankers Trust
Weeklies				
Business Week McGraw Hill **New York**	Europe: 40,935 **Asia: 20,989** **Latin America: 17,462** **Other: 1,696**	856,305	29,720	Citibank† **L.M. Ericsson** **Hewlett-Packard** **N.V. Philips** **Rothmans Int'l.**
Newsweek Newsweek Ltd. New York	Atlantic: 302,343 Pacific: 208,299 Latin Am.: 46,091	3,594,010	82,470	Rupperts/Rothmans† British American Tobacco Singapore Airlines L.M. Ericsson Rolex Watch
Time Time Inc. Publications New York	Atlantic: 525,122 Asia: 242,214 S. Pacific: 140,671 Latin Am.: 100,265	6,001,338	107,358	British American Tobacco† Distillers Co. Singapore Airlines Rolex Watches Nissan Motors
Monthlies				
National Geographic Nat'l. Geographic Society Washington, D.C.	Atlantic: 683,839 Pacific: 377,459 Latin Am.: 90,275 Other: 32,932	10,202,854	107,460	Canon Cameras AT&T Nikon Inc. Olympus Camera Corp. Nissan Motors

theaters, depending on a particular product's market. (See the Checklist for international media planning.)

▨ Economics of foreign media

As pointed out in Chapter 1, a major purpose of advertising is to communicate with customers less expensively than through the use of personal selling. In many underdeveloped countries, however, this is not necessarily true. Colgate-Palmolive found that in countries where labor is extremely cheap, it could send people around with baskets of samples twice a year.[13] This kind of personal contact is impossible in the United States so Colgate uses advertising to do the entire consumer selling job.

Title/publisher	Paid foreign circulation by region	Paid global circulation	Cost of worldwide full page B&W	Top worldwide advertisers
Monthlies (*continued*)				
Reader's Digest Reader's Digest Assn. Pleasantville, N.Y.	Atlantic: 7,302,000 Pacific: 2,181,000 Latin Am.: 1,265,000	30,283,000	187,215	Unilever† Toyota Motors Dart & Kraft N.V. Philips Franklin Mint
Scientific American Scientific American Inc. New York	Europe: 65,842 Asia/Pacific: 21,731 Cen. & S. Am.: 6,310 Africa: 2,580 Middle East: 1,513	652,832	20,000	MacDonnell-Douglas Hewlett-Packard Hughes Aircraft AT&T Rolex Watches
*WorldPaper** World Times Inc. Boston	Latin Am.: 309,000 East Asia: 301,000 Middle East: 119,500 Europe: 26,000	755,500	23,100	AT&T Pan American Xerox Corp. Overseas Private Inv. Corp. American Express
Other				
Fortune Time Inc. Publications New York	Europe: 55,310 Asia: 29,992 Other: 7,748	709,903	25,800	ITT Singapore Airlines General Foods Matsushita General Motors
Harvard Business Review Harvard Business Review Boston	Europe: 12,322 Asia/Pacific: 8,042 Cen. & S. Am.: 3,848 Africa: 2,214 Middle East: 1,496	240,046	6,315	General Motors Philips Business Systems IBM AT&T Barclays Bank

*Distributed as a newspaper supplement.
†All advertisers in category are for non-U.S. editions.

Checklist for international media planning

Basic Considerations (Who Does What?)

☐ What is the client's policy regarding supervision and placement of advertising? Make sure you know when, where, and to what degree client and/or client branch offices abroad want to get involved.

☐ Which client office is in charge of campaign? North American headquarters or local office or both? Who else has to be consulted? In what areas (creative or media selection, etc.)?

☐ Is there a predetermined media mix to be used? Are there any "must" media? Can international as well as foreign media be used?

☐ Who arranges for translation of copy if foreign media are to be used?

    ☐ Client headquarters in North America.

    ☐ Client office in foreign country

    ☐ Agency headquarters in North America.

    ☐ Foreign media rep in North America.

    ☐ Foreign media advertising department

    ☐ Other

☐ Who approves translated copy?

☐ Who checks on acceptability of ad copy in foreign country. Certain ads, especially those of financial character, sometimes need special approval by foreign government authorities.

☐ What is the advertising placement procedure?

    ☐ From agency branch office in foreign country, after consultation with agency headquarters, directly to foreign media

    ☐ From North American agency to American-based foreign media rep to foreign media

    ☐ From North American agency to American-based international media

    ☐ From North American agency to affiliated agency abroad to foreign media

    ☐ Other

☐ What are the pros and cons of each of these approaches? Is commission-split with foreign agency branch or affiliate office necessary or can campaign be equally well-placed directly from North America? Does the client save money by placing from North America to save certain ad taxes (in Belgium and the Netherlands, for instance)? Some publications quote local rates and higher U.S. dollar rates. In those instances local ad placement results in a lower rate. Therefore, in what currency does client want to pay?

☐ Who receives checking copies?

☐ Will advance payment be made to avoid currency fluctuation possibilities? What will the finance folks in the back room have to say about your choice?

☐ Who bills whom? In what currency? Who approves payment?

Budget Considerations

☐ Is budget predetermined by client?

☐ Is budget based on local branch or distributor recommendation?

☐ Is budget based on recommended media schedule of agency?

☐ Is budget based on relationship to sales in the foreign markets?

☐ What is the budget period?

☐ What is the budget breakdown for media, including ad taxes, sale promotion, translation, production and research costs?

☐ What are the tie-ins with local distributors, if any?

Media Considerations

☐ Availability of media to cover market: Are the desired media available in the particular area (e.g., business magazines, newsmagazines, trade and professional magazines, women's magazines, business and financial newspapers, TV, radio, etc.).

☐ Foreign media and/or international media: Should the campaign be in the press and language of a particular country, or should it be a combination of the two types?

☐ What media does competition use?

☐ Does medium fit?

    ☐ Optimum audience quality and quantity

    ☐ Desired image editorial content and design

    ☐ Suitable paper and color availability

    ☐ Justifiable rates and CPM (do not forget taxes on advertising which can vary by medium)

    ☐ Discount availability

    ☐ Closing dates at North American rep and at the publication headquarters abroad

    ☐ Type of circulation audit

    ☐ Agency commission (when placed locally abroad at the agency commission is sometimes less than when placed in North America.)

    ☐ Availability of special issues or editorial tie-ins

    ☐ For how long are contracted rates protected?

☐ Does foreign or international publication have North American representative to help with media evaluation and actual advertising placement?

Market Considerations

☐ What is your geographical target area?

    ☐ Africa and Middle East

    ☐ Asia, including Australasia

    ☐ Europe, including U.S.S.R.

    ☐ Latin America

    ☐ North America

☐ What are the major market factors in these areas?

    ☐ Local competition

    ☐ GNP growth over past four years and expected future growth

    ☐ Relationship of country's imports to total GNP in percent

    ☐ Membership of country in a common market or free trade association

    ☐ Literacy rate

    ☐ Attitude toward North American products or services

    ☐ Social and religious customs

☐ What is your basic target audience?

    ☐ Management executives across the board in business and industry

    ☐ Managers and buyers in certain businesses

    ☐ Military and government officials

    ☐ Consumers; potential buyers of foreign market goods

FIGURE   20–11

Internationally, the market for Care Bears is comprised of children. However, in some countries like England, the target audience is adults, and the advertising appeal is based on parental love—a universal motivation.

In North America the cost of labor has inhibited the growth of outdoor advertising. In most foreign markets, though, outdoor enjoys far greater coverage, since it costs less to have people paint the signs, and there is often less government restriction about placement of billboards. In Mexico, for example, almost every street seems to have a "Disfrute Coca-Cola" sign. In Nigeria billboards with the slogan "Guiness gives you power" next to the bulging biceps of an African arm kept Guiness stout ale the best seller for many years—despite an 80 percent illiteracy rate.

Of course, just as economics determines which medium is used, economics also determines the availability of media. We have just seen this in the case of outdoor advertising. Likewise, one factor that inhibits the growth of TV is its cost. This same factor, however, causes some countries to consider opening TV to commercial use to help pay for it. In 1986, for example, three direct broadcast satellites and several advertiser-supported channels will debut in Europe. We may expect, therefore, that as more countries allow commercial broadcasts, TV will proliferate. On the other hand, as labor rates increase, we may see reductions in the number of press and outdoor media available in foreign markets. Likewise, the use of personal selling and sales promotion may similarly become more restricted due to the costs involved.

Message Considerations

The final element of the creative mix, as we know, is the advertising message. But in developing the message strategy for foreign markets, there are numerous considerations. Advertising appeals must be based on the consumer's purchasing abilities, habits, and motivations. The whole question of language must be decided. And the issue of what can be legally advertised in each region will have to be resolved. We will consider each of these briefly here.

Purchasing characteristics in foreign markets

Advertising messages must be geared to the characteristics of the market that can afford to buy the product. In low-income countries where only the wealthy can afford to purchase automobiles, ads that stress a car's luxury qualities would logically find an interested audience. Where middle-class consumers exist in large numbers, though, the message will probably be more effective if the functional or economical aspects of the car are stressed. Just as in the domestic market, many of these middle-class consumers are hard pressed financially, and they welcome economy choices.

It is also important to consider *how* purchases are made and *when* they are normally made. Most important, though, is the question of *who* makes the buying decision. In North America and Europe, for instance, the balance of power between marriage partners is fairly equal. In Latin American countries, though, the wife often has a clearly subordinate role in major decision making. In the United States, children may even have a strong influencing voice (especially in the selection of breakfast cereals, snacks, toothpastes, and fast-food chains), but this is much less common in foreign markets.

These differences, though, vary from country to country and product to product, and the advertiser must consider the issues carefully before creating ads or buying media. One company introduced a new detergent in Holland by advertising solely in one magazine read by children under 10. A miniature sports car was offered as an in-pack premium. The success of the introduction indicated that, in this case at least, the children did have a strong influencing voice in the buying decision (Figure 20–11).

Consumer motives and appeals

In some countries certain appeals are logically more significant than others, and care must be taken to understand the particular personal motivations inherent to each market (Figure 20–12). Swiss women, for example, live under a social code that stresses hard work in the home. Advertising American dishwashers as labor- and time-saving devices only served to create guilt feelings. What proved more successful to the spic-and-span Swiss housewife was to communicate the sanitizing qualities of automatic dishwashers.[14]

Selling a deodorant in Japan is difficult because most Japanese don't think they have body odor—and they don't—due to their low-protein diets. A commercial for Feel Free deodorant, therefore, positioned the product as youthful, chic, and convenient rather than as a solution to odor problems. This was accomplished by simply showing a young girl, on her way out for a date, who suddenly remembers her deodorant and uses it quickly before leaving.

National pride is also an important consideration for foreign advertisers. Many lower-income, less developed nations envy American wealth and technology at the same time that they fear and profess disdain for it. Thus a strange paradox exists. On one hand they respect and desire American products. But, on the other hand, they may harbor hidden inferiority feelings and resent what they perceive as American influence and power. Many American advertisers, therefore, toe a careful line to avoid aggravating this understandable national sensitivity in certain foreign markets.

The Ford Motor Company discovered that Germans have a strong positive attitude toward their own technical product. Their research also showed that the Ford name had a strong American association. Many Germans wondered why they should buy an American car

FIGURE 20–12

In Italy the greatest wear and tear on automobiles is that experienced by taxicabs in heavy stop-and-go urban traffic and by turbos in wide-open mountain and freeway driving. Therefore, this is a unique appeal to the Italian motorist for a reliable motor oil that has been "tested to the limits of endurance."

when so many Americans who owned Volkswagens and Mercedes obviously thought German cars were better. By introducing the German Ford as an example of cooperation between American ingenuity and know-how and German thoroughness and efficiency, considerable sales success was achieved.

In industrial advertising, differences in taste and attitude may not be so apparent or important as in the marketing of consumer products. The businessperson's problems are fairly universal and so are the appeals (Figure 20–13). The difference in approach comes down to the economics of the area. Professor Levitt's global marketing disciples would probably echo this sentiment.

On the other hand, Paul Aass, the president of MarkCom, a Belgian advertising agency, says that "the only thing the European countries and Europe's submarkets have in common is the fact that they are different." This is certainly true when it comes to language.

■ The Question of Language and Campaign Transfer

In Western Europe at least 15 different languages and more than twice as many different dialects are still spoken today. This presents a problem of potentially enormous magnitude to the American marketer entering Europe for the first time. The same is true in Asia, to a lesser extent in South America, and to an even greater extent in Africa (Figure 20–14).

South Africa, for instance, has a complex multicultural society consisting of four major ethnic groups—white, black, colored, and Asian. These groups in turn are divided into various distinct subgroups, most of whom are catered to by separate, specifically directed media. For example, whites have two languages—English and Afrikaans—and most campaigns directed to the whites appear in both languages. Blacks have five basic languages. Radio and television sta-

FIGURE   20–13

A trade ad for a Norwegian company uses a testimonial headline in English but Norwegian copy to promote pilot training.

Entre na dimensão Pierre Cardin.
Um universo de moda muito exclusivo.

PIERRE CARDIN

FIGURE 20–14

In South America advertisers must be able to use Spanish, of course. But Portuguese is extremely important for the marketer wanting any share of the dynamic Brazilian business. In this Pierre Cardin ad created in Rio, avant-garde surrealism abounds: "Enter the Pierre Cardin dimension. A most exclusive universe of fashion."

tions, which are government owned, direct their programs on a carefully worked out time allocation basis—in two languages to whites and in five languages to blacks—and commercial content, by regulation, must correspond. An advertiser may not, for example, broadcast English-language ads on an Afrikaans program, or vice versa. The same applies in respect to the five black languages. In print media, nearly all campaigns directed to whites appear in English and Afrikaans and most campaigns directed to blacks appear in English.

For years a controversy has raged in international advertising circles over the transferability of campaigns. On one hand are those who feel it is too expensive to create a unique campaign for each national group. They believe it is acceptable to take one campaign and simply translate it into the necessary languages. This group has now been aided and abetted by the globalists who believe consumers have become so homogeneous that product and advertising standardization is possible around the world. Some cases seem to support their view. Shell Oil ran the same campaigns in five different countries. Each ad was produced in the language of that country. The campaigns scored equally well on recall, believability, and persuasion wherever they were used.

On the other hand, some feel this never works out right and that the only way to assure success is to create a special campaign for each market. In addition, there are a few who feel that both these solutions are uneconomical and unnecessary. They run their ads in English and don't concern themselves with the problems of local markets.

Obviously, no one of these solutions is always correct, and the problem of transferability of campaigns remains unsolved. Marketers probably don't have to create different campaigns for every country of the world. Moreover, the hard facts of life are that the economics of various promotional strategies must be weighed against the anticipated promotional objectives. Thus each situation must be looked at

FIGURE 20–15

A major hotel in Sofia, Bulgaria, informed its English-speaking visitors: "This elevator is broken. We regret to inform you that in the next few days you will be unbearable."

individually. Identifying the target audience and knowing the cultural preferences in that market are basic. However, even if we are talking to similar audiences and detailing similar product characteristics so that we could use the same basic campaign, we still have the translation problem.

Translating ads for foreign markets

One well-known story concerns Exxon Corporation's attempts to market gasoline in Japan under its old brand name, Enco. Exxon couldn't understand why sales were so low. It sent a team of executives to Japan to investigate the situation. After an exhaustive study of Japanese driving habits, gasoline consumption figures, and service station sites, the executives decided to interview Japanese consumers. The first person they could find that spoke English gave them a very simple answer to their question. He told them that, in Japanese, "Enco" means "stalled car."

A similar event occurred when General Motors introduced their new Chevrolet Nova to Puerto Rico. In Spanish, "no va" means "it doesn't go." Parker Pen attempted to translate its American billboard campaign in Latin America: "You'll never be embarrassed with a Parker Pen." Unfortunately, Parker was embarrassed when it discovered too late that in Spanish *embarazada* means "pregnant."

English is spoken in the United States, Canada, England, Australia, and South Africa, but among these five countries are wide variances of vocabulary, word usage, and syntax. Similarly, the difference in the French spoken in France, Canada, Vietnam, and even Belgium may be as great as the difference in English spoken by a high-brow Britisher and a sharecropper from Tennessee. Even within single countries there is wide variation in the language used.

In the Japanese language five "gears" are used, from haughty and condescending to fawning and servile, depending on the speaker's and the listener's respective stations in life. The Japanese translator must know when to change gears.

Suffice it to say that there are certain basic rules that must be followed when translating advertisements:

1. The translator must also be an effective copywriter. Just because the translator speaks a foreign language doesn't mean he or she can write advertising copy effectively. The logic of this should be clear. All of us can speak English, yet relatively few of us are good writers, and even fewer are good copywriters. Still, advertisers too often fall into the trap of simply having a translation service rewrite their advertisements in the foreign language—rarely a good solution (Figure 20–15).
2. The translator must have an understanding of the product, its features, and its market. It is always better to use a translator who is a specialist rather than a generalist for particular products or markets.
3. The translator should translate into his or her native tongue and should be a native resident of the country where the ad will appear. Only in this way can you be certain that the translator has a current understanding of the country's social attitudes, culture, and idiomatic use of the language.

4. The English copy submitted to the translator should be easily translatable. Double meanings and idiomatic expressions, which make English such an interesting language for advertising, are usually not translatable. They only make the translator's job more difficult.

Finally, remember the Italian proverb, "Tradutori, traditori," (Translators [are] traitors).[15] There is perhaps no greater insult to a national market than to misuse its language. The translation must be accurate, but it must also be good copy.

English is rapidly becoming the universal language used for corporate advertising campaigns directed to international businesspeople. However, some industrial firms, completely baffled by the translation problem, have printed their technical literature and brochures in English. This kind of poor solution may incite nationalistic feelings against the company. Worse yet, this approach automatically limits a product's use to those people who can read and understand technical English. It also greatly increases the probability of misunderstanding and thus additional ill will toward the company.

LEGAL RESTRAINTS ON INTERNATIONAL ADVERTISERS

No discussion of the creative message in international advertising is complete without some consideration of the problem of restrictions imposed by foreign cultures and governments on what may or may not be said, shown, or done in an ad. Some restrictions are legal ones; others are moral and ethical ones that determine the boundaries of good taste (Figure 20–16).

Advertising claims are strongly regulated in many countries. Superlatives of any kind are frequently outlawed. In Germany, for example, superlatives may be used only if they are scientifically provable, and no reference may be made to a competitive product. In the United States the seller is often in a more favorable position than the buyer. In many European countries just the reverse is true. Many countries bar practices such as two-for-the-price-of-one offers, coupons, premiums, one-cent sales, box-top gimmicks, and free tie-in offers.

Some countries tax advertising and not always at a standardized rate. Austria charges a 10 percent tax on newspaper and magazine advertising in all states except two. The 10 percent tax is also charged on radio and television ads in all but one state where the radio tax is 20 percent.

These restrictions can cause problems in international advertising. McCann-Erickson once tried to translate the old Coca-Cola slogan, "Refreshes you best," into foreign languages. In the United States this slogan would merely be considered harmless exaggeration. In Germany, however, it was outside the boundaries of the law. The agency, therefore, substituted "Das erfrischt richtig," or "Refreshes you right."

In Europe there are "Official Sales Periods," which are the only times price cuts may be advertised. These periods vary from country

FIGURE   20–16   Advertising regulations in selected countries of Western Europe

| Country | General regulations | | Limitations on specific products | | | Media regulations | |
	Comparative advertising	Advertising to children	Alcoholic beverages	Tobacco	Drugs and medicine	Restricted or banned media	Limitations on commercials
Austria	Banned if denigrating	Direct appeal forbidden	None	Voluntary ban on TV ads	Ads need approval of government	None	Maximum length of 30 seconds
Belgium	Banned if denigrating	Banned by law in all media	Ads for absinthe drinks banned	Cigarette ads banned in cinema, TV and radio	Banned by law in all general media	No commercial TV or radio	Not applicable
Denmark	Minor restrictions	None	None	Voluntary control over cigarette ads	Banned in all general media	No commercial television or radio	Not applicable
Finland	None	None	Banned on TV	Banned on TV and media directed at youth	Voluntary control over copy	No domestic radio	No television commercials on certain days
France	Banned	Prebroadcast screening of commercials	Hard liquor banned on all media, others on radio and TV	Cigarettes banned on TV and radio	Copy clearance needed	Total receipts from one advertiser limited to 8 percent of total TV	Blocks, or groups, of commercials only (no spots)
Germany	Banned	Voluntary for TV and radio	Voluntary limits by industry	Banned on TV and radio	Banned in all media	None	TV commercials between 6 and 8 P.M.; none on Sunday
Italy	Direct comparisons banned; indirect OK if substantiated	Cannot show children eating	Some restrictions on TV ads	All tobacco banned in all media	Copy clearance needed	None	Sold in broadcast packages
Netherlands	OK if comparison is fair, detailed	Voluntary restraints	Voluntary restraints on TV and radio	Voluntary restraints on TV and radio	None	None	No more than two TV commercials per week per product
Sweden	Banned if denigrating	Ban on showing children in danger	Voluntary control on ads for wine and hard liquor	Banned in all media	Prescription drug ads banned	No commercial TV or radio	Not applicable
Switzerland	None	None	Banned in all media	Banned in all media	Banned in all media	No commercial radio	No more than two TV commercials per week per product
United Kingdom	Banned if denigrating	Voluntary rules designed to protect children	No commercials before 9 P.M.	Cigarette ads banned on TV and radio	Voluntary control	None on major media	None

to country, but control is very strict and fines are extremely high. And before a sale ad may be published, it frequently must be approved by a government-controlled agency.

The only solution to these and the myriad other legal problems encountered by international advertisers is to have a good local lawyer on retainer.

Summary

Since the end of World War II, advertising has grown worldwide. As economic conditions and the standard of living have improved in foreign lands, the use of advertising has also increased. However the status of advertising varies from country to country depending on local attitudes toward promotional activities in general.

The way advertising activities are managed in foreign markets depends on the marketing structure and strategy of the firm and on the availability of qualified talent. Some companies are organized to market internationally, others multinationally, and some globally. Depending on the needs of their international advertising program, these companies may elect to use large American or foreign-based international agencies, local foreign agencies, export agencies, their normal domestic agencies, or even an in-house agency.

In overseas markets, companies often find it necessary to use different creative strategies than they use in their domestic campaigns. For one thing, foreign markets are different. They are characterized by different social, economic, technological, and political environments. And, in some developing countries, market research may not be as reliable as it is in North America, thereby making it more difficult to understand local customs, culture, and attitudes.

Second, the media in foreign markets are different. Some media may not be available, others may not be as effective, and still others may not be economical.

Third, advertising messages often must be different. They must be based on the purchasing ability, habits, and motivations of the consumer in the particular foreign market being approached. And, of course, they usually must be communicated in the consumer's language.

Finally, advertisers must be ever mindful of foreign cultural and governmental restrictions on what may or may not be said, shown, or done in an ad. Some restrictions are legal ones; others are moral and ethical ones that determine the boundaries of good taste.

Questions for review and discussion

1. How would you explain the impact of expanding technology on world advertising expenditures?
2. What is the relationship between expenditures for advertising and a country's per capita national income? Why?
3. What is the difference between an international firm and a multinational firm? How does this affect the way their advertising is managed?
4. What are the pros and cons of the global advertising debate? How would you evaluate each side's position?
5. What factors differentiate American or Canadian markets from foreign markets?
6. How would a country's political environment affect the local market for television sets or other major appliances? How would that affect advertising for these products?
7. What do you suppose is the primary advertising medium in most foreign countries? Why?
8. What major factors influence the creation of advertising messages in foreign markets?
9. What are "official sales periods," and why are they important?
10. Overall, what is the basic difference between advertising in the United States or Canada and advertising in overseas markets?

References

Chapter 1

1. "A New Look for Coca-Cola: A Synopsis of the 70's," Coca-Cola Company, July 1970.
2. Stanley M. Ulanoff, *Advertising in America* (New York: Hastings House, 1977), p. 27.
3. David A. Aaker and John G. Myers, *Advertising Management* (Englewood Cliffs, N.J.: Prentice-Hall, 1975), pp. 559–60.
4. *The Borden Co. vs. FTC,* 381F.2d 175, 5th Cir., 1967.
5. Walter Taplin, *Advertising: A New Approach* (Boston: Little Brown, 1963), p. 106.
6. Charles Yang, "Variations in the Cyclical Behavior of Advertising," *Journal of Marketing,* April 1964, pp. 25–30.

Chapter 2

1. "Afterword," *Madison Avenue,* May 1980, p. 98.
2. Vivian Gornich and Barbara K. Moran, *Women in Sexist Society* (New York: New American Library, 1971), p. 304.
3. "Dear***, Your Advertising Has Recently Come to the Attention of the National Advertising Division . . ." (New York: Council of Better Business Bureaus, 1983), p. 1.

Chapter 3

1. Christian McAdams, "Frank Perdue Is Chicken!" *Esquire,* April 1973, pp. 113–17. Copyright 1973 by Esquire Publishing, Inc., and "Frank Perdue," *Inc.,* February 1984, pp. 21–23.
2. Frederic R. Gamble, *What Advertising Agencies Are—What They Do and How They Do It,* 7th ed. (New York: American Association of Advertising Agencies, 1970), p. 4.
3. Ibid., p. 5.
4. Ibid., pp. 6 and 7.
5. *Communication Arts,* April 1973, pages unnumbered.
6. Franchellie Cadwell and Herman Davis, "Why Is It That Ad Agencies Don't Advertise?" *Advertising Age,* November 19, 1979, p. 51.
7. "Ted Turner Tackles TV News," *Newsweek,* June 16, 1980, pp. 58–66. Copyright 1980 by Newsweek, Inc. All rights reserved. Reprinted by permission.
8. *Current Biography* (New York: H. W. Wilson Company, 1979), pp. 408-11.

Chapter 4

1. "Lee Iacocca of Chrysler: Crisis Plans Paying Off," *Advertising Age,* January 2, 1984, pp. 1, 30–31.
2. Louis E. Boone and David L. Kurtz, *Contemporary Marketing,* 3d ed. (Hinsdale, Ill.: Dryden Press, 1980), pp. 142–144. Copyright 1980 by The Dryden Press, a division of Holt, Rinehart & Winston. Reprinted by permission.
3. Ibid., p. 199.
4. Philip Kotler, *Principles of Marketing* (Englewood Cliffs, N.J.: Prentice-Hall, 1980), p. 48. Copyright 1980 Prentice-Hall, Inc. Adapted by permission.
5. Boone and Kurtz, *Contemporary Marketing,* pp. 207–8.
6. Bert C. McCammon, Jr., *Marketing and Economic Development* (Chicago: American Marketing Association, 1965), pp. 496–515.

Chapter 5

1. Abraham H. Maslow, *Motivation and Personality,* 2d ed. (New York: Harper & Row, 1970), pp. 39–51. Copyright 1970 by Abraham H. Maslow. By permission of Harper & Row, Publishers, Inc.
2. Ben M. Enis, *Marketing Principles* (Santa Monica, Calif.: Goodyear Publishing, 1980), p. 287.
3. Edward L. Grubb and Gregg Hupp, "Perception of Self-Generalized Stereotypes and Brand Selection," *Journal of Marketing Research,* February 1968, pp. 58–63.
4. Bibi Wein, "Psychographics," *Omni,* July 1980, p. 97.
5. Edmund Faison, *Advertising: A Behavioral Approach for Managers* (New York: John Wiley & Sons, 1980), p. 132.
6. Leon Festinger, *A Theory of Cognitive Dissonance* (Evanston, Ill.: Row, Peterson, 1957), p. 83.
7. Marcus, Burton, et al., *Modern Marketing Management* (New York: Random House, 1980), p. 83. Copyright by Random House, Inc. Reprinted by permission of Random House.
8. Harold W. Berkman and Christopher C. Gilson, *Consumer Behavior* (Encino, Calif.: Dickenson Publishing, 1978), pp. 226–27.
9. Burton and Marcus, *Modern Marketing Management,* p. 86.
10. Peter W. Bernstein, "Psychographics Is Still an Issue on Madison Avenue," *Fortune,* January 16, 1978, pp. 78–84.
11. Everett Rogers, *Diffusion of Innovations* (New York: Free Press, 1962), pp. 168-71.
12. Joseph T. Plummer, "Life Style Patterns and Commercial Bank Credit Card Usage," *Journal of Marketing,* April 1971, pp. 35–41.
13. Philip Kotler, *Principles of Marketing* (Englewood Cliffs, N.J.: Prentice-Hall, 1980), p. 32. Copyright 1980 Prentice-Hall, Inc. Adapted by permission.
14. Ibid., p. 304.

15. William D. Wells and Douglas J. Tigert, "Activities, Interests and Opinions," *Journal of Marketing Research,* August 1971, pp. 27–35.
16. Louis E. Boone and David L. Kurtz, *Contemporary Marketing* (Hinsdale, Ill.: Dryden Press, 1980), pp. 91–92. Copyright 1980 by The Dryden Press, a division of Holt, Rinehart & Winston. Reprinted by permission.

Chapter 6

1. Edward Buxton, *Promise Them Anything* (New York: Stein and Day, 1972), pp. 218–19.
2. AMA Committee on Definitions, *Marketing Definitions: A Glossary of Marketing Terms* (Chicago: American Marketing Association, 1963), pp. 16–17.
3. Kenneth Longman, *Advertising* (New York: Harcourt Brace Jovanovich, 1971), pp. 177–78.
4. "Volks Called Biggest Success: Edsel Gets Booby Prize," *Advertising Age,* April 30, 1980, pp. 130–32.
5. Don E. Schultz and Dennis G. Martin, *Strategic Advertising Campaigns* (Chicago: Crain Books, 1979), p. 26.
6. Philip Kotler, *Principles of Marketing* (Englewood Cliffs, N.J.: Prentice-Hall, 1980), p. 145. Copyright 1980 Prentice-Hall, Inc. Adapted by permission.
7. Kenneth E. Runyon, *Advertising and the Practice of Marketing* (Columbus, Ohio: Charles E. Merrill Publishing, 1979), p. 108.
8. Pamela L. Alreck and Robert B. Settle, *The Survey Research Handbook* (Homewood, Ill., Richard D. Irwin, 1984), p. 98.
9. Robert M. Worcester, ed., *Consumer Market Research Handbook* (London: McGraw-Hill, 1972), p. 7.
10. Kotler, *Principles of Marketing,* p. 146.
11. Charles E. Overholser, "Advertising Strategy from Consumer Research," *Journal of Advertising Research,* November 1971, pp. 3–9.
12. Edward Faison, *Advertising: A Behavioral Approach for Managers* (New York: John Wiley & Sons, 1980), pp. 664–65.
13. Ibid., p. 665.
14. Ibid.

Chapter 7

1. Richard Stansfield, *Advertising Manager's Handbook* (Chicago: Dartnell Corporation, 1969), p. 84.
2. Philip Kotler, *Marketing Management: Analysis, Planning, and Control* (Englewood Cliffs, N.J.: Prentice-Hall, 1973), p. 369.
3. Marcus, Burton, et al., *Modern Marketing Management* (New York: Random House, 1980), p. 556. Reprinted by permission of Random House, Inc.
4. E. Jerome McCarthy, *Basic Marketing,* 6th ed. (Homewood, Ill.: Richard D. Irwin, 1978), pp. 35–39.
5. Kotler, *Marketing Management,* p. 89.

6. Kenneth Roman and Jane Maas, *How to Advertise* (New York: St. Martin's Press, 1976), p. 2.
7. Speech by Charles Fredericks, executive vice president, Ogilvy & Mather, before the American Association of Advertising Agencies. Eastern Annual Conference, New York, November 1974.
8. Kotler, *Marketing Management,* pp. 360–70.
9. Russell H. Colley, *Defining Advertising Goals for Measured Advertising Results* (New York: Association of National Advertisers, 1961), p. 1.
10. Speech by Fredericks.
11. Leo Bogart, *Strategy in Advertising* (New York: Harcourt Brace Jovanovich, 1967), p. 28. Reprinted by permission of the author.
12. Ibid., pp. 19–23.

Chapter 8

1. "Spreading the Word," *Advertising Techniques,"* September 1979, pp. 31–33; and "International Paper Update," *Advertising Techniques,* March 1980, p. 31.
2. F. Allen Foster, *Advertising: Ancient Market Place to Television* (New York: Criterion Books, 1967), pp. 166–67.
3. David Ogilvy, *Confessions of an Advertising Man* (New York: Atheneum Publishers, 1966), pp. 104–7.
4. Ibid., p. 108.
5. Philip Ward Burton, *Advertising Copyrighting* (Columbus, Ohio: Grid, 1974), p. 73. Reprinted with permission from Grid Publishing, Inc.

Chapter 9

1. "The Sweet Taste of Success," *Advertising Techniques,* pp. 8–10, 12, 13.
2. Joel G. Cahn, *Print Casebooks 3: 1978–79 Edition, The Best in Advertising* (Washington, D.C.: R. C. Publications, 1978), pp. 78–84.
3. J. Douglas Johnson, *Advertising Today* (Chicago: Science Research Associates, 1978), pp. 91–92.
4. Richard H. Stansfield, *Advertising Manager's Handbook* (Chicago: Dartnell Corporation, 1969), pp. 640–41.
5. Stephen Baker, *Advertising Layout and Art Direction* (New York: McGraw-Hill, 1959), pp. 246–47.
6. Walter P. Margulies, *Packaging Power* (New York: World Publishing, 1970), p. 62.
7. Ibid., pp. 62–67.

Chapter 11

1. "TV's Mr. Whipple, Dick Wilson, Wraps His 20th Year," *People,* December 12, 1984, p. 151.
2. Harry Wayne McMahan, "Levi's," *Advertising Age,* October 31, 1977, p. 58.
3. Joel G. Cahn, *Print Casebooks 3: 1978–79 Edition, The Best in Advertising* (Washington, D.C.: R. C. Publications, 1978), pp. 34–37.

4. Kenneth Roman and Jane Maas, *How to Advertise* (New York: St. Martin's Press, 1976), pp. 79–81.
5. Albert C. Book and Norman D. Cary, *The Radio and Television Commercial* (Chicago: Crain Books, 1978), p. 18.
6. Milton H. Biow, *Butting In—An Adman Speaks Out* (Garden City, N.Y.: Doubleday, 1964), p. 136.

Chapter 12

1. "Canon Clicks with AE-1 Camera Campaign," *Marketing Communications,* May 1980, pp. 73–74.
2. Kenneth Longman, *Advertising* (New York: Harcourt Brace Jovanovich, 1971), pp. 211–12.
3. Ibid., p. 351.
4. Ibid.
5. Ibid., pp. 207–10.
6. Ibid., pp. 371–72.

Chapter 13

1. Tom Gross, *Print Casebooks 6: 1984–85 Edition, The Best in Advertising* (Washington, D.C.: R. C. Publications, 1984), pp. 25–26.
2. "Ad Concepts '79," in *Creative Newspaper* (New York: Newspaper Advertising Bureau, 1979), p. 26.
3. Leo Bogart, "Newspapers Girth Off Broadcast Challenge, Survive and Prosper," *Advertising Age,* April 30, 1980, p. 176.
4. "Ad Concepts '79," p. 26.
5. *1984 Facts about Newspapers,* p. 7.
6. Tom Goss, *Print Casebooks 6: 1984–85 Edition, The Best in Advertising* (Washington, D.C.: R. C. Publications, 1980), p. 72.

Chapter 14

1. Daviel Burstein, "Using Yesterday to Sell Tomorrow," *Advertising Age,* April 11, 1983, pp. M-4, M-5, M-48.
2. *Nielsen Report on Television 1984* (Chicago: A. C. Nielsen, 1984), pp. 1–9.

Chapter 15

1. "National Geographic Sells 380M Journey to China Books," *Direct Marketing,* November 1983, p. 76.
2. "Direct Marketing: What Is It?," *Direct Marketing,* September 1983, p. 20.
3. Bob Stone, *Successful Direct Marketing Methods* (Chicago: Crain Books, 1979), p. 79.

Chapter 16

1. William A. Robinson, *Best Sales Promotions* (Chicago: Crain Books, 1982), p. 106.

2. William A. Robinson, *Best Sales Promotions* (Chicago: Crain Books, 1979), pp. 40–41.
3. "The Life of A Coupon," *Parade,* March 4, 1984, p. 24.

Chapter 17

1. "Kings of the Tacky Commercials," *Dun's Review,* May 1979, pp. 60–64.

Chapter 18

1. "Product Survival: Lessons of the Tylenol Terrorism" (Washington, D.C.: Washington Business Information, 1982), pp. 11–17.
2. *Corporate Advertising/Phase II,* An Expanded Study of Corporate Advertising Effectiveness, conducted for *Time* magazine by Yankelovich, Skelly & White, Inc., undated, pages unnumbered.
3. Doug Newsom and Alan Scott, *This Is PR, the Realities of Public Relations* (Belmont, Calif.: Wadsworth, 1981), pp. 12–13. Reprinted by permission of Wadsworth Publishing Company.

Chapter 20

1. E. Jerome McCarthy, *Basic Marketing* (Homewood, Ill.: Richard D. Irwin, 1984), p. 693.
2. John Fayerweather, *International Marketing* (Englewood Cliffs, N.J.: Prentice-Hall, 1970), p. 2.
3. "The Ad Biz Gloms Onto 'Global'," *Fortune,* November 12, 1984, p. 77.
4. "Efficacy of Global Ad Projects Is Questioned in Firm's Survey," *The Wall Street Journal,* September 13, 1984, p. 29.
5. Ernest Dichter, "The World Customer," *Harvard Business Review,* July–August, 1961, p. 116.
6. "Yankee Goods—and Know-How—Go Abroad," *Advertising Age,* May 17, 1982, pp. M-14, M-16.
7. "The Ad Biz Gloms Onto 'Global'," *Fortune,* November 12, 1984, p. 80.
8. Dean M. Peebles and John K. Ryans, *Management of International Advertising* (Boston: Allyn & Bacon, 1984), p. 145.
9. Ibid., p. 149.
10. Philip R. Cateora, *International Marketing* (Homewood, Ill.: Richard D. Irwin, 1983), p. 85–87.
11. "Culture Shocks: Pitfalls Lie Waiting for Unwary Marketers," *Advertising Age,* May 17, 1982, p. M-9.
12. Fayerweather, *International Marketing,* pp. 92–93.
13. Ibid., p. 90.
14. Ibid., p. 84.
15. Robert R. Roth, *International Marketing Communications* (Chicago: Crain Books, 1982), p. 21.

CREDITS AND ACKNOWLEDGMENTS

Chapter 1

Figures 1–1, 1–2, 1–3, 1–4, and Ad Lab 1–A Courtesy The Coca-Cola Company.

Figure 1–5 Dick Sutpen, *The Mad Old Ads* (New York: McGraw-Hill, 1966).

Figure 1–6 Courtesy Chiat/Day, Inc. Advertising.

Figure 1–7 Courtesy The Martin Agency.

Figure 1–8 Courtesy Dancer Fitzgerald Sample/New York.

Figure 1–9 Courtesy Grey Advertising Inc.

Figure 1–10 Courtesy J. Walter Thompson USA.

Figure 1–11 Courtesy Tracy-Locke, BBDO.

Figure 1–12 Courtesy McCann-Erickson/Toronto.

Figure 1–13 Adapted from Frank Presbey, *History and Development of Advertising* (Garden City, N.Y.: Doubleday, 1929), p. 361. Copyright 1929 by Frank Presbey. Reprinted by permission of Doubleday & Company, Inc.

Figure 1–14 Reprinted with permission from September 14, 1984, issue of *Advertising Age.* © 1984 by Crain Communications, Inc.

Figure 1–15 Dick Sutpen, *The Mad Old Ads* (New York: McGraw-Hill, 1966).

Figure 1–16 Reprinted with permission from April 30, 1980, issue of *Advertising Age.* © 1980 by Crain Communications, Inc.

Figure 1–17 Henry Ford Museum/Edison Institute.

Figure 1–19 Courtesy Volkswagen of America.

History of Advertising Portfolio Courtesy The Coca-Cola Company.

Figure 1–21 Courtesy Pepsi-Cola U.S.A.

Figure 1–22 Courtesy Union Oil of California.

Figure 1–23 Photograph by Gordon Wagner/Bookworks.

Figure 1–24 Courtesy Dana Perfumes Corp.

Chapter 2

Figure 2–1 Courtesy of HCM.

Figure 2–3 Courtesy Fallon McElligott Rice.

Figure 2–4 Courtesy Pepsico.

Figure 2–5 Courtesy Parfums de Coeur.

Figure 2–6 Courtesy Sosa & Associates.

Figure 2–9 Courtesy Scali, McCabe, Sloves, Inc.

Figure 2–10 Reprinted with permission from June 11, 1984 *Advertising Age.* © 1984 by Crain Communications, Inc.

Figure 2–16 Adapted from *The National Advertising Review Board, 1971–1976: A Five Year Review and Perspective on Advertising Industry Self-Regulation* (New York: National Advertising Review Board, 1977).

Chapter 3

Figure 3–1 Courtesy Scali, McCabe, Sloves, Inc.

Figure 3–2 Photograph by Sue Markson/Bookworks.

Figure 3–3 Courtesy Scali, McCabe, Sloves, Inc.

Checklist for Agency Review Adapted with permission from the March 30, 1981, issue of *Crain's Chicago Business.* © 1981 by Crain Communications, Inc.

Figure 3–4 Courtesy Revlon.

Ad Lab 3–A *Occupational Outlook Handbook* 1985.

Figure 3–5 Courtesy Benton & Bowles, Inc. and The Proctor & Gamble Company.

Figure 3–6 Courtesy Greycom Public Relations.

Checklist of Ways To Be A Better Client Adapted from Kenneth Roman and Jane Maas, *How to Advertise* (New York: St. Martin's Press, Inc., Macmillan & Co., Ltd., 1976), pp. 151–56.

Figure 3–7 Courtesy DCE Marketing/Graphic Design, University of Utah.

Figure 3–8 Courtesy Harris Carstens Amaral Advertising.

Ad Lab 3–B Reprinted with permission from the March 28, 1985 issue of *Advertising Age.* © 1985 by Crain Communications, Inc.

Figure 3–9 Courtesy Young & Rubicam Inc.

Figure 3–10 Courtesy Glidden & Boyles.

Figure 3–11 Courtesy Scali, McCabe, Sloves, Inc.

Figure 3–12 Courtesy Chiat/Day.

Ad Lab 3–C Adapted and updated from *Advertising: A Career of Action and Variety for Exceptional Men and Women* (New York: American Association of Advertising Agencies, no date), and *Advertising: A Guide to Careers in Advertising* (New York: American Association of Advertising Agencies, 1975).

Figure 3–13 Courtesy Scott Lancaster Mills Atha.

Figure 3–15 Adapted from American Association of Advertising Agencies data.

Figure 3–17 Courtesy Leo Burnett Company, Inc. Advertising.

Figure 3–18 Courtesy Jack Eagle.

Figure 3–19 Photograph by Mary Cairns/*Advertising Age.*

Figure 3–20 Courtesy Turner Broadcasting System, Inc.

Figure 3–21 Courtesy The Richards Group.

Figure 3–22 Courtesy Davis, Johnson, Mogul & Colombatto, Inc. Advertising.

Figure 3–23 Courtesy Bozell & Jacobs, Inc.

Figure 3–24 Courtesy Magazine Publishers Association.

Figure 3–25 Courtesy Union Tribune Publishing Co., San Diego.

Figure 3–26 Courtesy Noral Color Corporation

Chapter 4

Figure 4–1 Courtesy Kenyon & Eckhardt, Inc.

Ad Labs 4A–E Adapted from "Apple Computer Inc.", *Business Marketing*, November 1983, p. 50. "Apple Launches a Mac Attack," *Time*, January 30, 1984, p. 68. "Desktop Wars: Will Apple's Mac Trip the Dancing Elephant?", *Industry Week*, January 23, 1984, pp. 16–17. "IBM and Apple Battle for the Business Market," *Dun's Business Month*, April 1984, pp. 123–124. "Reviewing the Mac," *Newsweek*, January 30, 1984, p. 56. Photograph Courtesy Apple Computer, Inc.

Figure 4–4 Courtesy Clearwater Federal.

Figure 4–5 Courtesy Mark Oliver, Inc.

Figure 4–7 Courtesy Kenyon & Eckhardt, Inc. and Needham Harper Worldwide, Inc.

Figure 4–8 Courtesy Creative Software.

Figure 4–9 Courtesy Sidjakov Berman & Gomez Design Communications.

C

Figure 4–10 Adapted from Ben M. Enis, *Marketing Principles* (Santa Monica, Calif.: Goodyear Publishing, 1980), p. 351.

People in Advertising. Adapted with permission from *The Positioning Era* by Jack Trout and Al Ries, July 16, 1979, issue of *Advertising Age*. Copyright 1979 by Crain Communications, Inc.

Figure 4–11 Courtesy Panasonic.

Figure 4–12 Courtesy Benton & Bowles, Inc. and The Proctor & Gamble Company.

Figure 4–13 Adapted from Elwood S. Buffa and Barbara A. Pletcher, *Understanding Business Today* (Homewood, Ill.: Richard D. Irwin, 1980), p. 37.

Figure 4–14 Courtesy NW Ayer Incorporated.

Figure 4–15 Courtesy Ally & Gargano, Inc.

Figure 4–16 Courtesy Doyle Dane Bernback, Inc.

Figure 4–17 Courtesy Webb & Athey, Inc.

Figure 4–18 *Nation's Restaurant News*, August 13, 1984, p. 78.

Chapter 5

Figure 5–2 Courtesy J. Walter Thompson USA.

Figure 5–3 Adapted from Burton, Marcus et al., *Modern Marketing Management* (New York: Random House, 1980), p. 66.

Figure 5–4 Courtesy Jody Donohue Associates, Inc.

Figure 5–5 Adapted from William H. and Isabella C. M. Cunningham, *Marketing: A Managerial Approach* (Cincinnati: South-Western Publishing, 1981), p. 121, and data based on hierarchy of needs in "A Theory of Human Motivation," in *Motivation and Personality*, 2d. edition, by Abraham H. Maslow. Copyright © 1970 by Abraham H. Maslow. By permission of Harper & Row Publishers, Inc.

Ad Lab 5–A Left, Courtesy McKinney, Silver & Rockett. Middle, Courtesy Young & Rubicam, Chicago. Right, Courtesy Young & Rubicam, New York.

Ad Lab 5–B Adapted from Harold W. Berkman and Christopher C. Gilson, *Consumer Behavior: Concepts and Strategies*, 2d ed. (Boston: Kent Publishing Co., 1981), p. 249. Reprinted by permission of Kent Publishing, a Division of Wadsworth Inc. and Jack Haberstroh "Can't Ignore Subliminal Ad Charges," *Advertising Age*, p. 3, 42, and 44.

Figure 5–6 Courtesy Ogilvy & Mather/New York.

Figure 5–8 Courtesy Carder Gray Advertising/Toronto.

Figure 5–9 Adapted from W. Lloyd Warner, Marchia Meeker, Kenneth Eels, *Social Class in America* (New York: Harper & Row, 1960), pp. 6–32.

Figure 5–10 Courtesy Badillo/Compton, Inc.

Ad Lab 5–C Left, Courtesy Young & Rubicam. Middle, Courtesy McKinney, Silver & Rockett. Right, Courtesy Panasonic.

Figure 5–11 Courtesy Laurence, Charles & Free, Inc.

Figure 5–12 Philip Kotler, *Principles of Marketing* (Englewood Cliffs, N.J.: Prentice-Hall, 1980), p. 297. © Prentice-Hall, Inc. Adapted by permission.

Figure 5–13 Adapted from Niles Howard, "More Bang for the Ad Dollar." Reprinted with the special permission of *Dun's Review*, November 1978. Copyright 1978, Dun & Bradstreet Publication Corporation; data from Major Market Index 1977.

Figure 5–14 Adapted from David L. Kurtz and Louis E. Boone, *Marketing* (New York: Dryden Press, 1981), p. 146.

Figure 5–15 Courtesy Chiat/Day, Inc.

Figure 5–16 Adapted from Dik Warren Twedt, "How Important to Marketing Strategy Is the 'Heavy User'?" *Journal of Marketing*, January 1964, p. 72.

Figure 5–17 Adapted from Russell J. Haley, "Benefit Segmentation: A Decision Oriented Research Tool." *Journal of Marketing*, July 1963, pp. 30–35.

Ad Lab 5–E Adapted from: "Times and VALS Engineer A Psychographic Product Launch," *Ad Forum*, September 1984, pp. 12–15. Artwork courtesy Young & Rubicam, Inc.

Figure 5–18 Adapted from U.S. Department of Commerce, Bureau of the Census, *Census of Manufacturers, Area Statistics*

(Washington, D.C.: U.S. Government Printing Office, 1977) p. 749.

Figure 5–19 Adapted from E. Jerome McCarthy and William D. Perreault, Jr. *Basic Marketing*, 8th edition (Homewood, Il.: Richard D. Irwin, 1984), p. 299.

Chapter 6

Figure 6–1 Courtesy NW Ayer Incorporated.

Ad Lab 6–A Adapted from Steuart Henderson Britt, *Marketing Managers Handbook* (Chicago: The Dartnell Corporation, 1973), pp. 286–87.

Figure 6–2 Adapted from Dik Warren Twedt, ed., *1973 Survey of Marketing Research* (Chicago: American Marketing Association, 1973), p. 41.

Figure 6–3 Adapted from Philip Kotler, *Principles of Marketing* (Englewood Cliffs, N.J.: Prentice-Hall, 1980). © 1980 Prentice-Hall, Inc. Adapted by permission.

Ad Lab 6–B Adapted from Natalie Goldberg, "How to Use External Data in Marketing Research," *Marketing Communication*, March 1980, pp. 76–82.

Figures 6–4 and 6–5 Alreck, Pamela L. and Settle, Robert B., *The Survey Research Handbook*, (Homewood, Il.: Richard D. Irwin, Inc., 1985) pp. 41 and 65, © 1985 Richard D. Irwin, Inc.

Ad Lab 6–C Adapted from *Everything You've Always Wanted to Know about TV Ratings*, A. C. Nielsen Company, 1978.

Figure 6–6 Courtesy NW Ayer Incorporated.

Checklist for Developing an Effective Questionnaire From Don E. Schultz and Dennis G. Martin, *Strategic Advertising Campaigns* (Chicago: Crain Books, 1979).

Figure 6–8 Photograph courtesy of Kenneth Hollander Associates, Inc.

Figure 6–10 Adapted from Edmund W. J. Faison, *Advertising: A Behavioral Approach for Managers* (New York: John Wiley & Sons, 1980), p. 664.

Figures 6–11, 6–12, 6–13, and 6–14 Courtesy NW Ayer Incorporated.

Figure 6–15 Courtesy Bruzzone Research Company.

Figure 6–16 Courtesy J. Walter Thompson USA and Starch INRA Hooper

Figure 6–17 M. Wayne DeLozier, *The Marketing Communication Process*. © 1976 by M. Wayne DeLozier. Used with permission of McGraw-Hill Book Company.

Chapter 7

Ad Lab 7–A Jack Trout and Al Ries, "Marketing Warfare," *Southern Advertising*, July 1978. Photographs by Wayne Bladholm.

Checklist for Situation Analysis Adapted from Russel H. Colley, *Defining Advertising Goals for Measured Advertising Results* (New York: Association of National Advertisers, 1961), pp. 62–68.

Figures 7–5, 7–6, and 7–7 Courtesy NW Ayer Incorporated.

Figure 7–8 Courtesy Ogilvy & Mather, Inc.

Figure 7–9 Courtesy Scali, McCabe, Sloves, Inc.

Figure 7–13 Courtesy NW Ayer Incorporated.

Ad Lab 7–B Courtesy Hank Forssberg Advertising; Advertisement and photograph reproduced with the permission of General Foods Corporation; Courtesy Chiat/Day, Inc.; Courtesy Ogilvy & Mather/Houston; Courtesy Scali, McCabe, Sloves, Inc.; and Courtesy Bozell & Jacobs, Inc.

Ad Lab 7–C Adapted from William J. Baumol and Alan S. Blinder, *Economics: Principles and Policy*, 3d edition (New York: Harcourt Brace Jovanovich, 1985), p. 386.

Figure 7–14 *Printer's Ink*, December 16, 1960, p. 27.

Figure 7–15 Reprinted with permission from March 28, 1984, issue of *Advertising Age*. © 1984 by Crain Communications, Inc.

Figure 7–16 Courtesy Doyle Dane Bernbach

Chapter 8

Figure 8–1 Courtesy International Paper Company.
Checklist of Product Marketing Facts for Copywriters Adapted from *Advertising Today.* © 1978 by J. Douglas Johnson. Reprinted by permission of the publisher, Science Research Associates, Inc.
Figure 8–3 Courtesy Henry Ford Museum/Edison Institute.
Figure 8–4 Courtesy Apple Computer, Inc.
Figure 8–5 Courtesy Allstate Insurance.
Figure 8–6 Courtesy Citibank.
Figure 8–7 Courtesy Advertising au Gratin/Minneapolis.
Figure 8–8 Courtesy Qually & Company.
Figure 8–9 Courtesy Kresser/Craig.
Figure 8–10 Courtesy Ted Bates Advertising/New York.
Copywriter's Portfolio A. Courtesy Scali, McCabe, Sloves, Inc. B. Courtesy The Straw Hat Restaurant Corporation. C. Courtesy John Paul Itta. D. Courtesy Needham Harper Worldwide, Inc. E. Courtesy Fallon McElligott Rice. F. Courtesy Ally & Gargano, Inc. Advertising. G. Courtesy Chuck Ruhr Advertising, Inc.
Figure 8–11 Courtesy Foote, Cone & Belding; Jozef Sumichrast, illustrator.
Figure 8–12 Courtesy Doyle Dane Bernbach Inc. Advertising.
Checklist for Writing Effective Copy David L. Malickson and John W. Nason, excerpted from page 74 *Advertising: How to Write the Kind That Works.* © 1982 David L. Malickson and John W. Nason. Reprinted with the permission of Charles Scribner's Sons.
Ad Lab 8–A Adapted from Robert Gunning, *The Technique of Clear Writing,* rev. ed. (New York: McGraw-Hill, 1968), p. 38.
Figure 8–13 Courtesy Phillips-Ramsey.
Figure 8–14 Courtesy Polaroid Corp.

Chapter 9

Figure 9–1 Courtesy Margeotes/Fertitta & Weiss
Figure 9–2 Courtesy Doyle Dane Bernbach Inc.
Figure 9–3 Courtesy Ackerman & McQueen.
Figure 9–4 Courtesy Yamaha Motor Corporation, U.S.A.
Figure 9–5 Courtesy J. Walter Thompson USA.
Ad Lab 9–A Adapted from Mike Turner, "What Makes a Good Account Executive?" *Viewpoint* I (1980), pp. 27–28.
Figure 9–6 Courtesy Leo Burnett Company, Inc.
Figure 9–7 Courtesy Advertising au Gratin/Minneapolis.
Figure 9–8 Courtesy Greycom Public Relations.
Figure 9–9 Courtesy Leber Katz Partners, Advertising; Peter Paris, designer.
Checklist for Choosing Illustrations Left: Courtesy Austin Nichols & Co., Inc. Right: Courtesy The Martin Agency, Inc.
Figure 9–10 Courtesy Talon.
Ad Lab 9–B Adapted from Walter Margulies, "What Colors Should You Use?" *Media Decisions* (New York: Decision Publications).
Art Directors' Portfolio A. Courtesy C. J. Herrick Associates Creative Director: Mr. N. G. Marchica Photographer: Neil Barr. B. Courtesy Ally & Gargano, Inc. Advertising. C. Courtesy Mendelsohn/Zien Advertising. D. Courtesy Foote Cone & Belding, Ltd. and Sunkist Growers, Inc. E. Courtesy Doyle Dane Bernbach, Inc. F. Courtesy George Lois. G. Courtesy Kenyon & Eckhardt, Inc. and Bulgari.
Figure 9–11 Photograph by Frank Williams/Bookworks.
Figure 9–12 Courtesy Selame Design.
Ad Lab 9–C Courtesy General Mills.

Chapter 10

Figure 10–1 Courtesy Emilio Paccione, retoucher; Carl Fischer, photographer.
Figure 10–2 Courtesy Della Femina, Travisano & Partners, Inc.

Figure 10–3 Courtesy The Lehigh Press, Inc.
Figure 10–4 Courtesy Chiat-Day.
Ad Lab 10–A Courtesy Young & Rubicam, Inc. Courtesy Bozell & Jacobs, Inc. Courtesy Stimpson Associates. Courtesy Calet, Hirsch & Spector, Inc. Courtesy Doyle Dane Bernbach Inc.
Figure 10–7 Courtesy Scali, McCabe, Sloves, Inc.
Figure 10–10 Adapted from U&lc, International Journal of Typographics.
Figure 10–11 Courtesy AM Verityper, division of AM International.
Figure 10–15 Courtesy Heidelberg Eastern, Inc.
Figure 10–16 Courtesy Towne, Silverstein, Rotter Inc.
Creative Department Courtesy Young & Rubicam New York and Dr Pepper.

Chapter 11

Figure 11–1 Courtesy Benton & Bowles and Cunningham Walsh, Inc.
Figure 11–3 Courtesy Genesco Inc.
Figure 11–4 Courtesy Geers Gross.
Figure 11–5 Courtesy Ted Bates Advertising/New York.
Figure 11–6 Courtesy Foote, Cone & Belding.
Figure 11–7 Digital Scene Simulation ^{sm} by Digital Productions, Los Angeles, CA U.S.A. © 1985. All Rights Reserved.
Figure 11–8 Courtesy Leo Burnett Company, Inc. and The Pillsbury Company.
Figure 11–9 Courtesy KCBN, Inc.
Figure 11–10 Adapted with permission of Macmillan Publishing Co., Inc., from *Advertising,* by William M. Weilbacher, p. 273. © 1962 by The Free Press.
Creative Department Courtesy Dancer Fitzgerald Sample, Inc. and Wendy's International, Inc.
Figure 11–11 Photograph by Peter LeGrand.
Figure 11–12 Courtesy Della Femina, Travisano & Partners, Inc. Checklist for Creating Effective Radio Commercials, Peter Hochstein, "Ten Rules for Making Better Radio Commercials," *Viewpoint* III (1981).
Ad Lab 11–A Adapted from Wallace A. Ross and Bob Landers, "Commercial Categories," in *Radio Plays the Plaza* (New York: Radio Advertising Bureau, 1969).
Figure 11–13 Courtesy Inglehart and Partners, Inc., Chicago.
Figure 11–14 Adapted with permission of Macmillan Publishing Co., Inc., from *Advertising,* by William M. Weilbacher, p. 273. © 1962 by The Free Press.

Chapter 12

Figure 12–1 Courtesy GreyCom Inc.
Figure 12–2 Reprinted by permission from May 14, 1984, issue of *Advertising Age.* © 1984 by Crain Communications, Inc.
Figure 12–3 Adapted from Jack Z. Sissors and E. Reynold Petray, *Advertising Media Planning* (Chicago: Crain Books, 1976).
Figure 12–5 Reprinted with permission from September 14, 1984, issue of *Advertising Age.* © 1984 by Crain Communications, Inc.
Ad Lab 12–A Adapted from Stephen Baker, *Systematic Advertising Research Report* (New York: McGraw-Hill, 1979), p. 154.
Figure 12–6 Courtesy Saatchi & Saatchi Compton Inc.
Figure 12–7 Courtesy Worcester Controls.
Figure 12–8 and 12–9 Adapted from *Cahners Advertising Research Report.*
Figure 12–10 From Donald W. Jugenheimer and Peter B. Turk, *Advertising Media* (Columbus, Ohio: Grid Publishing, 1980), p. 90.
Ad Lab 12–B Stephen Baker, *Systematic Approach to Advertising Creativity* (New York: McGraw-Hill, 1979), pp. 176–83.

Chapter 17

Figure 17–1   Courtesy Action Real Estate.
Figure 17–2   Courtesy Ingalls, Boston.
Figure 17–3   Courtesy Chuck Ruhr Advertising Agency.
Figure 17–4   Courtesy Fallon McElligott Rice.
Figure 17–6   Courtesy Santa Barbara Bank & Trust.
Figure 17–7   Courtesy Mark Oliver, Inc.
Figure 17–8   Photograph by Frank Williams/Bookworks.
Figure 17–9   Courtesy Fallon McElligott Rice.
Figures 17–10, 17–11, and 17–12   Data from Newspaper Advertising Bureau, Inc.
Figure 17–14   Courtesy Ogilvy & Mather.
Figure 17–15   Courtesy Siddall, Matus & Coughter, Inc.
Figure 17–16   Courtesy Borders, Perrin and Norrander.
Figure 17–17   Courtesy The Martin Agency.
Figure 17–18   Courtesy KCBN, Inc.
Checklist for Creating Local Advertising   Data from Newspaper Advertising Bureau, Inc.
Figure 17–19   Courtesy Jason Grant Associates.
Figure 17–20   Courtesy Richard Urquhart. Illustration by Neville Smith.
Figure 17–21   Courtesy International Drapery Association.
Figure 17–23   Courtesy Cal Worthington Ford.

Chapter 18

Figure 18–1   Historical Picture Services, Chicago.
Figure 18–3   Courtesy Foote Cone & Belding.
Ad Lab 18–A   Adapted from David Ogilvy, "Corporate Advertising," *Viewpoint* 1 (1979). Illustration Courtesy Ogilvy & Mather.
Figure 18–4   Courtesy William Esty Company.
Figure 18–5   Courtesy HCM, Inc.
Figure 18–6   Courtesy Software Design Associates.
Figure 18–7   Courtesy Neiman-Marcus.
Figure 18–8   © 1978 Hans Wendt.
Figure 18–9   Courtesy Jonson Pedersen Hinrichs & Shakery.
Figure 18–10   Courtesy World Typeface Center.
Figure 18–11   Three A.D., Incorporated. Illustration by Larry Keith.
Portfolio of Corporate Advertising   A. Courtesy HBM/MacDonald. B. Courtesy EF Hutton & Company, Inc. C. Phillips-Ramsey. D. Courtesy Bozell & Jacobs and The Greyhound Corporation. E. Courtesy Lord, Geller, Federico, Einstein, Inc. and IBM Corp.
Figures 18–12 and 18–13   Adapted from Scott M. Cutlip, Allen H. Center, *Effective Public Relations*, 5th edition. © 1978, pp. 23 and 24. Reprinted by permission of Prentice-Hall, Inc., Englewood Cliffs, New Jersey.

Chapter 19

Figure 19–1   Courtesy Sierra Club.
Figure 19–2   Courtesy Diane Lozito.

Figure 19–4   Courtesy Christian Children's Fund, Inc.
Figure 19–5   Courtesy D'Arcy MacManus & Masius, Inc.
Figure 19–6   Courtesy U.S. Navy Recruiting Command.
Figure 19–7   Courtesy Camp Associates Advertising Limited.
Figure 19–8   Courtesy Ketchum Advertising/Pittsburgh and the Pennsylvania Committee for Effective Justice.
Figure 19–9   Courtesy The Advertising Council Inc.
Figure 19–10   Courtesy Cosimo Studios.
Figure 19–11   Courtesy Moral Majority Report.
Figure 19–12   Courtesy American Civil Liberties Union.
Figure 19–14   Courtesy Mission USA.
Figure 19–16   Fallon McElligott Rice.
Figure 19–17   Courtesy Cochrane Chase, Livingston & Company, Inc.
Ad Lab 19–A   Adapted from June 2, 1980, issue of *Television/Radio Age*.

Chapter 20

Figure 20–1   Courtesy Dentsu Incorporated.
Ad Lab 20–A   Reprinted with permission from the March 18, 1981, issue of *Advertising Age*. Copyright 1981 by Crain Communications, Inc.
Figure 20–2   Courtesy BBDO International, Inc.
Figure 20–3   Courtesy The Coca-Cola Company.
Figure 20–4   Courtesy GreyCom Inc.
Figure 20–5   Reprinted with permission from March 28, 1984, issue of *Advertising Age*. © 1984 Crain Communications, Inc.
Figure 20–6   Courtesy Saatchi & Saatchi Compton Inc.
Figure 20–7   Courtesy Ogilvy & Mather, International/London.
Figure 20–8   Courtesy Dancer Fitzgerald Sample, Inc.
Figure 20–9   Reprinted by permission of the Harvard Business Review. An exhibit from "The World Customer" by Ernest Dichter (July/August 1962). © 1962 by the President and Fellows of Harvard College; all rights reserved.
Figure 20–10   Reprinted with permission from the Dec. 3, 1984 issue of *Advertising Age*. © 1984 by Crain Communications, Inc.
Checklist for International Media Planning   Courtesy Directories International, Inc.
Figure 20–11   Courtesy Grey Advertising, Inc.
Figure 20–12   Courtesy D'Arcy MacManus Masius Worldwide.
Figure 20–13   Courtesy AB Bates a/s, Oslo.
Figure 20–14   Courtesy BBDO International, Inc.
Figure 20–15   Reprinted with permission from the May 17, 1982 issue of *Advertising Age*. © 1982 by Crain Communications, Inc.
Figure 20–16   Adapted from *Advertising: It's Role in Modern Marketing*, Fifth Edition, by S. Watson Dunn and Arnold M. Barban. Copyright © 1982 by The Dryden Press, a division of Holt, Rinehart and Winston, Publishers. Reprinted by permission of Holt, Rinehart and Winston.

Glossary*

AAAA (2)   The American Association of Advertising Agencies has members throughout the United States and controls agency practices by denying membership to any agency judged unethical.

AAF (2)   The American Advertising Federation is a nationwide association of advertising people. The AAF helped to establish the Federal Trade Commission, and its early "vigilance" committees were the forerunners of the Better Business Bureaus.

ABC (13)   See *Audit Bureau of Circulation.*

Account Executive (3)   The liaison between the agency and the client, the account executive is responsible on the one hand for mustering all the agency's services for the benefit of the client and on the other hand for representing the agency's point of view to the client.

A. C. Nielsen Company (6)   The largest market research company in the world and an important source of secondary data. Nielsen's numerous publications, available on a subscription basis, provide such information as the Nielsen retail store audits.

Action Programs (7)   The precise details of a company's marketing strategy that spell out the specific tactics it will use to achieve its marketing objectives.

ADI (14)   See *Area of Dominant Influence.*

Advertising (1)   Nonpersonal communication of usually persuasive information about products, services, or ideas. The information is communicated through the various media and paid for by identified sponsors.

Advertising Age (2)   The industry's leading trade publication. It continually champions the cause of more ethical and responsible advertising.

Advertising Agency (3)   An independent organization of creative people and businesspeople that specializes in the development and preparation of advertising plans, advertisements, and other promotional tools for advertisers.

Advertising Appeal (8)   The motive to which an ad is directed and which is intended to get a person to comply with the goal the advertiser has established.

Advertising Council (19)   A nonpartisan, nonpolitical volunteer organization supported by the American Association of Advertising Agencies which conducts campaigns of service to the nation at large, avoiding regional, sectarian, or special-interest drives of all kinds.

Advertising Manager (3)   Person in the advertiser's employ who is responsible for the administration, planning, and budgeting of advertising activities, supervi-

sion of outside advertising services, and coordination with other company departments.

Advertising Message (7)   What the company plans to say in its advertisements and how it plans to say it—verbally and nonverbally. The message strategy is determined by the copy, art, and production elements of the ad or the campaign.

Advertising Objectives (7)   The goals of the company's advertising campaign and a logical deduction from the firm's marketing plan. Objectives may include building awareness and appeal or promoting additional use.

Advertising Plan (7)   An overall statement of the company's advertising objectives and strategy, the plan tells the intended role of advertising in the marketing mix, defines target audiences, and describes how the elements of the creative mix will be used.

Advertising Pyramid (7)   A simple graphic method of understanding the tasks advertising can accomplish in preparing customers to act.

Advertising Research (6)   Types of research designed for advertising strategy determination, concept development, pretesting of ads and commercials, and campaign evaluation.

Advertising Specialty (16)   An inexpensive, but useful, goodwill gift—a reminder that carries the company or product name or logo—like a pen, key chain, coffee mug, cap, etc. (Also called *specialty advertising.*)

Advertising Strategy (7)   The methodology the advertiser will employ to achieve its stated advertising objectives. The strategy (also called creative strategy) is determined by the advertiser's use of the creative mix.

Affidavit of Performance (14)   A signed and notarized form sent by a television station to an advertiser or agency indicating what spots ran and when. It is the station's legal proof that the advertiser got what was paid for.

Agate Line (13)   In newspaper advertising, a unit of measurement for depth $\frac{1}{14}$ inch deep by one standard column wide.

Agency Commission (3)   Compensation paid by a medium to recognized advertising agencies, usually 15 percent ($16\frac{2}{3}$ percent for outdoor) for advertising placed with it.

Agency Network (20)   An affiliation of domestic and/or foreign advertising agencies organized to give and receive media counsel, translation services, production assistance, or other specialized services in unfamiliar markets.

Aided Recall (6)   A research technique of verifying readership, viewership, or listenership in which respondents

---

*Numbers in parentheses after term indicate chapter(s) where term is discussed.

are given the advertisement or other aids to help them remember.

All News (14) A radio station format in which national, international, regional, and local news is broadcast continuously throughout the day. Advertisers tend to favor all-news formats to reach older, upscale men and women who are interested in business and civic affairs.

ANA (2) The Association of National Advertisers is composed of 400 major manufacturing and service companies that are clients of member agencies of the AAAA. These companies, which are pledged to uphold the ANA code of advertising ethics, work with the ANA through a joint Committee for Improvement of Advertising Content.

Animatic (11) A rough television commercial produced by photographing storyboard sketches on a film strip with the audio portion synchronized on tape. It is used primarily for testing purposes.

Animation (11) The use of cartoons, puppet characters, or photo animation in television commercials to create a live effect in inanimate objects. Often used to communicate especially difficult messages or whimsical ideas to specialized markets like children.

Annual Report (18) A formal document issued yearly by a corporation to its stockholders to reflect the corporation's condition at the close of the business year. Annual reports contain financial statements and other information required by either generally accepted accounting principles or specific legal requirements.

Answer Print (11) The final print of a filmed commercial, along with all the required optical effects and titles, used for review and approval before duplicating.

Arbitron (14) A commonly used rating service that regularly publishes statistics on how many people, in what age groups, and of what sex are watching TV or listening to radio at various times of the day within a specific market area.

Area of Dominant Influence (ADI) (14) Arbitron's term for a television market—defined as "an exclusive geographic area consisting of all counties in which the Home Market stations receive a preponderance of total viewing hours." Thus, the Charlotte ADI is all counties in which the Charlotte TV stations are the most watched.

Art (9) The whole visual presentation of the commercial or advertisement including how the words in the ad are arranged, what size and style of type are used, whether photos or illustrations should be used, and, if so, how they should be organized. Art also refers to what style of photography or illustration is employed, how color is used, and how these elements are arranged in an ad and relate to one another in size and proportion. Art is the "body language" of advertising.

Art Director (3)(9) Art directors are responsible for the visual presentation of the ad. They are therefore nor-

mally involved with a copywriter in the initial concept of the ad.

Art Studios (3) Small firms of artists used to design and produce artwork and illustrations for advertisements.

Ascender (10) In typography, the stroke of the letter that rises above the x height; e.g., d, t, l.

Association Advertising (19) Advertising by nonprofit labor, professional, trade, and civic groups usually for the purpose of creating goodwill and a positive impression of the association's members.

Attention Value (12) A consideration in selecting media based on the degree of attention paid to ads in a particular medium by those exposed to them. Attention value relates to the advertising message and copy just as much as to the medium.

Attitude Tests (6) Type of posttest that usually seeks to measure the effectiveness of an advertising campaign in creating a favorable image for a company, its brand, or its products.

Audience (12) The total number of people who are reached by a particular medium.

Audio (8) (11) The right side of a script for a television commercial which indicates sound effects, spoken copy, and music. Also, the spoken dialogue or copy in broadcast advertising. The audio may be delivered as a *voice-over* by an announcer who is not seen but whose voice is heard. Or it may be delivered *on-camera* by an announcer, a spokesperson, or actors playing out a scene.

Audiovisual systems (16) A wide variety of equipment from portable sound-slide filmstrip projectors to small videotape monitors to complex multiscreen equipment used with small groups or audiences of thousands for sales training and demonstrations.

Audit Bureau of Circulation (13) An organization supported by advertising agencies, advertisers, and publishers that verifies circulation and other marketing data on newspapers and magazines for the benefit of its members.

Avails (14) An abbreviated term referring to the TV programs that are available to an advertiser. Media buyers contact the sales reps for the stations they are considering and ask them to supply a list of available time slots along with prices and estimated ratings.

Average Quarter Hour (14) A radio term referring to the average number of people who are listening to a specific station during any 15-minute period of any given daypart. A high average quarter-hour figure usually means that people are listening and staying tuned in.

Bait-and-Switch Advertising (2) The illegal practice of baiting customers with an unusually low advertised price on a product which they are then unable to buy or discouraged from buying.

Basic Bus (15) In transit advertising, all the inside space on a group of buses, which thereby gives the advertiser complete domination.

BBB (2) The Better Business Bureau, a volunteer group of over 100,000 member companies, monitors business and advertising practices to protect consumers against fraud and deception.

Behavioristics (5) Method of determining market segments by dividing consumers into product-related groups based on their knowledge, attitude, use, or response to actual products or product attributes.

Benefit Headline (8) Type of headline that makes a direct promise to the reader.

Benefits Sought (5) Method of segmenting markets by determining the major benefits consumers seek in a product (high quality, low price, status, speed, sex appeal, good taste, etc.).

Bleed Page (13) A magazine advertisement in which the dark or colored background of the ad extends to the edge of the page. Most magazines offer bleed pages, but they normally charge advertisers a 10 to 15 percent premium for them.

Body Copy (8) The text of an advertisement which tells the complete story and attempts to close the sale. It is a logical continuation of the headline and subheads and is usually set in a smaller type size than headlines or subheads.

Boxes and Panels (8) A *box* is copy around which a line has been drawn, while a *panel* is an elongated box that usually runs the whole length or width of an ad. Boxes and panels are generally used in advertisements to set apart coupons, special offers, contest rules, and order blanks.

Brand (2) Name that identifies one particular product or line of products from a single source.

Brand Manager (3) The advertiser's person responsible for the success of a particular brand. The brand manager works with the division's advertising department to coordinate sales promotion and merchandising programs and has the support of the corporate advertising department's media and research supervisors for statistical information and guidance. In addition each brand manager normally has an advertising agency, which creates and places the brand's media advertising.

Broadcast Media (3) The electronic media of radio, television, and cable TV.

Broadside (15) A form of direct mail advertisement, larger than folders and sometimes used as a window display or wall poster in stores, which can be folded to a compact size and fit into a mail bag.

Broadside Approach (12) A media scheduling theory or method in which an equal number of messages are sent to each target audience group without regard to priority.

Business Advertising (1) Advertising directed at people in business who buy or specify products for business use.

Business Magazine (13) A periodical directed to a particular industry, trade, profession, or occupation such as farming.

Business Markets (5) Business or industrial markets are composed of manufacturers, utilities, government agencies, contractors, wholesalers, retailers, banks, insurance companies, and institutions that buy goods and services to help them in their own business.

Business Periodicals Index (6) An index for finding articles in selected business magazines.

Business Reply Mail (15) A type of mail that enables the recipient of direct-mail advertising to respond without paying postage and thereby tends to increase the rate of response.

Bus-O-Rama (15) In transit advertising, a jumbo roof sign, which is actually a full-color transparency backlighted by fluorescent tubes, running the length of the bus, with space for two advertisers on each side of the bus.

Cable TV (also, **CATV**) (3) Television signals carried to households by cable and paid for by subscription.

Call-outs (9) Small captions placed next to and describing particular elements in a photo or illustration.

Campaign Issue (19) The subject of argument or debate in political campaigns. The candidate's position on the important political issues are, in effect, sales features. The selection of issues as well as one's record on past issues is therefore a major marketing consideration for most politicians.

Caption (8) The words under a picture that describe the illustration.

Casting off (10) See *Copy casting.*

Catalog (15) Reference books mailed to prospective customers that list, describe, and often picture the products sold by a manufacturer, wholesaler, jobber, or retailer.

Central Location Test (6) Type of pretest in which videotapes of test commercials are shown to respondents on a one-to-one basis, usually in shopping center locations.

Centralized Advertising Department (3) A staff of employees, usually located at corporate headquarters, responsible for all the organization's advertising. The department is often structured by product, advertising subfunction, end user, media, or geography.

Cents-off Coupon (16) A certificate with a stated value that is presented to a retail store for a price reduction on a specified item. Coupons may be distributed in newspapers, magazines, door-to-door, on packages, and by direct mail.

Cents-off Promotions (16) A common sales promotion device designed to induce trial and usage. Cents-off promotions take different forms including basic cents-off packages, one-cent sales, free offers, and boxtop refunds.

Certification Mark (2) Guarantees the origin, trade, or quality of the product; for example, Teflon II.

Channels of Distribution (4)   See *Distribution channels*.

Circulation (12)   Total number of copies of an average issue of a newspaper or periodical that are distributed through subscriptions and newsstand sales.

Classified Advertising (13)   Newspaper and magazine advertisements usually arranged under subheads that describe the class of goods or the need that the ads seek to satisfy. Rates are based on the amount of space purchased and on how long the ad is run. Most employment, housing, and automotive advertising run today is in the form of classified advertising.

Clearance Advertising (17)   A type of local advertising designed to make room for new product lines or new models, or to get rid of slow-moving product lines, floor samples, broken or distressed merchandise, or items that are no longer in season.

Clients (3)   The different sellers advertising agencies work for in an effort to find customers for their goods and services.

Closed-circuit TV (18)   A television system that enables the distribution of live pictures and sound to specific receivers rather than for broadcasting (e.g., private political telecasts for fund-raising dinners).

Close-up (11)   A television or film shot in which one object or face fills the screen.

Closing Date (13)   The final date for supplying printing material to a medium for an advertisement.

Cognitive Dissonance (5)   Theory that people try to justify their behavior by reducing the degree to which their impressions or beliefs are inconsistent with reality.

Cold Type (10)   Modern method of typesetting characterized by high-speed electronic photocomposition equipment and operators schooled in computer technology.

Collateral Materials (4)   All the accessory nonmedia advertising materials prepared by companies to help achieve marketing or public relations objectives.

Collective Mark (2)   A mark used to indicate membership in an organization.

Column Inch (13)   In newspaper advertising, a measurement of depth one inch deep by one column wide. It is equivalent to 14 agate lines. Most newspapers now sell advertising space by the column inch.

Combination Offers (16)   A sales promotion device in which two related products are packaged together at a special price; e.g., a razor and a package of blades. Sometimes a combination offer may be used to introduce a new product by tying its purchase to an established product at a special price.

Combination Rate (13)   A special newspaper advertising rate offered for placing a given ad in (1) morning and evening editions of the same newspaper; (2) two or more newspapers owned by the same publisher; and (3) in some cases, two or more newspapers affiliated in a syndicate or newspaper group.

Command Headline (8)   A type of headline that orders the reader to do something. Command headlines attempt to motivate action through fear or emotion, or because the reader understands the inherent correctness of the command.

Commercial Advertising (1)   Advertising that promotes goods, services, or ideas for a business with the expectation of making a profit.

Comparative Pricing (4)   Pricing strategy that involves comparing the advertised low price with "normal" list prices in order to give the impression of overall discount prices.

Competitive Parity Method (7)   A method of allocating advertising dollars according to the amounts spent by the firm's major competitors.

Competitive Pricing (4)   Pricing strategy aimed at meeting or beating the prices of all competitors.

Compiled Lists (15)   A kind of direct-mail list that has been compiled for one reason or another by another source; e.g., lists of automobile owners, new-house purchasers, business owners, etc. It is the most readily available in volume but offers the lowest expectation.

Comprehensive Layout (9)   A facsimile of a finished ad with copy set in type and pasted into position along with proposed illustrations. The "comp" is prepared so the advertiser can gauge the effect of the final ad.

Concept Testing (6)   A type of advertising research used to develop thematic concepts for ads or campaigns.

Constituency (19)   The people who make up the electorate and are served by elected representatives.

Consumer Advertising (1)   Advertising directed at the ultimate consumer of the product or at the person who will buy the product for someone else's use.

Consumer Magazine (13)   A periodical directed to individuals or ultimate consumers who buy products for personal or nonbusiness use.

Consumer Purchase Tests (6)   Tests designed to measure the retail sales of a product that result from a given advertising campaign normally run in newspapers, regional editions of magazines, or on spot TV or radio.

Consumerism (2)   Social action designed to dramatize the rights of the buying public.

Contests (16)   A sales promotion device for creating consumer involvement in which prizes are offered based on the skill of the entrants.

Continuity (9) (12)   A media planning objective referring to the length of an advertising campaign and the manner in which it is scheduled and sustained over an extended period of time.

Contract (14)   A legal document used by radio and television stations. It states the dates, times, and programs on which the advertiser's commercials will run, the length of the spots, the rate per spot, and the total amount, and it defines the terms of payment and the various obligations and responsibilities of the advertiser, the agency, and the station.

Contract Rate (13) A special rate for newspaper advertising usually offered to local advertisers who sign an annual contract for frequent or bulk space purchases. As the number of inches contracted for increases, the rate decreases.

Contrast (9) The degree of difference between the lightest and darkest tones in photographs or on television. Contrast can also be created with the use of color, size of type or elements in an ad, or style.

Controlled Circulation (13) Free subscriptions to business publications given to individuals the publisher feels are in a position to influence buying decisions. Subscribers must ordinarily qualify by providing their title, job function, purchasing responsibilities, and similar details.

Cooperative Advertising (4) (16) The sharing of advertising costs by the manufacturer and the distributor or retailer. The manufacturer may repay 50 or 100 percent of the dealer's advertising costs or some other amount based on sales. Under the Robinson-Patman Act, the same terms must be extended to all distributors and dealers.

Copy (3) The words that make up the headline and message of an advertisement or commercial.

Copy Casting (10) The act of fitting type into the space designated for it in the layout by determining the number of characters in the copy. The two methods used for this are the word-count method and the character-count method.

Copy Platform (8) A document that serves as a guide for writing an ad. It describes the most important issues that should be considered in writing the copy, including a definition and description of the target audience in terms of demographic, psychographic, and behavioristic qualities; the rational and emotional appeals to be used; the product features that will satisfy the customer's needs; the support for the product claim; the product's position; the product's personality or image; the style, approach, or tone that will be used in the copy; and generally what the copy will say either verbally or nonverbally.

Copyright (2) Exclusive right granted by the Copyright Act to authors and artists to protect their original work from being plagiarized, sold, or used by another without their express consent.

Copyright Act of 1978 (2) Law providing for the protection of copyrights during the lifetime of the author plus 50 years after his or her death.

Copywriters (3) People who create the words and concepts for ads and commercials.

Corporate Advertising (18) The broad area of nonproduct advertising aimed specifically at enhancing company reputation, familiarity, and overall impression and improving lagging awareness.

Corporate Identification Program (18) An advertising campaign designed to familiarize the public with the name, logos and corporate signatures of an organization and its products or services.

Corporate Identity Advertising (18) Type of corporate advertising used to communicate a change in corporate name, logos, trademarks, or corporate signatures. Also used when companies need to communicate an ownership change or a change in corporate personality, or when the company is suffering from generally lagging awareness.

Corporate Objectives (7) Goals of the company stated in terms of profit or return on investment. Goals may also be stated in terms of net worth, earnings ratios, growth, or corporate reputation.

Cost Efficiency (12) The cost of reaching the target audience through a particular medium as opposed to the cost of reaching the medium's total circulation.

Cost per Rating Point (CPP) (14) A simple computation used by media buyers to determine which shows are the most efficient ones in relation to the target audience; determined by dividing the cost of the show by the show's expected rating against the target audience.

Cost per Thousand (CPM) (12) A common term describing the cost of reaching 1,000 people in a medium's audience. It is used by media planners to compare the cost of various media vehicles.

Cover Position (13) A special magazine advertising position on the inside front, inside back, and outside back covers (called the second, third, and fourth covers, respectively), which is almost always sold at a premium.

CPM (12) See *Cost per Thousand.*

Creative Boutique (3) (17) Organization of creative specialists (like art directors, designers, and copywriters) that works for advertisers and occasionally advertising agencies to develop creative concepts, advertising messages, and specialized art. A boutique performs only the creative work.

Creative Department (3) The department in an advertising agency that provides creative services such as copy and art.

Creative Mix (7) Those advertising elements that the company controls to achieve its advertising objectives including the product concept, the target audience, the communications media, and the advertising message.

CRT Typesetter (10) A modern type of typesetting equipment based on cathode-ray tube technology in which characters are stored digitally, retrieved from the computer's memory, and passed to a print CRT (similar to a television receiver tube) where they are lined up and then exposed through a lens system onto photosensitive paper or film.

Cume Audience (14) The capsule term for cumulative audience which describes the total number of different people listening to a radio station for at least one 15-minute segment over the course of a given week, day, or daypart. The number gives an indication of the reach potential of a radio schedule since a high cume figure means that a lot of different people are tuning in to the station for at least 15 minutes.

Dailies (13) One of the two basic types of newspapers, dailies are published at least five times a week, Monday through Friday, as either morning or evening editions. Some are published on Saturday and Sunday as well.

Day-after Recall (6) Audience recall measured the day after an advertisement is shown.

Dealer Displays (16) In-store displays, counter stands, and special racks designed to provide the retailer with ready-made, professionally designed vehicles for selling more of the featured products. Also called *point-of-purchase* advertising.

Dealer Premiums (16) Prizes and gifts used to get retail dealers and salespeople to reach specific sales goals or to stock or display a certain product.

Deals (16) Limited discounts offered to dealers on the cost of the product, special displays at reduced charges, or other dollar inducements to sell the product. Trade deals must comply with the Robinson-Patman Act by being offered on an equal basis to all dealers.

Decentralized Advertising Department (3) The establishment of advertising departments in various divisions, subsidiaries, products, countries, regions, brands, or whatever other categories most suit the firm's needs.

Demarketing (1) The marketing and advertising techniques used by producers of energy and energy-consuming goods to slow the demand for their products.

Demographics (5) The study of the numerical characteristics of the population.

Descenders (10) In typography, the stroke of a letter that drops below the base line; e.g., *p, g, y.*

Designated Market Areas (DMA) (14) The concept of a television market area, according to the Nielsen Station Index, similar to Arbitron's ADI method.

Dialogue/Monologue Copy (8) A type of body copy in which the characters illustrated in the advertisement do the selling in their own words either through a testimonial technique or through a comic strip panel.

Dichotomous Question (6) A question with only two response alternatives, such as a yes-no question.

Direct-action Advertising (1) Advertising intended to bring about immediate action on the part of the reader or viewer.

Direct Advertising (15) Any form of advertising issued direct to the prospect through the use of the mails, salespeople, dealers, or other means. It does not involve the traditional mass media.

Direct-entry Typesetting (10) A modern typesetting system that has all the input and output capabilities in one device.

Direct Inducement (16) Things such as money, prizes, extra products, gifts, or specialized information, which provide extra incentive to buy, visit the store, request literature, or take some other action.

Direct Mail (3) (15) The advertising medium that includes all forms of advertising sent direct to prospects through the U.S. Postal Service or private services. In dollars spent, direct mail is the third-ranked advertising medium today, surpassed only by newspapers and television.

Direct Mail Test (6) Method of pretesting advertisements through the use of direct mail. For example, two or more alternative ads can be tested by mailing each ad to different prospects on mailing lists. By keying (coding) each ad, the sources of the responses can be determined. The ad that generates the largest volume of orders is presumed to be the most effective.

Direct Marketing (4) (15) A marketing system in which the seller does not rely on the traditional channels of distribution but rather builds and maintains its own database of customers and uses a variety of media to communicate directly with those customers.

Directories (16) Locators, buying guides, and mailing lists published by telephone companies, trade associations, state and city agencies, Chambers of Commerce, newspapers, industrial groups, advertising services, and others, which also carry advertising aimed at the publishers' specialized fields.

Direct Questioning (6) A method of pretesting designed to elicit a full range of responses to the advertising. Direct questioning is especially effective for testing alternative advertisements in the early stages of development.

Direct Response Advertising (15) An advertising message that asks the reader, listener, or viewer for an immediate response. Direct response advertising can take the form of direct mail, or it can use a wide range of other media, from matchbook covers or magazines to radio or TV.

Display Advertising (13) Newspaper and magazine ads that normally use illustrations as well as type. They may range in size from small boxes to one- and two-page ads.

Display Type (10) Large, bold type, heavier than text type, used in headlines, subheads, logos, addresses, or wherever there is a need for emphasis in an advertisement.

Distribution Channel (4) Network of all the firms and

individuals that take title to the product, or assist in taking title to the product, as it moves from the producer to the consumer.

DMA (14) See *Designated Market Areas.*

DMA (15) Direct Marketing Association.

Dogmatic Message (12) A simple, easy-to-understand statement presented in an advertising headline as an indisputable fact; e.g. "When E. F. Hutton talks, people listen."

Dummy (9) A layout of a brochure or other multipage advertising piece. It is put together, page for page, just like the finished product will eventually appear.

Dupes (11) Copies of a finished television commercial that are delivered to the networks or TV stations for airing. (Also called *dubs.*)

Earned Rate (13) A special newspaper advertising rate offered to local advertisers (1) as a frequency discount earned when a given ad is run repeatedly during a specific period of time or (2) as a volume discount earned as the number of inches used within one year increases.

Electronic Media (3) Radio, television, and cable TV, also called broadcast media.

Empirical Research (7) A method of allocating funds for advertising that uses experimentation to determine the best level of advertising expenditure. By running a series of tests in different markets with different budgets, companies determine the most efficient level of expenditure.

End Users (5) The final users or consumers of a product.

Euphemism (8) The substitution of an inoffensive, mild word for a word that is offensive, harsh, or blunt.

Exclusive Distribution (4) Distribution strategy used to maintain prestige image and premium prices by granting exclusive rights to a wholesaler or retailer to sell in one geographic region.

Experimental Method (6) A method of research designed to measure actual cause-and-effect relationships.

Exploratory Research (6) A type of initial research used to learn more about the market, the competition, the business environment, and the problem before any formal research is undertaken.

Export Agency (20) Agencies that specialize in creating ads for American companies engaged in international advertising.

Exposure Value (12) A consideration in selecting media based on the number of people who actually see an advertisement in a given medium as opposed to the total audience of that medium. (Or, from another perspective, how many people an ad sees in a given medium.)

Eye Movement Camera (6) Instrument used chiefly to track the subject's eye movement over the layout and copy of advertisements to obtain information on the placement of headlines, the proper length of copy, and the most satisfactory layout.

Fair Package and Label Act (2) A truth-in-labeling law requiring manufacturers to state the contents of the package, who made it, and how much it contains.

Farm Advertising (1) Advertising directed to farmers as businesspeople and to others in the agricultural business. Also referred to as *agricultural advertising.*

Favorable Attitude Score (6) Result of posttest aimed at learning whether the reader of an ad is more favorably disposed toward the company, product, or service. These tests may use direct questions, wholly unstructured questions, depth interviews, or semantic differential tests.

FCC (Federal Communications Commission) (2) Federal regulatory body with jurisdiction over radio, television, telephone, and telegraph industries. Through its authority to license broadcasting stations and to remove a license or deny license renewal, the FCC has indirect control over broadcast advertising.

FDA (Food and Drug Administration) (2) Federal agency that has authority over the advertising, labeling, packaging, and branding of packaged foods and therapeutic devices.

Fee/Commission Method (3) Compensation method whereby the agency establishes a fixed monthly fee for all its services to the client and retains any commissions earned for space or time purchased on behalf of the client.

Field Study (6) Also referred to as *field test.* Type of testing technique that takes place in a respondent's home or in a public place as opposed to a laboratory setting.

First Class Mail (15) A U.S. Postal Service classification of mail delivery used by direct-mail advertisers to assure fast delivery, mail forwarding (at no additional charge), and return of undeliverable mail.

Flat Size (13) A magazine size measuring 7 by 10 inches.

Flight (12) A media scheduling term that describes a period of advertising activity scheduled between periods of inactivity.

Flyer (15) A form of direct-mail advertising that is usually a single, standard-size (8½ by 11 inches) page printed on one or both sides and folded one or more times. It often accompanies a sales letter to supplement or expand the information it contains.

Focus Groups (6) One of the most useful qualitative methods of research in which 8 to 10 people, "typical" of the target market, are invited to discuss the product, the service, or the marketing situation with a trained moderator in a free-wheeling discussion lasting an hour or more.

Food, Drug, and Cosmetic Act (2) Law that forbids

interstate commerce of adulterated or misbranded foods, drugs, devices, and cosmetics. The Food and Drug Administration enforces this act.

Foreign Agency (20) An advertising agency based in a foreign country employing a local staff that understands local attitudes and customers as well as the local media.

Foreign International Agency (20) A large foreign-based advertising agency with offices in several countries.

Foreign Media (20) The local media of foreign countries that cater to their own local markets in the language of that market.

Formal Balance (9) Perfect graphic symmetry with matched elements on either side of an ad to achieve equal optical weight. This is often used to create a dignified, stable, conservative image.

Four-color Plates (10) The printing plates used in four-color process. Since a printing plate can print only one color at a time, the printer must prepare four different printing plates, one for each color. Therefore, four separate continuous-tone negatives are produced to make a set of four-color plates: one for yellow, one for magenta, one for cyan, and one for black.

Four-color Process (10) The method for printing color advertisements with tonal values, such as photographs and paintings. This process is based on the principle that all colors can be printed by combining the three primary colors—yellow, magenta (red), and cyan (blue)—plus black (which provides greater detail and density as well as shades of gray).

Frames (11) The blank television screens on a typical preprinted storyboard sheet which are sketched in by the art director to represent the video. Also, any single image of motion picture film. Since film is projected at 24 frames per second, this means 1,440 frames must be shot for each minute of activity.

Free lancers (17) Advertising specialists who act as free agents often working out of their homes preparing copy, art and layout, photography, or other services.

Frequency (12) A measure of the intensity of a specific media schedule, frequency describes the number of times an advertising message reaches the same person or household. Across a total audience, frequency is calculated as the *average* number of times individuals or homes are exposed to the advertising.

Fringe (14) Refers to television dayparts immediately before and after prime time. Early fringe runs from 4 to 8 P.M. EST, and late fringe covers the 11 P.M. to 1 A.M. time.

FTC (Federal Trade Commission) (2) The major but not the sole federal regulator of advertising used to promote products sold in interstate commerce.

Full Position (13) In newspaper advertising, the preferred position near the top of a page or on the top of a column next to reading matter. It is usually surrounded by editorial text and may cost the advertiser 25 to 50 percent more in many newspapers.

Full-service Agency (3) An agency equipped to serve its clients in all areas of communication and promotion. Its advertising services include planning, creating, and producing advertisements, as well as performing research and media selection services. Nonadvertising functions include producing sales promotion materials, publicity articles, annual reports, trade show exhibits, and sales training materials.

Fund Raising (18) The activity of soliciting money for an organization or for a cause the organization deems worthwhile, such as the United Way or a political action committee (PAC).

Galvanometer (6) A device used to measure changes in sweat gland activity as a subject looks at an advertisement. Best used for testing advertisements for products people have strong feelings about.

Games (16) A sales promotion activity conducted over some period of time in which prizes are offered based on chance. Games include local bingo-type games designed to build store traffic. Their big marketing advantage is that customers must make repeat visits to the dealer to continue playing.

Gatefold (13) A magazine cover or page extended and folded over to fit into the magazine. The gatefold may be a fraction of a page or two or more pages, and it is always sold at a premium.

General Advertising Rate (13) The rate charged to general (national) advertisers by most newspapers. The national rate averages 51 percent higher than the local rate.

General Agency (3) An agency that is willing to represent the widest variety of accounts but concentrates on companies that make goods purchased chiefly by consumers.

Generic-market Objectives (7) Type of marketing objectives that view the organization as a satisfier of market needs rather than a producer of products.

Geographic Segmentation (5) Method of dividing a market along geographic lines.

Gimmick Copy (8) A type of body copy that depends on word plays, humor, poetry, rhyming, great exaggeration, gags, and other trick devices.

Global Marketing (20) The theory that, thanks to cheap air travel and new telecommunications technology, the world is becoming a common marketplace in which people have the same tastes and desires and want the same products and lifestyles no matter where they live—thus allowing for world-standardized products at low prices sold the same way around the world.

Government Advertising (1) (19) Advertising placed by government organizations: the Army, Navy, Marine Corps, Postal Service, Social Security Administration, Internal Revenue Service, and various state Chambers of Commerce.

Graphic Designer (9)   Designers responsible for the shape, dimension, and placement of the elements in an ad. The initial design of the ad will dictate its artistic direction and eventually determine whether that ad is to be stunning, beautiful, a "work of art," or just another ad.

Gross Rating Points (12) (14)   The total audience delivery or weight of a specific media schedule computed by multiplying the reach, expressed as a percentage, by the average frequency. In television, gross rating points are the total weight of a media schedule against TV households. For example, a weekly schedule of five commercials with an average household rating of 20 would yield 100 GRPs, or a total audience equivalent to the total number of TV households in the area. In outdoor advertising, a 100 gross rating point showing (also called a number 100 showing) covers a market fully by reaching 9 out of 10 adults daily over a 30-day period.

Group System (3)   System in which the agency is divided into a number of little agencies or groups, each composed of an account executive, a copywriter, an artist, a media buyer, and any other specialists that are needed for the particular clients being served by the group.

GRP (12) (14)   See *Gross Rating Points.*

Guaranteed Circulation (13)   The number of copies of a magazine that the publisher guarantees to advertisers will be delivered. If this figure is not reached, the publisher must give a refund.

Gunning Fog Index (8)   A technique for evaluating the ease of reading of a text.

Habit (5)   The natural extension of learning—an acquired or developed behavior pattern that has become nearly or completely involuntary.

Halftone Plates (10)   Printing plates used for printing continuous-tone artwork such as photographs or illustrations. Whereas line plates print lines and solid areas (like type), halftone plates print from dots.

Halftone Screen (10)   A glass or plastic screen, crisscrossed with fine black lines at right angles like a window screen, which breaks continuous-tone artwork into dots. The key element in making halftone plates, this screen is placed in the camera between the lens and the negative holder and, in effect, converts the artwork being photographed into a series of black dots. In the dark areas of the (halftone) photograph the dots are large, in the gray areas they are small, and in the white areas they almost disappear. The combination of big and little dots with a little or a lot of white space between them produces the illusion of shading in the photograph.

Handbills (17)   Low-cost flyers or other simple brochures distributed by hand to offices, local residences, or cars in parking lots.

Headline (8)   The words in the leading position of the advertisement—that is, the words that will be read first or that are positioned to draw the most attention.

Hierarchy of Needs (5)   Maslow's theory that the lower biologic or survival needs are dominant in human behavior and must be satisfied before higher, socially acquired needs become meaningful.

High Assay Principle (12)   A method or theory of media scheduling based on the mining principle of working the richest claim first. This method suggests that, to maximize reach, the advertiser should start with the medium that produces the best return and then move to other media only when the first becomes unavailable or loses its effectiveness.

Horizontal Publications (13)   Business publications targeted at people with particular job functions that cut across industry lines, such as *Purchasing* magazine.

Hot Type (10)   An old and obsolete method of metal type composition that formed letters by pouring molten lead into brass molds.

House Lists (15)   A company's most important and valuable direct-mail list which may contain current customers, recent customers, and long past customers or future prospects.

House Organs (15) (18)   Internal and external publications produced by business organizations including stockholder reports, newsletters, consumer magazines, and dealer publications. Most are produced by a company's advertising or public relations department, or by its agency.

Households Using TV (HUT) (14)   The percentage of homes in a given area that have one or more TV sets turned on at any particular time. If there are 1,000 TV sets in the survey area and 500 are turned on, the HUT figure is 50 percent.

HUT (14)   See *Households Using TV.*

Identity (19)   The public awareness or perception of an organization, company, or person. In political advertising, identity is the same as *name I.D.*, the primary objective of unknown candidates.

Illustrator (9)   The artist who paints, sketches, or draws the pictures we see in advertising.

Image (19)   The sum of the impressions about an organization, company, or individual as they are perceived in the mind of the public. In politics, for example, image refers to what voters think or feel about a candidate, either rightly or wrongly.

Imperceptible Differences (4)   Method of differentiating products by means that are not readily apparent without close inspection or use.

Impressions (12)   The total of all the audiences delivered by a media plan. Also called *total exposures*, it is calculated by multiplying the number of people who receive a message by the number of times they receive it.

Independent Shopping Guides (17)   Local advertising publications, often called shoppers or pennysavers, which are published as a forum for local advertisers and normally distributed free of charge by direct mail or by hand.

Indirect-action Advertising (1)   Advertising that attempts to build the image of a product or familiarity with the name and package in order to influence the audience to purchase a specific brand at some future time when they are in the market for that product.

Indirect Marketing (4)   Distribution strategy involving use of a network of middlemen.

Induced Differences (4)   Method of differentiating a product through unique branding, packaging, distribution, merchandising, and advertising.

Industrial Advertising (1)   Advertising aimed at individuals in business who buy or influence the purchase of industrial goods.

Industrial Agency (3)   An agency which represents client companies that make goods to be sold to other businesses.

Industrial Goods (1)   Products and services that are used in the manufacture of other goods or that become a physical part of another product. Industrial goods also include products that are used to conduct business and that do not become part of another product, like capital goods (office machines, desks, operating supplies) and business services for which the user contracts.

Informal Balance (9)   A type of visually balanced presentation achieved by placing elements of different size, shape, intensity of color, or darkness at different distances from the optical center.

In-home Projection Test (6)   Often called the ''black box'' method, a type of pretest in which commercials are run on a 16-mm projector in the respondents' homes. Questions are asked before and after exposure to the commercials in an effort to detect weaknesses in the commercials and to measure the effectiveness of the commercials in increasing brand awareness.

In-house Advertising Agency (3)   Agency wholly owned by the company, set up and staffed to do all the work of an independent full-service agency.

In-pack Premiums (16)   Sales promotion device, popular in the food field, in which inexpensive gifts are placed inside the package for the buyer; e.g., plastic toys for children.

Inquiry Tests (6)   A test of advertising based on responses such as inquiries or returns of coupons.

Insertion Order (13)   A form submitted to a newspaper or magazine when an advertiser wants to run an advertisement. This form states the date(s) on which the ad is to run, its size, the requested position, and the rate. It also states whether finished art, mechanicals, Velox prints, or mats will be furnished with the ad.

Inside Cards (15)   A transit advertisement normally 11" by 28" placed in a wall rack above the windows. Four other widths are available in multiples of 14 inches (11" by 14", 11" by 42", 11" by 56", and 11" by 84").

Institutional Advertising (17) (18)   A type of advertising that attempts to obtain favorable attention for the business as a whole, not for a specific product or service that the store or business sells. The effects of institutional advertising are intended to be long rather than short range. (Also called *corporate advertising*.)

Institutional Copy (8)   A type of body copy in which the advertiser tries to sell an idea or the merits of the organization or service rather than the sales features of a particular product.

Integrated Commercial (11)   A straight television or radio commercial, usually delivered by one person, woven into a show or tailored to a given program to avoid any perceptible interruption.

Intensive Distribution (4)   Distribution strategy for heavily advertised, high-volume, low-profit items like convenience goods to make them available for purchase at every possible location with a minimum of effort.

Intensive Techniques (6)   An extension of the interview method of research designed to probe the deeper feelings of the respondent.

International Advertising (1)   Advertising directed at foreign markets.

International Agency (20)   A large advertising agency with overseas offices usually staffed with multilingual, multinational personnel in both creative and administrative positions.

International Media (20)   Media that offer substantial audiences in a variety of foreign countries.

International Structure (20)   Organization of companies with foreign marketing divisions, typically decentralized with autonomous units in various foreign countries.

Island Half (13)   A half page of magazine space that is surrounded on two or more sides by editorial matter. This type of ad is designed to dominate a page and is therefore sold at a premium price.

Jingle (11)   Musical commercials, usually sung with the sales message in the verse.

Junior Page (13)   A magazine advertisement produced in a single size, whose dimensions are a full page in some publications and a partial page in larger-size publications, with editorial matter on two or more sides.

King Size Posters (15)   Transit advertisements (30" by 144") placed on the sides of buses, printed on high-grade cardboard, and often varnished to be weather-resistant.

Large Size (13)   A magazine measuring 9⅜ × 12⅛ inches.

Laser Scanning (10)   A recently developed electronic method of performing two- or four-color separations and screening in one process, along with enlargement or reduction. In addition, scanners are now used in digital color pagination systems, which perform all positioning of illustrative and text elements as well as electronic retouching.

Laser Typesetting (10) A modern computer-laser method of setting type in which type fonts and software programs can be stored digitally in a computer that also controls the on/off action of the laser beam as it "writes" onto (exposes) the output paper on film. No CRT is used. Extremely high speeds are possible as well as great reliability and versatility. Laser typesetters are usually able to output graphics and halftones besides type.

Layout (9) A pencil design and orderly formation of the parts of the advertisement within the specified dimensions. The layout will include the headline, subheads, illustration, copy, picture captions, trademarks, slogans, and signature (or logotype). The layout serves a mechanical function, working as a blueprint, to show where the parts of the ad are to be placed. It also serves a psychological or symbolic function, creating a feeling for the product or company.

Leading (10) The space between lines of type. Art directors may vary this space to give a slightly more airy or condensed feeling.

Lead Time (13) The length of time between the closing date for the purchase of advertising space or time and the publication or broadcast of the ad. Advertising in magazines requires long lead time—sometimes as long as three months. And once the closing date has been reached, no changes in copy or art can be allowed.

Learning (5) A relatively permanent change in behavior that occurs as a result of reinforced practices.

Letterpress (10) The old process of printing in which the ink is applied to a raised (relief) surface on a metal or plastic printing plate and transferred to the paper similar to the way a rubber stamp works. Like a stamp, the image to be transferred is backward ("wrong reading").

Libel (8) A printed false statement or allegation about a person or holding a person up to contempt in print.

Library of Congress (2) Federal body that registers and protects all copyrighted material, including advertising.

Line Drawings (9) Sometimes referred to as pen-and-ink drawings because everything is either black or white with no shades of gray, line drawings provide clear detail and sharpness. They are also less costly than drawings with tonal values.

Line Plates (10) The plates used to print solid black and white images (not tonal values) such as typeset copy, pen-and-ink drawings, or charcoal illustrations. (In the letterpress process, these are also known as line cuts, line etchings, and line engravings.)

Live Action (11) The basic production technique in television that portrays people in everyday situations.

Live Telecast Test (6) Type of test conducted on closed-circuit television, CATV stations, or non-network UHF stations in which commercials being studied are substituted for regular commercials on established TV programs.

Local Advertising (1) Advertising directed to customers and prospects in only one city or local trading area.

Local Rates (13) The lower rate charged by newspapers for local display advertising. The largest source of newspaper display revenue is local retail merchants. About 85 percent of all newspaper display advertising is local.

Logotype (8) Special designs of the advertiser's name (or product name) which appear as a *signature* in all advertisements and are like trademarks because they give the advertiser individuality and provide quick recognition at the point of purchase.

Loss-leader Pricing (4) Pricing strategy involving use of items advertised below cost in order to create store traffic and sell other regularly priced merchandise.

Lottery (16) An illegal sales promotion device. In contests and sweepstakes, no purchase can be required as a condition for entry, or else the sweepstakes becomes a lottery and therefore illegal.

Lowercase (10) See *Upper- and Lowercase.*

Macroeconomics (1) The large world of national and international economics.

Mail-order Advertising (15) A form of direct response advertising and a method of selling in which the product or service is promoted through advertising and the prospect orders it. Mail-order advertising is usually received in three distinct forms: catalogs, advertisements in magazines and newspapers, and direct-mail advertising.

Mail Response Lists (15) Type of direct-mail list, comprised of people who have responded to the direct-mail solicitations of other companies, especially those whose efforts are complementary to the advertiser's.

Majority Fallacy (4) A common marketing misconception that, to be successful, a product or service must appeal to the majority of people.

Makegoods (14) TV spots that are aired to compensate for spots that were missed or run incorrectly.

Market (4) A group of potential customers who share a common interest, need, or desire. The group must be able to use the product or service that is offered to some advantage, and they must be able to afford the purchase price.

Market Concentration (5) Refers to the reduced geographic target and the limited number of buyers for most industrial marketing efforts.

Market Research (6) Information about the market: its size, composition, structure, etc.

Market Segmentation (4) (5) The process of (1) categorizing customers into meaningful segments to determine which groups would be potentially profitable markets, (2) designing products specifically for those segments, and (3) aiming all marketing activities at those groups.

Marketing (4)   An umbrella business process that includes all activities aimed at: (1) finding out who customers are and what they want, (2) developing products to satisfy those customers' needs and desires, and (3) getting the products into the customers' possession.

Marketing Mix (4) (1)   Four elements, called the four Ps (product, price, place, and promotion), that every company has the option of adding, subtracting, or changing in order to create a desired marketing strategy.

Marketing Objectives (7)   Goals of the marketing effort that may be expressed in terms of (1) the needs of specific target markets and (2) specific sales objectives.

Marketing-oriented Period (4)   The modern marketing era in which companies determine in advance what customers want and then make products that will satisfy those desires.

Marketing Plan (7)   The plan that directs the company's marketing effort. It assembles and brings up to date all the pertinent facts about the organization, the markets it serves, its products, services, customers, and competition. It sets goals and objectives to be attained within specified periods of time and lays out the precise strategies that will be used to achieve them.

Marketing Research (6)   The systematic gathering, recording, and analyzing of data about problems relating to the marketing of goods and services.

Marketing Strategy (7)   The statement of how the company is going to accomplish its marketing objectives. The strategy is the total directional thrust of the company, the "how-to" of the marketing plan. It identifies the company's target markets and presents a marketing mix for each of those targets.

Markup (3)   Traditionally, the 17.65 percent that agencies add to the net cost of outside purchases in order to obtain a commission of 15 percent of the new gross amount.

Mass Distribution System (1)   The huge network of warehouses, transportation facilities, wholesalers, distributors, dealers, packing plants, advertising media, salespersons, clerks, and stores organized to deliver the low-priced, mass-produced goods from the manufacturer to the consumer.

Master Tape (11)   The final recording of a radio commercial, with all the music, sound, and vocals mixed, from which dubs (duplicates) are recorded and sent to radio stations for broadcast.

Matched Consumer Samples (6)   The matching of two or more groups of consumers in terms of demographic characteristics such as age, education, or occupation for the purpose of conducting controlled experiments.

Mechanical (9)   A large piece of white cardboard with the set type and the illustrations or photographs pasted into the exact position in which they will appear in the final ad. Also called a *paste-up*, this is then used as a direct basis for the next step in the reproduction process.

Media (1)   Plural of *medium*, referring to the *paid* means used to present an advertisement to its target audience.

Media Buying Service (3)   Organization of media specialists experienced in purchasing and packaging radio and television time.

Media Commission (3)   See *Agency Commission.*

Media Director (3)   The person who evaluates media according to efficiency and cost and then recommends the best medium or media combination to use.

Message Strategy (8)   The specific determination of what an ad or campaign will say and how it will say it. The elements of the message strategy include: copy (what you're going to say and how you're going to say it), art (what you're going to show and how you're going to show it), and production (what you're going to create mechanically and how you're going to create it).

Media Kit (18)   A package of material used to gain publicity at staged events such as press conferences or open houses. It includes a basic fact sheet detailing the event, a program for the event or a schedule of the activities, a list of the participants with biographical data, brochures prepared for the event, a news story for the broadcast media, and news and feature stories for print media.

Microeconomics (1)   Issues dealing with particular aspects of economics such as the costs and revenues of individual enterprises.

Microencapsulation (13)   The storage of the smell or scent (microfragrance) of such things as perfume, soap, and cologne on paper and other substances so that when the paper is scratched, the odor is emitted.

Middleman (4)   A business firm that operates between the producer and the consumer or industrial purchaser.

Mixed Interlock (11)   The earliest edited version of a filmed television commercial mixed with the finished soundtrack. Used for initial review and approval prior to finishing the editing process.

Mnemonic Device (11)   Literally, a device used to assist the memory. Often a gimmick is used to dramatize the product benefit and make it memorable; e.g., the Imperial Margarine crown or the Avon doorbell.

Mock Magazine Test (6)   Type of test in which ads being studied are "stripped into" an actual magazine and left with respondents for a time. They are told to read the magazine, including the ads that interest them. Afterward the respondents are questioned about the test ads.

MOR (14)   Middle of the road. A radio programming format featuring popular music, past and present, that appeals to a somewhat older (25–49), more affluent audience.

Motivation (5)   The underlying drives that stem from the conscious or unconscious needs of the consumer and contribute to the individual consumer's purchasing actions.

Motivation Value (12)   A consideration in selecting

media based on the characteristics of a particular medium which might enhance that medium's ability to motivate its audience to action; e.g., good quality reproduction or timeliness.

Movement (9)   The principle of graphic design that causes the reader of an advertisement to read the material in the sequence desired.

MPA (13)   See *Magazine Publishers Association.*

Multinational Advertisers (20)   Corporations with full and integrated participation in world markets and a view toward business based on choices available anywhere in the world. The multinational's marketing activities are typically characterized by strong centralized control and coordination. (See also *International Structure.*)

NAB (2) (13)   See *Newspaper Advertising Bureau.*

NAD (2)   The National Advertising Division of the National Advertising Review Council, a self-regulatory body, investigates and monitors advertising industry practices.

Name I.D. (19)   In political advertising, having one's name known by or at least familiar to voters. (See also *Identity.*)

NARB (2)   The National Advertising Review Board is a five-member panel, composed of three advertisers, one agency representative, and one layperson, selected to review decisions of the NAD.

Narrative Copy (8)   A type of body copy that tells a story. It sets up a problem and then creates a solution using the particular sales features of the product or service as the key to the solution.

National Advertising (1)   Advertising aimed at customers in various parts of the country.

National Retail Merchants Association (17)   A national organization of retailers aimed at assisting the retail business. The Association publishes an extensive list of materials on research topics of interest to retailers.

Networks (3) (14)   Any of the national broadcasting chains or companies such as Columbia Broadcasting System (CBS), National Broadcasting Company (NBC), or American Broadcasting Company (ABC). Networks offer the large advertiser convenience and efficiency because the message can be broadcast simultaneously throughout the country.

News/Information Headline (8)   A type of headline that includes many of the "how-to" headlines as well as headlines that seek to gain identification for their sponsors by announcing some news or providing some promise of information.

News Release (18)   A typewritten sheet of information (usually 8½ by 11 inches) issued to print and broadcast outlets to generate publicity or shed light on a subject of interest.

Nielsen Station Index (14)   One of the most commonly

used rating services for TV which publishes a wide array of statistics on how many people, in what age groups, and of what sex are watching TV at various times of the day within a specific market area.

Nonbusiness Institutions (19)   Nonprofit organizations whose primary objective is noncommercial: churches, schools, universities, hospitals, charitable organizations, etc.

Noncommercial Advertising (1) (19)   Advertising sponsored by or for a charitable institution, civic group, religious order, political organization, or some other nonprofit group to promote an idea, a philosophy, an attitude, a social cause, or a political issue.

Nonprobability sample (6)   Research samples that do not provide every unit in the universe with an equal chance of being included. As a result, there is no guarantee that the sample will be representative; however, nonprobability samples are less expensive to conduct.

Nonproduct Advertising (1)   Advertising designed to sell ideas or a philosophy rather than products or services.

Observational Method (6)   A method of research used when researchers actually monitor the overt actions of the person being studied.

Offset Lithography (10)   A modern printing process in which the image is transferred from the printing plate to an intermediate rubber surface called a blanket, which comes in contact with the paper and enables the image to be printed.

On-camera (11)   Actually seen by the camera, as an announcer, a spokesperson, or actors playing out a scene.

On-pack Premium (16)   Premiums designed to have a good impulse value attached to the outside of the package. Sometimes they may encourage pilferage or make it difficult for the grocer to stack the product on the shelves.

Open House (18)   A public relations activity in which a company opens its doors to the public to build goodwill and give the community a greater understanding of its inner workings.

Open Rate (13)   The highest newspaper advertising rate for one-time insertions.

Opinion Leader (5)   Someone whose beliefs or attitudes are considered right by people who share an interest in some specific activity.

Order of Merit Tests (6)   Type of test in which two or more advertisements are shown to potential prospects with instructions to arrange the ads in rank order of preference.

Out-of-home Media (3)   Media like outdoor advertising (billboards) and transit advertising (bus and car cards) which reach prospects outside of their homes.

Outside Posters (15)   The variety of transit advertisements appearing on the outside of buses, including:

king size, queen size, traveling display, taillight spectacular, and headlights.

Overspill Media (20)   Foreign media aimed at a local national population that is inadvertently received by a substantial portion of the population of a neighboring country.

Painted Displays (15)   Large, outdoor painted bulletins and walls, normally 14' by 48' or larger, meant for long use and usually placed in only the best locations where traffic is heavy and visibility is good. Usually illuminated, painted displays often feature three-dimensional cutouts, plastic facing, back-lighting, moving messages, and other variations.

Paired Comparison Method (6)   Type of test in which each advertisement is compared with every other advertisement in the group. Only two ads are evaluated at any one time.

Participation (14)   The basis on which most network television advertising is sold. Advertisers can participate in a program once or several times on a regular or irregular basis by buying 30- or 60-second segments within the program. This allows the advertiser to spread out the budget and makes it easier to get in and out of a program without a long-term commitment.

Paste-up (9)   See *Mechanical* and *Production Artist.*

Patent and Trademark Office (2)   Federal office that registers and protects all patents and trademarks.

Peaking (19)   In political marketing and advertising, reaching the highest level of identity, image, and popularity. The objective of all timed activities is to "peak" the day before the election.

Penetration Pricing (4)   Pricing strategy often used by new businesses in which low prices are offered initially in order to penetrate the market quickly by creating immediate traffic and sales.

Percentage of Profit Method (7)   A method of advertising allocation similar to percentage of sales except that the proponents of this method deal with profit dollars rather than with before-profit dollars.

Percentage of Sales Method (7)   A method of advertising allocation based on a percentage of sales—either the previous year's, the anticipated sales for the next year, or a combination of the two.

Perceptible Differences (4)   Method of differentiating products by means that are visibly apparent to the consumer.

Perception (5)   The sensing of stimuli to which an individual is exposed—the act or process of comprehending the world in which the individual exists.

Perceptual Meaning Studies (PMS) (6)   Type of test in which ads are shown at controlled exposures using a tachistoscope. Respondents are questioned on recall of product, brand, illustration, copy, and the main idea of the ad.

Personal Selling (4)   Sales method based on person-to-person contact, such as by a salesperson at a retail establishment or by a telephone solicitor.

Photo Animation (11)   An animation technique that uses still photography instead of illustrations or puppets. By making slight movements of the photos from one frame to the next, the animated illusion is created. Especially effective for making titles move.

Photocomposition (10)   The most dominant method of producing typesetting materials today, photocomposition is a combination of computer technology and electronics. It offers an almost unlimited number of typefaces and sizes, faster reproduction at lower cost, and improved clarity and sharpness of image.

Photo-optic Typesetters (10)   Type of typesetting equipment that uses an electromechanical method of projecting characters through a lens, which magnifies the characters to the desired size. This image is then reflected off a mirror onto photosensitive paper or film, thus setting the characters.

Photoplatemaking (10)   A process for making printing plates, similar to taking a picture, in which an image is photographed, and the negative is printed in reverse on a sensitized metal plate rather than on paper. This plate is then used for printing.

Physiological Testing (6)   The use of pupilometric devices, eye-movement cameras, galvanometer, tachistoscopes, and electroencephalographs to measure unconscious responses to advertisements.

Pica (10)   The unit of measurement for the horizontal width of lines of type. There are six picas to the inch and 12 points to the pica.

Picture Caption Copy (8)   A type of body copy in which the story is told through a series of illustrations and captions rather than through the use of a copy block alone.

PMS (6)   See *Perceptual Meaning Studies.*

Pocket size (13)   A magazine size measuring 4½ by 6½ inches.

Point of Purchase (16)   Advertising or display materials set up at the retail location to build traffic, advertise the product, and promote impulse buying. Includes window displays, counter displays, floor and wall displays, streamers, and posters.

Point (10)   The unit of measurement for the depth (or height) of type. There are 72 points to the inch, so 1 point equals ½₂ of an inch.

P-O-P (16)   See *Point of Purchase.*

Portfolio Test (6)   A method of testing in which ads being studied are interspersed with other ads and editorial matter in an album-type portfolio. Consumers in an experimental group are shown this portfolio; consumers in a closely matched control group are shown the portfolio without the test ads. Afterward members of both groups are questioned to determine their recall of the portfolio contents and the advertisements being tested.

Position Paper (18)   A formal statement of a company's views on an issue of social, political, or public importance—often issued in conjunction with a speech. Occasions for position papers may be congressional hearings, annual stockholders' meetings, and important conferences and conventions.

Positioning (1)   The way in which a product is ranked in the consumer's mind in relation to the competition or certain target markets.

Poster Panels (15)   The basic form of outdoor advertising and the least costly per unit, a poster is a structure of blank panel with a standardized size and border, usually anchored in the ground, with its advertising message printed by lithography or silkscreen and mounted by hand on the panel.

Postproduction (11)   All the work done after the day of shooting to finish a television commercial. Includes editing, processing film, recording sound effects, mixing audio and video, and duplicating final films or tapes.

Posttesting (6)   The fourth stage of advertising research designed to determine the effectiveness of an advertisement or campaign *after* it runs. The findings obtained from posttesting can provide the advertiser with useful guidelines for future advertising.

Preferred Position (13)   A choice position for a newspaper or magazine ad for which a higher rate is charged.

Premium (16)   An item that is offered free or at a bargain price to encourage the consumer to buy an advertised product. Premiums are intended to produce quick sales.

Preprinted Inserts (13)   Newspaper advertisements printed in advance by the advertiser and then delivered to the newspaper plant to be inserted into a specific edition. Preprints are inserted into the fold of the newspaper and look like a separate, smaller section of the paper. Sizes range from a typical newspaper page to a piece no larger than a double postcard.

Preproduction (11)   All the work done prior to the actual day of filming a television commercial, including casting, arranging for locations, estimating costs, obtaining necessary permissions, selecting technical suppliers and production companies, and finding props and costumes.

Press Agentry (18)   The planning of activities and the staging of events in order to attract attention to new products or services and to generate publicity about the company or organization that will be of interest to the media.

Prestige Pricing (4)   Pricing strategy that aims at a select clientele who can afford to pay higher prices in exchange for convenience, service, and quality.

Pretesting (6)   The third stage of advertising research used to increase the likelihood of preparing the most effective advertising messages.

Price/Quality Differentiation (7)   A type of product differentiation strategy based on differences in price and quality. For example, a company could offer a better quality product at a higher price, or it could advertise the same quality at a lower price.

Primary Data (6)   Research information gained directly from the marketplace. There are basically three alternatives in collecting primary data: observation, experiment, and survey.

Primary Demand (4)   Type of marketing and advertising strategy aimed at stimulating consumer demand for a whole product category. To educate the consuming public about the new product, advertising will stress information about what the product does and how it works.

Prime Time (14)   The highest TV viewing time of the day, namely 7:30 to 11 P.M.

Print Media (3)   Any commercially published medium (like a newspaper or magazine) that sells advertising space to a variety of advertisers.

Probability Sample (6)   A sampling procedure in which every unit in the universe has an equal and known probability of being selected for the research.

Product Advertising (1)   Advertising intended to promote products and services.

Product Concept (4)   The "bundle" of values built into a product which are aimed at satisfying various functional, social, psychological, economic, and other consumer needs.

Product Differentiation (4)   A strategic, modern marketing concept based on building unique differences into products in order to satisfy consumer demand.

Product Life Cycle (4)   Progressive stages in the life of a product—including introduction, growth, maturity, and decline—that affect the way a product is marketed and advertised.

Production (10) (11)   The process of converting ideas, scripts, sketches, copy, etc., into finished advertisements, brochures, films, and commercials. Also, the actual day (or days) that a television commercial is filmed or videotaped.

Production Artist (9)   The person responsible for assembling the various elements of an ad and mechanically putting them together the way the art director or designer indicated. Also called *paste-up* artist.

Production Manager (3)   The person responsible for producing the finished advertisement or commercial according to the concept and direction of the copywriter and art director.

Production-oriented Period (4)   An era when there were few products and many consumers, and companies only had to worry about creating and producing enough products to satisfy the huge demand. At this time the emphasis in marketing was on distribution and transportation.

Professional Advertising (1)   Advertising directed at individuals who are normally licensed and operate under a code of ethics or professional set of standards.

Profile Matching (12)   A method or theory of media scheduling in which the schedule is split so that messages are delivered to each segment of the target audience in proportion to that segment's importance among all prospects.

Program Rating (14)   The percentage of TV households in an area that are tuned in to a specific program.

Programming (14)   The wide variety of radio station formats, like rock, easy listening, all news, middle of the road (MOR), sports, and classical music which are carefully planned in order to reach specific markets and capture as many listeners as possible. The larger its audience, the more a station can charge advertisers for commercial time.

Promotion (18)   The marketing-related communication between the seller and the buyer. For profit-making organizations, promotion means using advertising and public relations techniques as a means of selling a product or service as well as enhancing the reputation of an organization.

Promotion Element (4)   See *Promotional Mix.*

Promotional Mix (4)   Those activities usually considered elements of the promotional strategy including personal selling, advertising, public relations, sales promotion, and collateral materials.

Promotional Pricing (4)   Pricing strategy for introducing a new line of equipment or clearing out old lines by using typical retail efforts like two-for-one sales or end-of-month sales in order to maintain traffic, stimulate demand, or make room for new merchandise.

Promotional Pulse (12)   A method of media scheduling designed to support some special promotion of the advertiser or manufacturer so that buying will be heavier during the time of the promotion than at other times.

Proof Copy (13)   A copy of a newspaper-created ad provided to the advertiser for checking purposes before the ad runs.

Proportion (9)   The space accorded the elements in an advertisement. For best appearance, elements frequently use varying amounts of space to avoid the monotony of equal amounts of space for each element.

Provocative Headline (8)   A type of headline written to provoke the reader's curiosity so that, in order to learn more, the reader will read the body copy.

Psychographic Segmentation (5)   The classification of consumers into market segments on the basis of psychological makeup—namely, personality, attitude, and lifestyle.

Public Affairs (18)   All activities related to the community citizenship of an organization including dealing with community officials and working with regulatory bodies and legislative groups.

Public Relations (4)   Communications activities usually not overtly sponsored that act as supplements to advertising to inform various audiences about the company and its products and to help build corporate credibility and image.

Public Relations Advertising (18)   A type of advertising used to communicate directly with a company's important publics in order to express its feelings, enhance its point of view, promote a program sponsorship, or improve relations with labor, government, customers, or suppliers. This kind of advertising is designed to enhance the company's general community citizenship and create public goodwill.

Public Relations Specialist (3)   A person who is a public relations practitioner and acts as a communications link between an organization and its various publics.

Publicity (18)   The generation of news about a person, product, or service that appears in broadcast or print media and is usually thought of as being "free" because the medium has no publicity rate card.

Pull Strategy (16)   Marketing, advertising, and sales promotion activities aimed at inducing trial, purchase, and repurchase by consumers.

Pulse (12)   A periodic schedule of advertising interspersed between periods of inactivity, usually during peak selling periods.

Pupilometric Device (6)   A device that measures the dilation of the pupil of a subject's eye in an effort to gauge the subject's reaction to ads, graphic designs, and packages.

Purchase Cycle (12)   The period or space of time between consumer purchase and repurchase. In some cases, the purchase cycle is very regular, while in others it may be erratic but susceptible to influence by advertising; the advertiser's objective is to try to reduce the length of time between purchases.

Purchase Occasion (5)   Method of segmenting markets by *when* they buy and use a product or service.

Push Money (16)   An inducement for retail salespeople to push the sale of particular products. (Also called *Spiffs.*)

Push Strategy (16)   Marketing, advertising, and sales promotion activities aimed at getting products into the dealer pipeline and accelerating sales by offering inducements to dealers, retailers, and salespeople. Inducements might include introductory price allowances, distribution allowances, and advertising dollar allowances to stock the product and set up displays.

Qualitative Research (6)   A type of research that is usually exploratory or diagnostic in nature, involving small numbers of people surveyed on a nonprobability basis to gain impressions rather than definitions.

Quantitative Research (6)   A type of data collection method used by market researchers to develop hard numbers so they can completely and accurately measure a particular market situation.

Question Headline (8)   A type of headline that asks the reader a question.

RADAR Report (14)   Radio's All-Dimension Audience Research audience estimates (ratings) are based on daily telephone interviews that cover seven days of radio listening behavior.

Radio Dayparts (14)   The five basic dayparts into which the radio day is divided: morning drive, daytime, afternoon drive, nighttime, all night. The rating services measure the audiences for only the first four of these dayparts, as all-night listening is very limited and not highly competitive.

Rate Card (13)   A printed information form listing the newspaper's advertising rates, mechanical and copy requirements, advertising deadlines, and other information the advertiser needs to know before placing an order.

Rating Services (14)   The research organizations which, through various techniques, furnish data on the size and characteristics of the audiences that view or listen to radio and TV programs for advertisers and broadcasters. Companies interested in their findings subscribe to the service and use it as a basis in making media plans for advertising.

Reach (12)   The number of different people or households that are exposed to an advertising schedule during a given time, usually four weeks. Reach measures the *unduplicated extent* of audience exposure to a media vehicle and may be expressed either as a percentage or as a raw number.

Reading Notice (13)   A variation of a display ad designed to look like editorial matter. It is sometimes charged at a higher space rate than normal display advertising, and the law requires that the word "advertisement" appear at the top.

Ready-made Posters (15)   Stock 30-sheet posters made available by manufacturers at low cost to local advertisers such as florists, dairies, banks, bakeries, and others. They often feature the work of first-class artists and lithographers.

Reason-why Message (12)   An advertising approach that explains the product's advantages; e.g., "Lite. Everything you always wanted in a beer. And less."

Recruitment Advertising (18)   A special type of advertising, most frequently found in the classified sections of daily newspapers and typically the responsibility of the personnel department, aimed at attracting employment applications.

Reference Groups (5)   Groups of people we try to emulate or with whom we are concerned about our own appearance.

Regional Advertising (1)   Advertising for products sold in only one area or region of the country. The region might cover several states but not the entire nation.

Regular Price-line Advertising (17)   A type of retail advertising designed to inform consumers about the services available or the wide selection and quality of merchandise offered at regular prices.

Reliability (6)   An important characteristic of research test results. For a test to be reliable it must be repeatable, producing the same result each time it is administered.

Rep Firm (3)   Independent firms that contract with newspapers, magazines, and radio and television stations to represent them on the national level.

Reprints (15)   Duplications of publication articles that show the company or its products in a favorable light used as direct-mail enclosures and frequently sent by public relations agencies or departments.

Retoucher (10)   The artist who alters photographs used in advertising and on magazine covers in order to add desired elements or subtract undesired elements.

Robinson-Patman Act (2)   Law prohibiting price discrimination that lessens competition or tends to create a monopoly.

Roman Type (10)   The most popular type group, it is considered the most readable and offers the greatest number of designs, which means that contrast can be achieved without a basic design change. It is characterized by the serifs (or tails) that cross the ends of the main strokes and the variations in the thickness of the strokes.

ROP (13)   Run of paper. A term referring to the newspaper's normal discretionary right to place a given ad on any newspaper page or in any position it desires—in other words, where space permits. Most newspapers, however, make an effort to place an ad in the position requested by the advertiser.

Rotary Plan (15)   In outdoor advertising the rotation of painted bulletins to different choice locations in the market every 30, 60, or 90 days, giving the impression of wide coverage over time.

Rotogravure (10)   A printing process that works in the reverse of letterpress. Instead of the printing design being raised above the printing plate as in letterpress, the rotogravure process prints from a depressed surface. Ink in the tiny depressions is transferred to the paper by pressure and suction.

Rough Layout (9)   A pencil drawing of the proposed ad drawn to actual size. The headlines and subheads are lettered onto the layout, the artwork and intended photographs are drawn, and the body copy is simulated with pencil lines.

Sale Advertising (17)   A type of retail advertising designed to stimulate the movement of particular merchandise or generally increase store traffic by placing the emphasis on special reduced prices.

Sales Letters (15)   The most common form of direct mail, sales letters may be typewritten, typeset and printed, printed with a computer insert (such as your name), or fully computer-typed.

Sales-oriented Period (4)   An era when the marketplace was glutted with products and the selling function was characterized by business' use of extravagant advertising claims and an attitude of *caveat emptor* ("let the buyer beware").

Sales Promotion (4)   A direct inducement offering extra incentive all along the marketing route—from manufacturers through distribution channels to consumers—to accelerate the movement of the product from the producer to the consumer. A broad promotional category that covers nonmedia advertising activities like sweepstakes, contests, premiums, etc.

Sales-target Objectives (7)   Marketing objectives that relate to the company's sales. They should be specific as to product and market, quantified as to time and amount, and realistic. They may be expressed in terms of total sales volume; sales by product, market segment, or customer type; market share; growth rate in total or by product line; or even gross profit.

Sales Tests (6)   Methods used to obtain information on the sales-producing value of specific ads or whole campaigns. These include six types: measures of past sales, controlled experiments, matched samples of consumers, mail-order selling, consumer purchase tests, and store inventory audits.

Sample (6)   A portion of the population selected by marketing researchers to represent the appropriate targeted population. Theories of sampling are drawn from the mathematical theories of probability. If a sample is to be considered adequate, it must be large enough to achieve satisfactory precision or stability. Naturally, the larger the sample size, the more reliable the results.

Sampling (16) (17)   The most costly of all sales promotions, sampling offers consumers a free trial of the product, hoping to convert them to habitual use.

Sans Serif (10)   The second most popular type group, it is also referred to as *block, contemporary,* or *gothic*. This large group of typefaces is characterized by (1) the lack of serifs (thus the name, sans serif) and (2) the relatively uniform thickness of the strokes.

Satellite Station (14)   A special type of TV station like Ted Turner's WTBS (see Chapter 3) that originates some minor programming of its own but primarily duplicates a major portion of the broadcasts of a parent station by relaying it to a satellite which then broadcasts it nationally.

SBA (Small Business Administration) (17)   A governmental agency designed to assist small businesses, the SBA publishes a wealth of information, most of it free or available for only a nominal charge.

Scratchboard (9)   A distinctive and different type of illustration that gives the impression of fine workmanship. On a special paper with a surface specifically made for this art form, black ink is applied to the area of the illustration. With the use of a scratching device (a stylus or other sharp instrument), the ink is removed and a white line remains.

Screen Printing (10)   An old printing process that requires no plates and is based on the stencil principle. As ink is squeezed through a special stencil screen stretched tightly on a frame, the desired image is reproduced. For printing in color, a separate stencil is made for each color.

Seal (8)   A type of certification mark offered by such organizations as the Good Housekeeping Institute and Underwriters' Laboratories when a product meets standards established by these institutions. Seals provide an independent, valued endorsement for the advertised product.

Seasonal Pulse (12)   A media scheduling method based on seasonal buying patterns which dictate heavy media use during peak selling periods; e.g., suntan oil, snow tires.

Secondary Data (6)   Data that already exist somewhere, having been collected for some other purpose.

Selective Demand (4)   Type of marketing and advertising strategy aimed at impressing customers with the subtle advantages of one brand over another.

Selective Distribution (4)   Distribution strategy in which manufacturers can cut their costs of distribution and promotion by selling through only a limited number of outlets.

Selective Perception (5)   The ability of humans to select from the many sensations bombarding their central processing unit those that relate to their previous experiences, needs, or desires.

Self-concept (5)   The images we carry in our minds of who we are and who we want to be.

Self-liquidating Premiums (16)   A special offer in which the consumer pays the cost of the premium plus handling charges. The seller does not attempt to make a profit on such a premium but only tries to break even.

Self-mailers (15)   Any form of direct mail that can travel by mail without an envelope. Such mailers are usually folded and secured by a staple or seal with a special blank space for the prospect's name and address.

Semantic Differential (6)   A type of survey question often used in image profiling that employs a scaling device of several pairs of bipolar adjectives and asks the respondent to rate the topic or subject on each scale.

Serifs (10)   Delicate curved tails that cross the end of each letter stroke of roman type.

Service Mark (2)   The name or symbol that identifies a service rather than a product.

Share of Audience (12) (14)   The percentage of homes

that have sets in use (HUT) tuned in to a specific program. A program with only five viewers could have a 50 share if only 10 sets are turned on.

Share of Market Method (7) A method of allocating advertising funds based on determining the firm's goal for a certain share of the market and then applying the same percentage of industry advertising dollars to the firm's budget.

Sherman Antitrust Act (2) Law prohibiting monopolies or any attempts to monopolize as well as any contract, combination, or conspiracy in restraint of trade.

Short Rate (13) The rate charged to advertisers who, during the year, fail to fulfill the amount of space for which they have contracted. This is computed by determining the difference between the standard rate for the lines run and the discount rate contracted.

Showing (15) A traditional term referring to the relative number of outdoor posters used during a contract period indicating the intensity of market coverage. For example, a 100 showing provides an even and thorough coverage of the entire market.

Signature (8) See *Logotype.*

Simmons Report (14) One of the most commonly used services for demographic studies of TV audiences.

Situation Analysis (7) A statement in the marketing plan of where the organization is and how it got there. It includes relevant facts about the company's history, growth, products or services, sales volume, share of market, competitive status, market served, distribution system, past advertising programs, results of market research programs, company capabilities, and strengths and weaknesses.

Skimming Pricing (4) Pricing strategy that employs use of high prices in order to quickly recover the money invested by manufacturers in developing a new product or by retailers in furnishing, decorating, stocking, and promoting their store.

Slander (8) Defamation of a person in broadcast advertising or verbal statements.

Slice of Life (11) A type of commercial consisting of a short play that portrays a real-life situation in which the product is tried and becomes the solution to a problem.

Slogan (8) A standard company statement or tag line for advertisements, salespeople, and company employees. Slogans have two basic purposes: (1) to provide continuity for a campaign and (2) to reduce a key theme or idea the company wants associated with its product or itself to a brief, memorable positioning statement.

Special Events Management (18) The planning, staging, and supervision of activities such as the grand opening of a new store, an autograph party for an author, the announcement of a new product, or the groundbreaking for a new public library.

Specialty Advertising (16) See *Advertising Specialty.*

Speculative Presentation (3) A presentation by competing agencies of the advertisements they propose using in the event they are hired. These presentations are usually made at the request of a prospective client, but not paid for by the client, and are therefore generally considered unethical and unprofessional.

Split Run (13) A feature of many newspapers (as well as magazines) that allows advertisers to test the comparative effectiveness of two different advertising approaches by running two different ads of identical size, promoting the same product or service, in the same or different press runs on the same day.

Sponsorships (14) The presentation of a radio or TV program by a sole advertiser. The advertiser is responsible for the program content and the cost of production as well as the advertising. This is generally so costly that single sponsorships are usually limited to specials.

Spot Announcement (14) An individual commercial message run between programs but having no relationship to either.

Spot Radio (14) National advertisers' purchase of airtime on individual stations. Buying spot radio affords advertisers great flexibility in their choice of markets, stations, airtime, and copy. In addition, spot advertising enables the message to be tailored to the local market and presented to listeners at the most favorable times.

Spot Television (14) Individual television commercials sold either nationally or locally in segments of 10, 20, 30, or 60 seconds. National spot advertising offers the advertiser greater flexibility since commercials can be concentrated on the markets most likely to pay off, and they are less expensive than participations because they are run in clusters between programs. Advertisers with limited distribution and budgets find this advantageous. Most advertising time of network affiliates is sold in this way.

SRDS (13) See *Standard Rate and Data Service.*

Standard Advertising Unit (SAU) (13) A system of 25 standardized newspaper advertisement sizes that can be accepted by all standard-sized newspapers without consideration of their precise format or page size. This system allows advertisers to prepare one advertisement in a particular size or SAU and place it in various newspapers, regardless of the format.

Standard Rate and Data Service (13) (14) (15) A publisher of media information directories that eliminate the necessity for advertisers and their agencies to obtain rate cards for every publication.

Standard Size (13) A newspaper size generally 22 inches deep and 14 inches wide. This type of newspaper has usually been eight columns wide, although the recent trend has been toward a six-column layout and a slightly reduced page size.

Start-up Pulse (12) A media scheduling method designed to start off a campaign with a bang. Used to introduce new products, it is also seen every year when the new automobile models are introduced.

Statement Stuffers (15)   Advertisements that are enclosed in the monthly customer statements mailed by department stores, banks, or oil companies.

Stimulus-response Theory (5)   Theory that treats learning as a trial-and-error process whereby needs, motives, or drives are triggered by some cue to cause the individual to respond in an effort to satisfy the need.

Stop Motion (11)   An animation technique whereby objects and animals come to life—walk, run, dance, and do tricks—by means of stop-motion photography. Each frame of film is shot individually. An arm may be moved only $\frac{1}{32}$ of an inch on each frame, but when the frames are assembled the effect is smooth and natural.

Store Inventory Audit (6)   Type of sales test in which an inventory of retailers' stocks is conducted before and after an advertising campaign. Such an audit generally includes not only the advertiser's brands but competitors' brands as well.

Storyboard (3)   A layout in a comic-strip series of sequential frames to indicate the conception of a television commercial. A storyboard helps in estimating the expense, visualizing the message, revealing any weakness in concept, presenting for client approval, and guiding the actual shooting.

Straight Announcement (11)   The oldest type of television commercial in which an announcer delivers a sales message directly into the camera or off-screen while a slide or film is shown on screen.

Straight Fee Method (3)   The straight fee, or retainer, is based on a cost plus fixed fees formula. Under this system the agency estimates the amount of personnel time required by the client, determines the cost of that personnel, and multiplies by some factor.

Straight-line Copy (8)   A type of body copy in which the text immediately begins to explain or develop the headline and illustration, and the product's sales points are ticked off in the order of their importance, all in a clear attempt to sell the product.

Strike-on Composition (10)   A simple method of setting cold type, also called *direct-impression composition*, which can be done on either a regular typewriter or on electronic typewriters and word processors.

Stripping (10)   The assembly of the various line and halftone negatives into one single negative, which is then used to produce the combination plate.

Subheads (8)   Secondary headlines in advertisements that may appear above or below the headline or in the text of the ad. Subheads are usually set in a smaller type size than the headline but larger than the body copy or text type size. They may also appear in boldface type or in a different ink color.

Subvertising (19)   Derogatory term referring to advertising that subtracts from the total value of advertising.

Sunday Supplement (13)   A newspaper-distributed Sunday magazine. Sunday supplements are distinct from other sections of the newspaper since they are printed by rotogravure on smoother paper stock. This heavier, higher quality paper is more conducive to quality color printing. Therefore, it enables Sunday supplements to attract and feature higher quality national advertising.

Supers (11)   Words superimposed on the picture in a television commercial.

Suppliers (3)   People and organizations that specialize in some ancillary aspect of the advertising business.

Supply and Demand (4)   Law of economics stating that, in a free market, if the supply of a product stays the same and the desire (or demand) for it increases, the price will tend to rise. If the demand decreases below the available supply, then the price will tend to drop.

Survey Method (6)   The most common way to gather primary research data. By asking questions of current or prospective customers, the researcher hopes to obtain information on attitudes, opinions, or motivations.

Sweepstakes (16)   A sales promotion activity in which prizes are offered based on a chance drawing of entrants' names. The purpose is to encourage consumption of the product by creating consumer involvement.

Syndicated Art Services (17)   Low-cost artwork (also called *clip art*) available by subscription to local media and advertisers. Clip art is available for various types of businesses and is often tied in to seasons, holidays, and other promotional angles.

Tabloid (13)   A newspaper size generally about half as deep as a standard-size newspaper and usually about 14 inches deep and 10 inches wide. It is sold flat, without folding, and looks like an unbound magazine. Most tabloid pages have five columns, each about two inches wide.

Tachistoscope (6)   A device used to measure a subject's physical perception of an advertisement under varying conditions of speed, exposure, and illumination.

Taillight Spectacular (15)   A form of transit advertising usually 21″ by 72″ that appears on the rear of buses.

Take-ones (15)   In transit advertising, pads of business reply cards or coupons affixed to interior advertisements for an extra charge that allow passengers to request more detailed information, send in application blanks, or receive some other product benefit.

Target Audience (1) (7)   The specific group of individuals to whom the advertising message is directed.

Target Market (4)   The market segment or group within the market segment toward which all marketing activities will be directed.

Task Method (7)   Method of allocating advertising funds that defines the objectives sought and how advertising will be used to accomplish those objectives. The task method occurs in three steps: defining the objectives, determining strategy, and estimating the cost.

Tear Sheet (13)   The page of a newspaper or magazine where the advertiser's ad appears that is torn out and sent to the advertiser or forwarded through the Advertising Checking Bureau for verification purposes.

Terminal Posters (15)   One-sheet, two-sheet, and three-sheet posters in many bus, subway, and commuter train stations, as well as major train and airline terminals. These are usually custom designed and include such attention-getters as floor displays, island showcases, illuminated signs, dioramas (three-dimensional scenes), and clocks with special lighting and moving messages.

Testimonial (11)   The use of satisfied customers and celebrities to endorse a product in advertising.

Text Type (10)   The smaller type used in the body copy of an advertisement.

Theater Tests (6)   A captive audience technique for pretesting television commercials in which a variety of methods may be used. For example, electronic equipment may be used enabling respondents to press a button to indicate what they like and don't like as they view a commercial.

Third-class Mail (15)   The inexpensive classification of mail usually used for direct-mail advertising. There are four types of third-class mail: single piece, bulk, bound books or catalogs, and nonprofit organization mail.

Thumbnail Sketch (9)   Miniature pencil sketches, approximately one-fourth to one-eighth the size of the finished ad, that are used for trying out ideas.

Total Audience (14)   The total number of homes reached by some portion of a program. This figure is normally broken down to determine the distribution of audience into demographic categories.

Total Bus (15)   In transit advertising all the exterior space on a bus including the front, rear, sides, and top, giving the product message powerful exclusivity.

Trade Advertising (1)   The advertising of goods and services to middlemen—to stimulate wholesalers and retailers to buy goods for resale to their customers.

Trade Character (2)   People, birds, animals, or other objects that may or may not also be applied to the goods as a trademark.

Trade Name (2)   The name under which a company does business.

Trade Shows (16)   Exhibitions where manufacturers, dealers, and buyers of the industry's products can get together for demonstrations and discussion; expose new products, literature, and samples to customers; and meet potential new dealers for their products.

Trademark (2)   Any word, name, symbol, or device or any combination thereof adopted and used by manufacturers or merchants to identify their goods and distinguish them from those manufactured or sold by others.

Trading Stamps (16)   A once-popular sales promotion device for department stores, supermarkets, and service stations in which customers making purchases received stamps that could be redeemed for valuable products.

Traffic Manager (3)   Person responsible for coordinating all phases of production and seeing that everything is completed on time and that all ads and commercials are received by the media before the deadline.

Trailer Tests (6)   A type of test in which trailers are situated in shopping center parking lots and shoppers are invited in to be shown TV commercials. The impact of the commercials is measured in part by the difference in coupon redemption rates between shoppers exposed to the commercials and those who are not.

Transit Advertising (15)   An out-of-home medium that actually includes three separate media forms: inside cards; outside posters; and station, platform, and terminal posters.

Translator Stations (14)   A special type of TV station that rebroadcasts regular stations to fringe areas using the higher UHF frequencies but is usually incapable of originating local programming.

Traveling Display (15)   A form of transit advertising measuring 21″ by 72″ that appears on the sides of buses.

TV Dayparts (14)   The various parts of the day into which TV programming and viewing is divided. These include: daytime, early fringe, early news, prime access, prime time, late news, and late fringe.

TVHH (TV Households) (14)   The number of households in a market area that own television sets.

Type Director (10)   The person responsible for type specification and copy casting.

Type Families (10)   Related typefaces identified by such names as Cheltenham, Futura, and Goudy, in which the basic design remains the same but there are variations in the proportion, weight, and slant of the characters. Variations also commonly include light, medium, bold, extra bold, condensed, extended, and italic.

Type Groups (10)   Typefaces classified into various groups because of their similarity in design. There are five major type groups: roman, sans serif (or gothic), square serif, cursive (or script), and ornamental.

Typesetters (3)   The people who take the copywriter's words and the art director's layout and translate them into what appears in the ad.

Typography (10)   The art of selecting and setting type.

UHF (14)   The more than 250 ultra-high frequency (channels 14 through 83) television stations. To equalize coverage, a law was passed in 1965 requiring all new TV sets to be designed to receive UHF broadcasts. This, along with the tremendous growth of cable networks in the late 70s, brought many more UHF stations into existence.

Unaided Recall (6)   Respondents are questioned about

advertisements they have seen or read without any assistance from the interviewer about the brand or the advertising.

Unit of Sale Method (7)   A method of allocating advertising funds, also called the case-rate method, in which a specific dollar figure is set for each case, box, barrel, or carton produced or for each unit anticipated to be produced.

Unity (9)   The appearance or impression created when all the elements in an ad (such as balance, movement, proportion, contrast, and color) relate to one another in a harmonious way.

Upper- and Lowercase (10)   Capital letters are called *uppercase,* and small letters are called *lowercase.* Type directors may call for type to be set in all-upper, all-lower, or upper and lower.

Usage Rate (5)   Also called *volume segmentation,* usage rates are used to define consumers as light, medium, or heavy users of products.

User Status (5) Method of segmenting markets by types of product users including nonusers, ex-users, potential users, new users, and regular users.

USP (1)   The *unique selling proposition* of every product advertised. A concept developed by Rosser Reeves of the Ted Bates advertising agency.

Validity (6)   An important characteristic of a research test. For a test to be valid, it must reflect the true status of the market.

VALS (5)   Acronym meaning Values and Lifestyles—refers to a method of segmenting consumer markets based on certain psychographic attributes. These categories may also be used to govern aspects of a product's marketing strategy.

Vendor Sales (13)   Sales of magazines through newsstands and news racks.

Vertical Marketing Systems (4)   A system of marketing in which members of the distribution channel cooperate closely with one another in selling, pricing, promotion, and advertising.

Vertical Publication (13)   Type of business publication aimed at people in various job functions within a specific industry; e.g., *Retail Baking Today.*

VHF (14)   The more than 500 very high frequency (channels 2 through 13) television stations. Until 1952 all stations were VHF.

Video (11)   The left side of a television script indicating camera action, scenes, and instructions. Also, the visual part of a television commercial.

Videotape (11)   Magnetic tape used to record television programs and commercials. Videotape offers a brilliant picture, better fidelity, and more consistent quality than film stock. It also provides an immediate playback.

Visualization (9)   The task of analyzing the problem, assembling any and all pertinent information, and developing some verbal or visual concept of how to communicate what needs to be said. It is the creative point where the search for the "big idea" takes place.

Voice-over (11)   In television advertising, the spoken copy or dialogue delivered by an announcer who is not seen but whose voice is heard.

Wash Drawings (9)   The closest illustrative technique to a black and white photograph, this ink or water-color technique can overcome many of the limitations of a camera. There are two types of wash drawings: tight and loose. A tight drawing is quite detailed and is much more realistic than a loose drawing. A loose wash drawing is more impressionistic and is used extensively by fashion illustrators.

Weeklies (13)   A newspaper that is published once a week and characteristically serves readers in small urban or suburban areas or farm communities with exclusive emphasis on local news and advertising.

White Space (9)   The space in an advertisement unoccupied by text or illustration.

Work Print (11)   The first visual portion of a filmed commercial assembled without the extra effects of dissolves, titles, or supers. At this time, scenes may be substituted, music and sound effects added, or other changes made.

INDEX*

This book has been set Linotron 202 in 10 point Pala-tino, leaded 2 points. Part numbers are 20 and 50 point Palatino and part titles are 20 point Palatino. Chapter numbers are 40½ point Palatino and chapter titles are 14 point Palatino. The size of the type page is 40 by 58½ picas.